in Special and Gifted Education

Committee on Minority Representation in Special Education
M. Suzanne Donovan and Christopher T. Cross, *Editors*

Division of Behavioral and Social Sciences and Education
National Research Council

NATIONAL ACADEMY PRESS
Washington, DC

NATIONAL ACADEMY PRESS • 2101 Constitution Avenue, N.W. • Washington, DC 20418

NOTICE: The project that is the subject of this report was approved by the Governing Board of the National Research Council, whose members are drawn from the councils of the National Academy of Sciences, the National Academy of Engineering, and the Institute of Medicine. The members of the committee responsible for the report were chosen for their special competences and with regard for appropriate balance.

This study was supported by Contract/Grant No. H324A980001 between the National Academy of Sciences and the U.S. Department of Education. Any opinions, findings, conclusions, or recommendations expressed in this publication are those of the author(s) and do not necessarily reflect the views of the organizations or agencies that provided support for the project.

Library of Congress Cataloging-in-Publication Data

National Research Council (U.S.). Committee on Minority Representation in Special Education.
    Minority students in special and gifted education / Committee on Minority Representation in Special Education, Division of Behavioral and Social Sciences and Education, National Research Council; M. Suzanne Donovan and Christopher T. Cross, editors.
        p.   cm.
Includes bibliographical references (p.   ) and index.
    ISBN 0-309-07439-8
        1. Special education—Government policy—United States.
2. Minorities—Education—Government policy—United States.
3. Educational equalization—Government policy—United States.
I. Donovan, Suzanne. II. Cross, Christopher T. III. Title.
    LC3981 .N355 2002
    371.9'0973—dc21
                            2002005195
Additional copies of this report are available from National Academy Press, 2101 Constitution Avenue, N.W., Lockbox 285, Washington, DC 20055; (800) 624-6242 or (202) 334-3313 (in the Washington metropolitan area); Internet, http://www.nap.edu

Printed in the United States of America

Suggested citation: National Research Council (2002) *Minority Students in Special and Gifted Education*. Committee on Minority Representation in Special Education, M. Suzanne Donovan and Christopher T. Cross, editors. Division of Behavioral and Social Sciences and Education. Washington, DC: National Academy Press.

THE NATIONAL ACADEMIES

National Academy of Sciences
National Academy of Engineering
Institute of Medicine
National Research Council

The National Academy of Sciences is a private, nonprofit, self-perpetuating society of distinguished scholars engaged in scientific and engineering research, dedicated to the furtherance of science and technology and to their use for the general welfare. Upon the authority of the charter granted to it by the Congress in 1863, the Academy has a mandate that requires it to advise the federal government on scientific and technical matters. Dr. Bruce M. Alberts is president of the National Academy of Sciences.

The National Academy of Engineering was established in 1964, under the charter of the National Academy of Sciences, as a parallel organization of outstanding engineers. It is autonomous in its administration and in the selection of its members, sharing with the National Academy of Sciences the responsibility for advising the federal government. The National Academy of Engineering also sponsors engineering programs aimed at meeting national needs, encourages education and research, and recognizes the superior achievements of engineers. Dr. Wm. A. Wulf is president of the National Academy of Engineering.

The Institute of Medicine was established in 1970 by the National Academy of Sciences to secure the services of eminent members of appropriate professions in the examination of policy matters pertaining to the health of the public. The Institute acts under the responsibility given to the National Academy of Sciences by its congressional charter to be an adviser to the federal government and, upon its own initiative, to identify issues of medical care, research, and education. Dr. Harvey V. Fineberg is president of the Institute of Medicine.

The National Research Council was organized by the National Academy of Sciences in 1916 to associate the broad community of science and technology with the Academy's purposes of furthering knowledge and advising the federal government. Functioning in accordance with general policies determined by the Academy, the Council has become the principal operating agency of both the National Academy of Sciences and the National Academy of Engineering in providing services to the government, the public, and the scientific and engineering communities. The Council is administered jointly by both Academies and the Institute of Medicine. Dr. Bruce M. Alberts and Dr. Wm. A. Wulf are chairman and vice chairman, respectively, of the National Research Council.

Preface

There are few topics in education that are as politically and emotionally charged as the education of children with disabilities. Who we identify as gifted and talented does not tug at the heart or the conscience in quite the same way, but it nonetheless touches deeply held beliefs about ability and about privileged opportunity. When the focus is on whether minority children are being disproportionately assigned to special and gifted education programs, opportunities for separating evidence from emotion become rare. For the past two and one-half years the Committee on Minority Representation in Special Education of the National Research Council (NRC) has been engaged in one of those rare events—an analysis of the evidence that can inform public policy regarding these controversial issues.

The roots of our work trace back almost 20 years to a previous report of the National Research Council that dealt with many of the same issues. We began our deliberations with a review of that report, agreeing that in many respects its messages are as salient today as they were then. Why had the report not stimulated more change? Why were we being asked to revisit the issue? What should we do this time that would be different?

The previous committee focused primarily on defining a better set of rules for determining who needs special education, whether placement is beneficial, and when and how students would exit. Their concern was whether special education identification was operating fairly and to the benefit of students, and their treatment of those issues was laudable. In fact, many of that committee's suggestions are reflected in the amendments to the Individuals with Disabilities Education Act and federal guidelines and regulations. And their notion of a fair process is very consonant with our own.

In the last several decades, however, both the successes and failures of social policy in a variety of areas have gradually brought a shift in focus. We have learned that fair rules and regulations, important though they may be, are a point of departure and not a destination. When regulatory procedures require tests that are valid for the intended use, for example, the test instruments must be available and the capacity at the school level to use the instruments properly must be in place for the rules to matter. Similarly, both assessing and designing a program that is responsive to a student's individual needs requires a capacity at the school level to observe, understand, and design responses that are sensitive to student differences. And the incentives put in place by the monitoring process may overwhelm the influence of the regulations themselves, as might the balance of influence among parents, teachers, and administrators in any school or school district. Moreover, placement in special and gifted education is rooted in achievement differences. Even the most unbiased rules of the game will not substantially reduce disproportion if there are genuine underlying achievement differences unless the sources of those differences are addressed.

While our committee embraced the principles in the earlier report, we cast our net more widely. We looked at the regulations and guidelines, but we also looked at issues of school-level capacity, at the supports for achievement available to students from different racial and ethnic groups, and at environmental influences on the developmental trajectory of children in the years before they reach the schoolhouse door that make them more vulnerable to school failure.

Our work began as a congressionally mandated study of minority children in special education only. It was funded through the Office of Research in the Office of Special Education and Rehabilitation Services of the U.S. Department of Education. Shortly after we began our work, the Department's Office of Educational Research and Improvement asked that we expand our charge to include the study of minority representation in programs for gifted and talented students. While at first that combination might seem awkward, it soon became clear that the issues were often the mirror image of one another. However, the work of the committee regarding gifted and talented students was constrained by both the limited resources available for that part of the study and the paucity of data that were available.

Who is the audience for this report? Since our charge came from the U.S. Department of Education, we took it as our primary mission to inform federal policy makers regarding the complex knowledge base relevant to an understanding of minority representation in special and gifted education. The implications of our study reach into other federal departments that regulate the health and environmental safety of young children. But the report also has important implications for state education policy regarding general, special, and gifted education. We urge that policy makers who are concerned with these issues bridge the very artificial lines that have separated our consideration of the interrelationships that exist between general, special, and gifted education and between the developmental well-being of children both before and after they reach school age. The time for turf protection has long passed, and the time for thoughtful consideration of how best to support the success of all students is upon us.

ACKNOWLEDGMENTS

Many people contributed to the launching of this study, the work of the committee, and the completion of the report. The committee is most grateful for their efforts. The support of our sponsors at the Department of Education, and their patience with the process and time required to produce a consensus report of this magnitude, was essential. We are grateful to Louis Danielson and Grace Duran (Office of Special Education Programs), Patricia O'Connell Ross (Office of Education Research and Improvement), and Rebecca Fitch and Richard Foster (Office for Civil Rights).

The committee extends its appreciation to those who assisted in the sometimes arduous task of assembling the data. Many of the data used by the committee were provided by the Department of Education with the assistance of Judith Holt and Peter McCabe. Data from the National Center for Education Statistics were provided by Mark Glander at the National Education Resource Center. Daniel Cork at the National Research Council's Committee on National Statistics assisted with the translation of state data into figures.

In the course of our work, the committee drew on the expertise of many others. The committee commissioned six papers, and the authors of those papers met and discussed their work with the committee. These include Richard Figueroa, University of California, Davis; Patricia Gandara, University of California, Davis; Kathleen Hebbler, SRI International; L. Scott Miller, The College Board; Herbert Needleman, University of Pittsburgh; Mary Wagner, SRI International; and Richard Wagner, Florida State University. The committee also benefited from presentations given by Deborah Speece, University of Maryland, and Arthur Baroody, University of Illinois, Urbana-Champaign. Barbara Foorman, of the University of Texas, Houston, provided materials on the Texas Primary Reading Inventory, and the Texas Education Agency provided us with their complete TPRI tool kit for reading teachers. Reid Lyon and Margot Malakoff of the National Institute of Child Health and Human Development shared with the committee materials they had pulled together for a study of Head Start.

A special thanks to Janet Garton, who provided extensive research assistance and substantial support in attending to the detail required for accuracy throughout the report. Leah Nower spent a productive summer internship at the NRC providing research assistance for the project. The committee also benefited considerably from the research contributions provided to individual committee members by Vicki Marie Nishioka, University of Oregon at Eugene, Elizabeth Cramer, University of Miami, Kathleen Lane, Vanderbilt University, and John Hosp, Vanderbilt University.

Over the course of the two and a half years, the committee's work was supported by three senior project assistants. Wendell Grant provided administrative support through the project's launching, LaVone Wellman carried it through its midlife, and Allison Shoup ushered it to a close, handling the manuscript through its various stages.

The efforts of a committee are realized in a final report only with the help of those experienced in navigating the occasionally bumpy terrain of report preparation. Alexandra Wigdor helped launch the project in its early stages, and her careful reading and feedback in the final stages were invaluable. The committee's work was also improved in the eleventh hour by thoughtful contributions of Patricia Morison. Our final product was polished by the skilled, professional editing of Christine McShane.

This report has been reviewed in draft form by individuals chosen for their diverse perspectives and technical expertise, in accordance with procedures approved by the Report Review Committee of the National Research Council. The purpose of this independent review is to provide candid and critical comments that will assist the institution in making the published report as sound as possible and to ensure that the report meets institutional standards for objectivity, evidence, and responsiveness to the study charge. The review comments and draft manuscript remain confidential to protect the integrity of the deliberative process.

We thank the following individuals for the participation in the review of this report: Leonard Baca, BUENO Center For Multicultural Education, University of Colorado; Barbara Foorman, Center for Academic and Reading Skills, University of Texas-Houston Medical School; Lynn Fuchs, Peabody College, Vanderbilt University; Russell Gersten, College of Education, University of Oregon; Daniel P. Hallahan, Curry School of Education, University of Virginia; Barbara Keogh, Department of Psychiatry and Biobehavioral Sciences, UCLA School of Medicine; Lorraine McDonnell, Department of Political Science, University of California, Santa Barbara; Nancy Robinson, Department of Psychiatry and Behavioral Sciences, emerita, University of Washington; Fred R. Volkmar, Child Study Center, Yale University School of Medicine; and James Ysseldyke, Office of the Dean, University of Minnesota.

Although the reviewers listed above have provided many constructive comments and suggestions, they were not asked to endorse the conclusions or recommendations nor did they see the final draft of the report before its release. The review of this report was overseen by Arthur Goldberger, Department of Economics, University of Wisconsin, and Catherine Snow, Graduate School of Education, Harvard University. Appointed by the National Research Council, they were responsible for making certain that an independent examination of this report was carried out in accordance with institutional procedures and that all review comments were carefully considered. Responsibility for the final context of this report rests entirely with the authoring committee and the institution.

Christopher T. Cross, *Chair*
M. Suzanne Donovan, *Study Director*
Committee on Minority Representation
in Special Education

Contents

Executive Summary

From the enactment of the 1975 federal law requiring states to provide a free and appropriate education to all students with disabilities, children in some racial/ethnic groups have been identified for services in disproportionately large numbers. Public concern is aroused by the pattern of disproportion. In the low-incidence categories (deaf, blind, orthopedic impairment, etc.) in which the problem is observable outside the school context and is typically diagnosed by medical professionals, no marked disproportion exists. The higher representation of minority students occurs in the high-incidence categories of mild mental retardation (MMR), emotional disturbance (ED), and to a lesser extent learning disabilities (LD), categories in which the problem is often identified first in the school context and the disability diagnosis is typically given without confirmation of an organic cause.

The concern is not new. In 1979 the National Research Council (NRC) was asked to conduct a study to determine the factors accounting for the disproportionate representation of minority students and males in special education programs for students with mental retardation, and to identify placement criteria or practices that do not affect minority students and males disproportionately (NRC, 1982). Twenty years later, disproportion in special education persists: while about 5 percent of Asian/Pacific Islander students are identified for special education, the rate for Hispanics is 11 percent, for whites 12 percent, for American Indians 13 percent, and for

1

blacks over 14 percent. The NRC, at the request of Congress, has been asked to revisit the issue. In this case, however, the Office for Civil Rights in the U.S. Department of Education extended the committee's charge to include the representation of minority children in gifted and talented programs as well, where racial/ethnic disproportion patterns are, generally speaking, the reverse of those in special education.

CURRENT CONTEXT

Since the 1982 NRC report, much has changed in general education as well as in special education. The proportion of minority students in the population of school-age children has risen dramatically—to 35 percent in 2000—increasing the diversity of students and of primary languages spoken in many schools. And state standards have raised the bar for the achievement expected of all students. More than 1 in 10 students is now identified for special education services: in the past decade alone, there has been a 35 percent increase in the number of children served under the Individuals with Disabilities Education Act (IDEA). And many more of these students are receiving special education and related services in general education classrooms.

The distribution of students across special education categories has changed as well. Identification rates for students with mental retardation today are about a quarter lower than in 1979. While the decline has applied across racial/ethnic groups, disproportionate representation of black students in that category has persisted. Just over 1 percent of white students but 2.6 percent of black students fall into that category.

Two decades ago, fewer than 3 percent of students were identified with learning disabilities (LD). That number approaches 6 percent of all students today. Only American Indian students are represented in disproportionately large numbers in that category. But for all racial/ethnic groups, the LD category accounts both for the largest number of special education students and for the largest growth rate in special education placements.

While these demographic and policy changes create a somewhat different context today from that confronting the earlier NRC committee, the problems are conceptually quite similar. At the outset, both committees confronted a paradox: if IDEA provides extra resources and the right to a more individualized education program, why would one consider disproportionate representation of minority children a problem? The answer, as every parent of a child receiving special education services knows, is that in order to be eligible for the additional resources a child must be labeled as having a disability, a label that signals substandard performance. And while that label is intended to bring additional supports, it may also bring lowered expectations on the part of teachers, other children, and the identified student. When a child cannot learn without the additional supports, *and* when the supports improve outcomes for the child, that trade-off may well be worth making. But because there is a trade-off, both the need and the benefit should be established before the label and the cost are imposed. This committee, like its predecessor, does not view the desirable end necessarily as one in which no minority group is represented in disproportionate numbers, but rather one in which the children who receive special education or gifted program services are those who truly require them and who benefit from them.

Who requires specialized education? Answering that question has always posed a challenge. The historic notion of a child with an emotional or learning disability or a talent conveys a "fixed-trait" model, in which the observed performance is the consequence of characteristics internal to the child. Assessment processes have been designed as an attempt to isolate those children with internal traits that constitute a "disability" or a "gift." And clearly there can be within-child characteristics that underlie placement in one of the high-incidence categories. Neurobiological investigations, for example, reveal different patterns of brain activity in dyslexic and nondyslexic children while reading.

However, in the past few decades a growing body of research has pointed to the critical role that context can play in achievement and behavior. The same child can perform very differently depending on the level of teacher support, and aggressive behavior can be reversed or exacerbated by effective or ineffective classroom management. In practice, it can be quite difficult to distinguish internal child traits that require the ongoing support of special education from inadequate opportunity or contextual support for learning and behavior.

COMMITTEE'S APPROACH

The conceptual framework in which the committee considered the issue of minority disproportion in special education and gifted and talented programs, then, is one in which the achievement or behavior at issue is determined by the interaction of the child, the teacher, and the classroom environment. Internal child characteristics play a clear role: what the child brings to the interaction is a function both of biology and of experience in the family and the community. But the child's achievement and behavior outcomes will also reflect the effectiveness of instruction and the instructional environment.

The committee did not view the problem of disproportionate representation in special education as one of simply eliminating racial/ethnic differences in assignment. If special education services provide genuine individualized instruction and accountability for student learning, we consider it as serious a concern when students who need those supports are passed over (false negatives) as when they are inappropriately identified (false positives). Likewise with respect to gifted and talented programs, we consider it a problem if qualified minority students are overlooked in the identification process, but consider it an undesirable solution if minority students are selected when they are not adequately prepared for the demands of gifted and talented programs. The committee's goal, then, was to understand why disproportion occurs. To address our charge, the committee asked four questions:

1. Is there reason to believe that there is currently a higher incidence of special needs or giftedness among some racial/ethnic groups? Specifically, are there biological and social or contextual contributors to early development that differ by race or ethnicity?

Our answer to that question is a definitive "yes." We know that minority children are disproportionately poor, and poverty is associated with higher rates of exposure to harmful toxins, including lead, alcohol, and tobacco, in early stages of development. Poor children are also more likely to be born with low birthweight, to have poorer nutrition, and to have home and child care environments that are less supportive of early cognitive and emotional development than their majority counterparts. When poverty is deep and persistent, the number of risk factors rises, seriously jeopardizing development.

Some risk factors have a disproportionate impact on particular groups that goes beyond the poverty effect. In all income groups, black children are more likely to be born with low birthweight and are more likely to be exposed to harmful levels of lead, while American Indian/Alaskan Native children are more likely to be exposed prenatally to high levels of alcohol and tobacco. While the separate effect of each of these factors on school achievement and performance is difficult to determine, substantial differences by race/ethnicity on a variety of dimensions of school preparedness are documented at kindergarten entry.

2. Does schooling independently contribute to the incidence of special needs or giftedness among students in different racial/ethnic groups through the opportunities that it provides?

Again, our answer is "yes." Schools with higher concentrations of low-income, minority children are less likely to have experienced, well-trained teachers. Per-pupil expenditures in those schools are somewhat lower, while the needs of low-income student populations and the difficulty of attracting teachers to inner-city, urban schools suggest that supporting comparable levels of education would require higher levels of per-pupil expenditures. These schools are less likely to offer advanced courses for their students, providing less support for high academic achievement.

When children come to school from disadvantaged backgrounds, as a disproportionate number of minority students do, high-quality instruction that carefully puts the prerequisites for learning in place, combined with effective classroom management that minimizes chaos, can put students on a path to academic success. While some reform efforts suggest that such an outcome is possible, there are currently no assurances that children will be exposed to effective instruction or classroom management before they are placed in special education programs or are screened for gifted programs.

3. Does the current referral and assessment process reliably identify students with special needs and gifts? In particular, is there reason to believe that the current process is biased in terms of race or ethnicity?

The answer here is not as straightforward. The majority of children in special and gifted education are referred by teachers. If a teacher is biased in evaluating student performance and behavior, current procedures provide ample room for those biases to be reflected in referrals. Some experimental research suggests that teachers do hold such biases. But whether bias is maintained when teachers have direct contact with children in the classroom is not clear. For example, research that has compared groups of students who are referred by teachers find that minority students actually have greater academic and behavior problems than their majority counterparts.

Once students are referred for special education, they must be assessed as eligible or ineligible. Whether the assessment process is biased is as controversial as the referral process. However research shows that context, including familiarity with test taking and the norms and expectations of school, may depress the scores of students whose experiences prepare them less well for the demands of classrooms and standardized tests.

Whether the referral and assessment of students for special and gifted education is racially biased or not, are the right students being identified— students who need and can benefit from those programs? Here the committee's answer is "no." The subjectivity of the referral process allows for students with significant learning problems to be overlooked for referral, and the conceptual and procedural shortcomings of the assessment process for learning disabilities and emotional disturbance give little confidence that student need has been appropriately identified. Importantly, current procedures result in placements later in the educational process than is most effective or efficient.

4. Is placement in special education a benefit or a risk? Does the outcome differ by race or ethnic group?

The data that would allow us to answer these questions adequately do not exist. We do know that some specific special education and gifted and talented interventions have been demonstrated to have positive outcomes for students. But how widely those interventions are employed is not known. Nor do we know whether minority students are less likely to be exposed to those high-quality interventions than majority students. What evidence is available suggests that parent advocacy and teacher quality, both of which would be expected to correlate with higher-quality interventions, are less likely in higher-poverty school districts where minority children are concentrated.

At the core of our study is an observation that unites all four questions: *there is substantial evidence with regard to both behavior and achievement that early identification and intervention is more effective than later identification and intervention.* This is true for children of any race or ethnic group, and children with or without an identifiable "within-child" problem. Yet the current special education identification process relies on a "wait-to-fail" principle that both increases the likelihood that children will fail because they do not receive early supports and decreases the effectiveness of supports once they are received. Similarly, the practice of identifying gifted learners after several years of schooling is based on the "wait 'til they succeed" philosophy rather than a developmental orientation.

While this principle applies to *all* students, the impact is likely to be greatest on students from disadvantaged backgrounds because (a) their experience outside the school prepares them less well for the demands of schooling, placing them at greater risk for failure, and (b) the resources available to them in general education are more likely to be substandard. Early efforts to identify and intervene with children at risk for later failure will help all children who need additional supports. But we would expect a disproportionately large number of those students to be from disadvantaged backgrounds.

The vision we offer in the report is one in which general and special education services are more tightly integrated; one in which no child is judged by the school to have a learning or emotional disability or to lack exceptional talent until efforts to provide high-quality instructional and behavioral support in the general education context have been tried without success. The "earlier is better" principle applies even before the K-12 years. The more effective we are at curtailing early biological harms and injuries and providing children with the supports for normal cognitive and behavioral development in the earliest years of life, the fewer children will arrive at school at risk for failure.

CONCLUSIONS AND RECOMMENDATIONS

A discussion of all conclusions and recommendations appears in Chapter 10. Here we give the conclusions we consider key, along with the recommendations. They are organized here in the following major categories: referral and eligibility determination in special education (SE) and gifted and talented education (GT); teacher quality (TQ); biological and early childhood risk factors (EC); data collection (DC); and expanding the research and development base (RD).

Special Education Eligibility

From our review of the current knowledge base, several important conclusions have led the committee to rethink the current approach to special education:

1. Among the most frequent reasons for referral to special education are reading difficulties and behavior problems.

2. In recent years, interventions appropriate for the general education classroom to improve reading instruction and classroom management have been demonstrated to reduce the number of children who fail at reading or are later identified with behavior disorders.

3. There are currently no mechanisms in place to guarantee that students will be exposed to state-of-the-art reading instruction or classroom management before they are identified as having a "within-child" problem.

4. Referral for the high-incidence categories of special education currently requires student failure. However, screening mechanisms exist for early identification of children at risk for later reading and behavior problems. And the effectiveness of early intervention in both areas has been demonstrated to be considerably greater than the effectiveness of later, postfailure intervention.

These findings suggest that schools should be doing more and doing it earlier to ensure that students receive quality general education services to reduce the number of students with pronounced achievement and behavior problems. The committee's proposed alternative would require policy and regulatory changes at both the federal and state levels of government.

Federal-Level Recommendations

Recommendation SE.1: The committee recommends that federal guidelines for special education eligibility be changed in order to encourage better integrated general and special education services. We propose that eligibility ensue when a student exhibits large differences from typical levels of performance in one or more domain(s) *and* with evidence of insufficient response to high-quality interventions in the rel-

evant domain(s) of functioning in school settings. These domains include achievement (e.g., reading, writing, mathematics), social behavior, and emotional regulation. As is currently the case, eligibility determination would also require a judgment by a multidisciplinary team, including parents, that special education is needed.

The proposed approach would not negate the eligibility of any student who arrives at school with a disability determination, or who has a severe disability, from being served as they are currently. But for children with milder high-incidence disabilities, the implications for referral and assessment are considerable. Assessment for special education eligibility would be focused on gathering information that documents educationally relevant differences from typical levels of performance, and that is relevant to the design, monitoring, and evaluation of treatments.

While eligibility for special education would by law continue to depend on establishment of a disability, in the committee view, noncategorical conceptions and classification criteria that focus on matching a student's specific needs to an intervention strategy would obviate the need for the traditional high-incidence disability labels such as LD and ED. If traditional disability definitions are used, they would need to be revised to focus on characteristics directly related to classroom and school learning and behavior (e.g., reading failure, math failure, persistent inattention and disorganization).

State-Level Recommendations

Regulatory changes would be required in most states for implementation of a reformed special education program that uses functional assessment measures to promote positive outcomes for students with disabilities. Some states have already instituted changes that move in this direction and can serve as examples. These states' rules require a systematic problem-solving process that is centered around quality indicators associated with successful interventions.

Recommendation SE.2: The committee recommends that states adopt a universal screening and multitiered intervention strategy in general education to enable early identification and intervention with children at risk for reading problems. For students who continue to have difficulty even after intensive intervention, referral to special education and the development of an individualized education program (IEP) would follow. The data regarding student response to intervention would be used for eligibility determination.

Recommendation SE.3: The committee recommends that states launch large-scale pilot programs in conjunction with universities or research

centers to test the plausibility and productivity of universal behavior management interventions, early behavior screening, and techniques to work with children at risk for behavior problems. Research results suggest that these interventions can work. However, a large-scale pilot project would provide a firmer foundation of knowledge regarding scaling up the practices involved.

Federal Support of State Reform Efforts

Recommendation SE.4: While the United States has a strong tradition of state control of education, the committee recommends that the federal government support widespread adoption of early screening and intervention in the states.

Gifted and Talented Eligibility

The research base justifying alternative approaches for the screening, identification, and placement of gifted children is neither as extensive nor as informative as that for special education.

Recommendation GT.1: The committee recommends a research program oriented toward the development of a broader knowledge base on early identification and intervention with children who exhibit advanced performance in the verbal or quantitative realm, or who exhibit other advanced abilities.

This research program should be designed to determine whether there are reliable and valid indicators of current exceptional performance in language, mathematical, or other domains, or indicators of later exceptional performance. Research on classroom practice designed to encourage the early and continued development of gifted behaviors in underrepresented populations should be undertaken so that screening can be followed by effective intervention.

School Context and Student Performance

School resources, class size, and indicators of teacher quality are associated with learning and behavior outcomes. However, their influence is exerted primarily through teacher-student interactions. Moreover, in the prevention and eligibility determination model the committee is recommending, general education assessments and interventions not now in widespread use are proposed as standard practice. Key to our proposals, then, are sustained efforts at capacity building, and sufficient resources, time, and coordination among stakeholders to build that capacity.

State-Level Recommendations

Teacher Quality: General education teachers need improved teacher preparation and professional development to prepare them to address the needs of students with significant underachievement or giftedness.

> Recommendation TQ.1: State certification or licensure requirements for teachers should systematically require:
> • competency in understanding and implementing reasonable norms and expectations for students, and core competencies in instructional delivery of academic content;
> • coursework and practicum experience in understanding, creating, and modifying an educational environment to meet children's individual needs;
> • competency in behavior management in classroom and noninstructional school settings;
> • instruction in functional analysis and routine behavioral assessment of students;
> • instruction in effective intervention strategies for students who fail to meet minimal standards for successful educational performance, or who substantially exceed minimal standards;
> • coursework and practicum experience to prepare teachers to deliver culturally responsive instruction. More specifically, teachers should be familiar with the beliefs, values, cultural practices, discourse styles, and other features of students' lives that may have an impact on classroom participation and success and be prepared to use this information in designing instruction.

While a foundational knowledge base can be laid in preservice education, often classroom experience is needed before teachers can make the most of instructional experiences.

> • States should require rigorous professional development for all practicing teachers, administrators, and educational support personnel to assist them in addressing the varied needs of students who differ substantially from the norm in achievement and/or behavior.
> • The professional development of administrators and educational support personnel should include enhanced capabilities in the improvement and evaluation of teacher instruction with respect to meeting student's individual needs.

> Recommendation TQ.2: State or professional association approval for educator instructional programs should include requirements for faculty competence in the current literature and research on child and adolescent learning and development, and on successful assessment,

instructional, and intervention strategies, particularly for atypical learners and students with gifts and disabilities.

Recommendation TQ.3: A credential as a school psychologist or special education teacher should require instruction in classroom observation/assessment and in teacher support to work with a struggling student or with a gifted student. These skills should be considered as critical to their professional role as the administration and interpretation of tests are now considered.

Federal-Level Recommendations

This committee joins many others at the NRC and elsewhere in calling for improved teacher preparation. How to move from widespread agreement that change is needed to system reform is a challenge that will itself require careful study.

Recommendation TQ.4: The committee recommends that a national advisory panel be convened in an institutional environment that is protected from political influence to study the quality and currency of programs that now exist to train teachers for general, special, and gifted education. The panel should address:
- the mechanisms for keeping instructional programs current and of high quality;
- the standards and requirements of those programs;
- the applicability of instructional programs to the demands of classroom practice;
- the long-term influence of the programs in successfully promoting educational achievement for pre-K, elementary, and secondary students.

Direct comparison to other professional fields (e.g., medicine, nursing, law, engineering, accounting) may provide insight applicable to education.

Biological and Social Risk Factors in Early Childhood

Existing intervention programs to address early biological harms and injuries have demonstrated the potential to substantially improve developmental outcomes. The committee concludes that the number of children, particularly minority children, who require special education can be reduced if resources are devoted to this end. In particular, the committee calls attention to the recommendation of the President's Task Force on Environmental Health Risks and Safety Risks to Children to eliminate lead from the housing stock by 2010.

Federal-Level Recommendations

The committee also looked at social and environmental influences on development with no clear biological basis that might differ by race or ethnicity. Because there is evidence that early intervention on multiple fronts, *if it is of high quality*, can improve the school prospects for children with multiple risk factors and reduce the likelihood that they will require special education, the committee recommends a substantial expansion and improvement of current early intervention efforts. Our recommendation is addressed to federal and state governments, both of whom currently play a major role in early childhood education.

> **Recommendation EC.1: The committee recommends that all high-risk children have access to high-quality early childhood interventions.**
>
> • **For the children at highest risk, these interventions should include family support, health services, and sustained, high-quality care and cognitive stimulation right from birth.**
> • **Preschool children (ages 4 and 5) who are eligible for Head Start should have access to a Head Start or another publicly funded preschool program. These programs should provide exposure to learning opportunities that will prepare them for success in school. Intervention should target services to the level of individual need, including high cognitive challenge for the child who exceeds normative performance.**
> • **The proposed expansion should better coordinate existing federal programs, such as Head Start and Early Head Start, and IDEA parts C and B, as well as state-initiated programs that meet equal or higher standards.**

While much is known about the types of experiences young children need for healthy development, improving the quality of early childhood programs will require refinement of the knowledge base in ways that are directly useful to practice, and bridging the chasm between what is known from research and best practice and is done in common practice. This will require a sustained vision and a rigorous research and development effort that transforms knowledge about what works and what does not work into field-tested program content, supporting materials, and professional development.

> **Recommendation EC.2: The committee recommends that the federal government launch a large-scale, rigorous, sustained research and development program in an institutional environment that has the capacity to bring together excellent professionals in research, program development, professional development, and child care/preschool practice**

for students from all backgrounds and at all levels of exceptional performance.

Improving Data Collection and Expanding the Research Base

The data documenting disproportionate representation are difficult to interpret in a variety of respects that make them a weak foundation on which to build public policy. Moreover, the data provide little if any insight into factors that contribute to placement or services that students receive.

Federal-Level Recommendations

Recommendation DC.1: The committee recommends that the Department of Education conduct a single, well-designed data collection effort to monitor both the number of children receiving services through the Individuals with Disabilities Education Act or through programs for the gifted and talented, and the characteristics of those children of concern to civil rights enforcement efforts. A unified effort would eliminate the considerable redundancy, and the burden it places on schools, in the current data collection efforts of the Office for Civil Rights and the Office of Special Education Programs.

While a more careful data collection effort of the sort outlined here would improve the understanding of who is being assigned to special education and gifted and talented programs, it would do little to further understanding of the reasons for placement, the appropriateness of placement (or nonplacement), the services provided, or the consequences that ensue.

Recommendation DC.2: The committee recommends that a national advisory panel be convened to design the collection of nationally representative longitudinal data that would allow for more informed study of minority disproportion in special education and gifted and talented programs. The panel should include scholars in special education research as well as researchers experienced in national longitudinal data collection and analysts in a variety of allied fields, including anthropology, psychology, and sociology.

In our study of the issues related to the representation of minority children in special education and gifted and talented programs, the existing knowledge base revealed the potential for substantial progress. We know much about the kinds of experiences that promote children's early health, cognitive, and behavioral development and set them on a more positive trajectory for school success. We know intervention strategies that have demonstrated success with some of the key problems that end in referral to special education. And we know some features of programs that are correlated with successful outcomes for students in special education.

Between the articulation of what we know from research and best practice, and a change in everyday practice, lies a wide chasm. It is the distance between demonstrating that vocabulary development is key to later success in reading, and having every Head Start teacher trained and equipped with materials that will promote vocabulary development among Head Start children. It is the distance between knowing that classroom management affects a child's behavior, and the school psychologist knowing how to help a specific teacher work with a specific child in the classroom context. It is the distance between those who are most knowledgeable and experienced agreeing on what teachers need to know, and every school of education changing its curriculum. Bridging the chasm will require that we become better at accumulating knowledge, extending it in promising areas, incorporating the best of what is known in teacher training efforts and education curricula and materials, and rigorously testing effectiveness. It will require public policies that are aligned with the knowledge base and that provide the support for its widespread application.

> **Recommendation RD.1: We recommend that education research and development, including that related to special and gifted education, be substantially expanded to carry promising findings and validated practices through to classroom applicability. This includes research on scaling up promising practices from research sites to widespread use.**

For medical problems like cancer, federal research programs create a vision, focus research efforts on areas with promise for improving treatments, conduct extensive field tests to determine what works, and facilitate the movement of research findings into practice. If the nation is serious about reducing the number of children who are on a trajectory that leads to school failure and disability identification as well as increasing the number of minority students who are achieving at high levels, we will need to devote the minds and resources to that effort commensurate with the size and the importance of the enterprise.

Part I

Setting the Stage

Academic achievement, classroom behavior, race/ethnicity: three phrases that, when uttered together, communicate complexity and controversy. When the focus is on the extremes of the distribution—on students with pronounced achievement and behavior problems or students considered gifted and talented—complexity and controversy multiply.

In the opening two chapters, we sketch the dimensions of the complexity as we see them. In Chapter 1 we put the current study of minority disproportion in special and gifted education in historical context. We provide the conceptual framework that the committee used to capture that complexity, and a description of the current education context (political, financial, and demographic) in which it is manifest.

In Chapter 2 we provide an analysis of federal data on the representation of minority students in special and gifted programs during the past three decades, as well as a discussion of studies that use more disaggregated data to examine disproportion and its correlates. We make recommendations regarding data collection and usage at the end of Chapter 2.

Controversy will not be quelled by our data analysis, nor should it be. Analysis should inform understanding and decision making; it should not tyrannize it. A thorough grasp of what the numbers do and do not tell us, however, provides a point of departure for more productive discussion, investigation, and decision making.

1

The Context of
Special and Gifted Education

The history of universal public education in the United States is one in which marked student diversity has presented a persistent challenge. Universal K-12 education is founded on the notion that groups of children (typically 20, 30, or more) of similar chronological ages can be effectively taught together by a single teacher using a common curriculum. The greater the diversity of the students in the classroom, the greater the challenges posed by this model. The expectations and demands of the classroom may reinforce the familiar for many students yet be indecipherable for others. While some students may be hopelessly left behind, others may be frustratingly bored.

The evolution of special education programs in the public schools has been inextricably linked with the challenges presented by diverse learners in general education. For some children receiving special education, the diversity is defined by certain physical or medical conditions, such as visual or hearing impairments or a physical disability, that must be accommodated or supported for instruction to be effective. For other students, the ability to comprehend or learn required content at the same pace as others may be impaired to a level that requires both instructional and curricular modifications. For students at the other end of the learning continuum, who may learn at a pace exceeding that of typical classroom instruction, insufficient challenge in the general curriculum may lead to disengagement and underachievement. This report is concerned with the intersection of racial and ethnic diversity and achievement and with why certain children are over-represented in some special education programs and underrepresented in those for the gifted and talented.

Since the passage of the federal special education law in 1975, now called the Individuals with Disabilities Education Act (IDEA), there has been racial disproportion in the assignment of students to special education, most persistently in the category of mental retardation but also in the categories of emotional disturbance and, increasingly, learning disabilities. Studies conducted early in the history of Public Law 94-142 (Brewer and Kakalik, 1974) noted that one of the major implementation problems associated with federal policy on special education was the mislabeling of students as handicapped. These studies note the vague and varying definitions of disability used across states and the confusion regarding both type and severity of educational need. The reports concluded that a fundamental issue confronting special education administrators was to identify and use nondiscriminatory devices and procedures. A 1970 survey of the 50 special education directors across the nation conducted by Goldstein et al. (1975) indicated that 56 percent considered mislabeling of students to be "the major controversy in special education today" (p.11).

COMMITTEE CHARGE

In 1979 the National Academy of Sciences was asked to conduct a study to determine the factors accounting for the disproportionate representation of minority students and males in special education programs, specifically for students with mental retardation, and to identify placement criteria or practices that do not affect minority students and males disproportionately (National Research Council [NRC], 1982). Twenty years later, concern about the disproportionate representation of minority children in special education persists, and the NRC has been asked to revisit the issue.

Since the first NRC report, there have been a number of changes in general education as well as in special education. Increasing numbers of students are identified for special education services, and more students are receiving more of their special education and related services in general education classrooms. For example, between 1987-1988 and 1998-1999, there was a 35 percent increase in the number of students aged 6-21 served under the IDEA. Furthermore, 46 percent of all of these students spend less than 20 percent of their instructional time outside general education classrooms (U.S. Department of Education, 2000). For almost three decades, however, the basic tenets of the law covering the specific eligibility categories and criteria have remained virtually unchanged.

The country has also become increasingly diverse, changing the mix of children by race, ethnicity, and primary language in many school districts.

In 1950, 86 percent of the K-12 population was white. By 2000, that proportion dropped to 65 percent while the proportion of Hispanic students grew from 2 to 15 percent (U.S. Bureau of the Census, 1950, 2000). Furthermore, according to a 1995 Census Bureau report, 31 percent of minority students have difficulty speaking English.

At the time of the earlier report, the controversy surrounding overrepresentation focused almost exclusively on the category of mental retardation—and more specifically on the milder cases of "educable mentally retarded." In fact, the earlier NRC report is devoted almost exclusively to the mental retardation category (NRC, 1982). Since publication of that report, there has been a dramatic reduction in the rate at which children are classified by the public schools as mentally retarded (MacMillan et al., 1996d). In many states the label "mentally retarded" is being reserved for children with only the most patent disabilities. Most children receiving services are currently labeled "learning disabled," a category that has in recent years accounted for over 50 percent of all children served under IDEA (and over 5 percent of all children in the total school population). Moreover, attention has also shifted to the emotionally disturbed category, as surveys have noted a disproportionate enrollment of black students in that category.

This committee, unlike its predecessor, has been asked by the U.S. Department of Education's Office for Civil Rights to broaden its charge to consider the representation of minority children in gifted and talented programs. For students identified as gifted and talented, an almost inverse relationship to special education is observed, with minority student groups who are overrepresented in programs for those with disabilities being underrepresented in gifted and talented programs. The issues are clearly parallel in many respects. The committee agreed to take on this expanded charge with the understanding that the analysis would be far more limited in this area. In some part, the limitation was one of resources. Perhaps more importantly, however, the field of gifted education has been given far less attention than has the field of special education. Support for research on interventions for students with disabilities has not been matched in the field of gifted and talented education. Nor is there a parallel to federal law protecting children with disabilities. As a result, data collection and monitoring have been more limited. The research base on which the committee could draw was therefore a meager one. We accepted the expanded charge, however, because the issues overlap in many respects, and drawing the parallels can strengthen understanding of both arenas.

Paradox of Special Education

Like the earlier committee, we recognize the paradox inherent in a charge that posits disproportionate placement of minority students in special education as a problem. The same program that can separate disadvantaged students from their peers, distinguish them with a stigmatizing label, and subject them to a curriculum of low expectations can also provide additional resources, supports, and services without which they cannot benefit from education. Like the previous committee, we conclude that disproportionality in eligibility for special education many not be problematic when the effect is to enhance opportunity to learn and provide access to high-quality curriculum and instruction. However, disproportionality is a problem when it stigmatizes or otherwise identifies a student as inferior, results in lowered expectations, and leads to poor educational outcomes such as dropping out, failure to receive a meaningful diploma, or diminished chances of moving to productive postschool endeavors.

We also acknowledge that the problem confronted by the earlier NRC committee persists despite almost 20 years of public scrutiny and discussion. Nonetheless, we recognize that changes in understanding of how children learn as well as of effective special education assessment and instructional practices have increased and deserve reexamination. In addition, our view is that the questions that might be asked about special education identification are relevant to those pertaining to placement in gifted and talented programs.

Approach to the Charge

The data, which are discussed in more detail in Chapter 2, suggest that there is in fact disproportion in the representation of some racial/ethnic groups in the three special education categories of mental retardation, learning disabilities, and emotional disturbance, although for learning disabilities the proportions are still in flux. There is substantial disproportion by race in the assignment to gifted and talented programs as well. However, the data have no straightforward interpretation. In view of the profound developmental impact of adverse life circumstances on racial and ethnic groups in U.S. society, proportional representation of groups of children needing services might be inequitable. Without a measure of true incidence of special needs or giftedness, we cannot know whether there are too many or too few students in any racial/ethnic group assigned to any of the categories. Nor in the case of special education do the data indicate whether disproportion is a problem. As noted above, special education placement brings additional resources and individual attention to a student's needs that are potentially beneficial, at the same time that it potentially brings stigma, separation from peers, and other adverse effects. From the committee's perspective, it is problematic when a child does not receive needed services as well as when a child is inappropriately placed in special education or passed over for placement in gifted and talented programs. We therefore set out to understand why current placement patterns exist and how the outcomes for minority students might be improved.

To address our charge, the committee asked four questions:

1. Is there reason to believe that there is currently a higher incidence of special needs or giftedness among some racial/ethnic groups? Specifically, are there biological and social or contextual contributors to early development that differ by race or ethnic group?

2. Does schooling independently contribute to the incidence of special needs or giftedness among students in different racial/ethnic groups through the opportunities that it provides?

3. Does the current referral and assessment process reliably identify students with special needs and gifts? In particular, is there reason to believe that the current process is biased in terms of race or ethnicity?

4. Is placement in special or gifted and talented education a benefit or a risk? Does the outcome differ by racial/ethnic group?

To structure our deliberations, the committee adopted a conceptual framework that reflects the complexity of the issues pertinent to the identification of any child as an atypical learner. We recognize that designation of a child as having a disability or a gift is in part the result of what happens in general education. We therefore first sought to revisit how special education and gifted and talented programs have evolved within the larger public education context.

INTERSECTION OF GENERAL AND SPECIALIZED EDUCATION

The development of special education and gifted and talented programs in public schools corresponded to the establishment of compulsory attendance laws and the ideology of education as the central remedy for social and economic opportunity (Cohen, 1970). Coinciding with the influx of immigrants at the beginning of the 20th century, this philosophy resulted in a flood of students who differed ethnically, culturally, and linguistically.

However, with the initiation of universal public education, schools began to confront large numbers of children who were not succeeding in or conforming to the demands of general education classrooms. Cohen (1970) notes that many of these students were immigrants, notably central and southern non-Jewish Europeans. In response to schools' frustration and lack of understanding of how to cope with students exhibiting severe academic deficits as well as behavior problems (Hoffman, 1975), administrators began to develop educational alternatives, including ungraded classes.

Mental Retardation

The origins of disproportionate representation began with the classification of mental retardation, as we discuss further in Chapter 6. Prior to 1900, children with mental retardation were almost exclusively those with conditions of "severe" intellectual retardation associated with some biomedical conditions that resulted in central nervous system damage and inadequate functional levels in different contexts. Ungraded classes for children with significant learning difficulties predated the use of intelligence testing by more than 10 years (Hendrick and MacMillan, 1989). But increasingly the concept of mental retardation was broadened to include both cases of severe retardation with biological underpinnings and cases of milder mental retardation associated with poverty. In other words, there were qualitative differences in these two groups of mentally retarded individuals (Zigler, 1967). The expansion of the concept of mental retardation (see Clausen, 1967) during the first half of the 20th century resulted in ever-greater proportions of the general population being considered mentally retarded. At the same time, there was recognition that while there were no dramatic social class or racial differences in the prevalence of severe forms of mental retardation, low social class was highly implicated in the cases of mild retardation, which was estimated to account for 75 to 80 percent of all cases of mental retardation. The disproportionate numbers of some minority group families living in poverty, in turn, gave rise to the observation that certain minority group children were disproportionately represented in this group of mildly mentally retarded children (Robinson and Robinson, 1965).

Mackie (1969) reported that between 1948 and 1966 there was a 400 percent increase in the number of students identified as mentally retarded served in the public schools. By the time President Ford signed P.L. 94-142 into law in 1975, mild mental retardation had the highest count of any exceptional child diagnosis (Reschly, 1988a). Those working in the public schools, particularly in urban settings, were aware that a disproportionate number of poor and/or minority youngsters populated the burgeoning classes for educable mentally retarded (EMR) children. A number of forces would coalesce during the 1960s to bring the issue of overrepresentation of minority students in this category to the forefront. Publication of a highly influential article by Dunn (1968) noted the disproportionate enrollment of poor minority children in EMR programs, while questioning the benefits of such services and proposing a plan for changing the system. His position was joined by minority scholars (e.g., Johnson, 1969) who, in some cases, viewed the EMR programs as the public schools' means of excluding minority students from mainstream education.

Emotional Disturbance and Learning Disabilities

Like programs for mentally retarded children, school-based programs for children classified as emotionally disturbed also began with ungraded classes designed for truant, disobedient, and insubordinate children (Hoffman, 1975). Similarly, throughout the 20th century, the numbers of both school programs and residential psychiatric and clinical programs continued to grow and serve both students with clinically diagnosed emotional disorders and those for whom the initial ungraded classes were designed. Attempts to discriminate between "true" emotional disturbance and social maladjustment have marked the history of classification for emotional disturbance, but the distinction has not been supported by research (Forness and Knitzer, 1990).

The category of specific learning disabilities has been among the fastest growing and is as contentious in terms of diagnostic criteria as emotional disturbance. The term was coined in 1963 by Samuel Kirk to explain students who were experiencing significant academic difficulties and "developmental disorders [in a number of language areas]; that does not include sensory handicaps or mental retardation" (Kirk, 1963). Due to concerns voiced by Congress at the time of passage of P.L. 94-142 that the term was so broad as to potentially swell dramatically the numbers of students who would need special education, the definitional criteria require that the problems with academic achievement not be the result of visual, hearing, or motor impairments, mental retardation, emotional disturbance, or environmental, cultural, or economic disadvantage (34 C.F.R. §300.541(b) 1999).

Gifted and Talented Programs

The history of differentiated treatment of students at the high end of the achievement distribution also stretches back to the turn of the century. As the influx of immigrants and compulsory education laws summoned large numbers of children into the schools in the early 20th century, accelerated programs were "welcomed wholeheartedly as a policy by school administrators seeking to bring efficiency to their overpopulated schools" (Resnick and Goodman, 1994:113).

The federal government has no legal requirements concerning gifted students analogous to those for students with disabilities. As a result, most gifted children do not have a legal entitlement to an ability-appropriate education (Heim, 1998; Bittick, 1995; Marquardt and Karnes, 1989).

Among the states, definitions of giftedness and commitments to publicly funded special programs for gifted students vary widely (Zirkel and Stevens, 1986). Although some states have specific requirements for gifted education, most merely recommend offering such education, leaving the choice and funding up to local districts (Bittick, 1995).

For example, in Pennsylvania and Connecticut, gifted students are entitled to some of the same legal protections as students with disabilities under state special education laws (Marquardt and Karnes, 1996). In Pennsylvania, state courts have found that the state's special education statutes protect gifted and talented students as well as students with disabilities and that these protections include the right to appropriate individualized education and individualized education programs. However, these courts also determined that schools do not have to provide services that are not already available in their districts (Marquardt and Karnes, 1996). In Connecticut, state courts found that services to gifted students are discretionary on the part of schools and that while the state's constitution created a fundamental right to education, for gifted students the right is one of access to education, not a right to a particular kind of instruction (Marquardt and Karnes, 1996; Padula, 1997). These types of provisions mean that gifted and talented students in effect have only a few, if any, of the legal protections afforded to students with disabilities and that the protections that do exist are not available in all states.

The earliest federal legislation pertaining to gifted and talented students called for a study, which resulted in the first federal definition of giftedness establishing broad, general, and overlapping categories (P.L. 91-230). It provided the guideline that one could expect 3 to 5 percent of the population to be gifted. At that time, the task force that produced the "Marland Report" (U.S. Department of Health, Education, and Welfare, 1972) studied services to gifted and talented students in the United States estimated that only 3 to 5 percent of all gifted students were receiving any services at all. As an outgrowth of the Marland report, in 1976 Congress established the Office of Gifted and Talented in the U.S. Office of Education with authority to fund special projects to develop professional expertise and programs.

The limited funding for these programs was eliminated with the institution of block grants, and no federal money was allocated to gifted students again until the passage of the Jacob K. Javits Gifted and Talented Students Education Act in 1988. While it has been documented that the number of gifted programs and level of support for programs declined during that period (Purcell, 1994), no systematic national data were collected on the numbers or percentage of students identified or served. The federal report *National Excellence* (U.S Department of Education, 1993) documented the wide variation by state in percentages of gifted students identified. In 4 states more than 10 percent of their students were identified as gifted and talented, while in 21 states fewer than 5 percent were identified. In 1988 only 65 percent of public schools at the middle school/junior high level reported some opportunity for gifted and talented 8th graders (National Center for Education Statistics, 1998). Passage of the very modestly funded Javits Act (just under $10 million) was distinguished from the earlier funding by short-term support for demonstration projects on the identification of gifted students from populations of students traditionally underserved in gifted programs: students who are economically disadvantaged, students who speak limited English, young gifted children, and children with disabilities.

Interrelationship of General and Specialized Education

As this brief history suggests, who is classified as disabled or gifted at a point in time is in part a function of the diversity of students and the issues that diversity poses for general education. But it is also a function of social policy, the scientific and philosophical understandings that guide it and the resource allocation that is determined by it. For special education, entitlement to additional resources, specialized personnel and services, as well as unique civil rights protections, is dependent on an individual classification of disability. While federal law does not require the use of particular disability categorizations, the establishment of a recognized disability is a prerequisite for securing the entitlement. Thus, definitional criteria and assessment procedures become critical elements of special education. Yet, the line drawn between those who do and do not require special services is artificial and variable. Eli Bower, whose definition of emotional disturbance was partially incorporated into federal law, stated, "Definitions are usually clear and concise at the extremes of a condition . . . As one moves from the extreme . . . toward the mean, one reaches a point where the waters are sufficiently muddied to cause . . . problems. However where such definitions limit or prescribe who may or may not receive services, the definitional problem becomes significant for children, their families, and school systems" (Bower, 1982:55).

The historical concept of a student with a disability or of a gifted student suggests that the characteristics of concern are within the child—an individual or fixed-trait model of ability—and that the student with a disability or a gift is qualitatively different from peers. However, for the high-incidence disabilities with which we are concerned, as well as for giftedness, both of these propositions are called into question.

In terms of cognitive and behavioral competence, students fall along a continuum depicted in Figure 1-1 in shades of gray; there is no black-and-white distinction between those who have disabilities or gifts and those

Special Education	General Education	Gifted
	General education resources (including Title I, ESL, Sec 504, voc/tech)	
Special education resources		Gifted education resources
Higher standards	←	←
→		

Severely Disabled   *Highly Gifted*

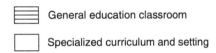 General education classroom

Specialized curriculum and setting

FIGURE 1-1 Student characteristics and school services and settings.

who do not. At the far ends of the continuum there is little dispute about a child's need for something different—for example, children who are severely mentally retarded, severely dyslexic, who have pronounced behavioral disorders, or whose cognitive function is years beyond that of peers. In Figure 1-1 these students fall at the far ends of the continuum where specialized curricula and instruction are required. Without special supports, placement of these children in a general education classroom is clearly inappropriate, and even with supports a separate educational environment may be required. But as one moves away from the extremes, where the line should be drawn between students who do and do not require special supports is unclear. A variety of forces push on the lines from opposing directions. As standards for students' performance rise, more students will appear to need special supports. As resources for remedial education or for students with limited English proficiency increase, the number of students whose needs can be addressed in the general education context applies an opposing force on that line.

While a line is drawn between those who do and do not receive special or gifted services, there is substantial variation in the type of service received. Placement in special education can occur even when a child requires only accommodations in the general education setting to learn the required curriculum. These accommodations can include increasing time and opportunity through multiple presentations, more intensive instruction, or more structured learning environments. Some students may need to learn certain meta-cognitive strategies. Other students may need more modifications and changes in the curriculum or entirely different sets of programs and services. In any event, the primary components of education are designed to aid the child in accessing and progressing in general education. The services may require additional personnel or specialized training, smaller groups, or specific settings that general educators are unable or unaccustomed to providing. For gifted students, accommodations in the classroom are not mandated by law and will occur at the teacher's discretion.

Figure 1-1 depicts the various settings in which services are provided. Like the line between general and special or gifted education, the line between those served in general education classrooms, and those served in separate settings speaks to the social policy and resource allocation at a point in time. For any individual student, the requirement for specialized supports and services can vary by age and by subject matter. It can even be teacher specific. The degree of diversity that can be accommodated in an individual classroom varies and represents an interaction between what the child brings to the learning environment and the characteristics of that environment.

CONCEPTUAL FRAMEWORK

The identification for special education or gifted and talented programs that we set out to understand has at its core the phenomenon of individual student achievement. We have argued that where along the continuum of achievement the lines are drawn for specialized education is artificial and variable. Perhaps of greater concern, however, are factors that affect where a student falls along the continuum. For students having difficulty in school who do not have a medically diagnosed disability, key aspects of the context of schooling itself, including administrative, curricular/instructional, and interpersonal factors, may contribute to their identification as having a disability and may contribute to the disproportionately high or low placements of minorities. The complexity of issues of culture and context in schools makes it nearly impossible to tease out the precise variables that affect patterns of special education placement. In a parallel vein, the child who may ultimately exhibit exceptionally high performance is a product of the interactions of those same variables of school context and interpersonal factors.

The extent to which the ability or behavior of concern in school performance is an intrinsic characteristic of the child or a consequence of the child's context is difficult to determine. The steady rise in IQ scores of about 3 points per decade—well publicized as the "Flynn effect" (Flynn, 1984, 1987)—has presented a significant challenge to those who argue for a fixed-trait model of intelligence (Neisser, 1998). The malleability of measured IQ scores with early intervention programs also suggests a powerful influence of environment on cognitive performance.

We attempt to capture relevant elements of the complexity that lies behind student achievement in Figure 1-2. What the child brings to the teaching-learning interaction is certainly influenced by individual biological traits or genetic endowment, as well as environmental and health influences on the child's biology. But it is also influenced by the child's family context, including the level of income and education of the parents and the family and community cultural environment.

As Figure 1-2 suggests, a student's achievement is the product of an instructional process and set of interactions that directly involve the teacher. Teachers differ in the individual characteristics (ability and temperament) they bring to the classroom just as students do. Teacher education and certification and several years of experience in the classroom have been demonstrated to positively influence student achievement (National Center for Education Statistics, 2001). The teacher's ability to manage the classroom has been shown to affect student achievement and behavior as well (Betts and Shkolnik, 1999; Levine and Ornstein, 1989; Martens and Kelly, 1993; Pierce, 1994; Wang et al., 1994). Other characteristics, such as the teacher's familiarity with students of various cultural backgrounds, may have an influence on teacher effectiveness with particular subgroups of children.

Finally, the classroom environment itself exerts an influence on individual student achievement. Salient features of the classroom include the size (number of students), the diversity of the student body including the cognitive and behavioral development of peers, the curriculum that the teacher is assigned or chooses, the materials and resources she or he has available to work with, and the other support personnel, such as school psychologists, administrators, and special education teachers, on whom she or he may rely for support.

In our effort to understand minority disproportion in special and gifted education, then, the committee set out to understand each of the three arenas that contribute to achievement. The domains of policy that we considered central to the task of addressing disproportion included not only those that define special and gifted education, but also those that affect the early developmental trajectories of children, the quality of teaching to which children are exposed, and the classroom environments in which children must learn. Our perspective is one in which special education and gifted education are viewed as integral parts of the general education system, and addressing disproportion in special and gifted education will require addressing the entire educational system.

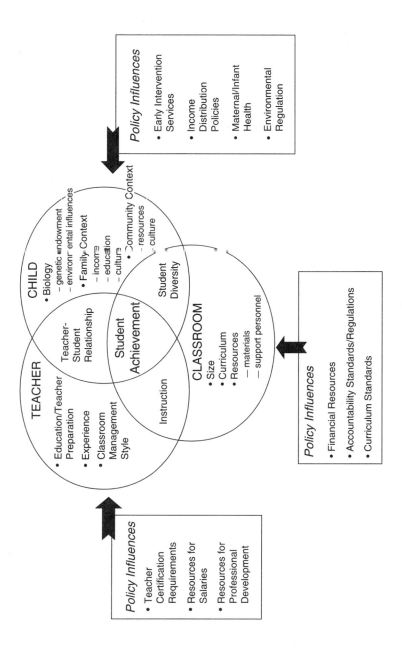

FIGURE 1-2 Contextual model of student achievement.

THE CURRENT EDUCATION CONTEXT

As noted earlier, the issues addressed by this committee are much like those confronted by the NRC panel in 1979; however, much has changed in public education in the intervening two decades. Medical advances mean that more children are living with medical conditions that can cause significant barriers to school achievement (Berman et al., 2001). The biological challenges brought by children to the classroom are thus different than they were two decades ago.

The past 20 years have brought considerable demographic and economic changes. As noted earlier in this chapter, the nation continues to become more ethnically diverse, changing the mix of children by race, ethnicity, and primary language in many school districts. Wealth and economic opportunities have increased for many, but disparities by race persist. Between 1980 and 1997, poverty levels among white, black, and Hispanic school-age children remained relatively constant. However, while the proportion of white students living in poverty hovered around 15 percent, the rates for Hispanic children were between 35 and 40 percent and for black children, rates varied between slightly below 40 and 45 percent (Lloyd et al., 2001).

Minority and poor children are increasingly concentrated in urban areas in which schools were constructed decades earlier and are poorly maintained and inadequately staffed by educators who are often poorly qualified. These children live in urban areas "characterized by a set of problems so severe that some see them as threatening the long-term viability of American society" (NRC, 1999a). Blacks and Hispanics are especially likely to live in neighborhoods where educational and economic opportunities are the most limited and where these problems are worsening, rather than improving with the nation's economic robustness (NRC, 1999a; Lloyd et al., 2001). The economic context affects the environmental influences on a child's development, and where poverty is concentrated, it affects the classroom influences as well.

Capacity of Educational Personnel

As Figure 1-2 suggests, teachers play a key role in student achievement. One of the greatest future challenges facing the effort to obtain appropriate educational opportunities for children in the nation's schools will be an unprecedented demand for new teachers to teach an increasingly pluralistic student population (Darling-Hammond, 1997; National Commission on Teaching and America's Future, 1996; Melnick and Pullin, 2000). There are 3.22 million teachers currently working in the nation's schools (Gerald and Hussar, 2000). But it is estimated that more than 2 million new teachers will be needed in the first decade of the 21st century (National Center for Education Statistics, 2001).

There is currently a severe shortage of special educators and related personnel (Council for Exceptional Children, 2001). Nearly 98 percent of public schools currently report a shortage of special education teachers (Boyer, 2000). According to the Bureau of Labor Statistics, employment of special education teachers is expected to increase faster than the average for all occupations through 2008. The Department of Labor attributes this employment growth to the increase in the enrollment of students with disabilities, legislation pertaining to the education and employment of people with disabilities, and education reform movements (National Clearinghouse for Professions in Special Education, 2001).

Changing Education Policies

The dividing lines between general education and special or gifted education, as we argue above, reflect the conditions of the entire educational system at any point in time. In the past two decades, several trends in public policy have exerted pressure on those lines, sometimes in competing directions. One of the more powerful influences is the political pressure for greater accountability and productivity in schools. While public commitment to the importance of elementary and secondary education as a social and economic equalizer remains strong, new strategies for achieving these goals have emerged.

Over the past two decades, there has been increasing emphasis on closing the achievement gaps between white and minority students and between the economically disadvantaged and the middle class. Previously, as Tyack and Cuban posited (1995), we tinkered with education reforms in a series of ongoing but unsuccessful efforts at achieving equality and excellence. Now there is increasing evidence that more substantial education reforms are needed, and many are being implemented. These include the imposition of high uniform standards and universal public accountability for student performance as well as increased flexibility and choice in how communities decide to educate students. New standards raise the bar for acceptable achievement and, all other things being equal, define the group of students who need special supports to meet expectations more broadly.

Accountability

While there was initially little consideration of the impact of standards-based reform on students with disabilities (see NRC, 1997a), recent efforts have begun to address this issue. Changes in Title 1 of the Elementary and Secondary Education Act and the 1997 amendments to IDEA include several new provisions that seek to align certain special education practices with a standards-driven reform model. These include the requirement that students with disabilities participate, with appropriate accommodations, in state and local tests of student achievement and public reporting of student scores. Changes to the IEP (individualized education program) process require greater attention to ensuring that individual students have access to the general education curriculum. But growing controversy over the depth of the nation's commitment to educating all children to high standards (NRC, 1999b) is even more salient for special education.

The Goals 2000: Educate America Act (20 U.S.C. § 5801 et seq.) and the Improving America's Schools Act of 1994 (20 U.S.C. § 6301 et seq.) require participating states to develop and implement state improvement plans that must include state content standards and state student performance standards for all students (20 U.S.C. § 5886 (c)(1)(A); see also 20 U.S.C. § 6311(b)(1)(A) (IASA)). The law explicitly defines "all students" as including students with disabilities (20 U.S.C. § 5802(a)(1); see also 20 U.S.C. § 6315(b)(2)(A)(i) (IASA)).

The new federal requirements were adopted as part of changes that also expanded the use of funds from the federal government's largest aid program for elementary and secondary schools: Title I (20 U.S.C. § 6315(b)(2)(A)(i)). Under Title I, a school must provide opportunities for "all" children, including those with disabilities, to meet the state's student performance standards (20 U.S.C. § 6315(b)(2)(A)(i); § 6315(c)(1)) and yearly assessments for accountability on how those standards are met. The requirements of the new law are designed to have several consequences for students with disabilities.

First, educational standards will be articulated and incorporated into special education. Second, there must be accountability for the education of students with disabilities. As in general education, the changes in special education law are motivated by the desire to improve educational outcomes of students with disabilities and to ensure that they have an equal opportunity to learn the same challenging and presumably essential and enduring content as all other students. Aligning special education with standards-driven reform offers an opportunity to refine the goals and functions of special education in contemporary public education but also exerts counterpressure on the special education/general education dividing line. On one hand, special education identification no longer exempts the school from accountability for an individual student's achievement; on the other hand, the demands of new content and performance standards can create conditions in classrooms that are less tolerant of children who are slower to learn.

While the above changes directed at raising achievement standards are likely to exert pressure on the line between general and special education in the direction of requiring additional supports for more students, some policy changes exert countervailing pressure. Proposed 2001 congressional reauthorizations of Title I and other sections of the Elementary and Secondary Education Act would affect the delivery of services to students at high risk of educational failure through the inclusion of new emphases on reading and limitations on bilingual education. The availability of additional resources for compensatory and bilingual education allows for the needs of more students to be addressed in the general education context, reducing pressure to expand the numbers of students requiring special education.

The impact of the standards movement and high-stakes testing on disproportionality in identification of and services for gifted students remains to be seen. The imposition of high-stakes testing may reduce the amount of time that is devoted to teaching high-end learning that will stimulate the talent and thinking of the gifted student, particularly in classes in which many students struggle to meet the standards.

PLAN OF THE REPORT

Our first task as a committee was to look at the data on students assigned to special education and gifted education by racial/ethnic groups to determine whether and to what extent disproportion exists. We present our analysis of the available data in Chapter 2. Part II of the report looks at early experience. To understand the observed disproportion, we address our first question in Chapter 3: "Is there reason to believe that there is currently a higher incidence of special needs or giftedness among some racial/ethnic groups?" We look at influences in the early childhood period that may affect the cognitive and behavioral development of children in ways that raise the probability of later special education placement—or lower the probability of being identified for gifted and talented programs. In Chapter 4 we look at early intervention programs designed to improve the developmental trajectory of disadvantaged children.

In Part III we look at the school experience, beginning with general education and then special and gifted education. In Chapter 5 we address our second question: "Does schooling independently contribute to the incidence of special needs or giftedness among students in different racial/ethnic groups through the opportunities that it provides?" The chapter spans issues of educational resources, potential bias toward minority students, and instructional and classroom management practices that may be helpful in placing at-risk students on a path to school success.

In the next three chapters we look at referral and assessment practices in special and gifted education. Here we address our third question: "Does the current referral and assessment process reliably identify students with special needs and gifts? In particular, is there reason to believe that the current process is biased in terms of race or ethnicity?" In Chapter 6 we focus on the legal context and the referral process. In Chapter 7 we discuss current assessment regulations and practices in the categories of learning disabilities, mental retardation, and emotional disturbance and assessment for gifted and talented students. In Chapter 8 we consider the major challenges to existing practices and alternative approaches to assessment.

In Part IV we look at improving student outcomes. In Chapter 9 we address our fourth questions: "Is placement in special or gifted and talented education a benefit or a risk? Does the outcome differ by racial/ethnic group?"

Throughout the report we present recommendations in context. Recommendations regarding data collection appear in Chapter 2, and those regarding early childhood intervention appear in Chapter 4. In Chapter 5 our recommendations focus on improving teacher quality, and in Chapter 8 we propose an alternative approach to special education identification, and research to support improved assessment and intervention in gifted and talented programs. Recommendations for additional research and development appear in Chapter 9.

The report covers a great deal of territory. In Chapter 10 we bring together the conclusions and recommendations as an integrated presentation of an approach to special and gifted education that begins early and focuses on continual efforts to identify and respond to children's needs as they arise. A central element of our proposal for change is the ongoing capacity building required to use the best of the existing knowledge base to support the achievement of children from all racial/ethnic groups, as well as continued research and development to extend the knowledge base in ways that are directly useful to educational practice.

2

Representation of Minority Students in Special and Gifted Education

Are minority children disproportionately represented in special and gifted education? On the surface, the question is straightforward. How "disproportion" is defined, however, determines whether the question can be answered. If the referent is the population of minority students, then one can simply compare the proportion identified with the proportion in the total student population. If, however, we are asking whether the number identified is in proportion to those whose achievement or behavior indicate a need for special supports, then the question is one for which no database currently exists. In this chapter, we compare the numbers of students of each race/ethnicity identified for special and gifted education with their representation in the student population. The reader should keep in mind, however, that these data cannot tell us about the appropriateness of assignment and, by themselves, they provide a very weak foundation for guiding public policy.

Some researchers have attempted to explain observed differences in placements by race/ethnicity using available data. Special education data at the district level have been analyzed, controlling for sociodemographic characteristics of the district, and conclusions have been drawn about the patterns that emerge. To understand differences in assignment to gifted programs, other data sets that provide information on socioeconomic characteristics of families have been correlated with high achievement data. We address the limitations of these data analyses before turning to conclusions and recommendations.

FEDERAL DATA SETS

Two federal agencies currently report data on enrollment of students in special education programs broken down by racial/ethnic group: the Office of Special Education Programs (OSEP) and the Office for Civil Rights (OCR), both in the U.S. Department of Education. OSEP has reported for over two decades to Congress on the implementation of Public Law 94-142 (and later, the Individuals with Disabilities Education Act [IDEA]), including data on the number of children served under the various disability categories. However, the child count data reported by OSEP were not broken down by racial/ethnic group until the last two reporting periods. OCR, in contrast, has consistently monitored minority representation, but only in the few disability categories with which it is concerned. Until 1994, these included mild mental retardation, emotional disturbance (ED), specific learning disabilities (LD), and speech and language impairments (SLI). Since that time, however, OCR has collected data on the broader category of mental retardation (MR), no longer differentiating "educable mental retardation" and "trainable mental retardation" (in earlier surveys) or among "mild mental retardation," "moderate mental retardation," and "severe mental retardation" (in the 1992 survey). In addition, in 1994 OCR discontinued monitoring of speech and language impairments and began monitoring enrollments in programs for gifted and talented students.

In federal reporting of data by race/ethnicity, five groups are specified: (1) American Indian/Alaskan Natives, (2) Asian/Pacific Islander, (3) Hispanics, (4) blacks, and (5) non-Hispanic whites. Using the OSEP and OCR datasets one is unable to examine rates for subgroups, such as Puerto Ricans, Cubans, or Mexican Americans as these are all aggregated into a single Hispanic category. And a student can be classified in only one group; "mixed race" is not an option.

Disability Categories of Concern in This Report

Concern about overrepresentation of certain minority group children in special education has focused almost exclusively on a few disability categories. In the earlier NRC report (National Research Council, 1982) the focus was exclusively on children classified as mildly mentally retarded (MMR), the category at issue in litigation challenging the fairness of intelligence testing as the "reason" behind disproportionately high enrollments of black and Hispanic children in special education programs (Reschly, 1988a). In the years since that report, the focus has broadened to include LD and ED. Concern has been raised as well over the underrepresentation of children from these same minority groups in programs for the gifted and talented. The categories MMR, LD, ED, and gifted and talented are sometimes referred to as the "judgmental" categories because the children so classified typically do not exhibit readily observable distinguishing features, and the authoritative diagnosis of medical professionals, which is common in assessment of many of the low-incidence disabilities, is absent. Categories like visual or auditory impairment may also involve judgment in more marginal cases regarding when the impairment becomes a disability, but the diagnosis of impairment by medical professionals is not called into question.

The potential importance of judgment is suggested in the wide variation in placement rates in the judgemental categories across states—variation that is substantially greater than in the low-incidence disability categories. MacMillan and Reschly (1998) found that the ranges of identification rates across states for LD, SLI, MR, and ED were considerable, far greater than one would expect for a given disability. For example, Massachusetts identified 3 times as many children as LD than did Georgia; New Jersey identified 3 times as many children with SLI than did Georgia; Alabama identified 10 times as many children with MR as did New Jersey; and Connecticut identified 41 times as many children with ED as did Mississippi.

Inadequacy of Datasets

At present, a considerable amount is spent on the data collection efforts of OSEP and OCR, yet the data reported are inadequate for informing policy. While the most fundamental limitation is the absence of data on incidence with which to compare placement rates, the placement numbers by race are themselves problematic. Neither disability status nor ethnicity is measured very precisely (MacMillan and Reschly, 1998).

Race/Ethnicity. The imprecision inherent in specifying a child's race/ethnicity in these datasets is apparent when one considers that the data are aggregated from the school building to the district to the state to the national level in the OSEP process. For OCR, race/ethnicity is recorded from district records. Any variation in practices for determining race/ethnicity at the school building or district level is obscured when considering state or national figures. One and only one box is checked on the school form, and the person making the decision varies from school district personnel to the child's parent. The Office of Management and Budget's Statistical Directive 15 urges that racial and ethnic categories should not be interpreted as scientific or anthropological in nature—yet the datasets summarized here are used in just this way (Hodgkinson, 1995). Phinney (1996) explains that "even within an ethnic group whose members share a relatively precise ethnic label there is tremendous heterogeneity" (p. 919). Variability in social class, income, education, generation of immigration, family structure, and geographical region is not captured by the racial/ethnic designation. Phinney goes on to note that "ethnicity cannot be treated like an independent variable that explains an outcome" (p. 924), yet that is precisely what is sought when one examines the bivariate relationship between ethnicity and disability status. In the case of biracial children, the confound is even more severe, as there has not been a "mixed" box for parents to check and a child is forced into one of the extant boxes, suggesting that "everyone in the category belongs completely in that box" (Hodgkinson, 1995:175).

Disability Status. In both the OSEP and OCR surveys, the disability status (i.e., the specific disability category) of a child is, in the vast majority of cases, taken directly from school records—that is, the children are "school identified" as qualifying for special education by virtue of qualifying for a specific disability category. In traditional epidemiological studies, the concepts of *prevalence* (total number of cases at a given point in time) and *incidence* (number of new cases) are employed. The figures reported in the surveys considered here are assumed to be *prevalence* figures; however, there is a lack of precision in the school's ability to detect "true" cases of disability, particularly in the judgmental categories. Stated differently, we do not know what the true prevalence of these conditions would be if specific criteria were applied rigorously in screening the population of children.

As a result, there are many *false positives* and *false negatives* in identification, introducing error of an unknown size (but known to be substantial, particularly in the LD area) (see Gottlieb et al., 1994; MacMillan et al., 1998a; Shaywitz et al., 1990; Shepard et al., 1983). Comparability across states is difficult, in part, because the states have differing criteria for eligibility. Mercer et al. (1996) surveyed state criteria for defining LD particularly in the method for calculating discrepancy (i.e., standard score discrepancy vs. regressed discrepancy) and the magnitude of the aptitude-achievement discrepancy (e.g., 1 SD, 1.5 SDs) required. Frankenberger and Fronzaglio (1991) and Denning et al. (2000) analyzed state guidelines for defining mental retardation and again reported considerable variability. On the criterion of intellectual level, Denning et al. (2000) reported that 13 states have no IQ cutoff score, Ohio and Pennsylvania use IQ 80 as the cutoff score, while most set the IQ cutoff score at IQ 70 or −2 SDs.

Giftedness. The issues plaguing the assignment of disability status also contaminate the collection of data on children identified as gifted and talented. The lack of national legislation governing the definition of, or services for, gifted and talented students has left each state with the prerogative of defining the construct. Even the definition suggested by the federal government and adopted by many states includes a wide variety of categories, which in some cases overlap and in others are presumably independent. For example, one would expect some overlap between creativity and exceptional performance in the arts, yet there is no reason to expect the same degree of overlap between those who are gifted in a specific academic area (e.g., mathematics) and those gifted in the domain of leadership. The definitions at the federal level and most state levels are also complicated by the phrases "children and youth with outstanding talent who *perform* or *show the potential for performing*" and "when compared with others of their age, experience or environment" (U.S. Department of Education, 1993:26, italics added), leaving the interpretation of potential open and making the category of giftedness relative to local school or school system populations. That relativity is rational regarding provision of services: a given student may need special services in a gifted program in a school in which the curriculum is not adequately challenging, but not in a school with a more challenging general curriculum. But a consequence of relativity is that the data on assignment to gifted and talented programs are far more difficult to interpret.

Denominators. OSEP requires states to report on the number of children in disability categories by age and (recently) race/ethnicity. They do not collect data on the total number of students (with and without a disability label) by age and race/ethnicity, however. The National Center for Education Statistics (NCES) collects data on student enrollment by race and grade, but not by age. The NCES data can be roughly, but not precisely, paired with the OSEP data. Of particular concern, children who are 6 years old may be in either kindergarten or first grade. They are not likely, however, to be in preschool. NCES provides numbers for preschool-12 enrollment, but these numbers are certainly too high. Subtracting out the preschool children would improve the count, but many states do not provide separate data for preschool, and the lack of uniformity in state counts of preschool children make these numbers hard to estimate reliably.

State-to-State Variations

The National Association of State Directors of Special Education (1999) reported on a survey of state practices in reporting child count data to the U.S. secretary of education. Findings of the survey illustrate variations and anomalies across states that potentially challenge the reliability and validity of the data reported. Variations in practices in the local education agencies similarly compromise the quality of the data reported to OCR, which gathers data at the district, rather than state, level. Among their findings were that some states use categories of disability that differ from the federal categories.

The most common difference was for the category of mental retardation. For example, alternative terms are used in several states: significant limited intellectual capacity in Colorado, cognitive delay in Montana, intellectual disabilities in Utah, and cognitively disabled in Wisconsin. Certain states that do not use one of the federal disability categories report zero children in their child count reports: West Virginia and Wisconsin do not use multiple disabilities, and Colorado does not use other health impaired. In Arizona, the category deaf-blind is not used: local education agencies report these cases in the category of multiple disabilities, while cases of deaf-blind children reported in the Arizona count are students identified as deaf-blind by the Arizona School for the Deaf-Blind. Local education agencies in Montana report *all* disabilities that each student is considered to have and the state education agency, in turn, assigns a single federal disability category to each child.

The survey also sought to explain "extreme" counts—that is, child counts for a specific disability or age group that were significantly higher or lower than the national average. Several states pointed to extreme poverty as contributing to high rates of mental retardation, multiple disabilities, and speech and language impairments. Aggressive and successful child find procedures were cited by directors in Maine, Rhode Island, and West Virginia for higher rates. Low child counts in the ED category were attributed to insufficient personnel in Arkansas and Mississippi, while these same states indicated that the stigma associated with the ED label is a contributor to lower counts.

States having noncategorical programs vary in how they report child count data. In Pennsylvania and Washington, a child is determined eligible under IDEA and then a disability category is assigned. In Iowa and Massachusetts, "formulas" are used to convert noncategorical counts to disability counts. "In Iowa, percentages for each federal disability category are based on incidence rates from 1986, 87, and 88, before the state became categorical. Massachusetts uses a formula based on disability category estimates from 98 percent of the LEAs, that was updated in 1992" (National Association of State Directors of Special Education, 1999:6).

For giftedness, the various states have adopted selected parts of the federal definition or created their own. Coleman and Gallagher (1992) report that 49 states include intelligence or general intellectual ability and achievement in their definitions, 40 states include creativity, 34 states include artistic ability, 28 states incorporate leadership ability, 15 states embrace critical thinking (not included in the federal definition), 26 establish leadership as a domain of giftedness, and 10 states include psychomotor abilities, although that category was dropped from the federal definition in 1978.

As might be expected, the states have widely varying laws, rules, guidelines, and regulations regarding the identification of gifted students. Some states, for example California, provide standards that are very general and might be considered only as principles to be followed. The California regulations include statements such as "methods and techniques for identification shall generate information as to a pupil's capacities and needs" (Passow and Rudnitski, 1993). Some states specify instruments to be used, while others go further to define scores required using specific instruments (such as a full-scale score of 130 on the Wechsler scales, 132 on the Stanford-Binet, or 130 on the Kaufman Assessment Battery for Children. Furthermore, some states have specified differing procedures or instruments to be used in identifying students who are considered "disadvantaged—'economically, culturally, and/or environmentally'" (Passow and Rudnitski, 1993). In the identification of a child as gifted and talented, there are not 50 differing approaches, but innumerable ones.

Whether for special or for gifted education, there are clearly sufficient variations and anomalies across states to urge extreme caution in interpreting data

Other Factors Compromising Interpretation of Data

A further consideration is that prior to 1997 states could be reimbursed for "up to 12 percent" of their school population under IDEA. While the precise influence of this cutoff point is unknown, it could have served to truncate identification in earlier years once the cap was approached. The quality of the data is potentially further compromised by variability in who reports the data at the local district. Differences in qualifications and familiarity with the district programs (a clerk at the district office vs. the director of special education for the district) could influence the accuracy of the data submitted.

In terms of state funding of services for gifted and talented students, Passow and Rudnitski (1993) have documented considerable diversity and complexity. Some services are tied to special education appropriations. In Alabama, funding "shall not exceed the average per pupil appropriation for all exceptional children in each school district, including allowances for teacher units, transportation, and all other aid for exceptional children (Passow and Rudnitski, 1993:64). Florida's funding formulas for gifted students are tied to "severity" of the giftedness and hence level of placement of the child, with those in homogeneous classrooms qualifying for greater funding. Other states base funding on a percentage of average daily attendance equivalency (e.g., "an amount not to exceed $100 per K-12 pupil for up to 5 percent of the district's or consortium's K-12 membership"). Some states reimburse only for the salary and benefits of the instructional personnel who provide services exclusively to gifted and talented students. In combination, these influences may have greater influence on the total number of students identified as gifted and talented than on the educational needs of students.

Efforts to collect reliable and valid data on gifted and talented enrollments have been stymied in various ways. Since federal efforts are limited to OCR data collection, the organization of state directors of gifted programs has attempted to collect data by surveying its membership. In their latest survey, only 43 states responded and data from many of the other states were incomplete. The conclusion of this group is that it is "quite apparent that complete, reliable data about gifted student education within states are not readily available" and "comprehensive information about gifted education throughout the United States is most difficult to produce" (Council of State Directors of Programs for the Gifted, 1999:9).

REVIEW OF THE DATA

Despite the limitations of the data, they are useful in some important respects. They provide an indicator of school placement rates in various categories of disability over time. While any individual figure may be imprecise, consistent patterns over time are informative. The numbers may indicate more about the variation in state and local practice than about differences in student populations, but this variation is of interest for policy monitoring. Comparison of placement rates for different racial/ethnic groups can appear quite different in magnitude when different indices are used to present identical data. One can report that in 1998 1.45 percent of black students, and 0.91 percent of white students were labeled ED, or one can report that black students were 17 percent of the student population, but 27 percent of the ED population. The underlying numbers are the same, but the impression is somewhat different. We present the OCR and OSEP data using three different indices, each of which communicates disproportion somewhat differently.

Calculations

Risk Index

The risk index (RI) is calculated by dividing the number of students in a given racial or ethnic category (e.g., Hispanic) served in a given disability category (e.g., LD) by the total enrollment for that racial or ethnic group in the school population. Hence, the "risk index" reveals the percentage of all students of a given racial/ethnic group identified in a given disability category. The 1998 risk index of 6.02 for white students in the LD category reveals that just over 6 percent of all white students were labeled LD.

Odds Ratio

The odds ratio (OR) divides the risk index of one racial/ethnic group (e.g., black) by the risk index of another racial/ethnic group (e.g., white) and thereby provides a comparative index of risk. All odds ratios reported here are relative to white students. If the risk index is identical for a particular minority group and white students, the odds ratio will equal 1.0. Odds ratios greater than 1.0 indicate that the minority group students are at greater risk for identification, while odds ratios of less than 1.0 indicate that they are less at risk.

The 1998 LD odds ratio for American Indian/Alaskan Natives is 1.24, revealing that they have a 24 percent greater likelihood of being assigned to LD than whites. This is obtained by dividing the American Indian/Alaskan Native risk index (7.45) by the white risk index (6.02). It should be noted, however, that the odds ratio does not reveal the absolute rate at which children from a given racial/ethnic group are identified by the schools in various disability categories.

Composition Index

The composition index (CI) is calculated by dividing the number of students of a given racial or ethnic group enrolled in a particular disability category by the total number of students (summed across all five racial/ethnic groups) enrolled in that same disability category. It therefore reflects the proportion of all children served under a given disability category who are members of a given racial/ethnic group. Note that the sum of composition indices for the five racial/ethnic groups will total 100 percent. The composition index does not control for the baseline enrollment of a given racial/ethnic group. Therefore, knowing that 53 percent of all MR students in a given state are white is not immediately interpretable without knowing the percentage of the total enrollment that is white. If, in a hypothetical state, whites constituted 85 percent of the total enrollment of students, one might conclude that whites are underrepresented in the MR category. Conversely, if whites constituted only 15 percent of the total enrollment, a very different conclusion would be warranted. We introduce this term because a variation of the composition index was used extensively in court cases concerned with overrepresentation. In *Larry P. v. Riles* (1972, 1974, 1979, 1984, 1986), for example, the plaintiffs presented the following figures to document overrepresentation of black students in the mild MR category: whereas 25 percent of the total mild MR enrollments were black, black students constituted only 10 percent of the California school enrollments.

Organization of Our Review

In the following sections we summarize data from OCR and OSEP on the relative participation of students from the five racial/ethnic groups in the various disability categories. Because the two data-collection efforts are separate, we look at the indices from both. While there are some differences between them, the discrepancies are small: the two datasets tell a very similar story. We begin by considering the three categories monitored by both OCR and OSEP (MR, LD, and ED), then report on the gifted and talented data monitored by OCR but not by OSEP. Finally, we report on the remaining disability categories recognized under IDEA and monitored only by OSEP.

For each category, we first present data on risk indices and odds ratios for 1998, then we show patterns over time. The time trends rely on the OCR data, as OSEP has only recently required that child count data be broken out by racial/ethnic group.

Mental Retardation

Recent Surveys

The most recent survey data available from OCR are for 1998, and for OSEP, 1999. For comparison purposes, we use indices calculated from 1998 data from both sources. The 1998 OCR survey using national projections (see Table 2-1) reveals that black students are most at risk for identification as MR (RI = 2.64 percent) with American Indian/Alaskan Natives the next highest (RI = 1.28 percent), followed by whites (RI = 1.18 percent). Hispanic students are at considerably less risk (RI = 0.92 percent) with Asian/Pacific Islander lower still (RI = 0.64 percent). The same pattern is evident in the 1998 OSEP data, although the risk indices based on actual child counts vary slightly.

Comparing these rates for the four racial/ethnic groups with that of white students reveals that black students are more than twice as likely to be identified as mentally retarded (OCR OR = 2.24; OSEP OR = 2.35), with American Indian/Alaskan Natives being identified at about the same rate as whites (OCR OR = 1.09; OSEP OR = 1.07). Both Hispanics (OCR OR = 0.78; OSEP OR = 0.87) and Asian/Pacific Islander (OCR OR = 0.54; OSEP OR = 0.51) are considerably less at risk than are whites for identification as MR.

The composition index for the racial/ethnic groups suggests that whites constitute approximately 54 percent of the total MR enrollments (compared with 63 percent of the student population), while blacks account for 33 percent of the MR enrollments but only 17 percent of the student population.

TABLE 2-1 Indices of Placement for Mental Retardation by Race/
Ethnicity: 1998 OCR and OSEP Data

	Risk Index		Odds Ratio		Composition Index	
Characteristic	OCR	OSEP	OCR	OSEP	OCR	OSEP
American Indian/Alaskan Native	1.28	1.20	1.09	1.07	1.04	1.03
Asian/Pacific Islander	0.64	0.57	0.54	0.51	1.90	1.67
Black	2.64	2.63	2.24	2.35	33.04	33.51
Hispanic	0.92	0.98	0.78	0.87	10.04	10.89
White	1.18	1.12			53.97	52.89
Total	1.37	1.32			100.00	100.00

NOTES: OCR placement and membership data are taken from the Fall 1998 Elementary and
Secondary School Civil Rights Compliance Report, National Projections. OSEP data are taken
from the 1998-1999 Child Count, and the indices were calculated using total enrollment data
for K-12 from the U.S. Department of Education, National Center for Education Statistics,
Common Core of Data, School Universe Study, 1998-1999, compiled by Mark Glander,
National Education Data Resource Center.

Trends Over Time

Over the past 25 years, there has been a substantial reduction in the
rate at which students are classified as mentally retarded by the schools
(MacMillan et al., 1996c). Examination of OCR survey national projections over time for MR (Table 2-2) suggests that rates for black children
have consistently been higher than rates for other racial/ethnic groups.
From a high of over 4 percent of black children identified as MR in 1976,
the risk index shows a gradual decline until it reaches 2.23 percent in 1998.
These data are also displayed in Figure 2-1.

Extremely low risk is evidenced for Asian/Pacific Islander students
across surveys, staying very close to 0.50 percent. Rates for whites consistently fell between 1 and 1.3 percent. Slightly higher risk indices were
recorded for American Indian/Alaskan Native children; however, the index
never exceeded 2 percent for this group. For Hispanic students the identification rate has fallen, and since the 1992 survey it has been below 1
percent. In 1997 it was half the rate of 1974.

The trends in odds ratios in the bottom half of Table 2-2 provide
another description of the same story. The ratios for Asian/Pacific Islander
have been steady and relatively low—well under half the rate for white
students in all but one year. For American Indian/Alaskan Natives, one
notes a considerable decline in the odds ratios. In 1974, American Indian/
Alaskan Native students were more than half again as likely to be classified

TABLE 2-2 Risk Indices and Odds Ratios for Mental Retardation by
Race/Ethnicity: 1974-1998 OCR Data

	American Indian/ Alaskan Native	Asian/ Pacific Islander	Hispanic	Black	White	Total
Risk Index						
1974	1.94	0.45	1.50	3.72	1.19	1.58
1976	1.99	0.55	1.36	4.07	1.30	1.73
1978	1.93	0.52	1.21	3.84	1.26	1.65
1980	1.92	0.45	1.02	3.76	1.26	1.63
1984	1.63	0.49	1.42	3.48	1.22	1.59
1986	1.39	0.38	0.78	2.69	1.07	1.28
1988	1.25	0.45	1.43	3.00	1.01	1.34
1990	1.25	0.50	1.28	2.81	1.05	1.35
1992	1.48	0.48	0.82	2.46	1.15	1.30
1994	1.61	0.52	0.92	2.65	1.25	1.42
1997	1.32	0.49	0.74	2.52	1.13	1.29
1998	1.28	0.64	0.92	2.64	1.18	1.37
Odds Ratios						
1974	1.63	0.38	1.26	3.12		
1976	1.53	0.42	1.04	3.12		
1978	1.54	0.41	0.96	3.06		
1980	1.52	0.36	0.81	2.98		
1984	1.35	0.40	1.17	2.86		
1986	1.30	0.35	0.73	2.53		
1988	1.24	0.44	1.41	2.96		
1990	1.19	0.47	1.21	2.67		
1992	1.28	0.41	0.71	2.14		
1994	1.29	0.41	0.74	2.12		
1997	1.16	0.43	0.65	2.23		
1998	1.09	0.54	0.78	2.24		

NOTE: OCR placement and membership data are taken from the Fall 1998 Elementary and
Secondary School Civil Rights Compliance Report, National Projections.

as MR as were white students (OR = 1.63), but by 1998 there was a narrow
difference in the identification rates (OR = 1.09). Odds ratios for Hispanic
students have fluctuated somewhat from year to year, but over time the
ratio has fallen considerably. From an identification rate for Hispanics that
was a quarter higher than that for whites in 1974 (OR = 1.26), surveys
from 1992 to the most current reveal an identification rate that is approximately a quarter lower for Hispanics than for whites.

For black students, there has been a consistent pattern of higher rates of
identification than for whites. The magnitude of the difference has diminished over time, but it is still considerable (1998 OR = 2.24).

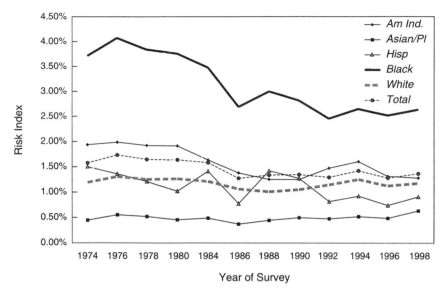

FIGURE 2-1 Risk indices for mental retardation: 1974-1998 OCR data.

Learning Disabilities

Recent Surveys

OCR survey data for 1998 reveal risk indices for all racial/ethnic groups that are dramatically higher for learning disabilities than those found for mental retardation. Asian/Pacific Islander have placement rates of 2.23 percent. Rates for all other racial/ethnic groups exceed 6 percent, and for American Indian/Alaskan Natives, the rate reached 7.45 percent (see Table 2-3). OSEP child count data for the same year track the OCR data very closely. Odds ratios, as expected, are low for Asian/Pacific Islander (0.37) and highest for American Indian/Alaskan Native (1.24). For Hispanics and blacks, they are close to 1.0.

Trends Over Time

The most significant pattern in the OCR national projections for the LD category is the dramatic ("epidemic") increase in the risk of children of all racial/ethnic groups except Asian/Pacific Islander. Table 2-4 shows summary data for national projections for LD, which are graphically displayed in Figure 2-2. The range for the non-Asian ethnic groups in 1974 was 1.03 to 1.60 percent. In 1998 the risk indices for the same four groups ranged from 6.02 percent to 7.45 percent.

TABLE 2-3 Indices of Placement for Learning Disabilities by Race/
Ethnicity: 1998 OCR and OSEP Data

Characteristic	Risk Index		Odds Ratio		Composition Index	
	OCR	OSEP	OCR	OSEP	OCR	OSEP
American Indian/Alaskan Native	7.45	7.30	1.24	1.20	1.38	1.37
Asian/Pacific Islander	2.23	2.25	0.37	0.37	1.51	1.43
Black	6.49	6.58	1.08	1.08	18.48	18.19
Hispanic	6.44	6.81	1.07	1.12	16.04	16.50
White	6.02	6.08			62.60	62.51
Total	6.02	6.07			100.00	100.00

NOTES: OCR placement and membership data are taken from the Fall 1998 Elementary and Secondary School Civil Rights Compliance Report, National Projections. OSEP data are taken from the 1998-1999 Child Count, and the indices were calculated using estimated K-12 total enrollment data from the U.S. Department of Education, National Center for Education Statistics, Common Core of Data, School Universe Study, 1998-1999, compiled by Mark Glander, National Education Data Resource Center.

Consistently higher risk indices are found for American Indian/Alaskan Native students in every survey, and their rate of increase parallels that found for black, Hispanic, and white students. Markedly lower risk indices are found for Asian/Pacific Islander students, and what increase in risk is shown is at a much lower rate than that seen for the other four racial/ethnic groups.

Odds ratios for classification as LD in Table 2-4 reveal a consistent pattern of somewhat higher rates of identification for American Indian/Alaskan Natives than for whites (OR between 1.15 and 1.58). For blacks and Hispanics, the ratio has fluctuated over time around 1.0. Since there is no significant overrepresentation of these two groups, the LD category has been of less concern in discussions of disproportionate representation. Yet the rate of increase in the risk indices indicates that *all* racial/ethnic groups have seen dramatic increases in the rate of identification as LD.

Emotional Disturbance

Recent Surveys

The 1998 OCR and OSEP data (see Table 2-5) reveal that children in all five racial/ethnic groups are less at risk for being identified as ED than for either MR or LD. Nevertheless, there is considerable variability in risk across racial/ethnic groups. Black students (OCR RI = 1.45 percent; OSEP RI = 1.56 percent) are at higher risk for ED identification than any other group. American Indian/Alaskan Natives and whites have rates close to 1

TABLE 2-4 Risk Indices and Odds Ratios for Learning Disabilities by Race/Ethnicity: 1974-1998 OCR Data

	American Indian/ Alaskan Native	Asian/ Pacific Islander	Hispanic	Black	White	Total
Risk Index						
1974	1.60	0.52	1.29	1.03	1.24	1.21
1976	3.18	0.98	2.32	1.86	2.05	2.04
1978	3.46	1.26	2.57	2.21	2.30	2.30
1980	4.05	1.43	3.22	3.14	3.20	5.93
1984	5.18	1.61	4.46	4.51	4.19	4.21
1986	5.68	1.56	4.31	4.43	4.29	4.25
1988	5.74	1.53	4.46	4.50	4.54	4.44
1990	6.04	1.60	4.68	4.95	4.97	4.83
1992	6.78	1.70	5.27	5.79	4.29	5.28
1994	7.28	2.01	5.68	5.67	5.66	5.55
1997	6.41	1.90	5.99	6.15	5.53	5.56
1998	7.45	2.23	6.44	6.49	6.02	6.02
Odds Ratio						
1974	1.29	0.42	1.04	0.84		
1976	1.55	0.48	1.13	0.90		
1978	1.51	0.55	1.12	0.96		
1980	1.77	0.45	1.01	0.98		
1984	1.24	0.39	1.07	1.08		
1986	1.32	0.36	1.00	1.03		
1988	1.27	0.34	0.98	0.99		
1990	1.22	0.32	0.94	1.00		
1992	1.58	0.40	1.23	1.35		
1994	1.29	0.36	1.00	1.00		
1997	1.16	0.34	1.08	1.11		
1998	1.24	0.37	1.07	1.08		

NOTE: OCR placement and membership data are taken from the Fall 1998 Elementary and Secondary School Civil Rights Compliance Report, National Projections.

percent. Hispanic children have considerably lower risk of ED placement (OCR RI: 0.55; OSEP RI: 0.68), and Asian/PacificIslander students have dramatically lower rates (OCR RI = 0.26; OSEP RI = 0.27) for this classification.

Odds ratios confirm the higher risk for black students (OCR and OSEP OR = 1.59), indicating they are half again as likely as white students to be classified as ED. As would be expected from the above data on risk, Asian/Pacific Islander are far less likely than whites (OCR OR = 0.29; OSEP OR = 0.27) to be classified as ED, and to a slightly lesser degree this is true for Hispanics (OCR OR = 0.60; OSEP OR = 0.69). The pattern for ED is similar to that for MR, though the magnitude of differences by race/ethnicity is not as great.

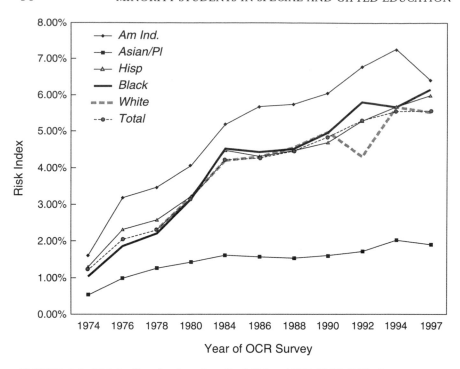

FIGURE 2-2 Risk indices for learning disabilities: 1974-1997 OCR data.

TABLE 2-5 Indices of Placement for Emotional Disturbance by Race/
Ethnicity: 1998 OCR and OSEP Data

Characteristic	Risk Index		Odds Ratio		Composition Index	
	OCR	OSEP	OCR	OSEP	OCR	OSEP
American Indian/Alaskan Native	1.03	1.00	1.12	1.02	1.23	1.14
Asian/Pacific Islander	0.26	0.27	0.29	0.27	1.16	1.04
Black	1.45	1.56	1.59	1.59	26.92	26.36
Hispanic	0.55	0.68	0.60	0.69	8.87	9.98
White	0.91	0.98			61.82	61.48
Total	0.93	1.00			100.00	100.00

NOTES: OCR placement and membership data are taken from the Fall 1998 Elementary and Secondary School Civil Rights Compliance Report, National Projections. OSEP data are taken from the 1998-1999 Child Count, and the indices were calculated using estimated K-12 total enrollment data from the U.S. Department of Education, National Center for Education Statistics, Common Core of Data, School Universe Study, 1998-1999, compiled by Mark Glander, National Education Data Resource Center.

Trends Over Time

For all five groups, the risk of being classified as ED has gradually increased over the years covered by the OCR survey (see Table 2-6 and Figure 2-3). At almost every data point, the rank order of risk is (from highest to lowest): black, American Indian/Alaskan Native, white, Hispanic, and Asian/Pacific Islander. The rate at which risk has increased appears somewhat parallel for black and American Indian/Alaskan Native students, and the rates of increase for these two groups is more rapid than is seen for white students. The rate at which risk has increased for Hispanic students is relatively slow and that for Asian/Pacific Islander is extremely slow.

Odds ratios tell the story of steady increases for all ethnic groups over the 22-year period. For blacks, American Indian/Alaskan Natives, and Asian/Pacific Islander, the odds ratio in 1998 was very similar to that in 1976. For Hispanics, the ratio declined from 0.97 to 0.60, reflecting a risk index that doubled, while that for other groups increased by three or more times.

GIFTED AND TALENTED DATA MONITORED BY OCR

Recent Surveys

Data on gifted and talented students come only from OCR surveys. The 1998 survey indicates that 6.2 percent of all children were placed in these programs (see Table 2-7), but placement rates for different racial/ethnic groups differ dramatically. The placement rate (risk index) for Asian/Pacific Islander students is 9.98 percent: 1 in 10 students in that group are in gifted programs. Relatively low risk indices are found for black (OCR RI = 3.04) and Hispanic (OCR RI = 3.57) students, with American Indian/Alaskan Native students (OCR RI = 4.86) also falling below the mean risk index for the total population. The risk index for whites (OCR RI = 7.47) is above the mean but not nearly as high as that found for Asian/Pacific Islander students. The odds ratios tell the same story with other numbers: Asian/Pacific Islander are one-third more likely than white students to be in gifted programs, while black and Hispanic students are less than half as likely. American Indian/Alaskan Natives (OCR OR = 0.65) fall between blacks and whites.

Trends Over Time

According to OCR data, in 1976 less than 1 percent of all schoolchildren were identified for gifted and talented programs, while in 1998 that

TABLE 2-6 Risk Indices and Odds Ratios for Emotional Disturbance by Race/Ethnicity: 1976-1998 OCR Data

	American Indian/ Alaskan Native	Asian/ Pacific Islander	Hispanic	Black	White	Total
Risk Index						
1976	0.29	0.08	0.25	0.42	0.26	0.28
1978	0.33	0.10	0.29	0.50	0.29	0.32
1980	0.46	0.09	0.37	0.72	0.42	0.46
1984	0.51	0.12	0.36	0.85	0.57	0.59
1986	0.54	0.11	0.46	1.04	0.58	0.63
1988	0.57	0.12	0.31	0.79	0.56	0.55
1990	0.68	0.13	0.33	0.89	0.69	0.66
1992	0.87	0.14	0.41	1.02	0.70	0.70
1994	0.95	0.18	0.47	1.12	0.76	0.77
1997	0.90	0.18	0.50	1.29	0.77	0.80
1998	1.03	0.26	0.55	1.45	0.91	0.93
Odds Ratio						
1976	1.12	0.30	0.97	1.63		
1978	1.13	0.34	1.00	1.71		
1980	1.09	0.23	0.89	1.71		
1984	0.89	0.21	0.64	1.48		
1986	0.94	0.19	0.79	1.81		
1988	1.03	0.22	0.57	1.42		
1990	0.99	0.19	0.48	1.30		
1992	1.23	0.20	0.59	1.46		
1994	1.24	0.23	0.62	1.46		
1997	1.17	0.24	0.66	1.69		
1998	1.12	0.29	0.6	1.59		

NOTE: OCR placement and membership data are taken from the Fall 1998 Elementary and Secondary School Civil Rights Compliance Report, National Projections.

number was 6.20 percent (see Table 2-8). These data are displayed graphically in Figure 2-4. While "risk" may not be the appropriate term to use for being classified as gifted and talented, the pattern of data is almost the mirror image of what was found for mental retardation in the OCR surveys.

Since 1976, there has been a steady increase in the rate at which children in each racial/ethnic group have been identified as gifted and talented (see Table 2-8). For all groups, the *rate* of change has been considerable; it has been greatest for American Indians and slowest for Asians. However, large differences in the initial placement rates leaves a distribution that is still very heavily weighted toward Asians and whites.

Reflecting these changes, the odds ratios for Asian/Pacific Islander students have dropped considerably: from 2.15 to 1.34. The ratio for Ameri-

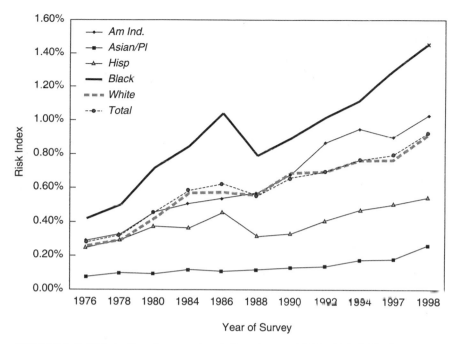

FIGURE 2-3 Risk indices for emotional disturbance: 1976-1998 OCR data.

[handwritten annotations: "% of stud. from ethnicity in TAG", "risk index white risk index", "% of students gifted in each ethnic group out of 100"]

TABLE 2-7 Indices of Placement in Gifted and Talented Programs by Race/Ethnicity: 1998 OCR Data

Characteristic	Risk Index OCR	Odds Ratio OCR	Composition Index OCR
American Indian/Alaskan Native	4.86	0.65	0.87
Asian/Pacific Islander	9.98	1.34	6.56
Black	3.04	0.41	8.40
Hispanic	3.57	0.48	8.64
White	7.47		75.53
Total	6.20		100.00

NOTES: OCR placement and membership data are taken from the Fall 1998 Elementary and Secondary School Civil Rights Compliance Report, National Projections.

TABLE 2-8 Risk Indices and Odds Ratios for Gifted and Talented
Students by Race/Ethnicity: 1976-1988 OCR Data

	American Indian/ Alaskan Native	Asian/ Pacific Islander	Hispanic	Black	White	Total
Risk Index						
1976	0.42	2.26	0.40	0.47	1.05	0.93
1978	0.76	4.60	1.47	1.27	2.08	1.94
1980	1.11	5.25	1.52	1.46	2.88	2.57
1984	1.97	8.28	2.12	2.16	4.75	4.15
1986	2.15	9.10	2.41	2.44	5.35	4.67
1988	2.45	9.63	2.50	2.57	5.65	4.96
1990	2.82	9.44	2.86	2.87	6.44	5.52
1992	3.13	9.99	2.98	2.96	6.15	5.35
1994	4.61	9.53	2.95	2.97	7.19	6.00
1997	4.43	9.41	3.38	2.43	6.79	5.64
1998	4.86	9.98	3.57	3.04	7.47	6.20
Odds Ratio						
1976	0.40	2.15	0.38	0.45		
1978	0.36	2.21	0.71	0.61		
1980	0.39	1.82	0.53	0.51		
1984	0.42	1.75	0.45	0.46		
1986	0.40	1.70	0.45	0.46		
1988	0.43	1.70	0.44	0.45		
1990	0.44	1.46	0.44	0.45		
1992	0.51	1.63	0.48	0.48		
1994	0.64	1.32	0.41	0.41		
1997	0.65	1.39	0.50	0.36		
1998	0.65	1.34	0.48	0.41		

Note: OCR placement and membership data are taken from the Fall 1998 Elementary and
Secondary School Civil Rights Compliance Report, National Projections.

can Indian/Alaskan Natives rose from 0.40 to 0.65, but that for Hispanics
and blacks showed no sustained rise.

NONJUDGMENTAL DISABILITY CATEGORIES

Our focus in this report is on the three high-incidence disability categories discussed above. We briefly examine the data for the other 10 categories, however, to provide a fuller picture of relative placement by race/
ethnicity. Only OSEP collects data on all 13 disability categories, and these
have been broken down by race/ethnicity only as of 1998. One of the
reasons these categories are not monitored by OCR is that for most of the
disabilities represented, few would question the professional judgment or

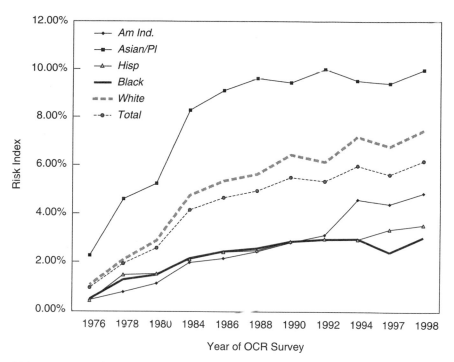

FIGURE 2-4 Risk indices for gifted and talented: 1976-1998 OCR data.

accuracy of a diagnosis in these cases. Moreover, the representation of racial/ethnic groups in these categories has not been at issue in the courts.

Table 2-9 contains 1998 summary data for all of the disability categories recognized under IDEA.[1] Since MR, ED, and LD were discussed previously, we focus on the other 10 categories here.

Speech and Language Impairments: Students served in the category of speech and language impairments constitute 2.33 percent of the nation's schoolchildren. Risk indices by racial/ethnic group reveal that Asian/Pacific Islander children are served at a much lower rate (RI = 1.42 percent), and Hispanic students at a somewhat lower rate (RI = 1.92 percent). American

---

[1]We call attention to the dramatic shift in the American Indian/Alaskan Native indices between the two years. This reflects both a substantial increase in the number of students in that category served in special education, and a substantial decrease in the total number of American Indian/Alaskan Native students in the population. But because NCES and OSEP conduct separate data collection efforts, the recorded change may be anomalous.

Indian/Alaskan Native, black, and white students are served at rates approximating the national average, with risk indices for these groups of, respectively, 2.41, 2.28, and 2.54 percent. Given that the risk index for white students is the highest, it comes as no surprise that the odds ratios for the other four racial/ethnic groups, when compared with that of whites, are less than 1.0.

The remaining disability categories recognized under IDEA are sometimes referred to as low-incidence disabilities, when compared with the ones considered above. The risk index for the total population under each of these disabilities ranges from a low of 0.003 percent (deaf-blindness) to a high of 0.46 percent (other health impairment).

Hearing Impairment: Risk indices for all racial/ethnic groups for hearing impairment are under 0.2 percent, with a national average of 0.15 percent. Odds ratios suggest slightly higher risk for American Indian/Alaskan Natives (OR = 1.23), Asian/Pacific Islander (OR = 1.21), and Hispanics (OR = 1.22) than is found for whites; however, only 0.18 percent of both American Indian/Alaskan Native and Asian/PacificIslander students are served in programs for the hearing impaired. The odds ratio for black students (OR = 1.03) suggests approximately the same rate as is found for white students.

Visual Impairment: All groups except American Indian/Alaskan Natives participate substantially less in programs for children with visual impairments than do white students. While this disability category has a very low prevalence (less than 0.07 percent for any racial/ethnic group), one might be tempted to speculate that issues of screening and the availability of routine medical care may be implicated here. The odds ratio for American Indian/Alaskan Natives is 1.27, suggesting higher identification rates for this group. For all other racial/ethnic groups, the odds ratios shown in Table 2-9 suggest comparable rates of identification.

Orthopedic Impairment: The national risk index for orthopedic impairment is 0.15 percent, with risk indices for all racial/ethnic groups ranging between 0.11 percent (American Indian/Alaskan Natives and Asian/Pacific Islander) and 0.16 percent (whites). Odds ratios reveal that in comparison to white students, all other racial/ethnic groups are just slightly less at risk for being served as orthopedically impaired. Odds ratios also reflect the slightly lower prevalence rates for all groups when compared with the rate for white students. Again, we raise the possibility of failure to detect as a factor in these figures.

TABLE 2-9 1998 OSEP Data by Disability and Ethnic Group: Composition Index, Risk Index, and Odds Ratio

Ethnicity	Total Number	N In Disability	Comp. Index	Risk Index	Odds Ratio
All Disabilities					
American Indian/ Alaskan Native	526,719	68,966	1.24	13.10%	1.08
Asian/Pacific Islander	1,794,189	95,343	1.72	5.31%	0.44
Black	7,785,863	1,111,650	20.03	14.28%	1.18
Hispanic	6,819,434	773,013	13.93	11.34%	0.94
White	28,937,632	3,500,911	63.08	12.10%	
Total	45,863,813	5,549,913		12.10%	
Mental Retardation					
American Indian/ Alaskan Native	526,719	6,295	1.03	1.20%	1.07
Asian/Pacific Islander	1,794,189	10,228	1.67	0.57%	0.51
Black	7,785,863	204,739	33.51	2.63%	2.35
Hispanic	6,819,434	66,543	10.89	0.98%	0.87
White	28,937,632	323,173	52.89	1.12%	
Total	45,863,813	610,978		1.33%	
Learning Disabilities					
American Indian/ Alaskan Native	526,719	38,455	1.37	7.30%	1.2
Asian/Pacific Islander	1,794,189	40,345	1.43	2.25%	0.37
Black	7,785,863	512,083	18.19	6.58%	1.08
Hispanic	6,819,434	464,458	16.5	6.81%	1.12
White	28,937,632	1,759,501	62.51	6.08%	
Total	45,863,813	2,814,842		6.14%	
Emotional Disturbance					
American Indian/ Alaskan Native	526,719	5,261	1.14	1.00%	1.02
Asian/Pacific Islander	1,794,189	4,796	1.04	0.27%	0.27
Black	7,785,863	121,800	26.36	1.56%	1.59
Hispanic	6,819,434	46,118	9.98	0.68%	0.69
White	28,937,632	284,062	61.48	0.98%	
Total	45,863,813	462,037		1.01%	
Speech and Language Impairment					
American Indian/ Alaskan Native	526,719	12,698	1.18	2.41%	0.95
Asian/Pacific Islander	1,794,189	25,408	2.35	1.42%	0.56
Black	7,785,863	177,484	16.43	2.28%	0.9
Hispanic	6,819,434	130,606	12.09	1.92%	0.75
White	28,937,632	734,339	67.96	2.54%	
Total	45,863,813	1,080,535		2.36%	
Multiple Disabilities					
American Indian/ Alaskan Native	526,719	1,474	1.36	0.28%	1.14

continues

TABLE 2-9 continued

Ethnicity	Total Number	N In Disability	Comp. Index	Risk Index	Odds Ratio
Asian/Pacific Islander	1,794,189	2,437	2.24	0.14%	0.55
Black	7,785,863	20,782	19.1	0.27%	1.09
Hispanic	6,819,434	13,000	11.95	0.19%	0.78
White	28,937,632	71,086	65.35	0.25%	
Total	45,863,813	108,779		0.24%	
Hearing Impairment					
American Indian/ Alaskan Native	526,719	952	1.35	0.18%	1.23
Asian/Pacific Islander	1,794,189	3,182	4.5	0.18%	1.21
Black	7,785,863	11,759	16.63	0.15%	1.03
Hispanic	6,819,434	12,243	17.32	0.18%	1.22
White	28,937,632	42,553	60.2	0.15%	
Total	45,863,813	70,689		0.15%	
Orthopedic Impairment					
American Indian/ Alaskan Native	526,719	563	0.81	0.11%	0.66
Asian/Pacific Islander	1,794,189	2,044	2.93	0.11%	0.71
Black	7,785,863	10,095	14.48	0.13%	0.81
Hispanic	6,819,434	10,471	15.02	0.15%	0.95
White	28,937,632	46,532	66.76	0.16%	
Total	45,863,813	69,705		0.15%	
Other Health Impairment					
American Indian/ Alaskan Native	526,719	2,233	1.01	0.42%	0.73
Asian/Pacific Islander	1,794,189	2,942	1.33	0.16%	0.28
Black	7,785,863	31,097	14.02	0.40%	0.69
Hispanic	6,819,434	18,268	8.24	0.27%	0.46
White	28,937,632	167,268	75.41	0.58%	
Total	45,863,813	221,808		0.48%	
Visual Impairment					
American Indian/ Alaskan Native	526,719	385	1.27	0.07%	1.02
Asian/Pacific Islander	1,794,189	907	2.99	0.05%	0.71
Black	7,785,863	4,413	14.55	0.06%	0.79
Hispanic	6,819,434	3,887	12.81	0.06%	0.8
White	28,937,632	20,741	68.38	0.07%	
Total	45,863,813	30,333		0.07%	
Autism					
American Indian/ Alaskan Native	526,719	363	0.67	0.07%	0.58
Asian/Pacific Islander	1,794,189	2,492	4.63	0.14%	1.17
Black	7,785,863	11,165	20.75	0.14%	1.21
Hispanic	6,819,434	5,405	10.04	0.08%	0.67
White	28,937,632	34,386	63.9	0.12%	
Total	45,863,813	53,811	99.99	0.12%	

continues

TABLE 2-9 continued

Ethnicity	Total Number	N In Disability	Comp. Index	Risk Index	Odds Ratio
Traumatic Brain Injury					
American Indian/ Alaskan Native	526,719	203	1.57	0.04%	1.23
Asian/Pacific Islander	1,794,189	294	2.27	0.02%	0.52
Black	7,785,863	2,050	15.84	0.03%	0.84
Hispanic	6,819,434	1,330	10.28	0.02%	0.62
White	28,937,632	9,063	70.04	0.03%	
Total	45,863,813	12,940		0.03%	
Deaf-Blind					
American Indian/ Alaskan Native	526,719	27	1.72	0.01%	1.52
Asian/Pacific Islander	1,794,189	174	11.08	0.01%	2.88
Black	7,785,863	178	11.34	0.00%	0.68
Hispanic	6,819,434	215	13.69	0.00%	0.93
White	28,937,632	976	62.17	0.00%	
Total	45,863,813	1,570	100	0.00%	
Developmental Delay					
American Indian/ Alaskan Native	526,719	57	0.48	0.01%	0.43
Asian/Pacific Islander	1,794,189	94	0.79	0.01%	0.21
Black	7,785,863	4,005	33.78	0.05%	2.06
Hispanic	6,819,434	469	3.96	0.01%	0.28
White	28,937,632	7,231	60.99	0.02%	
Total	45,863,813	11,856		0.03%	

NOTES: OSEP data are taken from the 1998-1999 child count, and indices were calculated using estimated K-12 total enrollment data from the U.S. Department of Education, National Center for Education Statistics, Common Core of Data, School Universe Survey, 1998-99, compiled by Mark Glander, National Education Data Resource Center, 4/26/01. Total enrollment for Idaho, estimated from total population, broken down by racial/ethnic category based on OSEP report for children ages 6-21 (AI = 1.26; API = 1.06; B = 0.43; Hisp. = 10.28; White = 86.98).

Other Health Impairment: The risk index across racial/ethnic groups for other health impairment is 0.48 percent. Risk indices range from 0.16 percent for Asian/Pacific Islander students to 0.58 percent for white students, who constitute over 75 percent of all children identified as having some other health impairment. Odds ratios reveal that in comparison to white students, all other racial/ethnic groups are less at risk for being served, with risk being far lower for Asian/Pacific Islander (OR = 0.28) and Hispanics (OR = 0.46). Interpretation of these figures may be compromised by the use of this category to serve some children diagnosed with attention deficit/hyperactivity disorder but not qualifying under the LD category.

Multiple Disabilities: The risk index across racial/ethnic groups for multiple disabilities is 0.23 percent, with lower risk for Hispanics (RI = 0.19 percent) and Asian/Pacific Islander (RI = 0.14 percent). Risks for all other groups are extremely similar (whites RI = 0.25 percent; blacks RI = 0.27 percent; American Indian/Alaskan Natives RI = 0.28 percent). Examination of the odds ratios contrasting the four racial/ethnic groups with white students suggests that American Indian/Alaskan Native and black students have about the same probability of being served in special education on the basis of qualifying as having multiple disabilities, with Hispanic students being slightly less likely (OR = 0.7). Asian/Pacific Islander students are approximately half as likely to be so served (OR = 0.55).

Deaf-Blindness: In this extremely low-incidence condition, fluctuations of only a few cases can result in higher risk. Only American Indian/Alaskan Native and Asian/Pacific Islander children have risk indices that reach 0.01 percent. The odds ratios for the two racial/ethnic groups suggest higher rates than that found for whites. Most pronounced is the odds ratio for Asian/Pacific Islander (2.88), yet, as noted previously, the risk index for this group is 0.01 percent. The odds ratio for American Indian/Alaskan Natives suggests approximately half again the proportion of cases (OR = 1.52) found among white students. The odds ratio for black students (OR = .68) reveals a lower rate of deaf-blindness than among white students, while the rate for Hispanic students (OR = .93) is comparable to that for white students. The very small numbers (smallest of any disability category) urge caution in interpreting these figures.

Autism: The national risk for autism across racial/ethnic groups is 0.12 percent. Risk indices range from a low of 0.07 percent (American Indian/Alaskan Natives) to 0.14 percent for Asian/Pacific Islander and black students. Odds ratios reveal slightly higher rates of autism for black (OR = 1.21) and Asian/Pacific Islander (OR = 1.17) students when compared with the rates for whites, while rates for American Indian/Alaskan Native and Hispanic students are considerably lower than is found among white students.

Traumatic Brain Injury: The national risk index across racial and ethnic groups for traumatic brain injury is 0.03 percent. Variability in risk across racial/ethnic groups is quite small, ranging from 0.02 percent (Asian/Pacific Islander) to 0.04 percent (American Indian/Alaskan Natives). Odds ratios indicate slightly higher rates of identification for American Indian/Alaskan Natives (OR = 1.23) than is found for white students, with rates for the other three groups being lower than that found among white students.

Developmental Delay: Caution is in order interpreting figures for children in this category. Not all states employ this category, and it cannot be used throughout the school years. The category includes primary grade students who are judged to need special education because their development is below expectations; these children must be placed into more specific categories to be served in special education in upper elementary grades. Very few American Indian/Alaskan Native or Asian/Pacific Islander children are served in this category nationwide (total numbers of 57 and 94 children, respectively). Highest risk indices are found for blacks (RI = 0.05 percent) and whites (RI = 0.03 percent). Odds ratios reveal rates substantially lower than that for white students for all racial/ethnic groups except for black students, who are over twice as likely as white students to be identified (OR = 2.06). Given the uneven use of this category across states, interpretation is difficult.

SUMMARY OF NATIONAL DATA ON
RACIAL AND ETHNIC REPRESENTATION

When OSEP participation data are aggregated across all 13 disability categories, one gets an overall impression of the relative participation of the five racial/ethnic groups in special education. In 1998 approximately 14 percent of all black students, 13 percent of American Indian/Alaskan Native students, 12 percent of white students, 11 percent of Hispanic students, and 5 percent of Asian/Pacific Islander students were served in special education in comparison to an overall (across the five racial/ethnic groups) rate of 12 percent.

When rates for minority children are considered in comparison to white students (i.e., odds ratios), one finds a higher risk for black students (OR = 1.18). But the biggest discrepancy is Asian/Pacific Islander students, whose risk index is less than half that of whites (OR = 0.44). Hispanic students have a slightly lower risk index than whites across all disabilities (OR = 0.94).

The OSEP data provide no evidence that minority children are systematically represented in low-incidence disability categories in numbers that are disproportionate to their representation in the population. While there is some variation in each category, no single race/ethnic group can be singled out as having higher or lower incidence across all categories.

There is evidence that disproportionate participation of black students continues in the categories of mental retardation and emotional disturbance. The magnitude of the disproportion in cases identified as mental retardation has been reduced over time, but the higher identification rate for black students persists. Given that many states reserve the term "mentally retarded" exclusively for students exhibiting patent disability (MacMillan et al., 1996d), interpretation of these numbers, as well as the ED numbers, requires more far-reaching analysis (see Chapters 3 and 5).

The LD category is both the largest and the fastest growing. Black, white, and Hispanic students are placed in that category at roughly the same rate. Asian/Pacific Islander students are represented at a much lower rate, and American Indian/Alaskan Native children at a somewhat higher risk of placement.

Because aggregating data nationally obscures much state-to-state variability, we turn in the sections that follow to disaggregated state data.

DATA ON STATE-TO-STATE VARIABILITY

States vary widely in both the total percentage of students and the percentage by race/ethnicity assigned to special education categories and gifted and talented programs. OCR data from the 1998 survey on all states for the high-incidence disabilities and gifted and talented programs are displayed in graphic form in Figures 2-5 to 2-8.

The interpretation of the box plots in the figures is as follows: the white line in the center denotes the median, and the shaded box is bounded by the first and third quartiles of the data distribution. Hence, the middle 50 percent of the data lies within the box. The "whiskers" of the plot are based on the interquartile range; points lying beyond the whiskers (denoted by the horizontal lines) are outlier points that are highly unusual given the distribution of the rest of the data. Side-by-side plots give a clear picture of central location across groups (comparing the median lines and location/ overlap of the boxes) but also the variability and skewness of the distributions (the vertical extent of the boxes and whiskers). Data for the 50 states and the District of Columbia for each of the five racial/ethnic groups are displayed by each disability group in these figures.

Figure 2-5 illustrates the higher median risk score for black students classified as MR and the relatively low rate for Asian/Pacific Islander students. The new information displayed here is the greater variability in the risk for black students across the states. In Figure 2-6, reflecting the distribution of LD risk indices, the median value for all groups except Asian/ Pacific Islander is roughly comparable: Asian/Pacific Islander students are at far lower risk for classification as LD than are students in the other four racial/ethnic groups. Considerable variability across states is seen for the American Indian/Alaskan Native population of students, with less variability observed for white students.

Figure 2-7 displays the risk indices for the ED category. Asian/Pacific Islander students show extremely low risk for this category, while the me-

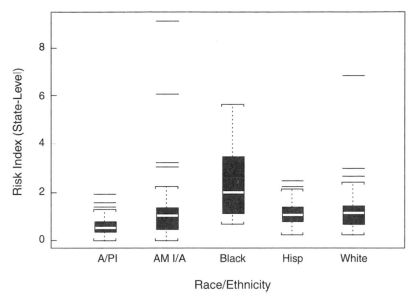

FIGURE 2-5 Variation in state-level risk indices for mental retardation.

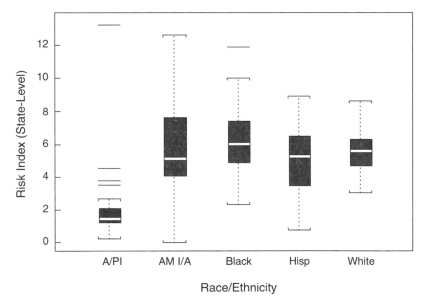

FIGURE 2-6 Variation in state-level risk indices for learning disabilities.

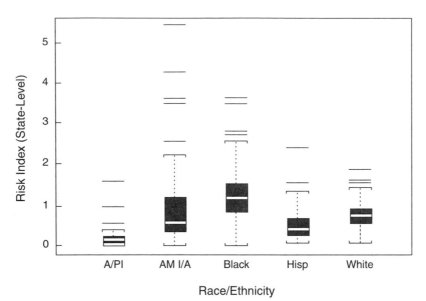

FIGURE 2-7 Variation in state-level risk indices for emotional disturbance.

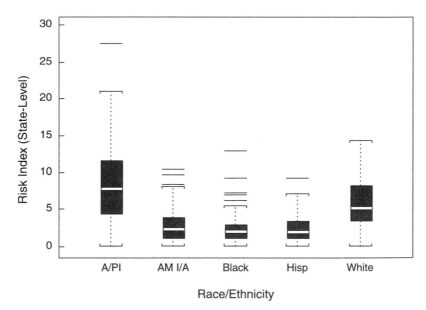

FIGURE 2-8 Variation in state-level risk indices for gifted and talented.

dian risk for black students is higher than is found for any other racial/ethnic group. The variability seen for Hispanic and white students across states is comparable, while that found for American Indian/Alaskan Native and black students is considerably greater. Several extreme values indicate high risk for American Indian/Alaskan Native and black students in certain states.

The findings for "risk" as gifted and talented appear in Figure 2-8 and record as expected the highest median risk for Asian/Pacific Islander students, for whom is also evident the greatest variability across states in classification for these services. Noticeably low-risk indices are evident for American Indian/Alaskan Native, black, and Hispanic students, and the variability in risk across states is considerably less for these groups than is found for Asian/Pacific Islander or white students.

To get a better grasp of the variability across states, the summary data from the OCR 1998 survey is highlighted for the subset of states that have the highest placement rates for blacks and Hispanics in the disabilities of concern, and the lowest placement rates for blacks and Hispanics in gifted and talented programs. We do not look at American Indian/Alaskan Natives by state because the small numbers in the population can cause the indices to be very unstable from year to year. We do look at the states in which the composition is highest for blacks and Hispanics. This provides insight into the placement rates in states that have large black and Hispanic populations. For each of the states we include the risk index for white students as well. By comparing the relative risk index for black and white students for a given state, one can get some insight into whether the state simply identifies high percentages of children (risk index for black and white being comparable) or whether one sees marked differences in a given state for children in different racial/ethnic groups.

Mental Retardation

We found nine states in which over 4 percent of black students were served in the mental retardation category (Alabama, Arkansas, Indiana, Iowa, Massachusetts, Nebraska, North Carolina, South Carolina, and West Virginia) while five states provided less than 1 percent of their black students with MR services (Alaska, Maine, New Hampshire, New Jersey, and New York). Table 2-10 shows the data on states with the highest risk index for black students in the top portion and the states with the highest composition index for black students in the lower portion.

Interestingly, these data do not tell a coherent story. In some states in which the black risk index is high, black students make up a large portion of the student body. This is true of Alabama and Arkansas. In Massachusetts and Indiana, the composition index is in the average range, and Iowa

TABLE 2-10 1998 Comparison of States with Highest Risk (RI) and Composition (CI) Indices for Black Students in the Category of Mental Retardation

State	RI	CI	White RI for State
Highest RI			
Massachusetts	6.28%	29.07%	1.32%
Alabama	5.49%	62.93%	1.80%
Arkansas	5.29%	43.87%	2.06%
Iowa	5.27%	6.14%	3.21%
Indiana	5.01%	23.67%	1.85%
Highest CI			
District of Columbia	1.74%	95.07%	.19%
Mississippi	2.27%	78.14%	.66%
South Carolina	4.35%	69.61%	1.41%
Louisiana	2.79%	69.58%	1.13%

has a low composition index because it has relatively few black children in the student body.

Turning to the composition index, the lack of pattern is reinforced. By virtue of its demographics, the District of Columbia has the largest percentage of black students in its school population. Black students make up over 95 percent of all MR placements. However, only 1.7 percent of black students are in that category—far below the national average for blacks. The risk index for whites in the District, however, is only 0.19 percent. While the District places relatively few children of any race in the MR category, the disproportion is very pronounced. The odds of a black student being placed in MR are over nine times those of white students. Looking at the four states with a high composition index for black students, the risk indices run from among the highest (South Carolina) to among the lowest (District of Columbia).

For Hispanic students, the highest risk indices are considerably below those for black students. Three of the states with higher risk indices for Hispanic students have relatively small Hispanic populations, and those with large Hispanic populations (high CI) have risk indices that are near the average. The national averages indicate that fewer Hispanic students than white students are labeled MR. But in all states in Table 2-11, one finds slightly higher risk for Hispanic students than for whites.

While these data give a flavor of the complexity involved in placement patterns, a single year's data for any state should be considered cautiously. While Alabama and Arkansas have consistently high placement rates for black students in MR, Massachusetts would not have ranked among the

TABLE 2-11 1998 Comparison of States with Highest Risk (RI) and Composition (CI) Indices for Hispanic Students in the Category of Mental Retardation

State	RI	CI	White RI for State
Highest RI			
Massachusetts	4.48%	22.54%	1.32%
Nebraska	2.68%	7.31%	1.99%
Hawaii	2.41%	3.70%	.96%
Indiana	2.23%	3.18%	1.85%
Highest CI			
New Mexico	1.06%	53.37%	0.84%
California	.78%	44.06%	0.66%
Arizona	1.04%	37.31%	0.72%
Texas	0.71%	35.42%	0.60%

top states in 1997. Yet in 1998 it had the highest placement rate in MR for both blacks and Hispanics. This may be explained by changes in reporting methodology.

Learning Disabilities

There is considerable variability in the rate at which states use the LD designation. For example, in 1998 Rhode Island identified 9.75 percent of its students as LD and Delaware 8.65 percent. Only 3.10 percent of the students in Georgia were classified as LD, and 3.36 percent in Kentucky. The nationally aggregated data have been interpreted to suggest no overrepresentation of either black or Hispanic students in LD. But state-level data tell a more complex story. For black students, for example, the risk index ranges from 2.33 percent in Georgia to 12.19 percent in Delaware. For Hispanic students, the risk index ranges from 2.43 in Georgia to 8.93 in Delaware. Clearly there is overrepresentation for these two minorities in the LD category *in some states*.

Tables 2-12 and 2-13 show states with the highest risk and composition indices for blacks and Hispanics, respectively. The RI for black students identified as LD in the top portion of the table are consistently and substantially higher than the RI for white students in three of the four states; the rate is high for both blacks and whites in Rhode Island. No discernible pattern emerges from these states, however. In Delaware, the high RI is associated with a high CI, while in the other states it is not. For states in which black students constitute the highest percentages of enroll-

TABLE 2-12 1998 Comparison of States with Highest Risk (RI) and Composition (CI) Indices for Black Students in the Category of Learning Disability

State	RI	CI	White RI for State
Highest RI			
Delaware	12.19%	43.26%	7.15%
Rhode Island	10.38%	7.75%	10.30%
New Mexico	9.99%	3.34%	6.83%
Montana	9.90%	.76%	5.80%
Highest CI			
District of Columbia	6.68%	91.94%	3.68%
Mississippi	6.39%	57.53%	4.87%
Louisiana	6.65%	55.57%	4.26%
South Carolina	5.82%	42.55%	5.86%

TABLE 2-13 1998 Comparison of States with Highest Risk (RI) and Composition (CI) Indices for Hispanic Students in the Category of Learning Disability

State	RI	CI	White RI for State
Highest RI			
Delaware	8.93%	3.60%	7.15%
New York	8.42%	21.72%	7.03%
New Mexico	8.21%	51.40%	6.83%
Highest CI			
New Mexico	8.21%	51.40%	6.83%
California	5.81%	41.65%	6.00%
Texas	7.05%	38.46%	6.59%
Arizona	5.90%	33.25%	5.44%

ment in LD (CI), we find RIs that are substantially higher for black students than white students in three states (District of Columbia, Louisiana, and Mississippi), and almost identical rates in South Carolina.

For Hispanic students, the states with the highest risk indices again show no pattern. They range from Delaware with 3.60 percent of LD students who are Hispanic, to New Mexico with 51.4 percent. In all three states, the risk index is higher for Hispanic students than for white students, but all three states identify white students at a rate higher than the national average.

Of the four states in which Hispanic students make up the largest share of the LD students, two (Arizona and California) identify those students at rates below the national average, and two (New Mexico and Texas) above. In the latter two states, white students are also identified at higher rates than they are nationally.

Emotional Disturbance

OCR national projections showed elevated identification rates for black students in the category of emotional disturbance. Again, we note the variability in the rates of ED identification across states. Minnesota, Ohio, Oklahoma, and Oregon identified more than 2 percent of their students as ED, while nine states identified under one half of one percent: Arkansas, California, Delaware, Idaho, Mississippi, Nevada, South Dakota, Tennessee, and Washington.

Among the states with the highest risk indices for black students are Iowa, Minnesota, Montana, and Vermont, all states in which black students claim a relatively small share of the total ED placements (see Table 2-14). The RI for black students in those states is markedly higher than for white students. In states in which black students make up the largest share of ED placements (District of Columbia, Louisiana, North Carolina, and South Carolina), the risk index is also substantially higher than that for whites, but it is less than half the rate in the states with the highest risk indices.

TABLE 2-14 1998 Comparison of States with Highest Risk (RI) and Composition (CI) Indices for Black Students in the Category of Emotional Disturbance

State	RI	CI	White RI for State
Highest RI			
Minnesota	3.88%	11.09%	1.88%
Montana	3.58%	2.05%	0.85%
Iowa	3.53%	11.81%	1.05%
Vermont	3.11%	1.42%	1.80%
Highest CI			
District of Columbia	1.25%	96.02%	0.41%
Louisiana	.97%	65.26%	0.48%
South Carolina	1.29%	57.04%	0.72%
North Carolina	1.38%	53.62%	0.58%

TABLE 2-15 1998 Comparison of States with Highest Risk (RI) and Composition (CI) Indices for Hispanic Students in the Category of Emotional Disturbance

State	RI	CI	White RI for State
Highest RI			
Hawaii	2.68%	4.09%	2.39%
Vermont	2.16%	0.49%	1.80%
Maine	1.99%	0.54%	1.73%
Minnesota	1.61%	1.95%	1.18%
Highest CI			
New Mexico	0.92%	43.68%	1.20%
Texas	0.62%	25.22%	1.09%
California	0.13%	19.81%	0.39%
Arizona	0.29%	15.36%	0.78%

States in which Hispanic students are most at risk for ED identification are Hawaii, Maine, Minnesota, and Vermont (Table 2-15). Hispanic students in these states constitute only a very small percentage of the total ED enrollment. While in all of these cases their placement rates are higher than those for whites, the discrepancies are relatively small. In states in which Hispanic students make up the largest percentage of the ED population (bottom of Table 2-15), placement rates for Hispanic students are uniformly below those for whites.

Gifted and Talented Category

For the gifted and talented category, the variations among states are even greater than are seen for the disability categories discussed above. At the upper end of the distribution, Oklahoma and Wisconsin serve over 13 percent of their students in these programs, while Massachusetts serves under 1 percent and the District of Columbia and Vermont just over 1 percent. Such variability is obscured when one cites a national projected average of 5.86 percent.

Since the concern in the area of gifted and talented students is underrepresentation of blacks and Hispanics, we have selected states with low placement rates indicated by low risk indices. Table 2-16 shows states low in placement rates for black students in the upper half of the table and states low in the percentage of gifted and talented who are black in the lower half. The low-RI states are all in New England. These states have placement rates for whites that are also far below the national average, although they are several times greater than the rate for black students. States in which the CI is lowest for black students are in the Midwest and

TABLE 2-16 1998 Comparison of States with Lowest Risk (RI) and Composition (CI) Indices for Black Students in the Category of Gifted and Talented

State	RI	CI	White RI for State
Lowest RI			
Vermont	0.36%	0.29%	1.06%
New Hampshire	0.39%	0.36%	1.34%
Massachusetts	0.39%	9.79%	0.83%
Lowest CI			
Montana	2.27%	0.22%	5.10%
Vermont	0.36%	0.29%	1.06%
New Hampshire	0.39%	0.36%	1.34%
Idaho	1.99%	0.39%	2.97%
Maine	1.45%	0.40%	3.65%

New England. In all of these states, the risk index is below the national average for both blacks and whites, but the differential between the two races is large.

Three of the four states with the lowest risk indices for Hispanic students in the gifted and talented category are in the Northeast. Table 2-17 shows the states along with RI data for white students. The magnitude of the differences in Hispanic-white RIs varies considerably, with white students about half again as likely to be served in Massachusetts, while the difference in New York is more than eight times. In states in which Hispanic students constitute a very small percentage of the overall enrollment

TABLE 2-17 1998 Comparison of States with Lowest Risk (RI) and Composition (CI) Indices for Hispanic Students in the Category of Gifted and Talented

State	RI	CI	White RI for State
Lowest RI			
District of Columbia	0.11%	0.39%	0.38%
New Hampshire	0.25%	0.43%	1.34%
New York	0.33%	2.50%	4.03%
Massachusetts	0.50%	4.84%	0.83%
Lowest CI			
Maine	1.99%	0.26%	3.65%
Vermont	0.72%	0.29%	1.06%
West Virginia	1.93%	0.29%	2.24%
District of Columbia	0.11%	0.39%	0.28%

in gifted and talented programs, one also finds a substantial difference in the RI for Hispanic and white students.

In summary, state-level data reveal the absence of a consistent pattern across states. No region of the country can be singled out as consistently placing greater or fewer percentages of minority students in special or gifted education. States with high proportions of minority students sometimes have higher placement rates, and sometimes lower. Some of the states with high placement rates for minority students also have high placement rates for white students, but this is not consistently the case. While federal IDEA legislation applies to all states, clearly the implementation is very much shaped by state-level policy and practice, just as gifted and talented programs are fundamentally different in conception and coverage in different states. We restate the caution, however, that state data fluctuate from year to year. The above tables using 1997 data appear in Appendix 2.A. The different configuration of states in some of these tables makes the point more concretely.

GENDER COMPARISONS

It is widely known that more boys than girls exhibit academic and behavioral problems. Furthermore, we have observed that for most disabilities, greater proportions of males are identified than females. OSEP does not report data broken down by gender; however OCR does, and it was noted in the 1982 National Research Council report that the overrepresentation in disability categories was a concern both for certain minority groups and for males (National Research Council, 1982). In analyzing the *Larry P.* decision from the perspective of the defense, Lambert (1981) commented that the magnitude of the overrepresentation of males in programs for educable mentally retarded children was far more egregious than the overrepresentation of black students. Figure 2-9 shows the proportion for males and females in each of the four categories monitored by OCR for the 1998 survey.

For the three disability groups, the overrepresentation of males is evident. The greatest gender disparity is found in ED, for which boys constitute almost 80 percent of all children served. In LD boys constitute close to 70 percent of the children served, while in mental retardation they constitute approximately 60 percent.

The 1998 survey data were plotted in Figure 2-10 to show differing risk of placement for ED by gender and ethnicity. What is evident from this figure is a main effect for males; for each racial/ethnic group, males are at over three times the risk for being classified as ED than are females in the same racial/ethnic group except for Asian/Pacific Islander (for whom males are still more than twice as likely). It is also interesting that the rank order

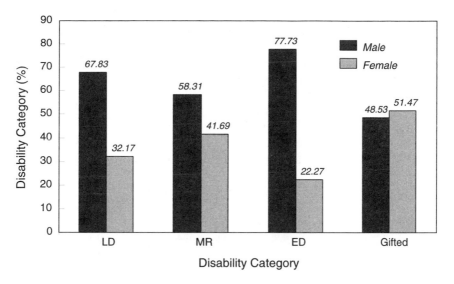

FIGURE 2-9 Gender breakdown by disability: 1998 OCR data.

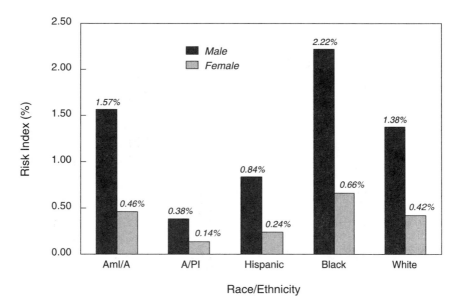

FIGURE 2-10 Ethnicity and gender breakdown for emotional disturbance: 1998 OCR data.

for risk by racial/ethnic group holds for both males and females. That is, black students (both male and female) are at higher risk than members of other racial/ethnic groups of the same gender. American Indian/Alaskan Native males and females are at next highest risk, followed by whites, Hispanics, and then Asian/Pacific Islander.

The same comparison is shown in Figure 2-11 for the category of mental retardation. In comparison to the pattern found for ED, the magnitude of the disparity in risk within each racial/ethnic group is smaller. Nevertheless, males are at greater risk for being classified as having mental retardation in every racial/ethnic group. As was found for ED, the racial/ethnic group rankings follow for both genders.

Data aggregated at the national level for gender, like the data on race/ethnicity, obscure variability. To illustrate, consider the gender breakdown in the disability category of mental retardation. Alabama has among the highest placement rates in that category, and New Jersey the lowest. Figure 2-12 shows the gender breakdown by racial/ethnic group in Alabama. While males exceed females in all five racial/ethnic groups, the risk for black females being served as MR is over twice as great as the risk for males in any of the other groups. In New Jersey, one finds a very different pattern shown in Figure 2-13. The risk for American Indian/Alaskan Native females is *greater* than the risk for American Indian/Alaskan Native males. There is no gender difference in risk for Hispanic students. The risk for

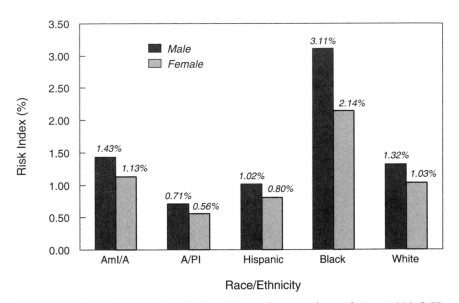

FIGURE 2-11 Ethnicity and gender breakdown for mental retardation: 1998 OCR data.

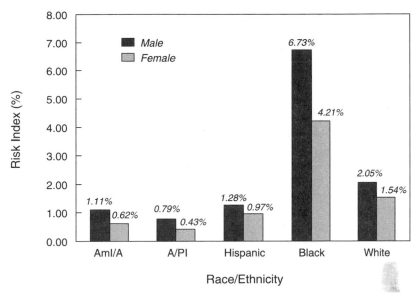

FIGURE 2-12 Ethnicity and gender breakdown for mental retardation in Alabama: 1998 OCR data.

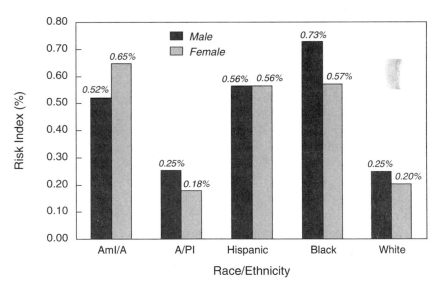

FIGURE 2-13 Ethnicity and gender breakdown for mental retardation in New Jersey: 1998 OCR data.

black females does not differ from Hispanic males or females, nor does it differ from American Indian/Alaskan Native females. Our point is simply that patterns that emerge at the national level fail to characterize the situation in many individual states. Moreover, the pattern in a given state probably fails to characterize the situation in individual school districts within that state.

EXPLAINING MINORITY REPRESENTATION

Special Education

OCR data are available at the school district level, and these data are sometimes analyzed to look for patterns in minority placement in special education. From the committee's perspective, the available data are not up to the task of explanation. As the discussion above suggests, what is captured in the disability variables (ED, LD, MR) varies widely. The meaning of placement—whether it involves a completely segregated program or additional supports in the general education classroom—is not captured at all. The accuracy of the data on race/ethnicity is questionable. As we discuss in more detail in later chapters, the number of students placed in special education will depend on the demands of the classroom, the resources to provide additional attention in the general education or compensatory education context, and the proclivities of teachers, administrators, and parents. When none of these variables are captured in the data analysis, one cannot have confidence in the results, even when they are statistically significant.

Some research has analyzed district-level data in a search for placement patterns (e.g., Oswald et al., 2000; 1998). These analyses look at the effect of the proportion of students who are poor, or who are from school districts with large numbers of minority students, as explanatory factors. Oswald et al. (2000), for example, point to several patterns in the identification of minority students: (a) black and Hispanic students are identified as LD and ED more often in school districts characterized as high-poverty districts, and (b) black and Hispanic students are identified as MR more often in school districts characterized as low-poverty districts. The authors conclude that a substantial number of black students are being labeled MR inappropriately. While the correlation between poverty level and placement may be entirely accurate, the conclusion does not necessarily follow. A competing hypothesis—that students who meet criteria for MR are being placed in LD classifications in high-poverty districts—cannot be ruled out. And without information on the LD and MR interventions in low- and high-poverty districts, which is the more appropriate placement is not known.

Since gender and ethnicity contributed to the likelihood of placement in special education when several sociodemographic variables were controlled, district-level findings were interpreted by Oswald et al. as lending indirect support to the "systematic bias hypothesis." In order for the correlation of gender and ethnicity with placement to signal systematic bias, it must be true that males and females, and students of all races, achieve and behave similarly in the classroom. If not, those achievement and behavior differences will be captured in the race and gender coefficients (absent control variables that were not available in the OCR data).

Other data, however, suggest that achievement and behavior cannot be assumed to be uncorrelated with race and gender. The recently published National Assessment of Educational Progress (NAEP) study of reading at the fourth-grade level reports percentages of students reading below the "basic" level by race/ethnicity: Asian = 22 percent, white = 27 percent, Hispanic = 58 percent, and black = 63 percent (Donohue et al., 2001). The students most likely to be referred for special education are those with low achievement, and there appear to be many more Hispanic and black students with low achievement in reading. Moreover, data from the Early Childhood Longitudinal Study (discussed in Chapter 3) suggest that, already at kindergarten entry, there are differences in classroom-relevant knowledge and behavior by race/ethnicity.

The interactions of minority and nonminority achievement levels with different levels of poverty and the composition of student enrollments are likely to be complex. It is plausible, however, that lower achievement by black or Hispanic students in a school context in which most of the white and/or Asian students are achieving at a higher level creates the circumstances that lead to greater disproportionate enrollment of the lower-achieving black or Hispanic students in special education. If there are smaller achievement differences between groups of students in districts with both high concentrations of minority students and high poverty, less disproportion may be observed as a consequence. We emphasize that data currently collected by OCR do not allow for a test of *either* the systematic bias or the achievement difference hypotheses. The need for different kinds of investigations that go beyond the establishment of correlation is apparent if one is to test these competing hypotheses.

One alternative approach is to conduct equal treatment studies of students referred for and either placed or not placed in special education. Hosp and Reschly (2001) compared black and white students placed in different special education programs, including part-time resource, full-time special class, etc. First, students in more restrictive placements, regardless of race, had more severe problems, a finding that is expected if there is any rationality associated with the continuum of special education program options. Second, for each placement, ranging from less to more restrictive, black students had a greater number of problems and more severe problems than white students. For example, the black students placed in part-time resource programs had lower achievement test scores and were more likely to exhibit behavior problems. Similarly, the black students in full-time placements had more severe problems than similarly situated white students. The findings in this equal treatment study suggest that minority students must demonstrate greater need in order to receive special supports. Similar findings were reported for black and white students placed in special education in the mild mental retardation category (Reschly and Kicklighter, 1985; Reschly and Ward, 1991). While these results are suggestive, independent replication in a variety of districts wold be required before any conclusions can be drawn.

It is not the position of the committee that no discrimination takes place in placement decisions, but rather that the evidence available is insufficient to support a claim that *either* discrimination does or does not play a significant role. And if discrimination is operative, whether its consequence is excessive placement of minority student in special education or denial of special education service to minority students is unclear. The data presented at the district level lend themselves to multiple interpretations. Whether discrimination, genuine achievement differences, or both are at play, the committee believes that a policy response is warranted. Later chapters draw on extensive literatures to better understand each hypothesis and provide policy recommendations.

Gifted and Talented

Analyses of race/ethnicity and high achievement in the gifted and talented area are relatively rare (College Board, 1999). At the committee's request, Miller (2000) examined existing datasets focusing on the representation of minority children at the upper end of the achievement distribution. He presented data (see Table 2-18) showing the percentage of children in 1st and 3rd grade performing above two cutoff scores in reading and math. Clearly, achievement differences are apparent early in the school years for minority children as a group. Table 2-19 suggests those patterns persist across subjects in 4th grade and apply to Native Americans/Alaskan Natives as well as blacks and Hispanics.

The complexity of this pattern becomes even more apparent when one considers differences between minority and majority children while attempting to control for social class differences (Table 2-20). In describing the above table, Miller points to two patterns:

> First, for whites, blacks, and Hispanics, scores go up as the education level of students' parents rises. Thus, within all three groups, the average

TABLE 2-18 Percentages of 1st Grade and 3rd Grade Cohorts in Prospects Study Who Scored At or Above the 50th and 75th Percentiles in Reading and Mathematics

| | First Grade Cohort | | | | Third Grade Cohort | | | |
| | Reading | | Mathematics | | Reading | | Mathematics | |
Race/Ethnicity	50th+	75th+	50th+	75th+	50th+	75th+	50th+	75th+
White	48	22	55	27	58	30	54	29
Black	23	7	25	8	19	6	22	8
Hispanic	25	8	29	12	24	7	27	10

SOURCE: Miller (2000).

TABLE 2-19   Percentages of 4th Grade Students Who Scored Within the Proficient and Advanced Ranges on the 1998 Reading, 1996 Math, 1996 Science, and 1998 Writing Tests of the National Assessment of Educational Progress

| | Proficient | | | | Advanced | | | |
Race/Ethnicity	Reading	Math	Science	Writing	Reading	Math	Science	Writing
White	29	25	33	27	10	3	4	2
Black	9	5	7	8	1	0	0	0
Hispanic	11	8	9	10	2	0	0	0
Asian/								
Pacific Islander	25	21	25	32	12	5	4	4
American Indian	12	7	24	11	2	1	2	1

SOURCES: Donahue (1999); Reece et al. (1997); Bourque et al. (1997); and Greenwald et al. (1999), compiled by Miller (2000).

> NAEP reading and history scores for students who have parents with college degrees are a great deal higher than for students who have no parent with a high school diploma or who have one or both parents with a high school degree but no more. This pattern of scores going up as social class rises is a consistent finding of educational research going back several decades. It also is an unsurprising finding (p. 14).

He went on to describe the more surprising pattern of results in this table as follows:

TABLE 2-20 1994 Average NAEP Reading and History Scores for 12th Graders, by Race/Ethnicity and Parent Education Level

Race/Ethnicity	1994 NAEP Reading Test Score Averages by Parent Education Level				1994 NAEP History Test Score Averages by Parent Education Level			
	Less than High School Degree	Graduated from High School	Some Post-Secondary Education	Graduated from College	Less than High School Degree	Graduated from High School	Some Post-Secondary Education	Graduated from College
White	274	283	294	302	271	281	291	300
Black	258	258	271	272	251	258	269	273
Hispanic	260	265	279	283	256	264	277	277
White – Black =	16	25	23	30	20	23	22	27
White – Hispanic =	14	17	15	19	14	17	14	23

NOTE: Differences in white and black scores and in white and Hispanic scores were calculated before rounding.

SOURCES: Campbell et al. (1996) and Beatty et al. (1996), compiled by Miller (2000).

The second important pattern in the data . . . is that, despite the tendency across the racial/ethnic groups for average scores to rise with parent education level, there are, nevertheless, large differences in average scores among the racial/ethnic groups at each parent education level. Indeed, there is a tendency for the gaps in average scores to be larger at high parent education levels than at low parent education levels. In any case, for both tests, black 12th graders with parents with college degrees had average scores that were about the same as for white students with no parent with a high school diploma. And Hispanics with parents with college degrees had average scores close to those of white students who had parents with a high school degree (pp. 14-15).

Data presented in his paper (see Table 2-20) were interpreted to support several important conclusions and generalizations about the pattern of minority underrepresentation among high-achieving students:

• The overall underrepresentation of several racial/ethnic minority groups among top students relative to the white majority is very extensive and long-standing.
• This limited minority presence among top students is found using virtually all traditional measures of academic achievement, including school grades, standardized test scores, and class rank.
• Extensive underrepresentation is present at all levels of the educational system, beginning in kindergarten.
• The limited presence of several minority groups among high-achieving students cuts across social class lines, that is, substantial minority-majority achievement gaps exist at all social class levels as measured by parent education and family income (Miller, 2000:1).

As with the special education analyses, data correlations cannot begin to suggest why the achievement distributions differ. Rather, they describe a situation in which available measures of student achievement place a smaller proportion of non-Asian minority children in the upper range from which gifted students are likely to be drawn.

CONCLUSIONS AND RECOMMENDATIONS

The national datasets provided by OCR and OSEP provide a snapshot of the relative participation in special education categories of children in different racial/ethnic groups. An important caveat that we have emphasized is that the figures aggregated at a national level obscure variations at the state and local levels and do not permit examination of other factors (e.g., social class, exposure to risk factors) that correlate with race and ethnicity. In addition, we have noted that weaknesses in the data temper the confidence with which conclusions can be drawn.

Nevertheless, these two large datasets suggest that both black and American Indian/Alaskan Native children are at heightened risk for identification as having mental retardation and emotional disturbance. In the most recent surveys, black children are twice as likely as their white counterparts to be classified as MR and half again as likely to be classified as ED. American Indian/Alaskan Native students are also at slightly higher risk than white students for being identified as MR and LD. Conversely, Asian/Pacific Islander students are least likely to be classified MR, LD, or ED.

Clearly, the LD category subsumes the vast majority of children classified into one of the judgmental high-incidence categories. The recent surveys find that over 6 percent of the children in all racial/ethnic groups, except Asian/Pacific Islander, are served in the category of LD. American Indian/Alaskan Native students are somewhat more at risk for identification as LD. Despite the high rates of assignment to the LD category, since the rate of participation of black and Hispanic students approximates that of white students overall, the issue of overrepresentation has generally not been raised.

The picture from the gifted and talented data is a mirror image of what is seen for mental retardation. The 1998 OCR survey reveals a rather high rate of participation of students in gifted programs: 6.20 percent of the nation's students are projected to be participating. Asian/Pacific Islander students are clearly the most likely to participate, with far lower placement rates for blacks and Hispanics.

There continues to be higher participation in the high-incidence disability categories for males. The greatest gender disparity in identification rates is found in the ED category (80-percent male), followed by LD (70-percent male) and MR (60-percent male).

Using the OCR surveys over time permits some examination of how participation by children in the racial/ethnic groups in certain disability categories has changed (see Table 2-21). Of the four categories considered (MR, LD, ED, and gifted and talented), only mental retardation shows a reduction in the percentage of children served between the mid-1970s and 1998.

Between the mid-1970s and 1998 the only category in which risk for identification fell is mental retardation. The racial/ethnic group in which there is the largest reduction is black students (–1.08 percent), while there has been a very slight increase for Asian/Pacific Islander students (0.19 percent). For the learning disability category, there has been a dramatic and uniform increase in the risk for identification. There are substantially more

TABLE 2-21 Changes in Participation Rates in Judgmental Categories by Ethnic Group (Percentage)

	AmI/A	A/PI	Hispanic	Black	White	Total
Mental Retardation						
1974	1.94	0.45	1.50	3.72	1.19	1.58
1998	1.28	0.64	0.92	2.64	1.18	1.37
	−0.65	0.19	−0.58	−1.08	−0.01	−0.21
Learning Disabilities						
1974	1.60	0.52	1.29	1.03	1.24	1.21
1998	7.45	2.23	6.44	6.49	6.02	6.02
	5.86	1.70	5.15	5.46	4.78	4.82
Emotionally Disturbed						
1976	0.29	0.08	0.25	0.42	0.26	0.28
1998	1.03	0.26	0.55	1.45	0.91	0.93
	0.74	0.18	0.30	1.03	0.66	0.65
Gifted and Talented						
1976	0.42	2.26	0.40	0.47	1.05	0.93
1998	4.86	9.98	3.57	3.04	7.47	6.20
	4.44	7.72	3.17	2.57	6.42	5.27

black and Hispanic students served as LD than are served in MR and ED combined, although placement in this category shows no disproportion for those groups.

For ED there has been an increase for all groups; however, the increase is far more modest than what has occurred in the LD category. The increase in placement rates ("risk") for gifted and talented programs is greater than for any of the three judgmental disability categories—5.27 percent across racial/ethnic groups; however, the increase for black and Hispanic students is substantially less than for the other racial/ethnic groups.

In the next few chapters we look at potential explanations for the patterns suggested by the data. But for the reasons described in this chapter, these data are a weak foundation on which to build public policy. The committee urges that policy decisions utilizing these datasets explicitly recognize the tenuous nature of the data.

Our recommendations with respect to data collection (DC) are directed at two goals: one is to improve the existing data collection process designed for monitoring program participation and civil rights compliance, and the other is to expand the collection of data to allow for research that would improve understanding of nonnormative achievement and behavior, as well as responses to intervention. Currently there is considerable redundancy in the reporting requirements placed on schools by the Office for Civil Rights and the Office of Special Education Programs. In response to the Paperwork Reduction Act of 1995 (44 U.S.C. Chapter 35), the Department of Education provided states with the option in 2001 of consolidated data collection on students with disabilities (Federal Register: March 8, 2001 (Vol. 66, Number 46)), an option that few states have chosen. While the efforts of the two agencies within the Department of Education to consolidate the collection are commendable, the committee believes a reexamination of survey design in the interest both of providing more reliable indicators, and of facilitating reporting from the perspective of local education agencies and states, is warranted.

> **Recommendation DC.1: The committee recommends that the Department of Education conduct a single, well-designed data collection effort to monitor both the number of children receiving services through the Individuals with Disabilities Education Act and the characteristics of those children of concern to civil rights enforcement efforts.**

Whether data collection responsibility is given to either of these offices, the National Center for Education Statistics, or some other entity, the shift in responsibility would require supporting changes:

> a. Data collected should meet all requirements for effective OCR monitoring, including disaggregated data by district and state, and they should be accessed easily by OCR and OSEP. This would require data collection to accommodate OCR's monitoring of data on assignment to gifted and talented programs and on limited English proficiency not currently collected by OSEP. The definitions in this category should allow for the distinction between "gifted" and "talented" to the extent that students are being served in different types of programs.
>
> b. In the reauthorization of IDEA, statutory authority should be given to those responsible for data collection to collect child count data for disability category by racial/ethnic group by gender for both special education and gifted and talented placements as well as by state and local district levels.

The committee urges the federal agency reporting on special education enrollments by racial/ethnic group do so by reporting *risk indices*—the proportion of a given racial/ethnic group's enrollment in the general school population that is enrolled in a given disability category. In order to accomplish this goal, steps must be taken to coordinate reporting child counts by age, currently done in the OSEP reporting by disability category, for ages 3-21, with the NCES Common Core of Data, which reports by grade level. This would remedy the current situation in which it is impossible to align the ages 3-5 and the 18-21 child count by OSEP with any meaningful count of the total population.

The committee also urges that the Office for Civil Rights monitor the impact of education reform initiatives, such as high-stakes testing programs, to ensure that implementation of these initiatives does not exacerbate minority representation problems in special or gifted education.

While a more careful data collection effort of the sort outlined above would improve the understanding of who is being assigned to special education and gifted and talented programs, it would do little to further understanding of the reasons for placement, the appropriateness of placement (or nonplacement), the services provided, or the consequences that ensue.

Moreover, the variation observed from one state to the next serves as a reminder that in special education or gifted and talented programs, we refer to practices that differ dramatically from one location to the next. While special education may be a set of well-targeted specialized classroom supports for children in need in one school, it may be a dead-end program in others—a last resort for teachers who can no longer work with a student. The data are not available to tell which it is, in which schools, and for which students. And while the data are poor with respect to special education, the data on gifted and talented students are even worse.

Recommendation DC.2: The committee recommends that a national advisory panel be convened to design the collection of nationally representative longitudinal data that would allow for more informed study of minority disproportion in special education and gifted and talented programs. The panel should include scholars in special education research as well as researchers experienced in national longitudinal data collection and analysts in a variety of allied fields, including anthropology, psychology, and sociology.

The panel should assess the cost of collecting data that could answer the following questions:

• What antecedents to special education placement are associated with students' assignment to special education services? Antecedents studied should include, but not be limited to: race (self-identified and school-identified), gender, and other socioeconomic and social background factors, and school factors, such as class size, teacher experience and preparation, instructional strategies, and school and classroom resources.

• How do schools differ in their categorization of students, and are these differences associated with differences in students' access to special education services?

• Are students who present with the same researcher-identified condition treated differently in different schools and, if so, what policy, resource, and individual-level factors are associated with these differences in treatment? What is the incidence of students who have the same research-identified conditions but are never referred for special education assessment? And is referral to special education assessment associated with severity of the researcher-identified condition or some other factors?

• If students who present with the same researcher-identified condition are treated differently, how is access or lack of access to a variety of special education services associated with later levels of cognitive achievement and behavioral adjustment?

The data would have improved value if the following additional information were included:

• how long the family has lived in the United States;
• birth country of students, their parents, and their grandparents;
• language proficiency (in both English and native language);
• education level of parents;
• level of acculturation; and
• experiences with literacy artifacts and practices.

Analysis for this report of the effect of race/ethnicity on special education placement or outcomes was made more difficult because many research studies did not specify the racial/ethnic composition of the sample or had too few minority children to measure effects by race/ethnicity. The committee urges that research funded by the Department of Education using these or other data require the careful description of samples as well as differential effects, to the extent feasible, by race, ethnicity, limited English proficiency, socioeconomic status, and gender.

APPENDIX 2-A

TABLE 2-A1 1997 Comparison of States by Highest Risk (RI) and Composition (CI) Indices for Black Students in the Category of Mental Retardation

State	RI	CI	White RI for State
Highest RI			
Arizona	5.62%	43.11%	0.69%
Alabama	5.58%	62.93%	1.90%
Iowa	4.92%	6.67%	2.58%
Nebraska	4.30%	11.46%	1.95%
Highest CI			
District of Columbia	1.21%	95.36%	0.13%
Mississippi	2.38%	78.45%	0.63%
Georgia	3.44%	64.19%	1.28%
Alabama	5.58%	62.93%	1.90%

TABLE 2-A2 1997 Comparison of States by Highest Risk (RI) and Composition (CI) Indices for Hispanic Students in the Category of Mental Retardation

State	RI	CI	White RI for State
Highest RI			
Nebraska	2.43%	5.52%	1.95%
Iowa	2.19%	2.08%	2.58%
Ohio	2.16%	1.43%	2.34%
Hawaii	2.06%	3.44%	6.78%
Highest CI			
New Mexico	0.81%	51.97%	0.56%
California	0.50%	43.50%	0.40%
Arizona	1.02%	34.94%	0.69%
Texas	0.72%	34.85%	0.60%

TABLE 2-A3 1997 Comparison of States by Highest Risk (RI) and Composition (CI) Indices for Black Students in the Category of Learning Disabilities

State	RI	CI	White RI for State
Highest RI			
Delaware	11.84%	43.72%	6.75%
New Mexico	9.99%	3.06%	6.83%
Nevada	9.61%	14.92%	6.19%
Alabama	9.47%	30.63%	5.79%
Highest CI			
District of Columbia	5.34%	90.97%	3.94%
Mississippi	6.83%	56.76%	5.15%
Louisiana	6.65%	53.83%	4.26%
South Carolina	4.96%	43.29%	5.03%

TABLE 2-A4 1997 Comparison of States by Highest Risk (RI) and Composition (CI) Indices for Hispanic Students in the Category of Learning Disability

State	RI	CI	White RI for State
Highest RI			
Delaware	8.88%	3.35%	6.75%
New York	8.41%	21.42%	6.63%
New Mexico	8.21%	52.79%	6.83%
	13.84%	6.89%	7.37%
Highest CI			
New Mexico	8.21%	52.79%	6.83%
California	5.27%	41.89%	4.92%
Texas	6.82%	36.62%	6.69%
Arizona	5.40%	31.80%	4.40%

TABLE 2-A5 1997 Comparison of States by Highest Risk (RI) and Composition (CI) Indices for Black Students in the Category of Emotional Disturbance

State	RI	CI	White RI for State
Highest RI			
Minnesota	3.64%	10.39%	1.84%
Iowa	3.49%	12.54%	0.92%
Nebraska	2.81%	19.79%	0.71%
Highest CI			
District of Columbia	0.97%	97.54%	0.19%
Louisiana	1.00%	59.65%	0.51%
South Carolina	0.93%	55.67%	0.58%
North Carolina	1.25%	50.92%	0.53%

TABLE 2-A6 1997 Comparison of States by Highest Risk (RI) and Composition (CI) Indices for Hispanic Students in the Category of Emotional Disturbance

State	RI	CI	White RI for State
Highest RI			
Vermont	2.38%	0.70%	1.40%
Minnesota	1.76%	2.16%	1.84%
Hawaii	1.53%	3.29%	1.52%
Highest CI			
New Mexico	0.85%	43.68%	1.10%
Texas	0.67%	26.15%	1.09%
New York	1.48%	21.26%	0.74%
California	0.08%	17.40%	0.24%

TABLE 2-A7 1997 Comparison of States by Lowest Risk (RI) and Composition (CI) Indices for Black Students in the Category of Gifted and Talented

State	RI	CI	White RI for State
Lowest RI			
Massachusetts	0.39%	3.94%	0.83%
New Hampshire	0.39%	0.28%	1.34%
Louisiana	0.72%	12.31%	3.81%
Kansas	0.80%	2.31%	3.37%
Lowest CI			
North Dakota	2.14%	0.39%	4.80%
Idaho	1.99%	0.42%	2.97%
Montana	6.42%	0.52%	6.57%
Wyoming	2.75%	0.52%	3.75%

TABLE 2-A8 1997 Comparison of States by Lowest Risk (RI) and Composition (CI) Indices for Hispanic Students in the Category of Gifted and Talented

State	RI	CI	White RI for State
Lowest RI			
New Hampshire	0.25%	0.27%	1.34%
Massachusetts	0.50%	5.62%	0.83%
New York	0.66%	3.74%	5.04%
Kansas	0.72%	1.59%	3.37%
Lowest CI			
West Virginia	0.77%	0.11%	2.31%
Maine	0.97%	0.14%	3.25%
New Hampshire	0.25%	0.27%	1.34%
Mississippi	2.92%	0.29%	7.70%

Part II

Pregnancy to Preschool:
Early Influences on
Cognition and Behavior

As Chapter 2 suggests, one can observe variation in the proportion of students from different ethnic groups assigned to special education and gifted and talented programs without knowing whether there are too many or too few members of any racial/ethnic group in any given category. To answer such a question, one would have to understand the source of the disproportion.

The committee considered three potential explanations, which are not mutually exclusive and which may well operate in tandem:

1. By the time they reach school age, children differ in the cognitive and behavioral characteristics that are related to placement in special education and gifted and talented programs. These differences may be distributed disproportionately among children in different racial/ethnic groups.

2. Schools may have an independent influence on the academic success and behavioral problems of students that varies with the racial/ethnic composition of students in the school, or with the race or ethnicity of the individual student.

3. Standards (or the implementation of standards) for referral and assessment of students for special education and gifted and talented programs may be biased, or they may be applied differentially across racial/ethnic groups to produce disproportion.

In this part we focus on the first explanation, asking whether characteristics that predict achievement and behavior problems differ across racial/ethnic groups. To do so, we ask what is known about factors that significantly contribute to variation in cognitive and behavioral function. Because such a review could itself span volumes, we focus in Chapter 3 on factors for which a research base is available to suggest both that the factor is significant in cognitive and behavioral development *and* that prevalence differs by race or ethnicity.

In Chapter 4 we review what is known from a now-extensive research base about early intervention programs and their potential to improve cognitive and behavioral outcomes for children at risk. We focus particularly on the more limited evidence available regarding the impact of early intervention on the placement of children in special education programs once they have entered school. Our early childhood recommendations appear at the end of Chapter 4.

3

Influences on Cognitive and Behavioral Development

CHANGING PERSPECTIVES ON
COGNITIVE AND BEHAVIORAL FUNCTION

Research in a variety of biological and social sciences in the past few decades has brought about substantial change in earlier understandings of the contributors to cognitive and behavioral function. In classic works by Galton (1869) and Burt et al. (1934), differences in intelligence were attributed to heredity, emphasizing a perception of the child as constitutionally separate from the environment. In the social sciences, however, a series of landmark studies in the 1930s and 1940s of infants and young children reared in institutions drew attention to the environmental and contextual contributors to child development (Ramey and Sackett, 2000). The research that ensued using animal models (Sackett et al., 1999), the study of children who experienced deprivation in institutional settings, and the proactive early intervention efforts in the 1960s collectively provided compelling evidence that early experience matters a great deal.

While genetic and physiological factors continue to play a central role in the understanding of cognitive and behavioral performance, the perception of the child as constitutionally separate from the environment no longer holds. Understanding the development of child behavior increasingly has required a focus on aspects of the environment that serve as moderators of performance (Sameroff, 1993; Ceci et al., 1997). The analytic lenses and

93

methods of different social sciences have focused attention on different correlates of achievement and behavior. Economics has focused on the role of family income and the education (or human capital) of parents; sociology looks more at the community, school, and family structure; and psychology focuses on the interactions among family members and other important individuals to understand social, emotional, and cognitive development. In seminal work that launched a line of research in social ecology, Bronfenbrenner (1979) suggested that the development of the child needs to be viewed as influenced by all of these factors. The current scientific task is to catalog and describe the relevant contributions of these dynamic components through time.

As the tools of the social sciences have become more powerful, so have those for studying the brain. We have come to understand that biological and environmental factors are not completely separate parts of the picture (Shore, 1997; Wahlsten and Gottlieb, 1997; Bidell and Fischer, 1997; Hunt, 1997). They combine as two pigments in a single paint, together determining a color that neither alone could create. Genetic and health influences themselves are no longer seen as purely biological (National Research Council [NRC], 2000b). Genetic expression is now understood not as a fixed and predetermined influence, but as a probabilistic propensity responsive in some degree to environmental influence (Plomin, 1997; Sameroff, 2000). Researchers can observe in animal studies and, to a more limited extent, in human studies that environmental experiences change the very physiology of the brain: encoding new experiences fosters new brain growth (Greenough and Black, 1992; Black and Greenough, 1986).

Contemporary genetics suggests further that the gene-environment dynamic is not one in which each has a distinct but separate role to play, nor that environment determines whether a gene does or does not exert the influence of its predetermined code. Rather, the function of the genetic system is itself context dependent (Bidell and Fischer, 1997). A dramatic instance is the case of a parasitic wasp that lays its eggs in two different hosts, a butterfly or a fly. Offspring that develop in the butterfly host have wings, but those that develop in the fly host do not, despite an identical genetic code (Gottlieb, 1992; Bidell and Fischer, 1997). While a substantial body of research has demonstrated the importance of genetics in explaining variation in cognitive and behavioral performance (Bouchard, 1997; Hunt, 1997), it is clear that genetic variation cannot be understood separately from context.

Figure 3-1 presents one schema that explicitly acknowledges the dynamic, reciprocal interplay between biology and experience (Ramey and Ramey, 2000). In this model, cognitive, social, and emotional development is an outgrowth of the transactions between children and the significant others in their environment. But a myriad of factors—biological, social,

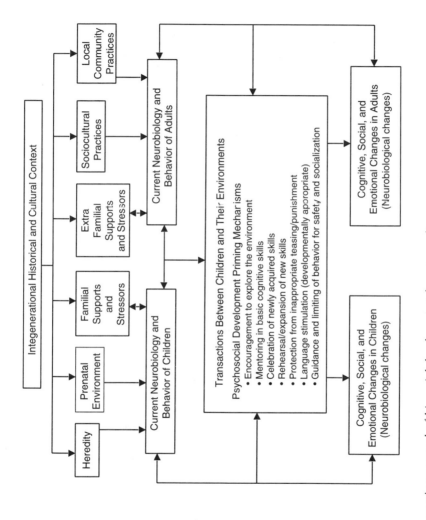

FIGURE 3-1 Schematic portrayal of biosocial developmental contextualism.
SOURCE: Ramey and Ramey (1998). Reprinted with permission.

economic, and cultural—influence the behaviors of both the child and the adults engaged in those interactions.

Below we review the current knowledge base regarding early influences on cognition and behavior by looking first at research regarding the biological influences on early development and then the research on environmental (social, emotional, economic) influences. The artificial nature of the dichotomy between biological and environmental influences is perhaps most evident when we discuss the role of poverty under the social and environmental context of development. Each of the biological factors discussed is found to vary with poverty status as well. Increasingly, research suggests that the biological and social worlds must be seen as tightly intertwined if the goal is to understand the cognitive and behavioral outcomes for children and the potential roles for social intervention (McLoyd and Lozoff, 2001; Ramey and Ramey, 1998). Despite the contemporary understanding of their inseparablity, the research enterprises regarding biological and social contributors have for the most part been conducted independently and from different disciplinary research traditions. We therefore look at each piece individually, after which we turn to their interactions.

Our focus in this chapter is, of necessity, on early harms and risk factors that impair normal development, as well as interventions that can diminish the impact of those risk factors. Our limited attention to issues regarding accelerated development reflects the research base, and the research base in turn reflects research opportunities (NRC, 2000c). Much of what we have learned about the developing brain, for example, we have learned because an abnormal event (premature birth, trauma, fetal alcohol syndrome) has occurred to call attention to the phenomenon. The group for study is clearly defined, and the contrasting case between the normal and the abnormal circumstance is clear. The group of high achievers is not so easily defined by an event. Moreover, the social policies designed to address the needs of disadvantaged children provide opportunities for research on the effects of physical and environmental risk, and of its amelioration, on development. No similar scaled, sustained research effort has been undertaken to better understand high achievement.

Nonetheless, the complex of factors that influence student achievement is likely to do so across the entire distribution. In Figure 3-2, achievement is plotted as a normal distribution, with the "main population" representing a hypothetical circumstance of a general population in which students differ in achievement because they themselves differ and because their environments differ within an average or low-risk range. The diagonal area of the distribution represents a hypothetical group of students who might require additional supports (special education at the lower end, gifted education at the upper end) when teaching targets students at the mean. We focus in this chapter on circumstances that diminish achievement—or shift the location

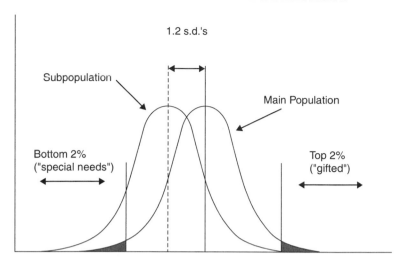

FIGURE 3-2 Idealized representation depicting displacement of subgroups with regard to main population on any variable that is normally distributed.
SOURCE: Case, Griffin, and Kelly (1999). Reprinted with permission.

of the curve back, as in the "subpopulation" for those developing in high-risk environments. This shift simultaneously increases the number of children with special needs at the lower end *and* decreases the number of high achievers who may be identified as gifted at the upper end. In a sense then, this chapter is about both groups, although those cases at the left tail of the distribution have been studied more because of their distinguishing characteristics than those in the right tail.

BIOLOGICAL CONTRIBUTORS TO COGNITION AND BEHAVIOR

The importance of the early years of life to development is incontrovertible (Ramey et al., 2000; Ramey and Ramey, 1999; NRC, 2000a). The unparalleled pace of brain growth and the development of fundamental cognitive, emotional, social, and motor processes make the period from conception through infancy one of exceptional opportunity and vulnerability (McLoyd and Lozoff, 2001). While the plasticity of the brain appears to extend well into adolescence, with growth in some areas of the brain as late as the third decade of life (NRC, 2000a), children who experience biological insults and stressors early in life are at greater risk for long-term developmental problems (McLoyd and Lozoff, 2001). Deprivation in the extreme can produce functional mental retardation and aberrant social and emotional behavior in animals born healthy and with good genetic endowment (Ramey and Ramey, 1999). In humans, mild mental retardation with

TABLE 3-1 Contributors to Early Brain Development

Conditions or substances needed for normal brain development:	Conditions and substances that are detrimental or toxic to the developing brain:
• Oxygen	• Alcohol
• Adequate protein and energy	• Lead
• Micronutrients, such as iron and zinc	• Tobacco
• Adequate gestation	• Prenatal infections (e.g., rubella,
• Iodine	plasmolysis, cytomegalovirus)
• Thyroid hormone	• Polychlorinated biphenyls (pcb)s
• Folic acid	• Ionizing radiation
• Essential fatty acids	• Cocaine
• Sensory stimulation	• Metabolic abnormalities (excess
• Activity	phenylalanine, ammonia)
• Social interaction	• Aluminum
	• Methylmercury
	• Chronic illness

SOURCE: NRC (2000).

no documented biomedical cause has been observed at elevated levels among very poor families (Garber, 1988).

For any individual child, genetic and experiential information come together in a process that organizes the brain to function. An NRC report on the science of early childhood development lists environmental factors that play a significant role in modulating prenatal and early postnatal brain development (see NRC, 2000a:199). The list, although not exhaustive, includes factors selected on the basis of clinical importance, the availability of basic research on brain effects, and/or the existence of relevant clinical studies (Table 3-1). In this report, we focus on a subset of these factors, which research suggests are implicated in *differential developmental outcomes for children by race:* premature birth (adequate gestation), fetal alcohol and nicotine exposure, and micronutrient deficiency, and exposure to lead. We do not suggest that these factors are uniquely important to healthy development. Other critical factors, such as the role of iodine in cognitive development, are not considered here because in this country they are unlikely to contribute to current developmental differences, since effective prevention measures have eliminated the iodine deficiency problem for children of all races (Stanbury, 1998).

Low Birthweight

In each year in the past decade, between 7 and 8 percent of babies were born at weights below 2,500 grams. The vast majority of low-birthweight children have normal outcomes. As a group, however, low-birthweight babies have higher rates of neurodevelopmental and behavioral problems (Hack et al., 1995; McLoyd and Lozoff, 2001). They are more likely to have lower IQ, cerebral palsy, less emotional maturity and social competence, and attentional difficulties (National Research Council, 2000a). A recent study of siblings found that those born weighing less than 5.5 pounds were almost four times less likely to graduate from high school by age 19 than their normal-birthweight siblings—15.2 percent of low-birthweight siblings, compared with 57.5 percent of normal-birthweight siblings graduated on time (Conley and Bennett, 2000).

The neurocognitive differences that are observed with low birthweight are more pronounced the lower the weight (Breslau et al., 1996). Similarly, the child's general developmental status and intelligence scores decrease with reductions in gestational age (Saigal et al., 1991).[1] At the borders of viability (22-24 weeks) where mortality is high, neurological damage to babies who survive is often sustained (Allen et al., 1993). But even lower-risk preterm babies (27-34 weeks) sometimes show cognitive lags compared with their full-term counterparts (de Haan et al., 2000).

Damage from premature birth arises in part due to the interruption of the normal process of brain development in utero, including the expected intrauterine stimuli and nutrients important for growth (NRC, 2000a). Recent research suggests that even when preterm infants have benign neonatal courses, they show poorer performance on elicited imitation tasks at 18 months (de Haan et al., 2000). But premature birth also increases the probability that infants will experience pathological events that directly injure the brain. Intracranial hemorrhage, for example, occurs in approximately 20 percent of 28- to 34-week infants and 60 percent of infants born between 24 and 28 weeks. The hemorrhage tends to be more severe at lower gestational ages, resulting in a higher likelihood of a major disability. Even with less severe hemorrhages, however, the risk of minor disabilities—including behavior problems, attention problems, and memory deficits—rises (Lowe and Papile, 1990; Ross et al., 1996; National Research Council 2000a; McLoyd and Lozoff, 2001).

In the United States, low birthweight is more common among blacks than any other racial/ethnic group (McLoyd and Lozoff, 2001; David and Collins, 1997; Foster, 1997) (see Table 3-2). Blacks are about twice as likely as whites to be born at low birthweights (see Figure 3-3), even controlling for socioeconomic status (Conley and Bennett, 2000; Foster, 1997). Interestingly, the incidence of low birthweight for babies of African-born

---

[1]While gestational age and birthweight are strongly correlated, babies can be small for gestational age.

black women more closely resembles that of U.S.-born whites than of U.S.-born blacks (David and Collins, 1997). Among whites there is a strong association between maternal education and low birthweight (National Center for Health Statistics, 1998; Guyer et al., 1997). While this is true of blacks as well, the rate for black mothers who have 16 or more years of education is still above that of whites with less than a high school education.

The link between income and the incidence of low birthweight has been well established (McLoyd and Lozoff, 2001; NRC, 2000a; Kiely et al., 1994). This relationship persists even when the mother's educational attainment, sex, birth order, and race/ethnicity are controlled (Conley and Bennett, 2000). In a recent provocative study, however, income lost its significance when parental birthweight status was controlled. The probability of having a low-birthweight child increased fourfold if the mother herself had low birthweight, and sixfold if the father had low birthweight (Conley and Bennett, 2000). This is a single study, however, and has not been replicated to our knowledge. At the same time that this study questioned the role of income in predicting the *incidence* of low birthweight, it found that an income-to-needs ratio of the family during the child's first five years was a significant predictor of the *effect* of low birthweight on timely high school graduation.

The incidence of low birthweight declined in the 1970s and early 1980s but has risen 10 percent since then—from a low of 6.7 in 1984 to 7.6 in 1998. Much of this is due to the increase in the odds of survival for low-birthweight babies due to increases in medical technologies (Seelman and Sweeney, 1995) and to a rise in multiple-birth rates among white women. The rate has declined overall for black mothers but has remained stable (at about 3 percent) for very small babies of 1,500 grams or less (McLoyd and Lozoff, 2001).

Several interventions have been shown to reduce the incidence of low birthweight: prenatal care, maternal nutrition and adequate weight gain during pregnancy, control of hypertension, and avoidance of long work hours and excessive physical exertion toward the end of pregnancy (Luke et al., 1995; McLoyd and Lozoff, 2001). Interventions focused on improving outcomes for low-birthweight babies have also demonstrated some effectiveness. These range from changes in the care these infants receive in neonatal intensive care units (Als, 1997; Hernandez-Reif and Field, 2000) to the Infant Health and Development Program, which provided comprehensive services to the infants and their families for several months after discharge (see Box 3-1). Additional stimulation of low-birthweight babies can reduce the cognitive impact, especially for the heavier babies in families with lower socioeconomic status (Hack et al., 1995; Ramey et al., 1992).

TABLE 3-2 Percentage of Low-Birthweight Births by Detailed Race and Hispanic Origin, 1980-1998

Race and Hispanic Origin	Low Birthweight (less than 2,500 grams, about 5.5 pounds)					Very Low Birthweight (less than 1,500 grams, about 3.25 pounds)				
	1980	1985	1990	1995	1998	1980	1985	1990	1995	1998
Total	6.8	6.8	7.0	7.3	7.6	1.15	1.21	1.27	1.35	1.45
White, non-Hispanic	5.7	5.6	5.6	6.2	6.6	.86	.90	.93	1.04	1.15
Black, non-Hispanic	12.7	12.6	13.3	13.2	13.2	2.46	2.66	2.93	2.98	3.11
Hispanic[a]	6.1	6.2	6.1	6.3	6.4	.98	1.01	1.03	1.11	1.15
Mexican American	5.6	5.8	5.5	5.8	6.0	.92	.97	.92	1.01	1.02
Puerto Rican	9.0	8.7	9.0	9.4	9.7	1.29	1.30	1.62	1.79	1.86
Cuban	5.6	6.0	5.7	6.5	6.5	1.02	1.18	1.20	1.19	1.33
Central and South American	5.8	5.7	5.8	6.2	6.5	.99	1.01	1.05	1.13	1.23
Other and unknown Hispanic	7.0	6.8	6.9	7.5	7.6	1.01	.96	1.09	1.28	1.38
Asian/Pacific Islander	6.7	6.2	6.5	6.9	7.4	.92	.85	.87	.91	1.10
Chinese	5.2	5.0	4.7	5.3	5.3	.66	.57	.51	.67	.75
Japanese	6.6	6.2	6.2	7.3	7.5	.94	.84	.73	.87	.84
Filipino	7.4	6.9	7.3	7.8	8.2	.99	.86	1.05	1.13	1.35
Hawaiian and part Hawaiian	7.2	6.5	7.2	6.8	7.2	1.05	1.03	.97	.94	1.53
Other Asian/ Pacific Islander	6.8	6.2	6.6	7.1	7.8	.96	.91	.92	.91	1.12
American Indian/ Alaska Native	6.4	5.9	6.1	6.6	6.8	.92	1.01	1.01	1.10	1.24

NOTES: Excludes live births with unknown birthweight. Low-birthweight infants weigh less than 2,500 grams at birth, about 5.5 pounds. Very-low-birthweight infants weigh less than 1,500 grams, about 3.25 pounds.

Trend data for births to Hispanics and non-Hispanic whites and blacks are affected by expansion of the reporting area in which an item on Hispanic origin is included on the birth certificate as well as by immigration. These two factors affect the numbers of events, the composition of the Hispanic population, and maternal and infant health characteristics. The number of states in the reporting area increased from 22 in 1980 to 23 and the District of Columbia (DC) in 1983-1987, 30 and DC in 1988, 47 and DC in 1989, 48 and DC in 1990, 49 and DC in 1991-1992, and all 50 states and DC from 1993 forward. Trend data for births to Asian/Pacific Islander and Hispanic women are also affected by immigration.

SOURCE: Ventura, Martin, Curtin, Mathews and Park (2000).

[a]Persons of Hispanic origin may be of any race.

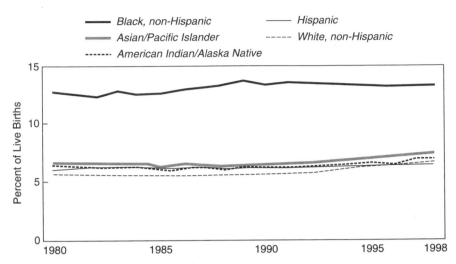

FIGURE 3-3 Percentage of infants born of low birthweight by race and Hispanic origin, 1980-1998.
Adapted from Centers for Disease Control and Prevention (2000) and National Center for Health Statistics (1998).

Exposure to Alcohol During Pregnancy

Maternal alcohol consumption during pregnancy can impair the physical and mental development of the fetus, although the vulnerability of individual fetuses varies for reasons that are not yet entirely understood (NRC, 1996). In its most serious form, fetal alcohol syndrome (FAS) causes craniofacial changes, growth retardation, and central nervous system impairment, including mental retardation and/or hyperactivity (NRC, 1996). Even among children who do not have FAS, however, moderate to heavy drinking during pregnancy has been associated with growth deficits and developmental lags (Streissguth et al., 1996).

National data on the effects of alcohol on fetuses are limited. Indeed, the potentially serious effects of alcohol have been recognized only in the past 30 years. Data collected in 1988 in the National Maternal and Infant Health Survey (Faden et al., 1997) suggest that heavy alcohol consumption during pregnancy (six or more drinks per week) is confined to a relatively small segment of the maternal population. But that rate is considerably higher for American Indian/Alaskan Native women (2.2 percent) and black women (1.2 percent), than for white (0.4 percent), Hispanic (0.3 percent), or Asian/Pacific Islander women (0.7 percent) (see Figure 3-4). The incidence of FAS births is approximately 10 times higher among blacks than among whites (Abel, 1995). No national data are available for other racial/ ethnic groups; however, a surveillance project in four communities (Duimstra et al., 1993) estimated that the rate may be 30 to 40 times higher

---

BOX 3-1
Infant Health and Development Program

The Infant Health and Development Program (IHDP) was designed to provide early intervention services to low-birthweight, premature babies with no severe impairments or illnesses. As both a demonstration program and a research project, the program targeted this population of infants because they are at higher risk of health and developmental problems than normal-weight infants.

IDHP was a large, randomized, multisite trial devised to test the effectiveness of child- and family-oriented intervention strategies to improve the health, behavioral, and intellectual outcomes for these at-risk children. The project included 985 infants who were enrolled from October 1984 through August 1985. Infants randomly assigned to the intervention group received services from the time they left the hospital until each child reached the age of 3. Children in both the intervention and follow-up only groups were assessed through age 8.

Multiple services were rendered to each child in the intervention group in the form of home visits, enrollment in a child development center (beginning at age 1) and health care. Specially trained home visitors regularly assigned to the same family facilitated good hygiene and health care. To ensure adequate health care, children received services at university based clinics or from private providers. Home visitors also enhanced parenting skills and provided a home education program.

Beginning at age 1, children attended a high-quality child development center 5 days a week, year round. Activities at the centers were geared to promoting the childrens' intellectual and social skill development.

Children in both the intervention and follow-up groups were assessed at the ages of 3, 5, and 8. At age 3, children in the intervention group showed higher IQ scores than children in the follow-up group, fewer behavioral problems, and little difference in overall health. The heavier low-birthweight children had cognitive test scores that were 13 points higher on average than the control group. The lighter low-birthweight group scored 6.6 points higher. At age 5, differences between the two groups diminished with only the heavier low-birthweight children showing a sustained IQ gain of 3.7 points. As at age 5, there were few differences between the two groups at age 8, except the heavier low-birthweight children scored 4 points higher than the heavier low-birthweight children from the follow-up group (Ramey et al., 1992).

---

for American Indians/Alaskan Natives than for whites (McLoyd and Lozoff, 2001).

While the reported number of women who drink during pregnancy has declined since the mid-1980s (Serdula et al., 1991), the overall change was driven by a decrease in light drinking (Hankin et al., 1993). In 1995 the Centers for Disease Control and Prevention (CDC) found the incidence of drinking at a level that put the fetus at risk for neurobiological damage was at 4.5 percent (Ebrahim et al., 1998). No data are available on differences by race/ethnicity over time.

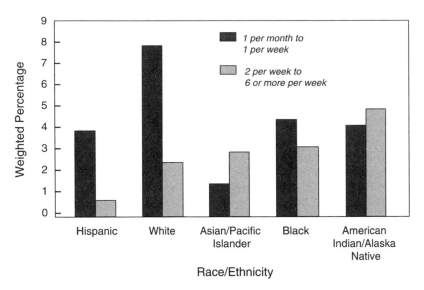

FIGURE 3-4 Alcohol consumption after finding out about pregnancy: Expectant mothers in the United States, 1988.
SOURCE: Faden, Graubard, and Dufour (1997). Reprinted with permission.

Tobacco Use and Drug Abuse

Alcohol is not alone in its harmful effects on a developing fetus. There is a substantial body of literature to suggest that nicotine has a detrimental impact (Levin and Slotkin, 1998), including increasing the probability of low birthweight (Aronson et al., 1993; Morrison et al., 1993) with the consequences described above. Long-term effects of maternal smoking during pregnancy on later child behavior, controlling for birthweight and other confounding effects, have been found in many studies (Williams et al., 1998; Weitzman et al., 1992; Fergusson et al., 1993), although some have found the effects to be substantial (Williams et al., 1998) and others small (McGee and Stanton, 1994). Mild attentional (Denson et al., 1975; Fried, 1992; Landesman-Dwyer and Emanuel, 1979; Picone et al., 1982a, b; Jacobson et al., 1984) and cognitive effects (Fergusson et al., 1993; Hardy and Mellits, 1972; Lefkowitz, 1981; Naeye and Peters, 1984; Keeping et al., 1989; Butler and Goldstein, 1973; Dunn and McBurney, 1977; Rantakallio, 1983; Gueguen et al., 1995) have been found as well. At 5 and 6 years of age, children exposed to tobacco prenatally had lower receptive language scores and poorer performance on memory tasks (Fried et al., 1992 a, b). Most effects occur at higher exposures (20 or more cigarettes a day) (Williams et al., 1998; Levin and Slotkin, 1998).

Because maternal smoking may be correlated with other maternal conditions and behaviors related to child outcomes, the causal connection between tobacco and those outcomes is difficult to establish with certainty, although some studies have been done on large-scale longitudinal data that allow for control of a great many confounding factors (Williams et al., 1998). As with lead exposure, research using animals allows for fuller experimental control. Such research confirms that prenatal exposure to nicotine is itself related to adverse consequences, including damage to the central nervous system (see Levin and Slotkin, 1998, for a review). Adverse effects on cognition and behavior are not as robust as the physiological effects. Levin and Slotkin hypothesize that redundancy in neural systems allows for the use of alternative pathways in order to compensate for damage. If this is the case, then higher levels of complexity should uncover the difference between exposed and unexposed rats. As with animal study of the effects of lead exposure, higher levels of complexity did reveal lower performance in exposed rats (Levin et al., 1996; Levin and Slotkin, 1998).

Tobacco Exposure Rates

Cigarette smoking is substantially higher among American Indian/Alaskan Native pregnant women than among any other racial/ethnic group. For Asians, blacks, and Hispanics, smoking rates during pregnancy are below that of whites (see Table 3-3). Several studies have found, however, that the biochemical measurement of serum cotinine, the primary metabolite of nicotine, is higher for non-Hispanic blacks than for non-Hispanic whites at the same exposure level (Caraballo et al., 1998; Clark et al., 1996; English et al., 1994; Wagenknecht et al., 1990; Pattishall et al., 1985). Serum cotinine is a widely used indicator of tobacco use and environmental tobacco exposure. In light of this finding, it is particularly encouraging that between 1983 and 1998 the number of young black women who smoke fell from almost 28 percent to under 10 percent—far below the rate for their white counterparts.

Cocaine Exposure

Exposure of a fetus to cocaine has been of increasing concern in the past 15 years as usage rates have risen. Careful research is complicated, however, because the illegal status of the drugs affects sampling, and because cocaine use is often accompanied by the use of other drugs and by alcohol and tobacco use. The independent contribution of the cocaine is thus difficult to determine (Msall et al., 1998). A recent attempt at a meta-analysis of the research on cocaine use concludes that available studies are sufficiently flawed to make any conclusions from them questionable (Lester

TABLE 3-3 Mothers Who Smoked Cigarettes During Pregnancy, According to Mother's Detailed Race, Hispanic Origin, Educational Attainment, and Age: Selected States, 1989-1996

Characteristic of Mother	Percent of Mothers Who Smoked[b]	
Race of Mother[a]	1989	1996
All races	19.5	13.6
White	20.4	14.7
Black	17.1	10.2
American Indian or Alaskan Native	23.0	21.3
Asian or Pacific Islander[c]	5.7	3.3
Chinese	2.7	.7
Japanese	8.2	4.8
Filipino	5.1	3.5
Hawaiian and part Hawaiian	19.3	15.3
Other Asian or Pacific Islander	4.2	2.7

[a]Includes data for 43 states and the District of Columbia (DC) in 1989, 45 states and DC in 1990, 46 states and DC in 1991-1993, and 46 states, DC, and New York City (NYC) in 1995-1996. Excludes data for California, Indiana, New York (but includes NYC in 1994-1996), and South Dakota (1989-1996), Oklahoma (1898-1990), and Louisiana and Nebraska (1989), which did not require the reporting of the mother's tobacco use during pregnancy on the birth certificate.

[b]Excludes live births for whom smoking status of the mother is unknown.

[c]Maternal tobacco use during pregnancy was not reported on the birth certificates of California and New York, which during 1989-1991 together accounted for 43-66 percent of the births in each Asian subgroup (except Hawaiian).

SOURCE: Data from Ventura et al. (1999), Centers for Disease Control and Prevention, Natoinal Vital Statistics System.

et al., 1998). Animal studies of cocaine exposure at very high levels show effects on growth, but behavioral and cognitive consequences have not yet been established (Paule, 1998).

Nutrition and Development

Children who are seriously malnourished tend to have low IQs (Stein and Kassab, 1970; Winick et al., 1975; Zeskind and Ramey, 1978, 1981). Malnourishment, however, is generally coincident with other stressors—including poverty, poor schooling, and neglect—that make it difficult to identify the impact of malnutrition alone (Sigman and Whaley, 1998). Moreover, malnutrition has been found in some studies to affect motivational and emotional responsiveness (Galler et al., 1983; Sigman and Whaley, 1998), suggesting that the effect on cognition may be mediated, at least in part, through reduced attention and interaction.

A few studies that have controlled for parental socioeconomic status have found positive associations between nutritional supplementation and IQ. One such study with Kenyan children (Sigman et al., 1989) found positive correlations with animal protein and fat intake. Several studies using random assignment experimental designs with pregnant women thought to be at risk found vitamin and mineral supplementation during pregnancy increased the child's IQ at age 1 (Rush et al., 1980) and age 4 (Harrel et al., 1955) compared with control children (Eysenck and Schoenthaler, 1997).

Vitamins and minerals in the diet play an important role in both physical and mental well-being (Essman, 1987). An association between nutritional supplementation and IQ scores has been found (Dean and Morgenthaler, 1990; Dean et al., 1993), as has an association between supplementation and behavior (Schoenthaler, 1991). One of the strongest claims for the impact of micronutrients is Lynn's (1990) argument that increases in the mean IQ of the population over time (Flynn, 1987) can be explained largely by improved nutrition. While some support Lynn's view of the importance of nutrition with caution regarding the ability to specifically isolate its contribution (Sigman and Whaley, 1998), others accept as incontrovertible the role of nutrition in cognitive development but caution that continued rises in IQ in countries like the United States and the Netherlands since 1970 are not likely to be explained by nutrition, suggesting other explanatory variables are important as well (Martorell, 1998).

Iron deficiency is one of the most common single-nutrient disorders (McLoyd and Lozoff, 2001). Its consequences are wide-ranging, including compromised cognitive and social development, short attention span, and impaired learning capacity (Viteri, 1998; Lozoff et al., 2000). The effects of iron deficiency interact with other developmental stressors because it increases the absorption of lead and impairs absorption of fat. There is considerable evidence that malnutrition and altered iron transport contribute to the detrimental effects of prenatal alcohol exposure (McLoyd and Lozoff, 2001). Iron deficiency in pregnant women is associated with poorer birth outcomes, including low birthweight (Viteri, 1998).

Iron affects cognition and behavior through its impact on brain structure and function. It plays a role in both myelin formation and in the operation of neurotransmitters. Roncagliolo et al. (1998) report direct evidence of its adverse effect on brain development in human infants.

Children with iron deficiency anemia during infancy have poorer scores on measures of behavior and development (Nokes et al., 1998). Of particular importance, the effects of early deficiencies extend well beyond early childhood. Even a full course of iron treatment does not appear to reverse the impact on mental or motor test scores or remediate behavior differences in most infants (Nokes et al., 1998), early school-age children (Lozoff et al.,

1991), or adolescents (Lozoff et al., 1997). The persistent consequences of iron deficiency long after it has been eliminated are not yet fully understood (Lozoff et al., 2000). One plausible explanation is that iron deficiency is correlated with other parent and home characteristics that affect development. Research by Lozoff et al. (2000) controlling for an array of such characteristics continued to find a substantial effect more than 10 years after iron deficiency therapy. In a longitudinal sample of 191 children who had been tested for iron deficiency during infancy and treated if found deficient, the outcomes on a variety of behavioral dimensions (see Figure 3-5 and on cognitive dimensions (see Figure 3-6) continued to differ for the 48 children who had chronic, severe iron deficiency in infancy. A greater proportion of the iron-deficient group had repeated a grade (26 vs. 12 percent, p = .04), and more of the iron-deficient group had been referred for special education services or tutoring (21 vs. 7 percent; p = .02), although at the time of the study there was no significant difference in the proportion receiving such services.

There are marked differences in the incidence of iron deficiency among racial/ethnic groups in the United States (Ogden, 1998). While iron deficiency among infants has been on the decline due to iron-fortified formula and baby cereal as well as to an increase in breast-feeding (McLoyd and Lozoff, 2001), the rate of decline has been substantially greater for whites than for blacks and Hispanics. About 5 percent of poor black and Mexican American children still suffer from iron deficiency anemia, about twice the rate for whites, and iron deficiency with or without anemia affects many more children in all racial/ethnic groups. As Figure 3-7 indicates, income is correlated with iron deficiency for all race groups. Since larger percentages of the minority groups fall below 185 percent of poverty, however, the proportions of minority children with iron deficiency are considerably higher than that of whites.

While the association of iron with variation in cognition and behavior appears to be pronounced, other nutritional influences on performance, particularly from vitamin supplementation, have been claimed as well. Eysenck and Schoenthaler (1997) provide a careful review of this literature, as do Sigman and Whaley (1998). Several conclusions can be drawn from their work that are highly relevant to our present concern:

1. Inadequate levels of vitamins and minerals in the bloodstream reduce a child's IQ, and supplementation of the child's standard diet can raise nonverbal IQ significantly.

2. A consistent effect of supplementation on young infants is on motor skills (Pollitt et al., 1994). Infant motor skills are predictive of later cognitive abilities among children in developing countries (Sigman and Whaley, 1998).

3. The younger the child, the greater the effects of supplementation. There is little effect beyond the teenage years.

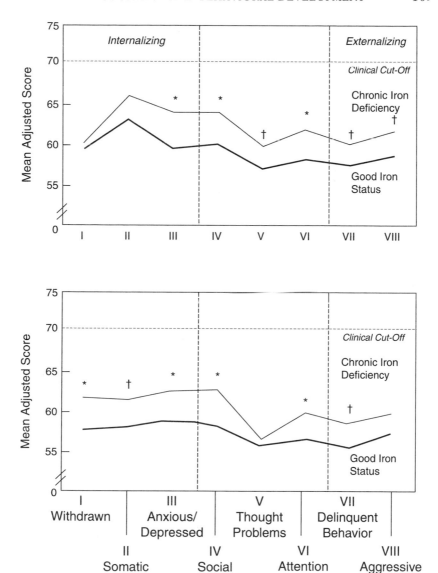

FIGURE 3-5 Behavior problem profiles.
SOURCE: Lozoff et al. (2000). Reprinted with permission.

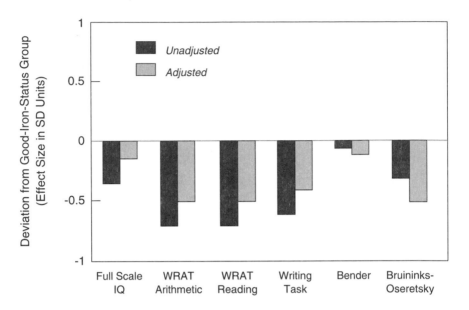

FIGURE 3-6 Standard test score differences at 11 to 14 years old.
SOURCE: Lozoff et al. (2000). Reprinted with permission.

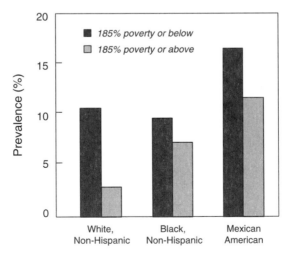

FIGURE 3-7 Iron deficiency among 1-to-2 year-old children by race and poverty status.
SOURCE: Ogden (1998), Centers for Disease Control and Prevention, unpublished analysis, Third National Health and Nutrition Examination Survey.

4. Approximately 20 percent of children in the United States respond to supplementation with IQ increases of 9+ points over test-retest increases in a placebo group. However, no effects are found for children with adequate levels of vitamins and minerals in their diets. The concentration of effects is likely to be greatest among disadvantaged children.

5. Effects of micronutrient supplementation have been demonstrated to continue for one year and may last longer.

One provocative natural experiment of the effect of dietary changes on academic performance took place in New York City public schools in the late 1970s and early 1980s. Schoenthaler et al. (1986a, b) analyzed the results of dietary modifications in the foods supplied to the schools. In school years 1979-1980, 1980-1981, and 1982-1983 there was a gradual elimination of synthetic colors, synthetic flavors, and selected preservatives. High-sucrose foods were gradually eliminated. When Schoenthaler and colleagues compared the student percentile rankings on the California Achievement Test, the results were striking (see Figure 3-8). The average ranking in the 41st percentile in the three years before the changes rose to 47th, 51st, and 55th in each of the three change years. In 1981-1982, when no new changes were introduced, the scores remained flat. Gains were largest for students doing worst academically. In 1979, 12.4 percent of students were performing two or more grades below level. At the end of 1983, that rate had dropped to 4.9 percent. While the precise nutritional change was not measured in this study, the authors argue that the foods eliminated tend to be low in the ratio of essential nutrients to calories, thus increasing the proportion of available foods with a higher ratio of nutrients to calories (Eysenck and Schoenthaler, 1997). The claim, however plausible, was not tested.

Exposure to Lead

Lead, a common element in the earth's crust, becomes harmful to humans only when it is bioavailable: that is, when it is ingested in paint chips or dust that contain lead, taken into the lungs via pollution from leaded gasoline, absorbed through foods that have been stored in lead soldered cans or ceramics (Rice, 1998), or consumed in drinking water that has flowed through lead-soldered pipes (NRC, 1993). Lead is both carried in the bloodstream and stored in bone and soft tissue. The fetal months and early childhood years of rapid bone and tissue growth therefore constitute a particularly vulnerable period for lead exposure.

Childhood lead poisoning was recognized only in the past century, a period that was marked by dramatic shifts in lead exposure. Widespread exposure to lead first rose, particularly with the addition of lead to gaso-

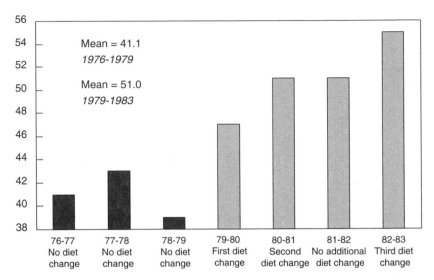

FIGURE 3-8 National ranking of 803 New York City public schools before and after diet changes.
SOURCE: Schoenthaler, Doraz, and Wakefield (1986a). Reprinted with permission.

line, in the 1920s (Elias et al., 1975). The latter half of the century was marked by a sharp decline in exposure as zinc and titanium oxide replaced lead in paint in the 1950s (Needleman, 2000). As consciousness of childhood lead poisoning grew, lead in paint was banned entirely in 1978 and was removed from gasoline in 1986. Blood lead levels responded. The average for young children in the United States and other industrialized countries has decreased dramatically from 15 mg/μ in the late 1970s to 4 mg/μ or less[2] currently (Rice, 1998).

The average decline in lead load in the last few decades, however, has not been shared evenly. From a 1991-1994 survey by the CDC of children ages 1-5, the U.S. Department of Health and Human Services estimated that about 4.4 percent of children in that age group had harmful levels of lead in their blood. However, more than 8 percent of children who participated in federal health care programs for low-income and uninsured families, including Medicaid, the Health Center Program,[3] and the Special

---

[2]Rice (1998) reports 4 mg/μ currently, and the U.S. General Accounting Office (1999) reports 2.7 mg/μ between 1991 and 1994.

[3]This program, administered by the Health Resources and Services Administration, awards grants to more than 3,000 sites in medically underserved areas. Children served include those covered by Medicaid and those who are uninsured.

Supplemental Nutrition Program for Women, Infants, and Children (WIC), had harmful lead levels (U.S. General Accounting Office, 1999).

Children in inner-city neighborhoods with older housing stocks tend to have higher lead exposure levels. And while children from all income and racial/ethnic groups live in houses built before the 1950s when lead in paint was common, children living in older, poorer, inner-city neighborhoods where maintenance of the housing stock is more limited are more likely to be exposed to lead from deteriorating paint (Centers for Disease Control and Prevention, 2000). The level of lead exposure is substantially higher for blacks than for whites, but in both race groups there is a dramatically higher incidence among children from low-income families: more than twice the incidence among low-income whites, and almost five times the incidence among low-income blacks (see Table 3-4). Mexican Americans have substantially higher incidence than do whites, but a rate that is approximately one-third that for blacks (Table 3-5).

At the same time that federal protections were reducing lead exposure, epidemiological research in this country and abroad was pointing to adverse effects from lead exposure at ever lower levels. Until the early 1970s, the acceptable concentration of blood lead in the United States was 60 mg/μ in children and 80 mg/μ in adults (NRC, 1993). Acceptable concentrations were lowered several times, until in 1990 the Science Advisory Board of the U.S. Environmental Protection Agency identified a blood lead concentration of 10 mg/μ as the maximum safe level for young children. CDC lowered its guideline to the same level, and the National Research Council concurred with the selection of 10 mg/μ as the concentration of concern in children in 1993 (NRC, 1993).

TABLE 3-4 Prevalence of Elevated Blood Lead Levels (>10 μg/dl), 1994

Category	Children with Blood Levels >10 μg/dl (%)
White	
Low income	9.8
Mid income	4.8
High	4.3
Black	
Low income	28.4
Mid income	8.9
High income	5.8

SOURCE: Needleman (2000).

TABLE 3-5 Prevalence of Elevated Blood Lead
Levels (>10 µg/dl), 1997

Category	Children with Blood Lead Levels >10 µg/dl (%)
Race	
Black	11.2
Mexican American	4.0
White	1.0
Income	
Low	8.0
Mid	1.9
High	1.0

SOURCE: Needleman (2000).

Lead levels at or above 10 mg/µ have been associated with a variety of adverse effects in infants, children, and pregnant women. We focus here on those associated with school performance. Research findings regarding the effect of lead on IQ have been somewhat controversial (Ernhart et al., 1993; Needleman, 1993). Most, though not all, studies find such an effect. Meta-analyses of both cross-sectional and longitudinal studies of lead on IQ conclude that there is a decline of 2-3 points when blood lead rises from 10 to 20 mg/µ (Rice, 1998). Perhaps more important for our purposes, numerous studies point to a relationship between lead and a variety of behaviors closely related to school success and the probability of being referred for special or gifted education, including impairment of attentional processes, impulsivity and hyperactivity, difficulty in changing response strategy, problems in social adjustment, and poor school performance more generally (Rice, 1998).

In a study of 2,000 1st and 2nd grade children in Boston, for example, teachers' ratings of children on measures of distractibility, lack of persistence, dependence, impulsivity, and ability to follow instructions rose in a dose-dependent fashion with the lead levels measured in the children's deciduous teeth (Needleman et al., 1979). Separate studies using measures of blood lead (Yule et al., 1984) and hair lead (Tuthill, 1996) concentrations on these same behaviors found similar dose-dependent responses. Graphic display of the striking results of these three studies appear in Figure 3-9. Other studies from New Zealand (Fergusson et al., 1988c; Silva et al., 1988), Mexico (Munoz et al., 1993), Yugoslavia (Wasserman et al., 1995), and the United States (Leviton et al., 1993) found similar adverse effects on behaviors related to social and academic success in the classroom. Several additional studies found an effect of lead on classroom behavior measurement scales (Yule et al., 1981; Yule and Lansdown, 1981) and on measures of internalizing behavior (like anxiety or withdrawal) and externalizing behavior (aggression, overreaction) (Sciarillo et al., 1992; Needleman et al., 1996; Needleman, 2000; Bellinger et al., 1994b; Rice, 1998).

Reaction time and flexible use of strategies—both characteristics associated with high achievement in school—were tested in several studies. Needleman et al. (1979) found longer reaction times in a simple task for children with higher dentine lead levels. These findings were replicated in a study done in London (Hunter et al., 1985) using blood lead concentration levels. Results of the two studies were later combined (blood lead levels were known for many of the children in the Needleman et al. study), showing an orderly dose-effect relationship between blood lead and reaction time. These findings were replicated in studies of Greek children (Hatzakis et al., 1987), German children (Winneke et al., 1983; Winneke and Kraemer, 1984), and a cohort of 1879 multiethnic European children (Winneke et al., 1990).

Two studies of strategy use employed the Wisconsin Cai Sorting Test, a test of abstract thinking, sustained attention, and ability to change response strategy as needed. Students with higher blood lead levels performed more poorly at age 10 (Stiles and Bellinger, 1993), perseverating in an old strategy even when a new one was required. A cohort of 79 19- and 20-year-olds showed an ability to select and respond to critical information and to shift focus adaptively that declined with increases in dentine lead levels (Bellinger et al., 1994a). These findings are consistent with those from a robust body of experimental research on animals exposed to low body burdens of lead found frequently in children (Winneke et al., 1977; Carson et al., 1974; Rice, 1998).

Several studies have looked at measures of students' school achievement directly. A study in Scotland (Fulton et al., 1987) found lead-related deficits in numeracy and literacy skills. The New Zealand study by Fergusson et al. (1988a, b, c) found deficits in reading, math, spelling, and handwriting. Similarly, Yule found deficits in school performance, including spelling and reading, and Leviton et al. (1993) found those deficits in girls but not boys in a Boston study.

Other measures of school outcome have been studied as well. A study in Denmark (Lyngbye et al., 1990) found an increased need for special education among 1st graders as a function of increased lead levels. Bellinger et al. (1984) found that the need for remedial education and the incidence of grade retention by 6th grade were associated with dentine lead levels of students measured in 1st grade. And a follow-up investigation of children studied by Needleman in 1976 found in young adulthood a dose-dependent

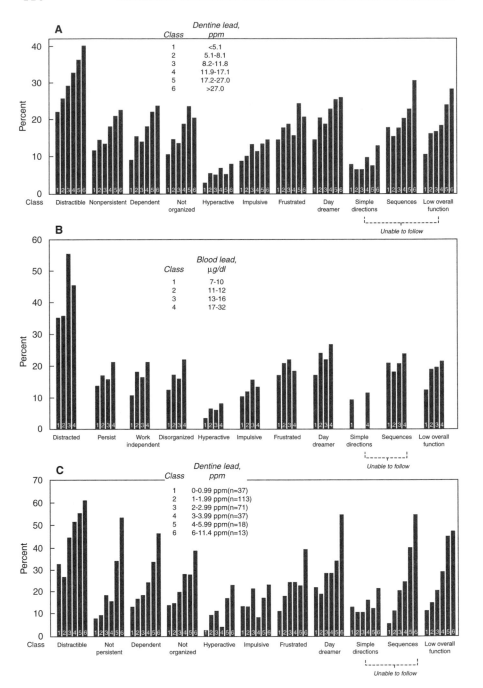

FIGURE 3-9 Lead levels and measured behavior: Results from three studies
SOURCE: Rice (1998). Reprinted with permission.

increase in reading disability (Needleman et al., 1990) and failure to complete high school associated with lead level.

When a child is identified with an elevated lead level, any treatment that does not eliminate the exposure is inadequate (Etzel and Balk, eds., 1999). Current federal policy requires that all state Medicaid programs cover a one-time environmental investigation to determine the lead source and necessary case management services.[4] But less than half of state Medicaid agencies reported covering these services in 1999 (Centers for Disease Control and Prevention, 2000).

If the first principle of intervention is to identify the source and limit exposure, it stands to reason that this effort should be undertaken before the child is initially exposed if the likely source of exposure can be targeted effectively. Because effective efforts to remove lead from paint, gasoline, drinking water, and food cans have largely eliminated new sources of toxic lead, substantial inroads into reducing the number of children with high lead levels will require limiting exposure to existing lead paint from the older housing stock, particularly in low-income neighborhoods. Lead abatement has been supported by several federal task forces (U.S. President's Task Force, 2000; Centers for Disease Control and Prevention, 1991, 2000).

In 1991, CDC argued in favor of lead abatement and estimated the cost of the effort at $32 billion—about half of the estimated benefits (at a 3 percent discount rate). In 2000, a President's Task Force on Environmental Health Risks and Safety Risks to Children again recommended elimination of lead from the housing stock by 2010. The technology for doing so has improved and become less expensive over the past decade. The task force estimated the cost and benefits of both a lead abatement effort and a more modest effort at interim control of exposure. They concluded that, in the long run, removal of lead through an abatement program is less expensive, although the stability of that result depends on the discount rate. While the cost of abatement was estimated at a total of $20.7 billion compared with $2.3 billion for interim controls, the *net quantifiable* benefits of abatement at discount rates at or near 3 percent were substantially larger.[5]

---

[4]It also prohibits coverage of certain costs of environmental laboratory analyses that are important to full investigation of exposure sources (Centers for Disease Control and Prevention, 2000).

[5]The discount rate reflects the value placed on money today compared with money in future years. The cost of interventions, particularly abatement, are paid up front, and the benefits extends for years into the future. If the value of those benefits in the out years is discounted at 3 percent, the net benefit of abatement is estimated at $17 billion, and the interim controls at $8.9 billion. As the discount rate rises and out year benefits are valued at a lower rate, the benefits drop. At a discount rate of 7 percent the benefits of abatement just surpass the costs, while those of interim controls exceed costs by $1.2 billion (U.S. President's Task Force, 2000).

SOCIAL AND ENVIRONMENTAL INFLUENCES
ON DEVELOPMENT

In the United States, racial/ethnic identification and poverty status are closely tied. While this is true for adults, it is even more so for children (see Figure 3-10). Decades of data collection and analysis have firmly established the strength and consistency of associations between socioeconomic status and cognitive, educational, emotional, occupational, and health outcomes (NRC, 2001b; Duncan and Brooks-Gunn, 1997a; Blank, 1994; Keating and Hertzman, 1999; Gottfried, 1984; Neisser et al., 1996; Stipek and Ryan, 1997).

A quarter of a century ago, a study by Broman et al. (1975) looked at the effects of 169 biomedical and behavioral variables during infancy on intellectual performance at age 4 in a sample of 26,760 children. Only 11 of the variables were social or family behavioral factors, but two of these— socioeconomic status (SES) and mother's education—were the most predictive of all the variables (Sameroff, 1993). The relationship between family socioeconomic status and school failure and behavior problems in children appears in other countries as well, including Britain, Finland, and Sweden (Pagani et al., 1997), although the gradients are not always as steep as in the United States (Case et al., 1999).

More recent research has taken a more refined look at poverty status, including the severity, duration, and timing of poverty (Brooks-Gunn and

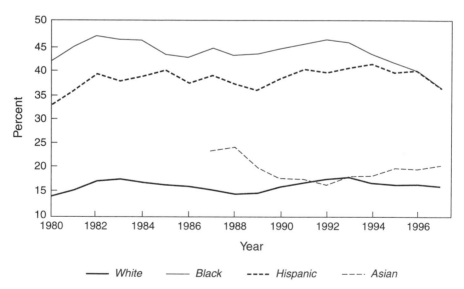

FIGURE 3-10 Children under 18 living in poverty: 1980-1997.
SOURCE: U.S. Bureau of the Census (1999b).

Duncan, 1997; Brooks-Gunn et al., 1999; Smith et al., 1997; Duncan and Brooks-Gunn, 1997a). A study by Smith et al. (1997) found that in two very different samples, the effect of poverty on cognitive ability (as measured by IQ, verbal ability, and achievement tests) varied dramatically depending on the severity of poverty. This has direct implications for minority children, since black children are four times as likely, and Hispanic children three times as likely as white children to live in families with income under 50 percent of the poverty threshold (see Table 3-6). A change of one unit in the family income-to-needs ratio in the Smith et al. study was associated with a 3.0 to 3.7 point increase in the child's score on the various cognitive assessments. A study by Brooks-Gunn et al. (1999) found similarly striking results. Graphs of income-to-needs ratios plotted against standardized IQ scores and Peabody Individual Achievement Test (PIAT) math scores appear in Figures 3-11 and 3-12. The math scores indicate that the depth of poverty (or the level of affluence) matters, and the results for ages 7-8 compared with ages 8-9 suggest that the magnitude of the effect increases over time. The stronger effect of poverty on cognitive scores with age is found by Smith et al. (1997) as well.

Not surprisingly, duration of poverty matters as well. The study by Smith et al. (1997) found that children who lived in persistently poor families scored on average 6-9 points lower on cognitive assessments, while those whose poverty was transient scored 4-5 points lower.

Does the timing of poverty matter? A review of the effect of the timing of poverty on child outcomes suggests that the income gradient is operating throughout the first two decades of life (Duncan and Brooks-Gunn, 1997b). But the effects of income on cognitive performance and school achievement appear to be particularly strong in the early years (Brooks-Gunn et al., 1999). In a study of the effects of poverty on completed schooling, much more powerful effects of income between birth and age 5 were found than at other points in childhood (Axinn et al., 1997). Since poverty is negatively correlated with school readiness on a variety of dimensions (National Center for Education Statistics, 2000, 2001), and low readiness is associated with grade failure, school disengagement, and school dropout (Barnett, 1995; Brooks-Gunn et al., 1993; Guo et al., 1996; Ramey and Ramey, 1994; Schweinhart and Weikart, 1997), this finding is not surprising.

Understanding SES Effects

That socioeconomic status—particularly income and mother's education—matters is beyond dispute. By itself, however, it tells us very little. More recent research has focused on understanding the ways in which poverty status and these outcomes may be linked (Sameroff, 2000; Duncan and Brooks Gunn, 1997a; Ramey et al., 1998).

TABLE 3-6 Child Poverty: Percentage of Related Children Under Age 18 Living Below Selected Poverty Levels by Age, Family Structure, Race, and Hispanic Origin, 1980-1998

Characteristic	1980	1990	1998
Under 100 percent of poverty			
Children in all families			
Related children	18	20	18
White, non-Hispanic	—	12	10
Black	42	44	36
Hispanic[a]	33	38	34
Related children under age 6	20	23	21
Related children ages 6-17	17	18	17
Under 50 percent of poverty			
Children in all families			
Related children	7	8	8
White, non-Hispanic	—	4	4
Black	17	22	17
Hispanic[a]	—	14	13

NOTES: Estimates refer to children who are related to the householder and who are under age 18. The poverty level is based on money income and does not include noncash benefits, such as food stamps. Poverty thresholds reflect family size and composition and are adjusted each year using the annual average consumer price index (CPI) level. The poverty threshold for a family of four was $16,660 in 1998. The levels shown here are derived from the ratio of the family's income to the family's poverty threshold. Related children include biological children, adopted children, and stepchildren of the householder and all other children in the household related to the householder (or reference person) by blood, adoption, or marriage. For more detail, see U.S. Census Bureau, Series P-60, No. 207.

[a]Persons of Hispanic origin may be of any race.

SOURCE: U.S. Census Bureau, March Current Population Survey, *Current Population Reports*, Consumer income, Series P-60, various years.

Why are child outcomes worse in families with low SES? An answer to this question requires more than the establishment of correlations; it requires an understanding of the supports for child development and the ways in which these supports are compromised in low-SES family circumstances.

Two recent NRC reports synthesized research on the development of young children. *From Neurons to Neighborhoods: The Science of Early Childhood Development* (NRC, 2000c) focuses on the period from birth to kindergarten entry, and *Eager to Learn: Educating Our Preschoolers* (NRC, 2001b) focuses on children ages 2-5. Both volumes emphasize the interconnectivity of cognitive, motor, and social-emotional development. And

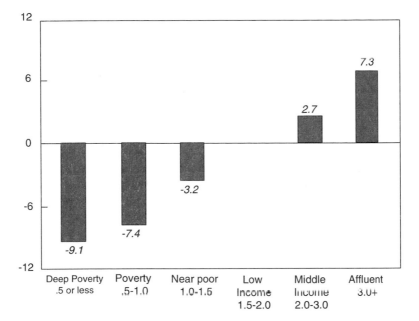

FIGURE 3-11 Income-to-needs ratios and child cognitive ability: Deep poverty and IQ scores, age 5, IHDP data set.
SOURCE: Brooks-Gunn, Duncan, and Britto (1999). Reprinted with permission of The Guilford Press, NY.

both argue that despite the enormous complexity of early development, one thing is abundantly clear: the weight of successful development in the early years falls most heavily on the child's relationships with primary adult caregivers.

Children, themselves tremendously diverse in the individual characteristics they bring into the world, develop in family and community contexts that vary widely. The committees that produced these reports were largely in agreement that despite this diversity, all children appear to require certain things from early abiding relationships in order to flourish:

a. a reliable, supporting relationship that establishes a sense of security and safety,

b. an affectionate relationship that supports the development of self-esteem,

c. responsiveness of the adult to the child that strengthens the child's sense of self-efficacy, and

d. support for the growth of new capabilities that are within the child's reach, including reciprocal interactions that promote language development and the ability to resolve conflicts cooperatively and respectfully.

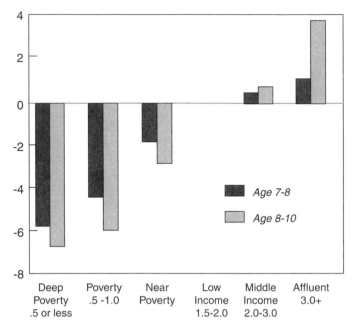

FIGURE 3-12 Income-to-needs and child cognitive ability: Deep poverty and math ability (PIAT-Math), NLSY-CS data set.
SOURCE: Brooks-Gunn, Duncan, and Britto (1999). Reprinted with permission of The Guilford Press, NY.

"In these ways, relationships shape the development of self-awareness, social competence, conscience, emotional growth and emotion regulation, learning and cognitive growth, and a variety of other foundational developmental accomplishments" (NRC, 2000c:265).

Each family and child has particular supports and stressors—from within the family and without—that affect the quality and quantity of the interactions among family members that are so critical to development. Poverty and maternal education can affect these supports in a number of ways, including maternal depression, differential knowledge and beliefs that shape parent-child interactions, resources available to access quality child care and other educational materials and resources, and exposure to stressful events. While the reciprocal interactions between the child and parent are the "engines that actually drive the outcome," parental knowledge and other resources influence the effectiveness of the process (Ceci et al., 1997). Moreover, poverty is highly correlated with single-parent status, decreasing the parental attention available to the child.

Parenting Interactions and the Home Environment

Numerous studies in the 1960s detected a strong association between the quality of a child's home environment—indexed by dimensions such as responsivity and sensitivity of the mother to her child, the amount and level of language stimulation, direct teaching and parenting styles—and children's intellectual and problem-solving competencies (Hunt, 1961; Vygotsky, 1962; Hess and Shipman, 1965; Bee et al., 1969). Over the next four decades, hundreds of additional studies have affirmed this strong association (reviews by Maccoby and Martin, 1983; Huston et al., 1994; Cowan et al., 1994). When Bee and her associates investigated early predictors of IQ and language development, they found that mother-infant interaction was one of the best predictors at every age tested, as good as actual child performance (Bee et al., 1982).

While the association between parenting style and cognitive development has been confirmed in a substantial body of literature, the shared genetic endowment of parents and children is the competing explanation for that association (Scarr, 1997). One study (Riksen-Walraven, 1978) of 100 Dutch mothers' interactions with their 9-month-old babies using a highly unusual experimental design did find that different styles of parenting cause differential cognitive development in children measured by exploratory behavior and speed of learning in a contingency task (see Box 3-2).

Poverty, especially persistent poverty, is strongly correlated with less optimal home environments (Garrett et al., 1994). Some studies have attributed as much as half of the gap in achievement test scores in preschool-age children and a third of the gap in school-age children to differences in the home learning environments of high-income and low-income children (Smith et al., 1997).

The effects of poverty on the home environment may be manifested in parenting practices. Findings from a large number of longitudinal studies accord in demonstrating strong and negative effects of social and economic hardships on parenting practices in the families of young children. In a study of young boys in grades K-2, Bank et al. (1993) found that social disadvantage predicted harsh parental discipline, which in turn predicted aggressive child behavior. In another study by Conger et al. (1997), harsh parenting and parental financial conflict mediated the relationship between both marital instability and poverty on child behavior and academic problems. A study by Repetti and Wood (1997) found that on days when mothers experienced increased stress at work, they responded by being more irritable and withdrawn in interactions with their children.

Poor parenting practices and a negative home learning environment may result in conduct problems. Studies have reported that 7 to 25 percent

BOX 3-2
Parenting Style and Child Development

Riksen-Walraven conducted a study of the interaction of 100 Dutch mothers with their 9-month-old babies, looking at the role of parental responsiveness and stimulation on development. The mothers were randomly assigned to one of four groups, and each group was given different instructions about the amount, quality, and timing of interaction.

One group of mothers was told not to be directive, to let the child find things out on his or her own and to praise the child's efforts. They were also to respond to the child's initiations of interactions. A second group of mothers was told to speak to and initiate interaction often, taking more of a directive role. A third group was told to engage in a mixture of the two strategies, and the fourth group were given no instructions.

After three months, the researchers determined that the mothers' behaviors differed significantly across groups in accordance with instructions. Babies were observed and tested. Babies of mothers encouraged to be responsive showed higher levels of exploratory behaviors than any other group. They also learned more quickly on a contingency task (Riksen-Walraven, 1978).

of preschool children meet the diagnostic criteria for what is called oppositional defiant disorder, with the highest rates found in low-income welfare families (Offord et al., 1986, 1987). During the preschool years, powerful antecedents of emotional and behavior problems are found in the interaction of children, their siblings and peers, and their parents in the home setting. In particular, coercive, irritable, and ineffective discipline and other parenting behaviors have been consistently implicated in the development of conduct problems throughout childhood (Patterson et al., 1992; Reid and Eddy, 1997). There is also abundant and consistent evidence that the early development of conduct problems is strongly predictive of behavioral problems in kindergarten, elementary school, and beyond (Patterson et al., 1992; Reid and Eddy, 1997; Ensminger et al., 1983; Goldstein et al., 1980; Walker et al., 1987).

Poverty and Language Development

Language development in the early years is particularly important to later school success in reading and acquiring content knowledge (Snow and Paez, in press). The best single predictor of reading success is vocabulary size (Anderson and Nagy, 1992). Substantial differences between the vocabulary size of children in low-income families and those in middle-class families have been well documented, as has the connection between the vocabulary of the child and the vocabulary used by the parent (NRC, 1998; Hart and Risley, 1992, 1995; Davidson, 1993). Higher-SES mothers have been found to talk to children more, sustain conversation longer, respond in a more contingent fashion to their children's speech, and elicit more response from the child (Hoff-Ginsberg and Tardif, 1995; Hart and Risley, 1995; Hoff-Ginsberg, 1991).

Other research has reported an association between parents' income and education level and their interactions with their children in ways that are relevant to mainstream schooling as well, including prompting infants to respond to books and pictures, and asking questions that require labeling and organizing knowledge into categories (Schieffelin and Ochs, 1983). They are also more likely to provide access to materials, time, and adult support for exploratory play that the child is encouraged to initiate (Bradley et al., 1994). Garrett et al. (1994) found that as the income-to-needs ratio rose, so did the quality of the home environment.

The National Center for Education Statistics is collecting longitudinal data on a nationally representative sample of children as they enter kindergarten and following them through 5th grade. The survey, called the Early Childhood Longitudinal Study (ECLS) also collects data on characteristics of the child's family and home environment. Among families with more than 100 children's books in the home, whites were represented at five times the rate of blacks or Hispanics, and among those with fewest books the proportions reversed. Asians were similar to other minority groups. Welfare status and a primary language other than English in the home were also associated with having fewer books and recordings (U.S. Department of Education, 1998).

Maternal Depression

An estimated 1 in 10 women with young children experiences depression (Dickstein et al., 1998; Gelfand et al., 1996). Estimated rates for mothers living in poverty, however, range from 13 to 28 percent (Danziger et al., 2000; Lennon et al., 1998; Moore et al., 1995; Olson and Pavetti, 1996). In two large samples of poor women in work and training programs, over 40 percent were found to have clinically significant depressive symptoms (Quint et al., 1997; U.S. Department of Health and Human Services, 1995). The higher prevalence is postulated to arise from the stress and loss of control that accompany persistent economic pressures (Brody et al., 1995; Brody and Flor, 1997; Caplovitz, 1979; Conger et al., 1992; Dressler, 1985; Kessler et al., 1987; McLoyd et al., 1994). While severe income constraints can serve as a catalyst to depression, it should be noted that most of the mothers in poor families are not depressed (Edin and Lein, 1997; Brody and Flor, 1997; NRC, 2000a).

Maternal depression has been consistently implicated in reducing the quality of parenting and disruptions in the emotional relationship between parent and child (NRC, 2000a). Particularly relevant to the development of children's emotional and behavioral problems, depressed mothers are less likely to be consistent with their children (McLoyd, 1997). They are more likely to withdraw and to respond with less emotion and energy and, when they do engage, they are more likely to do so in an intrusive or hostile manner (Brody and Forehand, 1986; Brody et al., 1994; Frankel and Harmon, 1996; Patterson, 1986; Tronick and Weinberg, 1997; Zeanah et al., 1997). Infants of depressed mothers are more likely to withdraw as well and show reduced levels of activity and dysphoria (Cummings and Davies, 1994, 1999; Dawson et al., 1992; Frankel and Harmon, 1996; Murray and Cooper, 1997; Seifer et al., 1996; van Ijzendoorn et al., 1992).

In a study by Bettes (1988), maternal depression was associated with linguistic as well as emotional development; 10 of 36 mothers studied were rated as depressed. Tape recordings indicated that when babies cooed, the nondepressed mothers quickly responded, whereas depressed mothers had a greater latency and their vocal patterns were not tied to their children's vocal output. At 3 to 4 months, there were no differences in the vocalization patterns of the infants, but after 6 to 9 months, the babies of depressed mothers vocalized much less.

As an isolated risk factor, maternal depression may have relatively little impact on development (Rutter, 1979; Cummings and Davies, 1994; Seifer et al., 1996; Zeanah et al., 1997). But since prevalence rates are much higher for mothers living in poverty, depression is often combined with other risks. As a group, children with depressed mothers are at higher risk of emotional and behavior problems, and these in turn are associated with difficulties in school, aggression, poor peer relationships, and reduced ability to exercise self-control (Campbell et al., 1995; Cummings and Davies, 1994; Dawson and Ashman, 2000; Zeanah et al., 1997). These children also have higher incidence of psychopathology themselves (Cummings and Davies, 1994; Downey and Coyne, 1990; Zeanah et al., 1997).

Child Care Quality

Because young children are far more likely to spend a significant amount of time in child care today than at any time in the past, a great deal of attention has been devoted in recent years to understanding the consequences of that care. The two NRC reports mentioned above review extensive literatures in this regard (NRC, 2000c, 2001b). The conclusions of relevance for our purposes are rather obvious: the consequences of child care depend largely on the quality of that care, and the characteristics of quality in child care are the same as those in home care. At its core, the quality of child care depends on the quality of the interactions between the caregiver and the child. Characteristics of those interactions that benefit the child—security, affection, responsiveness, and support for emerging abilities—are the same as those with a parent.

And as in relationships with parents, secure attachments to child care providers are associated with adaptive social development (Howes et al., 1992; Oppenheim et al., 1988; Peisner-Feinberg et al., 2000; Pianta and Nimetz, 1991; Sroufe et al., 1983), more competent interactions with adults, and more sophisticated play with peers (Howes and Smith, 1995; Howes et al., 1998, 1994), effects that last into the school years (Howes, 2000). And as with the home environment, quality interactions in child care have been positively associated with cognitive and linguistic development (Burchinal et al., 1996; Galinsky et al., 1994; National Institute of Child Health and Human Development, 1999; Peisner-Feinberg and Burchinal, 1997; Peisner-Feinberg et al., 2000).

Central to determining the quality of child care are the characteristics of the caregivers: their education, early childhood training, and attitudes about their job and the children in their charge. And the ability to carry out their work well is positively influenced by small child-adult ratios and small group size (NRC, 2000c, 2001b). Clearly, creating quality in a child care program is directly related to program cost.

Efforts to assess child care quality in the United States have concluded that from 10 to 20 percent of arrangements fall below minimal standards of adequacy (Cost, Quality, and Outcomes Study Team, 1995; Galinsky et al., 1994; Helburn, 1995; Whitebook et al., 1990). These settings are characterized by "caregivers who more often ignore than respond to young children's bids for attention and affection, a dearth of age-appropriate or educational toys, and children who spend much of their time wandering aimlessly around, unengaged with adults, other children, or materials" (NRC, 2000c:320). At the other extreme, fewer than 20 percent of toddlers and preschoolers were in settings considered to be of high quality (National Institute of Child Health and Human Development Early Child Care Research Network, 1996).

The gains from quality child care are often greatest for children from low-SES families (Peisner-Feinberg and Burchinal, 1997), but the higher cost of quality care means access for these families is restricted without government subsidy or provision of services. In the private marketplace, children from poorer, more stressed homes receive lower-quality care than other children (Howes and Olenick, 1986; National Institute of Child Health and Human Development, 1997b; Phillips et al., 1994). Families with low incomes spend a substantially higher proportion of that income on child care but are nonetheless priced out of higher cost forms of care in many areas of the country (U.S. Department of Health and Human Services, 1999; Giannarelli and Barsimantov, 2000).

There is an exception to the rule that quality of child care is directly related to income level. Poor families who receive subsidies for child care or access to early intervention programs like Head Start often receive care that is of higher quality than that obtainable by low-income families that are not eligible for these supports. Head Start programs (discussed below) are characterized by a relatively compressed range of quality. While there are few very high-quality Head Start centers, none is characterized by the substandard care found in the private child care market (Administration of Children, Youth, and Families, 2001).

As with other risk factors, it is important to maintain a broad perspective: poor-quality child care is not deterministic. A strong attachment relationship with a parent, and the benefits that ensue, appear in large measure to protect children from the negative effects of poor-quality child care (National Institute of Child Health and Human Development, 1997a; Roggman et al., 1994; Symons, 1998). However, the limited financial and human capital resources that are predictive of low-quality care often are accompanied by other stressors. Several studies have found that when young children are exposed to risk factors at home and are in poor-quality child care, they are also more likely to experience insensitive mothering (Belsky et al., 1996; Clarke et al., 1997; Tresch et al., 1988). It is worth noting as well that mothers in the National Institute of Child Health and Human Development study living at or near the poverty line whose children were in full-time, high-quality child care were more responsive and affectionate with their infants than low-income mothers raising their children at home or in lower-quality care (National Institute of Child Health and Human Development, 1997c). And other studies have found child care to be a protective factor for infants and children living in poverty (Caughy et al., 1994) or with depressed mothers (Cohn et al., 1986, 1991).

Multiple Risks

Since Bronfenbrenner published his influential article proposing an "ecological" model of development in 1979, substantial empirical research has examined the effect of a combination of risk factors that together determine a child's experience. Many of the factors described above had been shown to have a significant impact on development, but individually any one factor could explain only a small portion of the variation in outcome. While poverty or low birthweight has a measurable impact on average, clearly some children with those characteristics do well. The very notion of risk suggests an uncertain or probabilistic outcome.

In the same year that Bronfenbrenner published his article, Michael Rutter looked at risk factors that helped explain child psychiatric disorders. He included in his list of variables severe marital discord, low social status, overcrowding or large family size, paternal criminality, maternal psychiatric disorder, and admission into the care of the local authority (Rutter, 1979). At the time, Rutter described his results as "interesting and surprising." Children with any single risk factor were no more likely to have a psychiatric disorder than were children with no risk factors (see Figure 3-13). But when any two stresses occurred together, the risk went up fourfold, and with four stresses, tenfold.

The past two decades have witnessed research efforts to replicate and extend the multiple risk model to look at a wider array of both risks and outcomes. The results are no longer surprising; it is now quite widely accepted that the number of risk factors that children face is more important than the impact of any single factor (Sameroff, 2000; Williams et al., 1990; Fergusson et al., 1994). Indeed, it has been argued that the challenge posed by adversity may in fact be a necessary condition for life's achievements (Bandura, 1997; Lewis, 1997; Sameroff, 2000). Yet as the number of stresses increases, the chance for a positive outcome drops off precipitously. This can be seen quite dramatically in the Rochester Longitudinal Study of a group of children from the prenatal period through age 18 from a socially heterogeneous set of families (Sameroff, 2000).

The study measured the impact of risk factors at age 4 on both cognitive outcome (measured by the Weschler Preschool and Primary Scale of

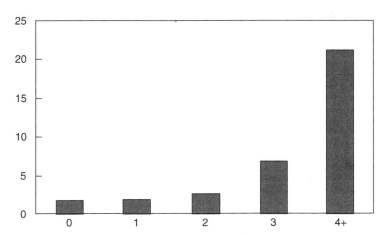

FIGURE 3-13 Multiplicity of risk factors and child psychiatric disorder. SOURCE: Rutter (1979). Reprinted with permission.

Intelligence verbal intelligence score) and mental health outcomes (measured by the Rochester Adaptive Behavior Inventory). The risk factors considered were maternal mental illness; high maternal anxiety; rigidity in the attitudes, beliefs, and values of mothers regarding the child's development; few positive maternal interactions with the child during infancy; less maternal education than high school; head of household in an unskilled occupation; disadvantaged minority status; single parenthood; stressful life events; and large family size. While each variable had a statistically significant negative impact by itself, no single variable was able to predict much of the variation. The total number of risk factors, however, was a powerful predictor. On the intelligence test, children with no environmental risks scored more than 30 points higher than children with eight or nine risk factors. No preschoolers in the zero-risk category had an IQ below 85, but 26 percent of those in the high-risk group did. And 4-year-olds with five or more risk factors were 12.3 times as likely to have clinical mental health symptoms as those with fewer risks (Sameroff, 2000).

Child development theory in recent years has incorporated the notion that children not only react to their environment, but also help create it as their behavior elicits responses from those around them (NRC, 2000c, 2001b). In an effort to determine the role played by the characteristics a child brings—including temperament, perinatal physical condition, interactive behaviors, and competence in motor behaviors and regulatory abilities—children were assessed during the first 12 months on a variety of development and behavior scales.[6] The children were assessed again at age 4 on both social-emotional competence (mental health) and on IQ. Infant competence scores were rendered insignificant compared with environmental risk. "High competent infants in high risk environments did worse as 4-year-olds than low competent infants in low risk environments . . . individual characteristics were not able to overcome the effects of environmental adversity. If one wants to predict the developmental course for infants, attention to the accumulation of environmental risk factors would be the best strategy" (Sameroff, 2000:26-27) (see Figure 3-14).

Effects of SES on School Readiness

Data from the National Center for Education Statistics on children entering kindergarten demonstrate how striking are the accumulated differences in knowledge and skill development across SES groups by the time

---

[6]These included scores from the infant's perinatal physical condition from the Research Obstetrical Scale (Sameroff et al., 1982), the Brazelton Neonatal Behavioral Assessment Scales (Brazelton, 1973), and the Bayley Scales of Infant Development (Sameroff, 2000).

children reach the schoolhouse door. The survey collects data on emergent literacy and numeracy skills and content knowledge. It also collects teacher and parent ratings on children's social skills (National Center for Education Statistics, 2000).

Table 3-7 displays differences by family and child characteristics in the skills that have been established to be prerequisites to learning to read: knowing that print reads left to right, knowing where to go when a line of print ends, and knowing where a story ends. Without a regression analysis, the independent effects of poverty, race, maternal education, marital status, and a primary language other than English cannot be disentangled. The simple correlations, however, are pronounced for each characteristic. At the extremes, 47 percent of white children with a mother who graduated from high school had all three skills, while only 11 percent of black children with mothers who did not graduate from high school had all three. The same pattern can be found for prereading skill level in letter recognition, beginning and ending sound identification, and identifying words by sight or in context and for early mathematics skills, including number and shape recognition, relative size comparison, ordinal sequencing, the ability to add, subtract, multiply, or divide small numbers.

Finally, social and emotional skills differ by SES as well. While these skills are of value in and of themselves, for the purposes of this report their relationship to later academic achievement and behavior is noteworthy (Swartz and Walker, 1984). While the Early Childhood Longitudinal Study collects data on a variety of measures, we focus here on self-regulatory and motivation characteristics and problem behaviors *as rated by the teacher.* Teacher ratings may incorporate bias (discussed in Chapter 5), but these are the ratings that are likely to influence special education placement.

Teachers see differences between boys and girls in the ability to attend, with only 58 percent of boys rated as being able to attend often, compared with 74 percent of girls. They also rate white and Asian children as better able to attend and as more persistent than black and Hispanic children. Children's ratings on all attributes rise with parents' education levels, and children in two-parent families are rated higher on average than those in one-parent families (see Table 3-8).

With respect to problem behaviors, the number of children who argue or fight with others is relatively small; most children can get along in the classroom. However, the differences by race are substantial, with Asians rated as exhibiting few problem behaviors and black children exhibiting the highest rate (see Table 3-9). Hispanic and white children receive similar ratings.

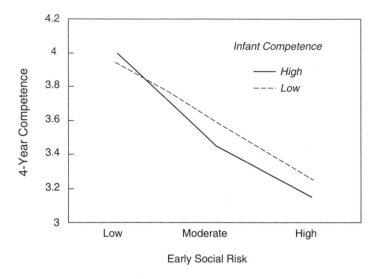

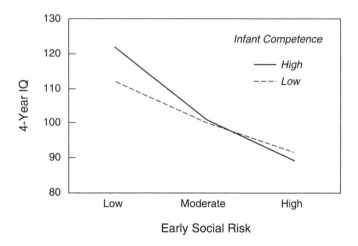

FIGURE 3-14 Relation of infant competence to competence and IQ scores at 4 years of age, controlling for early multiple environmental risk scores.
SOURCE: Sameroff (2000). Reprinted with permission of John Wiley & Sons.

Implications of School Readiness Differences

The early disparities in school readiness are of marked significance because they portend future achievement gaps. While gaps in the particular skills of letter and number identification close during the kindergarten year,

TABLE 3-7 Percentage Distribution of First-Time Kindergartners by Print Familiarity Scores, by Child and Family Characteristics: Fall 1998

Characteristic	0 Skills	1 Skill	2 Skills	3 Skills
Total	18	21	24	37
Child's sex				
Male	20	20	23	37
Female	17	21	25	38
Child's race/ethnicity				
White, non-Hispanic	14	18	24	45
Black, non-Hispanic	29	26	24	21
Asian	15	19	22	43
Hispanic	24	23	26	27
Hawaiian Native/Pacific Islander	30	27	19	23
American Indian/Alaska Native	38	27	18	17
More than one race, non-Hispanic	18	23	24	35
Child's race/ethnicity by maternal education				
Maternal education:				
High school diploma/equivalent or more				
White, non-Hispanic	12	17	24	47
Black, non-Hispanic	27	25	25	23
Asian	14	17	22	46
Hispanic	22	22	25	31
Maternal education:				
Less than high school diploma or equivalent				
White, non-Hispanic	26	26	25	22
Black, non-Hispanic	40	30	20	11
Asian	22	36	23	19
Hispanic	32	26	27	15
Welfare receipt				
Utilized welfare	32	27	22	19
Never utilized welfare	17	19	24	40
Primary language spoken in home				
Non-English	26	22	24	28
English	18	20	24	38

NOTES: Estimates based on first-time kindergartners who were assessed in English (approximately 19 percent of Asian children and approximately 30 percent of Hispanic children were not assessed). Percentages may not sum to 100 due to rounding.
SOURCE: U.S. Department of Education, National Center for Education Statistics, Early Childhood Longitudinal Study, Kindergarten Class of 1998-99, Fall 1998.

children who enter kindergarten with those skills already in place have made strides in other areas that take them beyond early skill development. Figure 3-15 shows the gains in reading scores over the course of the kindergarten year by maternal education level. While all children gained significantly over the course of the year, the gap did not narrow, even though

TABLE 3-8 Percentage Distribution of First-Time Kindergartners by the Frequency with Which Teachers Say They Persist at a Task, Are Eager to Learn New Things, and Pay Attention Well, by Child and Family Characteristics: Fall 1998

	Persist	
Characteristic	Never/Sometimes	Often/Very Often
Total	29	71
Child's sex		
Male	35	65
Female	22	78
Child's race/ethnicity		
White, non-Hispanic	25	75
Black, non-Hispanic	38	62
Asian	19	81
Hispanic	33	67
Hawaiian Native/Pacific Islander	36	64
American Indian/Alaska Native	36	64
More than one race, non-Hispanic	27	73
Child's race/ethnicity by maternal education		
Maternal education:		
High school diploma/equivalent or more		
White, non-Hispanic	23	77
Black, non-Hispanic	36	64
Asian	18	82
Hispanic	31	69
Maternal education:		
Less than high school diploma or equivalent		
White, non-Hispanic	39	61
Black, non-Hispanic	50	50
Asian	18	82
Hispanic	35	65
Welfare receipt		
Utilized welfare	41	59
Never utilized welfare	27	73
Primary language spoken in home		
Non-English	31	69
English	28	72

NOTE: Estimates based on first-time kindergartners. Percentages may not sum to 100 due to rounding.
SOURCE: U.S. Department of Education, National Center for Education Statistics, Early Childhood Longitudinal Study, Kindergarten Class of 1998-99, Fall 1998.

Eager to Learn		Attention	
Never/Sometimes	Often/Very Often	Never/Sometimes	Often/Very Often
25	75	34	66
29	71	42	58
22	78	26	74
22	78	30	70
34	66	45	55
20	80	29	71
30	70	38	62
32	68	41	59
28	72	48	52
28	72	33	67
20	80	28	72
31	69	42	58
18	82	28	72
27	73	36	64
35	65	44	56
47	53	58	42
23	77	32	68
36	64	41	59
38	62	47	53
24	76	32	68
32	68	37	63
25	75	34	66

TABLE 3-9 Percentage Distribution of First-Time Kindergartners by the Frequency with Which Teachers Say They Exhibit Antisocial Behavior, by Child and Family Characteristics: Fall 1998

	Argue with Others	
Characteristic	Never/Sometimes	Often/Very Often
Total	89	11
Child's sex		
Male	87	13
Female	92	8
Child's race/ethnicity		
White, non-Hispanic	90	10
Black, non-Hispanic	83	17
Asian	94	6
Hispanic	90	10
Hawaiian Native/Pacific Islander	86	14
American Indian/Alaska Native	86	14
More than one race, non-Hispanic	90	10
Child's race/ethnicity by maternal education		
Maternal education:		
High school diploma/equivalent or more		
White, non-Hispanic	91	9
Black, non-Hispanic	84	16
Asian	94	6
Hispanic	90	10
Maternal education:		
Less than high school diploma or equivalent		
White, non-Hispanic	87	13
Black, non-Hispanic	80	20
Asian	97	3
Hispanic	89	11
Welfare receipt		
Utilized welfare	84	16
Never utilized welfare	90	10
Primary language spoken in home		
Non-English	91	9
English	89	11

NOTE: Estimates based on first-time kindergartners. Percentages may not sum to 100 due to rounding.
SOURCE: U.S. Department of Education, National Center for Education Statistics, Early Childhood Longitudinal Study, Kindergarten Class of 1998-99, Fall 1998.

Fight with Others		Easily Get Angry	
Never/Sometimes	Often/Very Often	Never/Sometimes	Often/Very Often
90	10	89	11
89	11	86	14
92	8	91	9
92	8	90	10
86	14	85	15
93	7	91	9
89	11	88	12
89	11	88	12
85	15	87	13
90	10	88	12
92	8	90	10
87	13	85	15
92	8	90	10
90	10	89	11
88	12	87	13
83	17	85	15
97	3	95	5
86	14	86	14
85	15	85	15
91	9	89	11
89	11	88	12
90	10	89	11

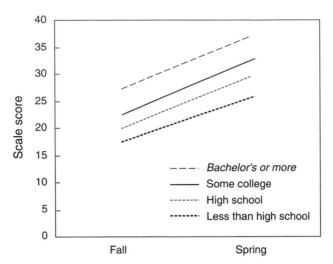

FIGURE 3-15 First-time kindergartners' reading mean scale scores, by mother's education: Fall 1998 and Spring 1999.
SOURCE: U.S. Department of Education, National Center for Education Statistics, Early Childhood Longitudinal Study, Kindergarten Class of 1998-1999.

almost all children had acquired letter recognition and print awareness skills (West et al., 2001). As children move through the school years, those who read well read more (Stanovich, 1986) and therefore acquire a larger knowledge base.

A similar pattern occurs in mathematics: children from low-SES groups acquire the same knowledge as those from higher-SES groups, but they acquire it later (West et al., 2001). Griffin et al. (1994) found that low-income 5- to 6-year-olds performed like middle-income 3- to 4-year-olds on a test of early math skills.

The implications of the lag apply not only to special education, but also to gifted education. At the upper end of the achievement distribution in the literacy domain are children who can recognize words by sight or can add and subtract in the spring of the kindergarten year. Figures 3-16 and 3-17 plot the percentage of such children by the number of risk characteristics present, including less maternal education than high school, family receiving welfare or food stamps, single-parent household, and primary language other than English. While about 1 in 5 children in families with none of those risk factors has mastered these skills, the representation of children with two or more risk factors in that category is very low.

Disparities in school readiness are also manifested in the development of peer and student-teacher relationships. We know from research on the development of behavior and emotional problems that young children who already exhibit aggressive, disruptive behaviors when they enter school are

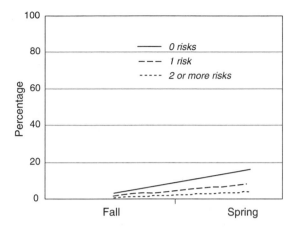

FIGURE 3-16 Percentage of first-time kindergartners recognizing the words by sight, by number of risk factors: Fall 1998 and Spring 1999.
SOURCE: U.S. Department of Education, National Center for Education Statistics, Early Childhood Longitudinal Study, Kindergarten Class of 1998-1999.

often not equipped with the necessary skills to develop healthy peer and adult relationships later on (Goldstein et al., 1980; Patterson, 1986; Patterson et al., 1992; Walker et al., 1987). We also know that aggressive and violent boys differ from less aggressive boys on measures of interpersonal problem solving, with the scores of aggressive and violent boys dem-

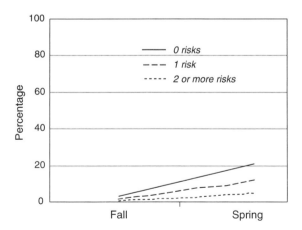

FIGURE 3-17 Percentage of first-time kindergartners adding and subtracting, by number of risk factors: Fall 1998 and Spring 1999.
SOURCE: U.S. Department of Education, National Center for Education Statistics, Early Childhood Longitudinal Study, Kindergarten Class of 1998-1999.

onstrating significantly poorer skills (Lochman and Dodge, 1994). This inability to appropriately solve problems, coupled with the use of coercive behaviors, makes it extremely difficult for antisocial students to attend, concentrate, and learn the basic academic skills necessary to function in school. These learning skill deficits, which often develop before school entry, cause students to have trouble moving successfully through the curriculum, because they usually need additional time and assistance to help them achieve mastery (Fuchs et al., 1993; Walker et al., 1995; Gleason et al., 1991).

The weight of the evidence reviewed above suggests that in order to have an education system in which non-Asian minority students (and disadvantaged students more generally) are not represented in disproportionately high numbers among those at the low end of the achievement distribution and in disproportionately low numbers at the high end of that distribution, efforts to support the cognitive, social, and emotional development of those children in the years before they arrive at kindergarten are critical. This is not to say that early experience sets a child on an unalterable course. We know, for example, that some schools do far better than others at promoting achievement among high-risk children (discussed in Chapter 5). Yet when children are exposed to many risk factors early on, promoting school success will be a much more difficult task for both the child and the school.

4

Early Intervention Programs

Interdisciplinary programs have been designed to address many of the threats to early development we have discussed. Most of these programs have had an impact, although in some areas gains are more modest (e.g., outcomes for children with very low birthweight) and harder to achieve (e.g., changes in parenting behavior) than in others (e.g., reduction in iron deficiency).

A number of early intervention demonstration programs were designed and implemented to test the effect of more comprehensive early intervention for children born into circumstances with a great many risk factors. These demonstration programs are of two types: one targets psychological development and mental health, emphasizing parenting interventions. The other targets cognitive and behavioral development as its primary purpose and usually includes direct provision of services to children in addition to family services. While the primary focus of those designing the programs is somewhat different and the research traditions tend to be separate, supporting the child in either domain is likely to have substantial spillover effects in the other domain. Early intervention policy for at-risk children can be best informed by looking at outcomes for both types of interventions, considering them as part of a single picture.

PARENTING PROGRAMS

Powerful risk and protective factors implicated in early emotional and behavioral development can be found in the relationship between parent and child (see Chapter 3). The parent plays a central role, for example, in teaching the child the critical social and emotional regulation skills that are essential for adjustment to the demands of elementary school and peer relationships. Parents also have an indirect effect on emotional development by the extent to which they buffer the child from the effects of poverty or neighborhood violence.

The quality of parenting practices specifically implicated in the development of emotional and behavioral problems is affected in turn by a myriad of contextual factors associated with poverty and, in many cases, with minority status (see Chapter 3). The effects on parenting and child emotional development of interventions to increase the incomes of poor families have not been evaluated in well-designed, randomized trials. Even among the numerous promising early intervention programs targeted directly at specific aspects of parenting, only about 1 in 20 has been evaluated, and many of these have methodological weaknesses (U.S. Department of Health and Human Services, 2001b).

In the findings summarized below, we emphasize randomized studies with objective or multiagent assessment. Trials without postintervention follow-up are cited for their value in establishing the causal status of antecedents to emotional disturbance.

Pregnancy Through the First Two Years

Early interventions directed at improving the parenting of young mothers appear highly promising for the prevention of emotional problems in children before they emerge at school entry. Importantly, the antecedents identified in developmental studies have been shown to be malleable in these intervention studies.

Early Home Visitation Programs

The most promising and carefully evaluated set of early interventions and randomized trials has been the nurse home visitation program developed by Olds and his colleagues (Olds et al., 1986, 1997, 1998). Beginning in the third trimester of pregnancy, women living in poverty with no previous live births were identified for a public health nurse visitation program that was targeted at specific and well-established early risk factors. Program targets included prenatal care, maternal diet, and reductions in cigarette smoking. The program provided mentoring and strong emotional support for the mother.

For two years after birth, maternal engagement with the child, maternal validation, and problem solving were central targets, as were parenting skills more generally. Parents were encouraged to utilize agencies and programs for financial, social, and educational support. Importantly, mothers were encouraged and assisted to develop job skills.

The program has been replicated in rigorous randomized studies, and follow-up studies have been conducted for up to 15 years. A wide variety of immediate impacts on early child behavior and cognitive development have been reported, as well as important long-term effects on behavioral adjustment. In addition to direct effects on child development and parenting, the mothers in the intervention groups had fewer and more widely spaced pregnancies and were significantly more likely to get paying jobs and to leave welfare. Beyond demonstrating the potential of early intervention with parents, the program also demonstrates the wide range of serious risk factors that are malleable in high-risk families with young children.

A variant of this model, called Healthy Start, originated in Hawaii and now operates in 37 or 38 states; it appears effective and feasible for large scale prevention efforts. To date there have been no randomized trials of Healthy Start.

Improving Mother-Infant Attachment

The basis for early and secure emotional attachment between mother and child has long been considered the foundation on which the psychological, emotional, and social development of the child is built. Insecure attachment has been implicated in both ineffective, harsh, and neglectful parenting and in the development of externalizing behavior by young children. A large number of studies of the efficacy of interventions designed to improve attachment has been carried out with mixed results. A classic study by van den Boom (1994) showed dramatic effects of early intervention both on the mother (contingent responsiveness, sensitivity) and on the infant (secure attachment, sociability, self-soothing, exploration). These findings were partially replicated by Toth et al. (2000) and by Wendland-Carro (1999). Although the long-term effects of attachment-focused interventions are not yet clear, they reliably increase maternal sensitivity and engagement, which are key factors in the prevention of emotional-behavioral problems. For a review and meta-analysis of relevant studies, see van Ijzendoorn et al. (1995).

Children Ages 3 to 5

The key developmental challenges during the preschool period expand to include demands for increased impulse control and compliance to social norms and parental expectations. Key risk factors during this period include parental reports of difficult child temperament, noncompliance, aggression, parental irritability and harshness, lack of discipline skills—particularly limit setting—and low parental warmth and playfulness. A substantial number of randomized trials of parent training and support interventions have targeted this constellation of risk factors. The most programmatic and successful work to date has been reported by Carolyn Webster-Stratton and her colleagues (Webster-Stratton, 1989, 1998; Webster-Stratton et al., 1988). Targeted at parents of children demonstrating severe conduct problems, these interventions focused on discipline, supervision, problem solving, praising, and positive interactions. Using both parent reports and direct observation data, they consistently report strong improvements in these skills, as well as improvements in children's social behavior, lower rates of problems and aggression, and better social skills. The parent training interventions are highly replicable and can be enhanced with videotapes and parenting manuals. Follow-up studies show persistence for up to two years.

An intriguing study by McNeil et al. (1991) demonstrated that improving parenting skills has direct and positive effects on young children's behavior in preschool classrooms (also see Sheeber and Johnson, 1994). As the next chapter discusses, these strategies can be integrated with school-based programs to produce truly integrated interventions for elementary school students.

CHILD DEVELOPMENT PROGRAMS

Demonstration programs that provide services directly to children to promote their cognitive and behavioral development have a history that stretches back 30 years. The effects of these programs have been reviewed thoroughly, frequently, and recently (Karoly et al., 1998; National Research Council [NRC], 2000a, 2000b; Ramey and Ramey, 1999; Guralnick, 1997; White and Boyce, 1993; Farran, 1990; Haskins, 1989; Karweit, 1989; Carnegie Task Force on Meeting the Needs of Young Children, 1994; Bryant and Maxwell, 1997; Currie, 2000). We do not undertake another review here. Rather, we summarize some of the major lessons from the programs characterized both by the provision of high-quality, intensive services and by the use of rigorous research designs to analyze outcomes (Ramey and Ramey, 1998). High quality refers to the nature of the transactions between caretakers and children, and is supported by the education and training of the caretakers, smaller child/adult ratios, and smaller group size. The findings synthesized below draw from prospective randomized trials targeted to children at risk for developmental delay, mental retardation, poor school achievement, or a combination of the three. A list of programs for which longitudinal studies were conducted to determine program effect appears in Table 4-1, along with program features.

We can conclude with confidence that early intervention programs can produce modest to large effects (effect sizes of 0.2 to over 1.0 standard deviation) on children's cognitive and social development. Larger effect sizes are associated with better subsequent performance in school, particularly when the schools are of good quality (Campbell and Ramey, 1994, 1995; Lazar et al., 1982). Variation in effect size and duration is associated with the particular program features reviewed below (Ramey and Ramey, 1992).

Developmental Timing

Interventions that begin early and continue for a longer duration result in greater benefits to participants. The five major studies that demonstrated some of the largest effects of early intervention on cognitive and social development all enrolled children during infancy (the Abecedarian Project, the Brookline Early Education Project, the Milwaukee Project, Project CARE, and the Infant Health and Development Program). Data on early cognitive development for program and control children in the Abecedarian Project displayed in Figure 4-1 suggest that, without intervention, high-risk children fall substantially behind as early as the second year of life. Since no experimental design has tested for a critical period or threshold effect, however, no precise timing for intervention can be supported empirically.

Program Intensity

Programs that provide more hours of service delivery produce larger positive effects than do less intensive interventions. Within programs, children and parents who participate the most actively and regularly are the ones who show the largest developmental gains. All of the programs mentioned as effective with regard to timing also provided intensive intervention services. In addition to these, the Perry Preschool Project (Weikart et al., 1978) and the Early Training Project (Gray et al., 1982), both of which began when children were 3 or 4 years old, also provided intensive services and registered substantial program impact. Numerous examples of early intervention programs that had little or no effect on cognitive, social, or later academic performance were less intensive.[1]

---

[1]The Utah State Early Intervention Research Institute (White, 1991), for example, found no significant effects in the 16 randomized trails of early interventions for children with developmental disabilities. None of these interventions provided full-day programs or multiple home visits per week. Similarly, a brief prenatal and postnatal program for urban teen mothers failed to affect their children's cognitive performance or social development (Brooks-Gunn and Furstenberg, 1987). For other examples, see Ramey and Ramey (1998).

TABLE 4-1 Longitudinal Studies of Child Development Programs

Researcher	Age Group	Ratio	Group size	Duration
Abecedarian Project (Campbell and Ramey, 1994)	Infants, preschool	1:3 1:6	14 12	5 years
Brookline Early Education Project (Hauser-Cram et al., 1991)	Infants, preschool	1:1 1:6	18	5 years
Early Childhood Education Project (Sigel et al., 1973; Cataldo, 1978)	2-3 years	1:7	22	3 years
Early Training Project (Gray et al., 1982)	Preschool	1:5	20	2 or 3 years
Family Development Research Program (Honig and Lally, 1982)	1-2 years Infants, preschool	1:4	8	5 years
Harlem Training Project (Palmer, 1983)	Preschool	1:1	NA	1-2 years
Infant Health and Development Program (Ramey et al., 1992; Infant Health and Development Program Consortium, 1990)	1-2 years 2-3 years	1:3 1:4	6 8	3 years
Milwaukee Project (Garber, 1988)	2 years 3 years preschool	1:2 1:3 1:7	?	6 years
Perry Preschool Project (Schweinhart and Weikart, 1993)	Preschool	1:5	20-25	2 years
Project CARE (Wasik et al., 1990)	Infants, preschool	1:3 1:6	14 12	5 years

SOURCES: Data from Frede (1998); Lazar et al. (1977); and NRC (2001b:134-135).

The principle that intensity matters applies to two-generation programs that work with parents as well. One home visit program (Powell and Grantham-McGregor, 1989) produced significant cognitive benefits with three visits per week but not with less frequent visits. Similarly, the Brookline Early Education Project (Hauser-Cram et al., 1991) reported significant cognitive and social benefits only from its most intensive two-generation interventions.

Intensity	Curriculum	Teacher Qualifications	Activities for Parents
Full-day	Interactive	Experienced paraprofessionals to certified teachers	Group meetings, home visits
Part- or full-day	Interactive	Certified teachers	Home visits, guided observation in classroom
Half-day	Interactive	Certified teachers and 2 paraprofessionals	None
Part-day 10 weeks summer	Structured Interactive	Certified teacher	Weekly home visits during academic year
Full-day	Interactive but less structured	Paraprofessional-home visitors/professional teachers	Weekly home visits, informal class visits, and daily notes home
2 weeks	2 tutoring approaches: concept training or discovery	Tutors change every 6 weeks high school to Ph.D. candidate	None
Full-day	Interactive	Bachelor's degree with early childhood education specialty	Home visits
Full-day	Cognitive curriculum	Paraprofessional/certified teacher at 4 years	Job training, social services, home visits
Half-day	Interactive	Certified teachers	Weekly home visits
Full-day	Interactive	Experienced paraprofessionals to certified teachers	Group meetings, home visits

To date, only one study has looked at program intensity at the level of the individual child: the Infant Health and Development Program. As indicated in the discussion of low birthweight in Chapter 3, the amount of intervention each child and family received, monitored daily over the first three years of life, had a strong, positive effect on the child's intellectual and social development at 36 months. Blair et al. (1995) found that children's yearly intellectual development was strongly linked to variations in yearly participation rates.

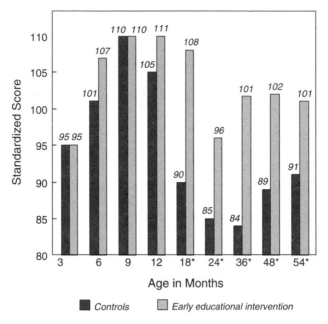

FIGURE 4-1 Intellectual performance of children in the Abecedarian Project during the preschool years.
SOURCE: Ramey and Ramey (1999). Reprinted with permission.

Direct Provision of Learning Experiences

Children who receive direct educational experiences show larger and more enduring benefits than do children in programs that rely only on the training of parents to change children's competencies. Variation in the delivery of services across programs between those that provide educational experiences to children directly and those that train caregivers (usually parents) to do so are clear: direct techniques are more powerful in enhancing children's intellectual and social experiences (e.g., Casto and Lewis, 1984; Madden et al., 1976; Scarr and McCartney, 1988; Wasik et al., 1990). Even when weekly home visits were sustained from birth to age 5 in a randomized, controlled trial with economically disadvantaged, high-risk children (Wasik et al., 1990), no measurable benefits on children's cognitive or social performance, parent attitudes or behavior, or the quality of the home environment were found. For the group that received both the weekly home visit and daily center-based intervention, there were significant cognitive gains for the children.

Planned Curriculum

Successful early intervention models have used a variety of curricula. But relatively little research has been done that allows for a direct comparison of curricular effects. No single curriculum has been demonstrated to be superior to others (Bryant and Maxwell, 1997), but this may reflect the difficulty of separating out the effects of curriculum, program intensity, and teacher quality. However, research does indicate the importance for learning outcomes of having a planned, well-integrated curriculum (NRC, 2001b).

Comprehensive Service Provision

The intervention programs that have produced relatively large early effects, including the Abecedarian Project, the Brookline Early Education Project, Project CARE, the Milwaukee Project, the Infant Health and Development Program, and the Mobil Unit for Child Health, all provided health and social services, transportation, practical assistance with meeting pressing family needs, neurodevelopmental therapies when needed, and parent services and training in addition to quality educational programs for children.

Benefits Vary with Type and Level of Risk

The idea that individuals respond differently to any kind of "treatment" is pervasive in many domains, including child development, medical interventions, and education. Indeed, a key mark of progress is the extent to which differential responses (or person by treatment interaction) are understood and incorporated into the intervention. Many of the early intervention programs viewed children as either disadvantaged or not, and the treatment for the disadvantaged ones was a program or service that differed often by site, but for reasons unrelated to the characteristics of the individual children.

Several studies, however, suggest relevant dimensions for distinguishing among children in the intervention required and the response anticipated. The Infant Health and Development Program (1990) found that very low birthweight babies did not benefit as much from the intervention as their heavier counterparts. In a study of educational interventions for children with disabilities, Cole et al. (1993) found that children who were higher performing at program entry benefited more from direct instruction techniques, while lower-performing students benefited more from the mediated learning treatment. Findings from the Abecedarian Project showed the largest gains for children whose mothers had the lowest IQ scores, findings reinforced by several other programs that showed larger program impact from intensive intervention for children whose mothers had low levels of education (Ramey and Ramey, 1998). Systematic attention to the match between the child's characteristics and the program provided holds promise for improvement in the efficiency and outcome of early intervention.

Sustained Cognitive, Social, and School Achievement Benefits

Long-term benefits of early intervention on school achievement, grade retention, and special education placement, as well as on behaviors outside school, have been identified (Campbell and Ramey, 1995; Lazar et al., 1982; Schweinhart and Weikart, 1993). Most studies also detect IQ benefits, but they generally diminish over time (Ramey and Ramey, 1998). Given that children in the studies live in high-risk environments and attend schools in high-risk neighborhoods, this result is not surprising. No theory of development would support an expectation of normative development in a high-risk environment without continued intervention.

One randomized study tested the effects of providing continued support into the elementary school years to children who received early intervention services. At age 8, children who received services for all eight years, children who received services for the first five years, and those who received services for three years were compared with control group children (Horacek et al., 1987). A strong positive association was found between the number of years that supports were maintained and reading and math scores at age 8. A nonrandomized study of Chicago Head Start children supports this finding (Reynolds, 1994). When resources are constrained, focusing supports on the early years, when children are putting into place the basic capacities and skills required for later functioning may be efficient. But if children are to continue to develop at a normative pace, it will not be sufficient.

Would Early Intervention Reduce Special Education Placement?

Since well-designed early intervention programs have been shown to affect cognitive and social functioning, one would expect that those improvements would move some number of students with mild disabilities over the threshold separating those who require special supports and those who do not. Several studies measure the effect directly.

Two model demonstration programs provide data on special education placements. The Perry Preschool project reports rates of special education placement of 17 percent for program participants compared with 37 percent for control children (Schweinhart et al., 1993). In the Abecedarian Project, special education placements rates differed even more dramatically for children who received the preschool program (12 percent) and the control group children (48 percent; P < .01).

The Chicago Child-Parent Center Program, unlike the demonstration programs reviewed above, is a large-scale federally funded program that provides education, family, and health services to low-income, mostly black children and their families. The program includes half-day preschool at ages 3 to 4, half- or full-day kindergarten, and services to children ages 6-9 linked to the elementary school. Outcomes for program children at a 15-year follow-up were compared with groups of matched children who were in alternative early childhood programs like full-day kindergarten, a subset of whom were in the program's kindergarten but who had not participated in the preschool program.

Preschool participation was associated with significantly lower rates of special education placement (14.4 vs. 24.6 percent; P < .001), and the program group spent on average 0.7 years in special education compared with 1.4 years for comparison students. Participation in the school-age program for at least a year was associated with lower rates of special education as well (15.4 vs. 21.3 percent, P - .02). Children with 5 or 6 years of participation had the lowest remediation (Reynolds et al., 2001). Preschool program participation was also associated with higher rates of high school completion (49.7 vs. 38.5 percent; P = .01) and lower juvenile arrest rates (16.9 vs. 25.1 percent; P = .003) and violent arrests (9.0 vs. 15.3 percent; P = .002) (Reynolds et al., 2001).

EXISTING FEDERAL EARLY INTERVENTION PROGRAMS

Federal legislation currently provides for funding to states for early intervention services for young children in low-income families through a variety of programs. Table 4-2 lists the largest of these programs, although the General Accounting Office has identified 69 in total that provided for or supported education and care for children birth to age 5 in fiscal year 1999 (U.S. General Accounting Office, 2000). We focus here on the intervention services for children diagnosed with or at risk of disability and on the largest of the early intervention programs—Head Start.

Early Intervention Under IDEA

IDEA Services for Infants and Toddlers

In 1986, the Individuals with Disabilities Education Act (IDEA) was expanded with the establishment of the Early Intervention Program for Infants and Toddlers with Disabilities (Part H, now Part C of IDEA). By 1994, all states and U.S. territories had programs in place. The states are

TABLE 4-2 Federal Spending on Education and Care of Children Under Age 5, Fiscal Year 1999

Program	Amount for Children Under age 5		
	FY 1999 Budget Authority	Estimated Amount	Percentage of Total Budget Authority
Head Start	$4,658,151,448	$4,378,662,000	94.0
Child Care Development Fund	3,166,000,000	2,216,200,000	70.0
Temporary Assistance to Needy Families	17,052,515,000	1,278,938,625	7.5
Special Education-Grants for Infants and Families with Disabilities	370,000,000	370,000,000	100.0
Special Education-Grants to States	4,310,700,000	258,642,000	6.0
Social Services Block Grant	1,900,000,000	209,000,000	11.0
Special Education-Preschool Grants (Individuals with Disabilities Education Act)	373,985,000	205,692,000	55.0

SOURCE: U.S. General Accounting Office (2000).

mandated to serve all children with developmental delay or confirmed conditions that, without intervention, are highly likely to result in developmental delay (e.g., cerebral palsy, blindness). States are also given the option to provide services to children at risk for developmental delay due to biological and environmental factors, such as low birthweight, respiratory difficulties, infections, malnutrition, and a history of abuse and neglect (U.S. Department of Education, 2000). Only 8 states[2] and one territory currently serve children in the at-risk category. In two states—California and Hawaii—well over half of all infants and toddlers served fall into the at-risk category.

The IDEA legislation grants a great deal of discretion to the states, with consequent wide variation in observed programs with respect to the state lead agency, the breadth of the program (proportion of children served), and the depth of the program (nature, intensity, and coordination of services). In 1998-1999, 1.63 percent of all infants and toddlers nationally were served under Part C of the legislation, but the variation among states

---

[2]California, Hawaii, Indiana, Massachusetts, New Hampshire, Nevada, New Mexico, North Carolina, West Virginia, and Guam.

ranged from less than 1 percent in Alabama, Illinois, Iowa, and Louisiana to 6.3 percent in Hawaii and 4.2 percent in Massachusetts (Table 4-3).

Children identified at this young age are likely to have the more obvious disabilities or delays that allow them to be identified early by the medical community or by parents (Kochanek et al., 1990). The largest group (41 percent) are identified as having impaired or delayed speech. These children are most likely to be identified at around age 2, by which time normally developing children would be expected to use some language. Another 19 percent of children who are provided with early intervention services experienced prenatal and perinatal abnormalities, most commonly low birthweight (11 percent). Only 4.9 percent of children receiving early intervention services did so because they were in high-risk social environments.

Representation in early intervention (risk index) by race appear in Figure 4-2. As is the case with later special education services, American Indian/Alaskan Native and black children are more likely to receive services than white children, and Asian/Pacific Islander and Hispanic children are less likely than white children to receive services. Unlike services to children in elementary and secondary education, however, disproportion in early intervention services does not pose a paradox. Children given assistance through Part C are not by virtue of that assistance removed from services generally available to other children (as in general education). Since services are an addition and not a substitution for the child with special needs, they are more likely to narrow the developmental gap. And because the services are provided outside the school context and before a child is highly self-aware, the effect of services on expectations for later school performance or on self-esteem is likely to be minimal. Early intervention services are given high ratings by parents of all races (Hebbeler and Wagner, 2000; McNaughton, 1994; McWilliam et al., 1995), suggesting that they view identification for services as helpful. In fact, the legislative concern is with underrepresentation of minorities, with a stated legislative intent "to enhance the capacity of State and local agencies and service providers to identify, evaluate, and meet the needs of historically underrepresented populations, particularly minority, low-income, inner-city, and rural populations" (sec. 631 (a)(5)).

A nationally representative, longitudinal study of children and families receiving early intervention services under Part C was begun in fall 1997. The National Early Intervention Longitudinal Study (NEILS) will follow children at least through age 5. At the committee's request, Hebbeler and Wagner (2000) analyzed the NEILS data that were available in winter 2000. Their analysis provides insights into the factors that contribute to disproportionate placement in early intervention services.

TABLE 4-3 Number of Infants and Toddlers Receiving Early
Intervention Services, 1998

State	Percentage of Population	American Indian/ Alaskan	Asian/ Pacific Islander	Black	Hispanic	White
Alabama	0.98	2.93	0.37	1.39	0.92	0.79
Alaska	1.71	2.59	1.64	2.58	1.37	1.33
Arizona	1.03	1.57	0.63	2.12	0.95	0.99
Arkansas	1.91	0.14	0.81	3.58	1.71	1.50
California	1.29	1.12	0.53	2.05	0.94	0.93
Colorado	1.91	2.59	1.72	3.21	1.93	1.83
Connecticut	2.74	5.88	2.07	4.11	3.02	2.52
Delaware	2.65	6.25	1.31	3.42	3.83	2.20
District of Columbia	1.40	0.00	0.50	1.51	2.21	0.23
Florida	2.08	0.93	0.61	2.77	1.59	2.06
Georgia	1.05	0.76	0.60	1.26	1.33	0.92
Hawaii	6.31	2.87	8.19	8.04	1.27	3.35
Idaho	1.93	1.75	0.13	2.78	1.91	1.90
Illinois	0.92	0.66	0.41	1.21	0.71	0.93
Indiana	2.26	1.10	1.81	2.48	1.42	2.28
Iowa	0.89	2.59	0.52	2.12	1.04	0.85
Kansas	1.73	2.18	1.38	2.74	2.09	1.61
Kentucky	2.15	.	.	.	.	.
Louisiana	0.91	1.93	0.51	1.09	0.37	0.82
Maine	1.92	2.18	1.34	1.66	0.52	1.95
Maryland	2.02	0.89	1.12	1.86	1.21	1.74
Massachusetts	4.21	5.96	1.91	4.07	6.44	4.05
Michigan	1.52	2.91	1.00	2.05	1.14	1.44
Minnesota	1.46	2.46	0.57	2.31	1.34	1.45
Mississippi	1.69	0.88	0.09	2.57	0.27	1.03
Missouri	1.16	5.35	0.53	1.25	0.55	1.16
Montana	1.85	3.54	2.48	5.10	1.60	1.62
Nebraska	1.21	1.55	0.68	1.85	0.92	1.21
Nevada	1.31	1.69	1.23	2.17	1.19	1.27
New Hampshire	2.07	11.48	1.55	3.76	1.56	2.05
New Jersey	1.36	1.27	0.60	1.90	1.11	1.40
New Mexico	1.47	2.32	0.58	2.48	1.28	1.49
New York	2.79	1.65	0.42	1.27	0.59	1.75
North Carolina	1.59	1.57	1.90	2.65	1.47	1.21
North Dakota	1.24	2.06	0.82	2.14	1.17	1.15
Ohio	1.17	1.36	0.63	1.26	0.97	1.11
Oklahoma	1.52	1.13	1.08	1.86	0.88	1.61
Oregon	1.25	2.31	0.55	1.29	1.29	1.27
Pennsylvania	1.75	3.54	0.49	2.24	1.59	1.45
Puerto Rico	1.36	.	.	.	.	.
Rhode Island	2.69	1.57	0.89	3.96	3.44	2.58
South Carolina	1.45	0.61	0.70	2.09	1.07	1.14
South Dakota	1.99	3.73	0.67	4.68	0.55	1.69

continues

TABLE 4-3 continued

State	Percentage of Population	American Indian/ Alaskan	Asian/ Pacific Islander	Black	Hispanic	White
Tennessee	1.56	2.61	1.34	1.25	1.72	1.44
Texas	1.32	1.13	0.95	1.85	1.18	1.25
Utah	1.46	6.61	1.08	3.53	1.22	1.41
Vermont	2.00	18.18	4.41	9.09	3.90	1.90
Virginia	1.00	1.20	0.41	1.28	0.92	0.95
Washington	1.06	1.67	0.36	1.49	1.28	0.92
West Virginia	3.00	4.44	0.58	1.27	0.15	3.14
Wisconsin	2.01	2.23	1.38	4.69	2.10	1.76
Wyoming	2.16	3.99	1.02	6.25	1.76	2.13
American Samoa	0.85	.	.	.	.	.
Guam	2.02	.	.	.	.	.
Northern Marianas	0.93	.	.	.	.	.
Palau	.	.	.	.	.	.
Virgin Islands	1.57	.	.	.	.	.
Bureau of Indian Affairs	.	.	.	.	,	,
U.S. and Outlying Areas	1.63	.	.	.	.	.
50 States, DC and Puerto Rico	1.63	2.04	1.18	1.89	1.17	1.42

NOTES: Population figures are July estimates from the Bureau of the Census. Population data for Puerto Rico and the outlying areas are projections from the Bureau of the Census, International Programs Center. The projections adjust the 1990 census annually based on the previous year's births and deaths. Resident population data are provided from Population Estimates Program, Population Division U.S. Census Bureau for July 1998. The percentage is based on the number of people within the specific race/ethnicity category in the resident population. Data based on the December 1, 1998, count, updated as of November 1, 1999.
SOURCE: U.S. Department of Education (2000).

For all racial/ethnic groups, placement in early intervention services varies with income. As Table 4-4 indicates, for the population as a whole and for each race group individually, the highest representation is of children from families with incomes below $15,000. While 17.6 percent of all children live in such families, 25.7 percent of children receiving early intervention services come from that group. And while 70.3 percent of children 0-3 live in families with income above $25,000, 58.9 percent of those receiving early intervention come form that income group. The disproportionate representation of children in families with incomes below $25,000 is similar for blacks and whites when the percentage in an income group receiving early intervention is compared with the percentage in the income group in the population at large. Hispanics are more likely to receive scr-

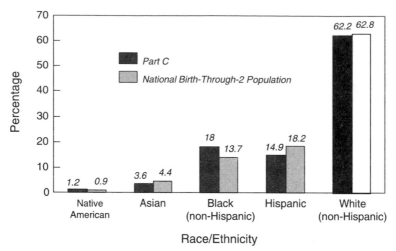

FIGURE 4-2 Race/ethnicity: National versus Part C percentages.
SOURCE: U.S. Department of Education (2000).

vices if they are in the $15,000-$25,000 income bracket than if they are in the lowest income bracket. With this exception, these data support the link between poverty and special needs discussed above: while children from all income groups have disabilities, the income status of the family is negatively correlated with the likelihood of disability.

The NEILS data also support more specific links between biological and environmental conditions more common in low-income (disproportionately minority) families and disability identification. Low-birthweight children were represented in the early intervention group in large numbers: 31 percent of early intervention children were low birthweight, and 17 percent were very low birthweight. These percentages far exceed those in the population as a whole, in which 7.5 percent are low birthweight and 1.4 percent are very low birthweight. A total of 42 percent of black children in the early intervention program were low birthweight, and 30.9 percent were very low birthweight—substantially higher than any for other racial/ ethnic group. But the rate at which black low-birthweight children are provided with early intervention services is just below the rate for white low-birthweight children, while the rate for Hispanic low-birthweight children is just above that of whites. The NEILS data also suggest that black children who were served under Part C were substantially more likely to have been in intensive care at birth than were the white and Asian children served, and they were less likely to be rated as in good or excellent health.

The risk models discussed above suggest that the challenges faced by children are compounded the greater the strain on the family and the fewer

TABLE 4-4 Household Income and Race/Ethnicity for Children Receiving Early Intervention

	All	EI/GP[a]	African American	EI/GP	Hispanic	EI/GP	Asian/Pacific Islander	White	EI/GP	Other
Early Intervention										
Percent with Income:										
$15,000 or less	25.7	1.46	48.1	1.37	34.6	1.14	20.1	15.5	1.36	24.4
	(1.8)		(3.5)		(3.4)		(8.4)	(2.0)		(2.5)
$15,001 to $25,000	15.4	1.26	20.1	1.18	27.0	1.37	7.1	10.6	1.10	20.6
	(.9)		(2.0)		(3.3)		(2.3)	(.8)		(34.4)
More than $25,000	58.9	.84	31.8	.67	38.4	.76	72.8	74.0	.94	45.0
	(2.1)		(2.9)		(4.0)		(8.6)	(2.6)		(4.6)
General Population—Families with Children under 18										
Percent with Income:										
$15,000 or less	17.6		35.2		29.9		11.4			
$15,001 to $25,000	12.2		17.6		19.7		9.6			
More than $25,000	70.3		47.2		50.4		79.0			

NOTE: Standard errors are in parenthesis. N for early intervention = 2,801. General population data not available for Asian/Pacific Islander and Other.

[a] EI/GP is the percentage of those receiving early intervention in the income group divided by the percentage of the population in that income group.

SOURCE: Hebbeler and Wagner (2000).

resources the family has available to cope with those strains. The glimpse of families served in early intervention provided by the NEILS data suggests that the strains are highest in black and Hispanic families, in which the number of children is on average greater, as is the likelihood that more than one child in the household will have special needs. The resources are fewest in the black families, in which the likelihood that only one adult lives in the household is more than double that of Hispanic families and five times greater than that for Asian and white families. In Hispanic and black families, the likelihood that the mother will have less than a high school education is 29 and 25 percent respectively, while that for whites and Asians falls below 10 percent.

A final, significant risk factor is foster care. Children in foster care are substantially more likely than other children to have disabilities (Gottlieb, 1999; Blatt and Simms, 1997; Klee et al., 1996). Almost 7 percent of the children in the NEILS dataset were in foster care—10 times that for the general population (U.S. Department of Health and Human Services, 1999). Over 18 percent of the black children were in foster care, however. In the general population, 45 percent of all children under 18 who are in foster care (less than 1 percent of the population) are black.

IDEA Services for Preschoolers

At the same time that the Early Intervention Program was added to IDEA, the Preschool Grants Program for Children with Disabilities was changed from an incentive program to a mandated program (U.S. Department of Education, 2000). By 1991, states were required to provide a "free and appropriate public education" to all eligible 3- to 5-year-olds. As Figure 4-3 indicates, the rate of identification increases with the child's age. The rapid increase in the number of children served in the early 1990s slowed substantially (to about 1.5 percent) by the end of the decade (U.S. Department of Education, 2000).

Data on the race/ethnicity of children served in the preschool program are available only as of 1998-1999. They differ considerably from either the early intervention proportions or the later population served under IDEA. In the preschool program, white children and American Indian children are represented in disproportionately large numbers (see Figure 4-4). The representation of black children is almost identical to the proportion in the population, and Hispanic and Asian children are served in less than proportional numbers. Most of these children (92 percent) receive special education services in regular public school settings (U.S. Department of Education, 2000).

Why is the racial composition of children in the preschool program different from the early intervention program and the special education

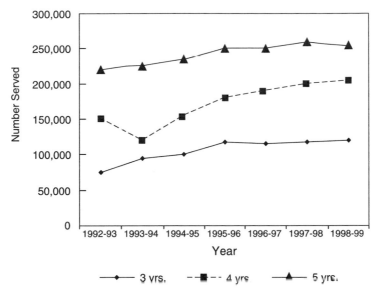

FIGURE 4-3 Number of preschool children with disabilities served under IDEA by age and year, 1992-1993 through 1998-1999.
SOURCE: U.S. Department of Education (2000).

program during the school years? An answer to that question is no more than speculation. One possibility is that the label serves the purpose of providing access to preschool services, and the Head Start program provides an alternate source of services for poor children. The disproportionate number of black children served in Head Start may shrink the proportion served under IDEA during those years.

Head Start

The Head Start program was created in 1965 to narrow the gap between disadvantaged children and their more advantaged peers by providing educational experiences, improved nutrition, parent involvement, and access to health and social services (U.S. General Accounting Office, 1998). In 1999-2000 the program served 857,664 children, primarily 3- and 4-year-olds. The program serves disproportionate numbers of black and Hispanic children, as one would expect given the targeted population of children living in poverty (see Table 4-5). About 12.7 percent of the children served were designated as disabled (see 2001 Head Start Fact Sheet: http://www2.acf.dhhs.gov/programs/hsb/about/fact2001.htm). Many of the Head Start programs provide home visitation services.

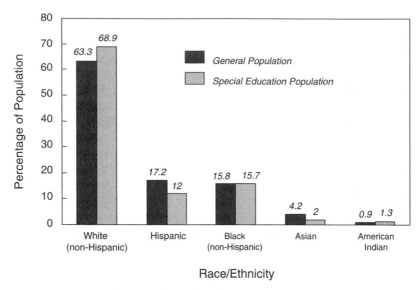

FIGURE 4-4 Race/ethnicity of preschoolers receiving special education and of the general preschool population, 1998-1999.
SOURCE: U.S. Department of Education (2000).

In all, 32 percent of Head Start staff are parents of children served or formerly served in the program. The program operates with a paid staff of 180,400, which is dwarfed by the volunteer staff of 1.25 million, about 0.8 million of whom are parents.

The average expenditure per child in Head Start in fiscal year 1999-2000 was $5,951, but the average conceals enormous variation both within and between states. In 1996-1997 the average in Texas was $1,081, while that in New York was $17,029. Within New York, the range between the lowest and highest expenditure per child was $16,206 (U.S. General Accounting Office, 1998a).

Little research using experimental design has been done to evaluate the effectiveness of Head Start in any of the services it provides (U.S. General Accounting Office, 1997). Unlike the efforts at evaluation of Early Head Start, Head Start has not yet been subject to randomized trials to determine its impact on school readiness or on health and nutrition. However, the Department of Health and Human Services recently awarded a contract for a Head Start Impact Study that will involve random assignment (see 2001 Head Start Fact Sheet: http://www2.acf.dhhs.gov/programs/hsb/about/fact2001.htm).

TABLE 4-5 Head Start: Fiscal Year 2000 Data

Enrollment	857,664
Ages:	
Number of 5-year-olds and older	5.0%
Number of 4-year-olds	56.0%
Number of 3-year-olds	33.0%
Number under 3 years of age	6.0%
Racial/Ethnic Composition	
American Indian	3.3%
Hispanic	28.7%
Black	34.5%
White	30.4%
Asian	2.0%
Hawaiian/Pacific Islander	1.0%
Number of Grantees	1,525
Number of Classrooms	46,225
Number of Centers	18,200
Average Cost per Child	$5,951
Paid Staff	180,400
Volunteers	1,252,000

SOURCE: 2001 Head Start Fact Sheet. Available: http://www2.acf.dhhs.gov/programs/hsb/about/fact2001.htm [accessed July 11, 2001].

Whether the program achieves the goal of narrowing the gap between disadvantaged children and their more advantaged peers in school readiness is difficult to say. The Family and Child Experiences Survey funded by Head Start is a nationally representative sample of families and children in the Head Start program designed to assess changes in children between the beginning and the end of the Head Start year. The analysis of the survey data shows conflicting results (Whitehurst and Massetti, in press), with possible small gains in word recognition and emergent writing. But without a control group, even these small gains cannot be attributed to the program. On measures of letter knowledge, book knowledge, and reports of the home reading environment, there were no improvements over the course of the Head Start year (Administration of Children, Youth, and Families, 2001).

The survey analyses are consistent with other studies that have shown that children participating in Head Start score very low in language development and preliteracy skills (Legislative Office of Education of Ohio,

1998; Robinson and Dixon, 1992; Snow and Paez, in press). However, two recent longitudinal studies of Head Start children in elementary school found that those children who had begun to learn about print, sounds, and writing during the preschool years were more likely to be reading successfully in elementary school (Lonigan et al., 2000; Storch and Whitehurst, 2001; Whitehurst and Fischel, 2000).

One recent study examining nonexperimental data suggests that Head Start may have long-run positive effects. Garces et al. (2000) analyzed data from the Panel Study of Income Dynamics, a longitudinal dataset that has collected data on a group of individuals for over a quarter-century. Data were examined for adults at age 30 who were asked whether they had participated in Head Start. The dataset contains information that allowed the study to control for family background and environmental characteristics. The findings suggest that for whites, Head Start is associated with a higher probability of completing high school and attending college, as well as with higher earnings in later years. Black males who had participated in Head Start were more likely than their siblings to have completed high school and less likely to have been charged with or convicted of a crime.

Early Head Start

The two-generation Early Head Start program, launched in 1995, provides services to low-income families with infants and toddlers. Currently the program provides services to 45,000 families at over 600 sites (U.S. Department of Health and Human Services, 2001a). A national random assignment evaluation of about 3,000 children in 17 sites was also begun in 1995 but has not yet been fully analyzed. Initial results, however, suggest that, compared with control groups, children in the program at age 2 performed significantly better on measures of cognitive, language, and social-emotional development, although the gains were relatively modest in magnitude. However, parents in the program scored higher than control parents on measures of home parenting behavior, home environment, and knowledge of infant and toddler development and were more likely to attend school or job training—outcomes that bode well for continued gains.

CONCLUSIONS AND RECOMMENDATIONS

Our review of biological and social/contextual contributors to early development brings us to the compelling conclusion that there are several factors that have a known detrimental impact on early cognitive and behavioral development that affect some groups of minority children disproportionately. The biological factors include low birthweight, alcohol and tobacco exposure, microneutrient deficiencies, and exposure to lead.

Existing intervention programs to address early biological harms have demonstrated the potential to substantially improve developmental outcomes. For example, prenatal health and nutrition programs that reduce the incidence of low-birthweight babies, and intervention strategies to stimulate development in low-birthweight babies, have had measured positive effects. Addressing these early biological risks has the potential to reduce the number of children, particularly minority children, with achievement and behavior problems. The strategies are neither unknown nor recently discovered. It is a matter of political priority whether resources are devoted to do so.

The committee calls particular attention to the recommendation of the President's Task Force on Environmental Health Risks and Safety Risks to Children to eliminate lead from the housing stock by 2010 (U.S. President's Task Force, 2000).

The committee also looked at social and environmental influences on development with no clear biological basis that might differ by race. Low socioeconomic status—both income and education level—is centrally implicated and is highly correlated with race/ethnicity. Poverty, especially persistent poverty, is associated with maternal depression, and with less optimal home environments on such dimensions as responsiveness and sensitivity of the mother to her child, the amount and level of language stimulation, direct teaching, and parenting styles. Income is also positively correlated with educational resources both inside and outside the home (child care and preschool). For both biological and social risk factors, the effect of any single factor is compounded by the presence of other risk factors.

Given the positive results of the research-based early interventions for high-risk children, the committee's view is that there is ample theoretical and empirical support to justify launching systematic prevention efforts. Indeed, both federal and state governments have acknowledged the importance of doing so in the variety of programs that have been put in place over the last several decades and expanded in recent years. But current policy falls short in terms of systematic prevention. Existing programs cover only a fraction of those eligible and at high risk.

IDEA Part C, for example, allows for services to be delivered to high-risk children, even if they have not been identified with a disability, in the at-risk category. In only eight states, however, is the at-risk category used.[3]

---

[3]Of the children receiving early services nationally, 64 percent had clearly identified developmental delays, 20 percent were diagnosed with a condition with a high probability of leading to a disability, and only 16 percent were served in the at-risk category (Hebbeler and Wagner, 2000).

The benefit of the IDEA legislative vehicle is that it allows for the targeting of children with the greatest need—i.e., children with a high number of risk factors whose chance of being referred to special education will be greatest without intervention. Given limited resources, the group that will require the most intensive interventions to ensure positive outcomes can be targeted through IDEA.

Similarly, Early Head Start provides an opportunity to serve high-risk children from birth, and without the connection to IDEA the services can be provided without establishing disability or risk of disability. But again, only a small number of children are currently served. A larger number of children are served in programs for 3- and 4-year-olds, including Head Start and IDEA Part B for preschoolers. Still, two-thirds of eligible children are not served, and the quality and effectiveness of the services provided to those who are served are questionable.

Because the committee regards the evidence on the benefits of early provision of services to children with multiple risk factors as compelling, we make the following recommendations:

Recommendation EC.1: The committee recommends that all high-risk children have access to high-quality early childhood intervention.

For children at highest risk, these interventions should include family support, health services, and sustained, high-quality care and cognitive stimulation right from birth.

- Preschool children (ages 4 and 5) who are eligible for Head Start should have access to a Head Start or other publicly funded preschool program. These programs should provide exposure to learning opportunities that will prepare children for success in school. The committee urges attention to the well-documented early learning practices recommended in two recent National Research Council reports that focus on early childhood pedagogy: *Preventing Reading Difficulties in Young Children*, and *Eager to Learn: Educating Our Preschoolers*. We also call attention to the finding that a critical requirement of the proposed change is raising the education requirements for preschool teachers.
- Intervention should target services to the level of individual need, including high cognitive challenge for the child who exceeds normative performance.
- The proposed expansion should better coordinate existing federal programs such as Head Start and Early Head Start, and IDEA parts C (for infants and toddlers) and B (for children 3-21), as well as state-initiated programs that meet equal or higher standards.

By high-quality early intervention services, we mean that early care and education provided to children through these programs should consistently reflect the current knowledge base regarding child development. It is important for all children to have quality child care and preschool services. However, to narrow the gap in school readiness among children at high risk for poor developmental outcomes and their lower-risk peers, carefully designed programs that support the development of self-regulation, social skills, and language and reasoning skills are critical.

While we know much about the types of experiences young children need for healthy development and we know that early intervention can improve outcomes, improving the quality of early childhood programs on a large scale will require that we refine our knowledge base in ways that are directly useful to early intervention efforts and bridge the chasm between what we know and what we do. This will require a sustained vision and a rigorous research and development effort that transforms knowledge about what works and what doesn't work into field-tested program content, supporting materials, and professional development. This is not likely to happen with current funding levels.

Recommendation EC.2: The committee recommends that the federal government launch a large-scale, rigorous, sustained research and development program in an institutional environment that has the capacity to bring together excellent professionals in research, program development, professional development, and child care/preschool practice.

Among its efforts, the research and development program should:

(a) fund projects to incorporate usable knowledge about early childhood development into field-tested curricula, educational tools, and professional development materials for early childhood teachers and classrooms;

(b) focus on areas with high potential for providing knowledge that can lead to prevention of disabilities and special education identification and the enhancement of gifted behaviors;

(c) systematically examine the comparative benefits associated with different early early intervention models and the developmental pathways through which those results were produced;

(d) conduct comprehensive re-analyses of longitudinal data sets to obtain clues about why some programs have succeeded and others have failed. While the results of longitudinal studies are now well known, the data have not been fully probed for an understanding of the components of both success and failure; and

e) explore whether some subgroups of participants in early intervention programs have benefited/are benefiting differentially.

The proposed expansion of early childhood services to disadvantaged children will, the committee acknowledges, require a substantial investment. Few programs collect longitudinal data that would allow for a careful cost-benefit analysis. Two programs—the Perry Preschool program and the Prenatal and Infancy Home Visitation by Nurses—have done longitudinal data collection that indicates benefits outweigh costs by several times when long run effects on crime and teenage pregnancy are considered (Karoly et al., 1998). Those results should not be projected onto large-scale intervention programs for many reasons, among them the change in both costs and benefits as program size increases dramatically and the characteristics of the population changes. The results do suggest, however, that up front investment in changing a developmental trajectory produces benefits over a life course with implications for government revenues as well as for individual success.

Part III

From General to Specialized Education: Why and How Students Are Placed

The research literature and the data from the National Early Intervention Longitudinal Study point to multiple reasons why minority children (other than Asian) would be expected to have higher incidence of disability and lower rates of high achievement. These children are more likely to experience multiple biological and environmental correlates of disability and low achievement. But while the committee considers the importance of early experiences to be incontrovertible, it is only one piece of a complex picture.

The notion that early biological and environmental experience is a critical contributor to the disproportionate representation of minority children in special and gifted education is entirely compatible with the notion that schools exert an important, sizable, independent influence on achievement and on special and gifted education placement of minority students. Case studies of schools in which student achievement is well above average despite a high representation of disadvantaged minority students, or of successful reform programs that raise achievement and lower special education placement in these schools, suggest the schools' effect can be substantial.

The most significant step in special[1] and gifted education placement is

---

[1]We refer here to the high-incidence categories of learning disabilities, mild mental retardation, and emotional disturbance.

the first: a student must be referred. Referral is most often done by the general education teacher. Special needs or gifts are therefore exhibited (or not) in the general education classroom. For this reason, the committee considers general education, and referral and assessment for special and gifted education, as parts of a single picture. In Chapter 5 we look at general education and its potential role in the disproportionate placement of minority students in special and gifted education. In Chapter 6 we look at special education referral and the law that guides special education practices. In Chapter 7 we look at the assessment process for the disabilities of concern and for gifted and talented programs.

In Chapter 8 the committee looks at major challenges to the existing system, and offers a set of recommendations for substantial reform. Our proposal rests on the conclusion that more effective referral and placement for all children require more closely integrated assessment, intervention, and monitoring in general education before students are placed in special and gifted programs. Therefore our recommendations for changes in general education, and for special and gifted education identification and placement, all appear in Chapter 8.

5

The General Education Context

This chapter focuses on various aspects of the context of general education and their contribution to minority children's achievement. Our motivation for considering these issues is threefold. First, it is the committee's contention that no coherent assessment of disproportion in special and gifted education can be conducted without a nuanced understanding of the factors leading to differences in measured achievement. This understanding is necessary because real achievement deficits are both the obvious competing explanation for any finding of racial disproportion, and because measured achievement differences are one means through which children are assigned to special and gifted education. Thus, in order to understand and potentially eliminate race-linked disproportion in special education and gifted and talented placements, one must understand the processes that can lead to measured achievement differences.

Second, the committee argues in this report that a key factor in addressing disproportion in special and gifted education is support for minority student achievement in general education. In order for such efforts to be successful, policy makers and practitioners need a thorough understanding of the kinds of factors that may matter for minority student achievement. Although we cannot provide a complete analysis of these issues here, we would be remiss to take this position yet provide no evidence to sustain it. We therefore suggest in this chapter the state of the literature in sufficient detail to further support this position.

Third, a wide variety of studies, from many different methodological, theoretical, and disciplinary traditions, point to the complex ways in which context matters. The widespread recognition of the importance of the context of education to student achievement is evidenced by standard inclusion of theories of context in teacher preparation programs. Such theories as Vygotsky's (1986) model of instruction within the zone of proximal development, Bronfenbrenner's (1979) model of nested ecological systems, Sameroff and Chandler's (1975) transactional model of child development, and others are commonly part of teacher training.

CONTEXT MATTERS

Perhaps the most persuasive evidence that context matters is the substantial difference in performance by the same student(s) in different contexts. In a 15-year line of research on the importance of context, Fischer et al. (1993) consistently demonstrated that children's skill levels in a range of social and classification tasks varied according to the degree and type of social support provided by the experimenter directing the task. The experiments were carried out on children ranging from 3 to 18 years of age.

The children were directed to carry out a variety of tasks, such as (for younger children) creating stories about "mean and nice" or sorting blocks into boxes. In low-support contexts, children performed the tasks spontaneously. In high-support contexts, there was direct modeling of high performance of the task. The children's independent performances were then rated on a developmental scale. Substantial differences were found between the functional level in the low-support context and the optimal level in the high-support context. In one study, in which 7-year-old children were asked to produce stories about mean and nice, their spontaneous responses were scored at or below stage 3 on the developmental scale, reflecting a rather shallow characterization of people as being either "mean" or "nice." After exposure to more complex stories in which mean and nice characterized particular actions with specific motivations, children's own stories were rated 3 stages higher, suggesting a very powerful influence of contextual support on performance (Fischer et al., 1993). Competence is "an emergent characteristic of a person-in-context, not a person alone," the authors concluded.

The quality of instruction and behavior management in a classroom and school are important contributors to the context in which student achievement and behavior problems arise. In a three-year ethnographic study utilizing extensive observations of classrooms and child study team meetings, Klingner and Harry (2001) noted that, while the child study process seldom included classroom observations, referred children were very often coming from classrooms in which teachers exhibited poor behavioral management and/or instructional skills.

The importance of the teacher's ability to manage the classroom is reinforced by findings in a longitudinal study of 1st grade students and teachers randomly assigned to classrooms in 19 schools. Boys who were aggressive in 1st grade were found to have a far higher probability of exhibiting behavior problems in later years if they were in poorly managed classrooms than boys who were similarly aggressive at the outset but were in well-managed classrooms (Kellam et al., 1998a). A study done some time ago by Rutter (1979) assessed the behavior of an entire cohort of students before they were assigned to high schools. Student behavior ratings were used to predict delinquency rates at the schools to which they were assigned. As Figure 5-1 shows, the rates deviated substantially from those predicted. "Some schools that had rather high proportions of children who had shown behavioral deviance in primary school, nevertheless had rather low delinquency rates. Good schools can and do exert an important protective effect" (Rutter, 1979:58-60). Given the growing body of research that points to the importance of context, the committee regards an examination of classroom and school context as critical to any serious effort to address race-linked disproportion in special and gifted education.

Although much of the research has focused on general education or special education placements, it suggests the importance of the general education context for eventual placement in both special education and gifted programs and may contribute to the possible racial-ethnic disproportion in both. Our concern is best understood in light of the observation that in the high-incidence disability categories, the majority of students who

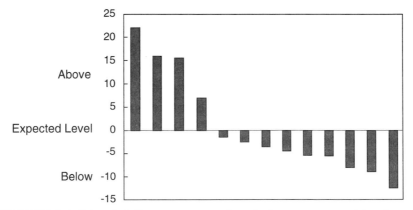

FIGURE 5-1 School delinquency rates in relation to expected level.
SOURCE: Rutter (1979). Reprinted with permission.

become eligible for special education services do not begin school with the label. Thus, schools are key actors in defining unmet instructional need; hence, they must be enabled to define it correctly and respond to it successfully.

Common sense understandings of the concept of context may make its meaning appear to be self-evident. However, there is a significant body of literature addressing the complex ways that concept may be defined and operationalized. Box 5-1 presents a range of formulations that influence our use of the concept. Although the theories cited are subtly different, we draw three insights that are consistently demonstrated in the work. First, the contextual factors surrounding all students, from the most proximal to the most distal, interact in a dynamic process that contributes to students' performance in school. Second, the notion of contextual factors includes the range of activities and interactions within which the student is expected to learn. Third, individuals, including students, parents, teachers, and other school personnel, make meaning as they interact with their environments, and this interaction, in turn, creates new contexts for learning and development.

We illustrate the importance of context by focusing on three broad areas: educational resources, intended and unintended bias in the design and delivery of schooling, and tested instructional and classroom management interventions.

EDUCATIONAL RESOURCES

The kind and quality of resources, and the way those resources are used, affect the context in which learning occurs. Although a comprehensive treatment of this topic is beyond the scope of this report, we discuss three issues that can affect the placement rates of minorities in special and gifted education: education personnel, class size, and school funding.

Education Personnel

Teacher Quality

Data directly linking teacher characteristics to student achievement are limited. In part, this is due to the difficulty of identifying measurable proxies for teacher quality (see National Research Council [NRC], 2001d). Although scores on teacher tests are very rough surrogates for teacher quality, some studies have used such scores to assess student access to effective instruction. For example, Ferguson (1991) studied 900 Texas school districts and found that teacher expertise (measured by scores on a licensing exam), master's degrees, and experience accounted for approxi-

BOX 5-1
Theories and Definitions of Context

Vygotsky's (1978) model of instruction within the zone of proximal development argues for the role of adults in supporting cognitive growth.

Bronfenbrenner's (1979) nested ecological systems suggest that the many contexts in which children live, including family, neighborhood, school, peer groups, etc., influence development.

Sameroff and Chandler (1975) argue the need for transactional models of child development, to take into account multidirectional influences of environment.

Many analysts have argued that ecological systems include both risk and protective factors (e.g., Barocas et al., 1985; Gabarino, 1982; Rutter, 1985).

Cazden (1986) and Phillips (1972, 1983) propose participation structures that implicitly or explicitly designate "the rights and obligations of participants with respect to who can say what, when and to whom."

Doyle (1986) describes "natural segments" that include (1) patterns for arranging participants, (2) roles and responsibilities for carrying out actions, (3) rules of appropriateness, and (4) props and resources used.

Tharp and Gallimore (1988) and Gallimore et al. (1993) focus on activities as the unit of analysis in describing context. "Activity settings" are comprised of five variables: (1) personnel present during an activity, (2) salient cultural values, (3) task demands of the activity, (4) cultural scripts for conduct that govern participants' actions, and (5) purposes or motives of the activity.

Engeström (1987, 1990) and Engeström et al. (1999) propose that these activity systems comprise subjects (including people, their viewpoints, and subjective perspectives); tools (a variety of cultural artifacts including skills, equipment, and ideas); the object (motives or objectives); desired outcomes (objects transformed toward some end); rules (formal and informal ways of working with the object); a community (which shares the object with the subject); and a division of labor—how actions are divied up in an activity.

Van Oers (1998) transcends "context" as merely situational influence, advocating a focus on information processing and meaning-making activities that translate situational influence into interpretation and action.

Spencer's (1995) Phenomenological Variant of Ecological Systems Theory analyzes the experiences of minority youth in the United States by combining ecological and phenomenological approaches. These perspectives suggest the key role of individual agency in responding to contextual influences.

mately 40 percent of the variance in students' reading and mathematics achievement, once socioeconomic status was controlled. Ferguson and Ladd (1996) found similar evidence in a smaller study in Alabama, and Strauss and Sawyer (1986) found a strong influence on student performance of teachers' scores on the National Teacher Examinations.

Evidence also suggests that poor and minority students are more likely to have teachers with less experience and expertise. The research of Ferguson (1991), Kain and Singleton (1996), and Ferguson and Ladd (1996) indicates that schools with concentrations of disadvantaged students are typically less successful than other schools in attracting teachers with strong cognitive skills (NRC, 1999a). Darling-Hammond and Post (2000) reviewed the influence of principals on school effectiveness, concluding that minority and low-income students are most likely to be in schools with inadequately prepared and inexperienced teachers and administrators. These authors note that impediments to hiring qualified teachers include differences in resources and salaries, teaching conditions (class size, autonomy), influence over school policy, mentoring, and district management. Sanders and Rivers (1996) report that black students are nearly twice as likely to be assigned to ineffective teachers.

A recent National Assessment of Title I documented that high-poverty schools have a greater percentage of inexperienced and uncertified teachers: 15 percent of elementary and 21 percent of secondary teachers in high-poverty schools had less than three years experience, compared with only 8 percent of elementary and 9 percent of secondary school teachers in low-poverty schools (U.S. Department of Education, 2001a). In high-poverty schools, temporary or emergency certification accounted for 12 percent and out-of-field teachers for 18 percent of teachers, compared with low-poverty schools in which less than 1 percent of secondary school teachers had temporary or emergency certification or were teaching out of field. The report also states that teachers in high-poverty schools are less likely to have opportunities for professional growth compared with low-poverty schools.

Another concern of the report was the widespread use of Title I funds for paraprofessionals as part of schools' instructional programs. These personnel account for half the instructional staff hired through Title I funds. Indeed, 84 percent of high-poverty schools reported using paraprofessionals, while only 54 percent of low-poverty schools reported using paraprofessionals. The report states, "although few Title I teacher aides have the educational background necessary to teach students, almost all (98 percent) reported that they were teaching or helping to teach students. Overall, providing instruction accounted for 60 percent of Title I aides' time, and 41 percent of aides reported that half or more of this time was spent working with students on their own, without a teacher present" (p. 35). The report points out that research shows no benefits of paraprofessionals, a finding consistent with the analyses of Project STAR data. The report recommends that the best uses of paraprofessional personnel are as translators/interpreters for limited English-speaking students and for liaison work with parents. However, only 3 percent of Title I paraprofessionals are employed as parent liaisons.

Similarly, Rothstein (2000) stated that one of the greatest inequities in education is the uneven distribution of teachers within urban districts. In most urban districts, union contracts allow greater choice according to seniority, so the inner-city schools are left with the most inexperienced teachers. Rothstein recommended financial incentives to attract senior teachers to inner-city schools.

Capacity

Increasing the supply of qualified teachers to urban schools is likely to be particularly challenging in the current labor market. There are 3.22 million teachers currently working in the nation's schools (Gerald and Hussar, 2000), but it is estimated that more than 2 million new teachers will be needed in the first decade of the 21st century (National Center for Education Statistics, 2001). The reasons for this increase are varied: enrollment growth due to increased births and migration, especially in the South and the West; the graying of America's teachers; and the persistent problems in attracting and retaining teachers in low-income urban and rural areas (Rodriguez, 1998; Melnick and Pullin, 1999).

The student population in the United States has become increasingly diverse. Future estimates suggest that the student population will become nearly one-half students of color—native, migrant, and immigrant—with an increasing number of white immigrant children from the former Soviet Union and Eastern Europe (National Center for Education Statistics, 1997b; National Commission on Teaching and America's Future, 1996).

At the same time that the proportion of minority students has been increasing, the proportion of minority teachers has been decreasing. For example, in 1993-1994, black non-Hispanics made up 16 percent of the public school population, but only 9 percent of the teaching force (National Commission on Teaching and America's Future 1996; National Center for Education Statistics, 1997a); while in 1998 black non-Hispanics made up 17 percent of the public school population and only 7.3 percent of the teaching force (National Center for Education Statistics, 2000; Digest of Education Statistics, 1999). In urban districts in which students of color make up 69 percent of the total enrollment, only 36 percent of the teaching force are minorities (Recruiting New Teachers, 2000). Almost 75 percent of these urban districts report an immediate need for minority teachers (Recruiting New Teachers, 2000). Furthermore, it is estimated that large urban districts alone will need to hire nearly 700,000 new teachers in the next decade (Recruiting New Teachers, 2000). Recognizing this problem, 36 states have special programs for minority teacher recruitment (Rodriguez, 1998). However, even with such minority recruiting efforts under way, nearly 75 percent of urban districts face *immediate* shortages in minority teacher placement and retention (Recruiting New Teachers, 2000).

These data suggest insufficient numbers of prospective minority teachers to radically alter current patterns of school staffing practices (Melnick and Pullin, 1999). In the coming years, students in public schools will be increasingly different in background from their teachers, who will be largely white, middle class, female, and monolingual speakers of English (Melnick and Pullin, 2000; Melnick and Zeichner, 1998). The potential consequence is highlighted in a recent study that found that students perform better (by 3 to 4 percentile points on average) in reading and math when taught by a teacher of the same race (Dee, 2001). As Gay (1990) noted, the changing demographic trends have the potential to create a significant social distance between students and teachers that will "make achieving educational equality even more unlikely in the existing structure of schooling" (1990:61).

Urban schools that enroll large numbers of poor minority students have difficulty in attracting new teachers because resources are typically more scarce than in suburban settings and teachers perceive social concerns, such as crime and high poverty, as making teaching and learning more difficult (Rodriguez, 1998).

Class Size

Current research provides evidence that reducing class size, especially in the elementary grades, improves student achievement and that these gains may be particularly pronounced for black and other minority students (Finn and Achilles, 1999; Molnar et al., 1999). Studies indicate that classes that have 20 or fewer students reduce the amount of time teachers devote to disruptive behavior and administrative or clerical tasks and lead to less teacher use of passive learning activities, such as teacher-led whole-group instruction (Achilles, 1996; Finn and Achilles, 1999; Glass and Smith, 1978). Thus, small class size allows students to devote more time to academic tasks, spend less time waiting for the teacher to begin instruction, receive more individualized instruction, and increase their time in active learning activities (Evertson and Randolph, 1989; Molnar et al.,1999; Robinson and Wittebols, 1986; Slavin, 1989).

In 1985, the Tennessee legislature and a consortium of Tennessee universities conducted a controlled statewide experiment to investigate the effects of small class size for students in kindergarten through 3rd grade

(Finn and Achilles, 1999). Project Student/Teacher Achievement Ratio (STAR) randomly assigned approximately 7,500 students in grades K-3 to (a) large classes (26 or more students), (b) regular size classes (22-26 students), and (c) regular size classes with an instructional assistant in 79 elementary schools across 42 school districts from 1985 to 1989. This four-year investigation found statistically significant academic gains in reading and math for students placed in small classes. Moreover, the magnitude of achievement gains for black and other minority students was, in many instances, twice as large as that of the academic gains made by nonminority students. Equally compelling was the similarity of students, regardless of ethnicity, across motivation measures and the lack of statistically significant interaction effects between class size, gender, age, and geographic region of the school.

Clearly, Project STAR provides important information regarding the impact of class size on student achievement during the early primary grades. Nye et al. (1999) conducted the Lasting Benefits Study, a five-year follow-along study that examined the long-term effects of the Project STAR small class intervention. The results of this study found that the academic benefits of small class size during K-3 persisted until at least 8th grade. Students who had been in small classes were also perceived as more motivated, as participating more, and as engaged in disruptive behavior less often than students who had been placed in regular-size classes. Krueger and Whitmore (2001a,b) found that black students in the experimental group had higher rates of taking ACT or SAT college entrance exams and lower rates of teen fatherhood for black males. These authors conclude that reduced class size should contribute to a significant reduction in the black-white test score gap and that "class size reductions will have the biggest bang for the buck if they are targeted to schools with relatively many minority students" (p. 32).

Wisconsin's Student Achievement Guarantee in Education (SAGE) program was a five-year pilot project that compared different models to reduce the number of pupils assigned to a regular classroom (Molnar et al., 1999). A total of 30 treatment schools and 14-17 comparison schools participated in the study. The treatment schools were required to reduce the pupil/teacher ratio to 12-15 students for each teacher. However, schools were allowed flexibility in implementation of this ratio, and classroom configurations ranged from one teacher for 12 students in a single classroom to 30 students taught by two certified teachers in a single classroom. The results of this study found the magnitude of academic gains for students, especially black students, who were placed in small classes was larger than that of their comparable peers placed in comparison schools.

The Project SAGE evaluation also investigated classroom and teacher characteristics related to student academic performance. Classroom changes reported by teachers included reduction and/or elimination of discipline problems, increased individualized instruction, use of student-centered learning activities as opposed to teacher-led activities, and increased knowledge about the student's personal and educational needs. Overall, teachers reported that students were learning more and interacting more with peers and the classroom environment was more cohesive and organized.

Project STAR, Project SAGE, and the Lasting Benefits Study provide strong evidence that reduction of class size to 20 or fewer students during the elementary grades can improve academic achievement and reduce classroom discipline problems for students regardless of ethnicity, socioeconomic background, or gender. Equally important is the growing documentation that students who attend small classes during their early primary years retain these academic and behavioral benefits at least through their middle-school years. As yet almost no data are available to examine the effects of smaller class size in grades 4 and up on achievement.

Reduction in class size in the above experiments brought academic and behavioral benefits for students without any explicit additional teacher training or orchestrated changes in classroom organization and teaching methods. Changes did occur spontaneously, however, as teachers shifted to more individualized instruction. However, recent studies offer caution that teachers may not change their teaching substantially in response to reduction in their class size.

Betts and Shkolnik (1999) investigated the impact of reduced class size on the type of instruction, pacing, and teaching methods used by 2,170 math teachers. This study used extant data from the Longitudinal Study of American Youth, which followed 100 nationally representative middle and high schools from fall 1987 to spring 1992. Study results indicate the largest effect of class size reduction was decreased time devoted to group instruction accompanied by increases in individualized instruction. However, reduced class size did not significantly increase the amount of new material taught by teachers, nor did teachers change their teaching methods, despite increased instructional time made available by reduced discipline, administrative, and clerical tasks. Instead, teachers, regardless of their education level or the ability level of their students, generally increased the amount of time spent on review activities.

An analysis by Murnane and Levy (1996) looked at a natural experiment occasioned by a desegregation agreement in Austin, Texas, in which 15 schools were given $300,000 above normal school spending for each of five years. Every one of the schools reduced class size. However, only two showed improvements in measured student achievement, and these two were the only ones to go beyond merely reducing class size. Among other changes, these schools also mainstreamed special needs children, exposed all children to a reading and math curriculum usually available only in gifted and talented programs, added health services to the school, and improved the involvement of parents.

Funding

Historically analysts have debated whether school funding matters. The evidentiary basis for the claim that money does not matter originates in *Equality of Educational Opportunity*, know as the Coleman Report (Coleman et al., 1966), which found limited impacts of school resources on student achievement. Drawing on the wealth of studies conducted in the wake of the Coleman Report, Hanushek (1997) conducted a widely known meta-analysis of studies of the effects of funding and also found no effect. He and other analysts have pointed to opposing trends in expenditures (rising) and achievement test scores (flat or falling) to question the influence of school resources (e.g., Hanushek, 1994).

The research producing these findings, however, is problematic. Analysts have long known that placing two time trends side-by-side is insufficient to establish a causal connection between them (e.g., Campbell and Stanley, 1963). Similarly, placing two trends that appear to run in opposite directions together cannot establish a lack of a causal connection. The reason such comparisons are rarely illuminating is that many factors, including changes in the population composition over time (e.g., rising numbers of students whose first language is not English), or changes in legal requirements for who the school must serve and how, may mask a possible underlying causal connection. Such competing explanations make it impossible to evaluate causality using gross time trend data.

Meta-analytic techniques are more promising for assessing the possible causal role of funding in student achievement, but decisions about what studies to include, and whether separate regressions run in a single study count as one or as multiple findings can influence the outcome. While Hanushek's analysis found no effect of funding, a similar study by Hedges et al. (1994) found a statistically significant and substantively important positive net effect of funding on achievement.

In the last two decades, well-designed studies that draw on the knowledge of learning, schools, and schooling have begun to show consistent effects of funding (NRC, 1999a). For example, Elliott (1998) analyzed National Education Longitudinal Study (NELS) data from the early 1990s and found that money matters for achievement gains, suggesting that more money allows districts to hire better-trained teachers who use more effective instructional strategies. The case of the 15 Austin school districts mentioned above suggests the rather obvious conclusion: money *can* matter. But how much it matters depends on how it is spent.

Documented resource inequities by race and income have received a great deal of attention (NRC, 1999a; Parrish et al., 1998). Currently the educational resources that affect student learning are not equitably distributed. As indicated above, poor and minority children are more likely to attend schools that are inadequately funded and staffed. Comparing per-pupil revenues for schools with low-poverty rates (< 8 percent) and high-poverty rates (25 percent or above), one finds that high-poverty schools have 89.4 percent of the per-pupil revenues of their low-poverty counterparts (NRC, 1999a:48-49).

Efforts to narrow per-pupil spending differentials though programs like Title I have made a difference. Schools with the highest concentrations of poverty (25 percent or more) now report per-pupil revenues that are higher than all but the wealthiest schools (those with less than 8 percent in poverty) (NRC, 1999a). And schools with less than 5 percent minority enrollment have, on average, 6 percent lower revenues per student than those with 50 percent or more minority enrollment. However, in recent years, attention has shifted from a focus on equity in education finance to "adequacy," in recognition that both education costs and student needs can be greater in urban schools with large numbers of disadvantaged students. Indeed, when the revenue-per-student data are adjusted to account for cost and need, low-minority schools have per-pupil revenues almost 4 percent *above* those of high minority schools (NRC, 1999a).

We echo here the theme that permeated the discussion of child development in Chapter 3: the impact of more distal factors like resources must be understood through their more proximal effects on interactions. The resources required to narrow achievement differences are those that will allow high-poverty schools to provide the teaching personnel and environments that support achievement. But the desired outcome will be ensured only if the resources are effectively used to those ends.

For example, schools in more affluent neighborhoods provide more rigorous college preparatory and honors courses than schools in lower-income communities. A recent study of California schools (Betts et al., 2000) found that 52 percent of classes in lower-income schools met college preparatory requirements, compared with 63 percent in the highest-income schools. The study also found that the median high-income school has over 50 percent more advanced placement courses than the median low-income school. Whether the issue involves funding, staffing, or the relationship between the two, if minority students are to have an equal opportunity to achieve, they must have access to the educational experience provided in more affluent neighborhoods.

BIAS IN THE DESIGN AND DELIVERY OF SCHOOLING

The experiences of minority children and youth in American schools are overlaid with a history of exclusion and oppression. It is important to remember that numbered among today's adults are the first black students to be educated in de jure desegregated schools. The historic exclusion of individuals on the basis of ethnicity has been accompanied by a stigmatizing process that has devalued those students associated with excluded minority groups. The work of Mickelson (1990), Steele and Aronson (1995), Steele (1997), Cunningham (1999), Spencer (1999), and others suggest that, at some point in the transition from childhood to adulthood, students become aware of the wider society's assessment of their racial/ethnic group. Claude Steele (1997) has advanced the theory of stereotype vulnerability to explain why many minority students may perform poorly or choose not to participate in academic endeavors in which they run the risk of confirming the stereotype that they are intellectually inferior. Through a series of experiments, Steele demonstrated that black students scored lower on tests when they were told that other ethnic groups routinely scored higher than they. Furthermore, Steele showed that students often disidentify (plead lack of interest) in an effort to protect themselves from stigmatization for low performance. Schools therefore face a daunting challenge. Not only must they be fair to all, but they must overcome the impediments placed in their way by the wider society to support higher achievement of minority students. Given this state of affairs, it is easy to understand the halting progress that has been made. Therefore, it is essential that whatever biases are present in schools be addressed.

Teacher Judgments, Expectations, and Potential Self-Fulfilling Prophecies

Given that wider context, the detrimental impact of a prejudicial school environment has been of concern to researchers for several decades. The intangible and often subtle nature of bias and prejudice, however, makes this issue difficult to study. In the 1980s several researchers used hypothetical or simulated situations, such as eliciting judgments and expectations from teachers in response to photographs or profiles of children of different ethnicities. DeMeis and Turner (1978) found significant evidence of negative judgments based on perceptions of race. Baron et al. (1985) conducted a meta-analysis of such studies and replicated the results of DeMeis and Turner. Studies using similar methodologies with Mexican American students found that teachers expected special class placement significantly more frequently for those students than for Anglo American students (Aloia, 1981; Prieto and Zucker, 1981). The findings were supported by Shinn et al. (1987).

Such simulations, however, are open to the criticism that they may not predict how teachers would actually behave in real situations. Several naturalistic studies have shown results such as higher rates of teacher attention and praise to Anglo American children (Buriel, 1983; Jackson and Cosca, 1974), as well as negative teacher attitudes to non-English-speaking students (Laosa, 1979). With regard to black students, Irvine (1990) found that teachers quickly formed lasting impressions of students' academic abilities that were often inaccurate, particularly with regard to black males.

Some studies of naturalistic settings, however, have shown that teacher's predictions about students' performance prove to be quite accurate (Brophy and Good, 1974; Egan and Archer, 1985; Evertson et al., 1972; Willis, 1972) for black students as well as for whites (Gaines, 1990; Haller, 1985; Irvine, 1990). Accurate teacher prediction, however, could also be explained as a self-fulfilling prophecy. This notion, developed by Merton (1948) and made famous by Rosenthal and Jacobson (1968), suggests that students will achieve in a manner consistent with the teacher's expectations. Evaluations of the self-fulfilling prophecy theory are mixed (Brophy, 1983; Jussim and Eccles, 1995; Smith, 1980).

An alternative explanation for the accuracy of teacher prediction involves potential race-linked differences in student sensitivity to teacher judgments. Jussim et al. (1996) compared teachers' perceptions of 1,664 6th graders' performance in mathematics, controlling for background factors such as students' previous grades, test scores, self-perception of mathematics ability, self-reported effort, and time spent on homework. They found no evidence of racial stereotype bias in teachers' perceptions. However, in examining how teacher perceptions influence students' future performance, they found significant differences in the impact of teacher perceptions on the students by race/ethnicity, with an impact on both test scores and grades for black students three times that of whites. This suggests that black students may be more vulnerable to teacher perceptions than are whites. Effects were also larger for girls and for children from low-income families.

Cultural Differences

The possible greater sensitivity, or perhaps vulnerability, of minority youngsters to teacher judgments and expectations is consistent with concerns that many researchers have raised about the role of culture in student success. Several analysts have proposed that racial and ethnic differences in measured achievement could be caused by cultural differences in attitudes toward school and achievement (e.g., Heath, 1982; Ogbu, 1987; Fordham, 1988). There are at least two different ways of articulating this argument. One prominent strand of the cultural argument contends that, for example, black students adopt an oppositional culture in relation to the school. A second perspective contends that minority students have different (but not necessarily oppositional) cultural practices that hinder their ability to learn in the school once they arrive.

This second strand is based on a long line of theorizing about schools. Bourdieu (1973) argues that every institution, including the school, has practices (or a culture) that are taken for granted. Children whose households are imbued with the very same culture as that of the school are likely to have an advantage once they enter school. This advantage is likely to be maintained over time because the very taken-for-granted nature of many school practices reduces the likelihood that school personnel will attempt to explicitly instruct disadvantaged students as to the cultural norms of the school. Indeed, school personnel may be unaware of the particularistic nature of their unspoken, taken-for-granted assumptions and the actions that flow from them.

Heath (1982) provides an example of such subtle cultural differences in her illuminating ethnography of language use at home and in school. Heath studied 1st graders and their teachers and interviewed parents during their daily routines as well. She notes that at the inception of her study, teachers reported that black students were unresponsive in class. Although all students were vocal when engaged in recess play, when asked direct questions in class, the black students did not respond. Notably for our concern with special education placement, teachers had even begun to wonder whether the black students were suffering from some mental defect.

Heath's analysis, however, suggests that cultural difference, not mental defect, is more likely to explain the teachers' experience. When interviewing the parents, Heath observed that white parents engaged their children by asking *inauthentic* questions, i.e., questions whose answers the parents knew (Nystrand and Gamoran, 1988). Thus, white parents would ask "What color is that truck?" or "What color is that car?" The asking of inauthentic questions is a staple of instruction in American schools (e.g., Nystrand and Gamoran, 1988), and thus when parents engage their children in such "discussion" prior to school entry, they prepare their children for becoming students in American schools. But there are other ways to teach language skills. For example, Heath found that black children learned language by sitting with their parents while the parents talked with other adults. When the child was invited to enter the conversation, the invitation came through the articulation of an *authentic* question, one whose answer the parent did not know. Parents and other adults might ask, "What is your favorite story?" or "What did you see at the store?" The answers to such questions were often complex, and children would often use their imagination to concoct fanciful stories in response to such questions.

Heath concluded that because black students operate at home in a culture that uses inauthentic questions relatively rarely, they were at a disadvantage upon entering school and encountering teachers who used such questions during instruction. Note that the disadvantage springs not from lack of preparation, but instead from *different* preparation. When Heath informed the teachers of these differences, they adjusted to incorporate a variety of teaching methods, and the measured achievements of black students increased.

For our purposes, the major point to Heath's research is that there may actually be many similarly subtle differences. Each subtle difference by itself may be small. Yet for students in racial and ethnic groups historically stereotyped as less intelligent, such cultural differences may set in motion a process of interaction and evaluation during which teachers may underestimate the abilities of students who are culturally different and may elicit confirming behavior. Given the pivotal—indeed, irreplaceable—role of teachers in nurturing excellence, such a process of cultural misunderstanding would be likely to undermine achievement. Students from cultures that prepare them for school may appear gifted and talented because of their responsiveness to instruction that is familiar in its delivery. Differential treatment of such students because they are believed to be more capable may, again, create a self-fulfilling prophecy. Indeed, the giftedness of students who do not come from cultures that prepare them for the particularistic demands of the school may be overlooked, and those students' gifts may go unnurtured.

Far more is known about the "oppositional culture" strand of the cultural argument. Ogbu (1987) divides minorities into voluntary and involuntary minorities. Briefly, involuntary minorities or their ancestors entered the country of residence by reason of conquest or enslavement; Ogbu contends that this history of contact makes it likely that involuntary minorities will develop an oppositional culture. For example, minority language styles may be both different from those of the dominant group and regarded by minority group members as a badge of solidarity. Adoption of majority group customs or language may be perceived as a betrayal of one's own group. Moreover, hostility by the dominant group is likely to be perceived as inescapable injustice, undercutting commitment to behaviors that might lead to upward mobility.

In contrast, voluntary minorities or their ancestors immigrated to the country of residence. They may have the option of returning to their ancestral home. Even if they remain, and even if return is not an option, their decision to immigrate to the new nation entails an acceptance of at least some period of adjustment. Thus, voluntary minority group members may explain the hostility of the dominant group as a passing phase, soon to be transcended once the members learn the ways of their new neighbors. In addition, familial customs from the old country may remain important, but they are unlikely to be practiced in *opposition* to the wider societal customs. Thus, voluntary minorities may maintain their language, but they also tend to learn the language of the new nation.

Some ethnographic evidence is consistent with Ogbu's thesis. Fordham (1988) alleged that successful black high school students endeavored to hide their academic success in order to avoid their peers' pejorative epithets. She reports that students were afraid of being labeled as "acting white" when they sought academic excellence.

However, more recent evidence raises questions about this claim. Using nationally representative data on 1990 high school sophomores, Ainsworth-Darnell and Downey (1998) found that high-achieving black students were more likely to be popular than similarly high-achieving white students. Cook and Ludwig (1998) show that the gaps between black and white students on a variety of important precursors to achievement (such as the amount of time spent on homework) and signals of achievement (such as the winning of academic awards) were sometimes trivial and sometimes favored black students. They conclude that there is little evidence in support of the oppositional culture thesis in the case of black students. Tyson (1998), analyzing data from observations of elementary school students, found little evidence of the racial differences in disdain for achievement that one might expect if the oppositional culture is based in community norms.

Research evidence does not support the proposition that minority students enter school opposed to what school has to offer. And if teachers engage in racial stereotype bias it is of a subtle and not a blatant variety. Notably, some research has suggested that teachers, counselors, and administrators are among the least prejudiced occupations in the United States (e.g., Lacy and Middleton, 1981). However, school personnel work in institutions with cultures and taken-for-granted pedagogical strategies that may be more harmonious with the home culture of larger numbers of majority children than minority children. Despite widespread good intentions, school personnel can engage in practices that are less supportive of the achievement of black, Hispanic, and other culturally different students. Subtle taken-for-granted assumptions that have become institutionalized may lead to a cultural mismatch that initiates a spiraling misunderstanding on the part of students and teachers. It is possible that the result of such misunderstanding might ultimately be the consignment of students to inappropriate special education treatments, or the failure to recognize and develop some students' gifts and talents.

Role of Parents

A number of studies have found that ethnic minority families have uniformly high aspirations for their children (Haro et al., 1994; Delgado-Gaitan, 1990; Steinberg, 1996). But many low-income and minority parents lack the cultural capital—knowledge of how the system works—and social capital—access to important social networks—that play an important role in supporting their children's academic success (Gandara, 2000). Research suggests that minority families have been less able than white families to emerge as successful advocates (Bennett, 1988; Connery, 1987; Harry et al., 1995; Harry, 1992; Lynch and Stein, 1987; Patton and Braithwaite, 1984; Tomlinson et al., 1977; Sharp, 1983). These differences can affect children's placement in both special and gifted education.

The role of parents in the referral, assessment, and placement of children in special education has been framed as one of advocacy. Due process procedures, including parental permission for evaluation and placement and parental participation in annual planning of the individualized education program (IEP), are designed to protect students against inappropriate placement decisions.

Certainly, ethnographic studies of middle-class parental advocacy in general education (Lareau, 1989) and of parental empowerment among low-income Spanish-speaking parents (Delgado-Gaitan, 1990) point to the positive influence of empowered parents. As documented in case studies of parental participation by Harry et al. (1999), a key mechanism through which parents may unknowingly exert their power is that when service providers *perceive* parents to be empowered, they may change their practices.

Yet a considerable body of research on this topic has suggested that most parents experience difficulty in meeting the challenge of advocacy (Turnbull and Turnbull, 2000). Indeed, these studies reveal that the decision-making process is far from the rational model espoused by the field. Mehan et al. (1986), in a 5-year ethnographic study, document that special education placement decisions were made on the basis of such factors as service providers' previous perceptions of students, information outside the range of the formal conference, and the availability of services rather than their appropriateness.

Parent advocacy is likely to be important for placement in gifted and talented programs as well, although their role is not formalized by law. Lareau (1989) found that middle-class parents effectively managed the school system and its resources through active engagement with school staff to afford the best opportunities for their children, while low-income parents tended to refrain from interactions with teachers and school administrators, accepting the school's decisions at face value. Useem (1992) found that well-educated parents, keenly aware of the implications of taking algebra versus basic math in junior high school, actively intervened when they disagreed with their children's placement. In contrast, parents with lower levels of education were largely unaware of the implications of being tracked into a low math course and tended to trust the school's placement decisions. Even among first-generation middle-class minority parents, cultural capital may not yet have accumulated (Miller, 1995). Attitudes, tastes, and dispositions develop over generations and result from exposure to particular cultural experiences specific to class categories (DiMaggio, 1982; Gandara, 2000).

The past two decades have seen a proliferation of studies examining the reasons for this discrepancy in parent participation. Marion (1981) argued that the historical mistrust of black parents of schools after desegregation was exacerbated by their awareness of minority overrepresentation in special education, and disrespectful and prejudicial treatment of parents by service providers. This line of research shows how black parents' low sense of efficacy in educational matters and stressful life circumstances combined with rejecting attitudes and procedures by school personnel to produce a picture of extreme parental alienation and low awareness of rights and procedures (Cassidy, 1988; Patton and Braithwaite, 1984; Sullivan, 1980; Lynch and Stein, 1987; Harry et al., 1995, 1999; Tomlinson et al., 1977; Lareau and Horvat, 1999). Studies of other minority groups yield a very similar picture, including a study of Puerto Rican parents (Harry, 1992), American Indians (Connery, 1987; Sharp, 1983), Chinese Americans (Smith and Ryan, 1987), Indochinese (Tran, 1982), Hmong (Trueba, 1990), Mexican Americans (Lynch and Stein, 1987), and a mixed nationality Hispanic group (Bennett, 1988). In addition to these studies, many theoretical explanations of the potential for cultural mismatch between families and the special education system have been offered (Correa, 1989; Chan, 1986; Cunningham et al., 1986; Leung, 1986; Sontag and Schact, 1994; Zetlin et al., 1996). Studies of parents' role in special education placement and in children's education as a whole indicate that the imbalance of power between school personnel and students or their parents is often exacerbated for minority and low-income parents. Impediments to the engagement of such students and parents include not only more limited resources, but also the difficulty of translating whatever resources they have into the currency of the school.

In light of this research, many have called for professionals to assume responsibility for the creation of effective parent-school partnerships (Epstein, 1996; Mlawer, 1993; Turnbull and Turnbull, 2000). Epstein's findings regarding parents' participation in general education suggest that their involvement is determined more by the teachers' encouragement than by family background variables, such as race or ethnicity, social class, marital status, and mother's work status. Moreover, family practices of involvement were found to be "more important than family background variables for determining whether and how students progress and succeed in school" (p. 217). Epstein also noted that teachers who involve parents typically rate parents more positively and stereotype them less.

Similarly, Trivette et al. (1996), in a study of 280 parents receiving early childhood services, found that child and family involvement in these programs was correlated with characteristics of the programs, rather than with such demographic characteristics as parental age, education, income, ethnicity, and marital status. Furthermore, the study found that family-centered programs were the most empowering.

Thus, while the literature suggests impediments to parent participation that are linked to cultural differences, it also indicates that school personnel can create participation structures that empower parents.

LESSONS FROM TESTED INTERVENTIONS

Few would argue with the claim that classroom instruction affects student achievement. At issue here, however, is a tougher question: Can improved instruction in the general education classroom change the number of minority students assigned to special or gifted education? Given the scope of this report, we cannot do a comprehensive review of the literature in this regard. Instead, we highlight several lines of research that suggest that general education instruction can indeed significantly raise minority student achievement at the lower end of the achievement distribution. These examples focus on preventing achievement problems, and the research base is primarily monolingual English-speaking students. We look briefly at the sparse literatures on English language learners and gifted and talented students. We then turn briefly to school-wide and community-wide approaches to intervention.

Mathematics

From a very early age, babies begin to develop an informal and rather sketchy understanding of number (National Research Council, 2001b). They can see there is more here than there, or that this is bigger than that. They realize that adding makes more cookies, and taking some away makes fewer. Before entering school, many children develop an intuitive understanding of number (Hiebert, 1986; Case, 1985; Siegler and Robinson, 1982) and operational definitions of addition and subtraction (Griffin and Case, 1998). These informal conceptions are the foundation for formal instruction.

From a series of research studies, Case and Sandieson (1987) argued that between ages 4 and 6, children typically develop a conceptual understanding of quantity. At age 4, children can usually solve problems that require bipolar distinctions (large vs. small, heavy vs. light) but a 6-year-old typically has developed a "central conceptual structure" that is more complex and entails the following abilities:

1. to verbally count from 1 to 10 forward and backward;

2. to understand the one-to-one correspondence with which the sequence of numbers is mapped onto objects;

3. to understand the cardinal value of each number (i.e., that 4 represents a set whose size is indicated by the number); and

4. to understand the relationship between adjacent values (that each adjacent number represents a size that is different by 1).

When this conceptual structure is in place, a child is able to solve problems as if she or he is using a mental number line. However, in tests of conceptual knowledge given to young children in low-income, inner-city communities, a significant number of them were found to lack the knowledge typical of their middle-come peers (Griffin et al., 1994, 1995; Griffin and Case, 1996, 1998; Case et al., 1999). Furthermore, students who have difficulty with the 1st grade mathematics curriculum—a disproportionate number of whom come from low-income families—appear not to have that conceptual structure in place. These children display a level of understanding that is about two years behind their peers. Case et al. (1999) provide evidence of an "SES gradient" in mathematics achievement in the United States (as well as in several other developed countries), and point to the potential consequences of the developmental lag (Case et al., 1999:139-140):

> Of course, the presence of these gradients does not mean that children from low-SES homes have some sort of neurological handicap. It does not even mean that they have some sort of psychological handicap. It simply means that their early home environment has not had such a strong numerical emphasis as has been present in middle class homes, and that they come to school with a knowledge base and a set of numerical capabilities that are less well developed. On the other hand, however, it seems clear that children from low-SES homes are at considerable risk that these early differences will be reified and that they will *develop into* a handicap. At the present moment, schools are not equipped to diagnose the subtle differences in knowledge with which children arrive at school.

One example of how instruction can be made sensitive to these developmental differences is a curriculum developed by Griffin and Case to deliberately teach the central conceptual structure outlined above to children before they reach 1st grade. The curriculum, originally called Rightstart, now incorporated into Number Worlds (Griffin and Case, 2000), was tested in multiple sites in California, Massachusetts, and Canada with multiple-sized groups of kindergarten children from inner-city, disproportionately minority schools. Children who were taught using the Rightstart curriculum were compared with matched control groups of children who were given an equal amount of attention but with a more traditional mathematics curriculum designed to provide a level of affective engagement commensurate with the Rightstart program. In tests of number knowledge and knowledge transfer, the Rightstart children significantly outperformed the control group. While almost all children in the sample failed the number knowledge test before the instruction, the vast majority of children who received the Rightstart training passed, while only a minority of children in the control group passed. Significant differences between the two groups persisted through 1st grade (Griffin et al., 1996).

The most dramatic results were obtained from a longitudinal study by Griffin, in which Rightstart children were traced over three years and given a follow-up program that was based on the same general principles as Rightstart. The treatment children were compared with two groups: (1) low-SES children who were originally tested as having superior achievement in mathematics, and (2) a mixed-SES group (largely middle class) who showed a higher level of performance at the outset and who attended a magnet school with an enriched mathematics program. The Rightstart children gradually outstripped both other groups. They also compared favorably with high-SES children from China and Japan who were tested on the same measures (Griffin and Case, 1997; Case et al., 1999).

In providing this example, our intention is to point to a clear case in which a disadvantaged student population may require an instructional response in general education to prevent disparities in early developmental experiences from being expressed in later years as an apparent learning disability. While other mathematics curricula may achieve this goal as well, we cite this example because the effect on minority student achievement in mathematics has been documented. These results suggest that curriculum and instruction targeted at the beginning of schooling can help to close academic gaps between children of differing SES levels.

Reading

Mastery of reading is perhaps the most important challenge for students in the elementary years. Just as early mathematics learning requires that children come to understand the mapping of quantity or set size onto "number," early reading requires that children pull apart the sounds of words and map individual phonemes or sounds onto letters. If young children do not engage in regular and consistent oral language and literacy interactions (e.g., bedtime reading, nursery rhymes, lap reading) that highlight the sounds in words through language usage and play, they are frequently phonemically unaware when they enter kindergarten or 1st grade (Lyon et al., 2001). As the Early Childhood Longitudinal Study suggests, there are substantial differences in mastery of early reading prerequisites by race (see Chapter 3), and data from the National Assessment of Educational Progress suggest substantial differences in reading achievement by race in 4th grade (Donahue et al., 2001).

The recent NRC (1998) report on reading, in summarizing decades of research, pointed to the interrelatedness of all components of reading instruction. In emphasizing the need for a multifaceted approach, the report pointed to three potential stumbling blocks that can interfere with children's acquisition of literacy: (1) failure to grasp the alphabetic principle, (2) failure to apply comprehension skills to reading, and (3) "the absence or loss of an initial motivation to read or failure to develop a mature appreciation of the rewards of reading" (p. 5).

Instructional methods aimed at helping emergent readers overcome these potential stumbling blocks are key. Both the NRC report and research funded by the National Institute for Child Health and Human Development (NICHD) converge on the recommendation that reading instruction in the early grades should involve direct instruction in the alphabetic code, vocabulary development, and reading for meaning. With frequent opportunities to practice reading with a variety of rich materials, reading instruction should reflect a balance between direct instruction and more holistic approaches.

There is converging evidence that English monolingual students who struggle with reading acquisition and are at risk for reading disabilities benefit from supplemental, intensive reading instruction (see O'Connor, 2000; Torgesen, 2000; Torgesen et al., 2001; Vellutino et al., 1996). The components of such instruction appear in Box 5-2.

Fletcher and Lyon's (1998) review of the NICHD studies suggests the research has *not* found qualitatively different processes underlying reading disability and proficiency. Rather, the findings suggest an "unbroken continuum of ability" (p. 62), with varying skills and deficiencies that contribute to good and poor reading. The challenge facing general education, then, is to move children as effectively as possible toward greater efficiency on the continuum of reading ability. The NRC (1998) review of early reading instruction supports this conclusion, recommending that "the same good early literacy environment and patterns of effective instruction are required for children who might fail for different reasons" (p. 2).

Because the rate at which individuals acquire the skills associated with reading mastery varies, and because the extent of exposure to a rich oral language environment varies significantly, some students may require more intensive instruction than others. National datasets cited and discussed in earlier chapters suggest that minority students will be represented disproportionately in this group (see Chapters 2 and 3). Torgesen (2000) and Wagner (2000) address the issue of how best to assist students who do not profit from proven effective interventions based on phonological processing and other direct word-level interventions. Based on reviews of major stud-

---

BOX 5-2
Components of Effective Reading Instruction

Major building blocks for reading instruction emphasized in the NICHD (2000) and NRC (1998) reports:

1.   *Phonological awareness.* Skilled readers possess and display a high degree of phonemic awareness (Morris, 1980; Scarborough et al., 1998), while students who are unaware of the sound structure of spoken words often demonstrate difficulty acquiring "decoding skills" that are necessary for proficient reading (Snowling, 1981). The same relationship exits between phonological awareness and reading in Spanish (Quiroga et al., 2002; Geva and Siegel, 2000). Furthermore, phonological awareness in Spanish is related to phonological awareness in English.

In a study of the developmental order of specific phonological awareness skills and their transfer across languages, Cisero and Royer (1995) found that both Spanish and English phonological awareness predicted English phonological awareness performance. Likewise, Quiroga and her colleagues (1999) found that phonological awareness in both Spanish and English predicted reading achievement in English and that English language learners benefited from explicit instruction in phonological awareness in English.

2.   *Reading fluency.* Students who struggle with reading often exhibit difficulty reading fluently (Adams, 1990; Mathes et al., 1992; Meyer and Felton, 1999). As a result, they must devote more attention to decoding individual words rather than to comprehending the text (Samuels, 1987; Sindelar, 1987). Interventions such as repeated reading (Knupp, 1988; Moyer, 1982; O'Shea et al., 1987; Rashotte and Torgesen, 1985; Samuels, 1987), classwide peer tutoring (Mathes and Fuchs, 1993; Mathes et al., 1994), and previewing (Rose, 1984; Salend and Nowak, 1988; Sindelar, 1987) can be used to improve reading fluency. Improved reading fluency and automatic word recognition allow students to focus on understanding and analyzing the content of the text. Repeated reading activities are also appropriate for English language learners. They provide the practice English language learners need to develop automatic recognition of English phonemes, high-frequency words, and word patterns, which in turn help them increase their fluency rate (Grabe, 1991; McLaughlin, 1987).

---

ies, these authors conclude that approximately 4-6 percent of children are likely to have weak word reading skills despite the interventions. Torgesen concludes that systematic, explicit instruction in phonemic awareness and phonetic decoding skills does promote reading growth for these children, but that they must also be taught to read for fluency and meaning. According to Torgesen, the question of how much instruction is most effective is still unanswered; the challenge currently facing the field is to determine the requisite intensity and duration of instruction needed by children "with the

3. *Comprehension and vocabulary development.* Reading comprehension is a complex skill that can be enhanced through the use of various strategies before, during, and after reading text (Palinscar and Brown, 1984; Pressley et al., 1995). Students benefit from instructional strategies that can be used to activate their previous knowledge, monitor understanding, self-question, distinguish between the main idea and supporting details, and summarize what has been read (Baker and Brown, 1984). Grabe (1991) found that providing English language learners a framework for drawing from background knowledge, utilizing prediction strategies, and summarizing and recalling important text events prior to, during, and after reading helped students comprehend text.

Vocabulary knowledge is necessary for reading comprehension. Students with limited vocabularies have difficulty with reading and comprehension. The goal of vocabulary instruction is to assist students to: (a) develop and apply vocabulary knowledge, (b) connect new vocabulary to existing knowledge, (c) understand text, and (d) increase their use of strategies for figuring out new vocabulary independently. Effective vocabulary instruction includes both definitional and contextual information about each word's meaning, involves students actively in word learning, and provides multiple exposures to meaningful information about the word, including the relationships between words (Baumann and Kame'enui, 1991; Stahl, 1999; Beck et al., 2002).

For English language learners, the following instructional practices are associated with improved outcomes in understanding text by building vocabulary: (a) explicit instruction in new, crucial, or multiple-meaning vocabulary (Au, 1993); (b) teaching word meanings in context and expanding on the context of words to build understanding of specific vocabulary or specific contexts in which certain multiple-meaning vocabulary is used (Anderson and Roit, 1998; Au, 1993; Grabe, 1991); and (c) addressing high-frequency vocabulary and vocabulary that is difficult to visualize (Anderson and Roit, 1998).

4. *Word study.* Word study refers to strategies that can be used to explore words and to make connection among and between words (Bear et al., 1996). Students with reading difficulties may have difficulty with spelling and benefit from word-level decoding instruction (Gaskins et al., 1997). Interventions that focus on increasing students' word study skills by teaching them to use high-frequency key words with common spelling patterns as models to read unknown words (Gaskins et al., 1997) or by using spelling (Zutell, 1996) have been validated empirically.

most severe phonological disabilities and most disabling environmental backgrounds" (p. 63).

Research by O'Connor (2000) of the effects of two years of increasingly intensive interventions with children in kindergarten through the 1st grade indicates that approximately 7 percent of the sample of 146 children demonstrated sustained reading problems despite participating in a tiered intervention that included large group, small group, and one-to-one tutoring. One-to-one tutoring has long been considered superior for students with serious reading difficulties (Wasik and Slavin, 1993). A meta-analysis of studies of the effects of one-to-one tutoring (Elbaum et al., 2000) concluded that this approach has been effective in improving reading levels by two-fifths of a standard deviation above the comparison group. While this would not raise performance to the average range, it may allow some students "to keep up with classroom instruction and to avoid academic failure" (p. 616). Tutoring by college students was found to be particularly successful.

Numerous reading curricula and programs have been developed that incorporate many of the features of effective reading instruction discussed above. Programs like Success for All, Open Court, and Reading Recovery focus specifically on placing a floor under reading achievement; that is, they are designed with particular attention to preventing reading difficulties and place less emphasis on promoting reading achievement at the highest level. Deductive reasoning suggests that these programs should have an impact on special education placements of minority students: as the data presented in Chapter 2 demonstrate, the largest number of students referred and placed in special education receive a designation as having a learning disability (LD), and most placements in the LD category involve reading problems (Lyon et al., 2001, estimated 80 percent). However, rigorous evaluation of special education outcomes when these reading curricula are implemented by regular classroom teachers (as opposed to researchers) have been rare.

Slavin and Madden (1999b) make the case that Success For All (SFA) has had a substantial impact in this regard. Success For All combines many of the features of high-quality reading instruction described above with careful monitoring of student success, and a timely response including one-to-one tutoring is initiated when students show signs of failure. The reading program is embedded in a school-wide program that includes teacher training, administrative facilitation, and parent involvement.

A study of two SFA schools in Ft. Wayne, Indiana, found a referral rate of 3.2 percent for LD or mild mental handicaps of students in grades K-1 and 1-2. The referral rate for students in matched control schools was 14.3 percent (Smith et al., 1994). A longitudinal study in Baltimore found special education placements for LD in the SFA schools were reduced by about half (Slavin et al., 1992). Since a goal of Success For All is to tackle reading failure in the general education classroom, a drop in referrals may not be tantamount to a drop in reading failure. However, other indicators in studies of the program also suggest that reading failure is reduced: only 2.2 percent of 3rd graders averaged two years behind grade level, compared with 8.8 percent of control children. And the effect sizes[1] for the students in

---

[1]Assessments include the Woodcock Reading Mastery Test, the Durrell Analysis of Reading Difficulty, and the Gray Oral Reading Test.

the lowest 25 percent of their grade—the group at highest risk for special education—were more than twice as high as for the full sample (Slavin and Madden, 1999b). The large majority of the SFA students in these schools were minorities (Slavin et al., 1996).

As with the mathematics program discussed previously, our intent is not to promote an individual program to the exclusion of others. Rather, we provide the example of a program that addresses the population of concern because there is empirical evidence of its effect. Like Number Worlds, SFA suggests the possibility of reducing special education placements for disadvantaged students by improving general education.

Instruction for English Language Learners

Students who enter school with limited proficiency in English are among those at highest risk for school failure. Many of these students come from families of low socioeconomic status, and their experience both inside and outside school is characterized by the consequences of diminished resources discussed here and in Chapter 3. Limited English proficiency is compounded with the effects of poverty.

Rigorous research on instructional interventions for English language learners has been sparse (NRC, 1997; Baker and Gersten, 1997). Much of what is available has focused on whether these students should be instructed in English or in their home language. Reviews of research on this issue have generally found benefits for native language instruction, with a gradual transition to English (Garcia, 1994; Meyer and Fienberg, 1992; Ramirez et al., 1991). The NRC report on preventing reading difficulties concluded that "the accumulated wisdom of research in the field of bilingualism and literacy tends to converge on the conclusion that initial literacy instruction in a second language can be successful, that it carries with it a higher risk of reading problems and of lower ultimate literacy attainment than initial literacy instruction in a first language" (NRC, 1998:234). The report points out that a grasp of the alphabetic principle requires oral familiarity with the words being read. This poses a challenge not only for non-English speakers, but also for those who speak English in a nonstandard dialect.

The conclusion from the research literature is supported by results of the Success For All program. Success For All has been adapted for students in English as a Second Language programs, and for those in bilingual programs for Spanish-speaking children (Slavin and Madden, 1999a). Although students taught using each of the approaches generally performed better than control students, the bilingual program students showed larger gains than the students in English as a Second Language programs.

Beyond the rather limited research on the acquisition of reading skills, quantitative research on the instructional approaches to teaching English language learners course content is essentially nonexistent (NRC, 1997; Gersten and Baker, 2000a). Gersten and Baker (2000) conducted a "multivocal synthesis" in which they reviewed qualitative studies and gathered information from professional work groups of researchers and teachers. Their work highlights a concern that teaching English through course content results in too little attention to language development. But they acknowledge that even the qualitative research base is thin.

Gifted Students

Research highlights the critical role of the family in supporting academic excellence (Coleman et al., 1966; Jencks et al., 1972; Entwisle and Alexander, 1992). While good schools can play an important role in supporting high achievement, it is not *the most important* role (Gandara, 2000). Yet for many students from disadvantaged backgrounds, limited resources in the home may mean that the school is the primary source of support for achievement. It is particularly troubling, therefore, that high-achieving students from low SES levels disengage from school early in the process.

The Prospects database was collected for a congressionally mandated study of the impact of Title I, the largest federal program aimed at providing supplemental services to low-income and low-achieving students (Puma et al., 1997). An analysis of these data (Borman et al., 2000) found that disengagement, defined as a downward trajectory of grades, begins early for these students, and "Black students who began third grade at or above the 50th percentile disengage at a significantly faster rate than comparable White students" (p. 79). Across the elementary school years, black and Hispanic students register a substantial achievement disadvantage (see Chapter 2).

Few interventions in K-12 schools target minority high achievement. Those programs that do focus primarily on helping minority students access college preparatory course work and honors and advanced placement classes (Gandara, 2000). Program activities include tutoring, summer academic bridge programs, special intensive curricular interventions, SAT and ACT test preparation, and peer study groups. Gandara and Bial (2001) reviewed a national sample of these programs and selected 13 with sufficiently rigorous evaluations to determine effectiveness. They conclude that when these programs are well implemented, they are able to at least double the college-going rate for participants. However, this is accomplished largely by raising the students' aspirations and helping them follow through on necessary steps for application, including test taking. They found no evidence that the programs are successful at raising test scores or grade point averages (Gandara, 2000). A few programs make efforts to engage students in more culturally relevant study: the Puente project, for example, engages Mexican American high school students in rigorous, college preparatory English classes with teachers trained to incorporate high-quality Latino literature (Gandara et al., 1998). But while these programs influence student engagement, there is not yet evidence that they raise high-end achievement.

Student Behavior

Many of today's classrooms demand that teachers accommodate a broad spectrum of student diversity across academic, behavioral, and cultural domains. The interaction of these three domains is evident, since children who do not experience academic success are more likely to engage in disturbing behavior, and behavior that is divergent from that expected in classrooms is likely to be seen as disturbing. A great deal of research indicates the capacity of behavioral interventions to modify children's behavior. However, it is important for educators to seek an understanding of the cultural and personal antecedents of children's behavior, as well as of the cultural assumptions that drive educators' interpretations of that behavior.

Culture and Classroom Behavior

There is no surprise in the statement that culture influences socialization. A review by Cartledge (1996) points to the effects of several processes, including child-rearing practices, sibling interaction, birth order, family stress, and family social interaction systems. Furthermore, as young people mature, they respond increasingly to societal pressures. As Spencer (1999) and Steele (1997) have shown, black youth, in particular, may respond negatively to their growing awareness of societal stereotypes and others' low expectations of them. Studies comparing teachers' perceptions of students indicate differential perceptions reflective of cultural stereotypes. For example, Keller (1988) found that teachers tended to give black children poorer behavioral ratings than white children; Feng and Cartledge (1996) found that teachers viewed black students as having more hyperactivity and externalizing than Asians, and more externalizing than whites; Wells et al. (1992) found that teachers overidentified and underidentified drug use among black and Asian students, respectively.

Because perceptions of behavioral appropriateness are colored by cultural expectations, it is difficult to operationalize and measure exactly what should be perceived as inappropriate. Even when an objective list of behaviors is used, it cannot be assumed that school personnel's perceptions are not further influenced by unmeasureable actions, such as a glance, a tone of voice, or a body posture. Checklists of behaviors, which provide the main sources of data on classroom behaviors, cannot take into account the effects these more subtle behaviors have on teachers' perceptions of children. Indeed, studies of rating scales completed by parents and teachers indicate differential impressions according to ethnicity (Elliott et al., 1989; Powless and Elliott, 1993).

In view of the significant disproportionate placement of black students, particularly males, in programs for behavioral disorders, any discussion of classroom management must take into account what is known about disciplinary practices experienced by many students of this group in general education. That these students are perceived as particularly troublesome is evident in the Office for Civil Rights' reports of very high rates of suspension and corporal punishment for black males in particular (U.S. Department of Education, 1997, 1999). Specifically, the 1997 report shows that while this group accounts for 9 percent of the total student body, they account for 30 percent of those receiving corporal punishment and 22 percent of those receiving out-of-school suspension. The rates for white males are the next highest, but far less disproportionate—33 percent of the total enrollment, 45 percent of those receiving corporal punishment, and 38 percent of those receiving out-of-school suspension. A study by McFadden et al. (1992) documented much higher rates of corporal punishment and out-of-school suspension and lower rates of in-school suspension for black students, even though disciplinary referral records gave no evidence that they engaged in more severe behavioral infractions than other groups. Several scholars have argued that the rates for blacks may reflect lower tolerance of behavioral infractions by black students as well as misinterpretation of behavioral styles that are cultural or reactive rather than pathological in nature (Harry and Anderson, 1994; Townsend, 2000).

A considerable body of literature has documented traditional socialization practices among blacks that may lead to a mismatch with school-prescribed behaviors (Boykin, 1986; Franklin, 1992; Gilbert and Gay, 1989; Irvine, 1990). Perhaps most illustrative of the mismatch hypothesis is what Boykin has called "verve" and what Gilbert and Gay have described as black children's propensity to "accompany their cognitive involvement with affective and physical involvement"(p. 279). These analysts argue that this tendency can be built on productively rather than seen as distracting and disruptive. When these behaviors are interpreted negatively, they become stereotypes on which school personnel may rely to explain children's behavior, rather than cultural patterns that may, quite appropriately, either be built on or modified as appropriate to the classroom context. Delpit (1988) addressed the mismatch hypothesis in terms of different ways that power and authority are expressed. Delpit argued that disciplinary practices in black families are traditionally explicit and directive, while the practices utilized by most teachers tend to camouflage authority in a style that invites rather than directs students to participate in the rules. Delpit called for teachers to explicitly teach the rules, rather than assume that children know them and then deem the children socially incompetent because of their lack of knowledge.

Another aspect of classroom management that is difficult to document is the role of teacher efficacy. Earlier in this chapter we cited several examples of literature addressing the power of teacher expectations; expectations for efficacy are another aspect of this. A study by Pang and Sablan (1995) found that preservice and inservice teachers' negative preconceptions about black family practices and values led the teachers to have low expectations regarding their potential efficacy with black students. Perhaps most difficult to document or measure is what Gay (2000) has referred to, simply, as "caring." However, Gay argues that caring is evident in the types, number, and direction of teacher-student interactions as well as in the display of teachers' expectations for students. Similarly, Ladson-Billings, in her qualitative study of the qualities shared by effective teachers of black students, noted high expectations, a sense of identity with students' communities, and a high sense of personal efficacy as a teacher. Furthermore, studies comparing affective-oriented teachers and task-oriented teachers found that the former were more effective with black students (Collins and Tamarkin, 1982; Dillon, 1989; St. John, 1971).

Our point here is that a great deal of what will determine effective classroom management springs not only from teacher skills but from teachers' ability to connect with their students in a manner that conveys respect and caring. As we argued earlier, students from devalued minority communities may be more influenced by negative teacher perceptions and biases. If this is so, then teacher attitudes and biases are as important as specific classroom management skills in improving behavioral outcomes for minority students.

Instruction, Curricula, and Classroom Management

Research indicates that schools with organized technical assistance teams providing consultation, support, and training to teachers experience a reduction in special education referrals (Nelson et al., 1991; Montague et al., 1997; Council for Children with Behavioral Disorders Executive Committee, 1989; Sprague et al., 1998). In the absence of context-sensitive technical assistance in regular education, potentially overwhelmed teachers are unable to accommodate student needs in meaningful ways that prevent academic failure and problem behaviors (Montague et al., 1997).

The ability of a teacher to manage a classroom effectively may be as critical to student performance as the ability to instruct effectively. Wang et al. (1994) investigated the direct and indirect influences on student learning through an analysis of 170 studies and reviews, 91 research syntheses, and 61 educational researcher surveys. They found that student aptitude, classroom management, and classroom instruction had significant and nearly equal influence on student learning—and were far more important than state, district, or school policies and district demographics.

Moreover, academic achievement and behavior are closely linked, although whether a causal connection exists or the direction of that connection is difficult to establish. Indeed, the research on early biological influences on development suggest that many of the factors that hinder cognitive development also hinder regulation of attention and emotion.

In the well-known Isle of Wight study (Rutter and Yule, 1970) behavioral information from both parents and teachers suggested that highly intelligent children were less likely to show behavioral deviance than children of average intelligence, and children of average intelligence with reading retardation had a much increased rate of conduct disorder. As the previous chapter suggests, disadvantage affects both behavior and academic achievement. Rutter and colleagues plot reading achievement and behavior problems for a sample of students stratified into two groups: those from high-risk and those from low-risk families (see Figure 5-2). As the figure suggests, behavior disorders are more prevalent among children from high-risk families. But mastery of reading appears to serve as a protective factor. For both groups of students, reading failure is correlated with a dramatically higher incidence of behavior problems.

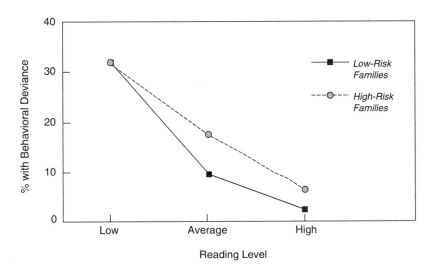

FIGURE 5-2 Reading skills, family adversity, and behavioral deviance. SOURCE: Rutter (1979). Reprinted with permission.

Effective classroom management is a critical element of effective classroom instruction. Students placed in orderly classroom environments devote more time to academic tasks, complete curricula at a faster pace, and achieve higher academic gains than students placed in poorly managed classrooms (Betts and Shkolnik, 1999; Levine and Ornstein, 1989; Martens and Kelly, 1993; Pierce, 1994; Wang et al., 1994).

The linkage between effective classroom management and reduction of the number of students considered at risk for emotional and behavioral disorders is emerging in current research. Aber et al. (1998) evaluated the efficacy of the Resolving Conflict Creatively Program violence prevention curriculum and the interaction effects of neighborhood and classroom contextual factors for 5,053 elementary students from predominantly black and Hispanic backgrounds. The results of this study suggest that students placed in disorderly classrooms had higher rates of aggression, were likely to associate hostile attributions in social interactions, used more aggressive strategies, and had lower levels of social competence than students placed in orderly classrooms.

In another study Kamps et al. (2000) examined the effectiveness of Head Start for 49 kindergarten and 1st grade students from predominantly minority backgrounds. The intervention consisted of social skills instruction, a classroom reinforcement (or feedback) system, peer tutoring, and parent support. Results at the 2-year follow-up were generally positive: students placed in classrooms with higher treatment fidelity showed higher gains in positive peer interactions and fewer problem behaviors in the classroom.

Classroom organization and behavior management systems that emphasize opportunities to teach and practice social and self-management skills are important prevention strategies for students who are academically at risk or who engage in chronic problem behaviors (Nelson et al., 1991; Hudley and Graham, 1993; Larson, 1989; Ruth, 1996; Todd et al., 1999). Examples of classroom behavioral interventions appear in Box 5-3.

Positive classroom management systems that promote social competence require positively stated rules and classroom routines (Colvin et al., 1993; Gottfredson, 1990; Mayer, 1995; Walker et al., 1995). Effective classroom teachers commit significant time to establishing: (a) behavior and academic expectations required in the classroom and school settings; (b) classroom routines, such as turning in completed work, lining up, getting teacher help, using the restroom, participating in class discussion, and completing independent seat work; and (c) a high percentage of teacher-student interactions (Brophy, 1983; Gettinger, 1988; Levine and Ornstein, 1989; Martens and Kelly, 1993; Montague et al., 1997; Waxman and Huang, 1997). Note how the effectiveness of explicitly teaching expecta-

BOX 5-3
Behavioral Interventions in General Education

A report on youth violence released by the U.S. Surgeon General in January, 2001 (U.S. Department of Health and Human Services, 2001a) contained an overview of model and promising programs that deter antisocial behaviors. These programs cover a wide range of intervention strategies, including family therapy, drug and alcohol awareness, parent training, and early childhood programs. Two of these programs are described below as examples of universal, school-based prevention with some form of parent involvement.

Bullying Prevention Program

This program is a school-wide prevention effort that originated in Norway and proved to be effective enough to reduce bully-victim problems by 50 percent. It also reduced vandalism, theft, and truancy, and students reported that it contributed to a better school climate. This program has been replicated in England, Germany, and the United States. It is an all-inclusive measure designed to heighten awareness and knowledge about bullying behavior by increasing the involvement of all responsible adults—teachers, parents, school bus drivers, administrators, counselors, and students.

The program establishes clear rules against bullying and provides support and protection for the victims. The first step in the process is the administration of the Olweus (the founder) Bully/Victim Questionnaire to students. This survey assesses the extent of the school's bullying problem and provides data against which improvement can be measured.

A committee consisting of representatives of teachers and other responsible adults, as well as students, is then set up to oversee the school's antiviolence efforts. In the classroom, students and teachers agree on a few simple rules—not bullying other students, helping those students who are bullied, including everyone in all activities. Teachers are given program materials and training to help students develop positive incentives to abide by the rules. All school staff receive training. Adults in the school are expected to intervene immediately if there is any indication of a bullying problem.

---

tions is consistent with the claims that analysts have made concerning culture (e.g., Heath, 1982).

Ineffective classroom management and instruction are certainly not the only reasons for classroom behavior problems. As Chapter 3 indicated, at kindergarten entry before academic demands are placed on students, some students are rated by parents and teachers as exhibiting more behavior problems. As with reading failure, some (but many fewer) students are likely to exhibit behavior problems even in the best-managed classrooms.

Sprague et al. (1998) organize student populations into three groups according to the level of behavior intervention they require. They recommend universal, school-wide social skills interventions for all students, concluding that most students (about 80 percent of the total) should be able to

Implementation costs are modest: staff time for the training sessions, $130 per school for the questionnaire and computer program, $60 per teacher for classroom materials, plus the cost of a part-time or full-time coordinator.

Promoting Alternative Thinking Strategies

The curriculum of Promoting Alternative Thinking Strategies (PATHS) was designed to promote the development of essential skills in positive peer relations, problem solving, and emotional awareness. The curriculum (Kusché and Greenberg, 1994) is for use by elementary school teachers from kindergarten through grade five. PATHS provides preventive interventions as part of the regular year-long curriculum. It is focused on a classroom setting, but there is information and activities for use with parents as well.

The goal of the program is to prevent or reduce behavioral and emotional problems by instructing students three times a week (20-30 minutes) with systematic, developmentally appropriate lessons that teach emotional awareness, self-control, social competence, positive peer relations, and problem-solving skills. Lessons include instruction in labeling and identifying feelings, managing feelings and their intensity, understanding the difference between feelings and behaviors, and controlling impulses. The children are taught to understand the perspective of others, use steps for problem solving and decision making, self-awareness, and communication skills. In order to accomplish this, teachers receive training in a two- to three-day workshop and in biweekly meetings with the curriculum consultant.

The program includes 131 lessons to be taught over a period of 5 years. Each lesson, however, may require multiple sessions. An evaluation of one version of PATHS that includes a longitudinal study compared schools with the program to schools without. In the PATHS schools they found:

- lower peer aggression scores based on peer ratings (sociometrics),
- lower teacher ratings of disruptive behavior (teacher report), and
- improved classroom atmosphere (assessed by independent observers).

Program costs range from $15 per student/per year to $45 per student/per year, depending on whether current staff was redeployed or a new on-site coordinator was hired. Costs are based on a three-year proposal.

maintain acceptable school behavior with the support of the regular school discipline system and this program. The second group consists of 7 to 10 percent of the student population considered at risk for discipline problems. More targeted interventions, such as anger management, are recommended for this group to maintain acceptable behavior. The third group, representing about 3 to 5 percent of the student population, will then require more individualized programs; analysis of discipline referrals for 16 elementary and 15 middle school discipline referrals indicated that students in this group account for 40 to 59 percent of all school discipline referrals. Given the behavioral issues for this group of students, early identification and intervention may help prevent academic failure and increased problem behavior.

An expanding research base points to intervention strategies to work with such students in the classroom and school setting. For example, Hudley and Graham (1993) investigated the effectiveness of an attributional intervention program designed to reduce peer-directed aggression among 101 aggressive and nonaggressive black elementary school boys. This study found statistically significant reductions in students assigning hostile intent to others and their preference for aggressive behavior in laboratory simulations. Moreover, teachers rated the aggressive and nonaggressive boys as less aggressive than the control group at the level of statistical significance. These effects suggest that behavioral interventions may be potentially important for constructing an environment in which all students can learn.

It is worth noting that the proportions of students who benefit directly from these interventions may be small. Yet because students are taught in group settings, a small set of students whose unmet needs result in their acting out may have deleterious effects on class-wide student achievement. A review of effective school-based prevention programs indicates that the most successful programs combined primary prevention skill building efforts in general education settings with secondary intermediate programs to manage the specialized needs of at-risk students (Kay, 1999; Miller et al., 1998; Tobin, 1992). Strategies used by successful prevention programs included social skills instruction, positive behavior management, quality classroom instruction, and school-wide discipline procedures. Evaluation research suggests that optimal benefits from a school-based prevention program for children with emotional disturbance may not be fully realized until after two or more years of the intervention; such a program requires quality implementation by trained teachers in the context of a well-organized classroom setting (Kamps et al., 2000; McConaughy et al., 2000; Van Acker and Talbott, 1999).

School-Wide Interventions

Instructional Interventions

We turn now to school-wide instructional models that take into account other factors that can affect learning, such as scheduling, the grouping of students, within-school communication processes, and school-home communication processes. Such a school-wide approach is consistent with our view that the context, the culture, and the resources embedded within them matter for student success. Indeed, a school culture and an organizational structure that support and reinforce instructional reform in the classroom are critical features of reforms that bring sustained improvement in student achievment (Elmore and Burney, 1997; Newmann and Associates, 1996).

Reauthorization of the Elementary and Secondary Education Act in 1994 provided for Title I funds to be made more flexible. They can now be used for systemic, school-wide programs, rather than retained only for stand-alone programs for disadvantaged students. In 1998, the Comprehensive School Reform Demonstration Program (P.L. 105-78) was enacted to help low-performing schools adopt whole-school strategies to improve student achievement. Funds were made available through this program for the adoption of research-based comprehensive school strategies, using nine specified components. A total of 17 models that met these specifications were suggested, although others were not precluded.

A report by the American Institutes for Research reviewed 24 whole-school reform programs and found 3 that provided strong evidence of positive effects on student achievement (Herman et al., 1999). These were Direct Instruction, High Schools that Work, and Success For All. Six others were evaluated as promising: Community for Learning, Core Knowledge, Different Ways of Knowing, Expeditionary Learning Outward Bound, and the (Comer) School Development Program. The ratings were compiled from reviews of available studies that were ranked by such criteria as sample size, duration of the study, appropriateness of the comparison groups, and relevance of measurement instruments. The highest rating required at least four rigorous studies showing positive achievement effects, and no more than 20 percent of studies showing no (or negative) effect. The "promising program" rating decreased the positive showings required by one, and increased allowable negative or null showings by 10 percentage points. The promising programs may not be less effective; they may simply have had fewer rigorous evaluations.

In a separate investigation of the three-year effects of 10 "promising programs," Stringfield et al. (1996) found strong evidence of the potential of school-wide models to affect significant academic improvement for students in high-poverty schools. The study concluded that while none of the programs provided a panacea for the difficulties of all children, the dramatic success of school-wide programs in some schools indicates the tremendous potential of these programs. However, they point out numerous challenges to the success of such efforts. In particular, they cite district, administrator, and faculty commitment in the context of careful consideration to the fit between the program and the school, the adequacy of materials and financial resources, the integrity of implementation of the program, and a concentration of effort in the early years of children's schooling.

Comprehensive school reform efforts targeted to low-income, low-performing schools have provided some indication, however, that these interventions can increase the number of minority students performing at high levels. Slavin et al. (1992) reported that in several Success For All schools in

Baltimore, 4.9 percent of 3rd graders performed at least two years above grade level on the Durrell Oral Reading Test compared with just 1.9 percent of the control students. Borman et al. (2000), in a review of the effectiveness of Special Strategies—several school-wide intervention programs in K-6—compared outcome data for students in those programs with data on other Title I students in the Prospects database. They found that black students in these programs learned at a faster rate than their counterparts in the control group. Of equal importance, they found that high-achieving black math students not only excelled at a faster rate, but also surpassed the achievement levels of the initially high-achieving math students in the control group. This suggests benefits at the upper end of the distribution of school-wide reform efforts. But whether these higher-achieving students are nurtured in programs for the gifted and talented, or whether these school-wide interventions are capable of stimulating very high achievement, is not known (Gandara, 2000).

Community-Wide Interventions

Schools are embedded within a wider context that may influence the challenges they face in educating the nation's youth. Some community-wide interventions exist that suggest the potential of harnessing community support where poverty imposes community challenges. Because such interventions are not tightly controlled, it is difficult to assign cause to a specific aspect, yet the overall impact remains of policy interest.

One example of a community intervention is the Juniper Gardens Children's Project, founded in 1964 as a collaboration between community residents and faculty at the University of Kansas. It has received continuous federal funding since that time. Serving a population of historically low-income, black housing project dwellers, the project has worked with parents and teachers on effective early intervention for students with and without special needs, on techniques for managing child behavior, developing communication skills (first and second language acquisition), strategies for overcoming discrimination, and the training of teachers and parents in effective practices. In addition to focusing on effective instruction, behavior management, and assessment, the project promotes increased use of pediatric services for low-income families. The Juniper Gardens research is particularly useful because of its exclusive focus on ethnic minority children in a low-SES community and its attention to both preventing, and intervening effectively with, special education needs.

One innovation studied in the Juniper Gardens research is the use of classwide peer tutoring, which, across a series of experimental studies, demonstrated superiority over conventional methods in its ability to increase students' levels of literacy and social competence by increasing their academic responding (Greenwood et al., 1990). It was also credited with successfully providing a range of learning styles and activities that matched the learning of ethnically diverse students (Garcia, 1992). Note, however, that this intervention occurred in the context of a wider community intervention, so the assignment of cause to peer tutoring must be questioned.

Still, a follow-along study of 90 students through the 6th grade showed that significantly fewer students who had participated in the peer tutoring intervention received special services than in the control group, and that the tutored students who did receive special services were placed in less restrictive environments (Greenwood et al., 1993). Overall, results indicated higher achievement, reduced special education services, less restrictive services, and lower dropout rates.

Another community program, the Start Making a Reader Today program (SMART), has been widely implemented throughout communities in Oregon. Currently in about 16 percent of the elementary schools in the state, most in low-income neighborhoods, the program pairs volunteer adults from the community with students who have been identified by their teachers as having difficulty learning to read. These students receive tutoring by an adult in two 30-minute sessions per week. From its inception, SMART attempted to reconnect communities and schools by promoting the advantages to both the adults and the students of time spent in tutoring. In order to implement it on a wide scale, training is kept brief and the program places minimal demands on the teachers whose students are being tutored. A two-year longitudinal evaluation of the program suggested that the performance of SMART students was statistically higher than those in a matched comparison sample on measures of word reading, reading fluency, and word comprehension. Although the difference was not statistically significant, fewer SMART (26 percent) than comparison-group (44 percent) students had been placed in special education by the fall of 3rd grade (Baker et al., 2000).

The Challenge of Change: A Cautionary Tale

Research on the effects of the wider context of schooling and of particular interventions to raise achievement indicate that context matters. But challenges attend any effort to change the school context. It is important to recognize the magnitude of the challenge, for at least two policy-relevant reasons. First, when a specific intervention fails, it is easy to conclude that the intervention itself is unwise. But such a conclusion may be inappropriate, especially if the intervention was not faithfully administered, if insufficient resources were available, or if the intervention was not conducted in a way sensitive to the wider context within which the instruction of students occurs. Second, if we downplay the magnitude of the challenge, the kinds and levels of resources needed for the intervention to succeed may be underestimated by policy makers.

The field of education is replete with examples of ostensibly failed interventions. One such contemporary example concerns the California class-size reduction initiative. In 1996, California legislators budgeted over $1 billion to reduce class size in K-3 schools. One impetus for this intervention was the evidence coming from analyses of Project STAR data, which showed that class size mattered. Despite the Tennessee experience, evidence suggests that California will not reap across-the-board gains in achievement. Indeed, there is some evidence that the intervention may ultimately increase some racial/ethnic gaps in achievement (e.g., Stecher et al., 2001).

There are important differences between the California and Tennessee experiences in reducing class size. In Tennessee, classes were reduced to 13-17 students, and control group students were in classes of 22-25 students. The California plan was to lower class size from 30 to 20—that is, the smallest class sizes in California were only slightly smaller than the largest class sizes in Tennessee. In addition, when California implemented the policy, they provided incentives for all schools to reduce class sizes, and the faster the school implemented the policy, the greater the reward they would receive. Yet schools that had larger classes at the inception of the program, particularly large urban districts with diverse student populations, had further to go to reduce their class sizes to the "magic" 20 student count. As Stecher et al. (2001) note, such schools were already dealing with shortages of space, teachers, and financial resources, all of which contributed to delays in implementing the program. The class size reduction policy exacerbated these problems.

Furthermore, the introduction of class size reduction seems to have led many teachers to flee urban districts, because it put every district into the job market for teachers. Again, the Stecher et al. analysis is instructive (2001:673):

> [Class size reduction] caused the K-3 teacher workforce to grow by at least 25,000 during its first three years, forcing school districts to compete for qualified teachers not only with one another but also with other sectors in the booming state economy. Consequently, a smaller proportion of California's current K-3 teachers have full credentials, education beyond a bachelor's degree, or three or more years' teaching experience.

> More disturbing, the decline in teacher qualifications has been greater for elementary schools serving minority, low-income, or EL students. . . . elementary schools serving the fewest low-income students saw the proportion of fully credentialed K-3 teachers drop 2 [percentage points] from 1995-96 to 1998-99, while schools serving the most low-income students experienced a 16 [percentage point] drop.

The moral of this unfolding story is that scaling up is challenging, and the complexity of the environment requires policy makers to consider the full environment as they attempt to address the issues of educational quality and equity.

CONCLUSIONS AND RECOMMENDATIONS

Children who are referred to the judgmental categories of special education[2] rarely come to school with a disability determination. They are referred to special education only after they have failed to achieve in the general education classroom. Similarly, gifted and talented students are generally identified only after they have excelled in the school context. Special education or gifted and talented identification takes place in the context of a child's performance in general education. While children come to schools with very different characteristics and levels of preparedness, how well any child meets the demands of schooling will be determined both by that child *and* by the school context itself. Several of the contributors to school context that have been shown to influence classroom achievement and behavior may be contributing to observed racial/ethnic differences in special education placement rates.

Financial resources are on average lower in schools with greater numbers of children who live in poverty. While there has been a debate regarding the role of financial resources in achievement outcomes, the evidence the committee reviewed suggests that resources can, and often do, have an impact. The critical issue, of course, is what those resources buy. Greater resources are required for class size reductions, which have been shown in some cases to improve the academic achievement of students in early grades, with benefits lasting at least through middle school. The largest gains from class size reduction have been for disadvantaged minority students. Resources can also be used to attract qualified teachers, which in turn would be expected to raise the level of teacher quality. For these reasons, the committee concludes that efforts to reduce the number of minority students with academic and behavioral problems and increase the number who excel will require a more equitable distribution of human and financial resources among states, school districts within states, and individual schools. The committee endorses the recommendation of the NRC's Committee on Education Finance that the distribution of resources take into account the higher cost of providing quality education in schools with disadvantaged student populations (NRC, 1999a).

---

[2]They do not include the speech and language category in which many young children are identified in preschool years.

While school resources, class size, and indicators of teacher quality are associated with learning and behavior outcomes, their influence must be exerted through teacher-student interactions. In this sense, what is true of cognitive and behavioral development in the earliest years continues to be true in the school years. Social, economic and environmental factors are important because they affect the nature of the interactions between children and the influential adults in their lives—in the current context, the teacher. The weight of the burden in improving school outcomes for minority students, then, falls on the interactions in the classroom.

Key to improving education outcomes for minority students is a sustained effort at capacity building, and sufficient time resources and coordination among stakeholders to build that capacity.

Teacher Quality: Recommendations for States

General education teachers need significantly improved teacher preparation and professional development to prepare them to address the needs of students with significant underachievement or giftedness, and to understand and work with the cultural differences among students that are relevant to school performance and behavior.

Recommendation TQ.1: State certification or licensure requirements for teachers should systematically require:

• **competency in understanding and implementing reasonable norms and expectations for students and core competencies in instructional delivery of academic content;**

• **coursework and practicum experience in understanding, creating, and modifying an educational environment to meet children's individual needs;**

• **competency in behavior management in classroom and noninstructional school settings;**

• **instruction in functional analysis and routine behavioral assessment of students;**

• **instruction in effective intervention strategies for students who fail to meet minimal standards for successful educational performance, or who substantially exceed those minimal standards; and**

• **coursework and practicum experience to prepare teachers to deliver culturally responsive instruction. More specifically, teachers should be familiar with the beliefs, values, cultural practices, discourse styles, and other features of students' lives that may have an impact on classroom** participation and success and be prepared to use this information in designing instruction.

While a foundational knowledge base can be laid in preservice education, often classroom experience is needed before teachers can make the most of instructional experiences.

- States should require rigorous professional development for all practicing teachers, administrators, and educational support personnel to assist them in addressing the varied needs of students who differ substantially from the norm in achievement and/or behavior.

- The professional development of administrators and educational support personnel should include enhanced capabilities in the improvement and evaluation of teacher instruction with respect to meeting student's individual needs.

In preparing teachers to deliver culturally responsive instruction, it is not our intention that the teacher recreate children's home lives at school, but rather that the teacher be prepared to incorporate this information into the classroom strategically to (a) improve instruction, as when a teacher is able to help children comprehend text by relating it to familiar cultural events, activities, practices, people, etc., and (b) ensure that all students feel comfortable and have a reasonable opportunity to participate in classroom activities.

Recommendation TQ.2: State or professional association approval for teacher instructional programs should include requirements for faculty competence in the current literature and research on child and adolescent learning and development, and on successful assessment, instructional, and intervention strategies, particularly for atypical learners, including students with gifts and disabilities.

Federal-Level Recommendations

Effective teaching practice requires not only well-prepared teachers but also high-quality, research-based curricula, educational tools and protocols, and tested interventions to support the work of well-trained teachers. We emphasize the need for expanded investments in a program of research *and development* focused on the needs of educational practice.

Recommendation RD.1: We recommend that education research and development, including that related to special and gifted education, be systematically expanded to carry promising findings and validated practices through to classroom applicability. This includes research on "scaling up" promising practices from research sites to widespread use.

In particular, the committee recommends:

• Strengthening research on educational improvement, particularly in schools with large numbers of children from low-income families. There are some promising models, but efforts are needed to accumulate knowledge, testing the dimensions of effectiveness (for whom and under what circumstances), and to make the best of what is known systematically available to school districts and teachers.

• Research on early interventions in general education settings.

• Research on what works in special education offers some important principles, but too few well-tested interventions with a solid evaluation of the conditions under which they work and for whom. In particular, the research base with respect to English-language learners needs to be strengthened.

• While there has been substantial progress on educational interventions for students who are having difficulty learning to read, little is currently known that can guide educational interventions for the non-responders to reading interventions. Research needs to attend now to this group of students.

• For the education of gifted and talented students, we have given relatively little attention either in research or in program development of any sort. This research base needs to be strengthened substantially.

• Features of cultural sensitivity that have an impact on learning outcomes for minority students have not been rigorously researched and evaluated in classroom settings. While a significant amount has been written about culturally appropriate accommodations, many of the recommendations have no empirical basis (such as matching learning styles) and should be avoided. Shoring up the empirical foundation for culturally sensitive teaching practice should be a research priority.

• Development is needed of effective mechanisms for communication of research findings to practitioner, policy, and teacher educator communities.

6

The Legal Context and the Referral Process

T he assessment of students for the purpose of determining eligibility for special education or gifted and talented services is complex and often controversial. The complexities and controversies multiply when the students considered for special education come from disadvantaged minority populations or non-English-speaking families. Indeed, some have asserted that the principal reason for disproportionate placement in special and gifted and talented education is inappropriate and biased referral, assessment, and eligibility determination processes. In this chapter we first discuss the legal context for referral, assessment, and eligibility determination. We then turn to an analysis of the literature on referrals for consideration of eligibility for special education.

LEGAL CONTEXT

Determination of eligibility for special education is a complex process that is governed by extensive legal requirements at the federal and state levels. Eligibility for gifted and talented programs is less regulated, especially at the federal level; we therefore discuss the legal context for the two domains.

Federal Disability Legal Requirements

In special education, legal requirements exist at the federal level in the form of statute and regulation (Individuals with Disabilities Education Act

1997, 1999). All of the major principles in the Education of All Handicapped Children Act (EHA) (1975, 1977), the forerunner of the Individuals with Disabilities Education Act (IDEA), have significant implications for assessment activities related to the determination of eligibility and the development of appropriate educational programs. For example, the most basic of the EHA/IDEA principles, access to appropriate educational services at public expense, vastly increased the number, complexity, and severity of students with disabilities in public school settings. Other principles, such as least restrictive environment, due process procedural protections, individualized educational programs, and confidentiality and parental access to records have similar vast implications for assessment that are beyond the discussion here (Reschly, 2000).

The greatest legal influences on the determination of special education need and eligibility for disability status are the regulations governing assessment and decision making with children and youth with disabilities, first promulgated on August 23, 1977, as the Protection in Evaluation Procedures Provisions (PEP) (Education of All Handicapped Children Act, 1975, 1977). Specific features of these regulations were derived, often verbatim, from the previous consent decrees that settled class action court cases (*Diana v. State Board of Education [Diana]*, 1970; *Guadalupe Organization v. Tempe Elementary School District No. 3 [Guadalupe]*, 1972; *Mills v. Board of Education [Mills]*, 1972; *Pennsylvania Association for Retarded Children v. Commonwealth of Pennsylvania [PARC]*, 1972). Incorporated into the PEP from these cases were regulations that required: (1) a comprehensive, individualized evaluation; (2) nondiscrimination regarding ethnic and cultural minorities; (3) consideration of multiple domains of behavior and not just a single measure such as IQ; and (4) decision making by a team of professionals with the participation of parents. The dual purposes of the PEP regulations were to ensure that all students with genuine disabilities were considered for special education and, conversely, those students with learning patterns and behaviors that appeared to be disabilities but were, in fact, due to cultural differences were not determined to be eligible for special education due to a disability. Not surprisingly untangling the differences between individual factors and cultural influences has been nearly impossible.

The PEP regulations were not changed from 1977 until March 12, 1999, when the regulations for IDEA 1997 were published as the Procedures for Evaluation and Determination of Eligibility (PEDE) (34 CFR 300.530 to 34 CFR 300.543 (see Appendix 6-A at the end of this chapter). The change in title was accompanied by expansion from approximately 1,100 to approximately 1,900 words. The section of the regulations devoted to Additional Procedures for Evaluating Children with Specific Learning Disabilities (34 CFR 300.541 through 300.543) did not change and has not changed since first published in 1977. All of the PEP regulations were incorporated into PEDE, along with several new regulations that reflect increasing concerns with the quality and usefulness of the information gathered during the full and individual evaluation related to eligibility determination and program development.

In Appendix 6-A, the changes and additions that are new in the 1999 PEDE regulations appear in bold type. All of the regulations represent important decisions by Congress regarding the characteristics of the evaluation and decision making provided by schools to children and youth with disabilities. All have the force of law. Moreover, the boldface content represents recent efforts to improve the nature of the evaluation and decision making provided to students considered for disability classification and special education services.

Continuing Regulations

In this section, the IDEA PEDE regulations that were continued from the EHA (1977) regulations are discussed. Like EHA, IDEA 1997 continues to place responsibility on states to ensure that the PEDE regulations are implemented by local educational agencies.

Full and Individual Evaluation

The EHA regulations regarding assessment, eligibility, and placement provide the essential background for consideration of the new IDEA PEDE regulations. Perhaps the most important provision is the continuing requirement that every child must receive a *full and individual evaluation* prior to the provision of special education and related services (for a description of related services, see 34 CFR 300.24). The implication of this regulation continues to be that a thorough evaluation, tailored to the individual child, is needed prior to decisions about determination of disability or the development of an individualized education program (IEP).

Best practice requires the individualization of the evaluation, which involves matching it carefully and precisely to referral concerns and the student's learning and behavior patterns. These requirements imply the avoidance of standard batteries of tests or the use of a common set of procedures for all children, such as an IQ test, a test of visual-motor perception, and a brief screening test of achievement. Recent survey data suggest that a standard battery is still prominent in schools, although perhaps less common in the 1990s than in previous decades (Hosp and Reschly, 2002a). Such standard evaluation approaches do not adequately implement the ideas of a full and *individualized* evaluation.

Multiple Domains

Other regulations continued in IDEA 1997 from the EHA regulations include the requirements that multiple domains of behavior be considered and, if appropriate, assessed thoroughly (34 CFR 300.532). The domains mentioned in this regulation are health, vision, hearing, social and emotional status, general intelligence, academic performance, communicative status, and motor abilities. This regulation, as well as many other parts of IDEA, requires professional judgments and individualization. The regulation does not require that every domain of functioning—intelligence, vision, health—be assessed with every child; rather, that all relevant domains be considered.

Team Decision Making

In addition to individualization and multiple domains of behavior, the IDEA continues the EHA requirements that a team, including professionals, parents, and, if appropriate, the child, is involved in the full and individual evaluation (34 CFR 300.533). Eligibility and placement decisions are viewed in the law as being too complex and important to allow reliance on a single specialty, such as school psychology, or on professionals generally without the involvement of parents. A continuing challenge is to adopt strategies that fully capitalize on the expertise of different professional specialties and the insights of parents in special education eligibility and intervention decisions.

IDEA 1997 also continues the EHA regulations that (a) tests must be valid for the specific purpose for which they are used, (b) tests and evaluation procedures must be nondiscriminatory and administered in the child's native language unless it is clearly not feasible to do so (see below), (c) no single test or procedure can be the sole basis for eligibility or placement, (d) tests are administered by trained and knowledgeable persons consistent with the instructions of the test publisher, (e) an IEP must be developed that meets extensive requirements if the child is eligible for special education, and (f) annual reviews of progress and triennial reviews of eligibility and program placements must be conducted. It is important to note that these regulations have been in place without any changes since 1977.

New Regulations

IDEA 1997 added several important regulations regarding assessment and decision making. Study of these regulations provides insight into areas seen by Congress as problematic in the implementation of mandatory special education legislation.

Disproportionality and Nondiscrimination

Nondiscrimination and consideration of the child's native language clearly receive greater emphasis in IDEA 1997, requiring additional practitioner efforts to avoid discriminatory practices or unwise decisions with children with limited English-speaking ability. The nondiscrimination clause has been and continues to be problematic. There is no consensus in the law or in the professional literature on a definition of discrimination or on criteria to judge specific practices as discriminatory (Reschly and Bersoff, 1999; Reynolds et al., 1999; special issue of the Journal of Special Education, 1998, vol. 32, no. 1). A subtle form of further direction to the states regarding nondiscrimination is provided in IDEA 1997 through a set of regulations dealing with disproportionality (34 CFR 300.755), signaling that disproportionate minority enrollment in special education should be investigated to determine if discriminatory practices exist (e.g., MacMillan and Reschly, 1998; Patton, 1998). The new regulation is also ambiguous. States are required to investigate "significant disproportion," but no guidance is given about the degree of difference that in considered significant.

Concerns about inappropriate decisions are reflected in 34 CFR 300.534, in which the "determinant factor" for eligibility cannot be the absence of instruction in basic academic skills or limited English proficiency. The latter provision undoubtedly reflects the concern that children and youth with limited English-speaking ability are penalized on tests due to language differences that can result in inappropriate eligibility and placement decisions.

Greater scrutiny of the "fairness" of assessment, eligibility determination, and placement is likely over the next decade. Special education is not seen positively by many professionals, who view disability status and special education placement as continuations of historical patterns of racial discrimination. Strident criticism is often directed at special educators suggesting that eligibility is determined by discriminatory tests and that the programs are stigmatizing and ineffective (Patton, 1998).

Minority overrepresentation in special education is seen increasingly as a symptom that provokes additional scrutiny by state and federal agencies. That scrutiny is taking the form of questioning traditional assessment practices, especially those tied to standardized intelligence and achievement tests, along with demands that the effectiveness of special education programs be documented for individuals and groups. Several subsequent regulations appear to be directed specifically to the concerns about fairness of assessment and effectiveness of programs. Generally, assessment procedures that do not rely on IQ tests and instead focus directly on educational needs and intervention design may be more acceptable to critics of current special education practices.

Functional Assessment and IEP Relevance

Part b of Regulation 532 (see Appendix 6-A) is new and significant. First, a clear emphasis is placed on functional and developmental information gathered from a variety of sources, including parents. The *functional* requirement implies greater emphasis on gathering information in the natural setting that is directly relevant to the problem behavior and to interventions addressing the problem behavior. The requirement that the evaluation procedures address progress in the general education curriculum further solidifies the emphasis on natural setting and interventions. Although the term "functional" has varied meanings (see Tilly et al., 2000), all of the meanings in the literature have important implications for the implementation of the law.

Practitioners are challenged to develop and tailor assessment procedures to more clearly reflect the problem behavior in the classroom, other school, and home settings. Behavior assessment and curriculum-based measurement methodologies typically provide information from the natural setting that is directly relevant to problem definition, special education need, and the design and evaluation of interventions. This section of the regulations, along with other sections discussed shortly, push the field toward problem-solving approaches featuring behavioral and curriculum-based assessment with less emphasis on standardized tests (Reschly, 1988b; Reschly and Tilly, 1999; Reschly and Ysseldyke, 1995; Tilly et al., 1999). These approaches have the advantages of being more acceptable to critics of special education and more closely related to ensuring effective programs.

The three new regulations at the end of this section, 532 (h), (i), and (j), are directed toward ensuring that the assessment procedures are closely related to the development of the special education program. Emphasis is placed on identifying all of the child's special education needs, assessment of the relative contribution of cognitive and behavioral factors and, most important, the collection of "relevant information that directly assists persons in determining the educational needs of the child." Clearly, IDEA 1997 places significant emphasis on determining educational needs, not just disability classification and eligibility determination.

Determination of Eligibility

Several new regulations stress the procedures by which children may be diagnosed as having a disability. First, according to 34 CFR 300.534, the diagnosis has to be made by a "group of qualified professionals and the parent of the child." Second, the school or other public agency must share with parents an evaluation report and the documentation regarding eligibility determination (whether or not the child is eligible). The reporting requirement was regarded as best professional practice for many years, although the kinds and amounts of information that are shared with parents are sometimes disputed.

Integration of PEDE with Other IDEA Regulations

The PEDE regulations do not stand alone. A good illustration of the interconnectedness of all of the IDEA (1997, 1999) regulations is apparent from studying the PEDE regulations in conjunction with the IEP regulations (34 CFR 300.340 to 300.350). First, the IEP regulations require the participation of someone on the IEP team who can interpret the *instructional* implications of the evaluation results. That person typically is a related services professional, such as a school psychologist. The IEP must include a statement of the child or youth's present levels of *educational* performance, including how the disability affects involvement with and progress in the general education curriculum. The IEP also must address the student's participation in the state and district-wide assessment programs, including any modifications of the assessment procedures to accommodate the needs of a student with a disability. Finally, the IEP must include information on the annual goals, short-term objectives, and measurement of progress toward these goals and objectives. IDEA 1997 suggests that all of the IEP requirements should be addressed in the full and individual evaluation governed by the PEDE regulations.

Although all states are obligated to comply with federal regulations regarding assessment, broad discretion to states is permitted in the implementation of the regulations (see later discussion). For example, all states must implement a full and individual evaluation, but whether a test of general intellectual functioning is part of that evaluation is a matter of state discretion. The principal influences on what domains of behavior are assessed and how they are assessed reside not in the general assessment regulations, but in the conceptual definitions and classification criteria for specific categories of disabilities.

Legal Requirements for Disability Classification

Definitions in the federal regulations for the 13 disability categories have changed only slightly since the 1991 revisions to IDEA when two categories were added, traumatic brain injury and autism. Conceptual definitions are provided for each of the categories in the regulations; however, specific classification criteria are not provided (34 CFR 300.7). In fact, the federal definitions do not constitute a national classification system, since the states are permitted wide discretion in the names and numbers of disability categories, conceptual definitions, and classification criteria (Denning et al., 2000; Frankenberger and Fronzaglio, 1991; Mercer et al., 1996; Patrick and Reschly, 1982).

The identification of a child as needing special education is a two-pronged determination: (a) a disability in obtaining an education must be documented and (b) need for special education must be established. Meeting one prong without meeting the other renders the child not eligible for special education and related services. The federal definitions generally include the phrase "adversely affects educational performance" to communicate the latter requirement as well as the language ". . . and who by reason thereof, needs special education and related services" [See Table 6-1, 34 CFR 300.7(a)(1)]. Future practices are likely to place additional emphasis on the special education need component of eligibility. This may be done by (1) strengthening interventions prior to referral and (2) determining empirically that well-designed and properly implemented interventions in general education are not sufficient to enable the student to receive an appropriate education.

Social System and Medical Models

The current disability classification system involves a mixture of underlying conceptual frameworks described by Jane Mercer as the social system and medical models (Mercer, 1979a; Reschly, 1996). Neither model is pure—that is, some students with social system disabilities show subtle biological disorders, and social system factors influence the expression and treatment of disabilities regarded as medical. Medical model disabilities include the nine disabilities that are regarded as low incidence, all with prevalence rates of well under 1 percent of the overall student population (e.g., multiple disabilities, hearing impaired). For virtually all of the students in these categories, there are clearly identifiable disorders of the central nervous system, sensory status, or neuromotor capabilities that can be said to cause the disability. Medical personnel identify most persons with medical model disorders prior to school entrance (see referral discussion in this chapter). The medical model disabilities recognized in IDEA are autism, deafness, deaf-blindness, hearing impairment, multiple disabilities, orthopedic disability, other health impairment, traumatic brain injury, and vision.

The vast majority of students classified with disabilities, however, are in 4 of the 13 categories that are generally described as social system model disabilities. A special problem exists with mental retardation (MR), in that the mild level is typically a social system disability, while the more severe levels of MR are more consistent with a medical model (see the discussion of MR in the next chapter). Social system disabilities typically involve

TABLE 6-1 Distribution of Disabilities by Category:1998

Category	Age 6-17 Number	Age 6-17 % of Enrollment	Age 6-17 % of SWD	State: Lowest Percent	State: Highest Percent	Factor
High Incidence						
Learning Disability	2,536,359	5.53	51.07	GA 2.94	RI 9.09	3.09
Emotional Disturbance	421,701	0.92	8.49	MS 0.06	MN 1.98	33.00
Mental Retardation	530,116	1.16	10.67	NJ 0.31	AL 2.85	9.19
Speech/Language Impairment	1,044,616	2.28	21.03	HI 1.25	NJ 3.86	3.09
Total High Incidence	4,532,792	9.89	91.26			
Low Incidence						
Autism	31,456	0.07	0.63	CO/OH 0.02	OR 0.24	12
Hearing Impairment	64,042	0.14	1.29	ND 0.08	WA 0.21	2.63
Visual Impairment	23,938	0.05	0.48	7 AT 0.03	TN 0.09	3
Orthopedic Impairment	62,110	0.14	1.25	AR/UT 0.03	MI 0.51	17
Other Health Impairment	155,249	0.34	3.13	4 AT 0.00	WA 1.44	144
Multiple Disabilities	86,946	0.19	1.75	9 AT 0.00	NJ 0.99	99
Deaf-Blindness	1,077	0.00	0.02	40 AT 0.00	ND 0.04	4
Traumatic Brain Injury	9,166	0.02	0.18	3 AT 0.00	PA/WY 0.07	7
Total Low Incidence	433,984	0.95	8.73			
Grand Totals	4,966,776	10.84	99.99	HI 7.94	RI 15.09	

NOTE: The categories of deaf and hearing impaired are combined for reporting purposes.
SOURCE: U.S. Department of Education, Office of Special Education Programs (1998).

students for whom there are no underlying identifiable biological structures or functions that can reasonably be said to cause the disability. These disabilities are subtler and typically are not diagnosed until after school entrance. The disabilities that fit best into the social system model are specific learning disability (LD), mild mental retardation (MMR), emotional disturbance (ED), and speech and language impairments (SLI). The issue of disproportionality is acute in two of the four social system model disabilities, MMR and ED. Disproportionality is much less of an issue with LD and SLI (see Chapter 2).

Disability Classification Policy

Contrary to the interpretation of many professionals, IDEA does not now, nor arguably has it ever required the use of the federal definitions or even a disability classification scheme using traditional categories. In a policy clarification letter from the Office of Special Education Programs, Hehir (1996) noted the following as federal interpretation of the regulations regarding disability identification (23 IDELR 341) (emphasis added):

> Part B does not require States to label children. The definitions of "children with disabilities" at 34 CFR §300.7 must be used by States to prepare annual data reports for the U.S. Department of Education regarding the number of children in the State receiving "special education" and "related services" under the Part B program requirements. The Department has no objection to a State's use of categories which differ from those specified in Part B or, if it elects, the use of a noncategorical approach *so long as those children eligible under Part B are appropriately identified and served.*

Requirements regarding the categorical designation of students eligible for special education were made even more explicit in the following new regulation in IDEA (1999): "Nothing in the Act requires that children be classified by their disability so long as each child who has a disability listed in §300.7 and who, by reason of that disability, needs special education and related services is regarded as a child with a disability under Part B of the Act" (34 CFR 300.125).

States and local districts must serve all children with disabilities who are in need of special education, but they do not have to use disability labels or categories. System change to a noncategorical approach to special education eligibility along with other reforms is made more feasible by recent clarifications of federal legal requirements (Graden et al., 1988; Reschly, 1988b; Reschly et al., 1999; Reschly and Ysseldyke, 1995).

State Discretion

As mentioned earlier in this report, states do, in fact, use broad discretion in the disability category names, definitions, and classification criteria. Some states do not use disability categories at all, only the broad designation that the child is eligible for special education based on educational need and very low performance in relevant domains of behavior (Tilly et al., 1999). As noted in Chapter 2, further evidence of state variations in the use of disability categories is apparent from a review of prevalence data reported by the states to the U.S. Department of Education (see Tables 2-10 to 2-15, Figures 2-5 to 2-8). In 1998 there were 33 times as many children eligible under the category of ED in Minnesota as in Mississippi (U.S. Department of Education, 1998). There were about nine times as many children reported under the category of MR in Alabama as in New Jersey, although that pattern is likely to change dramatically due to an Office for Civil Rights agreement with Alabama that changes substantially the identification of students as MR in that state.

These huge variations in prevalence show definitively that the categories are used differently and inconsistently by the states (also see Chapter 2 on patterns of disproportionality). These differences occur due to idiosyncratic state funding mechanisms, variations in state classification criteria for the various disabilities, and other local, poorly understood influences. The classification criteria beyond the category name or the conceptual definition for the disability also are important influences. For example, some states require a discrepancy of 15 standard score points between intellectual ability and achievement as part of their LD classification criteria, while other states use discrepancy criteria such as 12 or 22 points (Mercer et al., 1996). The maximum IQ score used by states for determination of MR varies from 69 to 80. Other state variations of this kind exist, leading to large differences in the prevalence of different categories. Clearly, it is possible for a student to be classified as eligible for special education in one state and not in another or (which is more likely) for the disability category to change with a move across state lines (Denning et al., 2000; Frankenberger and Fronzaglio, 1991; Mercer et al., 1996; Patrick and Reschly, 1982).

Although less well documented, in-state variability in the prevalence of different categories of disabilities also exists. Some of the variations may reflect different levels of performance in urban and suburban districts (Gottlieb et al., 1994, 1999), while others may be explained by the degree of rigor in applying state classification criteria in decisions about eligibility. Some of the intrastate variations are likely to reflect real differences in district student populations, while others cannot be easily explained.

For the reasons described above, practitioners must focus primarily on state rules regarding the use (or nonuse) of disability categories, definitions of disabilities, and classification criteria. This information typically appears in the State Department of Education Special Education Rules and also in policy interpretation or guidelines documents.

Summary

Legal requirements have vast influences on how disabilities are conceptualized and assessed for special education eligibility. Federal regulations establish general principles for assessment practices, including the two-pronged criteria of eligibility for a disability designation and the need for special education services. General principles are established, such as assessment over broad domains of functioning potentially related to the disability, team decision making, and determination of specific educational needs. Recent changes in federal regulations place more emphasis on gathering functional information directly related to interventions, analyses of environments in which problem behaviors occur, and development of positive behavioral interventions as well as assessment of progress in the general education curriculum. The recent changes appear to be directed toward improving the results of special education interventions for students with disabilities.

REFERRAL PROCESS

There are two fundamental routes that students traverse to enter the special education services system. Children with severe or biologically involved disability (referred to above as medical model disabilities) are usually identified well before entering school at age 5 or 6 and are typically identified with a disability by physicians. Sometimes these children participate in preschool programs while being identified as having a disability and enter the public schools with a diagnosis, which the public schools simply accept or confirm. The second route is relevant to children with judgmental, or social system, disabilities, who enter school, in Mercer's (1973a) sociological terms, as fulfilling the role of the "normal" student. As Mercer notes, such children at some point in time "violate" the normative expectations of normal student in the eyes of someone—for example, a teacher, parent, physician, family court. The person perceiving a problem refers the child because of the discrepancies between the child's learning rates or social behaviors compared with age or grade level expectations for his or her peers.

While the emphasis of the next two chapters is on assessment, it is important to recognize a crucial sequence of events leading up to entrance into the special education system. Only students *referred* are ever given a psychoeducational assessment, that is, the full and individual evaluation mandated by state legislated regulations. Those who are referred and given a psychoeducational assessment are ultimately deemed eligible or ineligible by a multidisciplinary team charged with considering all of the evidence brought before them. Therefore, decisions *not* to refer or failure to detect a child who "should be referred" result in false-negative cases. In addition, cases that are referred and assessed but not recommended for special education services despite meeting eligibility criteria by the multidisciplinary committee may add to the number of false-negative cases. Attention has been focused on assessment as the step in the sequence responsible for overrepresentation of minority group children in court cases and even in the 1982 National Research Council report (Reschly, 1988a, b, c). This was largely due to the evidence reported by Mercer (1973a) in her book on mental retardation.

Influence of Mercer's Analysis

Mercer (1973a) provided a description of the stages students pass through in the process of being identified as in the category of MMR; specifically, she identified eight stages. Her model describes the process involved in the second route noted above, in which students enroll in school as normal students. She found that 62.5 percent of the students ultimately placed as MMR had repeated at least one grade before being labeled and, despite that "intervention" (i.e., grade repetition), failed to perform academically at an acceptable level in general education. Social promotion or referrals for a psychoeducational assessment were at that point the available options. Those cases referred by teachers for an evaluation were examined, and Mercer reported no disproportion of minority group students. Yet when she examined actual placements in MMR programs there was clear evidence of overrepresentation of both black and Hispanic students. Black students constituted 32 percent of the MMR enrollment yet only 9.5 percent of the total school enrollment; Hispanic students constituted 12 percent of the children in the MMR program but only 7 percent of the total enrollment. These figures led Mercer to reason that if there were proportionate numbers at the time of referral and *dis*proportionate numbers in placements, the explanation must lie in the intervening step—psychoeducational assessment.

Mercer's data were subsequently reanalyzed by Gordon (1980), who made a revealing discovery. The referred cases included not only those children who were encountering difficulty, but also those children who teachers thought might be gifted. That is, Mercer had failed to distinguish between referrals for problems and referrals for academic excellence. At the time these data were collected (early 1960s), the program for the gifted enrolled primarily white students, for which it would subsequently be faulted. Were Mercer to have exclusively studied those referred for academic difficulties or behavior problems (i.e., excluding cases referred for suspected gifted students), she might have found disproportion *prior to psychoeducational assessment*. Gordon's reanalysis came after the *Diana* and *Larry P.* cases, in which Mercer's findings had considerable influence and resulted in litigation focusing on the fairness of intelligence tests for use with minority group children, with precious little attention devoted to referral behavior as a plausible contributor to the disproportion evident in enrollments (MacMillan and Forness, 1998).

Referrals by Classroom Teachers

There is no screening using nationally normed scales in determining which students will, and will not, be formally evaluated for special education eligibility. In the context of public school classrooms, those children ultimately administered a psychoeducational battery are screened by classroom teachers as being at risk, and only after interventions in the general education classroom have been attempted. That is to say, referral for formal evaluation is not an initial response to a child encountering difficulty; rather, it typically comes only after less intensive efforts fail to resolve the difficulty encountered by the child. Moreover, it can be undertaken only with the approval of the child's parent or guardian under current IDEA regulations.

We have long recognized the primacy of referral in understanding who gets classified as MMR (Ashurst and Meyers, 1973; MacMillan et al., 1980; Meyers et al., 1974) and LD (Ysseldyke and Algozzine, 1983; Zigmond, 1993). In fact, Ysseldyke and Algozzine asserted that the decision by the regular class teacher to refer is *the most important decision in the assignment of children to LD programs*. The general education teacher makes the determination that the child's academic progress is not acceptable or their behavior is unacceptable. Zigmond (1993) describes the situation as follows: "The referral is a signal that the teacher has reached the limits of his or her tolerance of individual differences, is no longer optimistic about his or her capacity to deal effectively with a particular student in the context of the larger group, and no longer perceives that the student is teachable by him- or herself" (pp. 262-263). As noted in regard to Mercer's (1973a) findings, retention in grade is commonly employed; in some schools Title I funds are available for remediation, and under current IDEA guidelines prereferral intervention efforts as part of general education are to precede formal evaluation for eligibility. A point to be emphasized here is that when a teacher reaches the decision that he or she cannot successfully cope with a child, referral is *not* for LD or MMR. At this point in the sequence, one of the questions unanswered is why the efforts tried have failed. Is it because the child has low general aptitude (i.e., may be MMR) or a domain-specific achievement problem, such as reading or math, that may be accompanied by a cognitive processing deficit (i.e., may be LD)? Are there circumstances at home that prevent that child from focusing on school work, or are the child's behavior problems so severe that they interfere with attending to instruction (i.e., may be ED)? Any and all of these outcomes are plausible—the teacher only knows that he or she has been unable to be successful with that child.

Teacher referral, however, is subjective. Whether a teacher perceives the child's level of achievement as acceptable or unacceptable varies as a function of the typical or average level of achievement in the immediate classroom. That is, local norms are applied in making the judgment that achievement is acceptable or unacceptable. Take a hypothetical child with a reading achievement score on a standardized achievement test of 75. If that child is enrolled in a class in which the average level of achievement in reading is 115, he or she stands out with a level of performance far below that of classmates. Conversely, if that same child is enrolled in a class of students whose average achievement level is 80, he or she is at about the class average and does not stand out. Hence, the risk for referral is relative to the performance level of classroom peers. It is the classroom teacher who makes that comparison and decides whether referral is appropriate. Let us turn to consider evidence concerning factors that may influence whether a teacher decides to refer a particular child.

Race and Gender Influences on Referrals

Studies using simulation methodologies have investigated whether teachers exhibit racial or gender bias in their referral behavior. Zucker and his colleagues (Prieto and Zucker, 1981; Zucker and Prieto, 1977; Zucker et al., 1979) presented vignettes portraying a child in terms of achievement and behavior to a sample of teachers, asking them to judge whether special education placement was appropriate. It is crucial to note that the only information that teachers had about the students they rated in these studies was from a brief written vignette describing the child. Using teacher ratings of hypothetical children, the investigators manipulated the race/ethnicity of the child, having some teachers judge the appropriateness of special education believing the child was portrayed as white, other teachers believing the child was black, and yet others thinking the child was Hispanic. This series of investigations yielded results that showed that when the teacher thought the child was either black or Hispanic, he or she more often judged special education placement as appropriate compared with when the teacher believed the child was white. These investigations did not find a gender bias in the teacher ratings. In a study conducted by Shinn et al. (1987), racial and gender bias were presented as evident in findings for referral behavior of elementary school teachers concerning students with severe reading problems. Studies using real children with whom the teacher has interacted directly or providing extended video information on the children did not find the kind of biases reported in studies using simulated methodologies (e.g., Reschly and Lamprecht, 1979).

Another approach to examining potential bias sought to determine whether the race of the child in question interacts with the race of the teacher making the referral decision. Tobias et al. (1983) presented teachers with a vignette describing a 10-year-old student with both academic and behavior problems. As in the Zucker studies, the race of the child was manipulated by alternating the race of the child from white to black to Hispanic. In this investigation, neither the race of the child nor the race of the teacher was found to exert a significant effect on the placement recommendation.

A variation of this design was employed by Bahr et al. (1991); however, it contained an important difference from previously described studies. Instead of using vignettes, Bahr et al. had 40 classroom teachers nominate their most "difficult-to-teach" (DTT) student who was "at risk for referral and special education placement" (p. 601). This design obviously fails to control child characteristics to the extent that the vignette could, yet it examines classroom situations more realistically. Half of the 40 male students nominated were black and half were white. The study revealed that black students were rated as more appropriate for placement than were white students (i.e., a significant main effect for race of the child); however, the race of the teacher making the recommendation did not exert a significant effect, and the interaction of race of child by race of teacher was not significant. As noted above, the inability to control actual achievement or behavior problems exhibited by the students could influence recommendations independent of the race of the child. In fact, achievement data on the children revealed that the black DTT students had significantly lower achievement than did the white DTT students; moreover, significantly more of the black DTT students had been retained in grade one or more times. Attribution of the recommendations solicited from teachers solely to the race of the child must be qualified in light of significant behavioral differences between the black and white DTT samples.

MacMillan et al. (1996b) reported on 150 students actually referred by their general education teacher for prereferral interventions. These children were not referred for formal psychoeducational assessments; nevertheless, their teachers perceived them as having difficulties unresponsive to interventions used in general education. The question addressed by this study was whether the behaviors prompting referral differ by domain (e.g., academic vs. behavior) or by degree for children differing by ethnicity or gender. The total sample of 150 children (55 white, 43 black, and 52 Hispanic) was selected using a stratified random sampling design. While the design sought to compare these groups, it should be noted, children from all three ethnic groups who had been referred exhibited intellectual, achievement, and behavioral measures indicative of students with real problems. For example, the mean score in reading and spelling for all three ethnic groups was approximately 2 standard deviations (SD) below the general population mean. On the Critical Events Index (Walker and Severson, 1990), tapping "behavioral earthquakes," the authors reported, "relative to the CEI standardization sample mean and SD (M = 0.12, SD = 0.46), the effect size for males was 5.20 and for females 2.30, indicating a level of differentiation of greater than 99 percent" (p. 147). Clearly teachers referred a group of children who presented significant achievement and behavior problems. The number of children presenting problems of similar severity who were not referred cannot be ascertained from this study.

Returning to comparisons of referred students on the basis of ethnicity and gender, there were differences on the basis of ethnicity. White referred students differed significantly from black referred students on the Wechsler verbal IQ, performance IQ, and reading achievement and differed from Hispanic referred students on verbal IQ, reading, and spelling. In all instances, white students scored significantly higher. Comparison of black and Hispanic referred students failed to detect any significant differences on intellectual or achievement measures. On problem behaviors and social skills, racial/ethnic comparisons revealed only one difference—black referred students exhibited more problem behaviors than did Hispanic referred students.

Gender comparisons failed to reveal any significant differences on either IQ or measures of achievement. However, in the behavioral domain, referred males were rated significantly higher on problem behaviors (i.e., conduct problems), critical events (low frequency, high salience—e.g., fire setting), and hyperactivity, while they were rated significantly lower on social skills. One intriguing finding is the failure to find male-female differences in academic achievement using standardized measures. However, teacher ratings of overall academic competence yielded significantly higher ratings for females than for males, despite the finding of no differences on the standardized measures.

MacMillan et al. (1996b) concluded that the students referred by teachers exhibited severe academic and behavioral deficiencies, validating "teachers as tests" in the referral process. This held across gender and racial/ethnic groups. Contrary to the fear that teachers indiscriminately and unfairly refer minority group children who are actually doing well, the findings from this project indicated that teacher referral of minority group students required more severe academic deficiencies than was evident for white referred students.

A second cohort of 179 students in the same project was evaluated recently by Dolstra (2000). The second cohort contained 57 white, 49 black, and 73 Hispanic students referred by their general education teacher for prereferral intervention. Again, white students scored significantly higher on verbal IQ than black and Hispanic referred students, and both white and Hispanic referred students scored significantly higher than black students on performance IQ. With this second cohort, using a different achievement test, no significant racial/ethnic differences were found on achievement. Contrary to the first cohort, however, a significant gender effect was found for achievement, with referred males scoring significantly higher on the math subscale. Findings regarding conduct problems mirrored those found with the first cohort—black referred students differed significantly from white and Hispanic students on conduct problems. On the Critical Events Index the only comparison that was significant was between black and white referred students—with black students exhibiting more critical events. This finding suggests a much greater rate of significant behavioral incidents. Finally, gender differences indicating more behavior problems for males and lower ratings on social skills for females paralleled the findings on the first cohort.

Hosp and Reschly (in press) conducted a meta-analysis of 10 studies of referrals to special education. Studies were selected if they reported on at least two of three groups (black, Hispanic, white) and the frequency of referrals and student population numbers by group. Black students were referred in disproportionate numbers compared with white and Hispanic groups, and Hispanic students were referred disproportionately compared with white students. One of the most controversial issues in disproportionality analyses is the actual effect of the psychoeducational assessment in the full and individual evaluation. The results from this meta-analysis suggest that psychoeducational assessment reduced the degree of disproportionality in the referrals. The vast majority of students from the three groups were referred for academic or a combination of academic and behavioral problems.

The apparent strong influence of academic achievement on referrals is consistent with national data on achievement patterns. Black and Hispanic students obtain lower achievement ratings or scores at all grade levels from kindergarten through high school (Campbell et al., 2000; West et al., 2000). Differences in average achievement levels, which in most cases are of the magnitude of 0.5 to 1.0 SD, have a marked effect on the incidence of low achievement, assuming relatively equal variations in achievement within each group (see Chapter 3).

Teacher Versus Parent Referral

While the majority of referrals for children enrolling in school as "normal" students come from teachers, others can and do make such referrals. Guidance counselors, principals, family court or other social agencies, and physicians are also the source of referrals. There is a limited research base addressing how referrals from sources other than teachers might differ in terms of the severity of the problem, the nature of the problem, and the probability that such referrals ultimately result in special education services. One investigation of this topic was reported by Gottlieb et al. (1991), who found that teachers made 74.7 percent of the referrals for psycho-educational assessments, while parents referred 25.3 percent of the cases. The reason given by the referring agent (combining teacher and parent) usually involved the academic performance of the child (59.2 percent were for academics alone, while an additional 30.5 percent were for both academic and behavioral reasons). There were pronounced differences in the race/ethnicity of the children referred by parents. White parents were far more likely to be the source of referral for their child than were black or Hispanic parents.

It is apparent from the above that, based on limited evidence, white parents appear to more frequently avail themselves of the legislative intent behind IDEA to be active in seeking assistance for their child than are minority parents. Gottlieb et al. (1991) also noted differences between the reasons parents and teachers referred. Parents referred a higher percentage of cases for academic reasons only, and children referred by their parents appeared to be higher-functioning academically than were those referred by teachers based on IQ scores and reading and math achievement. An additional finding was that a higher percentage of children referred by their parents were not placed in special education. This suggests that either teachers are more accurate in referring students who will qualify or that teachers exert greater influence in the multidisciplinary committee meetings than do parents, thereby ensuring higher placement rates for those they (the teachers) see as problematic. Another possibility is that teachers, fearing they will be perceived as incompetent if they cannot teach a particular child or one later to be found ineligible, refer only the clear-cut cases for evaluation. Again, the Gottlieb et al. (1991) study design does not permit testing of these competing hypotheses.

While more research is needed clarifying the nuances of referral, the Gottlieb et al. (1991) study conducted in a large urban district suggests the need to examine the extent to which urban special education and suburban special education are different enterprises. We suspect that parents in more affluent districts are alerted when they perceive that their child is not performing at desired levels or below a level that parent believes they are capable of. This prompts the parent to request an assessment and seek assistance for their child. In urban districts, a greater percentage of referrals are hypothesized to be initiated by teachers, who tend to refer on the basis of absolute, not relative, level of achievement (i.e., discrepant low achievement). This difference in rate of referral by parents from differing socioeconomic circumstances may also reflect different perceptions of the value of special education and differences in the type of peers a child will have in the special education program at a specific school site.

When Gottlieb et al. (1991) examined the source of referral and reason for referral as related to the ultimate special education classification, their findings were dramatic for those ultimately classified ED. While the schools classified 25 percent of the Hispanic children referred by their parents as ED, only 8.7 percent of those referred by teachers were classified as ED. A very different pattern was found for referred black students. Only 6.9 percent of black children referred by parents, but 29.5 percent of those referred by teachers, were ultimately classified as ED. Finally, 9.5 percent of parents' referrals of white students and 5.9 percent of teachers' referrals were classified as ED. Gottlieb et al. (1991) addressed the racial/ethnic disparities in ED enrollments as follows: "They are due in part to the fact that black children are more than three times as likely as white or Hispanic children referred by teachers to be labeled as emotionally handicapped" (p. 166).

Referred and Not Referred Students

Since referral is a necessary if insufficient step for receiving special education services, one question that arises is whether those students referred differ from those who go unreferred. Stated differently, are there students in the regular class with similar levels of achievement or behavior problems who do not get referred (false-negatives)? If so, how, if at all, do they differ from those referred? Gottlieb and Weinberg (1999) conducted a prospective study on this issue by asking teachers to complete two questionnaires for up to eight students who had never been in special education in their classes who were the lowest-functioning, either academically or behaviorally. Identification numbers for 376 students on whom ratings were completed were given to the chair of the multidisciplinary team at each school site, who notified the investigators within two days of referral of any problem student. A structured interview was then conducted with referring teachers after referral, but prior to the disposition of the child's eligibility.

A total of 36 (of the original 376 on whom ratings were completed) were referred for special education evaluation. Each of the 36 was paired with the child rated most similar on academic and behavior ratings completed at the beginning of the project. Referred students differed from not referred (but at risk) on reading achievement, mobility (number of times a family moved prior to referral), and the number of times the child was late to school. The narrative interview data revealed that teachers agreed that the two groups of students performed similarly at the beginning of the school year and that the problem children were on their "watch" list for possible referral. Teachers described one group of referred students in terms of their having "given up and not making an attempt to learn," while those they did not refer still seemed motivated to learn. Finally, students whose behavioral problems prompted referral were characterized as having a history of misbehavior, but a single episode ("the last straw"), a critical event, precipitated the referral. It should be noted that one-eighth of the teachers made two-thirds of the referrals, suggesting differences among teachers in their tolerance for low achievement or misbehavior.

What has been clear for many years is that the public schools do not screen with tests to "catch" children with disabilities. We have long recognized that many children presenting similar psychometric profiles (IQ scores below a cutoff score, IQ-achievement discrepancies) are never referred by classroom teachers or parents and are never at risk for special education identification. Few datasets illustrate this more clearly than that of Mercer (1970) in the Riverside Desegregation Study. In addition to her description of the stages that children went through at that time on the way to being labeled mentally retarded, she also surveyed classrooms from which referred students came. Individual tests of intelligence (WISC) were administered to all Spanish-surname ($n = 509$) and black ($n = 289$) children in three segregated elementary schools and a random sample of white ($n = 500$) students in predominantly white schools. None of the students assessed was identified as having a disability or referred for evaluation. At the time of this study, the upper cutoff score used in California for MR was 80. The percentage of each racial/ethnic group scoring below IQ 80 in these samples was as follows: white, 1.2 percent; black, 12.2 percent; and Spanish-surname, 15.3 percent. Were the schools to have screened with IQ tests, very few additional white students would be "caught," but had IQ alone defined MR, substantially more black and Hispanic students would have been identified as mentally retarded, but were not. While Judge Peckham opined in his famous trial opinion (*Larry P.*, 1979) that IQ was "primary and determinative" in the identification process for MR, clearly professional judgment of teachers in deciding which children to refer reduced the number of minority group children formally considered for eligibility, even at a time when minority overrepresentation was much higher than it is today.

Summary

Referral for a full and individual evaluation to determine educational needs and special education eligibility determination is a crucial influence in disproportionate minority representation. The available evidence suggests that referrals occur because of significant problems with school achievement, often complicated by social skills and behavior difficulties in the classroom. There is no evidence to support the idea that some of the children referred to special education are normal achievers who have no classroom learning or behavior problems.

APPENDIX 6-A
IDEA Procedures for Evaluation and
Determination of Eligibility

§300.530 General.
Each SEA shall ensure that each public agency establishes and implements procedures that meet the requirements of §§300.531-300.536.

§300.531 Initial evaluation.
Each public agency shall conduct a full and individual initial evaluation, in accordance with §§300.532 and 300.533, before the initial provision of special education **and related services** to a child with a disability under Part B of the Act.
(Authority: 20 U.S.C. 1414(a)(1))

§300.532 Evaluation procedures.
Each public agency shall ensure, at a minimum, that the following requirements are met:
(a)(1) Tests and other evaluation materials used to assess a child under Part B of the Act—
(i) Are selected and administered so as not to be discriminatory on a racial or cultural basis; and
(ii) Are provided and administered in the child's native language or other mode of communication, unless it is clearly not feasible to do so; and
(2) **Materials and procedures used to assess a child with limited English proficiency are selected and administered to ensure that they measure the extent to which the child has a disability and needs special education, rather than measuring the child's English language skills.**
(b) **A variety of assessment tools and strategies are used to gather relevant functional and developmental information about the child, including information provided by the parent, and information related to enabling the child to be involved in and progress in the general curriculum (or for a**

preschool child, to participate in appropriate activities), that may assist in determining—

(1) Whether the child is a child with a disability under §300.7; and

(2) The content of the child's IEP.

(c)(1) Any standardized tests that are given to a child—

(i) Have been validated for the specific purpose for which they are used; and

(ii) Are administered by trained and knowledgeable personnel in accordance with any instructions provided by the producer of the tests.

(2) If an assessment is not conducted under standard conditions, a description of the extent to which it varied from standard conditions (e.g., the qualifications of the person administering the test, or the method of test administration) must be included in the evaluation report.

(d) Tests and other evaluation materials include those tailored to assess specific areas of educational need and not merely those that are designed to provide a single general intelligence quotient.

(e) Tests are selected and administered so as best to ensure that if a test is administered to a child with impaired sensory, manual, or speaking skills, the test results accurately reflect the child's aptitude or achievement level or whatever other factors the test purports to measure, rather than reflecting the child's impaired sensory, manual, or speaking skills (unless those skills are the factors that the test purports to measure).

(f) No single procedure is used as the sole criterion for determining whether a child is a child with a disability and for determining an appropriate educational program for the child.

(g) The child is assessed in all areas related to the suspected disability, including, if appropriate, health, vision, hearing, social and emotional status, general intelligence, academic performance, communicative status, and motor abilities.

(h) In evaluating each child with a disability under §§300.531-300.536, the evaluation is sufficiently comprehensive to identify all of the child's special education and related services needs, whether or not commonly linked to the disability category in which the child has been classified.

(i) The public agency uses technically sound instruments that may assess the relative contribution of cognitive and behavioral factors, in addition to physical or developmental factors.

(j) The public agency uses assessment tools and strategies that provide relevant information that directly assists persons in determining the educational needs of the child.

(Authority: 20 U.S.C. 1412(a)(6)(B), 1414(b)(2) and (3))

§300.533 Determination of needed evaluation data.

(a) Review of existing evaluation data. As part of an initial evaluation (if appropriate) and as part of any reevaluation under Part B of the Act, a group that includes the individuals described in §300.344, and other qualified professionals, as appropriate, shall—

(1) Review existing evaluation data on the child, including—

(i) Evaluations and information provided by the parents of the child;

(ii) Current classroom-based assessments and observations; and

(iii) Observations by teachers and related services providers; and

(2) On the basis of that review, and input from the child's parents, identify what additional data, if any, are needed to determine—

(i) Whether the child has a particular category of disability, as described in §300.7, or, in case of a reevaluation of a child, whether the child continues to have such a disability;

(ii) The present levels of performance and educational needs of the child;

(iii) Whether the child needs special education and related services, or in the case of a reevaluation of a child, whether the child continues to need special education and related services; and

(iv) Whether any additions or modifications to the special education and related services are needed to enable the child to meet the measurable annual goals set out in the IEP of the child and to participate, as appropriate, in the general curriculum.

(b) Conduct of review. The group described in paragraph (a) of this section may conduct its review without a meeting.

(c) Need for additional data. The public agency shall administer tests and other evaluation materials as may be needed to produce the data identified under paragraph (a) of this section.

(d) Requirements if additional data are not needed.

(1) If the determination under paragraph (a) of this section is that no additional data are needed to determine whether the child continues to be a child with a disability, the public agency shall notify the child's parents—

(i) Of that determination and the reasons for it; and

(ii) Of the right of the parents to request an assessment to determine whether, for purposes of services under this part, the child continues to be a child with a disability.

(2) The public agency is not required to conduct the assessment described in paragraph (d)(1)(ii) of this section unless requested to do so by the child's parents.

(Authority: 20 U.S.C. 1414(c)(1), (2), and (4))

§300.534 Determination of eligibility.

(a) Upon completing the administration of tests and other evaluation materials—

(1) A group of qualified professionals and the parent of the child must determine whether the child is a child with a disability, as defined in §300.7; and

(2) The public agency must provide a copy of the evaluation report and the documentation of determination of eligibility to the parent.

(b) A child may not be determined to be eligible under this part if—

(1) The determinant factor for that eligibility determination is—

(i) Lack of instruction in reading or math; or

(ii) Limited English proficiency; and

(2) The child does not otherwise meet the eligibility criteria under §300.7(a).

(c)(1) A public agency must evaluate a child with a disability in accordance with §§300.532 and 300.533 before determining that the child is no longer a child with a disability.

(2) The evaluation described in paragraph (c)(1) of this section is not required before the termination of a student's eligibility under Part B of the Act due to graduation with a regular high school diploma, or exceeding the age eligibility for FAPE under State law.

(Authority: 20 U.S.C. 1414(b)(4) and (5), (c)(5))

§300.535 Procedures for determining eligibility and placement.

(a) In interpreting evaluation data for the purpose of determining if a child is a child with a disability under §300.7, and the educational needs of the child, each public agency shall—

(1) Draw upon information from a variety of sources, including aptitude and achievement tests, parent input, teacher recommendations, physical condition, social or cultural background, and adaptive behavior; and

(2) Ensure that information obtained from all of these sources is documented and carefully considered.

(b) If a determination is made that a child has a disability and needs special education and related services, an IEP must be developed for the child in accordance with §§300.340-300.350.

(Authority: 20 U.S.C. 1412(a)(6), 1414(b)(4))

§300.536 Reevaluation.

Each public agency shall ensure—

(a) That the IEP of each child with a disability is reviewed in accordance with §§300.340-300.350; and

(b) That a reevaluation of each child, in accordance with §§300.532-300.535, is conducted if conditions warrant a reevaluation, or if the child's parent or teacher requests a reevaluation, but at least once every three years.

(Authority: 20 U.S.C. 1414(a)(2))

Additional Procedures for Evaluating Children with Specific Learning Disabilities

§300.540 Additional team members.
The determination of whether a child suspected of having a specific learning disability is a child with a disability as defined in §300.7, must be made by the child's parents and a team of qualified professionals which must include—
(a)(1) The child's regular teacher; or
(2) If the child does not have a regular teacher, a regular classroom teacher qualified to teach a child of his or her age; or
(3) For a child of less than school age, an individual qualified by the SEA to teach a child of his or her age; and
(b) At least one person qualified to conduct individual diagnostic examinations of children, such as a school psychologist, speech-language pathologist, or remedial reading teacher.

§300.541 Criteria for determining the existence of a specific learning disability.
(a) A team may determine that a child has a specific learning disability if—
(1) The child does not achieve commensurate with his or her age and ability levels in one or more of the areas listed in paragraph (a)(2) of this section, if provided with learning experiences appropriate for the child's age and ability levels; and
(2) The team finds that a child has a severe discrepancy between achievement and intellectual ability in one or more of the following areas:
(i) Oral expression.
(ii) Listening comprehension.
(iii) Written expression.
(iv) Basic reading skill.
(v) Reading comprehension.
(vi) Mathematics calculation.
(vii) Mathematics reasoning.
(b) The team may not identify a child as having a specific learning disability if the severe discrepancy between ability and achievement is primarily the result of—
(1) A visual, hearing, or motor impairment;
(2) Mental retardation;
(3) Emotional disturbance; or
(4) Environmental, cultural, or economic disadvantage.

§300.542 Observation.

(a) At least one team member other than the child's regular teacher shall observe the child's academic performance in the regular classroom setting.

(b) In the case of a child of less than school age or out of school, a team member shall observe the child in an environment appropriate for a child of that age.

(Authority: Sec. 5(b), P.L. 94-142)

§300.543 Written report.

(a) For a child suspected of having a specific learning disability, the documentation of the team's determination of eligibility, as required by §300.534(a)(2), must include a statement of—

(1) Whether the child has a specific learning disability;

(2) The basis for making the determination;

(3) The relevant behavior noted during the observation of the child;

(4) The relationship of that behavior to the child's academic functioning;

(5) The educationally relevant medical findings, if any;

(6) Whether there is a severe discrepancy between achievement and ability that is not correctable without special education and related services; and

(7) The determination of the team concerning the effects of environmental, cultural, or economic disadvantage.

(b) Each team member shall certify in writing whether the report reflects his or her conclusion. If it does not reflect his or her conclusion, the team member must submit a separate statement presenting his or her conclusions.

NOTES: The Procedures for Evaluation and Determination of Eligibility regulations (PEDE) first appeared on March 12, 1999, in the *Federal Register*, 64(48). The forerunner to PEDE was the Protection in Evaluation Procedures (PEP) Provisions, which first appeared on August 23, 1977, in the *Federal Register*, 42(163) as part of the regulations implementing the Education for All Handicapped Children Act of 1975 (P.L. 94-142). The PEP regulations were not changed from 1977 to 1999.

The Procedures for Evaluating Specific Learning Disabilities, section 300.540 through 300.543, first appeared in the *Federal Register*, 1977, December 29, 42(250), pp. 65082-65085. These provisions remain the same in the IDEA (1997) Regulations (*Federal Register*, 1999, March 12, 1999, vol. 64 (48)).

APPENDIX 6-B
IDEA Definitions of Disabilities

§300.7 Child with a disability.

(a) General.

(1) As used in this part, the term child with a disability means a child evaluated in accordance with §§300.530-300.536 as having mental retardation, a hearing impairment including deafness, a speech or language impairment, a visual impairment including blindness, serious emotional disturbance (hereafter referred to as emotional disturbance), an orthopedic impairment, autism, traumatic brain injury, another health impairment, a specific learning disability, deaf-blindness, or multiple disabilities, and who, by reason thereof, needs special education and related services.

(2)(i) Subject to paragraph (a)(2)(ii) of this section, if it is determined, through an appropriate evaluation under §§300.530-300.536, that a child has one of the disabilities identified in paragraph (a)(1) of this section, but only needs a related service and not special education, the child is not a child with a disability under this part.

(ii) If, consistent with §300.26(a)(2), the related service required by the child is considered special education rather than a related service under State standards, the child would be determined to be a child with a disability under paragraph (a)(1) of this section.

(b) Children aged 3 through 9 experiencing developmental delays. The term child with a disability for children aged 3 through 9 may, at the discretion of the State and LEA and in accordance with §300.313, include a child—

(1) Who is experiencing developmental delays, as defined by the State and as measured by appropriate diagnostic instruments and procedures, in one or more of the following areas: physical development, cognitive development, communication development, social or emotional development, or adaptive development; and

(2) Who, by reason thereof, needs special education and related services.

(c) Definitions of disability terms. The terms used in this definition are defined as follows:

(1)(i) Autism means a developmental disability significantly affecting verbal and nonverbal communication and social interaction, generally evident before age 3, that adversely affects a child's educational performance. Other characteristics often associated with autism are engagement in repetitive activities and stereotyped movements, resistance to environmental change or change in daily routines, and unusual responses to sensory experiences. The term does not apply if a child's educational performance is adversely affected primarily because the child has an emotional disturbance, as defined in paragraph (b)(4) of this section.

(ii) A child who manifests the characteristics of "autism" after age 3 could be diagnosed as having "autism" if the criteria in paragraph (c)(1)(i) of this section are satisfied.

(2) Deaf-blindness means concomitant hearing and visual impairments, the combination of which causes such severe communication and other developmental and educational needs that they cannot be accommodated in special education programs solely for children with deafness or children with blindness.

(3) Deafness means a hearing impairment that is so severe that the child is impaired in processing linguistic information through hearing, with or without amplification, that adversely affects a child's educational performance.

(4) Emotional disturbance is defined as follows:

(i) The term means a condition exhibiting one or more of the following characteristics over a long period of time and to a marked degree that adversely affects a child's educational performance:

(A) An inability to learn that cannot be explained by intellectual, sensory, or health factors.

(B) An inability to build or maintain satisfactory interpersonal relationships with peers and teachers.

(C) Inappropriate types of behavior or feelings under normal circumstances.

(D) A general pervasive mood of unhappiness or depression.

(E) A tendency to develop physical symptoms or fears associated with personal or school problems.

(ii) The term includes schizophrenia. The term does not apply to children who are socially maladjusted, unless it is determined that they have an emotional disturbance.

(5) Hearing impairment means an impairment in hearing, whether permanent or fluctuating, that adversely affects a child's educational performance but that is not included under the definition of deafness in this section.

(6) Mental retardation means significantly subaverage general intellectual functioning, existing concurrently with deficits in adaptive behavior and manifested during the developmental period, that adversely affects a child's educational performance.

(7) Multiple disabilities means concomitant impairments (such as mental retardation-blindness, mental retardation-orthopedic impairment, etc.), the combination of which causes such severe educational needs that they cannot be accommodated in special education programs solely for one of the impairments. The term does not include deaf-blindness.

(8) Orthopedic impairment means a severe orthopedic impairment that adversely affects a child's educational performance. The term includes impairments caused by congenital anomaly (e.g., clubfoot, absence of some member, etc.), impairments caused by disease (e.g., poliomyelitis, bone

tuberculosis, etc.), and impairments from other causes (e.g., cerebral palsy, amputations, and fractures or burns that cause contractures).

(9) Other health impairment means having limited strength, vitality, or alertness, including a heightened alertness to environmental stimuli that results in limited alertness with respect to the educational environment, that—

(i) Is due to chronic or acute health problems such as asthma, attention deficit disorder or attention deficit hyperactivity disorder, diabetes, epilepsy, a heart condition, hemophilia, lead poisoning, leukemia, nephritis, rheumatic fever, and sickle cell anemia; and

(ii) Adversely affects a child's educational performance.

(10) Specific learning disability is defined as follows:

(i) General. The term means a disorder in one or more of the basic psychological processes involved in understanding or in using language, spoken or written, that may manifest itself in an imperfect ability to listen, think, speak, read, write, spell, or to do mathematical calculations, including conditions such as perceptual disabilities, brain injury, minimal brain dysfunction, dyslexia, and developmental aphasia.

(ii) Disorders not included. The term does not include learning problems that are primarily the result of visual, hearing, or motor disabilities, of mental retardation, of emotional disturbance, or of environmental, cultural, or economic disadvantage.

(11) Speech or language impairment means a communication disorder, such as stuttering, impaired articulation, a language impairment, or a voice impairment, that adversely affects a child's educational performance.

(12) Traumatic brain injury means an acquired injury to the brain caused by an external physical force, resulting in total or partial functional disability or psychosocial impairment, or both, that adversely affects a child's educational performance. The term applies to open or closed head injuries resulting in impairments in one or more areas, such as cognition; language; memory; attention; reasoning; abstract thinking; judgment; problem solving; sensory, perceptual, and motor abilities; psychosocial behavior; physical functions; information processing; and speech. The term does not apply to brain injuries that are congenital or degenerative, or to brain injuries induced by birth trauma.

(13) Visual impairment including blindness means an impairment in vision that, even with correction, adversely affects a child's educational performance. The term includes both partial sight and blindness.

(Authority: 20 U.S.C. 1401(3)(A) and (B); 1401(26))

7

Assessment Practices, Definitions, and Classification Criteria

In this chapter we discuss the influence of conceptual definitions, classification criteria, and assessment practices on the four educational classifications of concern here: mental retardation, emotional disturbance, specific learning disability, and giftedness. We begin with the disability classifications.

Conceptual definitions and classification criteria have enormous influence on the assessment procedures applied during the determination of eligibility and special education needs. Although general assessment requirements are applicable to all disabilities (see Appendix 6-A), there are also specific requirements for each of the disability classifications considered in this chapter.

SPECIFIC LEARNING DISABILITY

Learning disabilities (LD) are a group of disorders that involve more than half the children in special education programs. LD prevalence has risen rapidly over the past 25 years. Disproportionate minority representation in LD occurs for Asian/Pacific Islanders, who are underrepresented by 2.7 times the rate of white students and for American Indian/Alaskan Natives, who are overrepresented by a factor of 1.2 times the white rate. All other groups are represented at or very close to the rate for white students.

Concept of Learning Disabilities

The notion of learning disabilities and the attendant terminology arose in the mid-1960s when a psychologist, Samuel Kirk, first used the term "learning disability." Kirk used the term as a catchall phrase to describe a number of different problems affecting the ability of certain children to learn. He noted that these problems manifested themselves in children who were otherwise capable, but were underachieving. There was a variance between the child's level of achievement and the child's presumed capabilities. Kirk defined learning disabilities as "a retardation, disorder, or delayed development in one or more of the processes of speech, language, reading, spelling, writing, or arithmetic resulting from a possible cerebral dysfunction and not from mental retardation, sensory deprivation, or cultural or instructional factors" (Kirk, 1962:263).

This was a new concept, even though unexpected underachievement in otherwise capable children had been reported much earlier in association with dyslexia, word blindness, dysgraphia, and dyscalculia (Doris, 1993; Hallgren, 1950; Hinshelwood, 1917; Orton, 1925; Strauss and Werner, 1942). Parents, educators, and policy makers embraced the new term "learning disabilities" because it fulfilled a need to provide special education services to children whose failure to learn could not be explained by mental retardation, visual impairments, hearing impairments, or emotional disturbance. The new term represented a new category for describing children with learning impairments that were not attributable to obvious physical, emotional, or psychological shortcomings. There was no stigma attached because "Their difficulties in learning to read, write, and/or calculate occurred despite adequate intelligence, sensory integrity, healthy emotional development, and cultural and environmental advantage" (Lyon et al., 2001).

Prior to Kirk's revelation, children with learning disabilities were simply not being served. The new concept catalyzed parents and educators to act. In 1969 these children were eligible for services with passage of the Learning Disabilities Act. Eligibility continued in the Education of the Handicapped Act (EHA) (1975, 1977) and in the Individuals with Disabilities Education Act (IDEA) (1997, 1999).

Legal Context

Additional rules were formulated in 1977 specifically for the LD category (34 CFR 300.541). These rules were a compromise that no one particularly liked or supported at the time, but they have survived as an apparently objective method used to solve a difficult problem: determining which students among those with achievement problems should be eligible for special education services in the category of LD. The objectivity and appropriateness of the method suggested in the 1977 regulations have been questioned over the past 15 years.

The 1977 federal regulations established classification criteria that were not entirely consistent with the LD conceptual definition (see Appendix 6-B), which implied an underlying cognitive processing disorder as the core feature of the disability. The classification criteria had three broad components (see Regulation 540 in Appendix 6-A). The first was low achievement in one of seven areas. The second was "a severe discrepancy between achievement and intellectual ability" in one or more of the seven achievement areas. The third involved what are known as the exclusion criteria: LD could not be the result of inappropriate educational programming; visual, hearing, or motor impairment; mental retardation; emotional disturbance; or environmental, cultural, or economic disadvantage. These criteria could be summarized as defining LD as unexpected low achievement that cannot be explained by low ability, absence of an opportunity to learn, or other factors.

State requirements for determining eligibility generally apply the discrepancy and exclusion factors, although there are substantial variations. The most recent national survey of state criteria (Mercer et al., 1996) indicated that 94 percent of states mentioned a processing disorder in the conceptual definition, but processing factors were included in only 33 percent of the states' classification criteria. Virtually all states applied the exclusion factors (98 percent), and all included the achievement areas of reading, writing, and math. Dissatisfaction with the achievement-ability severe discrepancy criterion has led to consideration of achievement-domain-specific criteria for eligibility (see Chapter 8 for a discussion of problems with the severe discrepancy method).

Domain-Specific Definitions

Federal law defines LD not as a single disability, but as a group of disabilities that are expressed in one or more skill domains. The disabilities are manifested in the areas of: (1) listening; (2) speaking; (3) basic reading (decoding and word recognition); (4) reading comprehension; (5) arithmetic calculation; (6) mathematics reasoning; and (7) written expression. The broadness of this definition encompasses a wide range of learning difficulties eligible for treatment. However, the complexity of each skill domain and the overlap between the domains compromise diagnostic precision. Diagnosis is further complicated by the fact that disabilities in these areas may be accompanied by other disorders, which are not the cause of the LD.

Because definitional clarity is so elusive, developing a set of specific operational criteria for identifying individual children has been problematic. Some advocate modification of generic definitions to reflect separate evidence-based definitions of domain-specific disabilities. The development of operational definitions and criteria relevant to each domain would guide procedures to determine which students are eligible for reading disabilities or mathematics disabilities, etc. A great deal is now known about the most common of the learning disabilities—dyslexia or reading disability—and using this domain-specific definitional strategy, investigators have now begun to examine other common learning disabilities, for example, mathematics disability. In the following section we review the significant advances in understanding reading and reading disabilities.

Reading Disability

Dyslexia is characterized by an unexpected difficulty in reading in children and adults who otherwise possess the intelligence, motivation, and schooling considered necessary for accurate and fluent reading (Shaywitz, 1998). Recent epidemiological data indicate that like hypertension and obesity, dyslexia fits a dimensional model. In other words, within the population, reading ability and reading disability occur along a continuum, with reading disability representing the lower tail of a normal distribution of reading ability (Gilger et al., 1996; Shaywitz et al., 1992; B. Shaywitz et al., 2001; S. Shaywitz et al., in press).

Dyslexia is one of the most common of childhood disorders, with a public school prevalence rate of approximately 6 percent (see Chapter 2). Previously, it was believed that dyslexia affected boys primarily (Finucci and Childs, 1981); however, more recent data (Flynn and Rahbar, 1994; Shaywitz et al., 1990; Wadsworth et al., 1992) indicate similar numbers of affected boys and girls. Longitudinal studies, both prospective (Francis et al., 1996; Shaywitz et al., 1995) and retrospective (Bruck, 1992; Felton et al., 1990; Scarborough, 1984), indicate that dyslexia is a persistent, chronic condition; it does not represent a transient developmental lag. Over time, poor readers and good readers tend to maintain their relative positions along the spectrum of reading ability (Shaywitz et al., 1995).

Dyslexia is both familial and heritable (Pennington and Gilger, 1996). Family history is one of the most important risk factors; between 23 and 65 percent of children who have a parent with dyslexia are reported to have the disorder (Scarborough, 1990). Rates among siblings of affected persons of approximately 40 percent and among parents of 27 to 49 percent (Pennington and Gilger, 1996) provide opportunities for early identification of affected siblings and often for delayed but helpful identification of affected adults. Linkage studies implicate loci on chromosomes 6 and 15 for reading disability (Cardon et al., 1994, 1995; Grigorenko et al., 1997) and most recently on chromosome 2 (Fagerheim et al., 1999).

Theories of dyslexia have been proposed that are based on the visual system (Demb et al., 1998; Eden et al., 1996; Stein and Walsh, 1997) and other factors, such as temporal processing of stimuli within these systems (Talcott et al., 2000; Tallal, 2000). Although other systems and processes may also contribute to the difficulty, there is now a strong consensus among investigators in the field that the central difficulty in dyslexia reflects a deficit in the language system. Investigators have long known that speech enables its users to create an indefinitely large number of words by combining and permuting a small number of phonological segments, the consonants and vowels that serve as the natural constituents of the biological specialization for language. An alphabetic transcription (reading) brings this same ability to readers, but only as they connect its arbitrary characters (letters) to the phonological segments they represent. Making that connection requires awareness that all words, in fact, can be decomposed into phonological segments. It is this awareness that allows the reader to connect the letter strings (the orthography) to the corresponding units of speech (phonological constituents) they represent. The awareness that all words can be decomposed into these basic elements of language (phonemes) allows the reader to decipher the reading code.

In order to read, a child has to develop the insight that spoken words can be pulled apart into phonemes and that the letters in a written word represent these sounds. As numerous studies have shown, however, such awareness is largely missing in dyslexic children and adults (Brady and Shankweiler, 1991; Bruck, 1992; Fletcher et al., 1994; Liberman and Shankweiler, 1991; Rieben and Perfetti, 1991; Shankweiler et al., 1995, 1979; Share, 1995; Shaywitz, 1998, 1996; Stanovich and Siegel, 1994; Torgesen, 1995; Wagner and Torgesen, 1987). Results from large and well-studied populations with reading disability confirm that in young school-age children (Fletcher et al., 1994; Stanovich and Siegel, 1994) as well as in adolescents (Shaywitz et al., 1999), a deficit in phonology represents the most robust and specific (Morris et al., 1998) correlate of reading disability. Such findings form the basis for the most successful and evidence-based interventions designed to improve reading (National Institute of Child Health and Human Development, 2000).

Implications of the Phonological Model of Dyslexia

Basically, reading comprises two main processes—decoding and comprehension (Gough and Tunmer, 1986). In dyslexia, a deficit at the level of the phonological module impairs the ability to segment the written word into its underlying phonological elements. As a result, the reader experiences difficulty, first in decoding the word and then in identifying it. The phonologic deficit is domain-specific; that is, it is independent of other, nonphonological, abilities. In particular, the higher-order cognitive and linguistic functions involved in comprehension, such as general intelligence and reasoning, vocabulary (Share and Stanovich, 1995), and syntax (Shankweiler et al., 1995), are generally intact. This pattern—a deficit in phonological analysis contrasted with intact higher-order cognitive abilities—offers an explanation for the paradox of otherwise intelligent people who experience great difficulty in reading (Shaywitz, 1996).

According to the model, a circumscribed deficit in a lower-order linguistic (phonological) function blocks access to higher-order processes and to the ability to draw meaning from text. The problem is that the affected reader cannot use his or her higher-order linguistic skills to access the meaning until the printed word has first been decoded and identified. Suppose, for example, that an individual knows the precise meaning of the spoken word "apparition"; however, until he can decode and identify the printed word on the page, he will not be able to use his knowledge of the meaning of the word, and it will appear that he does not know the word's meaning.

Phonological Deficit in Adolescence and Adult Life

Deficits in phonological coding continue to characterize dyslexic readers even in adolescence; performance on phonological processing measures contributes most to discriminating dyslexic and average readers, as well as average and superior readers (Shaywitz et al., 1999). Children with dyslexia neither spontaneously remit nor do they demonstrate a lag mechanism for catching up in the development of reading skills. In adolescents, fluency, defined as rapid, accurate *oral* reading with good comprehension, as well as facility with spelling may be most useful clinically in differentiating average from poor readers. From a clinical perspective, these data indicate that as children approach adolescence, a manifestation of dyslexia may be a very slow reading rate; in fact, children may learn to read words accurately, but they will not be fluent or automatic, reflecting the lingering effects of a phonological deficit (Lefly and Pennington, 1991). Because they are able to read words accurately (albeit very slowly) dyslexic adolescents and young adults may mistakenly be assumed to have "outgrown" their dyslexia. Data from studies of children with dyslexia who have been followed prospectively support the notion that the ability to read aloud accurately and rapidly as well as facility with spelling may be most useful clinically in differentiating average from poor readers in students in secondary school, college, and graduate school. It is important to remember that these older dyslexic students may be similar to their unimpaired peers on untimed measures of word recognition yet continue to suffer from the phonological deficit that makes reading less automatic, more effortful, and slow. For readers with dyslexia, the provision of extra time is an essential accommodation; it allows them the time to decode each word and to apply their unimpaired higher-order cognitive and linguistic skills to the surrounding context to get at the meaning of words that they cannot entirely or rapidly decode. Other accommodations useful to adolescents with reading difficulties include note-takers, taping classroom lectures, using recordings to access texts and other books they have difficulty reading, and the opportunity to take tests in alternate formats, such as short essays or even orally (Shaywitz, 1998).

Neurobiological Studies

To a large degree, advances in understanding dyslexia have informed and facilitated studies examining the neurobiological underpinnings of reading and dyslexia. Thus, a range of neurobiological investigations using postmortem brain specimens (Galaburda et al., 1985) and, more recently, brain morphometry (Filipek, 1996), and diffusion tensor MRI imaging (Klingberg et al., 2000) suggest that there are differences in the temporo-parieto-occipital brain regions between dyslexic and nonimpaired readers.

Rather than being limited to examining the brain in an autopsy specimen or measuring the size of brain regions using static morphometric indices based on CT or MRI, functional imaging offers the possibility of examining brain function during performance of a cognitive task. In principle, functional brain imaging is quite simple. When an individual is asked to perform a discrete cognitive task, that task places processing demands on particular neural systems in the brain. To meet those demands requires activation of neural systems in specific brain regions, and those changes in neural activity are, in turn, reflected by changes in brain metabolic activity, which in turn are reflected, for example, by changes in cerebral blood flow and in the cerebral utilization of metabolic substrates such as glucose. The term *functional imaging* has also been applied to the technology of magnetic source imaging using magnetoencephalography, an electrophysiological method with strengths in resolving the temporal sequences of cognitive processes.

Recent findings using fMRI may help reconcile the seemingly contradictory findings of previous imaging studies of dyslexic readers (Shaywitz, B. et al., in press; Brunswick et al., 1999; Helenius et al., 1999; Horwitz et al., 1998; Paulesu et al., 2001; Rumsey et al., 1992, 1997; Salmelin et al., 1996; Shaywitz et al., 1998, submitted; Simos et al., 2000). In addition, some functional brain imaging studies show a relative increase in brain activation in frontal regions and right hemisphere systems in dyslexics compared with nonimpaired readers (Shaywitz, B. et al., in press; Brunswick et al., 1999; Rumsey et al., 1997; Shaywitz et al., 1998, submitted; Georgiewa et al., 1999).The involvement of the posterior region centered about the angular gyrus is of particular interest, since this portion of association cortex is considered pivotal in carrying out those cross-modal integrations necessary for reading—that is, mapping the visual percept of the print onto the phonological structures of the language (Benson, 1994; Black and Behrmann, 1994; Geschwind, 1965). Consistent with this study of developmental dyslexia, a large literature on acquired inability to read (alexia) describes neuroanatomic lesions most prominently centered about the angular gyrus (Damasio and Damasio, 1983; Dejerine, 1891; Friedman et al., 1993).

It should not be surprising that both the acquired and the developmental disorders affecting reading have in common a disruption in the neural systems serving to link the visual representations of the letters to the phonological structures they represent. While reading difficulty is the primary symptom in both acquired alexia and developmental dyslexia, associated symptoms and findings in the two disorders would be expected to differ somewhat, reflecting the differences between an acquired and a developmental disorder. In acquired alexia, a structural lesion resulting from an injury, such as stroke or tumor, disrupts a component of an already functioning neural system, and the lesion may extend to involve other brain regions and systems. In developmental dyslexia, as a result of a constitutionally based functional disruption, the system never develops normally so that the symptoms reflect the emanative effects of an early disruption to the phonological system. In either case, the disruption is within the same neuroanatomic system. A number of studies of young adults with childhood histories of dyslexia indicate that although they may develop some accuracy in reading words, they remain slow, nonautomatic readers (Bruck, 1992; Felton et al., 1990).

The model used to study reading and reading disability has now been extended to the study of mathematics and mathematics disability. Though these studies are still in their infancy, the indications are that within the next decade, understanding of the underlying cognitive and neurobiological underpinnings of mathematics disability will be elucidated.

Current Identification Procedures

The concept of unexpected underachievement remains the central diagnostic criterion for designating a child as LD. Because the definition of LD in EHA/IDEA provided insufficient criteria for identifying eligible children, in 1977 the Department of Education published guidelines for the identification of an unexpected underachievement, settling on an operational definition of a severe discrepancy between achievement and intellectual ability, that is, an IQ-achievement discrepancy. Over time, it has become apparent that the use of the IQ-achievement discrepancy has the effect of delaying identification until the child falls below a predicated level of performance. Waiting for a child to exhibit failure sufficient to signal a significant discrepancy between IQ and achievement level takes time. This type of discrepancy cannot be measured until a child reaches approximately age 9 and by that time the student has been experiencing the frustration of academic failure for two to three years. A significant number of epidemiological data show clearly that the majority of children who are poor readers at age 9 continue to have reading difficulties into adulthood (Shaywitz et al., 1999). Thus, a reliance on the IQ-achievement discrepancy, when employed as the principal criterion for the identification of reading disability, possibly harms more children than it helps. Furthermore, good evidence indicates that it is possible to screen children as young as 4-5 years of age and identify those at risk for reading disability, an identification based on poor reading relative to chronological age, that is, poor reading defined solely on the basis of low reading achievement.

The results of several studies indicate that there are no significant differences in cognitive characteristics (other than verbal ability) between children who are poor readers relative only to chronological age (i.e., poor readers defined by low achievement) and children defined as reading disabled on the basis of unexpected underachievement (i.e., on the basis of an IQ-achievement discrepancy) (Fletcher et al., 1994; Stanovich and Siegel, 1994). In addition, neurobiological evidence using sophisticated brain imaging technology supports the cognitive data in indicating similar patterns of brain organization in children defined as having a reading disability on the basis of unexpected underachievement and on the basis of low achievement for chronological age (Shaywitz, B. et al., in press). Important for future policy development, the IQ test results and whether or not a child shows a discrepancy between IQ and reading achievement have little significance for understanding or treating a reading disability.

MENTAL RETARDATION

Disproportionate representation in the mental retardation (MR) category, especially the mild level (MMR), is a long-standing concern in discussions of the participation of minority students in special education (Dunn, 1968; National Research Council [NRC], 1982). Although the numbers of and the degree of disproportionality in minority and nonminority students classified as MR and participating in special education have declined substantially over the past 25 years, the greatest degrees of special education disproportionality continue to occur in this category. Currently,

2.63 percent of all black students receive special education services due to the MR disability, a rate that is 2.35 times the rate for white students. White and American Indian/Alaskan Native students are in MR programs at very close to the same rates, while Hispanic students have slight underrepresentation and Asian/Pacific Islanders have substantial underrepresentation (see Chapter 2). Disproportionate MR representation has been the most controversial and intractable pattern over the past few decades.

Many changes in MMR have occurred since the 1982 NRC report. While MR was the disability category of interest in that report, during the intervening period many of the mild cases have ceased to be identified as mentally retarded in many states (MacMillan et al., 1996d). It is instructive to note the "vacillating prevalence" of MR among schoolchildren in the past half century (Mackie, 1969). Mackie reports that between 1948 and 1966 there was a 400 percent increase in the number of children served in public school programs for students with MR. During the latter phase of that time period, the American Association on Mental Deficiency adopted the Heber (1959, 1961) definition that set the upper IQ cutoff score at −1 SD (roughly IQ 85), leading Clausen (1967) to note that this was the most liberal, inclusive definition ever of the concept of mental deficiency. In the mid-1960s there was no LD category recognized in federal law, and public schools encountering a youngster with severe and chronic low achievement had few options for helping that child—either they classified him or her as MMR, or services were restricted to the interventions available in general education.

The existence of two groups of individuals with MR has long been recognized (Dingman and Tarjan, 1960; Zigler, 1967). One is a more patently disabled group of individuals whose MR more often has a biological basis (referred to as "organic" by some) and whose IQ is commonly very low (i.e., below 50). Zigler (1967) proposed that this group of individuals represents a separate IQ distribution with a mean of approximately 35 and ranges from an untestable level up to an IQ of about 70. Zigler said that the intellectual functioning of this group of mentally retarded children reflected "factors other than the normal polygenic expression"—that these people had an "identifiable physiological defect." A second group of individuals, referred to as "familial cases of mental retardation" evidence no organic impairment and are believed by Zigler to represent the lowest portion of the normal curve of intelligence. Predictions derived from these hypotheses generated by Dingman et al. were tested by Mercer (1973b), examining the presence of physical disabilities (e.g., seizures, ambulation, vision, and hearing problems) in individuals clinically identified as MR with IQ scores in the range of about 55-75, i.e., the familial type. She concluded: "Clearly, persons whose IQs are more than 3 standard deviations below the mean of the population suffer from significantly more physical disabilities than persons whose scores fall within the normal curve (Mercer, 1973b:15).

The two groups of individuals with MR are important to the issue of assessment. Physicians typically diagnose the organic cases (i.e., those with IQs below about 55-60), very early in childhood using clinical and laboratory tests, medical histories, and other evidence employed in medical diagnoses. As described in the discussion of referral in Chapter 6, more severe cases of MR are commonly enrolled in preschool programs and arrive for public school enrollment already classified as mentally retarded. The MMR or familial cases, however, have traditionally arrived for enrollment in school undiagnosed with any disability. Diagnosis as MMR occurs only after chronic and severe achievement problems are found, marked by failure to respond to normative instructional materials and methods and leading ultimately to referral and psychoeducational assessment in an effort to determine: (a) if the child has a disability and (b) a prescription for educational treatment. It is this second group of children ultimately classified as MMR over whom the role of educational assessment is most relevant.

Behavioral Dimensions Defining Mental Retardation

The dimensions of intellectual functioning and social competence (i.e., adaptive behavior) have been fundamental to most definitions of MR. The relative importance of these two dimensions, however, has varied in the different classification schemes proposed (MacMillan and Reschly, 1996). Definitions of MR adopted by the American Association on Mental Retardation (AAMR) have historically been the most influential in terms of being adopted in federal legislation and state education codes (Frankenberger and Fronzaglio, 1991). Moreover, the various AAMR definitions adopted since that of Heber (1961) reflect modest, but not insignificant, variations of that original definition, which read: "MR refers to subaverage general intellectual functioning which originates during the developmental period and is associated with impairment in adaptive behavior" (Heber, 1961:3). In subsequent revisions of the AAMR definition (Grossman, 1973, 1977, 1983; Luckasson, 1992), the importance of adaptive behavior vis-à-vis intelligence was enhanced, and the cutoff score on tests of intelligence defining "subaverage general functioning" has also varied.

Intellectual Dimension

Under Heber (1961), the criterion for subaverage general intellectual functioning was –1 SD (approximately IQ 85); however it was dropped to –2 SDs by Grossman (1973) (approximately IQ 70). Later, guidelines for employing IQ cutoff scores were adjusted, permitting identification of children with IQ scores up to 75, a change explained as follows: "This particularly applies in schools and similar settings if behavior is impaired and clinically determined to be due to deficits in reasoning and judgment" (Grossman, 1983:11). The most recent AAMR definition (Luckasson, 1992) has continued with "a version" of the IQ 75 upper limit: "a score of approximately 70 or 75 or below" (p. 14). This imprecision has been criticized (MacMillan et al., 1993, 1995) on the basis of the proportion of cases falling between IQ 70 and 75 (even ignoring the standard error of measurement). MacMillan and Reschly (1996) argue that while setting the upper cutoff score is arbitrary, the imprecision reflected in the Luckasson guidelines reflects a lack of awareness of psychometrics. Table 7-1 shows the consequences of these subtle shifts in IQ scores for the proportion of children eligible on the intellectual dimension defining MR alone. Very slight shifts in cutoff scores have rather dramatic consequences in terms of the percentage of the general population eligible. The proportion eligible using IQ 70 and below is only half as large as the proportion eligible using a criterion of IQ 75 and below.

The application of more or less stringent cutoff scores clearly influences the degree of overrepresentation of disadvantaged minority children in the MR category. The degree of overrepresentation would be expected to be larger when higher, rather than lower, IQ cutoff scores are employed due to the nature of the distributions of intellectual performance. Reschly and Jipson (1976) studied the effects of different IQ cutoff scores (IQ 70 and IQ 75) on the potential overrepresentation of black, Hispanic, and American Indian children. Greater overrepresentation occurred at IQ 75 and below than at IQ 70 and below. Moreover, the fact that tests of intelligence yield

TABLE 7-1 Proportion of the Population Falling Below Certain IQ Cutoffs and Falling Within Certain IQ Intervals

IQ	Normal Curve Percentage
Below 70	2.28
70 and below	2.68
Below 75	4.75
75 and below	5.48

IQ Interval	Percentage Within Interval
56-60	0.30
61-65	0.69
66-70	1.52
71-75	2.80

different distributions for different groups results in higher risk of being identified as MR for those groups whose distributions yield a lower mean score. For example, Kaufman and Doppelt (1976) examined the standardization data for the WISC-R and reported for white subjects a mean IQ of 102.26 (SD = 14.04) and a mean IQ of 86.43 (SD = 12.70) for black subjects in the standardization sample. Clearly, on the IQ-test dimension alone, a higher percentage of black students are at risk for being classified as MR.

In addition to the influence of the cutoff score adopted to define general intellectual functioning, the type of intellectual measure also influences the rate of eligibility for certain racial/ethnic groups. The *Diana* (1970) and *Guadalupe* (1972) consent decrees were directed at reducing the overrepresentation of American Indian and Hispanic students in special education programs for students with MMR. Both consent decrees required adoption of non-English language or performance IQ measures in future evaluations of American Indian and Hispanic students. In the Reschly and Jipson (1976) study, the prevalence rates for Hispanic and Native American children were considerably higher if one used verbal IQ scores to define aptitude. When the nonverbal (i.e., performance IQ) measure was used, the overrepresentation of Hispanic and Native American children was virtually eliminated; however, the overrepresentation of black children was about the same regardless of the type of intellectual measure. MacMillan et al. (1998b) contrasted eligibility decisions that would be reached for a referred sample of children, stratified on the basis of ethnic group (i.e., white, black, Hispanic) using psychometric criteria. Referred Hispanic students scored on average 8 points higher on performance IQ than on verbal IQ using the WISC-III, which was not found for either white or black samples of referred students. The eligibility decisions based exclusively on psychometric data (i.e., no clinical or other evidence considered) were then contrasted using full-scale IQ (FSIQ) or performance IQ (PIQ), (Table 7-2). Consistent with the Reschly and Jipson (1976) findings, use of PIQ dramatically alters the percent of Hispanic students scoring below the IQ cutoff that defines MR. Using PIQ as the estimate of aptitude, 11 fewer Hispanic students scored 75 or below than did so on the FSIQ. Only one Hispanic child qualified as MR on the PIQ who did not qualify on the FSIQ. To a lesser degree PIQ also reduced the number of black students by four who qualified as MR in comparison to the number qualifying when FSIQ was used. For white students, however, a slightly different pattern emerged. Use of PIQ instead of FSIQ resulted in three children moving out of the MR classification, while four additional students who did not qualify as MR using FSIQ did qualify using PIQ as the estimate of aptitude. Clearly, the use of PIQ would reduce the percentage of black and Hispanic students referred to special education who would qualify as MMR.

TABLE 7-2 Comparison of Classification as MR, LD, and Ineligible Using FSIQ and PIQ to Estimate Aptitude by Ethnic Group

FSIQ Classification	PIQ Classification			TOTAL	Kappa
	MR	Ineligible	LD		
White					
MR	7	1	2	10	
Ineligible	3	15	6	24	
LD	1	0	20	21	
Total	11	16	28	55	0.63
Black					
MR	10	4	0	14	
Ineligible	0	16	2	18	
LD	0	0	10	10	
Total	10	20	12	42	0.78
Hispanic					
MR	7	7	5	19	
Ineligible	1	6	11	18	
LD	0	1	15	16	
Total	8	14	31	53	0.31

There is somewhat of a paradox in this classification exercise. While the use of performance IQ as the estimate of aptitude reduced the number of Hispanic students qualifying as MMR by 11, it also resulted in increasing the number of Hispanic students qualifying as LD by a total of 16. By optimizing the aptitude estimate while the measure of achievement remained constant, the total number of LD cases for Hispanics more than offset the reduction in the number of children who moved out of the MR classification.

The construct of intelligence has historically been fundamental to defining MR. As discussed elsewhere in this report, tests of intelligence have very limited curricular validity and, when routinely administered to establish the eligibility of students as MR or LD, add considerably to the cost of assessment. Nevertheless, in the context of MR, "subaverage general intelligence" is a defining feature of the disability and using measures other than tests of intelligence or resistance to treatment as criteria for eligibility raises some perplexing possibilities. For students who are referred for psychoeducational assessment, the charge is to identify those cases whose "failure to thrive" in the best clinical judgment of the individual education program (IEP) committee is "due to low general intelligence" as opposed to competing hypotheses, such as a specific processing problem (i.e., LD) or emotional or behavioral problems that are so severe that they interfere with adaptation or academic achievement (i.e., emotional disturbance). Making that differential diagnosis without using tests of intelligence raises a host of issues. We turn now to the second behavioral dimension defining MR, adaptive behavior.

Adaptive Behavior Dimension

The second behavioral dimension defining MR, impairments in adaptive behavior or adaptive skills, presents more serious psychometric problems to those conducting the assessment, particularly when applied to those with MMR. Even when the Heber definition was dominant, which would permit approximately 16 percent of the general population having IQ scores of 85 or below to be classified as MR, no more than 1 percent of the general population was identified as MR (Mercer, 1973a, b; Tarjan et al., 1973). The reason for the discrepancy was that the schools and other clinicians never used IQ alone to define MR; two dimensions were always considered in making a diagnosis (impairments in adaptive behavior *and* subaverage general intellectual functioning). In fact, these two criteria were applied sequentially: (a) impairments in adaptation and *then* (b) subaverage general intellectual functioning. Only children referred by their classroom teachers were ever evaluated on the intellectual dimension. A huge percentage of those who would have scored below IQ 85 were never referred, and even among those who were, only a small percentage were ever certified as eligible for services. In fact, some of those referred were *protected* from certification as a result of the psychoeducational assessment provided.

Ashurst and Meyers (1973) also examined data from the Riverside study reported by Mercer (1973a). They examined 269 cases of children referred for severe and persistent academic underachievement. Of interest to the current discussion is how referred cases were deemed eligible or ineligible by school psychologists and then how admissions and dismissal committees arrived at decisions in light of: (a) teacher referral data, and (b) psychologist certification that the child was eligible or ineligible. Five different results were identified and the number of cases fitting a given "result" noted:

1. Teacher referred, psychologist found child eligible, child placed as MMR (86 children).
2. Teacher referred, psychologist found child eligible, child not placed (63 children).
3. Teacher referred, psychologist found child ineligible, child not placed (116 children).

4. Teacher referred for reason other than academic problems, psychologist found child eligible as MMR, child placed (1 child).

5. Teacher referred for reason other than academic problems, psychologist found child eligible as MMR, child not placed (3 children).

Of 269 children referred by teachers, only 87 (32 percent) were actually placed. In 116 cases (43 percent), the IQ score secured by the psychologist actually prevented certification, being above the cutoff score for MR. Finally, in 63 cases (23 percent) of all referred children, the child was not placed *despite having an IQ score permitting eligibility.* Of the 153 referred children with IQ scores permitting placement in programs for MMR, less than three-fifths were actually placed (57 percent). Clearly, IQ alone did not preordain placement as MR. These data were collected in the early 1960s, when the more inclusive Heber definition was in effect in the California education code. To quote Mercer (1973b): "Clinicians are apparently assessing more than IQ test scores in making diagnoses" (p. 15). Something akin to adaptive behavior enters into the placement formula as well as numerous contextual factors including, but not limited to, parental opposition, perceived competence of the special education teacher, issues of second language acquisition, and the like.

The inclusion of adaptive behavior as a dimension defining MR has been controversial since introduced by Heber (see Clausen, 1967, 1968, 1972; Zigler et al., 1984; Zigler and Hodapp, 1986) due to the subjectivity (i.e., unreliability) it introduces into the diagnostic process. These concerns are particularly salient to the segment of children considered MMR, the category in which overrepresentation is most prominent, because the domains measured by extant scales do not tap the behaviors that prompt referral of cases of MMR. Instead, a ceiling effect is noted. Paradoxically, the segment of children for whom diagnosis is most difficult is the same segment for which the existing scales are least appropriate.

State definitions of MR continue to use the Grossman (1983) definition as a model, opting not to adopt the more current AAMR version (Luckasson, 1992). Denning et al. (2000) summarized existing state definitions and classification practices, reporting that 44 states use the Grossman definition while three used the Luckasson definition. Only one state (Massachusetts) reported that consideration of adaptive behavior was *not* required in diagnosing MR. However, only 14 states actually listed specific practices that needed to be considered for eligibility. This is consistent with an earlier survey by Frankenberger and Fronzaglio (1991:318), who reported:

> Even though states appear to be moving toward agreement on IQ cutoffs, there is little agreement in the states' methods of identifying deficits in adaptive behavior and academic achievement. In the current study, only 7 states delineated cutoff scores indicative of deficits in adaptive behavior.

In fact, clinical judgment has usually been employed to supplement the information on the severe and chronic achievement problems that prompted the referral in arriving at the conclusion that adaptive behavior is impaired. Garber (1988) described the situation as follows: "Definition may require that both intellectual and adaptive skill levels be ascertained . . . . It is the low IQ scores that cause the label of mental retardation to be applied" (p. 10). Reschly (1992) observed that prior to about 1980, for school-age children and youth who accounted for the majority of detected cases of MR, "low achievement as assessed by standardized measures of achievement along with referral for academic difficulties was sufficient to constitute a deficit in adaptive behavior" (p. 33). Over the past two decades, considerable effort has been devoted to the more precise measurement of adaptive behavior in multiple contexts (Harrison and Robinson, 1995).

Disagreements over the key domains have complicated the use of adaptive behavior in decisions about MR eligibility in schools, as has uncertainty about appropriate cutoff scores to define a deficit in adaptive behavior. Adaptive behavior measures differ in underlying conceptions of adaptive behavior (e.g., the degree to which learning and achievement are important dimensions for children and youth), methods of obtaining information (e.g., third-party respondent vs. direct observation), the key contexts (e.g., home, school, neighborhood), and appropriate respondent (e.g., parent, teacher, peers, or the child himself or herself). A most vexing but enormously important issue is the selection of a cutoff score to define a deficit in adaptive behavior. The modern MR definitions refer to a deficit in adaptive behavior or deficits in adaptive skills. They include the modifier, "significantly subaverage" that is the basis for the IQ of approximately 70 to 75 on the intellectual functioning dimension. There is no modifying wording applied to adaptive behavior that provides the basis for a specific, required cutoff score for adaptive behavior. Consistent with these definitions, the deficit might be more appropriately defined through clinical judgment or a criterion such as 1 SD below the mean rather than the 2 SD criterion applied to the intellectual dimension.

The issues concerning adaptive behavior measurement are more than sterile academic debates. Research in the 1980s showed that MR was essentially eliminated if the adaptive behavior measure focused on nonschool settings, eliminated practical cognitive skills, and used parents as the sole respondents (Heflinger et al., 1987; Kazimour and Reschly, 1981). Recently developed adaptive behavior instruments generally suggest a more moderate view, in which the adaptive behavior cutoff score is somewhat flexible and decisions about the existence of deficits are based on consideration of performance over several domains (Harrison and Oakland, 2000). The evidence to date clearly supports the conclusion that the measurement of adaptive behavior is not as well developed as the measurement of general intellectual functioning.

Changes in the MMR Construct

There is an extensive literature documenting the changes that have occurred in the population of children served by the public schools as MR. It was commonly stated in the 1970s that 75-80 percent of all individuals with MR were at the mild level (IQ 55-70 to 75) who did not display physical or other identifiable signs of biological anomaly. Such statements persisted even later (e.g., Grossman and Tarjan, 1987). However, criticisms and legal challenges to the process whereby children were classified as MMR coupled with the changes brought about with the enactment of EHA/IDEA were successful in reducing the number of schoolchildren classified as MMR—largely because of the reluctance on the part of schools to use the MR classification for students in the mild range (MacMillan et al., 1996c). While MR was the disability category accounting for the largest number of children served in special education when President Ford signed EHA into law in 1975, by 1993-1994 there had been a 38 percent decline (a reduction of over 335,000 children) in the number of students so served. In the 1996-1997 school year, the percent of schoolchildren classified as MR was 1.16 percent. During the same period, the number of children served as learning disabled increased by 207 percent (an increase of over 1.5 million children).

Since 1970 the borderline MR subgroup (those with IQ scores between 70 or 75 and 85) has been excluded from the MR category. Moreover, in many states there is reluctance to classify able-bodied students as MR, with the result that the MR population in 2000 in comparison to that of 1970 is more patently disabled. During the 1980s, a number of investigators noted the "change" in the MMR population. For example, MacMillan and Borthwick (1980) described the MMR population as including many children who prior to that time would have been served in programs for students with moderate levels of MR (IQ 40 to 55) (e.g., children with Down syndrome). Epstein et al. (1989) questioned whether the cultural-familial subgroup of MR children, as traditionally defined, is to be found today in MMR classes. Their survey found that 90 percent of the post-EHA/IDEA MMR students they studied needed speech and language assistance and multiple handicaps were frequently evident (convulsive disorders, serious levels of visual impairments, history of significant behavior disorders). Polloway et al. (1986) noted that the younger MMR students "were identified virtually at the initiation of their school careers" (p. 7), a situation that differs markedly from that described by Mercer (1973a, b) earlier, when initial enrollment was in general education and referral came only after failure to keep up academically for three or more years. As Gottlieb (1981) noted, "the category of mild MR appears reserved for the lower end of the mild MR range usually for children having an IQ of about 65 or lower" (p. 124).

The assessment of children who are ultimately classified as MR has changed dramatically since the period addressed in the previous National Research Council report (1982). Increasingly, a greater percentage of the children come to school already classified by the medical profession, rendering the issue of IQ moot. As MacMillan et al. (1996c) found, most children referred and given psychoeducational assessments and who score below IQ 75 are currently classified in many schools as LD, not MR. The discrepancy between who qualifies as MR according to specified criteria and who is administratively labeled MR by the schools is considerable. This explains, in part, the decline in the number of children identified in school as MR—a phenomenon that is on the way to rendering MR a low-incidence disability.

EMOTIONAL DISTURBANCE

In 1997, 446,835 students between ages 6 and 21 were receiving services under the category of emotional disturbance (ED). Although the theoretical prevalence estimates for students with ED range from 3 to 6 percent of the student population (Brandenberg et al., 1990; Forness et al., 1983; Skiba et al., 1994), enrollment statistics indicate that approximately 1 percent of the school-age population is certified with ED as a primary disability (Forness, 1992b; see Chapter 2). Furthermore, there is substantial variability in ED prevalence rates from state to state, with estimates ranging from 6 per 10,000 in Mississippi to 2 per 100 in Minnesota (see Table 6-1).

The risk of ED classification for black students is 1.56 percent, a rate that is approximately 1.6 times the white rate of approximately 1.0 percent. The ED classification risk is the same for white and American Indian/ Alaskan Native students. The white risk is approximately 1.4 times the Hispanic rate and 3.6 times the Asian/Pacific Islander rate. The ED risk, like the MR risk, is highest for black students, nearly equal for white and American Indian/Alaskan Native students, slightly lower for Hispanic students, and markedly lower for Asian/Pacific Islander students.

These findings—underidentification of children and youth with emotional disturbances and overrepresentation of black students in the ED category—suggest that relatively few students with behavior problems are being served under the ED category and that the procedures currently employed for identifying and screening students for possible inclusion in this category require examination. Moreover, the lack of definitional clarity and reactive school practices in addressing emotional and behavioral disorders may, in part, contribute to the varying ED prevalence rates and overrepresentation of black students.

Definitional Dilemma:
Perspectives on Emotional and Behavioral Disorders

There are three main perspectives on emotional and behavioral disorders: clinical, empirical, and educational (Hallahan and Kauffman, 1997; Kauffman, 1997). Childhood behavior disorders have been most often conceptualized from a clinical, medical-model perspective. The *Diagnostic and Statistical Manual of Mental Disorders 4th ed.* (DSM IV; American Psychiatric Association, 1994) has used professional judgment to identify and assign psychiatric diagnoses such as oppositional defiant disorder (ODD), conduct disorder (CD), and antisocial personality disorders (APD). Some researchers contend that there may be a developmental progression from less severe disorders (e.g., ODD) to more severe disorders (e.g., CD) noting that prevalence rates of these disorders decrease as the severity of the disorder increases (Frick et al., 1992; Frick, 1998; Lahey and Loeber, 1994). Yet this clinical classification system suffers from problems of reliability and validity due to the heavy reliance on professional judgment (Gresham, 1985).

Empirical approaches to behavior disorders, in contrast, employ factor analytic procedures for identifying behavior patterns and thereby afford improved reliability and validity relative to clinical classification systems. Examples of such tools include Achenbach's (1991) Child Behavior Checklist, Quay and Peterson's (1983) Revised Behavior Problem Checklist, and Gresham and Elliott's (1990) Social Skills Rating System. These instruments can be used to identify broad-band (e.g., externalzing and internalizing behaviors) and narrow-band syndromes (e.g., aggressive, delinquent behaviors vs. withdrawn, immature behaviors). One dilemma with the use of empirical classification schemes, however, is how to interpret reliable data in which multiple informant perspectives (e.g., parents, teachers) do not converge.

The final perspective is that of education. The federal definition of ED first came into being as part of the Education of the Handicapped Act in 1975 and has not changed substantially in the past 25 years. Congress constructed the federal definition of ED from a study conducted by Eli Bower that identified the following five dimensions of maladaptive behavior as characteristics of ED (Bower, 1960):

a. inability to learn that cannot be explained by intellectual, sensory, or health factors;

b. inability to build or maintain satisfactory relationships with peers or teachers;

c. inappropriate types of behavior or feelings under normal circumstances;

d. general pervasive mood of unhappiness or depression; and

e. tendency to develop physical symptoms or fears associated with school problems.

In essence, the federal definition requires at least one of Bower's five characteristics to adversely affect a student's academic performance across "a long period of time" and to a "marked degree" (Individuals with Disabilities Education Act, 1997).

Furthermore, the federal definition requires states to exclude students labeled socially maladjusted (SM) from special education eligibility. To date, the five characteristics in the definition of ED lack specificity and represent a variety of behavioral and emotional disorders with different etiologies and implications for interventions. Likewise, the distinction between students who are emotionally disturbed and those who are socially maladjusted is not operationally defined or empirically validated by federal legislatures, educators, or research (Center, 1990; Forness and Knitzer, 1992; Webber, 1992), although some professionals equate social maladjustment, an education term, with conduct disorder, a clinical term (see Forness, 1992a). Moreover, the exclusion of students labeled socially maladjusted appears unwarranted given the similarity between students labeled ED and SM across behavior, social competence, academic, and contextual factors (Council for Children with Behavioral Disorders, 1987; Forness 1992b; Skiba and Grizzle, 1991; Walker et al., 2000).

Finally, the federal definition of ED does not consider important behavioral differences associated with gender, ethnicity, developmental level, or contextual factors in defining and assessing each of these characteristics. Research by Forness (1992b) suggests that the allocation of services to students with conduct problems largely depends on the presence of comorbidity with other disorders (e.g., depression or attention deficit hyperactivity disorder). Findings also indicate that it is not until a specific learning disability is diagnosed that students with conduct problems become eligible for special education services.

Thus, the lack of consistent terminology across clinical, empirical, and education perspectives is problematic. First, lack of definitional uniformity hinders effective communication between professions in the clinical, research, and school settings. This is particularly troublesome given that many of today's students who have or are at risk for behavior disorders are likely to require services from the educational and mental health systems (Walker et al., 1999). Second, without a clear, reliable definition, design and implementation of identification, assessment, and intervention procedures are at best challenging. From inspection of the prevalence rates for CD (3-6 percent of the school-age population) and ED (less than 1 percent of the school-age population) it is clear that many students who exhibit problem behaviors will not ultimately receive special education services under the label of ED. While some students with specific psychiatric problems (e.g., depression) may require only mental health services and many not necessarily benefit from special education services under the ED label, other students with conduct problems may be going unidentified (false negatives) for ED.

Accordingly, Forness and Knitzer (1992) called for a new, broader definition: emotional and behavioral disorder (E/DB), a term that has been largely adopted by the research community. This new term, posed initially by the National Mental Heath and Special Education coalition, is defined as follows (Forness and Knitzer, 1992:13):

(i) The term emotional and behavioral disorder means a disability characterized by behavioral or emotional responses in school so different from appropriate age, cultural, or ethnic norms that they adversely affect educational performance. Educational performance includes academic, social, vocational, and personal skills. Such a disability:

(A) is more than a temporary, expected response to stressful events in the environment;

(B) is consistently exhibited in two different settings, at least one of which is school related; and

(C) is unresponsive to direct intervention in general education, or the child's condition is such that general education interventions would be insufficient.

(ii) Emotional and behavioral disorders can co-exist with other disabilities.

(iii) This category may include children or youths with schizophrenic disorders, affective disorders, anxiety disorder, or other sustained disorders of conduct or adjustment when they adversely affect educational performance in accordance with section (i).

The benefits of this new definition include (a) addressing disorders of emotion and behavior while recognizing that they may co-occur or occur independently, (b) establishing a school-based definition that acknowledges that disorders demonstrated beyond the school day are also relevant, (c) sensitivity to ethnic and cultural differences, (d) acknowledging the importance of prereferral interventions, (e) recognizing that disabilities can co-occur, and (d) eliminating arbitrary exlusions (Hallahan and Kauffman, 1997; Webber and Scheuermann, 1997). Unfortunately, the legal definition guiding eligibility and service delivery is still that of emotional disturbance.

Students' Characteristics

Students with ED, by definition, are characterized by behavioral and academic problems that negatively influence school-, teacher-, and peer-related adjustment (Hersh and Walker, 1983; Walker et al., 1995). The ED label addresses both externalizing (e.g., aggression, delinquency) and internalizing (anxiety, depression, withdrawal) behaviors (Achenbach, 1991). Externalizing behavior, which is characteristic of the majority of students served under the ED label, tends to be more stable over time, less amenable to intervention and therefore faces a worse prognosis for remediation relative to internalizing behavior (Gresham et al., 1999; Hinshaw, 1992a, b). Students with externalizing behavior patterns also tend to function at a lower level in social, cognitive, and academic arenas and are more likely to attract teacher attention in comparison to students with internalizing behaviors (Dodge, 1993; McConaughy and Skiba, 1993). It is important to note that, in addition to the aggressive, coercive behavior patterns typical of these students, students with ED are also characterized by acquisition and performance deficits in academic areas as well as low rates of time academically engaged (Coie and Jacobs, 1993).

Evidence suggests that the coexistence of learning and problem behaviors is evident during the preschool years and is predictive of a wide range of pejorative outcomes, which include academic underachievement, truancy, school dropout, motor vehicle accidents, unemployment, substance abuse, criminality, and welfare receipt (Walker et al., 1995; Walker and Severson, 2001). To prevent these deleterious outcomes, early intervention is essential and has been the focus of recent efforts in the research community (Conduct Problems Prevention Research Group, 1999a, b). In order to serve these students more effectively, intervention needs to occur early in a child's schooling when he or she is less resistant to intervention efforts (Kazdin, 1987; Walker and Severson, 2001) and when less intensive interventions are more likely to produce the desired changes in a student's behavioral and academic performance (Lane, 1999).

Yet the focus of intervention efforts has not been empirically validated. Three hypothetical models have described the relationship between externalizing behavior patterns and academic underachievement (Hinshaw, 1992a, b; Lane, 1999; Lane et al., 2001a). The first model suggests that academic underachievement leads to externalizing behavior. Students who lack the skills or motivation to participate in the requisite instructional tasks may act out to escape the task demand. The second model hypothesizes that externalizing behavior problems lead to academic underachievement. According to this model, students who engage in disruptive classroom behaviors do not benefit from participation in essential instructional activities. Over time, this lack of participation may lead to academic underachievement. The final model poses a transactional relationship between these two domains. These models have direct implications for intervention. If the first model is accurate, intervention efforts should target increased academic achievement. If the second model is correct, intervention should focus on decreasing problem behaviors. If the transaction model is accurate, then intervention would need to focus on both domains.

Although the relationship between externalizing behavior patterns and academic underachievement has been explored for more than a quarter of a century (Berger et al., 1975; Hinshaw 1992a, b; Richards et al., 1995; Rutter and Yule, 1970), only a handful of treatment-outcome studies have been conducted to examine the validity of these hypothetical causal models (Ayllon et al., 1975; Ayllon and Roberts, 1974; Coie and Krehbiel, 1984; Lane, 1999; Lane and Wehby, in press). Although few in number, intervention studies conducted to date provide preliminary support for the first causal model: academic underachievement leads to externalizing behaviors (Ayllon et al., 1975; Ayllon and Roberts, 1974; Coie and Krehbiel, 1984; Lane and Wehby, in press). In the studies mentioned, when students experienced academic improvement in either acquisition or performance deficits (Frentz et al., 1991), collateral improvement on behaviors was observed. However, these findings must be interpreted with extreme caution given that interventions have not been conducted systematically across students of varying ages. Clearly, additional treatment outcome research is warranted.

Educating Students with Emotional Disturbances

Schools are challenged by the task of identifying, assessing, and educating students with ED; several interrelated issues collectively influence educational outcomes negatively (Lane, 1999). These issues, or challenges, exist at federal, state, and local levels (Council for Children with Behavioral Disorders, 1990; Lane, 1999; Maag and Howell, 1992; McIntyre, 1993) and include reactive school practices in identification, resistance to intervention, current educational practices, and current screening and assessment practices.

Reactive School Practices in Identification

Due to a lack of definitional clarity and reactive approaches to addressing problem behaviors, students who begin school with behavior problems typically do not receive services until such time as a disability is diagnosed or significant academic underachievement is apparent (Forness, 1992b). Studies indicate that teacher referral for special education frequently occurs in the early primary grades, but the time delay between first documentation of a problem and first placement for ED services may be five years or more (Duncan et al., 1995, Nishioka, 2001) much like the wait-to-fail model utilized to identify students with LD (Fletcher et al., 1998). Forness and colleagues (1983) suggest that a trimorbidity of social maladjustment, emotional or behavior disorders, and a learning disability appears to be the only way to obtain a label of ED. Until the diagnosis of ED is made, schools often rely on punitive procedures (e.g., office referral, in- and out-of-school suspensions) to control the behavior of these students. Unfortunately, most research would suggest that these tactics are ineffectual in meeting the needs of students with ED (Lewis and Daniels, 2000).

This population becomes increasingly resistant to intervention efforts over time (Kazdin, 1987, 1993; Walker and McConnell, 1995). If comprehensive interventions are implemented prior to 3rd grade, it is possible to prevent the development of antisocial behavior, the cornerstone of conduct disorder. However, after approximately 8 years of age, the behavior patterns are relatively stable and intervention efforts move from prevention to remediation (Bullis and Walker, 1994; Kazdin, 1987). Furthermore, interventions implemented after 3rd grade require greater intensity and would be more ideographic in nature—as in functional assessment-based interventions—relative to those interventions implemented earlier in a child's educational career. While functional assessment-based interventions have been quite successful with students with behavior disorders (Lane et al., 1999), these interventions are often time- and labor-intensive, a fact that necessarily limits the number of students who can receive them (Lane, 1999). Accordingly, proactive efforts, such as early detection and early intervention, are essential in order to better serve these students.

Current Educational Practices

Current educational practices for students with ED have been sharply criticized (Knitzer et al., 1990; Steinberg and Knitzer, 1992) for creating barriers that impede effective educational programming. In particular, barriers pertaining to curricular content, classroom management practices, and services delivery (Peacock Hill Working Group, 1991; Webber and Scheuermann, 1997) have been cited as problematic.

Curricular content. The primary concerns regarding curricular content of ED classrooms range from not addressing both academic and sociobehavioral domains to an overall lack of systematic programming (Wehby et al., 1998). Kauffman (1997) contends that instruction in irrelevant, nonfunctional skills actually contributes to the development of emotional and behavioral problems. And some researchers voice concern about an absence of a strong academic focus in ED classrooms (Lane and Wehby, in press), whereas others contend that the curricular content too closely parallels general education curriculum, with little attention afforded to the students' emotional needs (Webber and Scheuermann, 1997). One possible explanation for this lack of attention to students' emotional needs is the decline in availability of mental health and school-based counseling (Knitzer et al., 1990).

Another concern in the area of service delivery is the tendency to implement ED curriculum and programs that have not been empirically validated. Program and material selection does not seem to be guided by data-driven outcomes (Peacock Hill Working Group, 1991). Instead, it would appear that programs and procedures that produce short-term behavioral changes are sought to address immediate rather than long-term needs (Webber and Scheuermann, 1997). To compound the problem even further, there is a shortage of certified teachers to work with ED students (Wald, 1996). Thus, untrained teachers are left to educate very difficult-to-teach students (Rockwell, 1993). When ED students employ the coercive tactics learned at home (albeit unintentionally) in the school setting with teachers who are ill prepared to manage such behavior patterns (Reid and Patterson, 1989), the result is an aversive series of student-teacher interactions that lead to classroom environments with low rates of praise delivery, positive student recognition, and instruction (Shores et al., 1993; Webber and Scheuermann, 1997; Wehby et al., 1998). Consequently, ED programs often feature a curriculum that is neither empirically validated sufficiently nor comprehensive enough to address the students' academic and socio-behavioral needs—and, to compound the difficulties further, it is implemented by educators without the proper training.

Classroom management practices. Classroom management practices have been widely criticized for what is referred to as a "curriculum of control" (Knitzer et al., 1990; Zable, 1992). A study conducted by Zable (1992) suggests that this emphasis on control has stemmed from administrative pressure, a mandate to emulate general education curricula, and a lack of options. It would appear that little emphasis is placed on identifying the function of the maladaptive behavior and then teaching appropriate replacement behaviors that meet the same functional need (Mace, 1994). Proactive procedures such as precorrection plans (Walker and McConnell, 1995) and rich praise delivery schedules (Wehby et al., 1998) are not being employed to enhance classroom instruction or to prevent behavior problems from occurring during instruction.

Screening and Assessment Practices

The field of behavior disorders has been influenced by the recent shootings that have occurred in schools across the nation (Walker et al., 1999). This tragic series of events has highlighted the need for proactive approaches to identify and assess troubled youth who may be at risk for committing such atrocities. At first glance, screening and early detection appear to be rather simplistic; however, most emotional and behavioral disorders of childhood are not so extreme that they are easily detected by the untrained observer (Kauffman, 1997; Webber and Scheuermann, 1997). However, the field of emotional and behavioral disorders has made substantial progress over the past 20 years, particularly in the area of early detection and intervention.

Researchers have established the importance of utilizing school-wide screenings to detect students at risk for ED, employing a variety of assessment tools and procedures based on the principle of multioperationalism, and designing and implementing comprehensive interventions that are linked to assessment results (Gresham, 1985; Gresham et al., 2000; Lane, 1999; Walker and McConnell, 1995). Programs and instruments such as the Systematic Screening for Behavior Disorders (Walker and Severson, 1992) and the Student Risk Screening Scale (Drummond, 1994) are now available for use in schools to identify students who may be at risk for emotional and behavioral disturbances.

Over the past 10 years there has been a tremendous increase in the availability of assessment instruments and practices to assess the various domains of emotional and behavior disorders. Some of the more recent advances in assessment include: (a) the use of conditional probabilities methodology (Milich et al., 1987; Pelham et al., 1992); (b) functional assessment methodologies (Horner, 1994; Umbreit, 1995); (c) the notion of resistance to intervention (Gresham, 1991, 2001); (d) direct observation systems, such as the Multiple Option Observation System for Experimental Studies (Tapp et al., 1995); (e) the School Archival Records Search (Walker et al., 1991); (f) curriculum-based assessment (Shinn, 1989); and (g) psychometrically sound rating scales, such as the Child Behavior Checklist (Achenbach and Edelbrock, 1991) and the Social Skills Rating System (Gresham and Elliott, 1990), which can be completed by multiple informants (e.g., parents, teachers, and, in some instances, students).

Federal regulations mandate that assessments be conducted by a multidisciplinary team of qualified specialists, given that the assessment results will not only influence eligibility and placement decisions, but also will help guide instructional programming. However, theory and practice do not always converge. Too often the teams have not embraced the advances in screening and assessment and therefore they do not function as intended.

Diagnostic, placement, and curricular decisions are frequently made based on limited, rather subjective information (Kauffman, 1997).

DISABILITY ASSESSMENT PRACTICES

Current assessment practices related to the determination of eligibility for disabilities are heavily influenced by legal requirements, as noted in Chapter 6. These requirements determine the kind of assessment that must be provided to all students considered for special education, including LD, MR, and ED. Compliance with these legal requirements is prompted by professional ethics and federal and state compliance monitoring activities, which typically focus on sample cases of students placed in special education. During these monitoring activities, careful scrutiny of the assessment practices and the domains of behavior examined establishes strong incentives for school district personnel to follow general assessment requirements and specific disability classification criteria, although at least some studies suggest that the criteria are applied loosely, especially in the determination of LD.

The typical assessment battery for nearly all students with disabilities includes the administration of a comprehensive, individually administered test of current intellectual functioning (IQ test), an individually administered general achievement test, classroom observation of student behavior, and one or more behavioral checklists or rating scales typically completed by the teacher or parent. In some regions, various tests of underlying processes are utilized (e.g., visual-motor, auditory processing). This battery is used with virtually all students with disabilities. The only exceptions occur with students with severe or marked sensory disabilities, which may render psychological and educational assessment impossible. Medical specialists typically diagnose students with severe disabilities of these kinds, and special education eligibility determination is not the primary focus of the evaluation.

The relative emphasis placed on the domains above—that is, current intellectual function, achievement, and behavior ratings—depends on the disability that is being considered by the multidisciplinary team. For students considered for the diagnosis of LD, there typically is in-depth consideration of achievement in one or more of the domains identified as problematic in the referral. For example, for a student referred due to low reading achievement, administration of several reading tests and additional formal and informal assessments of reading skills are likely in order to establish more precisely the degree and nature of the reading difficulty. Depending on state classification criteria and local practices, students considered for LD may also receive one or more tests of underlying psychological processes. Currently, measures of phonological processes are nearly always part of an LD evaluation if the referral involves reading concerns. The intellectual ability/achievement discrepancy, in current practice, is the most fundamental part of the LD eligibility determination in most states, virtually necessitating the administration of individual IQ and achievement tests.

Determination of eligibility in the category of MR is similar to that for the LD category in that tests of current intellectual functioning and achievement are nearly always involved. The MR diagnostic construct, as noted earlier, involves the dimensions of current intellectual functioning and adaptive behavior. Intellectual functioning is almost always assessed through the administration of individual IQ tests. The adaptive behavior domain, when it can be assessed formally, typically involves the results of one or more inventories in which the teacher, parent, or both serve as reporters on the child's adaptive functioning. A general achievement test is almost always used with MR, as are other measures such as teacher- or parent-completed rating scales or checklists. However, the fundamental feature of MR eligibility determination is the IQ score, with confirming or supportive evidence from formal and informal measures of adaptive behavior.

The assessment procedures for ED have the same general characteristics as those for MR and LD. An individually administered IQ test and one or more standardized achievement tests almost always are included in the evaluation for ED eligibility. In addition, the ED evaluation should, and sometimes does, emphasize measures of behaviors across different social contexts, as well as assessment of social skills—including peer relations and interactions with significant adults. Formal rating scales that focus on key behavioral dimensions, such as aggression, attention, hyperactivity, and depression, are nearly always used along with direct observations in relevant settings and interviews with the student, the teacher, and the parents.

Depending on the region, students considered for the category of ED may or may not receive projective instruments, such as Rorschach, human figure drawings, and incomplete sentence techniques. Use of highly subjective projective approaches with dubious technical characteristics is more common in the states on the East and West coasts of the United States (Hosp and Reschly, 2002a). Although IQ and achievement tests are typically used with an ED assessment, the fundamental eligibility determination rests typically on reviews of behavioral incidents, social skills measures, and behavior/personality ratings completed by various respondents, who may include teachers, parents, and the student.

GIFTED AND TALENTED

Because eligibility to receive services as a gifted or talented student is not regulated by federal statutes, the process is usually guided by state-level policies that range from law, to rule, to guidelines, to administrative code. In some states, identification of gifted students is not mandated at all. And existing policies on identification stem from widely varying definitions of giftedness and include widely disparate requirements. In some states, local school districts are not required to use the state definition or state guidelines and recommended identification processes. This results in widely different proportions of identified students. In the report of the Council of State Directors of Gifted Education (1999), the percentage of total students identified in those states reporting this statistic ranged from 0.22 percent in Nevada to 22.9 percent in Maryland.[1] In Massachusetts only 14 percent of local education agencies identify gifted students.

The age at which identification of gifted students begins is also determined at the state level. At least two states report that identification begins as early as pre-K (Council of State Directors of Programs for the Gifted, 1999) while 16 states simply recommend prekindergarten screening (Coleman and Gallagher, 1992). In some states, policies do not mandate identification until grade 4, and in some states the onset of the process is left to local discretion (Council of State Directors of Programs for the Gifted, 1999). The later the identification and screening process occurs, the less likely a student from a minority or low-income population is to be identified using criteria that rely heavily on academic achievement on standardized assessments. As Chapters 2 and 3 suggest, the pattern of lower achievement on standardized assessments of black, Hispanic, and Native American students is at least partially established by the beginning of kindergarten. By 4th grade, the percentages of whites scoring in the advanced range on the National Assessment of Educational Progress on reading, math, science, and writing were from two to five times as large as those for the underrepresented minorities, with 0 percent of black and Hispanic students scoring in the advanced range in math, science, and writing (Donahue et al., 2001).

The discrepancies among definitions, policies, and implementation of policy at the local school district level result in considerable variation from school to school in the creation of a pool of identified gifted and talented students. Even when a particular definition has been adopted—for example, outstanding academic performance—the subjective judgment of what represents outstanding performance is influenced by the normative performance of students in a given school or school district.

---

[1]Many state directors of gifted programs did not report the percentage of students identified as gifted in their states.

Identification of Giftedness

Many of the suggested practices in the literature on identification of gifted and talented students mirror those suggested for the identification of students with disabilities. There is widespread agreement that assessment tools must validly and reliably measure the construct of giftedness, using separate and appropriate identification strategies to identify different aspects of giftedness, using multiple criteria for identification, and including criteria that are appropriate for underserved populations (Callahan et al., 1995). Current identification practice, however, does not widely adhere to these principles.

Perhaps the greatest challenge in determining the validity and reliability of an instrument to measure the construct of giftedness is defining the construct itself. There are some who believe that academic giftedness can be captured in the measure of general intellectual function, often referred to as "g," that underlies all adaptive behavior (Sternberg, 1999; Jensen, 1998). Jensen (1998) explains: "the g factor reflects individual differences in information processing as manifested in functions such as attending, selecting, searching, internalizing, deciding, discriminating, generalizing, learning, remembering, and using incoming and past-acquired information to solve problems and cope with the exigencies of the environment" (p. 117).

The hypothesis of a unitary intelligence factor is generally supported with evidence that g underlies performance across a broad range of tests. However, this interpretation is challenged by those who argue that separate dimensions of intelligence are identifiable, and students who demonstrate exceptionality on one dimension often are unexceptional on others (e.g., Gagne, 1985; Gardner, 1983; Stanley, 1984). Sternberg (1997) considers that analytic, creative, and practical intelligence are three different, largely uncorrelated dimensions that are expressed as different abilities both inside and outside the classroom. Gardner (1999) argues for eight separate intelligences, although there are no predictive empirical data to support his argument. Benbow and Minor (1990) studied extremely precocious 13-year-old students and found that mathematical and verbal giftedness were entirely distinct. Moreover, within-individual discrepancies are typically much greater for high-ability than low-ability students (Detterman and Daniel, 1989).

As with disability determination, aligning assessment with the construct being measured provides just two legs of a table. The third leg required for functionality is alignment of the program or intervention. It does little good to broaden the definition of giftedness to include creativity, leadership, or musical ability if the program a school has to offer gifted students is advanced mathematics. Yet Callahan et al. (1995) found schools using intelligence tests to assess creativity and musical aptitude.

In their survey of school districts regarding identification of gifted and talented students, Callahan et al. (1995) found that despite contemporary understandings, most school divisions subscribed to the original federal definition found in the Marland report (U.S. Department of Health, Education, and Welfare, 1972). The construct of general intellectual ability in the federal definition of giftedness was the most frequently used construct guiding identification.

Referral and Identification Procedures

The initiation of the identification process in many localities is a call to teachers to simply nominate all students they believe to be gifted. In other school divisions, the initial consideration for gifted services may be initiated through a process of asking teachers to complete a checklist or rating scale on all students in the class or only those from the class judged to be gifted. In most cases, these nomination forms or checklists are based on a set of characteristics rather than on specific assessments of educational need. Widespread use of teacher judgment has been identified as a potential explanation for the disproportionate representation of minority students (other than Asians) as gifted and talented (e.g., Ford, 1995, 1996). Some scholars argue that teacher nominations are compromised by the generally low expectations that they hold for culturally and linguistically diverse learners (Clasen, 1994; Dusek and Joseph, 1983; Jones, 1988; McCarty et al., 1991) and their inability to recognize characteristics of giftedness when exhibited in nontraditional behaviors of minority children (Bermudez and Rakow, 1990). As discussed in Chapter 6, empirical findings regarding teacher bias in natural settings are inconclusive.

It is not uncommon for schools to also collect nominations of parents, but parents of Hispanic and black students tend to refer their children at lower rates than white parents (Colangelo, 1985; Scott et al., 1992; Woods and Achey, 1990). The potential significance of teacher and parent involvement was suggested by the results of a program designed to increase minority participation in gifted programs that was launched some time ago in Greensboro, North Carolina (Woods and Achey, 1990). Although the program study was done in 1986-1989, its findings are noteworthy. Identification for the gifted program in grades 2 through 5 relied on a combination of standardized test scores and parent, teacher, peer, or self-nomination. Once nominated, a student was eligible for up to three rounds of aptitude and achievement testing: the first two were group evaluations, and the third was an individual evaluation. After testing, parents were notified of the test results. A qualifying score would admit the child to the program. If the child scored below the cutoff point, the parent or a school committee could request retesting. Students were required to reach a cutoff score that combined achievement test scores, aptitude test score, and (with a much lower weight) scholastic performance. The highest scores from the three rounds were used to determine eligibility.

The standards for determining giftedness were not altered in the program that targeted minority students. Rather, when a minority student was identified as at or above the 85th percentile on the school-wide standardized tests, the three-step evaluation was begun; no nomination was required. Two professionals were assigned to the program to administer individual tests, monitor test scores, track data, and ensure follow-through for the targeted students. Parents were notified after each round, but testing proceeded through the full battery unless there was a specific parent request to discontinue. Without altering standards for entry, the number of minority students in the gifted program increased by 181 percent, from 99 to 278 students. Minority students' share of the gifted program increased from 13.2 to 27.5 percent. Only 15 percent of the minority students ultimately identified were identified on the first round of testing.

In some school systems, the referral pool comes from reviewing group-administered tests and selecting those who score above some predetermined score. Archambault et al. (1993) report that 79 percent of teachers in a national survey claimed that achievement tests are used to identify the gifted in their schools, 72 percent use IQ tests, and 70 percent use teacher nomination. Not surprisingly, intelligence tests were the most frequently cited tests for measuring the construct of general intellectual ability, with general reliance on group tests. Individual tests were most often used only for further data gathering in borderline cases.

School divisions with specific provisions for identifying gifted students from minority populations most often relied on traditional measures to accomplish this goal. Often the school districts listed individual intelligence tests as the vehicle for most effective identification of minority students. Screening by reviewing test scores is sometimes carried out in combination with teacher nominations, parent nominations, and/or peer nominations and sometimes as the sole source used in creating a screening pool.

The next step in the decision process resulting in classification as gifted is sometimes based on a single score derived from the tests or the teacher nominations used in the screening process. In other cases, identification may entail the collection of a specified range of data, including scores derived from group or individually administered ability or achievement tests, creativity tests, teacher ratings, portfolio reviews, or interview data. While in 34 policy statements states recommended the use of multiple criteria for identification (Coleman and Gallagher, 1992), a survey of schools in 50 states found only very limited applications of this principle in practice (Patton et al., 1990).

The data that are collected in the assessment process may be reviewed by a team of educators, or students may be identified by the entry of the scores on a matrix that assigns arbitrary weights to particular scores or ratings; it assigns a prescribed number of the highest-scoring students or students meeting a preassigned total score to the gifted program. The use of such matrices has been criticized for presenting the illusion of being more culturally unbiased while, in truth, using a procedure that still gives greatest weight to the scores with most variability—test scores (Callahan and McIntire, 1994). In other identification procedures used in schools, students whose scores or other characteristics meet a set of prescribed criteria on the indicators are selected. Finally, a case study approach may be used, in which the data are used to describe educational needs and to assign program and curricular modifications.

Screening and Identification in Underserved Populations

The underrepresentation of American Indian/Alaskan Native, black, and Hispanic students in gifted and talented programs was reviewed in Chapter 2, using data from the periodic surveys of school districts conducted by the Office for Civil Rights. Concern with disproportionality is reflected in the federal Jacob K. Javits Gifted and Talented Students Education Act of 1988, which gave highest priority to "the identification of gifted and talented students who may not be identified through traditional assessment methods (including economically disadvantaged individuals, individuals of limited English proficiency, and individuals with handicaps" (p. 238). It is also reflected in court cases (e.g., *Coalition to Save Our Children v. State Board of Education*, 1995): racial discrimination has been the focus of suits brought against local school districts, often as a component of more general charges of discrimination within a school division (Karnes and Marquardt, 2000).

Coleman and Gallagher (1992) reported that 38 state policies make some reference to issues of identifying gifted students from "culturally diverse populations, economically disadvantaged students and disabled students" (p. 11). In some states, there are specific guidelines for selecting tests or carrying out the identification process to help schools identify greater numbers of minority students; in other states, specific instruments are recommended (e.g., the Raven's Progressive Matrices Test, the Matrix Analogies Test, the Torrance Test of Creative Thinking). These tests emphasize reasoning ability or "fluid" intelligence and de-emphasize information acquisition or "crystallized knowledge," which is likely to be more culturally specific.

The Raven's Progressive Matrices, for example, assess nonverbal, abstract reasoning by having students select which pattern pieces fit best into an overall array or matrix. While the cultural neutrality of the abstract patterns is appealing, its usefulness for gifted and talented identification has not been fully tested. One study found that scores on the test were not related to school performance (Mills et al., 1993), and it does less well at predicting academic achievement than most intelligence tests or specific ability measures (Baska, 1986; Raven, 1990). This does not suggest that the Raven's is less able to identify exceptional ability; it may be that the students who score well are exceptional in respects not well tapped by school programs. The validity of these alternative methods and their effects on disproportionality are largely unknown, although nonminority and high-income students tend to perform better than their minority, low-income counterparts (Mills et al., 1993).

Noting that state policies have not resulted in uniform adoption of procedures effective in increasing identification of low-income or minority students, Coleman and Gallagher (1992) investigated the factors that inhibited the adoption and implementation at the local level of more flexible and permissive identification policies. They found two major constraints to implementation. The first was a fear that increased numbers of identified students would not be accompanied by an increase in financial resources, and the second was a fear of legal suits that would be filed by parents whose children might have higher test scores but were not selected for the programs (reverse discrimination suits).

While the literature is replete with suggestions for increasing the numbers of black, Hispanic, American Indian/Alaskan Native students, it is much more limited in the documentation of success of alternative strategies in recruiting and retaining such students in gifted and talented programs. However, several innovative efforts have been documented.

One model focused on interactive staff development using core attributes of intellectual giftedness, corresponding observable behaviors (as they might be manifest in low-income and minority populations), and group decision making using multiple assessment tools. It was successful in generating greatly increased numbers of teacher nominations and subsequent identification as gifted (Frasier et al., 1995). A complex system (described by the authors as labor-intensive and time-consuming) using classroom observation, multicultural curriculum-based enrichment activities, standardized assessments, portfolio assessments, teacher nominations for screening and a dynamic assessment tool, literature-based performance assessment, standardized tests, and child interviews demonstrated that academically gifted students could be found "even in the most beleaguered schools" (Borland and Wright, 1994:170). A comprehensive screening of kindergarten children in an urban environment increased the identified 1st grade students in that school division from 0.2 percent to 2 percent (Feiring et al., 1997).

All the approaches noted above focused on identification and traditional conceptions of giftedness. Other nontraditional strategies with promise for identification are based on alternative conceptions of intellectual ability and include studies of the effects of curricular adaptations on identified students. One strategy, based on adopting an alternative conception of giftedness derived from Howard Gardner's model of intellectual functioning and employing a set of performance assessment tasks, provided evidence that minority or economically disadvantaged students selected using this model during kindergarten *and provided with systematic curricular intervention* were more likely to be selected for programs for the gifted in 3rd grade (Callahan et al., 1995). Students at the high school level identified using Sternberg's triarchic conception of intelligence and students who were instructed using strategies that matched their patterns of identified areas of strength performed better than students who were mismatched across a broad range of assessments (Sternberg et al., 1996).

CONCLUSION

A theme that runs through this chapter and, indeed, through the entire report warrants repeating here: addressing disproportion is far more complex than changing the participation numbers by adopting assessment tools that will identify a different racial/ethnic mix of students. The goal must be to better serve the educational needs of all students. Success in that endeavor will depend first on the alignment of program interventions to the educational needs of students, and only then on crafting better assessment tools and procedures. While the tools must be valid, reliable, and culturally unbiased, they must also effectively identify those students who need and can profit from the interventions made available at the school. Certainly as the needs of atypical learners are better understood, the interventions we design may, and should, change. Assessment practices must then evolve to serve the purpose of linking student need to program intervention.

The research base that highlights the challenge of designing and administering assessments for students from very different cultures and socioeconomic backgrounds suggests, however, that persistent attention to the ability of the assessment tool to reliably identify educational need is warranted. In the next chapter we look at the major challenges to current assessment practices in this regard, and at alternatives that in the committee's view would better serve the end of linking educational need to special and gifted program interventions.

8

Alternative Approaches to Assessment

While the vision in the Individuals with Disabilities Education Act (IDEA) and associated state guidelines is of a program that looks carefully at the individual needs of a student who is referred for special education, both the state guidelines implemented at the school level and traditional special education assessment rely heavily on standardized batteries of tests. Those same standardized test scores are frequently the primary determinant of eligibility for gifted and talented programs. In this chapter, we review the major challenges to these standardized testing practices, including challenges to the very notion of context-free measures of intellectual ability, as well as challenges to the usefulness and efficiency of standardized scores in providing information that is relevant to intervention. We then discuss alternative approaches to assessment that are tied more closely to intervention and present our recommendations for policy change.

CONTEXT, CULTURE, AND ASSESSMENT

Approaches to assessing intellectual ability used widely in special and gifted education placement (see Chapter 7) are rooted in a conception of intelligence as a general factor (often labeled g), which underlies all adaptive behavior (Sternberg, 1999; Jensen, 1998). The very notion of decontextualized intelligence is challenged by two lines of work that highlight the role of culture and context in the development and assessment of intellectual abilities. One line of work, termed here *cross-cultural psychological research*, has focused on the influence of factors related to culture and context on testing and on cognition more generally. The other line of work is from a more traditional psychological or psychometric orientation and is focused somewhat more directly on issues of test bias and cultural bias in standardized assessment batteries, including IQ and intellectual ability measures.

Cross-Cultural Psychological Research on Cognitive and Intellectual Ability

Rogoff and Chavajay (1995) have traced the development of cross-cultural psychological research over the past three decades. Initially much attention was directed at the exploration in other cultural settings of the robustness of cognitive tasks developed in the United States and in Europe. Emanating from a Piagetian perspective, a great deal of this work investigated the claims of universality of the stages of intellectual and cognitive development (Dasen, 1977a, b; Dasen and Heron, 1981). A clear finding is that people in many cultures did not reach what is called the formal operational stage without having had extensive experience in school (Ashton, 1975; Goodnow, 1962; Super, 1979). Characteristics assumed intrinsic to child development were found to be context dependent.

In the attempt to understand this variation, many investigators began to examine the power of situational contexts of testing and the issue of subjects' familiarity with test materials and concepts (Irwin and McLaughlin, 1970; Price-Williams et al., 1969; Ceci, 1996; Gardner, 1983; Lave, 1988; Nuñes et al., 1993). Cross-cultural settings were particularly productive for this purpose (Posner and Barody, 1979; Dasen, 1975; Carraher et al., 1985; Ceci and Roazzi, 1994; Nuñes, 1994). Several studies documented clear differences across cultures in people's ability to sort objects into taxonomic categories (Cole et al., 1971; Hall, 1972; Scribner, 1974; Sharp and Cole, 1972; Sharp et al., 1979). Those whose experiences were not rooted in Western schooling tended to sort objects into functional categories rather than into more abstract conceptual taxonomies. In tasks thought to tap into logical thinking, often employing logical syllogisms, non-Western subjects often refused to accept the premise of the task, preferring to confine reasoning and deduction to immediate practical experience rather than hypothetical situations (Cole et al., 1971; Fobih, 1979; Scribner, 1975, 1977; Sharp et al., 1979). When the task was modified to focus on immediate and familiar everyday experience, non-Western subjects were able to make judgments, draw conclusions, and exhibit other features of logical thinking and memory that appeared absent in hypothetical problem solving (Cole et al., 1971; Cole and Scribner, 1977; Dube, 1982; Kagan et al., 1979; Kearins, 1981; Lancy, 1983; Mandler et al., 1980; Neisser, 1982; Price-Williams et al., 1967; Rogoff and Waddell, 1982; Ross and Millsom, 1970; Scribner, 1974, 1975, 1977).

This body of work led many investigators to challenge the assumption that cognitive tasks or batteries developed in a specific cultural setting were context-free measures of cognitive abilities (Cole et al., 1976; Ceci, 1996, Gardner, 1983; Lave, 1988; Nuñes et al., 1993). Research focused on analogues of standardized cognitive tasks that were embedded in people's everyday lives, such as weaving patterns, the calculating of change in the store, and personal narration (Cole et al., 1976; Greenfield, 1974; Greenfield and Childs, 1977; Lave, 1977; Serpell, 1977). In many of these studies, "native" subjects were shown to perform better than Western subjects when the materials and tasks reflected some correspondence to the more familiar, everyday versions of the tasks. During this same period, increasing attention was directed to the social context surrounding standardized testing situations and the study of testing as a unique context in itself with its own discourse and interactional rules for what constitutes appropriate behavioral expectations (Goodnow, 1976; Miller-Jones, 1989; Rogoff and Mistry, 1985).

In more recent research challenging a universal *g* factor, Sternberg and Grigorenko (1997b) tested Kenyan children using several different instruments: one measured tacit knowledge of appropriate use of natural herbal medicines, including their source, their use, and dosage. Two other instruments designed to measure reasoning ability (Raven's Coloured Progressive Matrices Test) and formal knowledge-based abilities (Mill Hill Vocabulary Scale) were administered as well. The findings showed no correlation between the "practical intelligence" measured by the herbal medicine test and the test scores for reasoning ability, as well as a *negative* correlation with the formal knowledge-based test. Ethnographic work with the families suggested to the authors that they saw either formal schooling or practical knowledge as relevant to a child's future and so emphasized only one. The implication drawn by the authors is that variation in performance on intelligence tests may capture what is valued in the home environment rather than what is intrinsic to the child's intellectual ability (Sternberg, 1999).

International research results have been supported in research done more locally. Housewives in Berkeley, California who successfully did mathematics when comparison shopping were unable to do the same mathematics when placed in a classroom and given isomorphic problems presented abstractly (Lave, 1988; Sternberg, 1999). A similar result was found with weight watchers' strategies for solving mathematical measurement problems related to dieting (de la Rocha, 1986). Men who successfully handicapped horse races could not apply the same skill to securities in the stock market (Ceci and Liker, 1986; Ceci, 1996).

In short, the available cross-cultural literature suggests that variations from the cultural norms embedded in tests and testing situations may significantly influence the judgments about intellectual ability and performance resulting from their use. Researchers have documented how these sociocultural contexts in the homes of different ethnic, racial, and linguistic groups in the United States can vary significantly from those of mainstream homes (Goldenberg et al., 1992; Heath, 1983, 1989). In light of differences in the fit between home and school culture for many minority children and the difference in the school experiences provided (see Chapter 5), these results bear directly on IQ testing of minority children.

Psychometric Views of Culture and Context: Research on Test Bias

In contrast to the cross-cultural and sociocultural research just described, work from a psychometric framework has centered on the issue of test bias. As early as the mid-1970s, questions were raised about the effects of cultural differences on standardized tests and their interpretation (Mercer, 1973a). Some researchers have considered the long-standing patterns of disproportionate representation of certain racial, ethnic, and English language learner groups in special education as de facto evidence of test bias (Bermudez and Rakow, 1990; Hilliard, 1992; Patton, 1992). The general argument has been that the content, structure, format, or language of standardized tests tends to be biased in favor of individuals from mainstream or middle- and upper-class backgrounds. Miller (1997) argues that all measures of intelligence are culturally grounded because performance depends on individual interpretations of the meaning of situations and their background presuppositions, rather than on pure g.

A contrasting approach to test bias is based on a more statistical or psychometric view. That is, a test is considered biased if quantitative indicators of validity differ for different groups (Jensen, 1980). A common procedure has been to conduct item analysis of specific tests to examine construct validity. A specific test would be considered to be biased if there is a significant "item by group interaction," suggesting that a specific item deviates significantly from the overall profile for any group. Several researchers have concluded that there is no evidence for test bias using such procedures (Jensen, 1974; Sandoval, 1979), a view that was embraced by the 1982 National Research Council (NRC) committee (1982). Other investigators have noted, however, that cultural factors may serve to depress the scores of a particular group in a more generalized or comprehensive fashion so that individual items would not stand out, even though cultural effects may still be present (Figueroa, 1983). This would be the case if familiarity with testing itself were at issue.

Another psychometric indicator of bias that has been used is predictive validity. Normally this involves correlating measures of intellectual functioning with academic achievement, such as grades. Generally moderate to high correlation coefficients are obtained in these analyses. Critics such as Hilliard (1992) point out that the same biases that operate on standardized tests also are likely to operate in institutions such as schools. Moreover, Reschly et al. (1988) have suggested that these analyses when applied to students referred to special education are not predictive in a true sense, since the standardized measure is normally administered only after low achievement has been demonstrated.

There is also a long tradition of investigation into the social and contextual factors embedded in standardized testing situations, in particular those conducted one-on-one with an unfamiliar examiner. Perhaps because it is easier to demonstrate these effects empirically, it has been argued that effects such as examiner familiarity differentially affect Hispanic and black children (Fuchs and Fuchs, 1989). However, efforts to determine whether white examiners impede the test performance of black children have found no evidence that they do (Sattler and Gwynne, 1982; Moore and Retish, 1974).

A recent, more comprehensive treatment of the issues raised here is presented by Valencia and Suzuki (in press). In addition, discussion of issues specific to English language learners is found in Valdés and Figueroa (1994) and elsewhere in this volume. It is important to note, however, that many have begun to question the utility of the debate, at least with respect to designing meaningful interventions for students. That is, even if the ideal standardized test could be created that minimized the incorrect categorization or labeling of individual students, the question still remains: What does such an approach have to offer in terms of designing appropriate interventions that will maximize achievement and academic outcomes (Reschly and Tilly, 1999)? For this reason, many have begun to turn attention to more academically meaningful assessment approaches, such as performance-based assessment, curriculum-based measures, and other approaches more closely tied to instruction and classroom practice.

Problems with IQ-Based Disability Determination

Objections to IQ testing and strong reactions to the interpretation of IQ test differences as reflecting hereditary differences among groups continue to complicate discussions of the meaning, appropriate uses, and possible biases in tests of general intellectual functioning. In addition to the limitations of IQ tests from the perspectives of cultural psychology, it is questionable whether the costs of IQ tests are worth the benefits in special education eligibility determination. The costs of the testing alone are several hundred dollars in the form of the time of related services professionals such as psychologists and do not include either an estimate of the costs in the time of the students or an analysis of the usefulness of what might be done in place of IQ tests (MacMillan et al., 1998a).

Treatment validity. Perhaps the most convincing of the arguments against IQ tests is that the results are largely unrelated to the design, implementation, and evaluation of interventions designed to overcome learning and behavioral problems in school settings. For example, IQ is not a good predictor either of the kind of reading problem that a student exhibits or of the student's response to treatments designed to overcome that reading problem (Fletcher et al., 1994). The same general interventions appear to work with basic skills problems regardless of whether the student is classified with mild mental retardation (MMR), learning disability (LD), or emotional disturbance (ED) (Gresham and Witt, 1997; Reschly, 1997). The differentiation between LD and MMR that is done primarily with IQ test results does not lead to unique treatments or to more effective treatments. Moreover, it is noted by MacMillan and colleagues (1998a) that significant numbers of students now classified as LD are in the borderline range of ability of about 70-85 or, in some cases, functioning in the MR range defined by an IQ of approximately 75 or below.

Misuse and racism. Further objections to the use of IQ-based disability determination come from the literature documenting the misuse of IQ tests to justify racist interpretations of individual differences among groups. No contemporary test author or publisher endorses the notion that IQ tests are direct measures of innate ability. Yet misconceptions that the tests reflect genetically determined, innate ability that is fixed throughout the life span remain prominent with the public, many educators, and some social scientists. These myths about the meaning of such results markedly complicate rational discussion of the proper role that IQ tests results might play in disability determination in school settings.

Mercer (1979b) provided a useful discussion of the very narrow conditions under which differences among individuals on IQ tests might properly be interpreted as indicating differences in genetic bases for intellectual performance. The necessary conditions never occur with groups that differ by economic resources, cultural practices, and educational achievement. Moreover, test authors and test publishers all acknowledge that IQ tests are measures of what individuals have learned—that is, it is useful to think of them as tests of general achievement, reflecting broad culturally rooted ways of thinking and problem solving. The tests are only indirect measures of success with the school curriculum and imperfect predictors of school achievement.

LD classification criteria. The most frequent use of IQ tests today is in determining whether a "severe discrepancy between achievement and intellectual ability" exists as per the federal criteria for LD (34 CFR 300.541) and state LD classification criteria. Several problems exist with this procedure. First and most fundamental, there is no "bright line" in performance that can be used to determine the appropriate size of the discrepancy; the size required is arbitrary. Some states use more stringent criteria (e.g., 23 standard score points), others more lenient ones (15 points). Second, serious technical problems exist with the methodologies for discrepancy determination used in most states that do not account for the phenomenon of regression to the mean, a special problem with extreme scores (Mercer et al., 1996; Reynolds, 1985). Failure to account for regression effects penalizes lower-scoring students in decreasing the likelihood of being diagnosed as LD rather than MMR. A third problem with the discrepancy method is that its intended objectivity may not be realized if multidisciplinary teams that are willing to administer a large number of achievement tests until the requisite discrepancy is attained without careful consideration of which test is most valid for a particular child and achievement problem. This activity is often predicated on the altruistic-sounding motive of making sure that students with achievement problems get services designed to ameliorate their difficulties; however, it seriously undermines the purpose of having an eligibility criterion.

A fourth and more fundamental problem with the intellectual ability/ achievement discrepancy is that the discrepancy is inherently unreliable in a single measurement occasion and notoriously unstable in repeated measurement occasions (Shinn et al., 1999). Moreover, the vast majority of students evaluated for LD and special education placement have discrepancies that just meet or just fail to meet the discrepancy criterion. The instability of the discrepancy means that if they were assessed again, the discrepancy status for many would change. It is important to remember that these problems occur with students with low achievement, some of whom are found eligible for LD and others of whom, with equally low achievement, especially those with IQs in the 70s and 80s, often are found ineligible. Is this a valid distinction?

Validity of LD Discrepancies

The case against using the "severe discrepancy between achievement and intellectual ability" criterion is further strengthened by a series of studies funded by the National Institute of Child Health and Human Development (NICHD) (Lyon, 1996), which reached a number of conclusions about the use and validity of IQ in defining LD in the area of reading:

> Results do not support the validity of discrepancy versus low achievement definitions. Although differences between children with impaired reading and children without impaired reading were large, differences between those children with impaired reading who met IQ-based discrepancy definitions and those who met low reading achievement definitions were small or not significant (Fletcher et al., 1994:6).

> The present study suggests that the concept of discrepancy operationalized using IQ scores does not produce a unique subgroup of children with reading disabilities when a chronological age design is used; rather, it simply provides an arbitrary subdivision of the reading-IQ distribution that is fraught with statistical and other interpretative problems (Fletcher et al., 1994:20).

Poor readers who make up 70 to 80 percent of the current LD population seem to have the same needs and the same cognitive processing profiles, and they respond to the same treatments regardless of their IQ status (it should be noted that children with IQs less than 80 generally were excluded from the NICHD studies). Therefore, arbitrarily dividing poor readers into subgroups with higher IQs (those who meet the current LD criteria) and those with IQs similar to their reading achievement levels is invalid. With regard to reading-related characteristics, these subgroups are much more similar than different, calling into serious question the current LD diagnostic practices.

These practices have an even more serious side effect: the wait-to-fail phenomenon. Learning to read in the early grades is crucial. The evidence suggests that a student's status as a poor or good reader at the end of 3rd grade is highly stable through adolescence (Coyne et al., 2001; Juel, 1988). To be effective, intervention needs to occur early with poor readers; otherwise, there are grave barriers to changing from learning to read (in the kindergarten to 3rd grade period) to reading to learn (in 4th grade and beyond).

Special education services for students with reading and math achievement problems are typically *delayed* until 2nd, 3rd, or 4th grade by the intellectual ability/achievement discrepancy criterion for LD. As noted by Fletcher and colleagues, "For treatment, the use of the discrepancy models forces identification to an older age when interventions are demonstrably less effective" (Fletcher et al., 1998:201). This effect of the IQ-achievement discrepancy method greatly diminishes the potential positive effects of LD services because they are initiated after two or more years of failure (Fletcher, 1998), not when it first is apparent that a student is having significant problems in acquiring reading or math skills. The wait-to-fail effects are markedly damaging to students and equally negative regarding the potential positive effects of special education. Significant changes in how LD is diagnosed, along with universal early interventions for children with reading problems, are crucial to improving the current system and to improving the achievement of minority children and youth.

Problems with Abandoning IQ-Based Disability Determination

Before leaving the topic of IQ-based disability determination, the long tradition associated with the use of IQ in determining disabilities and the current practices involving IQ across a variety of contexts must be acknowledged. If IQ-based conceptions and classification criteria for LD and MMR were abandoned, significant retraining of existing special education and related services personnel would be required. Even more daunting is the change required in the thinking of professionals and the public about disabilities—a change from assumptions of fixed abilities and internal child traits to new assumptions about the malleability of skills and the powerful effects of instruction and positive environments. Belief changes of this magnitude do not occur immediately or easily, but they are supported by research understanding and are likely to be beneficial to children.

Abandoning IQ-based disability determination will complicate articulation of eligibility and service delivery across different settings and agencies. The largest problem is likely to occur with MR, a disability category recognized in the laws pertaining to a number of agencies, including law enforcement and social security. For example, a person with an IQ below 60 is presumptively eligible for Social Security Income Maintenance benefits, and persons with IQs in the 60 to 70 range are eligible pending an evaluation of intellectual functioning and confirmation of deficits in adaptive behavior (as well as meeting income requirements). Examination of school records is often part of the process of identifying deficits in adaptive behavior. School practices over the past 25 years involving increasing reluctance to identify MMR and the apparent practice of diagnosing some students as LD who meet criteria for MMR compromise the usefulness of school records and potentially undermine an individual's access to services and protections that should be accorded to persons with MR. Today, IQ data typically are available for persons classified as LD, and those data assist with determination of adult eligibility for services. In the future, such data may not be available.

A counterargument, however, is that schools should not identify disabilities to meet the needs of other agencies. The goal of the schools is to assist children and youth in developing the academic skills, problem-solving capabilities, social understanding, and moral values that promote successful adult lives. The use of IQ tests and IQ-based disability determination does not promote the achievement of those critical goals; therefore, IQ should be abandoned, even if that action complicates the work of other agencies. It seems entirely reasonable to expect the other agencies to collect data relevant to their eligibility and to learn how to use the kinds of school data described in the last section.

Use of the diagnostic construct of MR without IQ is problematic. Intellectual functioning is critical to all contemporary conceptions of MR and has been a part of the construct since it first was differentiated from mental illness by John Locke in the 17th century (Kanner, 1964; Doll, 1962, 1967). No one has developed alternative criteria for this diagnostic construct that do not use intellectual functioning either implicitly or explicitly. Before classifying someone as MR, given all of the classification schemes that currently exist (American Psychiatric Association, 1994; Luckasson et al., 1992; World Health Organization, 1992), use of a comprehensive and reliable test of general intellectual functioning is mandatory. Some children may be incorrectly classified as MR if IQ is eliminated from the MR conceptual definition and classification criteria (Lambert, 1981; Reschly, 1981, 1988d); IQ tests results can protect children from the more subjective judgments of adults.

It also is important to recognize what will *not* occur with an elimination of IQ-based disability determination and the use of IQ tests in the full and individual evaluation of students suspected of having disabilities. First, current patterns of over- and underrepresentation in special education and for gifted and talented services are likely to continue unless substantial improvements in levels of minority students' achievement are realized. As noted in the 1982 NRC report, IQ tests are not mechanically applied to all students in the general population. If they were, "the resulting minority overrepresentation would be almost 8 to 1" (NRC, 1982:42). At the time of that report, the actual overrepresentation in MR was slightly over 3 to 1. Further evidence of continued overrepresentation even though IQ testing was eliminated is available from California, where federal Judge Robert Peckham issued a ban on IQ testing in 1986 that was in effect until 1992, when it was modified by the same judge. The ban had no effect on disproportionate special education representation.

The IQ issue in the context of special education was never the principal issue to the *Larry P. v. Riles* court, which in 1979 and 1986 ordered first a limitation of the use of IQ tests with black students and then a complete ban on such use. The judge clarified his views of the meaning of the case in 1992 with the following comments: "First, the case was, . . . clearly limited to the use of IQ tests in the assessment and placement of African-American students in dead end programs such as MMR" (*Larry P.*, 1992, also cited as *Crawford et al. v. Honig* [*Crawford et al.*], 1992:15). Furthermore,

"Despite the Defendants' attempts to characterize the court's 1979 order as a referendum on the discriminatory nature of IQ testing, this court's review of the decision reveals that the decision was largely concerned with the harm to African-American children resulting from improper placement in dead-end educational programs" (*Crawford et al.*, 1992:23).

The real *Larry P.* issue, according to the judge who adjudicated the case over a 20-year period from 1972 to 1994, was the effectiveness of special education programs for black students. Without data confirming effectiveness, Judge Peckham regarded overrepresentation as highly suspicious. The 1992 order required the California Department of Education to inform the court regarding which of the 1990s special education programs in California were "substantially equivalent" to the dead-end programs of concern to the court in the 1979 opinion. Instead of responding to that order, the department appealed the decision to the 9th Circuit. The appeal was rejected, leaving Judge Peckham's 1992 order to stand. No further action in the *Larry P.* case has occurred since 1994, although the 1992 order to the California Department of Education is still in effect.

Perhaps the most important lesson from *Larry P.* is that the outcomes of special education matter a great deal in judging fairness to the minority students who are overrepresented in programs. Demonstratably effective outcomes would probably have changed the original ban on IQ tests and would greatly diminish if not eliminate contemporary concerns about disproportionate representation. This leads to a useful reframing of the IQ issue, providing as well the foundation of the next section on alternatives to the current system of special education. Are IQ tests useful in promoting positive outcomes for children and youth with severe achievement and social behavior problems? In the committee's view, the balance of the evidence does not provide continued support for the use of IQ tests in special education decision making.

The major advantages of eliminating IQ-based disability determination and use of IQ in the full and individual evaluations have to do with focusing the efforts of parents, students, teachers, and related services personnel on promoting greater competence in academic skills and social behaviors. The use of IQ tests detracts from efforts to analyze environments carefully and develop effective interventions. The time and cost of IQ testing during the full and individual evaluation and reevaluations could be put to better use if they were devoted to more thorough analyses of reading, math, written language, or other achievement deficits, as well as analyses and development of interventions for classroom behaviors that interfere with effective instruction and achievement of positive learning outcomes. Abandoning IQ testing does not automatically produce more appropriate assessment. Accomplishment of the latter will require significant changes in state and local practices as well as substantial continuing education efforts. The promise, however, of better outcomes justifies the difficulties and costs associated with making these changes.

IQ Tests and Gifted and Talented Determination

Programs for the gifted and talented can be academic programs, leadership programs, or arts (including music) programs. IQ testing is relevant only to the first. Identification for academically gifted programs, to be responsive to available interventions, should identify those students in a discipline who require and can profit from instruction that moves at a quicker pace, and that explores topics in more depth and complexity *if* that is what gifted programs have to offer.

While objections to IQ as a measure of innate intelligence are many, few would contest the evidence that IQ predicts school success. It may well be that IQ tests capture the same skills and abilities as are captured by successful school performance, and that neither is a measure of innate intelligence. Even so, IQ tests may successfully identify students who are most likely to succeed in programs for the academically gifted. Snow (1995) argued that despite its many drawbacks, IQ tests do successfully identify the ability to deal with complexity. To the extent that gifted programs provide access to accelerated and more complex curricula, IQ test results may be relevant to placement. Scores for verbal and quantitative subtests should be considered separately, however, since mathematical and verbal giftedness are separate dimensions (Benbow and Minor, 1990), and a single score should never be used in isolation.

In a homogeneous, middle-class, suburban school, the above arguments may be persuasive. The more diverse the tested population, however, the greater the challenge to those arguments. Student who do not excel on IQ tests, as argued above, may be less familiar with testing procedures, and for reasons of background and culture they may have less familiarity with the types of items on the test. As the body of research reviewed above suggests, their reasoning capacity and skilled performance may be exceptional when the referents are familiar, but unexceptional in the context of the test. If the characteristic that distinguishes academically gifted students from their peers is advanced ability to learn, unfamiliarity with test taking and with test items may obscure that ability.

Research done by Sternberg and colleagues (1999, 2001) in Tanzania lends empirical support for this concern. A sample of 358 schoolchildren were given intelligence tests. They were then given a 5 to 10 minute period of instruction in which they were able to learn skills that would potentially enable them to improve their scores. When they were retested, the students registered on average small, statistically significant gains. Importantly, scores on the pretest showed only weak correlations with scores on the posttest. This suggests that for populations inexperienced with test taking, a small amount of training can change scores significantly. More importantly, it suggests that initially high-scoring students are not necessarily those who learned most from instruction. The authors found that the posttraining scores were better predictors of transfer to other cognitive performance tasks than were the pretraining scores.

The research base, in the committee's view, is not sufficiently developed to permit either a complete embrace or a complete rejection of IQ testing for placement in gifted and talented programs. The lack of a consensus, coupled with well-reasoned questions concerning the validity of psychometric intelligence tests, provides sufficient warrant for supporting multiple means of assessment at this time.

But multiple means of assessment, based on a lack of scholarly consensus, should be considered only a temporary measure. The committee regards it as a priority matter that the findings from research on the contextual basis of test performance, as well as other aspects articulated in the wide-ranging scholarly critique of decontextualized intelligence testing, be engaged in an effort to study the implications of culture and context on efforts to assess children for gifted and talented placement. As with assessment for special education, assessment alternatives should be anchored in an understanding of the characteristics of students that constitute a need for a different educational program, and should be valid with respect to the gifted programs available to students.

The short-term resolution of this dilemma is crafted in light of the existing state of knowledge and the desirability of continuing to provide exceptional learners with interventions that support their genuinely different educational needs. The short-term resolution should not, however, become the de facto appropriate means of assessment.

ALTERNATIVES TO TRADITIONAL
CLASSIFICATION AND PLACEMENT

We now turn to alternative approaches to assessment that would better match student need to program interventions. It is important to emphasize that the current methods of identifying students with low-incidence disabilities are not the focus of this discussion; it is assumed that the current practices regarding determining eligibility and special education needs for these students will continue. The overarching theme in this discussion is improving achievement and social learning outcomes for all children and youth, including the minority students currently disproportionately represented in the MR, ED, and gifted and talented categories.

Universal Screening, Prevention, and Early Intervention

In considering alternatives to the current identification process, the committee considered two goals paramount: (1) assuring that the pool of children identified are those who need and can benefit from special or gifted education, and (2) assuring that the assessment procedures maximize the opportunity for effective intervention. Both concerns point us to early, universal screening.

Universal screening of young children to detect problems in the early development of academic and behavioral skills is increasingly recognized as crucial to achieving better school outcomes and preventing achievement and behavior problems. Evidence suggests that effective and reliable screening of young children by ages 4-6 can identify those most at risk for later achievement and behavioral problems (Coyne et al., 2001; Fuchs and Fuchs, 2001; Graham et al., 2001; NICHD, 2000; Kellam et al., 1998b), including those most likely to be referred and placed in special education programs. Cost-effective screening measures use structured interviews, rating scales, and checklists completed by teachers and parents as well as simple, brief measures of skills administered directly to children (Good and Kaminski, 1996; Walker and McConnell, 1995; Achenbach and Edelbrock, 1986; Werthamer-Larsson et al., 1991).

Early screening is rather futile, however, if it is not followed by effective interventions. In fact, instructional and social training programs for parents and teachers are available that can produce significant gains for many children showing at-risk characteristics at ages 4-6 (for reading interventions, see NICHD, 2000; NRC, 1998; for behavioral interventions, see McNeil et al., 1991; Reid et al., 1999; Hawkins et al., 1992; Kellam et al., 1998b; U.S. Department of Health and Human Services, 2001b). It is important to recognize that the nearly inevitable effect of universal early screening will be higher identification of disadvantaged students, a disproportionate number of whom are members of minorities. West et al. (2000) reported rates of mastery of skills that are early predictors of later reading success. Black and Hispanic students were behind Asian and white children both at the beginning and at the end of kindergarten, and the lower-scoring groups made slightly smaller gains over the course of the year (see Chapter 3). Studies of achievement at kindergarten and 4th grade through the National Assessment of Education Progress (NAEP) (Donahue et al., 2001; West et al., 2001) and other national measures of achievement provide a basis for anticipating the probable patterns and degrees of disproportionality likely to result from early screening. According to the most recent NAEP results for 4th grade reading, 63 percent of black students had scores that are below the basic level in reading. In contrast, 27 percent of white and 22 percent of Asian/Pacific Islander students scored at below the basic level. The results of universal screening are likely to parallel those differences. Universal screening will be beneficial, however, if it identifies schools, classrooms, and individual teachers and children who need additional sup ports and provides effective interventions. Otherwise, the same problems with disproportionate representation in special education will accompany universal screening efforts. Furthermore, universal screening may uncover children with learning disabilities, particularly girls, who are presently underidentified.

Many of the children who are referred to special education exhibit reading problems, behavior problems, or both (Bussing et al., 1998). In both these areas, screening tools are available that would allow for early identification of children at risk for later problems, and existing intervention strategies hold promise for improving outcomes for those identified.

Early Screening and Intervention in Reading

There are a number of working models for screening all children in kindergarten, 1st, and 2nd grade for reading problems. Examples include the Observation Survey developed in New Zealand (Clay, 1993), the South Brunswick, New Jersey, Early Literacy Portfolio (Salinger and Chittenden, 1994), the Primary Language Record (Barr et al., 1988), the Work Sampling System (Meisels, 1996-1997), and the Phonological Awareness and Literacy Screening developed at the University of Virginia (see Foorman et al., 2001, for summaries of all of these programs). Most are attempts to engage teachers in collecting evidence on which to base curricular decisions about individual children. Some of these are more standardized, formal assessments that have attempted to address important psychometric issues such as test reliability and validity; others are more informal. Some have been implemented on a large-scale basis.

Perhaps the most fully researched and implemented model for universal screening is that currently being used in Texas. Beginning in 1998-1999, all school districts in Texas were required by law to administer an early diagnostic reading instrument for K-2. Although the specific assessment instrument was not mandated, the Texas Education Agency contracted for the development of the Texas Primary Reading Inventory (TPRI). This instrument (described in more detail in Box 8-1) was designed to be used on a large scale, to bring psychometric rigor to informal assessment, and to be aligned with state curriculum standards. By the 2000-2001 school year, over 90 percent of Texas's 1,000 school districts had adopted the TPRI and its Spanish reconstruction, known as the Tejas Lee.

The TPRI consists of two parts, beginning with a screening instrument, which is administered to each child in grades K-2. Phonological awareness

BOX 8-1
The Texas Primary Reading Inventory

Carefully developed and revised through field trials and several years of use with thousands of students, the Texas Primary Reading Inventory (TPRI) is a two-part tool that helps teachers diagnose the kinds of reading problems students may be having and plan instruction accordingly. A screening test is first administered to all K-2 students by their teachers; this is followed by a more in-depth inventory for those students who do not show complete mastery of the questions on the screening test.

The concepts assessed by the screening test were selected because they were found to be good predictors of successful reading at the end of grades 1, 2, and 3. Screening is done at four keys points in time (i.e., middle and end of kindergarten, beginning of 1st grade, beginning of 2nd grade) with questions that focus on the critical reading skills that should be "developed" at that time. The TPRI screening helps teachers quickly identify those students who are on track to become successful readers one or two years later. The teacher can then administer the more time-consuming inventory only to those students who are potentially not on track—i.e., at risk for developing difficulties in learning to read. The inventory section provides information about the child's strengths and weaknesses that can then be used by the teacher to plan reading instruction and monitor progress.

For example, midway through the year, a kindergarten teacher using the TPRI would individually administer the screening portion of the TPRI to each student in her class. She begins with a series of questions that assess the child's letter-sound (or graphophonemic) knowledge—showing the child a letter and asking for its name and sound. Then she asks a set of questions focused on phonemic awareness. For example: "If the puppet says s-it, I know the word is sit. What would the word be if the puppet says c-ake?" If the child does not answer enough of these questions correctly, the teacher would proceed to administer the whole inventory portion of the TPRI.

The inventory portion of the TPRI consists of the following conceptual domains:

Book and print awareness (K only)—knowledge of the function of print and of the characteristics of books and other print materials (e.g., the child is asked to point out a sentence in text and show where it starts and ends).

Phonemic awareness (K and 1st grade)—the ability to detect and identify individual sounds within spoken words. Tasks include asking for rhyming words (tell me another word that rhymes with stop, shop, hop) or repeating words without the initial consonant sound (say the word "cake" without the "c").

Graphophonemic knowledge (K, 1st, and 2nd grades)—recognition of letters of the alphabet and understanding of sound-symbol relationships. (e.g., for kindergarteners, questions like "What is the first sound in the word man?" for 2nd graders asking them to spell in writing words spoken by the teacher).

Reading accuracy (1st and 2nd grades)—the ability to read grade-appropriate text accurately (i.e., the child is asked to read a passage aloud and the teacher keeps track of the types of errors made by the child and scores the overall accuracy).

Reading fluency (1st and 2nd grades)— the ability to read connected text accurately, quickly, and automatically (e.g., the teacher times the reading of the passage above and calculates a fluency rate that includes only words read correctly).

Reading comprehension (1st and 2nd grades)—the understanding of what has been read (e.g., the teacher asks the child to answer implicit and explicit questions about the passage that the child has read aloud). For K-1 students unable to read aloud by themselves, listening comprehension is assessed, i.e., the ability to understand what has been read aloud (e.g., the teacher reads a short passage and asks the child both explicit and implicit questions about the events in the story).

According to the researchers who helped develop the test, "the most cost-effective early intervention is prevention—prevention in the form of differentiated classroom instruction" (Foorman and Schatschneider, in press). This means that teachers who use the TPRI to identify risk must also be able to translate the results of the assessment into instruction. To this end, an *Intervention Activities Guide*, provided to each teacher, has activities and sample lessons geared toward each of the major concepts assessed by the TPRI. Teachers can use it to plan supplementary lessons that focus on the specific skills in need of development. Developers of the test do note, however, that many teachers will need some professional development to help them learn to administer the test systematically and to use it to plan instruction effectively (Foorman et al., 2001).

The TPRI is notable for the attention paid to collecting empirical data about its psychometric properties. Items were selected for the screening test from a larger battery of items that were found to distinguish statistically between successful and unsuccessful readers at the ends of grades 1 and 2. In addition, field test data were collected to examine interrater reliability (the accuracy, agreement, and objectivity of scoring across teachers) as well as the validity of the TPRI scores compared with other well-known measures of word recognition and comprehension.

Cutoff points for the screening instrument have been purposely set low so that overidentification of those at risk occurs instead of underidentification (i.e., teachers err on the side of administering the complete inventory to some students who might not really be at risk rather than not administering it to some who truly are at risk). In this case, the main consequence of overidentification is that the teacher proceeds to administer the more comprehensive inventory to the child. Although the false-positive rate for the screening instrument is relatively large in kindergarten (38 percent) and 1st grade, it drops below 15 percent by the beginning of 2nd grade. Results of this test have been explicitly excluded by legislation from use in the Texas accountability system or its teacher appraisal and incentive system.

For more information on the TPRI, visit www.tpri.org or the web site of the Center for Academic and Reading Skills, developers of the instrument for the Texas Education Agency, at http://cars.uth.tmc.edu.

NOTE: This box describes TPRI as revised for 2001-2002.

and letter-sound knowledge are the focus of this screening in kindergarten and the beginning of grade 1, while word reading is the focus of the screening at the end of grade 1 and the beginning of grade 2. If the screening test suggests that a child is still developing these key concepts, then a more comprehensive inventory is administered by the teacher to help identify each child's strengths and weaknesses and to help target intervention strategies to use with each child. The scores on the TPRI are designed to provide a concrete demonstration of the knowledge and skills covered in the classroom curriculum. As expected, early identification through universal screening does yield a higher number of false positives (i.e., children who will be identified as at risk but will not end up experiencing difficulties learning to read). For example, about 38 percent of second-semester kindergartners are misidentified by the TPRI screen as needing further help. However, most of these students can get the support they need to be successful readers through supplemental small-group reading instruction from the teacher for about 20-30 minutes a day.

By the end of 2nd grade, if a child still does not meet the criterion of successful mastery on the TPRI, they are referred for further evaluation and intervention. Thus, use of the TPRI not only signals the need for more intensive intervention by 2nd grade, but it also holds promise for preventing reading difficulties by the use of ongoing assessment and targeted interventions while children are still learning to read in kindergarten and 1st grade.

Early Screening and Intervention for Behavior Problems

There now exist feasible and inexpensive tools to systematically assess the reading skills of all students. Currently there is no parallel emphasis on the systematic, continual tracking of emotional or behavioral problems, even though they commonly figure into reading and other learning problems (Bussing et al., 1998). Since identification and referral by teachers for emotional disturbance or behavior disorders is often unsystematic, idiosyncratic, and late in the development of a behavioral problem (see Chapter 6), early systematic screening could bring large improvements.

Existing identification procedures that rely on intrapersonal psychiatric assessments or standardized tests (e.g., Achenbach and Edelbrock, 1986) do reveal problems in emotional and behavioral adjustment. But they do not take into account possible problems in teacher practices or classroom or school-wide issues that may be critical in understanding the child's problems and in formulating a corrective intervention strategy. This point is driven home by findings from a recent longitudinal study by Kellam et al. (1998a). On average, across 19 schools, 1st grade children who were assessed to be in the top quartile in aggression were four times more likely than other students to demonstrate significant behavior problems in middle school. However, the subset of 1st grade children scoring in the top quartile who were in poorly managed 1st grade classrooms was over 50 times more likely to have conduct problems in middle school. This suggests a very powerful, independent influence of the teacher's classroom management skills on child behavior outcomes.

Universal and repeated assessments of children and settings in schools have the potential to provide information on the behavioral adjustment of each child, both individually and in relation to other children in a class, school, or district. It also has the potential to provide systematic information on the effects of individual, classroom, or school-wide interventions. Several well-developed and validated assessment tools are available for the classroom settings. Instruments such as the Teacher Observation of Child Adjustment (TOCA; Werthamer-Larsson et al., 1991) and the Scale of Social Competence and School Adjustment (SSCSA; Walker and McConnell, 1995) are appropriate for all students. They provide specific and relevant information to enable teachers to assess the adjustment of every child in their classroom (see Box 8-2). Instruments such as the Child Behavior Checklist Report Form (Achenbach and Edelbrock, 1986), and the Systematic Screening for Behavior Disorders (SSBD) (Walker and Severson, 1992) provide scores and norms on several relevant behavioral and emotional dimensions. Although such instruments are used widely, they were designed and validated on clinical populations and provide useful information only at the extreme end of the continuum of disturbance (i.e., clinical cutoff scores). As such they are less than optimal universal assessment tools.

Direct observational tools that teachers can use with minimal training can be tailored to assess individualized behavioral and emotional adjustment (see Walker et al., 1995). Direct observational strategies are also available for noninstructional school settings (playgrounds, hallways, etc.) in which many behavioral and emotional problems are demonstrated.

As illustrated in the study by Kellam et al. (1998a), children scoring in the top quartile in aggression or conduct problems are at significant risk for subsequent behavior problems. For these children, a second-stage assessment that is individualized to take into account contextual factors should be considered. Such a multiple gating procedure, including three or more graduated assessments, is highly effective, allowing the integration of universal and clinical assessment strategies in a cost-sensitive way (Loeber et al., 1984; Walker and Severson, 1992).

The first level can be used to assess the adjustment, or progress, or response to new school-wide interventions of all students in a classroom, school, or district. The data can then be used to identify a smaller subset for further assessment to determine the appropriateness and then effectiveness

---

BOX 8-2
Universal Assessment

Behavioral Adjustment: Universal Assessment and Multiple Gating

There is a growing body of evidence that systematic teacher ratings of student behavior in the early grades is highly predictive of both short-term and long-term emotional adjustment (e.g., Kellam et al., 1998a). One instrument for such a systematic assessment is the Teacher Observation of Child Adjustment (TOCA). It is a relatively short and structured interview that can be conducted by a school psychologist or counselor, which systematically assesses a child's adjustment in the classroom, particularly issues around aggressiveness/disruptiveness and shyness/social isolation. Assessment of all children in a typical classroom can be conducted in under two hours, including time for a short discussion of teacher concerns about individual children. Teachers typically see the process as worthwhile, particularly if they are provided time within the school day to complete the process.

The TOCA yields quantitative scores and can be used to identify children with the most serious adjustment problems. Kellam et al. (1998a) found that 1st grade children in the top 15 percent in rated adjustment problems were at very high risk of serious discipline problems in middle school. One could use such a cutoff point to trigger a teacher consultation with the school psychologist and more intensive assessment to decide whether or not to institute an evidence-based, individualized program in the classroom (e.g., First Steps to Success; Walker et al., 1998).

This two-step assessment process—a universal assessment systematically triggering a more intensive assessment—is an example of "multiple gating." If the teacher and students were really struggling and reported average scores in a classroom were much higher than in other classes in a given school, then an effective classroom-wide intervention (e.g., Webster-Stratton et al., 2001) might be considered to help the teacher more effectively deal with behavior and classroom management issues.

---

of individualized interventions. Examples of this type of program intervention for children whose screening suggests they are at risk of later behavior problems appear in Boxes 8-3, 8-4, and 8-5.

Direct observational tools that school psychologists, counselors, or teachers could use, given appropriate preservice or inservice training, can be tailored to assess behavioral dimensions, to further define and specify the targets and measure the effects of individualized interventions (see Walker et al., 1995; Horner, 1994). Both rating and direct observational procedures and associated interventions are available to conduct analogous assessments in key noninstructional settings that are less well structured and supervised than classrooms and in which student-to-student aggression

---

BOX 8-3
First Step to Success

The First Step to Success program targets at-risk kindergartners who show the soft, early signs of an antisocial pattern of behavior (e.g., aggression, oppositional-defiant behavior, severe tantrums, victimization of others). First Step to Success consists of three interconnected modules: (a) proactive, universal screening of all kindergartners; (b) school intervention involving the teacher, peers, and the target child; and (c) parent/caregiver training and involvement to support the child's school adjustment. The major goal of the program is to divert at-risk kindergartners from an antisocial path in their subsequent school careers.

Multiple waitlist control studies (Golly et al., 1998; Walker et al., 1998) have documented the effects of First Step to Success. Effects include observed reductions in classroom problem behavior and increases in on-task behaviors. Teacher and parent ratings indicate:

decreased disruptive behavior (teacher report),

decreased withdrawn behaviors,

improved classroom atmosphere (assessed by independent observers), and

improved ratio of positive to negative interactions with the student.

---

and bullying often occur at very high levels (Olweus, 1991; Walker et al., 1995; Stoolmiller et al., 2000).

Interventions and Referral Decisions

It is the responsibility of teachers in the regular classroom to engage in multiple educational interventions and to note the effects of such interventions on a child experiencing academic failure before referring the child for special education assessment. It is the responsibility of school boards and administrators to ensure that needed alternative instructional resources are available (NRC, 1982:94).

Improved universal screening, prevention, and early intervention processes such as those described above should, in the committee's view, be essential prerequisites to any consideration of student referral to special education. The current literature indicates, however, that some students do not respond to even the best early interventions in reading and other achievement areas (Torgesen, 2000; Wagner, 2000). The proportion of a general population that does not respond adequately is unknown because universal screening followed by early intervention procedures has not been applied broadly in any general population. Research with relatively small groups of students suggests that the nonresponse rate may be as high as 4 percent of

BOX 8-4
Incredible Years Series: Parent, Teacher, and Child Training

The Incredible Years Series is a set of three comprehensive, multifaceted, and developmentally based curricula for parents, teachers, and children designed to dovetail in order to promote emotional and social competence and to prevent, reduce, and treat behavior and emotional problems in young children (ages 2-8). In a report that emerged from the Division 12 Task Force on Effective Psychosocial Interventions (1995), the series was identified as one of two well-established treatments for conduct disorder (Brestan and Eyberg, 1998) and was selected by the Office for Juvenile Justice and Delinquency Prevention (OJJDP) as 1 of 11 model violence prevention programs (Webster-Stratton et al., 2001).

This series of programs addresses multiple risk factors across settings (school and home) known to be related to the development of conduct disorders in children. In all three training programs, trained facilitators use videotape scenes to structure the content, stimulate group discussion and problem solving, and promote the sharing of ideas among participants.

Incredible Years Training for Parents. The Incredible Years parenting series includes three types of parent programs. The Basic program emphasizes parenting skills known to promote children's social competence and reduce behavior problems, such as: how to play with children, helping children learn, effective praise and use of incentives, effective limit-setting, and strategies to handle misbehavior. The Advance program emphasizes parental interpersonal skills, such as: effective communication skills, anger management, problem-solving between adults, and ways to give and get support. The Supporting Your Child's Education (known as SCHOOL) emphasizes parenting approaches designed to promote children's academic skills, such as: reading skills, parental involvement in setting up predictable homework routines, and building collaborative relationships with teachers.

Incredible Years Training for Teachers. This series emphasizes effective classroom management skills, such as: the effective use of teacher attention, praise, and encouragement, the use of incentives for difficult behavior problems, proactive teaching strategies, how to manage inappropriate classroom behaviors, and the importance of building positive relationships with students. In addition, a series of training videotapes are used to train teachers how to implement the Dinosaur Social Skills and Problem-Solving Curriculum as a prevention program in the classroom with all children. There is both a preschool/kindergarten and grade 1-2 version of this training.

Incredible Years Training for Children. The Dinosaur Child Curriculum emphasizes training children in such skills as emotional literacy, empathy or perspective taking, friendship skills, anger management, interpersonal problem solving, school rules, and how to be successful at school. It is designed for use as a pull-out treatment program for small groups of children exhibiting conduct problems or can be offered to the entire classroom in circle time discussions combined with small-group activities. There are 90 lessons designed to be offered twice a week over a period of 1 to 3 years.

BOX 8-5
Linking the Interests of Families and Teachers

Listed as a promising program in the Surgeon General's Report on Youth Violence (U.S. Department of Health and Human Services, 2001a) Linking the Interests of Families and Teachers (LIFT) is a universal school-based program that targets two major factors that put children at risk for subsequent behavior problems and delinquency: aggressive and other problem behaviors with teachers and peers at school and ineffective parenting, including inconsistent and inappropriate discipline and lax supervision. LIFT has 3 main components: (1) child social skills training, (2) a playground behavior game, and (3) parent management training.

Child social skills training in the program consists of 20 sessions of 1 hour each conducted across a 10-week period. Sessions are held during the regular school day. Each week, the sessions include five parts: (1) classroom instruction and discussion on specific social and problem-solving skills, (2) skills practice, (3) free play in the context of a group cooperation game, (4) a formal problem-solving session, and (5) review and presentation of daily rewards. The curriculum is similar for all elementary school students, but the delivery format, group exercises, and content emphasis are modified to address normative developmental issues depending on the grade level of participants.

The playground behavior game takes place during recess. During the game, rewards can be earned by individual children for the demonstration of both effective problem-solving skills and other positive behaviors with peers as well as the inhibition of negative behaviors. These rewards are then pooled with a small group of students as well as his or her entire class. When a sufficient number of armbands are earned by a group or by the class, simple rewards are given (e.g., an extra recess, a pizza party). The key to this aspect of the game is to have adults roaming throughout the playground, immediately terminating negative confrontations and handing out colorful nylon armbands as a reward to individual students for positive behavior towards peers. Playground monitors, required in most schools, can be taught to fill this role.

The parenting classes are conducted in groups of 10 to 15 parents and consist of 6 sessions scheduled once per week for approximately 2.5 hours each. The sessions are held during the same period of time as the child social skills training. Session content focuses on positive encouragement, discipline, monitoring, problem solving, and parental involvement in the school. Counselors, teachers, or psychologists can conduct the groups, as the curriculum is designed to accommodate varying levels of instructor education and expertise. Teachers and parents give the program extremely positive evaluations.

The surgeon general's report documents evidence of the program's effectiveness: "In short-term evaluations, LIFT decreased children's physical aggression on the playground (particularly children rated by their teachers as most aggressive at the start of the study), increased children's social skills, and decreased aversive behavior in mothers rated most aversive at baseline, relative to controls. Three years after participation in the program, 1st-grade participants had fewer increases in attention-deficit disorder-related behaviors (inattentiveness, impulsivity, and hyperactivity) than controls. At follow-up, 5th-grade participants had fewer associations with delinquent peers, were less likely to initiate patterned alcohol use, and were significantly less likely than controls to have been arrested."

the general population (Wagner, 2000). The students who do not respond adequately to the very targeted, intensive interventions described above would then be eligible for an individualized education program (IEP), which would stipulate the ongoing supports required.

The proposed tiered intervention strategy is consistent with a broad consensus in the literature that high-quality interventions should be applied prior to consideration of special education eligibility and placement. Current special education rules and guidelines in the states nearly always require such prereferral interventions (although it may have another name) or school-based problem solving. Unfortunately, the quality of these interventions is often poor (Flugum and Reschly, 1994; Telzrow et al., 2000). For example, the vast majority lack critical features of effective interventions, such as: (a) behavioral definition of the problem; (b) development of a direct measure of the problem in the natural classroom or other setting that is of concern; (c) baseline data indicating the nature and severity of the problem; (d) analysis of the problem (task analysis with identification of prerequisite skills, analysis of environmental conditions, including instructional features); (e) development of an explicit, written intervention plan based on principles of instructional design and behavior change; (f) frequent checks on whether the plan is implemented as intended; (g) frequent progress monitoring with changes in the plan as needed; and (h) evaluation of results in terms of whether the gap is reduced sufficiently between peer and age-grade expectations (Tilly et al., 1999).

According to self-report information and examination of special education case files, approximately 80 to 90 percent of current prereferral interventions are missing three or more of these indices of quality (Flugum and Reschly, 1994; Telzrow et al., 2000). Studies indicate that 80 percent or more of the students receiving prereferral interventions as they are implemented today are also considered for special education eligibility. Poor quality is a major reason for the failure of prereferral interventions to resolve more problems in general education settings. Many of the prereferral interventions are guided by very popular models of "collaborative consultation" (e.g., Idol and West, 1987; West and Idol, 1987), which do not require data collection or several of the other critical features identified above (Fuchs and Fuchs, 1992; Tilly et al., 1999). Changing the quality of the interventions prior to the consideration of special education eligibility is crucial. Key special education and related services personnel (e.g., school psychologists) need substantial retraining and reorientation in order for this step in the special education services process to have its intended effect.

Children and youth who do not respond to high-quality interventions should be considered for special education, but only after high-quality interventions are provided. We reiterate that special education should not be considered unless there are effective general education programs, preferably supported by universal screening and early high-quality interventions prior to referral. Improving the interventions before considering special education placement is essential to implementing more effective general and special education programs.

Eligibility Decisions and System Reform

Eligibility decisions are markedly influenced by legal requirements, including conceptual definitions for disabilities (see Appendix 6-B) and classification criteria that are determined by the states. The conceptual definitions and classification criteria have an enormous impact on how professionals and the public think about disabilities; they determine rather directly the kind of assessment that is conducted during the full and individual evaluation, a mandated part of eligibility determination. If conceptual definitions and classification criteria use such concepts as general intellectual functioning or intellectual ability, it is nearly impossible to avoid the use of individually administered IQ tests and other measures of internal child traits or states. As noted previously, the information from measures of internal child traits have little application to interventions, are costly, and are objectionable to many constituencies.

Design alternatives that address some of the problems with the current special education system exist and have been implemented successfully (Ikeda et al., 1996; Reschly et al., 1999). Box 8-6 provides a brief description of the alternative approach used in the State of Iowa. Changes in the design and organization of the special education delivery system are consistent with current legal requirements, but they utilize quite different conceptions of disabilities and apply different assessment methods. The overall purpose of these systems is to improve outcomes through application of direct assessment methods and effective instruction and behavior change principles in a problem-solving framework.

Problem-Solving Approach

To be effective, the problem-solving approach for eligibility determination and the design of interventions in special education must be pervasive in the system, governing the behavior of professionals and others from the first indication of problems with learning or behavior through early intervention, prereferral interventions, eligibility determination, IEP development, annual review of progress, and triennial consideration of eligibility and programming.

There are several problem-solving models, all requiring systematic problem solving with data collection is essential (Upah and Tilly, 2002; Tilly et al., 1999). Problem solving should be a consistent set of activities involving

BOX 8-6
Special Education without IQ: The Case of Iowa

General intellectual functioning and IQ tests are used nearly universally as part of eligibility criteria and comprehensive evaluations for students suspected of having disabilities in educational settings. Many critics have pointed out limitations and flaws in IQ testing and in decision making highly influenced by IQ test results. Is IQ essential to special education?

Clearly, the answer is "no." The Iowa reform plan that has been adopted in most of the state led to the complete abandonment of IQ testing. The Iowa reform was motivated by a commitment to improve the educational outcomes in special and general education programs. Educational leaders in Iowa focused on using the existing resources in general and special education more effectively and forging a close relationship between what special educators did in eligibility determination with educational programming.

Since 1995 the official State of Iowa Department of Education Rules of Special Education have permitted the adoption of a problem-solving approach to special education eligibility and programming that eliminates categorical eligibility and programming in the high-incidence disabilities. Instead of using IQ-achievement discrepancies and IQ cutoff scores, the Iowa Problem Solving Rules emphasize functional assessment that is related directly to the interventions that children and youth need. Moreover, traditional categorical labels for high-incidence disabilities are no longer used, leading to a focus on what children need and their degree of need rather than application of formulae for determining eligibility.

In the Iowa alternative model, traditional standardized IQ and achievement tests are replaced by direct measures of academic, behavioral, and emotional regulation in natural classroom and school settings. Local norms are used as the primary basis to determine degree of need for interventions. But special education eligibility is not based solely on degree of need. In addition, a problem-solving process is implemented to determine if the patterns of learning, behavior, or emotional regulation can be altered significantly in general education.

Rigorous criteria are established to guide the problem-solving process that requires a minimum of several weeks to implement properly. For example, the presenting problem must be defined in terms of observable behavior, a goal must be established that represents significant improvement, a direct measure of the behavior is developed and implemented, an intervention plan tailored to the problem is developed using experi-

behavioral definitions of learning and behavior goals, collection of data in natural settings, application of research-based principles of learning and behavior, monitoring progress with changes in interventions as needed, and evaluation of outcomes. This framework is, in the committee's view, the most promising approach currently available ensure the effectiveness of special and remedial education programs.

mentally validated principles of instructional design and behavior change, implementation of the intervention is monitored to ensure that it is carried out as intended, and the student's progress is monitored frequently (often, twice or more per week). Improvements in the intervention are implemented if the results are falling short of goals and the overall effects are evaluated.

Special education eligibility may be considered after the results of one or more high-quality interventions are implemented and evaluated. If the student's progress has improved significantly, special education is not likely to be considered further. If the intervention is not sufficient to bring the student into a broadly defined range of normal achievement, behavior, or emotional regulation, special education need is considered. Special education need is evaluated according to judgments of whether the specially designed instruction with necessary supports and services are likely to address the problem effectively.

In Iowa, students are simply designated as eligible or not eligible for special education services. The eligibility criteria for the high-incidence disabilities are: (a) a large difference from average levels of achievement, behavior, or emotional regulation that interferes significantly with school performance, (b) insufficient response to high-quality, rigorous interventions, and (c) demonstrated need for special education.

No IQ tests are used; there are no eligibility criteria specifying the need for an assessment of intellectual functioning or ability. Standardized tests of achievement and behavior rating scales are used sparingly. Direct measures in the natural setting, such as curriculum-based measurement in academic skills domains and behavior observation and interview, are used instead, with local norms used to decide degree of need. That is, students are compared with peers in the same classroom, school, and district to determine degree of need.

Special education is changed. Resources are redirected from expensive eligibility evaluations to the development of high-quality interventions in general and special education. Moreover, greater emphasis on early intervention and prevention is possible because the focus is on delivering effective programs, not on waiting until students fail badly enough to qualify for special education.

Finally, the Iowa reform has not resulted in greater numbers or proportions of students placed in special education. It has changed how special education is done in order to improve outcomes for children and youth. For more information see Ikeda et al. (1996) and Reschly et al. (1999).

Assessment

Application of assessment measures that provide the foundation for problem-solving interventions was recognized as crucial in the 1982 NRC report: "It is the responsibility of assessment specialists to demonstrate that the measures employed validly assess the functional needs of the individual child for which there are potentially effective interventions" (p. 94). The report noted that much of the data collected then within the context of special education had little or no relationship to interventions. The main change over the past two decades is the development of a much richer and relevant knowledge base to provide the kind of assessment that is related to interventions to achieve the goal. That is, problem-solving approaches, assessment methods, and techniques are determined by what is needed in each of the problem-solving steps. The measures used must reflect the problem in the natural setting in which it occurs (e.g., number of words read correctly, number of disruptive events that interfere with the child's learning as well as the learning of other children) and be conducive to frequent assessment of progress. The kinds of measures that meet these criteria typically come from a behavioral assessment tradition (e.g., Gresham, 1999; Gresham and Noell, 1999; Mash and Terdal, 1998; Shapiro and Kratochwill, 2000; Shinn, 1998). The measures are direct reflections of the problem behavior, applied in the natural setting typically as part of the ongoing classroom routine, through observation in natural settings, or in very brief interactions with children.

Using direct measures, "problems" are defined typically as large differences between the performance of individual or small groups of children and that of other children in the same environment. For example, disruptive behaviors (further defined into specific behaviors that are observable, such as number of inappropriate verbalizations or number of physically aggressive behaviors) are observed in a classroom, focusing on a specific child or a small group of children as well as other children. A "problem" exists when the disruptive behavior of one child or a small group of children is substantially different from others in the same environment in a domain of achievement or behavior that is developmentally important. For referred children these differences typically are large.

Classification Decisions

Before considering alternatives to the traditional classification system, it is important to consider goals for a classification system. The NRC report (1982:94) established important criteria for a child disability classification scheme:

> It is the responsibility of the placement team that labels and places a child in a special program to demonstrate that any differential label used is related to a distinctive prescription for educational practices and that these practices are likely to lead to improved outcomes not achievable in the regular classroom. . . .

> It is the responsibility of the special education and evaluation staff to demonstrate systematically that high-quality, effective special instruction is being provided and that the goals of the special education program could not be achieved as effectively within the regular classroom.

Among the most important goals for a classification scheme are those of reliability and validity (Cromwell et al., 1975). Current disability classifications for special education have dubious reliability (see previous discussion of LD) and undocumented validity with regard to the design, implementation, and evaluation of treatments. The measures used in traditional classification schemes are not directly related to treatment, meaning that valuable time and resources are lost that could be used if direct measures of performance were used more widely.

As noted previously, classification decisions are strongly influenced by federal and state legal requirements. The direct measures described above are useful in classification decisions regardless of the classification scheme used, traditional or noncategorical. The direct measures focus on relevant domains of behavior in natural settings—specifically, achievement and school social behaviors. These behaviors are directly linked to general schooling goals and specifically to state accountability programs.

Two alternatives exist for the development of a classification scheme that focuses on direct measures of child performance. One is noncategorical designation of students as eligible for special education, and the other is changing the definitions and classification criteria for traditional disability categories. The first is preferable in the committee's view, but it requires the greater amount of change. As noted previously, categorical designation of students as eligible for special education is not required by federal law (see 34 CFR 300.125); noncategorical designation is legal at the federal level. The states vary significantly in their requirements regarding the categorical designation of students as eligible. Some states in full compliance with IDEA (1997, 1999) do not use categorical disability schemes for special education (e.g., Iowa).

The committee's support for noncategorical designations was arrived at in recognition of what has occurred in the public schools over the past four decades. The challenges leveled at the labeling and educational treatment of children with mild mental retardation (usually referred to as "educable mentally retarded" [EMR]) in the late 1960s and 1970s was highlighted in the 1982 report (NRC, 1982) and is significant to the understanding of what has occurred. It is our contention that the assessment process *at that time* was a "high-stakes enterprise" in the sense that the psychometric profile of the child had consequences for: (a) the label that was appended to the child, and as a result, (b) the curriculum and/or services, along with (c) the administrative arrangement or placement of the child. Recall that this predates passage of P.L. 94-142 and the applications of "free appropriate public education," "least restrictive environment," or "individualized education plans" (IEP).

Classification as EMR dictated, in turn, in what kind of administrative placement the child would receive services. To quote Robinson and

Robinson (1965) in describing education services for EMR students in that era, "The consensus of special educators today definitely favors special class placement for the mildly retarded" (p. 466). Essentially, diagnosis as EMR carried with it a "packaged program"—and the package almost inevitably was an alternative, functional curriculum that differed markedly from the curriculum taught in general education. In fact, the position taken by special educators then was that for children with mental retardation, unlike virtually every other disability, special education services modified not only how children were taught, but also what they were taught. The various EMR curricula" (e.g., Hungerford's New York program, the Cincinnati curriculum) shared an emphasis on promoting prevocational and later vocational skills, social and interpersonal skills, and functional academics. Hence, diagnosis as EMR in the 1960s resulted in a child's being taught a "different" curriculum, which would subsequently be faulted by critics who observed that it made return to the general education population difficult, if not impossible, and made the assumption that all EMR children should receive the same curriculum. In addition, that curriculum was almost invariably taught in a self-contained special class, or special day class. Hence, diagnosis as EMR carried with it placement consequences—i.e., placement in a special day class.

In a similar fashion, diagnosis as LD had program and placement consequences as well. Typically, children diagnosed as LD continued to receive the general education curriculum and services were designed to assist the child with processing problems by pulling them out of a regular class to a resource room for remedial assistance from the resource teacher. Hence, the differences between being diagnosed as EMR and LD were several. One diagnosis conveyed the belief that the general curriculum was appropriate (i.e., LD), while the other diagnosis (EMR) was predicated on the belief that an alternative curriculum was needed. Placement consequences were also noted, as LD students were typically served in a resource room pull-out program.

When one examines the consequences today of diagnosing a child as EMR or LD, it is a very different situation than existed prior to P.L. 94-142. At present, a child must be qualified as eligible for special education and related services by meeting one of the existing disability categories. However, no longer does categorical eligibility carry with it either curricular or placement consequences. Instead, IDEA requires that once a child is deemed eligible for special education by qualifying for a disability category, the IEP process will be the means by which the "appropriate" portion of the free, appropriate public education is negotiated. In the IEP process, short-term and long-term goals are denoted and the supports and services needed to accomplish those goals specified. Hence, program or placement is negotiated during the IEP process. Being found eligible by virtue of qualifying as LD entitles a child only to have an IEP drawn up, but it carries with it no particular programmatic or placement consequences. As a result, diagnosis into one of the disability categories is no longer a high-stakes venture.

As explained in the discussion of referral, public school personnel in many, if not most, states are reserving the label "mental retardation" for only patently disabled children (Gottlieb et al., 1994; MacMillan et al., 1996c) and are knowingly labeling low aptitude (i.e., those with IQ scores below the cutoff score for mental retardation) as learning disabled (MacMillan et al., 1998b). The rationale for doing so is that there is no advantage to labeling able-bodied children "mentally retarded" when an appropriate curriculum and placement can be designated in the IEP process in which the least restrictive environment is specifically considered.

Rational classification criteria have been developed to guide eligibility decisions for special education without using categories or traditional measures (Tilly et al., 1999). These schemes apply all of the due process requirements associated with IDEA as well as establish strong parental involvement programs. The two crucial features of these eligibility criteria are: (a) documented large differences in performance in relevant domains of behavior using peers as a comparison group and (b) documented insufficient response to well-designed, appropriately implemented interventions in general education. The student can then be designated as "eligible for special education," assuming that all of the due process protections are implemented. This approach finds the "right" kids—that is, those who need additional supports in order to achieve—is legally defensible in due process hearings, and is politically acceptable in that it does not lead to excessive numbers of students qualifying for special education (Ikeda et al., 1996; Reschly et al., 1999). The "hit rate" using the less than perfect traditional system as a criterion is very high (Wilson et al., 1992).

A second and less desirable alternative to the current classification system is to redefine the criteria for the high-incidence disabilities of LD, MR, and ED. Changing the classification criteria for LD and ED is feasible; however, changes in MR are less feasible due to the perspective of several centuries that it involves very low intellectual ability. LD, MR, and ED could, however, be defined in terms of functional deficits in relevant domains using direct measures of academic skills and social behaviors. The changes in LD, MR, and ED classification criteria have the advantage of eliminating assessment procedures having little relevance to treatment, but also the large disadvantage of being associated with ideas of internal child deficits that are difficult if not impossible to change. Moreover, the negative connotations of traditional categories, especially MR, would not be avoided to the same extent as is possible with a noncategorical system.

Accountability

It is clear that the original framers of Education of All Handicapped Act (1975) were concerned with making sure that special education programs were effective. The various procedural requirements, such as due process, IEP development, full and individual evaluation, annual review, and triennial reevaluation, were all designed to ensure that the services would be effective. The framers established "process or procedural" protections to ensure accountability.

Although a great deal has been accomplished with the procedural requirements, accountability for results was not achieved. IDEA (1997, 1999) placed more emphasis on accountability and moved special education for students with disabilities into the mainstream of educational reform. The system now demands accountability without adjustments in the classification practices and assessment requirements to make accountability feasible.

Research on the effectiveness of special education overwhelming supports changes away from IQ-based disability determination to functional assessment and problem-solving interventions. One aspect of problem solving is particularly important: formative evaluation. Formative evaluation methods involve establishing goals, gathering baseline data to reflect current performance, instruction or behavioral interventions, with monitoring of progress frequently (daily, twice per week), and with changes made in interventions depending on the ongoing results of that intervention. If goals are met, typically the goal is raised to ensure that the student always has a challenging but achievable goal to guide and motivate efforts. If goals are not met, instructional and behavior change interventions are analyzed further and changed to foster better outcomes and efforts to improve instruction are implemented (Fuchs and Fuchs, 1986; Kavale and Forness, 1999). Interventions guided by this kind of problem solving are more effective by 0.75 to 1.0 SD over typical special education interventions.

Gifted and Talented Identification

It is far more difficult to make a case for early identification and intervention for gifted and talented students, because no research base currently provides guidance in this regard. There has been an absence of public support for gifted programs for the very young, resulting in few opportunities to conduct research on program features that promote achievement at the highest end of the distribution. This is perhaps not surprising given the well-known problems of reliability of traditional instruments for assessing intellectual function in young children. "Readiness tests" used as screening instruments for intellectual competence and traditional tests of intelligence and aptitude have been soundly criticized for their inappropriateness for young children generally, and with minority children in particular (Meisels, 1987; Anastasi, 1988, Gandara, 2000). Thus, while many of the predictors of academic failure are well established even for the very young, there is currently no consensus regarding predictors of giftedness.

For elementary and secondary students, limited programs of identification and services for gifted and talented students have been carried out under the auspices of the Jacob K. Javits Gifted and Talented Students Education Program. But the collection of data in the framework of any systematic research paradigm has been limited. Yet the importance of early identification and opportunity to learn is likely to be as critical to the success of students at the upper end of the achievement distribution as it is for those at the lower end. And the problem of disentangling the child's abilities from the previous opportunities to learn strikes a clear parallel. Nevertheless, the existing research base provides too weak a foundation for proposing an alternative assessment approach similar to that proposed for special education.

CONCLUSIONS AND RECOMMENDATIONS

Assessment in special education is guided by complex legal requirements that are responsible in part for the gap between current practices and the state of the art. Direct measures of skills in natural settings, along with the application of problem-solving methodologies, have the promise of significantly improving the outcomes for students in special education and for those considered for but not placed in special education. Traditional disability conceptions and classification criteria interfere with the implementation of systematic problem solving, functional assessment, formative evaluation, and accountability for outcomes. The system changes discussed here and in the recommendations were anticipated in the 1982 National Research Council report. Over the last two decades, significant system changes have become more feasible due to advances in assessment and intervention knowledge. It now is time to implement these changes more widely as a means to protect all children from inappropriate classification and placement, as well as from ineffective special education programs.

The proposed change would focus attention away from efforts to uncover unobservable child traits ,the identification of which gives little insight into instructional response, and toward the problems encountered in the classroom and appropriate responses. The role of instruction and classroom management in student performance is explicitly acknowledged, and effort is devoted first to ensuring the opportunity to succeed in general education.

Federal Level Changes

Recommendation SE.1: The committee recommends that federal guidelines for special education eligibility be changed in order to encourage better integrated general and special education services. We propose that eligibility ensue when a student exhibits large differences from typical levels of performance in one or more domain(s) *and* with evidence of insufficient response to high-quality interventions in the relevant domain(s) of functioning in school settings. These domains include achievement (e.g., reading, writing, mathematics), social behavior, and emotional regulation. As is currently the case, eligibility determination would also require a judgement by a multidisciplinary team, including parents, that special education is needed.

We provide more detail regarding our intended meaning below:

Eligibility

• The proposed approach would not negate the eligibility of any student who arrives at school with a disability determination, or who has a severe disability, from being served as they are currently. Our concern here is only with the categories of disability that are defined in the school context in response to student achievement and behavior problems.

• While eligibility for special education would by law continue to depend on establishment of a disability, in the committee's view noncategorical conceptions and classification criteria that focus on matching a student's specific needs to an intervention strategy would obviate the need for the traditional high-incidence disability labels such as LD and ED. If traditional disability definitions are used, they would need to be revised to focus on behaviors directly related to classroom and school learning and behavior (e.g., reading failure, math failure, persistent inattention and disorganization).

Assessment

• By high-quality interventions we mean evidence-based treatments that are implemented properly over a sufficient period to allow for significant gains, with frequent progress monitoring and intervention revisions based on data. Research-based features of intervention quality are known and must be implemented rigorously including:

　　a. an explicit definition of the target behavior in observable, behavioral language;

　　b. collection of data on current performance;

      c. establishment of goals that define an acceptable level of performance;

      d. development and implementation of an instructional or behavioral intervention that is generally effective according to research results;

      e. assessment and monitoring of the implementation of the intervention to ensure that it is being delivered as designed, frequent data collection to monitor the effects of the intervention, revisions of the intervention depending on progress toward goals, and evaluation of intervention outcomes through comparison of postintervention competencies with baseline data.

Several sources detail these procedures (Flugum and Reschly, 1994; Reschly et al., 1999; Shinn, 1998; Upah and Tilly, 2002).

- Assessment for special education eligibility would be focused on the information gathered that documents educationally relevant differences from typical levels of performance and is relevant to the design, monitoring, and evaluation of treatments. Competencies would be assessed in natural classroom settings, preferably on multiple occasions.
- While an IQ test may provide supplemental information, no IQ test would be required, and results of an IQ test would not be a primary criterion on which eligibility rests. Because of the irreducible importance of context in the recognition and nurturance of achievement, the committee regards the effort to assess students' decontextualized potential or ability as inappropriate and scientifically invalid.

Reporting and Monitoring

- Current federal requirements regarding reporting by states of the overall numbers of students served as disabled and the program placements used to provide an appropriate education would not change with these recommendations. Moreover, the reporting of the nine low-incidence disabilities would continue to be done by category. Reporting of the numbers of students currently diagnosed with high-incidence disabilities would become noncategorical, with the loss of very little useful information due to the enormous variations in the operational definition of the high-incidence categories used currently. The reporting by states concerning students now classified in high-incidence categories could be made more meaningful if the reporting also included the nature of the learning or behavioral problem as reflected in the top 2-4 IEP goals for each student, that is, the number of students with IEP goals in basic reading, reading comprehension, math calculation, self-help skills, social skills, math reasoning, etc. The latter information would provide more accurate information on the actual needs of students with disabilities than the current information indicating unreliable categorical diagnoses.

• Consistent with IDEA 1997 and 1999, federal compliance monitoring should move in the direction of examining the quality of special education interventions and the outcomes for students with disabilities. Current compliance monitoring focuses on important, but limited, characteristics of the delivery of special education programs, particularly implementation of the due process procedural safeguards and the mandated components of the IEP. Compliance monitoring by the Federal Office of Special Education Programs and the state departments of education must assume an outcomes focus in addition to the traditional process considerations.

State-Level Changes

State regulatory changes would be required for implementation of a reformed special education program that uses functional assessment measures to promote positive outcomes for students with disabilities. Some states have already instituted changes that move in this direction. In Iowa, noncategorical special education for students with high-incidence disabilities has been implemented since the early 1990s. Several other states have approved "rule replacement" programs that allow school districts to implement special education systems that do not require categorical designation of students with high-incidence disabilities (e.g., Illinois, Kansas, South Carolina). These state rules require a systematic problem-solving process that is centered around quality indicators associated with successful interventions (see previous section). The rules are explicit about each of these quality indicators, and compliance monitoring is focused on their implementation. Several features of rules in the majority of states can be omitted in a noncategorical system, including the requirements regarding IQ testing.

The changes in federal regulations and state rules toward greater emphasis on producing positive outcomes and away from an eligibility determination process that is largely unrelated to interventions are consistent with the greater emphasis in IDEA (1997, 1999) on positive outcomes for students with disabilities. Positive outcomes are enhanced by the implementation of high-quality interventions; no such claim can be made for conducting the assessments required to assign students with significant learning and behavior problems to the high-incidence categories of LD, ED, and MMR.

Early Screening

Universal screening of young children for prerequisities to and the early development of academic and behavioral skills is increasingly recognized as crucial to achieving better outcomes in schools and preventing achievement and behavior problems. While this is true for all children, a disproportionate number of disadvantaged children are on a developmental trajectory that is flatter than their more advantaged counterparts. Evidence suggests that effective and reliable screening of young children by age 4 to 6 can identify those most at risk for later achievement and behavior problems, including those most likely to be referred to special education programs.

In two arenas—reading and behavior—the knowledge base exists to screen and intervene in general education both systematically and early. Less attention has been devoted to early identification and intervention for mathematics problems. However, the NICHD has launched a research program in this area. Other efforts to develop early screening mechanisms in mathematics have been developed, but their psychometric properties have not yet been widely tested (Ginsberg and Baroody, 2002; Griffin and Case, 1997).

While early reading is only one of the areas in which students struggle, it is an important one because failure in early reading makes learning in the many subject areas that require reading more difficult. Moreover, there is a great deal of comorbidity between reading problems and other difficulties (attentional, behavioral) that results in special education referral.

As indicated above, early screening and intervention would help to identify children who may be missed in a wait-to-fail model. It may obviate the need for placement in special education for some children, and it would provide the evidence of response or lack of response to high-quality instruction that we proposed be written into federal regulations.

Recommendation SE.2: The committee recommends that states adopt a universal screening and multitiered intervention strategy in general education to enable early identification and intervention with children at risk for reading problems.

The committee's model for prereferral reading intervention is as follows:

• All children should be screened early (late kindergarten or early 1st grade) and then monitored through 2nd grade on indicators that predict later reading failure.

• Those students identified through screening as at risk for reading problems should be provided with supplemental small-group reading instruction by the classroom teacher for about 20-30 minutes per day, and progress should be closely monitored.

• For those students who continue to display reading difficulties and for whom supplemental small-group instruction is not associated with improved outcomes, more intensive instruction should be provided by other support personnel, such as the special education teacher and/or reading support teacher in school.

• For students who continue to have difficulty, referral to special education and the development of an IEP would follow. The data regarding student response to intervention would be used for eligibility determination.

• State guidelines should direct that the screening process be undertaken early, and the instructional response follow in a very timely fashion. The requirement for general education interventions should not be used to delay attention to a student in need of specialized services.

The committee's recommendation to adopt a universal screening and multitiered intervention *strategy* is meant to acknowledge that there is some distance to travel between the knowledge base that has been accumulated and the capacity to use that knowledge on a widespread basis. There are early examples in Texas and Virginia of taking screening to scale. But making the tools available to teachers, preparing teachers both to assess students and to respond productively to the assessment results, and supporting teachers to work with the instructional demands of intervening differently for subgroups of students at different skill levels require the careful development of capacity and infrastructure.

At the same time that the committee acknowledges the investment required to adopt this recommendation, we call attention to the potential return on the investment and the consequences of not making such an investment. When early screening and intervention is not undertaken, more students suffer failure. The demands on the school to invest in a support structure for those students is simply postponed to a later age, when the response to intervention is less promising and when the capacity of teachers to intervene effectively is made even more difficult by a weaker knowledge base and limited teacher skill. The consequences of school failure for the student and for society go well beyond the cost to the school, of course.

Behavior Management

Current understanding of early reading problems is the outcome of a sustained research and development effort that has not been undertaken on a similar scale with respect to other learning and behavior problems. In the committee's view, however, there is enough evidence regarding universal behavior management interventions, behavior screening, and techniques to work with children at risk for behavior problems to better prevent later serious behavior problems. Research results suggest that these interventions can work. However a large-scale pilot project would provide a firmer foundation of knowledge regarding scaling up the practices involved.

Recommendation SE.3: The committee recommends that states launch large-scale pilot programs in conjunction with universities or research centers to test the plausibility and productivity of universal behavior management interventions, early behavior screening, and techniques to work with children at risk for behavior problems.

We propose a model for experimentation similar to that proposed for reading:

- Assessment of the classroom and of noninstructional school settings (hallways, playgrounds) should be made yearly.
- Behavioral adjustment of all children in grades K-3 should be screened yearly to provide teachers with information regarding individual children. The assessments should be reviewed yearly by a school-level committee (comprised of administrative and teaching staff, specialists, and parents) to ensure that school-wide interventions are implemented when indicated in a timely fashion and to ensure that individual children are given special services quickly when needed.
- Because characteristics of the classroom and school can increase risk for serious emotional problems, the first step in the determination of an emotional or behavioral disability is the assessment of the classroom and school-wide context. Key contextual factors should be assessed and ruled out as explanations before intervention at the individual child level is considered.
- If it is determined that contextual factors are not significantly involved in the child's problem, then individualized measures should be taken to help the child adjust *in the standard classroom/school setting*. Only those interventions with empirical evidence supporting their effectiveness should be considered. For example, common features of emotional and behavioral problems are off-task and disruptive behaviors. Well documented interventions with demonstrated effectiveness at reducing these behaviors should be employed before the child is considered disabled.
- Because the most serious and developmentally predictive emotional and behavioral problems in children tend to be manifested across settings, and because family issues and solutions tend to overlap with those at school, every effort should be made to include parents and guardians as partners in the educational effort. To the extent that this is done, early and accurate identification of serious problems should be facilitated, and parents can be enlisted to collaborate with teachers in both standard education and in solving emerging academic, emotional, and behavioral problems.
- For children who do not respond to standard interventions, the intensity of the interventions should be increased through the use of behavioral consultants, more intensive collaborations with parents, or through

adjunct interventions to address various skill or emotional deficits (e.g., anger control, social skills instruction). Such individualized programs should be carefully articulated through the use of IEPs, coupled with systematic assessments of the child's behavioral response to the interventions.

Teacher Quality

To support the proposed changes, school psychologists and special education teachers would need preparation that is different in some respects from that now required.

> **Recommendation TQ.3: A credential as a school psychologist or special education teacher should require instruction in classroom observation/assessment and in teacher support to work with a struggling student or with a gifted student. These skills should be considered as critical to their professional role as the administration and interpretation of tests are now considered.**

• Instruction should prepare the professional to provide regular behavioral assessment and support for teachers who need assistance to understand and work effectively with a broad range of student behavior and achievement.

• Recognizing and working with implicit and explicit racial stereotypes should be incorporated.

The proposed reform of special education that would focus on response to intervention in general education would require substantial changes in the current relationship between general and special education. It would put in place a universal prevention element that does not now exist on a widespread basis with the purpose of: (a) providing assistance to children who may now be missed and (b) obviating the need for the special education referrals that can be remedied by early high-quality intervention in the general education context. In the final analysis, the committee cannot predict the effect of this approach on the number of special education students nor on racial/ethnic disproportion, but the result, in our judgment, would be that children identified for special education services would be those truly in need of ongoing support. And if the effect of the classroom context and opportunity to learn is successfully disentangled from the student's need for additional supports, in our view that disproportion in identification would not be as problematic as it is currently.

Federal Support of State Reform Efforts

Recommendation SE.4: While the United States has a strong tradition of state control of education, the committee recommends that the federal government support widespread adoption of early screening and intervention in the states.

In particular:

• Technical assistance and information dissemination should be coordinated at the federal level. This might be done through the Department of Education, the NICHD, a cooperative effort of the two, or through some other designated agent. Accumulation and dissemination of information and research findings has "public good" properties and economies of scale that make a federal effort more efficient than many state efforts.

• The federal government can encourage the use of Title I funds to implement early screening and intervention in both reading and behavior for schools currently receiving those funds. Funds provided in the Reading Excellence Act might also support this effort under the existing mandate.

Gifted and Talented Eligibility

The research base justifying alternative approaches for the screening, identification, and placement of gifted children is neither as extensive nor as informative as that for special education. While limited programs of identification and services for gifted students have been carried out under the auspices of the Jacob K. Javits Gifted and Talented Students Education Program, the collection of data in the framework of any systematic research paradigm has been limited. Yet the importance of early opportunity to learn is likely to be as important for the success of students at the upper end of the achievement distribution as it is for those at the lower end. And the problem of disentangling the children's abilities from their previous opportunities to learn strikes a clear parallel. Nevertheless, the existing research base restricts our understanding and therefore our recommendations: rather than proposing a specific approach to screening or identification for gifted and talented students, we propose research that may allow for better informed decision making in the future.

Recommendation GT.1: The committee recommends a research program oriented toward the development of a broader knowledge base on early identification and intervention with children who exhibit advanced performance in the verbal or quantitative realm, or who exhibit other advanced abilities.

This research program should be designed to determine whether there are reliable and valid indicators of current exceptional performance in language, mathematical, or other domains, or indicators of later exceptional performance. To the extent that the assessments described above provide information relevant to the identification of gifted students, they should be used for that purpose.

In addition to research to support the development of identification instruments, research on classroom practice designed to encourage the early and continued development of gifted behaviors in underrepresented populations should be undertaken so that screening can be followed by effective intervention. That research should be designed to identify:

• Opportunities that can be provided during the kindergarten year to engage children in high-interest learning activities that allow development of complex, advanced reasoning, accelerated learning pace, and advanced content and skill learning capabilities.
• Interventions in later school years with children who demonstrate advanced learning capabilities and their impact on the performance of these children over time.
• The effect of curricular differentiation through various options, such as resource room instruction, independent study, and acceleration, and the interaction of treatments with individual student profiles. Group size, instructional method, and complexity of the curriculum should all be variables under study.

An enriched curriculum designed for gifted students may well improve educational outcomes for all children. As mentioned in Chapter 5, when class size was reduced in 15 schools in Austin, Texas, the two that showed improved student achievement were schools that made other changes as well, including making the curriculum for gifted students in reading and mathematics available to all students (NRC, 1999a). This does not imply, however, that the pace of instruction or the level of student independence is necessarily the same for all students. We recommend that research be conducted using control groups to determine the impact of interventions designed for children identified as gifted on children who have not been so identified.

Part IV

Improving Outcomes

I n this section we turn our attention away from the processes that lead
to special education placement and toward the outcomes for students
once they are assigned. Is special education a benefit for the students
who are placed in it? Do the additional resources improve students' educational prospects? Are the benefits similar for students of different races/
ethnicities? The answer to these questions signals the level of concern that is
warranted regarding the disproportionate representation of minority children. If the educational achievement and life prospects of special education
children is advanced through program placement, then disproportionate
representation is less alarming than if the reverse is true. The ultimate goal
of reducing the disparities in early experiences that generate disproportionate need for services may still be a social policy priority. But special education would nonetheless be a helpful mechanism for responding to the need
for additional supports for school success. Without evidence of educational
benefit, however, assignment to special education warrants close scrutiny.

We ask the same questions for gifted and talented programs. Are there
interventions that make a difference for students placed in these programs?
Our concern here is different in nature. The more effective interventions for
gifted student prove to be, the greater the concern when minority children
who may benefit from that education are not identified. In contrast to
special education, the "gifted" label itself may confer a benefit through

higher expectation and positive perceptions of teachers, peers, and placed students.

In Chapter 9 we review the literature on what works for special education and gifted students. While the research literature provides encouraging findings regarding effective interventions, evidence that looks at racial/ ethnic groups separately was virtually absent. Similarly, there is a paucity of research on the extent to which interventions with documented positive outcomes are used and the difference in utilization among schools in districts with widely differing financial and demographic characteristics.

Our report has covered many different topics, and our recommendations appear in several different chapters. In a final chapter, we revisit the major conclusions of the report. We summarize our answers to the four questions that have structured this inquiry. We then present our recommendations as a consolidated proposal for policy change.

9

Weighing the Benefits of Placement

Placement in a gifted and talented program is widely viewed as beneficial. In addition to providing instruction that is closely tailored to the students served, eligibility signals positive judgment of the student as highly capable. At the outset of this report, we noted a paradox in special education that is not present in gifted education. Special education provides additional resources to support the achievement of eligible students, yet eligibility singles out the student's achievement or behavior as substandard in some respect. And while instruction that is tailored to the needs of high-achieving students raises expectations for their performance, instruction tailored to low-achieving students has the potential to undermine their performance by lowering expectations. Whether placement of minority students in special education in disproportionate numbers should be viewed as a problem depends in part on whether the trade-off is worthwhile. Is special education beneficial to the students it serves? Does the benefit of special education differ for students in different racial/ethnic groups?

DO STUDENTS BENEFIT FROM
SPECIAL EDUCATION INTERVENTIONS?

A rapidly growing body of research details what interventions *have been demonstrated* to work with students who are identified for special education. We summarize these findings below, emphasizing at the outset that the extent to which effective practices are used among students of any race or ethnicity is largely unknown.

The findings reviewed here are drawn from research conducted primarily with students with learning disabilities (LD) and to a lesser extent students with emotional and behavioral disorder (ED/BD). This emphasis reflects the bulk of the research conducted in the past 20 years. Little research on curriculum and instruction has been conducted in that period with students with mild mental retardation (MMR). Most of the research on moderate and severely mentally retarded children has addressed issues of where and not how to teach them, with the debate often being more philosophical than empirical in nature.

Features of Effective Interventions

Considerable progress has been made over the past two decades in designing, implementing, and evaluating effective academic and behavioral interventions for students with disabilities (Gerber, 1999-2000). These interventions have been closely linked to models of learning and to providing access for students with disabilities to the general education curriculum. With the support of the U.S. Department of Education, the Office of Special Education Programs, and the National Center for Learning Disabilities, research syntheses have been completed to examine the converging findings related to intervention studies for children with LD. These syntheses have addressed the overall effectiveness of interventions for students with learning disabilities (Swanson et al., 1999), specific findings for reading comprehension (Gersten et al., 2001) and written expression (Gersten and Baker, 2001), higher-order processing (Swanson, 1999), grouping practices that are associated with improved outcomes in reading (Elbaum et al., 1999), behavioral interventions (Marquis et al., 2000), and interventions for students with learning disabilities associated with improved outcomes in self-concept (Vaughn and Elbaum, 1999). For summaries of the above-stated syntheses, see Gersten and Baker (2000a, b) and Swanson et al. (1999).

Initially presented in Vaughn et al. (2000), the following principles of instruction associated with effective outcomes for students with LD are drawn from the above described syntheses in special education. It is reasonable to assume that the best intervention practices would be hybrids that capitalize on as many of these findings as is sensible.

1. *Research on effective interventions for students with LD has demonstrated success with both general and special education.* All the research conducted thus far demonstrating significantly positive effects for students with LD has also resulted in at least as high (often higher) effect sizes for all other students in the class, including average and high-achieving students.

Given the increasing numbers of students with LD who are provided instruction in the general education classroom, this is a very important finding. Teachers and parents need not be concerned that effective interventions provided for students with disabilities will provide less than effective outcomes for students without disabilities. In addition, it demonstrates that effective interventions for students with disabilities can be generalized and effective in the broader learning community. Thus, intervention practices associated with positive outcomes for individuals with LD have educational benefits for all learners.

It is important to note, however, that it is unclear how these interventions influence students identified as gifted. While many of the interventions and features of instruction designed to improve outcomes for students with disabilities have overall positive outcomes for most students, this should not suggest that students who are gifted or those with severe learning disabilities would not benefit from instruction and curriculum that is even further differentiated. In the case of students who are gifted, more complex curriculum that provides extensive opportunities to extend learning would be needed. For many students with learning disabilities, this may include highly specialized instruction that is provided one-on-one or in very small groups, extended time to learn the building blocks of literacy and math, greater specificity in pacing instruction, additional practice, and continuous feedback.

2. Explicit instruction is a consistent feature of effective interventions (Elbaum et al., 1999; Gersten and Baker, 1998; National Institute of Child Health and Human Development, 2000; National Research Council [NRC], 1998; Swanson, 1999). Students with disabilities reach mastery more quickly when overt strategies for completing tasks are identified and taught. Examples of overt strategies are the explicit teaching of the steps in the writing process (see for review, Swanson et al., 1999; Wong, 1999) or the use of "think alouds" as a means for teaching reading comprehension strategies. The benefit to making instruction explicit and overt is twofold. First, students are given an opportunity to learn how to think about completing a task in a way that they would probably not discover on their own. Second, overt instruction allows teachers and peers to provide students with feedback during the learning process.

The utility of direct instruction has been considered effective for students with ED (Coleman and Vaughn, 2000). In one study, direct instruction was more effective than another approach (i.e., Language Master and independent practice) in terms of increasing sight word acquisition of students with behavioral and emotional disorders (Yell, 1992). A study using focus groups of ED teachers demonstrated that they perceived direct instruction to be effective for these students (Coleman and Vaughn, 2000). In addition, direct instruction was more likely to increase on-task behavior and decrease disruptive behaviors of students with behavioral problems than cooperative learning or independent practice (Nelson et al., 1996).

3. *Interactive dialogue between teacher and student and between students is a feature of effective reading and writing programs.* The role of the teacher and the other students is to provide ongoing and systematic feedback to assist in repairing misunderstandings or revising text, giving students an opportunity to learn from each other and to expand their knowing by linking it to the constructs and thinking of fellow students. For example, Wong (1999) concluded that the quality of feedback and verbal interaction between teacher and student leads to improved outcomes in the quality of written expression.

4. *Basic or fundamental elements of reading and writing, such as sounding out words in reading and handwriting in writing, are essential elements for students with LD.* For example, Berninger and colleagues (1998) found that students' speed of writing is linked with improved outcomes in writing. Word-level reading and decoding of sight words are interventions that are associated with high effect sizes in reading (Swanson et al., 1999). Consequently, effective intervention approaches in reading and writing build skills and knowledge both specifically and broadly using both top-down and bottom-up instruction.

5. *Small-group instruction and pairs are connected with improved outcomes in reading and writing.* As stated earlier, a critical component of effective interventions in reading and writing is interactive dialogue between teacher and student (Gersten and Baker, 1998). For example, in reading, Englert and colleagues (1994) promoted teacher-student dialogue in ways that mediated students' performance and facilitated their use of cognitive strategies while reading. Likewise, interaction between students in the form of peer tutoring has shown effectiveness with all students (Mathes and Fuchs, 1994) and particularly for students with disabilities when they serve as the tutor (Elbaum et al., 1999). These benefits seem to reach beyond academic outcomes. In fact, in a synthesis of intervention studies for elementary students with LD that included self-concept as one of the outcome measures (Elbaum and Vaughn, 2001), interventions focusing on academic skills within cooperative group structures also showed gains in self-concept.

Similarly, students with ED/BD increased their academic performance in various areas (e.g., reading, math) by tutoring (Lock and Fuchs, 1995; Maher, 1982, 1984; Scruggs and Osguthorpe, 1986). Tutoring interventions in special education usually take two formats, cross-age tutoring and peer tutoring (Scruggs and Osguthorpe, 1986). In cross-age tutoring, an older student tutor serves as "expert" providing instruction to a younger student (Durrer and McLaughlin, 1995; Scruggs and Osguthorpe, 1986). Peer tutoring consists of same-age pairs of students working together (Scruggs and Osguthorpe, 1986).

The effectiveness of cross-age tutoring on academic outcomes for students with ED/BD has been well established by many researchers. A recent synthesis on reading intervention for students with ED/BD revealed that cross-age tutoring was the most distinct practice associated with improved reading outcomes for students with ED/BD (Coleman and Vaughn, 2000). Studies by Maher (1982, 1984) reported that cross-age tutoring in which adolescents with BD tutored elementary students with MR yielded increased academic performance (in social science and mathematics) for both tutors and tutees. Top and Osguthorpe (1987) implemented cross-age tutoring by assigning 4th- to 6th graders with BD as tutors for 1st graders without disabilities in reading. Both tutors and tutees increased their reading performance, and tutors with BD improved their self esteem as well. Similarly, cross-age tutoring was associated with social gains for students with BD (Scruggs and Osguthorpe, 1986).

The effectiveness of peer tutoring on academic outcomes yields lower effect sizes than cross-age tutoring, but it is a promising practice for students with ED/BD. Adolescents with BD in roles of both tutor and tutee improved their mathematics outcomes after participating in peer tutoring (Franca et al., 1990). Similarly, peer tutoring yielded improved spelling outcomes for adolescents with BD (Stowitschek et al., 1982). Partner reading, which is a component of class-wide peer tutoring, yielded enhanced on-task behavior and positive social interaction for students with ED/BD (Lock and Fuchs, 1995).

6. *Motivation to learn, task difficulty, and task persistence influence intervention effectiveness.* As early as 1982, Keogh noted that "the organization of curricular content, and the order and sequence of presentation, may have important consequences for children's accomplishments" (p. 33). Planning instruction around task difficulty to ensure students experience success and persist in learning activities has long been recognized as a critical feature of effective instruction for students with LD (Gersten et al. 1984). In addition, "time on task" has been established as an essential factor linked to improved academic outcomes. However, time on task and persistence with tasks is affected by students' motivation to learn and their working on tasks that are challenging, meaningful, and within their capabilities. Most of the instructional activities in which students with LD are engaged are at inappropriate levels of task difficulty. Students who experience some successes in school are much more likely to participate actively in

educational or work experiences following school (SRI International, 1995). Conscious attention to task difficulty is likely to be linked to higher levels of student achievement (Swanson and Hoskyn, 1998). To date, research in instructional areas such as reading comprehension, expressive writing, and problem solving has rarely addressed these issues of task difficulty, persistence, and motivation in a systematic fashion. In part, this is because the domains of these topics have not been well systematized (Kucan and Beck, 1997), especially in terms of task difficulty and measurement. This may well be a productive direction for future research.

Maintaining motivation to learn for students with BD/ED was identified as a challenge for teachers (Coleman and Vaughn, 2000). These students lack interest in school and tend to attribute their failure in school to their inability rather than the need for increased practice (Cutler, 1982; Luchow et al., 1985). Kim (1999) found that students with BD showed higher rates of off-task behaviors under learning conditions that provided difficult tasks and low adult attention.

7. *Procedural facilitators or strategies help students develop a plan to guide their learning in the areas of reading comprehension, written expression, and general higher-order processing.* Students with LD are not likely to discover these plans of action on their own, and therefore it is necessary that they be explicitly taught. For example, although students with LD may possess the conceptual and background knowledge to generate texts about a particular topic (e.g., the American Revolution), they may appear to have little of this foundation knowledge because they do not have a strategy for generating the categories and structure of expository text about the American Revolution, including setting, key characters, plot, etc. (Englert and Raphael, 1988). By teaching students strategies, the teacher provides them with "their culture's best kept secret about how to obtain academic success" (Harris and Pressley, 1991:395).

With practice, proficiency with the strategy develops, and there is an increased likelihood that students will apply the strategy on their own in new contexts. To facilitate the spontaneous application of strategies, it would seem that students must be explicitly taught where, when, and how to use a particular strategy. Once students have this metacognitive knowledge, they can take ownership of the strategies and modify them for use in different situations. Some of the research in science on using self-assessment procedures to monitor task and progress may be particularly useful for students with disabilities (White and Frederiksen, 1998).

Evidence of Effectiveness

According to Kavale and Forness (2000), who reported findings from meta-analyses of the effectiveness of many interventions in special education, the following types of interventions have been highly effective with students with disabilities (the number in parentheses is the mean effect size): computer-assisted instruction (0.52), peer tutoring (0.56), direct instruction (0.84), behavior modification (0.93), reading comprehension (0.98, 0.113), and mnemonic strategies (0.162).

Hockenbury et al. (1999-2000) also comment on the effectiveness of special education:

> Special education has a considerable history of devising and testing effective instructional methods for atypical students. These include, for example, direct instruction (e.g., Gersten, 1985; White, 1988), self-monitoring (e.g., Lloyd et al., 1989; Webber et al., 1993), mnemonic instruction (e.g., Mastropieri and Scruggs, 1998; Scruggs and Mastropieri, 1990), strategy training (e.g., Deshler and Schumaker, 1986; Ellis et al., 1991; Hughes and Schumaker, 1992), curriculum-based measurement (e.g., Deno and Fuchs, 1987; Fuchs and Fuchs, 1996), applied behavior analysis (e.g., Jenson et al., 1988; Wolery et al., 1988), and functional assessment (e.g., Arndorfer and Miltenberger, 1993; Horner and Carr, 1997). Some of these instructional methods are applicable in some form to many students in general education. This does not, however, preclude the need for special education. One thing that is right about special education is that it includes devising and testing empirically methods of instruction that are effective with atypical students, whose instruction often must be different in content or be made more explicit, carefully controlled, carefully monitored, intensive, and sustained than instruction for typical learners (p. 6).

Minority Students with Learning Disabilities and Behavior Disorders

Minority students are often represented in intervention research. However, findings for minority students are rarely, if ever, disaggregated and compared to majority students with LD or BD. The assumption is that the performance of minority students with disabilities is comparable to majority students with disabilities.

Recently, a synthesis on instructional practices for English language learners was reported (Gersten and Baker, 2000a). Combining both a multivocal synthesis and a more traditional meta-analysis, results provide minimal guidelines for instruction of students who are English language learners. Eight studies that provided both an experimental and a control group were located. Effect sizes ranged from –0.56 to 1.95, with a median effect size of 0.25. This documents the frequently held belief that there is little empirical data on the effectiveness of interventions with English language learners. Even these studies were often unclear about how interventions were implemented and the language of instruction.

In any study with diverse populations, there are certain variables akin to Keogh's "marker variables" for LD (Keogh et al., 1978). For minority students and English language learners, these would include, at a minimum, socioeconomic status (SES), ethnicity or race, and language proficiency in both languages if bilingualism is involved. These variables are particularly salient to consider when interpreting results from intervention studies. Of the 180 intervention studies of students with LD that were synthesized by Swanson et al. (1999:78), the majority did not report ethnicity; however, of the studies that did report it, 7 studies included Asians/Pacific Islanders, (4.71, 6.01), 25 studies included blacks (7.42, 7.97), 36 studies included whites (11.67, 8.45), 11 studies included Hispanics (9.36, 10.11), 2 studies included Native Americans/Alaskan Natives (1.0, —). (Note: The first number in parentheses represents the mean number of students and the second number the standard deviation.) Findings disaggregated by ethnicity were neither provided nor possible to calculate.

Special Education Settings Versus the General Education Classroom

Interventions that are designed to be implemented in the general education classroom for students whose primary disabilities are in learning and behavior demonstrate improved outcomes for all participants, even those who are average to high achieving. However, the overall outcomes, even of the most effective class-wide interventions implemented in general education classrooms, demonstrate low to modest effects for students with disabilities that are unlikely to significantly improve academic and social outcomes in ways that will adequately compensate for how far behind they are.

For most students with disabilities, overall improvements in general education classroom instruction are a necessary but insufficient means to adequate instruction (Zigmond and Baker, 1994; Zigmond et al., 1995). This is not a commentary on where students are taught (general education classroom, resource room, special education setting), but rather a recognition that additional intensive and specifically designed instruction is necessary to enhance their outcomes.

Since students with reading disabilities are the subgroup for whom there are the most converging data, we provide a brief discussion of their response to treatment. The effectiveness of intervention strategies for children at risk for, or having, reading problems has been examined in several recent meta-analyses.

Group Size. One of the most significant ways to improve the intensity and effectiveness of instruction is to modify dramatically the size of the group taught. For students with reading disabilities, this means that students need to be instructed in groups of four or fewer.

Elbaum et al. (2000) carried out a meta-analysis of the effects of one-to-one tutoring in reading for students at risk for reading problems. They cumulated the results of 31 studies that contained a total of 219 effect sizes reported from 44 independent samples of children. The main results of interest were that the average weighted effect size was 0.39. The average weighted effect size for Reading Recovery of 0.60 was significantly greater than that for the other interventions of 0.27. However, the average weighted effect size for Reading Recovery is biased positively because many studies do not report results for all children who received the intervention. When intervention is provided by volunteers rather than professional educators, training and supervision were critical. Amount of intervention provided was not a predictor of variability in effect sizes across studies. In another meta-analysis, Elbaum and her colleagues (1999) cumulated studies that examined the effects of peer tutoring in reading. The average weighted effect size for peer tutoring in reading was 0.40.

Similarly, Russ and her colleagues (2001) synthesized the research about class size for students with disabilities. The findings revealed that students' engagement in tasks increased when group size decreased, regardless of age or type of disability. In addition, small group sizes were associated with higher academic performance of students with mild disabilities.

Focus of Instruction. Swanson (1999) carried out a meta-analysis of the effects of various reading interventions for children and adolescents who were identified as having a learning disability. They cumulated the results of 54 studies that contained a total of 159 effect sizes for word recognition and 58 studies that contained a total of 176 effect sizes for reading comprehension. The average weighted effect sizes were .57 for word identification and .72 for reading comprehension. Variability in effect sizes across studies was not predicted by number of treatment sessions. Larger effect sizes for word recognition were associated with interventions that featured segmentation and sequencing as tools for simplifying complex or difficult tasks and metacognitive instruction in the form of advance organizers.

R.K. Wagner (2000) carried out a meta-analysis of the effects of phonological awareness training on seven reading-related outcome measures: phonemic decoding (word attack), word identification, word-level decoding (a composite of phonemic decoding and word identification), fluency, comprehension, spelling, and phonological awareness. Results presented in Table 9-1 show that average weighted effect sizes ranged from a low of 0.36 for fluency to 0.84 for phonological awareness. Various moderators

TABLE 9-1 Effect Sizes from Meta-Analysis of the Effects of
Phonological Awareness Training

Outcome	Average Weighted Effect Size	95 percent CI
Word-level decoding	0.46	0.39-0.54
Phonemic decoding	0.79	0.69-0.90
Word identification	0.38	0.31-0.46
Fluency	0.36	0.13-0.59
Comprehension	0.48	0.34-0.62
Spelling	0.47	0.40-0.55
Phonological awareness	0.84	0.77-0.91

SOURCE: Wagner (2000).

predicted variability in effect sizes across studies, but these moderators varied across the seven outcome measures.

The studies that reported posttraining follow-up data were used in a separate meta-analysis to assess maintenance of effects after training. Unlike most treatments, for which dissipation of training effects is expected over time, an intriguing possibility is that the effects of phonological awareness training may actually increase over time. Empirical support for this idea is provided by a study reported by Lundberg et al. (1988), in which the effects of phonological awareness training done in preschool appear to become larger from 1st to 2nd grade in the absence of any additional phonological awareness training. Theoretical support for the possibility of maintenance or even increase in posttraining effects is provided by idea of Matthew effects in reading (Stanovich, 1986). The reference is to the biblical notion of the rich getting richer and the poorer getting poorer, which in the present context translates into the widening gap between good and poor readers that is observed as children move through their elementary school years. One explanation of Matthew effects is differences in the instructional experience provided to good and poor readers. It has been estimated that within a regular classroom, children in the top reading group read an *order of magnitude* more words in school per week than do children in the bottom reading group. A second explanation is motivational differences, which derive from whether reading is easy and enjoyable or difficult and painful. Children who experience success at early reading may be more likely to read more both in and out of school than children who experience early failure.

Alternatively, it may be the case that the effects of phonological awareness lessen over time after completion of the training program, as is characteristic of the effects of most interventions. This possibility is even more likely if it is the case that the effects of phonological awareness training are largely to "hot-house" beginning readers by enabling them to read sooner that they would otherwise, but ultimately no better overall. Consider the question of when to commence reading instruction. The conventional wisdom is that although it is possible to teach many children to read in kindergarten or even in preschool, there is no advantage in doing so because children who are taught to read in 1st grade soon will catch up with those taught to read earlier. Might the same outcome be expected for phonological awareness training? If so, no long-term effects of training are expected.

The results on maintenance of effects of training are presented in Table 9-2. Negative values for weighted mean are interpreted as dissipation of training effects after treatment ends, whereas positive values are interpreted as enhanced training effects upon follow-up. All of the weighted means were either significantly negative or not reliably different from zero. Clearly, training effects are not magnified over time once training has ended. At best they are maintained or diminish considerably.

Numbers of Children Who Appear to Benefit

Substantial effect sizes, which reflect the average performance of an intervention group relative to a control group, can be obtained even when, for example, a third of the group fails to respond to the intervention at all.

These issues can be illustrated by an intervention study carried out by Torgesen et al. (2001): 60 children with severe reading problems were randomly assigned to two instructional programs. Both programs incorporated principles of effective instruction. They differed in whether articulatory-based cues were used in training phonemic awareness and in amount of decontextualized training in phonemic awareness and phonemic decoding skills. An Auditory Discrimination in Depth (ADD) program provided considerable decontextualized training using articulatory-based cues. An Embedded Phonics (EP) program provided less decontextualized training,

TABLE 9-2 Maintenance of Effects of Training

Outcome	Average Weighted Effect Size	Z	p
Phonemic decoding	−0.148	−1.53	n.s
Word identification	−0.221	−4.66	<0.001
Fluency	0.199	1.24	n.s.
Comprehension	−0.092	−1.05	n.s.
Spelling	−0.154	−3.12	<0.001
Phonological awareness	−0.560	−10.0	<0.001

SOURCE: Wagner (2000).

did not use articulatory-based cues, but provided more practice reading connected text. All children received 67.5 hours of one-to-one intervention and were followed for two years after the intervention was completed. The performance of both groups was compared to growth they had made during their previous 16 months in LD resource rooms before the intervention began, yielding effect sizes of 4.4 and 3.9 for the two interventions.

Group averages for eight reading outcomes are presented in Table 9-3 for the ADD group and Table 9-4 for the EP group. Performance is expressed in standard scores with the average represented by scores of 90 or above. Note that group performance reaches the average range for word attack accuracy (phonemic decoding), remains a bit lower for word identification accuracy, and is lower for rate or efficiency than for accuracy. Percentages of children who had scores that were below the average range, and conversely, the percentage of children whose performance reached the average range (percentage normalized) are presented in Tables 9-5 and 9-6 for the two intervention groups. The key results for our purposes are that although these were powerful interventions, a substantial number of children remained below average, especially for measures of rate or efficiency.

Torgesen (2000) provided estimates of the number of treatment resisters, defined as falling below the 30 percentile after completion of the intervention. These results are presented in Tables 9-5 and 9-6. Based on these results, between 4 and 5 percent of children would continue to need help if the best existing interventions were given to all who needed them. These results are consistent with evaluations of other interventions. For example, as previously discussed, evaluating the success of Reading Recovery is com-

TABLE 9-3 Outcomes for Eight Reading Measures Expressed in Standard Scores: Additory Discrimination in Depth (N = 30)

	Pre	Post	1 Yr	2 Yrs
Decoding measures				
Word attack	68.5	96.4	90.7	91.8
Nonword efficiency	74.3	83.3	81.6	84.3
Word identification	68.9	82.4	82.7	87.0
Sight-word efficiency	69.7	74.5	79.3	82.1
Gray oral				
Accuracy	73.8	89.4	93.7	91.3
Rate	71.3	75.4	75.0	72.7
Comprehension measures				
Passage comprehension	80.1	91.0	92.8	94.7
Gray oral	73.3	85.6	90.2	87.9

SOURCE: Wagner (2000).

TABLE 9-4 Outcomes for Eight Reading Measures Expressed in Standard Scores: Embedded Phonics (N = 30)

	Pre	Post	1 Yr	2 Yrs
Decoding measures				
Word attack	70.1	90.3	87.0	89.9
Nonword efficiency	75.7	83.7	80.6	82.7
Word identification	66.4	80.5	78.2	83.9
Sight-word efficiency	67.3	72.7	74.4	77.8
Gray Oral				
Accuracy	77.5	87.5	90.8	90.4
Rate	71.5	72.1	72.1	70.7
Comprehension measures				
Passage comprehension	82.2	88.2	91.5	96.9
Gray oral	79.4	86.0	88.1	87.2

SOURCE: Wagner (2000).

plicated by the fact that some children who are not successful in the program are not included in evaluation reports. However, at least one-third of children who complete Reading Recovery successfully make insufficient progress in subsequent years to maintain adequate reading skills (Center et al., 1995). An extensive evaluation of the program Success for All determined that 16 percent of children from schools in which the program had been implemented for three years remained at least one year below grade level, and 3.9 percent were at least two years behind.

Ironically, the estimate that between 4 and 5 percent of children would continue to need help if the best existing interventions were given to all who need them is similar to the percentage of children currently who are receiving special education services for reading problems. Recall that 5.8 percent of school-age children are served under the Individuals with Disabilities Education Act (IDEA) for specific learning disabilities. Using the estimate that reading is the primary problem for 80 percent of children with specific learning disabilities results in an estimate of 4.8 percent currently receiving special education services for specific reading disabilities. Thus, the number of children who need continued help is not likely to diminish even if a program were put in place so that children with reading problems could receive the best available treatments. However, because of bias in the referral and placement process that results in an abundance of boys with concomitant behavior and attention problems receiving services, many of the 4 to 5 percent of children who would need continued help do not overlap with the 4 to 5 percent of children currently being served. We would expect

TABLE 9-5 Percentage of Children in Embedded Phonics Program with Standard Scores Below 90 (Percentage Normalized)

	Pre	Post	2 Yrs	
Decoding measures				
Word attack	100	54	46	(54)
Nonword efficiency	100	83	83	(17)
Word identification	100	83	67	(33)
Sight-word efficiency	100	100	87	(13)
Gray Oral				
Accuracy	79	62	35	(44)
Rate	100	100	91	(09)
Comprehension measures				
Passage comprehension	75	46	21	(54)
Gray oral	71	50	52	(19)

SOURCE: Wagner (2000).

more girls, for example, to be identified in this group. In addition, the impact would vary by state, given their marked differences in rates of identification and placement of children with reading problems.

While the behavioral problems of students with ED/BD are well documented (Kauffman, 1993; Kerr and Nelson, 1989; Russell and Ann, 1985), the academic difficulties of this population often have not been the focus of research. However, students with ED/BD have demonstrated severe aca-

TABLE 9-6 Percentage of Children in Auditory Discrimination in Depth Program with Standard Scores Below 90 (Percentage Normalized)

	Pre	Post	2 Yrs	
Decoding measures				
Word attack	100	16	31	(69)
Nonword efficiency	100	92	73	(27)
Word identification	100	72	61	(39)
Sight-word efficiency	100	100	88	(12)
Gray Oral				
Accuracy	92	40	35	(57)
Rate	100	96	88	(12)
Comprehension measures				
Passage comprehension	65	40	15	(50)
Gray oral	92	64	46	(46)

SOURCE: Wagner (2000).

demic difficulties. According to Kauffman (1993), more than two-thirds of students with ED/BD fall below their grade level. Reading is one of the areas in which they demonstrate significant difficulties (Coleman and Vaughn, 2000; Mastropieri et al., 1985). Despite needs for effective reading instruction, there are very few intervention studies in reading for students with BD/ED (Coleman and Vaughn, 2000).

Current Classroom Practice

Current classroom practice deviates far too extensively from the knowledge of best practice to enhance outcomes for students with disabilities, and the quality of teacher preparation for both special and general education teachers with respect to instructing youngsters with disabilities is seriously inadequate. While there are indeed educators for whom this is not true—they are the exceptions.

To what extent is knowledge about effective instructional practices actually part of district and school recommendations and actually imple mented in classrooms? The answer "it depends on the school or teacher" is both apparent and true, but less than useful in addressing the issue of adequacy of implementation of educational and behavioral practices for students with disabilities.

There is general consensus that considerably more is known about effective instruction than is implemented (Carnine, 2000; Chall, 2000). There is a range of explanations for why this is the case and what should be done about it, but little disagreement that research-based practices are not broadly implemented. And students who have the most to lose by not being provided with the most effective practices are students with disabilities and minority students.

Prior to the IDEA requirement for access to the general education curriculum, observational studies of students with LD in general education settings revealed that many students were not provided access to the general education curriculum and that meaningful participation often did not occur. For example, in a year-long study that was conducted in 60 general education classrooms during social studies and science classes in which a student with LD was present during the lesson: (a) instruction for students with disabilities was not differentiated; (b) students with disabilities were provided little instruction or support that allowed them to have meaningful access to the general education curriculum, despite significant gaps in reading and study skills; (c) students with disabilities demonstrated significantly low levels of interaction, including not asking for or receiving instructional assistance; and (d) students with disabilities did not respond to questions from the teacher (McIntosh et al., 1993).

Across multiple sites and settings (e.g., Zigmond et al., 1995), studies have confirmed the undifferentiated instruction provided for students with disabilities (Baker and Zigmond, 1990). This does not necessarily mean that students with LD were not receiving an appropriate education, so long as their progress was being monitored appropriately. These studies as well as others have resulted in questions about how to ensure that students with disabilities are provided with access to the general education curriculum and how their progress should be monitored. The notion of monitoring students' progress is a direct result of the lack of sufficient data for determining that placement in special education was associated with improved outcomes for students with disabilities.

There has been a convergence of the knowledge base about effective interventions for teaching reading to struggling readers (NRC, 1998); however, too little of this knowledge has been woven into the instruction provided for students with disabilities. For example, instruction in reading for students with difficulties is often provided as a whole class format, even when group sizes are as small as three to six (Allington et al., 1986). Although most agree that "children learn best when instruction corresponds to their current reading level, and may not learn well if the instruction is not attuned to their stage in learning to read" (Brady and Moats, 1997:9), students with LD are often provided with the same reading instruction, even though their abilities cut across a broad range (i.e., 3 to 5 grade levels; Vaughn et al., 1998). Students with disabilities are not provided instruction tailored to meet their individual needs in large part because teachers are responsible for teaching too many students at one time (Moody et al., 2000). Thus, many students with disabilities are not provided the explicit intensive instruction they need (Zigmond and Baker, 1995).

Minority Students in Special Education

The committee is not aware of any published studies that compare the quality of special education programs or the efficacy of specific instructional practices among various racial/ethnic groups. However, from what is known of the context of schools that serve minority children from low-income communities, it is reasonable to suspect that certain aspects of these schools will not be conducive to state-of-the-art practice. Two particular aspects that are likely to be detrimental to special education efficacy in such settings are low parental empowerment and lower levels of education and experience of school personnel.

In Chapter 5 we referred to the fact that parent advocacy is considered a factor that should protect children from inappropriate placement or treatment. The literature on parent advocacy, however, shows that minority parents with low incomes tend to be perceived by school personnel as generally passive and uninvolved in the special education process. Qualitative studies of interaction between school personnel and family members indicate that the responsibility for this pattern lies as much in the way discourse is structured by school personnel as in various logistical barriers faced by such parents (Bennett, 1988; Connery, 1987; Harry et al., 1995; Harry, 1992; Lynch and Stein, 1987; Patton and Braithwaite, 1984; Tomlinson et al., 1977; Sharp, 1983). In the study by Harry et al., for example, participant observations and interviews in an inner-city school district serving black students revealed little effort to encourage parental presence at individualized education program (IEP) conferences. Parents were frequently told that it would be all right if they couldn't attend and that the "paperwork" would be sent to them to sign and return. Interviews with parents revealed that many did not understand the importance of the conferences or that their input could influence the outcomes.

Also as discussed in Chapter 5, it is known that schools serving low-income minorities are staffed with less qualified and less experienced personnel (Darling-Hammond and Post, 2000; U.S. Department of Education, 2001a). It is evident that in special education specific expertise and high-quality personnel preparation is particularly important. It is also one of the tenets of special education that children should receive individualized instruction and that, to accomplish this, small class sizes should be expected. Yet in a three-year ethnographic study of 12 elementary schools in a large urban school district in a southern state, Klingner and Harry (2001) found that it was common for classes for children with high-incidence disabilities to have between 18 and 24 students with one teacher. In the research sample, however, the two schools that served higher-income populations had much smaller class sizes, typically between 6 and 10 students. The findings of this study also reflected the pattern of less skilled teachers in the schools that served low-income populations.

There is currently a severe shortage of special educators and related personnel (Council for Exceptional Children, 2001). Nearly 98 percent of public schools currently report a shortage of special education teachers (Boyer, 2000). According to the Bureau of Labor Statistics, employment of special education teachers is expected to increase faster than the average for all occupations through 2008.

These severe personnel shortages will present significant challenges to the nation's capacity to deliver appropriate education, intervention, and supportive services to students with special needs. Since school districts with the highest concentrations of minority students have more difficulty attracting and retaining teachers (see Chapter 5), services are likely to suffer most in those school districts. A key focus of concern should be teacher preparation programs.

These findings point to the likelihood of rather discrepant patterns of parental influence as well as instructional quality in special education programs serving low-income, minority populations.

The *National Longitudinal Transition Study of Students in Special Education* (SRI International, 1995) revealed that after high school, only 73 percent of students with LD were involved in work or educational activities. Furthermore, only 50 percent of students with BD/ED were employed (SRI International, 1995). Dropout rates are particularly high for BD/ED and LD students. As Figure 9-1 shows, almost a third of students in these two categories fail to graduate. This highlights the need for continued attention to instructional research in this area to enhance outcomes for these students.

On a positive note, appropriate interventions that enhance outcomes for students with LD have been identified, and there is substantial research documenting their effectiveness. These findings have brought the field a long way from the "process approaches" to instruction that characterized early research efforts. However, there is still a long way to go. For example, understanding of the importance of task persistence on learning is still emerging. Similarly, strategy instruction is known to be effective, but surprisingly little is known about how to get students to "own" strategies, adapt them, and apply them spontaneously to new contexts. Investigation of these areas and others must continue in order take the field and the students to the next level.

The big principles of instruction presented earlier are not revolutionary. Certainly, these principles are both intuitively reasonable and well recognized as effective instructional practices for students with LD. However, these principles are rarely implemented in classrooms (McIntosh et al., 1993) and certainly less than consistently. The future challenge is to increase the sustained implementation of these documented effective practices in all classrooms.

WHAT WORKS FOR GIFTED STUDENTS?

Most gifted and talented students spend the majority of their time at school in the general education classroom. Relatively little is known about the extent to which instruction is differentiated for them. Westberg and colleagues (1993) conducted structured observations in a national sample of 46 3rd and 4th grade classrooms. The study found very little differentiation of curriculum in any area; in 84 percent of the activities in which students participated, there was no difference at all. The greatest amount of differentiation occurred in mathematics, in which advanced content instruction constituted 11 percent of the mathematics activities (Westberg et al., 1993).

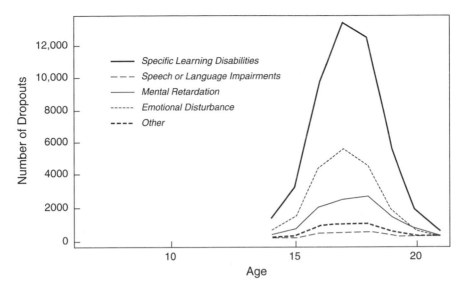

FIGURE 9-1a Number with disability label dropping out by age, 1997-1998.
SOURCE: Data from U.S. Department of Education (2000).

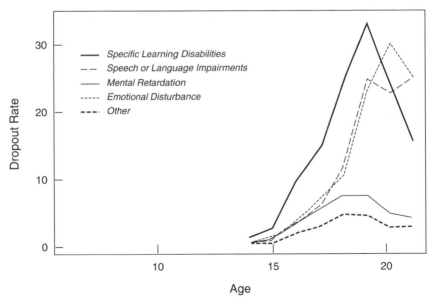

FIGURE 9-1b Dropout rate among students with disability label by age, 1997-1998.
SOURCE: Data from U.S. Department of Education (2000).

Any evaluation of the relative effectiveness of services or curricular options offered to students identified as gifted, and particularly to minority students who are identified as gifted, is hampered by the relative lack of empirical research on intervention effects. As noted throughout this report, the field of gifted education is characterized by a literature with a very small research base. Rogers (1989) concluded from her review of the major databases that only 32 percent of all citations were reports of research. In 1990, Carter and Swanson identified 1,700 articles focusing on giftedness, winnowed them to prominent, frequently cited articles, and found that only 29 percent were based on data compared with 78 percent of a similarly devised list of articles on learning disabilities. More recent reviews by Ziegler and Raul (2000) of articles published in 1997 and 1998 in the five journals addressing gifted education and by Heller and Schofield (2000), of six journals published between 1992 and 1998 reaffirmed that only a small proportion of publications in gifted education are data based (33 percent in the Ziegler and Raul study and 23 percent in the Heller and Schofield analysis).

Shore et al. (1991) concluded that of 110 recommended practices in gifted education, only 40 percent were supported by empirical evidence in the literature, "most of them marginally, and few of these directly address curriculum, programming or pedagogy" (p. 279). While there has been a body of research that has addressed many of these pedagogical issues related to the gifted population since that time, problems surrounding interpretation of the results prevail. Among those problems is the wide variability in definition of giftedness used in the studies, making comparison and generalization difficult.

A methodological shortcoming of many of the studies is the use of single-sample reporting (lack of control groups or comparison groups) or equal quality control in qualitative studies, which limits interpretation of the findings. For example, Ziegler and Raul (2000) report that only 20 of 90 data-based articles they reviewed included control group information. Furthermore, in many cases the populations studied were derived from groups determined by identification procedures of local school divisions rather than researcher-imposed criteria for giftedness or researcher assessment, leaving exact determination of the groups served as gifted somewhat vague and indeterminate.

The drawing of clear, sound conclusions from the research base is hampered by the intertwined variables of differing program delivery options and curricular offerings and the assessment of broad curricular models with multiple and varied expected outcomes rather than specific instructional strategies. For example, the term "acceleration" may refer to early entrance to kindergarten, grade skipping, or early entrance to college, or it may mean acceleration of the curriculum while maintaining age-expected grade placement (e.g., independently studying algebra while in third grade). While all of these options involve delivering content that is more advanced than grade-level expectations, the environment for delivery may have widely differing effects on social and emotional adjustment. Similarly, curricular options entitled "enrichment" may use curricular options ranging from a specific curricular model, such as the Schoolwide Enrichment Model (Renzulli and Reis, 1985), to activities structured around a set of guidelines for curricular modification, such as those that grew out of the work of the National/State Leadership Training Institute (Kaplan, 1979), or models for differentiation in the regular classroom (Tomlinson, 1999; Winebrenner, 2000).

Nonetheless, the meta-analyses of grouping programs for gifted students that involve a substantial adjustment of curriculum to match identified student strengths have shown clear positive effects on gifted children (Kulik, 1992; Kulik and Kulik, 1997). Rogers (1991) also concluded that ability grouping for curriculum extension in a pull-out program produces an academic effect size of 0.65.

Research on Curriculum Models

Research studies on several of the major curriculum models has yielded some evidence of success in achieving the goals specified by the models for a particular type of gifted student. We briefly discuss acceleration, school-wide enrichment, triarchic components, and integrated curriculum models.

Acceleration

Perhaps no other curriculum or programming model has been more widely investigated than acceleration. In this report, acceleration is considered a curriculum model in the sense that whatever the placement of the child, he or she will either be studying the content at a more rapid pace or at a more advanced level than might be expected of a child of that age or normal grade placement. As one example of this model, the effects of the Study of Mathematically Precocious Youth on students who score exceptionally high on the quantitative portion of the SAT as middle-school students have been reported in more than 300 published articles, journals, and books. These reports have ranged from case studies of individual children to long-term follow-ups of the effects on groups of students who had been enrolled in the program. Outcome variables that are assessed in control group studies are represented by a study that compared students who participated in the Johns Hopkins University Center for Talented Youth academic programs with nonparticipating eligible students over a 5-year time period. In general, the Johns Hopkins model has been an out-of-school model with instruction offered through colleges and universities during the summer. Both groups exhibited high academic achievement, but the center youth took more advanced courses at an earlier age and enrolled in more college courses while in high school (Barnett and Durden, 1993). While many of the other studies do not include control samples, reviewers of this literature conclude that the model garners "long-term positive repeated impacts" (VanTassel-Baska, 2000).

Kulik and Kulik (1984) examined the more general model of acceleration in a meta-analysis of 26 controlled studies in which the achievement of accelerated students in school settings was directly compared with non-accelerated students. The achievement of the accelerants exceeded that of the nonaccelerants by nearly one full grade level. Shore et al. (1991) conclude from their qualitative analysis of the literature that "the academic benefits of acceleration are clear" (p. 79). Many of the same authors that extol the academic benefits of acceleration also point to a lack of evidence that acceleration has deleterious emotional effects. Cornell et al. (1991), however, question that assertion, noting that studies of acceleration have failed to use control groups or have failed to assess adjustment prior to the implementation of acceleration.

School-wide Enrichment Model

Research on the Enrichment Triad Model (Renzulli, 1977), which evolved into the Schoolwide Enrichment Model, has documented that students and teachers both hold positive perceptions of the program (Cooper, 1983; Olenchak and Renzulli, 1989; Reis, 1981). The more liberal definition of giftedness espoused by the model and the more inclusive nature of many of the instructional activities are considered a strong base for talent development (Renzulli and Reis, 1994). The limited research on outcomes has compared only the products of students identified for the program with those identified by more traditional methods (finding no difference in quality) (Reis, 1981) and has documented that students who complete the products characteristic of the model more often initiate similar projects both inside and outside the school setting than did similar students who did not receive such instruction (Starko, 1986).

The Triarchic Model

The Triarchic Componential Model (Sternberg, 1981) was not developed as a curriculum model, but rather as a model of intellectual functioning. In this model, Sternberg (1988) posits that intellectual ability is made up of three components: memory-analytic, creative-synthetic, and practical-contextual. Sternberg and his colleagues have demonstrated that elementary, middle school, and high school students who are instructed in curricular and instructional formats that match exceptional strength in one of the triarchic areas or who excelled in all three perform better on measures of achievement than students who do not receive matched instruction. (Sternberg and Clinkenbeard 1994; Sternberg et al., 1996, 1998a, b).

Integrated Curriculum Model

A specific unit of science instruction based on another curriculum model (Integrated Curriculum Model) has shown promise for the development of integrated science process skills in gifted children (VanTassel-Baska et al., 1998). Gifted students in classrooms (including homogeneous self-contained classrooms, pull-out classes, cluster-grouped gifted students within heterogeneous classrooms, and heterogeneous classrooms) instructed for 20-36 hours using a problem-based unit earned significantly higher scores (on an assessment of specific skills in the process of designing, collecting data and analyzing data) than an "equally able" (p. 200) comparison group. While the size of the differences between means was quite small, the effect size of 1.3 suggests that this model warrants further consideration. The type of gifted students who benefit from this unit are not described, as they were identified by the schools in which the classrooms were located. Staff of the curriculum development project scored the test protocols, and no independent verification of the model has been conducted. As in the last model, the developers or advocates of the model have done the evaluation. In addition, no systematic investigation of the effects on minority students has been included either within general studies of the model or with designs that specifically included minority students.

Specific Instructional Practices

Compacting

One of the most widely recommended practices for use with academically gifted students is called "compacting." In this strategy, students are preassessed to determine what parts of a particular unit of instruction (content or skill) a child has already mastered. Then instruction is designed so that students with mastery may extend their learning or accelerate to new learning. For those areas in which mastery is not demonstrated, the students either receive individual instruction or are included in the whole-class instruction on that topic or in that skill. The success of compacting was documented in a study in which treatment students who had had between 40 and 50 percent of their curriculum eliminated did not score significantly differently on achievement measures than students who had experienced the full range of the curriculum. Examination of trends indicates that ceiling effects on the one-year-out-of-level tests may have masked greater gains by the treatment group.

In another out-of-school instructional intervention, young mathematically precocious children began receiving treatment as kindergarteners or 1st graders. Collecting data over a 2-year period, Robinson et al. (1997) demonstrated that a constructivist curriculum (problem posing, multiple solution paths, translating math concepts from one domain to another, solution sharing) delivered 14 times per academic year on Saturday mornings resulted in greater gains by the treatment group on measures of quantitative achievement.

Direct Instruction and Inquiry Development

While any studies of direct instruction versus other models conducted in classroom settings are most likely to include gifted students, the literature most often fails to analyze relative effects of the instructional model on that particular subgroup of students. Judy et al. (1988) investigated the relative effects of direct instruction versus inquiry approaches to learning about analogical reasoning. They found that gifted students benefited more from direct instruction but suggested that the difference may have been because of its novelty to the students. An earlier study of the efficacy of the inquiry development materials developed by Suchman (1962) compared with traditional science activities with high-IQ 7th grade students found no significant differences on measures of critical thinking or science achievement (Youngs and Jones, 1969).

Peer Tutoring

Peer tutoring is a strategy used in many classrooms based on the assumption that all students benefit from the experience. Higher-achieving students, including those who are gifted, presumably gain greater and deeper understanding of the content area taught by virtue of the teaching experience. Feldman et al. (1976) reviewed the empirical data on the effects of peer tutoring on tutors and tutees and found that while the positive effects on low-achieving student tutors were documented, the effects on high-achieving students were not, and the effects on tutees were inconclusive. A review by Arreaga-Mayer et al. (1998) points to the benefits of peer tutoring for several at-risk groups, but no evidence is presented on benefits to the gifted student. The research of Judy et al. (1988) did include gifted students in tutoring situations, who did not benefit from the tutoring experience. Wiegmann et al. (1992), in contrast, found that high-ability students benefited most from playing the student role. Other studies of peer tutoring do not contribute to the understanding of effects on students at the highest level of performance for a variety of reasons (e.g., consideration of the "high" group as those above the median in a class—Depaulo et al., 1989—or samples of college students).

Training in Mnemonic Strategies

In a comparison of free study and the use of high, medium, and low structure mnemonic strategies with gifted students, their learning of low-level factual recall of information was enhanced by the provision of complex mnemonic strategies. Gifted students transferred those strategies to new learning situations, albeit more effectively with minimal prompting (Scruggs and Mastropieri, 1988; Scruggs et al., 1986).

Grouping Arrangements

The practice of tracking has been much debated. Since the work of Oakes was published in 1985 suggesting that ability grouping "does not appear to be related to either improving academic achievement or promoting positive attitudes and behavior," and that "poor and minoirty students seem to have suffered most from tracking," (p. 191), tracking is widely considered an unacceptable practice. Mosteller et al. (1996) challenge that conclusion. Tracking can refer to very different practices—some of which involve instruction that is carefully tailored to each group, and some involving no instructional differentiation. In their review of the literature, Mosteller and colleagues find some studies that show positive effects when curriculum is differentiated. They argue that more careful experimental research needs to be conducted before firm conclusions can be drawn regarding when and for whom tracking does and does not provide benefits.

Educators in the field of gifted education still recommend "cluster grouping" (ensuring that small groups of gifted students are placed in the context of one classroom) and within-class grouping on the basis of student achievement in specific academic domains for instruction in that content area. Since 1987, there have been four major reviews of the literature on grouping practices (Kulik and Kulik, 1987, 1982; Lou et al., 1996; Slavin, 1987).

Mixed Results of Within-Class Grouping

The earlier meta-analyses of the literature on the relative effects of within-class grouping versus whole-class instruction reported positive effects of grouping practices (Kulik and Kulik, 1987, 1991; Slavin, 1987). The average effect sizes reported in those reviews ranged from 0.32 (Slavin, 1987) to 0.17 (Kulik and Kulik, 1987) in studies that compared grouping with no-grouping arrangements. In a more recent review of the literature on grouping practices, Lou et al. (1996) examined effect sizes of studies of small-group instruction versus no grouping on several outcome variables and the effects of heterogeneous grouping versus homogeneous grouping on achievement outcomes. They concluded that the overall effect size of small group instruction on achievement was 0.17. "On average, student learning in small groups within classrooms, achieved significantly more than students not learning in small groups" (p. 439).

They also noted that the range of effect sizes indicated great heterogeneity in results. Their analysis of factors affecting the range of effect sizes on achievement produced the finding that in grouping/no-grouping comparisons, the high- and low-ability groups of students demonstrated larger effect sizes than the medium-ability students. Grouping was more effective when the group composition was based on mixed sources of information for assigning groups, when grouping was based on specific or general ability plus other factors, when groups were composed of small numbers (3-4 members), when teachers received extensive or even different training, and when class sizes were either small (less than 25) or large (more than 35). In their analysis of student attitudes and self-concept, they found that within-class grouping resulted in more positive attitudes toward the subject matter and significantly higher general, but not academic, self-concept (d = 0.16).

Furthermore, comparisons of homogeneous versus heterogeneous groupings revealed "no evidence that one form of grouping was *uniformly* superior for promoting the achievement of all students" (p. 450). The average learner benefited significantly overall from homogeneous groupings; however, the researchers noted that the degree to which instructional materials were tailored appropriately to the groups' readiness to learn and the peer influences greatly influence student performance in small-group learning situations.

In a comparative study of grouping arrangements, Delcourt et al. (1994) found that students in special schools, separate class programs, and pull-out programs showed higher levels of achievement than students served in within-class programs and students not served in gifted programs. The performance of black students in this study indicated that that program type did not have a differential effect on this subgroup compared with white students. There were no differences across program type or race/ethnicity for social acceptance. Students from the gifted comparison group, the pull-out programs, and the within-class programs had high perceptions of scholastic abilities. Again, there were no differences between white and black students on this variable. Similarly, Lockart (1996) found significantly higher reading achievement gains among gifted students in homogeneous classrooms or those receiving weekly enrichment in pull-out programs than the gains among gifted students in heterogeneous grouping arrangements. In both of these studies, initial achievement levels served as covariates in the analyses.

In a study of cluster grouping in one school division, the researchers found positive effects on the achievement of all students in the schools studied compared with a comparison group of students in another district (Gentry and Owen, 1999) but noted that cluster grouping was accompanied by a variety of other factors, such as regrouping for math and reading instruction, that probably also influenced achievement.

Reviews of the practice of cross-age or cross-grade-level grouping also support this practice in general, pointing out that specific practices, for example, grouping in specific content areas such as reading or mathematics, are the most effective (Gutierrez and Slavin, 1992; Kulik, 1992). Kulik notes that the average effect size for gifted students in the two studies that reported separately for ability level was only 0.12.

In an exploratory study of the effects of training in metacognitive awareness in homogeneous and heterogeneous grouping of gifted students, Sheppard and Kanevsky (1999) reported greater awareness of complexity of thinking and greater awareness of differences in thinking related to differences in tasks in both groups. Furthermore, the gifted students in the homogeneous group showed a greater increase in metacognitive awareness; they offered more sophisticated and creative responses; and they spontaneously made connections to and extended each other's ideas. Students in the heterogeneous group were more hesitant and conforming.

In two studies of attributional retraining of gifted females, Heller and Ziegler (1996) found that in German junior high and college students' attributions for success and failure in mathematical domains could be modified by systematic feedback, both direct and indirect, and that the changes in attributions resulted in significantly greater gain scores in the domain in which the students were studying. Recent work by Carol Dweck (2000) also suggests the potential of attributional retraining.

Cooperative Learning

One of the commonly accepted guides to classroom practice relies on the assumption that what is good for all students is good for the gifted. And the literature on certain instructional strategies leads the reader to accept that conclusion when it may or may not be an appropriate interpretation. One case in point is the instructional strategy of cooperative learning.

This particular instructional strategy gained widespread recognition as the middle school movement sought ways of maintaining the philosophical principles accompanying heterogeneous classrooms. Claims were made that cooperative grouping provides a vehicle through which all students, including the gifted, benefit academically and socially. This overgeneralization is typified by an article in *Educational Leadership* (a publication widely read by administrators, curriculum supervisors, and teachers) stating that "cooperative learning can benefit all students even those who are low achieving, gifted, or mainstreamed" (Augustine et al., 1990). Middle school educators have accepted the instructional strategy as integral to their classroom practice, despite reported uncertainty and lack of clarity in appropriate practice of the strategy (Tomlinson et al., 1997b).

While numerous studies have shown that, in general, cooperative learning positively affects student achievement and self-esteem, critics have questioned the appropriateness of the practice with gifted students (e.g., Kenny et al., 1995; Robinson, 1991). Their skepticism is based on the paucity of research evidence that supports using cooperative learning with this population, the "basic skill" measures used in most studies, and the use of only traditional classroom instruction for control conditions rather than educational treatments considered more appropriate for gifted students. In some studies, the top 25 percent of the class is considered the high-ability group (e.g., Johnson et al., 1993; Lucker et al., 1976), or high ability is defined as a score above the median on a teacher-made placement test (Mervasch, 1991) or is based on teacher judgement only (Johnson and Johnson, 1981; Johnson et al., 1983).

Furthermore, the practice of heterogeneously grouping students for cooperative learning activities has been questioned. One controlled field experiment assessed the effect on both gifted and nongifted students of both heterogeneous and homogeneous grouping in cooperative learning settings (Kenny et al., 1995). Gifted students outperformed their nongifted peers in all groups and worked at a faster pace and produced more work in homogenous groups, but achievement differed significantly based on group composition. Materials were not tailored for student level of achievement, however, perhaps limiting possible gains. Gifted students' self-concept did not differ based on group arrangement, but students grouped with gifted students experienced a significant decrease in social but not academic or general self-concept. In this study, students overall perceived each other to be less friendly, less of a teammate, less smart, less likeable, and less of a leader after working in cooperative groups regardless of ability or type of grouping arrangement. Nongifted students were perceived by their peers as less competent on task-related dimensions after being in heterogeneous groups with gifted students.

Minority and Low-Income Students

The literature on curricular or programming options that have been successful in the development of the talents of minority and low-income students in particular is very limited. The dearth of research on specific interventions is consistent with funding patterns to support identification of and programming for these populations. Patton et al. (1990) surveyed state directors of gifted programs and found that 82.6 percent (43 states) had no specific funds allocated for disadvantaged but gifted students. No state indicated separate program standards. Although most of the model projects funded by the Jacob K. Javits Gifted and Talented Students Education Program focused on the identification and development of giftedness in underserved populations (Ross, 1994), the collection of data with control or comparison groups was rare.

Qualitative analysis of teacher and parent responses has been conducted in case studies of low-income and minority children (Tomlinson et al., 1997a). It indicates that even modest affirmation of talent and intervention, using a model of instruction based on structuring learning experiences to address student interests and cultural differences, which focused on hands-on learning and recognizing varied learning strengths (verbal, spatial, linguistic), brought about transformations in student learning behaviors as perceived by parents and teachers. This approach also resulted in greater identification of these students as gifted in later years.

Initial research using a language arts unit of the Integrated Curriculum Model (discussed in an earlier section) provides preliminary data on effectiveness for lower-SES groups (VanTassel-Baska et al., 2002). It demonstrated equal gains between high-SES students and a low-SES group composed of 72 percent of students on free or reduced lunch status and 67 percent minority (unspecified).

The early intervention projects designed to close the achievement gap between minority and low-SES children have largely focused on the general success of the programs, not on the issue of giftedness. However, Gandara (2000) concludes that these programs in general have an impact on higher-level functioning for children who are not at serous risk (p. 24). In one study that examined the factors associated with particularly high levels of academic achievement of Head Start students in 1st grade, the authors attributed the outcome to features of the home environment (Robinson et al., 1998). Gandara (2000) also concludes from her review of the school reform initiatives at the elementary school level that "school-wide reform efforts directed toward strengthening the curriculum (among other things) can have an impact on raising the achievement of high achieving African-Americans to even higher levels, conceivably to a level commensurate with gifted performance, at least in math" (p. 26). The conclusion she reaches about precollege programs, such as A Better Chance, Upward Bound, and I Have a Dream, is that while these programs are successful in increasing college attendance rates, there is striking "absence of evidence that these programs have a significant impact on academic performance" (p. 29).

There is little evidence of intervention programs at the high school level focused on producing exceptionally high achievers from minority groups (Gandara, 2000). One program showing promise is the Puente project. Larger proportions of students in this program attended college and they "demonstrated significantly higher interest in intellectual activity and in being a good student than matched control students from the same schools" (Gandara et al., 1998).

Benefits of Gifted and Talented Assignment[1]

Adelman (1999) argues that the rigor of the curriculum to which students are exposed is the best predictor of their long-term outcomes (college attendance and completion) irrespective of race or ethnicity. If he is correct, then one of the most important roles that programs for gifted and talented students can play is in preparing and channeling them into upper-level curricula. As Adelman points out, the best proxy for a rigorous curriculum is taking math courses beyond two years of algebra. Students who take beginning algebra in the 8th grade are on track to take high-level math courses later in high school; those who postpone algebra will have a more difficult time reaching higher-level math in the time remaining to them in high school. Therefore, being assigned to algebra in the 8th grade is an important marker of a student's assignment to a rigorous curriculum and a good predictor of future academic attainment. Using 8th grade data from the National Education Longitudinal Study database, Rumberger and Gándara (in preparation) asked if students from different ethnic groups who were in gifted programs had an equal chance of being assigned to algebra in the 8th grade. Table 9-7 displays the percentages of students from each major ethnic group who were in gifted and talented programs in the 8th grade and who were also assigned to algebra. All data are based on student self-report.

Evidently being in a gifted and talented program is highly associated with being assigned to algebra in the 8th grade, suggesting that students who have been identified as gifted are generally perceived as being more academically able, at least in mathematics. Students in gifted and talented programs were two to three times more likely to be assigned to algebra than those students who were not in the program. For students not in a gifted program, differences among racial/ethnic groups in the percentage of students assigned to algebra were relatively small. However, there are considerable discrepancies by race/ethnicity in assignment to algebra for students

---

[1]This section is drawn from the paper written for the committee by Patricia Gandara (2000).

TABLE 9-7 Percentage of Students in Gifted and Nongifted Programs Who Are Assigned to Algebra in Grade 8 (Percentage)

Ethnicity	Gifted in Grade 8 Algebra	Nongifted in Grade 8 Algebra
White	73	28
Hispanic	52	26
Black	60	27
Asian	83	35

SOURCE: Data from National Education Longitudinal Study of 1988, U.S. Department of Education, National Center for Education Statistics (Gandara, 2000).

who are in a gifted and talented program. Asian and white students are much more likely to be assigned to algebra than are black or Hispanic students. Hispanic students have the least likelihood of being in algebra, whether they are in the program or not. To consider why would this be, Gandara (2000) then examined grades and achievement test scores for each of the groups to determine if students' grades or test scores were responsible for the discrepancies in algebra placement. Table 9-8 displays the percentages of students falling into each test score quartile and at each of four levels of grade point average by ethnicity.

Grades and test scores probably explain a fair amount of the variance in assignment to algebra in the 8th grade by race/ethnicity. For white students, 82.4 percent had overall grades of 3.0 or higher, and for Asians, 90.4

TABLE 9-8 Percent of Students with Specified Grades and Test Scores by Ethnicity for 8th Grade Gifted and Talented Students

Ethnicity	Test Score 1st Quartile (Low)	Test Score 2nd Quartile	Test Score 3rd Quartile	Test Score 4th Quartile (High)	Grades Less Than 2.0	Grades 2.0–2.99	Grades 3.0–3.49	Grades 3.5+
White	18.1	25.8	30.3	23.0	2.2	15.3	20.0	62.4
Hispanic	29.7	22.6	22.9	20.9	6.9	24.8	28.3	40.1
Black	39.6	19.1	13.7	18.9	17.7	30.4	22.6	29.3
Asian	11.4	7.7	17.0	37.9	2.2	7.5	21.7	68.7

SOURCE: Data from National Education Longitudinal Study of 1988, U.S. Department of Education, National Center for Education Statistics (Gandara, 2000).

had 3.0 or higher, and grades correlate highly with assignment to upper track classes. However, the fact that Hispanic students were less likely than blacks to be assigned to algebra is not explained by grades or test scores, inasmuch as both were higher for Hispanics than for black students. This may be related to other findings noted earlier that teachers are somewhat less likely to identify Hispanic students for gifted classes and that even training in identification procedures does not appear to reduce this problem substantially. The discrepancies in grades among different racial/ethnic groups does raise another fundamental concern, however: Are students from different racial/ethnic groups being selected into gifted and talented programs on the basis of very different criteria? And, if this is the case, does the curriculum to which they are exposed in the program meet their needs equally? Put another way, does the experience of being in a gifted program contribute significantly to closing the high achievement gap between groups? The labeling effect of being identified as gifted may be a factor in some black and Hispanic students being assigned to algebra (given their overall lower grades and test scores). However, it is difficult to know to what extent the benefits of the program extend beyond the label for these under-represented students.

CONCLUSIONS AND RECOMMENDATIONS

Throughout this chapter we have highlighted what we know about effective instruction for special needs students, particularly those identified as having learning disabilities or emotional disturbance and those identified as gifted and talented. The principles of what constitutes good instruction apply across all students. The generally applicable principle of managing task difficulty might require that the pace of instruction, the amount of repetition, and the speed at which complexity or abstraction can be introduced be made different for students at opposite ends of the achievement spectrum. But all students benefit when, for example, the goals of instruction are explicit and metacognition is incorporated into instruction.

Instructional practices that have been verified as effective in research are not widely used. Making those practices more common is likely to require a research and development effort that does not end with promising findings—but rather begins with them. Those findings will need to be translated into effective curricula and other teaching tools, field-tested in classroom practice, and carefully scaled up when appropriate in a studied fashion. We repeat our recommendation for research and development from Chapter 5, but specify several additional areas that the research and development program should cover.

Federal-Level Recommendations

> **Recommendation RD.1:** We recommend that education research and development, including that related to special and gifted education, be systematically expanded to carry promising findings and validated practices through to classroom applicability. This includes research on scaling up promising practices from research sites to widespread use.

• Research on what works in special education offers some important principles, but too few well-tested interventions with a solid evaluation of the conditions under which they work and for whom. In particular, the research base with respect to English language learners needs to be strengthened.

• While there has been substantial progress on educational interventions for students who are having difficulty learning to read, little is currently known that can guide educational interventions for the nonresponders to reading interventions. Research needs to attend now to this group of students.

• We have given relatively little attention either in research or in program development to the education of gifted and talented students. This research base needs to be strengthened substantially.

• Features of cultural sensitivity that have an impact on learning outcomes for minority students have not been rigorously researched and evaluated in classroom settings. While a significant amount has been written about culturally appropriate accommodations, many of the recommendations have no empirical basis (such as matching learning styles) and should be avoided. Shoring up the empirical foundation for culturally sensitive teaching practice should be a research priority.

Development is needed of effective mechanisms for communication of research findings to practitioner, policy, and teacher educator communities.

Successful teaching of all students requires a substantive and complex knowledge base in the subject matter being taught, in how children learn, and in pedagogical strategies to promote learning. Understanding the cultural, gender, and other differences in how individual students learn is also an essential skill for effective teaching. Successful in-school implementation of the types of assessments and interventions the committee proposes to maximize educational effectiveness for all students—including the gifted and talented—those who are low achieving and those with disabilities—requires intensive training based on the scientific evidence supporting those strategies. The changes the committee recommends in this report can occur only if there is a significant cadre of well-prepared education professionals and paraprofessionals to implement them. There is ample evidence, however, that the growth in knowledge about effective teaching and learning has not begun to significantly impact the practices of educators, administrators, and support services personnel in many schools (National Research Council, 1999c). There is also evidence that part of the reason for the failure of local educators to embrace scientific advances in teaching and learning is the inadequacy of educator preparation programs and professional development activities (Clifford and Guthrie, 1988; Goodlad et al., 1990; National Commission for Teaching and America's Future, 1996; Orlosky, 1988; Roth, 1999; Zeichner et al., 1996).

Many commentators have asserted that higher education-based educator preparation programs are particularly unresponsive to the scientific advances of the past several decades concerning teaching and learning (Clifford and Guthrie, 1988; Goodlad et al., 1990; Murnane et.al., 1991; National Commission for Teaching and America's Future, 1996). In fact, many states have begun to rely on alternate routes to educator certification in an effort both to bypass traditional college and university teacher preparation programs and to address a shortage of people interested in education jobs.

These three significant challenges—unresponsive educator preparation programs, a failure to infuse scientific advances into local practice, and the impending shortage of individuals willing to work in education settings—present the potential for significant barriers to the effective implementation of the committee's recommendations.

> **Recommendation TQ.4: The committee recommends that a panel be convened in an institutional environment that is protected from political influence to study the variety of programs that now exist to train teachers for general, special, and gifted education; the mechanisms for keeping training programs current and of high quality; the standards and requirements of those programs; the applicability of training to the demands of classroom practice; and the long-term impact of the programs in successfully promoting educational achievement for pre-K, elementary, and secondary students.** Direct comparison with other professional fields (e.g., medicine, nursing, law, engineering, accounting) may provide insight in this endeavor applicable to education.

The marketplace will demand responses to the staffing shortage. The need for an assessment of the current state of the nation's educator preparation mechanisms and recommendations for improvement could be a useful first step toward linking research and practice via effective professional training.

10

Recommendations

Minority children, particularly black and American Indian/Alaskan Native children, are represented in disproportionately large numbers in some high-incidence special education categories. All minority children except Asian/Pacific Islanders are represented in disproportionately small numbers in gifted and talented programs. As we noted at the outset, however, disproportionate representation itself tells us very little. A judgment as to whether disproportionate placement is inappropriate or problematic depends both on the reasons for the disproportion and on the consequences of placement.

The committee considered three potential explanations for minority disproportion. **First, we asked whether there are biological and social/contextual contributors to early development that differ by race and that leave students differentially prepared to meet the cognitive and behavioral demands of schooling.** Our answer to that question is a definitive "yes."

We know that minority children are disproportionately poor, and poverty is associated with higher rates of exposure to harmful toxins, including lead, alcohol, and tobacco, in early stages of development. Poor children are also more likely to be born with low birthweight, to have poorer nutrition, and to have home and child care environments that are less supportive of early cognitive and emotional development than their majority counterparts. When poverty is deep and persistent the number of risk factors rise, seriously jeopardizing development. Some risk factors have a disproportionate impact on particular race groups that goes beyond the poverty effect. Across all income groups, black children are more likely to be born with low birthweight and are more likely to be exposed to harmful levels of lead, while American Indian/Alaskan Native children are more likely to be exposed prenatally to high levels of alcohol and tobacco. While the separate effect of each of these factors on school achievement and performance is difficult to determine, substantial differences by race/ethnicity on a variety of dimensions of school preparedness are documented at kindergarten entry.

Second, we asked whether the school experience itself contributes to racial disproportion in academic outcomes and behavioral problems that lead to placement in special and gifted education. Again, our answer is "yes."

Schools with higher concentrations of low-income, minority children are less likely to have experienced, well-trained teachers. Per-pupil expenditures in those schools are somewhat lower, while the needs of low-income student populations and the difficulty of attracting teachers to inner-city, urban schools suggest that supporting comparable levels of education would require higher levels of per-pupil expenditures. These schools are less likely to offer advanced courses for their students, providing less support for high academic achievement.

When children come to school from disadvantaged backgrounds, as a disproportionate number of minority students do, high-quality instruction that carefully puts the prerequisites for learning in place, combined with effective classroom management that minimizes chaos in the classroom, can put students on a path to academic success. While some reform efforts suggest that such an outcome is possible, there are currently no assurances that children will be exposed to effective instruction or classroom management before they are placed in special education programs.

Third, we asked whether existing referral and assessment practices are racially biased and, furthermore, whether they are likely to successfully identify those at either end of the achievement distribution who need specialized supports or services. The answer here is not as straightforward. The majority of children in special and gifted education are referred by teachers. If a teacher is biased in evaluating student performance and behavior, those biases may well be reflected in referrals. Some experimental research suggests that teachers do hold such biases. But whether bias is maintained when teachers have direct contact with children in the classroom is not clear. For example, research that has compared groups of students who are referred by teachers find that minority students actually have greater academic and behavior problems than their majority counterparts. The interpretation of such a finding is not obvious, however. It may be that teachers are more reluctant to refer minority students than white students with similar problems. Or it may be that teacher referral practices compensate for inadequate measurement tools.

Once students are referred for special education, they must be assessed as eligible or ineligible. Whether the assessment process is biased is as controversial as the referral process. A long-standing debate on IQ scores has no definitive resolution. Tests of "item bias" that examine whether the same questions differentiate high and low scorers across races generally find that they do. And the tests do have predictive validity with regard to school success. However, research on the effect of context, including familiarity with test taking and the norms and expectations of school, may depress the scores of students whose experiences prepare them least well for the demands of classrooms and standardized tests. To the extent that this is the case, test scores may be depressed overall, even if no item bias exists.

Whether the referral and assessment of students for special and gifted education are racially biased or not, we asked whether the right students are identified—students who need and can benefit from those programs. Here the committee's answer is a more confident "no." The subjectivity of the referral process, as well as the conceptual and procedural shortcomings of the assessment process for learning disabilities and emotional disturbance give little confidence that student needs have been appropriately identified. Moreover, current referral and assessment processes result in placements later in the education process than is most effective, providing a weak link between assessment and intervention.

Beyond understanding why there is disproportion, the committee was concerned with why disproportion is a problem. To address this issue, we asked a fourth question: **Does special education and gifted education provide a benefit to students, and is that benefit different for different racial/ ethnic groups?** However, the data that would allow us to answer the question adequately do not exist. We do know that some specific special education and gifted and talented interventions have been demonstrated to have positive outcomes for students. But how widely those interventions are employed is not known. Nor do we know whether minority students are less likely than majority students to be exposed to those high-quality interventions. What evidence there is suggests that parent advocacy and teacher instruction and experience, both of which would be expected to correlate with higher-quality interventions, are less likely to happen in higher-poverty school districts where minority children are concentrated.

A VISION FOR CHANGE

Twenty years ago, the National Research Council (NRC) report, *Placing Children in Special Education: A Strategy for Equity* based its recommendations on six principles that are as efficacious and insightful today as they were then. We quote from several that are closely aligned with our own (NRC, 1982:94-95):

1. "It is the responsibility of teachers in the regular classroom to engage in multiple educational interventions and to note the effects of such interventions on a child experiencing academic failure before referring the child for special education assessment."

2. "It is the responsibility of assessment specialists to demonstrate that the measures employed validly assess the functional needs of the individual child for which there are potentially effective interventions."

3. "It is the responsibility of the placement team that labels and places a child in a special program to demonstrate that any differential label used is related to a distinctive prescription for educational practices and that these practices are likely to lead to improved outcomes not achievable in the regular classroom."

4. "It is the responsibility of the special education and evaluation staff to demonstrate systematically that high-quality, effective special instruction is being provided and that the goals of the special education program could not be achieved as effectively within the regular classroom."

Twenty years later, we can say that those principles continue to express the vision of a well-functioning, equitable special education system. They can readily be adapted to assessment for gifted and talented education as well. Our concerns today do not differ substantially from those of 20 years ago.

In many respects the school system is in a better position to make the required changes today than in 1982 because it has the benefit of two additional decades of research on effective interventions in general and special education, and to a lesser extent on gifted and talented education. But realizing that vision requires far more than a conceptual understanding of what should be done and more than the practical knowledge of how to teach children to read or to moderate behavior. It will take an investment in building the capacity of teachers and other education professionals to effectively assess and intervene with children across the spectrum of achievement and behavior before they are ever considered for special or gifted education, and to use the best of the current knowledge base as standard practice in instruction for children once they are identified for special or gifted education. It will take changing incentives and standard practices in the assessment process so that children are identified early, when they can be helped most effectively, and so that the link between the student's functional needs, the assessment, and the potential intervention is more closely tied. And it will take compliance monitoring that focuses on treatments and response to treatment in both general and special education rather than on procedural compliance that is unrelated to the services provided.

Some of the required changes, like new regulatory guidelines, can be made quickly. Others, like changing the knowledge base of teachers with respect to classroom management and behavior assessment, will take years. Our hope is that decisions made today will take us down a different path, so that 20 years from now we will look back and see that we have moved substantially closer to the desired outcome.

The conclusions and recommendations that appear throughout the report are organized here in the following major categories: referral and eligibility determination in special education (SE) and gifted and talented education (GT); teacher quality (TQ); biological and early childhood risk factors (EC); improving data collection (DC); and expanding the research and development base (RD).

REFERRAL AND ELIGIBILITY DETERMINATION

Special Education Eligibility

From our review of the current knowledge base, several important findings have led the committee to rethink the current approach to identification and assignment to special education:

1. Among the most frequent reasons for referral to special education are reading difficulties and behavior problems.

2. In recent years, interventions appropriate for the general education classroom to improve reading mastery and to improve classroom management have been demonstrated to reduce the number of children who fail at reading or are later identified with behavior disorders.

3. There are currently no mechanisms in place to guarantee that students will be exposed to state-of-the-art reading instruction or classroom management before they are identified as having a "within-child" problem.

4. Referral for the high-incidence categories of special education with which we are concerned currently requires student failure. However, screening mechanisms exist for early identification of children at risk for later reading and behavior problems. And the effectiveness of early intervention in both areas has been demonstrated to be considerably greater than the effectiveness of later, postfailure intervention.

These findings lead the committee to conclude that schools should be doing more and doing it earlier to ensure that students receive quality general education services to obviate the need for special education, particularly in the areas of reading and behavior management. The committee's concerns, however, extend beyond missed opportunities to several questionable features of existing referral and evaluation regulations and practices:

1. Teacher referral requires that a student be called to the teacher's attention. This initial screening device is subjective, and the perception of a student's performance and behavior may interact with the teacher's instructional and classroom management approach.

2. Once referred for special education, the assessment process often involves features that are problematic, including questionable exclusionary clauses and definitions that are neither supported by the research literature nor sensitive to gender, ethnicity, developmental level, or contextual factors.

3. Most state regulations for determining a learning disability currently require a discrepancy between a student's ability and achievement (varying in the magnitude of the requisite discrepancy and the manner in which it is computed) as measured by an IQ test, although this criterion neither identifies a group with a unique problem, nor provides information useful to intervention.

The missed opportunities to identify children who need help early on and to provide help in the general education context that might obviate the need for referral, combined with the flaws in the current referral and assessment system, lead the committee to recommend an alternative model to the one now in effect. The proposed change would focus attention away from efforts to uncover unobservable child traits, the identification of which gives little insight into instructional response, and toward the problems encountered in the classroom and appropriate responses. The role of instruction and classroom management in student performance is explicitly acknowledged, and effort is devoted first to ensuring the opportunity to succeed in general education. The alternative would require policy and regulatory changes at both the federal and the state levels of government.

Federal-Level Changes

Recommendation SE.1: The committee recommends that federal guidelines for special education eligibility be changed in order to encourage better integrated general and special education services. We propose that eligibility ensue when a student exhibits large differences from typical levels of performance in one or more domain(s) *and* with evidence of insufficient response to high-quality interventions in the relevant domain(s) of functioning in school settings. These domains include achievement (e.g., reading, writing, mathematics), social behavior, and emotional regulation. As is currently the case, eligibility determination would also require a judgment by a multidisciplinary team, including parents, that special education is needed.

We provide more detail regarding our intended meaning below:

Eligibility

• The proposed approach would not negate the eligibility of any student who arrives at school with a disability determination, or who has a severe disability, from being served as they are currently. Our concern here is only with the categories of disability that are defined in the school context in response to student achievement and behavior problems.

• While eligibility for special education would by law continue to depend on establishment of a disability, in the committee's view, noncategorical conceptions and classification criteria that focus on matching a student's specific needs to an intervention strategy would obviate the need for the traditional high-incidence disability labels such as learning disability (LD) and emotional disturbance (ED). If traditional disability definitions are used, they would need to be revised to focus on behaviors directly related to classroom and school learning and behavior (e.g., reading failure, math failure, persistent inattention, and disorganization).

Assessment

• By high-quality interventions we mean evidence-based treatments that are implemented properly over a sufficient period to allow for significant gains, with frequent progress monitoring and intervention revisions based on data. Research-based features of intervention quality are known and must be implemented rigorously, including:

a. an explicit definition of the target behavior in observable, behavioral language;

b. collection of data on current performance;

c. establishment of goals that define an acceptable level of performance;

d. development and implementation of an instructional or behavioral intervention that is generally effective according to research results;

e. assessment and monitoring of the implementation of the intervention to ensure that it is being delivered as designed, frequent data collection to monitor the effects of the intervention, revisions of the intervention depending on progress toward goals, and evaluation of intervention outcomes through comparison of post-intervention competencies with baseline data.

• Assessment for special education eligibility would be focused on the information gathered that documents educationally relevant differences from typical levels of performance and is relevant to the design, monitoring, and evaluation of treatments. Competencies would be assessed in natural classroom settings, preferably on multiple occasions.

• While an IQ test may provide supplemental information, no IQ test would be required, and results of an IQ test would not be a primary criterion on which eligibility rests. Because of the irreducible importance of context in the recognition and nurturance of achievement, the committee regards the effort to assess students' decontextualized potential or ability as inappropriate and scientifically invalid.

Reporting and Monitoring

• Current federal requirements regarding reporting by states of the overall numbers of students served as disabled and the program placements used to provide an appropriate education would not change with these recommendations. Moreover, the reporting of the nine low-incidence disabilities would continue to be done by category. Reporting of the numbers of students currently diagnosed with high-incidence disabilities would become noncategorical, with the loss of very little useful information due to the enormous variations in the operational definition of the high-incidence categories used currently. The reporting by states concerning students now classified in high-incidence categories could be made more meaningful if the reporting also included the nature of the learning or behavioral problem as reflected in the top 2-4 individualized education program (IEP) goals for each student, that is, the number of students with IEP goals in basic reading, reading comprehension, math calculation, self-help skills, social skills, math reasoning, etc. The latter information would provide more accurate information on the actual needs of students with disabilities than the current information indicating unreliable categorical diagnoses.

• Consistent with the Individuals with Disabilities Education Act (IDEA) (1997 and 1999), federal compliance monitoring should move in the direction of examining the quality of special education interventions and the outcomes for students with disabilities. Current compliance monitoring focuses on important, but limited, characteristics of the delivery of special education programs, particularly implementation of the due process procedural safeguards and the mandated components of the IEP. Compliance monitoring by the Federal Office of Special Education Programs and the state departments of education must assume an outcomes focus in addition to the traditional process considerations.

State-Level Changes

State regulatory changes would be required for implementation of a reformed special education program that uses functional assessment measures to promote positive outcomes for students with disabilities. Some states have already instituted changes that move in this direction. Special education rules for the State of Iowa serve as an example; in Iowa, non-categorical special education for students with high-incidence disabilities has been implemented since the early 1990s. Several other states have approved "rule replacement" programs that allow school districts to implement special education systems that do not require categorical designation of students with high-incidence disabilities (e.g., Illinois, Kansas, South Carolina). These state rules require a systematic problem-solving process that is centered around quality indicators associated with successful interventions. The rules are explicit about each of these quality indicators, and compliance monitoring is focused on their implementation. Several features of rules in the majority of states can be omitted in a noncategorical system, including the requirements regarding IQ testing.

The changes in federal regulations and state rules toward greater emphasis on producing positive outcomes and away from an eligibility determination process that is largely unrelated to interventions are consistent with the greater emphasis in IDEA (1997, 1999) on positive outcomes for students with disabilities. Positive outcomes are enhanced by the implementation of high-quality interventions; no such claim can be made for conducting the assessments required to assign students with significant learning and behavior problems to the high-incidence categories of LD, ED, and MMR.

Early Intervention. Universal screening of young children for prerequisites to and the early development of academic and behavioral skills is increasingly recognized as crucial to achieving better outcomes in schools and preventing achievement and behavior problems. While this is true for all children, a disproportionate number of disadvantaged children are on a developmental trajectory that is flatter than their more advantaged counterparts. Evidence suggests that effective and reliable screening of young children by age 4 to 6 can identify those most at risk for later achievement and behavior problems, including those most likely to be referred to special education programs.

In two arenas—reading and behavior—the knowledge base exists to screen and intervene in general education both systematically and early. Less attention has been devoted to early identification and intervention for mathematics problems. However, the National Institute of Child Health and Human Development has launched a research program in this area.

Other efforts to develop early screening mechanisms in mathematics have been developed, but their psychometric properties have not yet been widely tested (Ginsburg and Baroody, 2002; Griffin and Case, 1997).

While early reading is only one of the areas in which students struggle, it is an important one because failure in early reading makes learning in the many subject areas that require reading more difficult. Moreover, there is a great deal of comorbidity between reading problems and other difficulties (attentional, behavioral) that results in special education referral. As indicated above, early screening and intervention would help to identify children who may be missed in a wait-to-fail model. It may obviate the need for placement in special education for some children, and it would provide the evidence of response or lack of response to high-quality instruction that we proposed be written into federal regulations.

> **Recommendation SE.2: The committee recommends that states adopt a universal screening and multitiered intervention strategy in general education to enable early identification and intervention with children at risk for reading problems.**

The committee's model for prereferral reading intervention is as follows:

- All children should be screened early (late kindergarten or early 1st grade) and then monitored through 2nd grade on indicators that predict later reading failure.
- Those students identified through screening as at risk for reading problems should be provided with supplemental small-group reading instruction provided by the classroom teacher for about 20-30 minutes per day, and progress should be closely monitored.
- For those students who continue to display reading difficulties and for whom supplemental small-group instruction is not associated with improved outcomes, more intensive instruction should be provided by other support personnel, such as the special education teacher and/or reading support teacher in school.
- For students who continue to have difficulty, referral to special education and the development of an IEP would follow. The data regarding student response to intervention would be used for eligibility determination.
- State guidelines should direct that the screening process be undertaken early, and the instructional response follow in a very timely fashion. The requirement for general education interventions should not be used to delay attention to a student in need of specialized services.

The committee's recommendation to adopt a universal screening and multitiered intervention *strategy* is meant to acknowledge that there is some distance to travel between the knowledge base that has been accumulated and the capacity to use that knowledge on a widespread basis. There are examples in Texas and Virginia of taking screening to scale. But making the tools available to teachers, preparing teachers both to assess students and to respond productively to the assessment results, and supporting teachers to work with the instructional demands of intervening differently for subgroups of students at different skill levels require the careful development of capacity and infrastructure.

At the same time that the committee acknowledges the investment required to adopt this recommendation, we call attention to the potential return on the investment and the consequences of not making such an investment. When early screening and intervention is not undertaken, more students suffer failure. The demands on the school to invest in a support structure for those students is simply postponed to a later age when the response to intervention is less promising and when the capacity of teachers to intervene effectively is made even more difficult by a weaker knowledge base and limited teacher skill. The consequences of school failure for the student and for society go well beyond the cost to the school, of course.

Behavior Management. Current understanding of early reading problems is the outcome of a sustained research and development effort that has not been undertaken on a similar scale with respect to other learning and behavior problems. In the committee's view, however, there is enough evidence regarding universal behavior management interventions, behavior screening, and techniques to work with children at risk for behavior problems to better prevent later serious behavior problems. Research results suggest that these interventions can work. However, a large-scale pilot project would provide a firmer foundation of knowledge regarding scaling-up the practices involved.

> **Recommendation SE.3: The committee recommends that states launch large-scale pilot programs in conjunction with universities or research centers to test the plausibility and productivity of universal behavior management interventions, early behavior screening, and techniques to work with children at risk for behavior problems.**

We propose a model for experimentation similar to that proposed for reading:

- Assessment of the classroom and of noninstructional school settings (hallways, playgrounds) should be made yearly.
- Behavioral adjustment of all children in grades K-3 should be screened yearly to provide teachers with information regarding individual

children. The assessments should be reviewed yearly by a school-level committee (comprised of administrative and teaching staff, specialists, and parents) to ensure that school-wide interventions are implemented when indicated in a timely fashion and to ensure that individual children are given special services quickly when needed.

• Because characteristics of the classroom and school can increase risk for serious emotional problems, the first step in the determination of an emotional or behavioral disability is the assessment of the classroom and school-wide context. Key contextual factors should be assessed and ruled out as explanations before intervention at the individual child level is considered.

• If it is determined that contextual factors are not significantly involved in the child's problem, then individualized measures should be taken to help the child adjust *in the standard classroom/school setting*. Only those interventions with empirical evidence supporting their effectiveness should be considered. For example, common features of emotional and behavioral problems are off-task and disruptive behaviors. Well-documented interventions with demonstrated effectiveness at reducing these behaviors (see Chapter 8) should be employed before the child is considered disabled.

• Because the most serious and developmentally predictive emotional and behavioral problems in children tend to be manifested across settings, and because family issues and solutions tend to overlap with those at school, every effort should be made to include parents and guardians as partners in the educational effort. To the extent that this is done, early and accurate identification of serious problems should be facilitated, and parents can be enlisted to collaborate with teachers in both standard education and in solving emerging academic, emotional, and behavioral problems.

• For children who do not respond to standard interventions, the intensity of the interventions should be increased through the use of behavioral consultants, more intensive collaborations with parents, or through adjunct interventions to address various skill or emotional deficits (e.g., anger control, social skills instruction). Such individualized programs should be carefully articulated through the use of IEPs, coupled with systematic assessments of the child's behavioral response to the interventions.

The proposed reform of special education that would focus on response to intervention in general education would require substantial changes in the current relationship between general and special education. It would put in place a universal prevention element that does not now exist on a widespread basis with the purpose of: (a) providing assistance to children who may now be missed and (b) obviating the need for the special education referrals that can be remedied by early high-quality intervention in the general education context. In the final analysis, the committee cannot predict the effect of this approach on the number of special education students nor on racial/ethnic disproportion, but the result, in our judgment, would be that children identified for special education services would be those truly in need of ongoing support. And if the effect of the classroom context and opportunity to learn is successfully disentangled from the student's need for additional supports, the committee believes that disproportion in identification would not be as problematic as it is currently.

Federal Support of State Reform Efforts

> **Recommendation SE.4: While the United States has a strong tradition of state control of education, the committee recommends that the federal government support widespread adoption of early screening and intervention in the states.**

In particular:

- Technical assistance and information dissemination should be coordinated at the federal level. This might be done through the U.S. Department of Education, the National Institute of Child Health and Human Development, a cooperative effort of the two, or though some other designated agent. Accumulation and dissemination of information and research findings has "public good" properties and economies of scale that make a federal effort more efficient than many state efforts.
- The federal government can encourage the use of Title I funds to implement early screening and intervention in both reading and behavior for schools currently receiving those funds. Funds provided in the Reading Excellence Act might also support this effort under the existing mandate.

Gifted and Talented Eligibility

The research base justifying alternative approaches for the screening, identification, and placement of gifted children is neither as extensive nor as informative as that for special education. While limited programs of identification and services for gifted students have been carried out under the auspices of the Jacob K. Javits Gifted and Talented Students Education Program, the collection of data in the framework of any systematic research paradigm has been limited. Yet the importance of early opportunity to learn is likely to be as important for the success of students at the upper end of the achievement distribution as it is for those at the lower end. And the problem of disentangling the children's abilities from their previous opportunities to learn strikes a clear parallel. Nevertheless, the existing research base restricts our understanding and therefore our recommendations: rather than proposing a specific approach to screening or identification for gifted and talented students, we propose research that may allow for better informed decision making in the future.

> **Recommendation GT.1: The committee recommends a research program oriented toward the development of a broader knowledge base on early identification and intervention with children who exhibit advanced performance in the verbal or quantitative realm, or who exhibit other advanced abilities.**

This research program should be designed to determine whether there are reliable and valid indicators of current exceptional performance in language, mathematical, or other domains, or indicators of later exceptional performance. To the extent that the assessments described above provide information relevant to the identification of gifted students, they should be used for that purpose.

In addition to research to support the development of identification instruments, research on classroom practice designed to encourage the early and continued development of gifted behaviors in underrepresented populations should be undertaken so that screening can be followed by effective intervention. That research should be designed to identify:

- Opportunities that can be provided during the kindergarten year to engage children in high-interest learning activities that allow development of complex, advanced reasoning, accelerated learning pace, and advanced content and skill learning capabilities.
- Interventions in later school years with children who demonstrate advanced learning capabilities and their impact on the performance of these children over time.
- The effect of curricular differentiation through various options, such as resource room instruction, independent study, and acceleration, and the interaction of treatments with individual student profiles. Group size, instructional method, and complexity of the curriculum should all be variables under study.

An enriched curriculum designed for gifted students may well improve educational outcomes for all children. As mentioned in Chapter 5, when class size was reduced in 15 schools in Austin, Texas, the two that showed improved student achievement were schools that made other changes as well, including making the curriculum for gifted students in reading and mathematics available to all students. This does not imply, however, that the pace of instruction or level of student independence is necessarily the same for all students. We recommend that research be conducted using control groups to determine the impact of interventions designed for children identified as gifted on children who have not been so identified.

SCHOOL SOCIAL, CULTURAL, AND CONTEXTUAL ISSUES INFLUENCING ACHIEVEMENT AND BEHAVIOR

Children in the high-incidence special education categories with which we are concerned[1] rarely come to school with a disability determination. They are referred to special education only after they have failed to achieve within the general classroom. Similarly, gifted and talented students are generally identified only after they have excelled in the school context. Special education or gifted and talented identification takes place in the context of performance in general education. While children come to schools with very different characteristics and levels of preparedness, how well any child meets the demands of schooling will be determined both by that child and by the school context itself. Several of the contributors to school context that have been shown to influence classroom achievement and behavior are implicated in observed racial differences.

Among the committees findings are the following:

• Financial resources are on average lower in schools with greater numbers of children who live in poverty.
• Because more minority children live in families with incomes below the poverty level, the lower resource schools generally have greater numbers of minority children.
• Teacher quality, as measured by years of teaching experience, education, and certification, influences student achievement and student behavioral problems. Minority children are more likely to be taught by unlicensed teachers and teachers with less experience.

While there has been a debate regarding the role of financial resources in achievement outcomes, the evidence reviewed leads the committee to conclude that resources can, and often do, have an impact. In particular, greater resources are required for reductions in class size, which have been shown in some cases to improve the academic achievement of students in early grades, with larger gains for disadvantaged minority students. Resources can also allow for improved salaries and teaching conditions for teachers, which in turn would be expected to raise the level of teacher

---

[1]They do not include the speech and language category in which many young children are identified in preschool years.

quality. For these reasons, the committee concludes that efforts to reduce the number of minority students with academic and behavioral problems and increase the number who excel will require a more equitable distribution of human and financial resources among states, school districts within states, and individual schools. The committee endorses the recommendation of the NRC's Committee on Education Finance that the distribution of resources take into account the higher cost of providing quality education in schools with disadvantaged student populations.

While school resources, class size, and indicators of teacher quality are associated with learning and behavior outcomes, their influence must be exerted through teacher-student interactions. In this sense, what is true of cognitive and behavioral development in the earliest years continues to be true in the school years. Social, economic and environmental factors are important because they affect the nature of the interactions between children and the influential adults in their lives—in the current context, the teacher. The weight of the burden in improving school outcomes for minority students, then, falls on the interactions in the classroom.

Moreover, in the new prevention and eligibility determining model the committee is proposing, it is not the child alone who is assessed, but the classroom and the instructional opportunities given the child as well. And it is not the child's innate characteristics that are being measured, but the specific dimensions of the achievement or behavior problem. This implies new aspects to the role played by general and special education teachers as well as school psychologists. Before special education is considered, general education assessments and interventions not now commonly in place are proposed as standard practice.

The committee is convinced that the approach we propose would be far more effective at supporting the classroom success of a broader range of students than practices now in place, but these needed changes will rest substantially on the capability of individual educators. The need for highly capable educators is made even more compelling by the current shortage of qualified educators, particularly qualified special educators in urban schools. Key to our proposals are sustained efforts at capacity building, sufficient resources and coordination among stakeholders to build that capacity, and the time necessary to build capacity.

TEACHER QUALITY

Recommendations for States

General education teachers need significantly improved teacher preparation and professional development to prepare them to address the needs of students with significant underachievement or giftedness.

Recommendation TQ.1: State certification or licensure requirements for teachers should systematically require:

• competency in understanding and implementing reasonable norms and expectations for students and core competencies in instructional delivery of academic content;

• course work and practicum experience in understanding, creating, and modifying an educational environment to meet children's individual needs;

• competency in behavior management in classroom and non-instructional school settings;

• instruction in functional analysis and routine behavioral assessment of students;

• instruction in effective intervention strategies for students who fail to meet minimal standards for successful educational performance, or who substantially exceed those minimal standards;

• course work and practicum experience to prepare teachers to deliver culturally responsive instruction. More specifically, teachers should be familiar with the beliefs, values, cultural practices, discourse styles, and other features of students' lives that may have an impact on classroom participation and success and be prepared to use this information in designing instruction.

While a foundational knowledge base can be laid in preservice education, often classroom experience is needed before teachers can make the most of instructional experiences.

• States should require rigorous professional development for all practicing teachers, administrators, and educational support personnel to assist them in addressing the varied needs of students who differ substantially from the norm in achievement and/or behavior.

• The professional development of administrators and educational support personnel should include enhanced capabilities in the improvement and evaluation of teacher instruction with respect to meeting student's individual needs.

In preparing teachers to deliver culturally responsive instruction, it is not our intention that the teacher recreate children's home lives at school, but rather that the teacher be prepared to incorporate this information into the classroom strategically to (a) improve instruction, as when a teacher is able to help children comprehend text by relating it to familiar cultural events, activities, practices, people, etc., and (b) ensure that all students feel comfortable and have a reasonable opportunity to participate in classroom activities.

Recommendation TQ.2: State or professional association approval for educator instructional programs should include requirements for faculty competence in the current literature and research on child and adolescent learning and development, and on successful assessment, instructional, and intervention strategies, particularly for atypical learners and students with gifts and disabilities.

Recommendation TQ.3: A credential as a school psychologist or special education teacher should require instruction in classroom observation/assessment and in teacher support to work with a struggling student or with a gifted student. These skills should be considered as critical to their professional role as the administration and interpretation of tests are now considered.

• Instruction should prepare the professional to provide regular behavioral assessment and support for teachers who need assistance to understand and work effectively with a broad range of student behavior and achievement.
• Recognizing and working with implicit and explicit racial/ethnic stereotypes should be incorporated.

Finally, successful teaching of all students requires a substantive and complex knowledge base in the subject matter being taught, in how children learn, and in pedagogical strategies to promote learning. Understanding the cultural, gender, and other differences in how individual students learn is also an essential skill for effective teaching. Successful in-school implementation of the types of assessments and interventions the committee recommends to maximize educational effectiveness for all students, including gifted and talented ones, those who are low achieving, and those with disabilities, requires intensive instruction based on the scientific evidence supporting those strategies. The changes the committee recommends in this report can occur only if there is a significant cadre of well-prepared education professionals and paraprofessionals to implement the recommendations. There is, however, ample evidence that the growth in knowledge on effective teaching and learning has not begun to significantly impact the practices of educators, administrators, and support services personnel in many schools. There is also evidence that part of the reason for the failure of local educators to embrace scientific advances in teaching and learning is the inadequacy of educator preparation programs and professional development activities.

Many commentators have asserted that higher education-based educator preparation programs are unresponsive to the scientific advances of the past several decades concerning teaching and learning. In fact, many states have begun to rely on alternate routes to educator certification in an effort to both bypass traditional college and university teacher preparation programs and address a shortage of people interested in education jobs.

These three significant challenges—unresponsive educator preparation programs, a failure to infuse scientific advances into local practice, and the impending shortage of qualified individuals willing to work in education settings—present the potential for significant barriers to the effective implementation of the committee's recommendations.

Federal-Level Recommendation

Recommendation TQ.4: The committee recommends that a national advisory panel be convened in an institutional environment that is protected from political influence to study the quality and currency of programs that now exist to train teachers for general, special, and gifted education. The panel should address:

- the mechanisms for keeping instructional programs current and of high quality;
- the standards and requirements of those programs;
- the applicability of instructional programs to the demands of classroom practice;
- the long-term impact of the programs in successfully promoting educational achievement for pre-K, elementary, and secondary students.

Direct comparison to other professional fields (e.g., medicine, nursing, law, engineering, accounting) may provide insight applicable to education.

BIOLOGICAL AND EARLY CHILDHOOD RISK FACTORS

Our review of biological and social/contextual contributors to early development brings us to the compelling conclusion that there are several factors that have a known detrimental impact on early cognitive and behavioral development that affect some groups of minority children disproportionately. For example,

- Low birthweight, which has been demonstrated to affect IQ, emotional maturity, social competence, and attentional processes, is more prevalent among black children than among children of any other racial/ethnic group, reaching double the rate for white children.
- Fetal exposure to alcohol and tobacco has been associated with growth, cognitive, and self-regulatory deficits. The incidence of exposure to high doses of alcohol or nicotine is considerably higher among American

Indian/Alaskan Natives. While alcohol consumption among black pregnant women is higher than that for whites or Hispanics, cigarette smoking prevalence is lower.

• Micronutrient deficiencies, particularly iron deficiency, affect cognitive and behavioral self-regulatory development. About 5 percent of black and Mexican-American children suffer from iron deficiency anemia—about twice the rate for whites.

• Exposure to lead has been demonstrated to have detrimental effects on attentional processes, impulsivity, and hyperactivity, difficulty in changing response strategy, problems in social adjustment, and poor school performance generally. While lead levels have declined precipitously for the population as a whole, 11.2 percent of black children and 4 percent of Mexican American children have blood lead levels above 10 mg/μ, compared with 1 percent of white children.

While each of these factors has an independent effect on cognition and behavior, in combination the effect is magnified. Lead absorption is higher among children with iron deficiency. And the consequences of low birthweight are exacerbated by poor nutrition. For this reason, poverty has a particularly pernicious effect. While the influence of each factor is detrimental regardless of income, the incidence of each rises as income level drops, increasing the risk that a child living in poverty will experience multiple biological insults.

Existing intervention programs to address early biological harms have demonstrated the potential to substantially improve developmental outcomes. These include, for example, prenatal health and nutrition programs that reduce the incidence of low-birthweight babies, and intervention strategies to stimulate development in low-birthweight babies have had measured positive effects. Addressing these early biological risks has the potential to reduce the number of children, particularly minority children, with achievement and behavior problems. The strategies are neither unknown nor recently discovered. It is a matter of political priority whether resources are devoted to do so. In particular, the committee calls attention to the recommendation of the President's Task Force on Environmental Health Risks and Safety Risks to Children to eliminate lead from the housing stock by 2010.

The committee also looked at social and environmental influences on development with no clear biological basis that might differ by race or ethnicity. Once again, low socioeconomic status—both income and education level—is centrally implicated and is highly correlated with race/ethnicity. Poverty, especially persistent poverty, is associated with maternal depression, and with less optimal home environments on such dimensions as responsiveness and sensitivity of the mother to her child, the amount and level of language stimulation, direct teaching, and parenting styles. Income is also positively correlated with educational resources both inside and outside the home (child care and preschool). As with the biological risk factors, the effect of any single social or environmental risk factor is compounded by the presence of other risk factors.

Given the likelihood that multiple biological and social risk factors will attend poverty, children who live in poor families in their early years are more likely to arrive at school poorly prepared for its cognitive and behavioral demands. Because there is evidence that early intervention on multiple fronts, if it is of high quality, can improve the school prospects for these children and reduce the likelihood that they will end up in special education, the committee recommends a substantial expansion and improvement of current early intervention efforts:

Recommendation EC.1: The committee recommends that all high-risk children have access to high-quality early childhood interventions.

• For children at highest risk, these interventions should include family support, health services, and sustained, high-quality care and cognitive stimulation right from birth.

• Preschool children (ages 4 and 5) who are eligible for Head Start should have access to a Head Start or other publicly funded preschool program. These programs should provide exposure to learning opportunities that will prepare them for success in school. The committee urges attention to the well-documented early learning practices recommended in two recent NRC reports that focus on early childhood pedagogy: *Preventing Reading Difficulties in Young Children* (1998), and *Eager to Learn: Educating Our Preschoolers* (2001b). We also call attention to the finding that a critical requirement of the proposed change is raising the education requirements for preschool teachers.

• Intervention should target services to the level of individual need, including high cognitive challenge for the child who exceeds normative performance.

• The proposed expansion should better coordinate existing federal programs, such as Head Start and Early Head Start, and IDEA parts C and B, as well as state-initiated programs that meet equal or higher standards.

By high-quality early intervention services, we mean that early care and education provided to children through these programs should consistently reflect the current knowledge base regarding child development. It is important for all children to have quality child care and preschool services. However, to narrow the gap in school readiness among children at high risk for poor developmental outcomes and their lower-risk peers, carefully designed programs that support the development of self-regulation, social skills, and language and reasoning skills are critical.

While we know much about the types of experiences young children need for healthy development, improving the quality of early childhood programs requires that we refine our knowledge base in ways that are directly useful to practice and bridge the chasm between what we know from research and best practice and what we do in common practice. This will require a sustained vision and a rigorous research and development effort that transforms knowledge about what works and what does not work into field-tested program content, supporting materials, and professional development. This is not likely to happen with current funding levels.

Recommendation EC.2: The committee recommends that the federal government launch a largescale, rigorous, sustained research *and* development program in an institutional environment that has the capacity to bring together excellent professionals in research, program development, professional development, and child care/preschool practice.

Among its efforts, the research and development program should:

a. fund projects to incorporate usable knowledge about early childhood development into field-tested curricula, educational tools, and professional development materials for early childhood teachers and classrooms;

b. focus on areas with high potential for providing knowledge that can lead to prevention of disabilities and special education identification and the enhancement of gifted behaviors;

c. systematically examine the comparative benefits associated with different early intervention models and the developmental pathways through which those results were produced;

d. conduct comprehensive reanalyses of longitudinal data sets to obtain clues about why some programs have succeeded and others have failed. While the results of longitudinal studies are now well known, the data have not been fully probed for an understanding of the components of both success and failure; and

e. explore whether some subgroups of participants in early intervention programs have benefited/are benefiting differentially.

IMPROVING AND EXPANDING THE RESEARCH BASE

Data Collection

The data documenting disproportionate representation, as we discussed in Chapter 2, provide a weak foundation on which to build public policy.

Because of the unreliability of the data resulting from the Office for Civil Rights (OCR) surveys and the Office of Special Education Programs (OSEP) child counts, the committee urges that policy decisions utilizing these datasets explicitly recognize the tenuous nature of the data.

Our recommendations are directed at two goals: one is to improve the existing data collection process designed for monitoring program participation and civil rights compliance, and the other is to expand the collection of data to allow for research that would improve understanding of nonnormative achievement and behavior, as well as responses to intervention.

Currently there is considerable redundancy in the reporting requirements placed on schools by the OCR and the OSEP. The option of combining reports offered recently by the Department, though commendable, does not in the committee's view go far enough to improve the process and quality of data collection.

> **Recommendation DC.1: The committee recommends that the Department of Education conduct a single, well-designed data collection effort to monitor both the number of children receiving services through the Individuals with Disabilities Education Act or through programs for the gifted and talented and the characteristics of those children of concern to civil rights enforcement efforts.**

Whether data collection responsibility is given to either of these offices, the National Center for Education Statistics, or some other entity, the shift in responsibility would require supporting changes:

a. Data collected should meet all requirements for effective OCR monitoring, including disaggregated data by district and state, and they should be accessed easily by OCR and OSEP. This would require data collection to accommodate OCR's monitoring of data on assignment to gifted and talented programs and on limited English proficiency not currently collected by OSEP. The definitions in this category should allow for the distinction between "gifted" and "talented" to the extent that students are being served in different types of programs.

b. In the reauthorization of IDEA, statutory authority should be given to those responsible for data collection to collect child count data for disability category by racial/ethnic group by gender for both special education and gifted and talented placements as well as by state and local district levels.

The committee urges the federal agency reporting on special education enrollments by racial/ethnic group do so by reporting *risk indices*—the proportion of a given racial/ethnic group's enrollment in the general school population that is enrolled in a given disability category. In order to accomplish this goal, steps must be taken to coordinate reporting child counts by age, currently done in the OSEP reporting by disability category, for ages 3 to 21, with the National Center for Education Statistics Common Core of Data, which reports by grade level. This would remedy the current situation in which it is impossible to align the ages 3 to 5 and the 18 to 21 child count by OSEP with any meaningful count of the total population.

The committee also urges that the OCR monitor the impact of education reform initiatives, such as high-stakes testing programs, to ensure that implementation of these initiatives does not exacerbate minority representation problems in special or gifted education.

While a more careful data collection effort of the sort outlined here would improve the understanding of who is being assigned to special education and gifted and talented programs, it would do little to further understanding of the reasons for placement, the appropriateness of placement (or nonplacement), the services provided, or the consequences that ensue. Moreover, the variation observed from one state to the next serves as a reminder that in discussing special education or gifted and talented programs, we refer to practices that differ dramatically from one location to the next. While special education may be a set of well-targeted specialized classroom supports for children in need in one school, it may be a dead-end program in others—a last resort for teachers who can no longer work with a student. The data are not available to tell which it is, in which schools, and for which students. And while the data are poor with respect to special education, the data on gifted and talented students are even worse. Currently the U.S. Department of Education has several longitudinal studies under way or completed that look at children in special education during certain ages or grades. These data are considerably more informative than the incidence numbers collected for monitoring purposes. However, these data do not allow for an understanding of how children got into the special education system in the first place.

Recommendation DC.2: The committee recommends that a national advisory panel be convened to design the collection of nationally representative longitudinal data that would allow for more informed study of minority disproportion in special education and gifted and talented programs. The panel should include scholars in special education research as well as researchers experienced in national longitudinal data collection and analysts in a variety of allied fields, including anthropology, psychology, and sociology.

The panel should assess the cost of collecting data that could answer the following questions:

• What antecedents to special education placement are associated with students' assignment to special education services? Antecedents studied should include, but not be limited to: race (self-identified and school-identified), sex, and other socioeconomic and social background factors, and school factors, such as class size, teacher experience and preparation, instructional strategies, and school and classroom resources.

• How do schools differ in their categorization of students, and are these differences associated with differences in students' access to special education services?

• Are students who present with the same researcher-identified condition treated differently in different schools and, if so, what policy, resource, and individual-level factors are associated with these differences in treatment? What is the incidence of students who have the same research-identified conditions but are never referred for special education assessment? And is referral to special education assessment associated with severity of the researcher-identified condition or some other factors?

• If students who present with the same researcher-identified condition are treated differently, how is access or lack of access to a variety of special education services associated with later levels of cognitive achievement and behavioral adjustment?

The data would have improved value if the following additional information were included:

• how long the family has lived in the United States;
• birth country of students, their parents, and their grandparents;
• language proficiency (in both English and native language);
• education level of parents;
• level of acculturation; and
• experiences with literacy artificats and practices.

The committee acknowledges that the more detailed the data collection, and the greater the number of subgroups that are represented, the more expensive the undertaking. However, the questions posed to this committee, and to the NRC panel in 1979, cannot be answered adequately without these data. If we hope to have a better understanding 20 years in the future, increasing the current investment and improving the rigor of the data collection now is required.

Even with more limited existing data, analysis for this report of the effect of race/ethnicity on special education placement or outcomes was made more difficult because many research studies did not specify the racial/ethnic composition of the sample or had too few minority children to measure effects by race/ethnicity. The committee urges that research funded by the U.S. Department of Education using these or other data require the careful description of samples as well as differential effects, to the extent feasible, by race, ethnicity, limited English proficiency, socioeconomic status, and gender.

Expanding the Research Base

In our study of the issues related to the representation of minority children in special education and gifted and talented programs, the existing knowledge base revealed the potential for substantial progress. We know many of the early biological and environmental factors that threaten healthy development, and we know something about effective intervention. We know the kinds of experiences that promote children's early cognitive and behavioral development and set them on a more positive trajectory for school success. We know intervention strategies that have demonstrated success with some of the key problems that end in referral to special education. And we know some features of programs that are correlated with successful outcomes for students in special education.

Between the articulation of what we know from research and best practice and a change in everyday practice lies a wide chasm. It is the distance between demonstrating that vocabulary development is key to later success in reading, and having every Head Start teacher trained and equipped with materials that will promote vocabulary development among Head Start children. It is the distance between knowing that classroom management affects a child's behavior, and the school psychologist knowing how to help a specific teacher work with a specific child in the classroom context. It is the distance between those who are most knowledgeable and experienced agreeing on what teachers need to know, and every school of education changing its curriculum. Bridging the chasm will require that we become better at accumulating knowledge, extending it in promising areas, incorporating the best of what is known in teacher instruction efforts and education curricula and materials, and rigorously testing effectiveness. It will require public policies that are aligned with the knowledge base and that provide the support for its widespread application.

> **Recommendation RD.1: We recommend that education research and development, including that related to special and gifted education, be systematically expanded to carry promising findings and validated practices through to classroom applicability. This includes research on scaling up promising practices from research sites to widespread use.**

In particular, the committee recommends:

- Strengthening research on educational improvement, particularly in schools with large numbers of children from low-income families. There are some promising models, but efforts are needed to accumulate knowledge, testing the dimensions of effectiveness (for whom and under what circumstances), and to make the best of what is known systematically available to school districts and teachers.
- Research on early interventions in general education settings.
- Research on what works in special education offers some important principles, but too few well-tested interventions with a solid evaluation of the conditions under which they work and for whom. In particular, the research base with respect to English language learners needs to be strengthened.
- While there has been substantial progress on educational interventions for students who are having difficulty learning to read, little is currently known that can guide educational interventions for the non-responders to reading interventions. Research needs to attend now to this group of students.
- We have given relatively little attention either in research or in program development to the education of gifted and talented students. This research base needs to be strengthened substantially.
- Features of cultural sensitivity that have an impact on learning outcomes for minority students have not been rigorously researched and evaluated in classroom settings. While a significant amount has been written about culturally appropriate accommodations, many of the recommendations have no empirical basis (such as matching learning styles) and should be avoided. Shoring up the empirical foundation for culturally sensitive teaching practice should be a research priority.
- Development is needed of effective mechanisms for communication of research findings to practitioner, policy, and teacher educator communities.

THE COST OF REFORM

The committee's recommendations are broad. An obvious and fair question is: At what price? While we have neither the resources nor the expertise to carry out a cost-benefit analysis, a few considerations are worth noting with regard to our major recommendations. First, some of our proposals have no obvious price tag. We recommend that teachers and school psychologists be trained differently so that they are better prepared to address the diversity among the children they will teach. Teacher training is already required, as is licensing of teacher training programs. The change in content that we recommend need not impose long-run costs. The proposal is not to do more, but to do what is now done differently.

A similar argument can be made for special education referral and assessment, though in this case some new costs are implied. Early universal screening and intervention for reading problems would impose additional costs. While the tests themselves are short and easy to administer during a regular class period, the training required for teachers to properly administer and interpret the test results, and to learn to work effectively in a classroom with multiple reading groups, represents a considerable up-front cost. Texas currently provides two days of training to every teacher administering the TPRI.[2] We would point out, however, that this training could become a standard requirement of pre-service teacher education in the future. School districts currently spend resources on professional development. Were the proposed program adopted, some portion of existing in-service training resources could be devoted to this training. The same is true of training in classroom management and universal behavior interventions. And offsetting the costs of new assessment techniques are the savings from replacing a time-intensive assessment process centered around IQ testing.

The largest sustained cost of our recommendations is likely to be quality early intervention services for the highest risk children that begins before birth and is maintained throughout childhood. Experience with these interventions suggests that doing them well is expensive—on the order of $7,000 to $12,000 per child per year. Provision of quality preschool services to children from poor families would also require substantial resources, since only about one-third of those children now receive Head Start services. As Chapter 4 indicates, the average cost per child of Head Start services is approaching $6,000 per year. But the upfront cost of the program would be offset by reduced special education and grade repetition, and long-term benefits to society from higher reading and mathematics achievement, increased employment and earnings, and reduction in teen pregnancy and crime.

Similarly, changing the data collection done by the U.S. Department of Education need not cost more in the long run. If the data collected are expanded as we recommend, one would expect higher costs of additional reporting. However, duplication of reporting that currently exists would be eliminated, potentially offsetting any increase in cost.

Lastly, the research we propose both with regard to early childhood programs and general, special, and gifted education is not an incremental increase in existing efforts. Rather, it is a substantial investment in carrying through important research findings to classroom applicability; an effort that is likely to require substantial new resources. In virtually every other sector of the economy, research plays a substantially larger role in improv-

---

[2]Personal communication with Barbara Forman, September, 2001.

ing and informing practice than in education (NRC, 1999c). While the size of the increase needed to substantially change the relationship between research and practice is significant, as a fraction of education spending, it is very small.

For medical problems like cancer, we have created federal research programs that create a vision, focus research efforts on areas with promise for improving treatments, conduct extensive field tests to determine "what works," and facilitate the movement of research findings into practice (National Cancer Institute, 2000). And those programs have been funded at impressive levels: The National Cancer Institute budget in fiscal year 2000 exceeded $3.3 billion. If we are serious about a research program that would support efforts to reduce the number of children who are on a trajectory that leads to school failure and disability identification and to increase the number of minority students who are achieving at high levels, then we will need to devote the minds and resources to that effort commensurate with the size and the importance of the enterprise.

References

Abel, E.L.
    1995   An update on incidence of FAS: FAS is not an equal opportunity birth defect. *Neurotoxicology and Teratology* 17(4):437-443.

Aber, J.L., S.M. Jones, J.L. Brown, N. Chaudry, and F. Samples
    1998   Resolving conflict creatively: Evaluating the developmental effects of a school-based violence prevention program in neighborhood and classroom context. *Development and Psychopathology* 10:187-213.

Achenbach, T.M.
    1991   *The Child Behavior Checklist: Manual for the Teacher's Report Form.* Burlington: University of Vermont, Department of Psychiatry.

Achenbach, T.M., and C.S. Edelbrock
    1986   *Manual for the Teacher's Report Form and Teacher Version of the Child Behavior Profile.* Burlington, VT: University of Vermont, Department of Psychiatry.
    1991   *Manual for the Child Behavior Checklist and Revised Child Behavior Profile.* Burlington, VT: University Associates in Psychiatry.

Achilles, C.M.
    1996   Students achieve more in smaller classes. *Educational Leadership* 53:76-77.

Adams, M.J.
    1990   *Beginning to Read.* Cambridge, MA: MIT Press.

Adelman, C.
    1999   *Answers in the Tool Box: Academic Intensity, Attendance Patterns, and Bachelor's Degree Attainment.* Washington, DC: U.S. Department of Education, Office of Educational Research and Development.

Administration of Children, Youth, and Families
    2001   *Head Start FACES: Longitudinal Findings on Program Performance, Third Progress Report to Commissionís Office of Research and Evaluation and he Head Start Bureau.* Washington, DC: U.S. Department of Health and Human Services.

Ainsworth-Darnell, J.W. and D.B. Downey
   1998   Assessing the oppositional culture explanation for racial/ethnic differences in school performance. *American Sociological Review* 63:536-553.
Alexander, K.L., M. Cook, and E. McDill
   1978   Curriculum tracking and educational stratification: Some further evidence. *American Sociological Review* 43: 47-66.
Allen, M.C., P.K. Donohue, and A.E. Dusman
   1993   The limit of viability—Neonatal outcome of infants born at 22 to 25 weeks' gestation. *New England Journal of Medicine* 329(22):1597 1601.
Allington, R., H. Stuetzel, M. Shake, and S. Lamarche
   1986   What is remedial reading: A descriptive study. *Reading Research Quarterly* 26:15-30.
Aloia, G.F.
   1981   Influence of a child's race and the EMR label on initial impressions of regular classroom teachers. *American Journal on Mental Deficiency* 85(6):619-623.
Als, H.
   1997   Earliest intervention for preterm infants in the newborn intensive care unit. Pp. 47-76 in *The Effectiveness of Early Intervention*, M.J. Guralnick, ed. Baltimore, MD: Paul H. Brookes.
American Psychiatric Association
   1994   *Diagnostic and statistical manual of mental disorders* (4th ed.). Washington, DC: American Psychiatric Association.
Anastasi, A.
   1988   *Psychological Testing, Sixth Edition.* New York: Macmillan.
Anderson, J.C., and W.E. Nagy
   1992   The vocabulary conundrum. *American Educator* 16:44-48.
Anderson, V. and M. Roit
   1993   Planning and implementing collaborative strategy instruction for delayed readers in grades 6-10. Special Issue: Strategies Instruction, *Elementary School Journal* 94(2): 121-137.
Archambault, Jr., F.X., K.L. Westberg, S.W. Brown, B.W. Hallmark, C.L. Emmons, and W. Zhang
   1993   *Regular Classroom Practices eith Gifted Students: Results of a National Survey of Classroom Teachers.* Research Monograph 93102. The National Research Center on the Gifted and Talented. Storrs, CT: University of Connecticut.
Arndorfer, R.W., and R.G. Miltenberger
   1993   Functional assessment and treatment of challenging behavior. *Topics in Early Childhood Special Education* 9:106-126.
Aronson, R.A, S. Uttech, and M. Soref
   1993   The effect of maternal cigarette smoking on low birth weight and preterm birth in Wisconsin, 1991. *Wisconsin Medical Journal* 92:613-617.
Arreaga-Mayer, C., B.J. Terry, and C.R. Greenwood
   1998   Classwide peer tutoring. Pp. 105-199 in *Peer-Assisted Learning*, K. Topping and S. Ehly, eds. Mahwah, NJ: Erlbuam.
Ashton, P.T.
   1975   Cross-cultural Piagetian research: An experimental perspective. *Harvard Educational Review* 45:475-506.
Ashurst, D.I., and C.E. Meyers
   1973   Social system and clinical model in the identification of the educable mentally retarded. Pp. 150-163 in *Socio-behavioral Studies in Mental Retardation: Papers in Honor of Harvey F. Dingman. Monographs of the American Association on Men-*

tal Deficiency, G. Tarjan, R.K. Eyman, and C.E. Meyers, eds. Washington, DC: American Association of Mental Deficiency.

Au, K.
1993   *Literacy Instruction in Multicultural Settings*. Belmont, CA: Wadsworth/ Thomson Learning.

Augustine, D.K., K.D. Gruber, and L.R. Hansen
1990   Cooperation works! *Educational Leadership* 47:4-7.

Axinn, W., G. Duncan, and A. Thornton
1997   The effects of parental income, wealth and attitudes on children's completed schooling and self-esteem. Pp. 518-540 in *Consequences of Growing Up Poor*, G.J. Duncan and J. Brooks-Gunn, eds. New York: Russell Sage Foundation.

Ayllon, T., and M. Roberts
1974   Eliminating discipline problems by strengthening academic performance. *Journal of Applied Behavior Analysis* 7:71-76.

Ayllon, T., D. Layman, and H. Kandel
1975   A behavioral-educational alternative to drug control of hyperactive children. *Journal of Applied Behavior Analysis* 8:137-146.

Bahr, M.W., D. Fuchs, P.M. Stecker, and L.S. Fuchs
1991   Are teachers' perceptions of difficult-to-teach students racially biased? *School Psychology Review* 20:599-608.

Baker, J., and N. Zigmond
1990   Are regular education classes equipped to accommodate students with learning disabilities? *Exceptional Children* 56:516-526.

Baker, L., and A.L. Brown
1984   Metacognitive skills and reading. Pp. 353-394 in *Handbook of Reading*, Pearson, R. Barr, M.L. Kamil, and P. Mosenthal, eds. White Plains, NY: Longman.

Baker, S., and R. Gersten
1997   *Exploratory meta-analysis of instructional practices for English-language learners.* (Tech. Rep. No. 97-01). Eugene, OR: Eugene Research Institute.

Baker, S., R. Gersten, and T. Keating
2000   When less may be more: A 2-year longitudinal evaluation of a volunteer tutoring program requiring minimal training. *Reading Research Quarterly* 35(4):494-519.

Bandura, A.
1997   *Self-efficacy: The Exercise of Control*. New York: W.H. Freeman.

Bank, L., M.S. Forgatch, G.R. Patterson, and R. Fetrow
1993   Parenting practices of single mothers: Mediators of negative contextual factors. *Journal of Marriage and the Family* 55:371-384.

Barnett, L.B., and W.G. Durden
1993   Education patterns of academically talented youth. *Gifted Child Quarterly* 37:161-168.

Barnett, W.S.
1995   Long-term effects of early childhood programs on cognitive and social outcomes. *The Future of Children* 5(3):25-50.

Barocas, R., R. Seifer, and A.J. Sameroff
1985   Defining environmental risk: Multiple dimensions of psychological vulnerability. *American Journal of Community Psychology* 13:433-447.

Baron, R., D.Y.H. Tom, and H.M. Cooper
1985   Social class, race, and teacher expectations. In *Teacher Expectancies*, J.B. Dusek, ed. Hillsdale, NJ: Lawrence Erlbaum.

Barr, M.A., S. Ellis, H. Tester, and A. Thomas
1988   *The Primary Language Record: Handbook for Teachers*. Portsmouth, NH: Heinemann.

Baska, L.
   1986   Alternatives to traditional testing. *Roeper Review*, 8(3):181-184.
Baumann, J.F. and E.J. Kameenui
   1991   Research on vocabulary instruction: Ode to Voltaire. Pp. 604-632 in *Handbook of Research on Teaching the English Language Arts*, J. Flood, D. Lapp, and J.R. Squire, eds. New York: Macmillan.
Bear, D.R., M. Invernizzi, S. Templeton, and F. Johnston
   1996   *Words Their Way*. Upper Saddle River, NJ: Merrill.
Beatty, A.S. et al.
   1996   *NAEP 1994 U.S. History Report Card: Findings from the National Assessment of Educational Progress*. Washington, DC: U.S. Department of Education.
Beck, I., M. McKeown, and L. Kucan
   2002   *Bringing Words to Life: Robust Vocabulary Instruction*. New York: Guilford Press.
Bee, H.L., L.F. Egeren, A.P. Streissguth, B.A. Nyman, and M.S. Leckie
   1969   Social class differences in maternal teaching strategies and speech patterns. *Developmental Psychology* 1:726-734.
Bee, H.L., K.E. Barnard, S.J. Eyres, C.A. Gray, M.A. Hammond, A.L. Speitz, C. Snyder, and B. Clark
   1982   Prediction of IQ and language skill from perinatal status, child performance, family characteristics, and mother-infant interaction. *Child Development* 53:1134-1156.
Bellinger, D., H.L. Needleman, R. Bromfield, and M. Mintz
   1984   A followup study of the academic attainment and classroom behavior of children with elevated dentine lead levels. *Biological Trace Element Research* 6(3):207-223.
Bellinger, D., H. Hu, L. Titlebaum, and H.L. Needleman
   1994a   Attentional correlates of dentine and bone lead levels in adolescents. *Archives of Environmental Health* 49(2):98-105.
Bellinger, D., A. Leviton, E. Allred, and M. Rabinowitz
   1994b   Pre- and post-natal lead exposure and behavior problems in school-age children. *Environmental Research* 66(1):12-30.
Belsky, J., S. Woodworth, and K. Crnic
   1996   Trouble in the second year: Three questions about family interaction. *Child Development* 67(2):556-578.
Benbow, C.P., and L.L. Minor
   1990   Cognitive profiles of verbally and mathematically precocious students: Implications for identification of the gifted. *Gifted Child Quarterly* 34(1):21-26.
Bennett, A.T.
   1988   Gateways to powerlessness: Incorporating Hispanic deaf children and families into formal schooling. *Disability, Handicap, and Society* 3(2):119-151.
Benson, D.F.
   1994   *The Neurology of Thinking*. New York: Oxford University Press.
Berger, M., W. Yule, and M. Rutter
   1975   Attainment and adjustment in two geographical areas: II. The prevalence of specific reading retardation. *British Journal of Psychiatry* 126:510-519.
Berman, S., P. Davis, A. Koufman-Frederick, and D. Union
   2001   The rising costs of special education in Massachusetts: Causes and effects. Ch. 9 in *Rethinking Special Education for a New Century*. C.E. Finn, A.J. Rotherham, and C. Hokanson, Jr., eds. Washington, DC: Thomas B. Fordham Foundation.
Bermudez, A.B., and S.J. Rakow
   1990   Analyzing teachers' perceptions of identification procedures for gifted and talented Hispanic limited English proficient students at-risk. *Journal of Educational Issues of Language Minority Students* 7:21-33.

Berninger, V., R. Abbott, L. Rogan, E. Reed, S. Abbott, A. Brooks, K. Vaughan, and S. Graham
   1998   Teaching spelling to children with specific learning disabilities: The mind's ear and eye beat the computer or pencil. *Learning Disability Quarterly* 21:1-17.

Bettes, B.A.
   1988   Maternal depression and motherese: Temporal and intonational features. *Child Development* 59(4):1089-1096.

Betts, J.R., K.S. Rueben, and A. Danenberg
   2000   *Equal Resources, Equal Outcomes? The Distribution of School Resources and Student Achievement in California.* San Francisco: Public Policy Institute of California.

Betts, J.R., and J.L. Shkolnik
   1999   The behavioral effects of variations in class size: The case of math teachers. *Educational Evaluation and Policy Analysis* 21(2):193-213.

Bidell, T.R., and K.W. Fischer
   1997   Between nature and nurture: The role of human agency in the epigenesis of intelligence. Pp. 193-242 in *Intelligence, Heredity, and Environment*, R.J. Sternberg and E. Grigorenko, eds. Cambridge, UK: Cambridge University Press.

Bittick, P.S.
   1995   Equality and excellence: Equal education opportunity for gifted and talented children. *South Texas Law Review* 36:119.

Black, J.E., and W.T. Greenough
   1986   Induction of pattern in neural structure by experience: Implications for cognitive development. Pp. 1-50 in *Advances in Developmental Psychology*, Volume 4, M.E. Lamb, A.L. Brown, and B. Rogoff, eds. Hillsdale, NJ: Lawrence Erlbaum.

Black, S.E., and M. Behrmann
   1994   Localization in alexia. Pp. 331-376 in *Localization and Neuroimaging in Neuropsychology*, A. Kertesz, ed. New York: Academic Press.

Blair, C., C.T. Ramey, and M. Hardin
   1995   Early intervention for low birth weight premature infants: Participation and intellectual development. *American Journal of Mental Retardation* 99:542-554.

Blank, R.
   1994   Outlook for the U.S. Labor Market and Prospects for Low-Wage Entry Jobs. Paper presented at the Urban Institute Conference on Self-Sufficiency and the Low-Wage Labor Market: A Reality Check for Welfare Reform, Washington, DC.

Blatt, S.D., and S. Simms
   1997   Foster care: Special children, special needs. *Contemporary Pediatrics* 14(4):109-129.

Borland, J.H., and L. Wright
   1994   Identifying young, potentially gifted, economically disadvantaged students. *Gifted Child Quarterly* 38:164-171.

Borman, G., S. Stringfield, and L. Rachuba
   2000   *Advancing Minority High Achievement: National Trends and Promising Programs and Practices.* New York: The College Board.

Bouchard, Jr., T.
   1997   IQ similarities in twins reared apart: Findings and responses to critics. Pp. 126-160 in *Intelligence, Heredity, and Environment*, R.J. Sternberg and E. Grigorenko, eds. Cambridge, UK: Cambridge University Press.

Bourdieu, P.
   1973   Cultural reproduction and social reproduction. Pp. 71-112 in *Knowledge, Education, and Cultural Change*. R. Brown, ed. London: Tavistock.

Bourque, M.J. et al.
  1997 *1996 Science Performance Standards: Achievement Results for the Nation and the States.* Washington, DC: National Assessment Governing Board.
Bower, E.M.
  1960 *Early Identification of Emotionally Handicapped Children in School.* Springfield, IL: Charles C. Thomas.
  1982 Defining emotional disturbance: Public policy and research. *Psychology in the Schools* 19:55-60.
Boyer, L.
  2000 Establishing the supply and demand for special educators. *Connections Newsletter,* 4. [Online]. Available: http://www.cec.sped.org/cl/whats_new/newsletter/v4_n2/1.html [Accessed March 17, 2001].
Boykin, A.W.
  1986 The triple quandary and the schooling of Afro-American children. Pp. 57-92 in Ulric Neisser, ed., *The School Achievement of Minority Children.* Hillsdale, NJ: Lawrence Erlbaum.
Bradley, R.H., L. Whiteside, D.J. Mundform, P.H. Casey, K.J. Kelleher, and S.K. Pope
  1994 Early indications of resilience and their relation to experiences in the home environments of low birthweight babies. *Child Development* 65:346-360.
Brady, S., and L. Moats
  1997 *Informed Instruction for Reading Success: Foundations for Teacher Preparation* (ERIC Document Reproduction Services No. ED 411 646). Columbus, OH: ERIC.
Brady, S.A., and D.P. Shankweiler, eds.
  1991 *PhonologicAl Processes In Literacy: A Tribute to Isabelle Y. Liberman.* Hillsdale, NJ: Lawrence Erlbaum.
Brandenberg, N.A., R.M. Friedman, and S.E. Silver
  1990 The epidemiology of childhood psychiatric disorders: Prevalence findings from recent studies. *Journal of the American Academy of Child and Adolescent Psychiatry* 29:76-83.
Brazelton, T.B.
  1973 *Neonatal Behavioral Assessment Scale.* London: Heinemann.
Breslau, N., H. Chilcoat, J. DelDotto, P. Andreski, and G. Brown
  1996 Low birth weight and neurocognitive status at six years of age. *Biological Psychiatry* 40:389-397.
Brestan, E.V., and S.M. Eyberg
  1998 Effective psychosocial treatments of conduct-disordered children and adolescents: 29 years, 82 studies, and 5,272 kids. *Journal of Clinical Child Psychology* 27(2): 180-189.
Brewer, G.D., and J.S. Kakalik
  1974 Serving Handicapped Children: The Road Ahead. RAND Paper No. 5304 presented at Child Welfare League Executives Conference, August 1974.
Brody, D.J., J.L. Pirkle, R.A. Kramer, K.M. Flegal, T.D. Matte, E.W. Gunter, and D.C. Paschal
  1994 Blood lead levels in the US population: Phase 1 of the Third National Health and Nutrition Examination Survey (NHANES III, 1988 to 1991). *Journal of the American Medical Association* 272:277-283.
Brody, G.H., and D.L. Flor
  1997 Maternal psychological functioning, family processes, and child adjustment in rural, single-parent, African American families. *Developmental Psychology* 33(6): 1000-1011.

Brody, G.H., and R. Forehand
   1986   Maternal perceptions of child maladjustment as a function of the combined influ-
            ence of child behavior and maternal depression. *Journal of Consulting and Clinical
            Psychology* 54:237-240.
Brody, G.H., Z. Stoneman, and D. Flor
   1995   Linking family processes, parental education, and family financial resources to
            academic competence among rural African American youths living in two-parent
            families. *Journal of Marriage and the Family* 57:567-579.
Broman, S.H., P.L. Nichols, and W.A. Kennedy
   1975   *Preschool IQ: Prenatal and Early Development Correlates.* Hillsdale, NJ: Lawrence
            Erlbaum.
Brooks-Gunn, J., and G.J. Duncan
   1997   The effects of poverty on children. *The Future of Children* 7(2):55-71.
Brooks-Gunn, J., G.J. Duncan, and P.R. Britto
   1999   Are socioeconomic gradients for children similar to those for adults? Pp. 94-124 in
            *Developmental Health and the Wealth of Nations: Social, Biological, and Educa-
            tional Dynamics*, D.P. Keating and C. Hertzman, eds. New York: Guilford Press.
Brooks-Gunn, J., and F. Furstenberg
   1987   Continuity and change in the context of poverty. Pp. 171-187 in *The Malleability
            of Children*, J. Gallagher and C. Ramey, eds. Baltimore: Brookes.
Brooks-Gunn, J., G. Guo, and F.F. Furstenberg, Jr.
   1993   Who drops out of and who continues beyond high school?: A 20-year follow-up of
            black urban youth. *Journal of Research on Adolescence* 3(3):271-294.
Brophy, J.
   1983   Research on the self-fulfilling prophecy and teacher perceptions. *Journal of Educa-
            tional Psychology* 75:631-661.
Brophy, J.E., and T.L. Good
   1974   *Teacher-Student Relationships: Causes and Consequences.* New York: Holt,
            Rinehart, and Winston.
Bruck, M.
   1992   Persistence of dyslexics' phonological awareness deficits. *Developmental Psychol-
            ogy* 28(5):874-886.
Brunswick, N., E. McCrory, C.J. Price, C.D. Frith, and U. Frith
   1999   Explicit and implicit processing of words and pseudowords by adult developmental
            dyslexics: A search for Wernicke's Wortschatz. *Brain* 122:1901-1917.
Bryant, D.M., and K. Maxwell
   1997   The effectiveness of early intervention for disadvantaged children. Pp. 23-46 in *The
            Effectiveness of Early Intervention*. M.J. Guralnick, ed. Baltimore, MD: Paul H.
            Brooks.
Bullis, M., and H.M. Walker
   1994   *Comprehensive School-Based Systems forTroubled Youth.* Eugene: University of
            Oregon, Center on Human Development.
Burchinal, M.R., J.E. Roberts, L.A. Nabors, and D.M. Bryant
   1996   Quality of center child care and infant cognitive and language development. *Child
            Development* 67:606-620.
Buriel, R.
   1983   Teacher-student interactions and their relationship to student achievement: A com-
            parison of Mexican-American children. *Journal of Educational Psychology* 75(6):
            889-897.
Burt, C., E. Jones, E. Miller, and W. Moodle
   1934   *How the Mind Works.* New York: Appleton-Century-Crofts.

Bussing, R., B.T. Zima, T.R. Belin, and S.R. Forness
  1998   Children who qualify for LD and SED programs: Do they differ in level of ADHD symptoms and comorbid psychiatric conditions? *Behavioral Disorders* 20:51-60.
Butler, N.R., and H. Goldstein
  1973   Smoking in pregnancy and subsequent child development. *British Medicine* 4:573-575.
Callahan, C.M., S.L. Hunsaker, C.M. Adams, S.D. Moore, and L.C. Bland
  1995   *Instruments Used in the Identification of Gifted And Talented Students.* (Research Monograph # 95130). Storrs, CT: University of Connecticut, National Research Center on the Gifted and Talented.
Callahan, C.M., and J.A. McIntire
  1994   *Identifying Outstanding Talent in American Indian and Alaska Native Students.* Washington, DC: U. S. Department of Education.
Callahan, C.M., C.A. Tomlinson, T.R. Moon, E.M. Tomchin, and J.A. Plucker
  1995   *Project START: Using a Multiple Intelligences Model in Identifying and Promoting Talent in High-risk Students.* (Research Monograph # 95136). Storrs, CT: University of Connecticut, National Research Center on the Gifted and Talented.
Campbell, D.T., and J.C. Stanley
  1963   *Experimental and Quasi-Experimental Designs for Research.* Boston: Houghton Mifflin.
Campbell, F.A., and C.T. Ramey
  1994   Effects of early intervention on intellectual and academic achievement: A follow-up study of children from low-income families. *Child Development* 65:684-698.
  1995   Cognitive and school outcomes for high risk students at middle adolescence: Positive effects of early intervention. *American Educational Research Journal* 32:743-772.
Campbell, J.R. et al.
  1996   *NAEP 1994 Reading Report Card for the Nation and the States: Findings from the National Assessment of Educational Progress and Trial State Assessments.* Washington, DC: U.S. Department of Education.
Campbell, J.R., C.M. Hombo, and J. Mazzeo
  2000   *NAEP 1999 Trends in Academic Progress: Three dDecades of Student Performance.* (NCES 2000-469). Washington, DC: National Center for Educational Statistics.
Campbell, S.B., J.F. Cohn, and T. Meyers
  1995   Depression in first-time mothers: Mother-infant interaction and depression chronicity. *Developmental Psychology* 31(3):349-357.
Caplovitz, D.
  1979   *Making Ends Meet: How Families Cope with Inflation and Recession.* Beverly Hills, CA: Sage.
Caraballo, R.S., G.A. Giovino, T.F. Pechacek, P.D. Mowery, P.A. Richter, W.J. Strauss, D.J. Sharp, M.P. Eriksen, J.L. Pirkle, and K.R. Maurer
  1998   Racial and ethnic differences in serum cotinine levels of cigarette smokers. *Journal of the American Medical Association* 280(2):135-139.
Cardon, L.R., S.D. Smith, D.W. Fulker, W.J. Kimberling, B.F. Pennington, and J.C. DeFries
  1994   Quantitative trait locus for reading disability on chromosome 6. *Science* 266:276-279.
  1995   Quantitative trait locus for reading disability: Correction. *Science* 268(5217):1553.
Carnegie Task Force on Meeting the Needs of Young Children
  1994   *Starting Points: Meeting the Needs of Our Youngest Children.* New York: Carnegie Corporation of New York.

Carnine, D.
    2000   *Why Education Experts Resist Effective Practices.* Report of the Thomas B.
            Fordham Foundation. Washington, DC: Thomas B. Fordham Foundation.
Carraher, T.N., D.W. Carraher, and A.D. Schliemann
    1985   Mathematics in the streets and in schools. *British Journal of Developmental Psychology* 3:21-29.
Carson, T.L., G.A. Van Gelder, G.C. Karas, and W.B. Buck
    1974   Slowed learning in lambs prenatally exposed to lead. *Archives of Environmental Health* 29:154-156.
Carter, K.R., and H.L. Swanson
    1990   An analysis of the most prominent gifted journal articles since the Marland report: Implications for researchers. *Gifted Child Quarterly* 34:116-123.
Cartledge, G.
    1996   *Cultural Diversity and Social Skills Instruction: Understanding Ethnic and Gender Differences.* Champaign, IL: Research Press.
Case, R.
    1985   *Intellectual Development: Birth to Adulthood.* New York: Academic.
Case, R., S. Griffin, and W. Kelly
    1999   Socioeconomic gradients in mathematical ability and their responsiveness to intervention during early childhood. Pp. 125-149 in *Developmental Health and the Wealth of Nations: Social, Biological, and Educational Dynamics*, D.P. Keating and C. Hertzman, eds. New York: Guilford Press.
Case, R., and R. Sandieson
    1987   General Developmental Constraints on the Acquisition of Special Procedures (and vice versa). Paper presented at the annual meeting of the American Educational Research Association, Baltimore, April.
Cassidy, E.
    1988   *Reaching and Involving Black Parents of Handicapped Children in Their Child's Education Program.* Lansing, MI: CAUSE Inc. (ERIC Document Reproduction Service No. ED 302 982).
Casto, G., and A. Lewis
    1984   Parent involvement in infant and pre-school programs. *Division of Early Childhood* 9:49-56.
Cataldo, C.Z.
    1978   A follow-up study of early intervention. *Dissertation Abstracts International* 39: 657A (University Microfilms No. 7813990).
Caughy, M.O., J. DiPietro, and D.M. Strobino
    1994   Day-care participation as a protective factor in the development of low-income children. *Child Development* 65(Special Issue: Children and Poverty):457-471.
Cazden, C.
    1986   Classroom discourse. Pp. 432-463 in *Handbook of Research on Teaching (3rd ed.)* M.C. Wittrock, ed. New York: Macmillan.
Ceci, S.J.
    1996   *On Intelligence: A Bioecological Treatise on Intellectual Development* (expanded ed.). Cambridge, MA: Harvard University Press.
Ceci, S.J., and J.K. Liker
    1986   A day at the races: A study of IQ, expertise, and cognitive complexity. *Journal of Experimental Psychology* 115(3):255-266.
Ceci, S.J., and A. Roazzi
    1994   The effects of context on cognition: Postcards from Brazil. Pp. 74-101 in R. J. Sternberg & R. K. Wagner, eds., *Mind in Context: Interactionist Perspectives on Human Intelligence.* New York: Cambridge University Press.

Ceci, S.J., T. Rosenblum, E. de Bruyn, and D.Y. Lee
   1997   A bio-ecological model of intellectual development: moving beyond $h2$. Pp. 303-322 in *Intelligence, Heredity, and Environment*, R.J. Sternberg and E. Grigorenko, eds. Cambridge, UK: Cambridge University Press.
Center, D.B.
   1990   Social maladjustment: An interpretation. *Behavioral Disorders* 15:141-148.
Center, Y., K. Wheldall, L. Freeman, L. Outhred, and M. McNaught
   1995   An evaluation of reading recovery. *Reading Research Quarterly* 30(2):240-263.
Centers for Disease Control and Prevention
   1991   *Strategic Plan for the Elimination of Childhood Lead Poisoning*. Atlanta, GA: Centers for Disease Control, U.S. Department of Health and Human Services.
   2000   Recommendations for blood lead screening of young children enrolled in medicaid: targeting a group at high risk. *Morbidity and Mortality Weekly Report*, 49.
Chall, J.S.
   2000   *The Academic Achievement Challenge*. New York: Guilford.
Chan, S.
   1986   Parents of exceptional Asian children. Pp. 36-53 in *Exceptional Asian Children and Youth*, M.K. Kitano and P.C. Chinn, eds. Reston, VA: Council for Exceptional Children and Youth.
Cisero, C., and J. Royer
   1995   The development and cross language transfer of phonological awareness. *Contemporary Educational Psychology* 20:275-303.
Clark, P.I., S. Gautam, and L. Gerson
   1996   Effect of menthol cigarettes on biochemical markers of smoke exposure among black and white smokers. *Chest* 110:1194-1198.
Clarke, R., J. Shibley Hyde, M.J. Essex, and M.H. Klein
   1997   Length of maternity leave and quality of mother-infant interactions. *Child Development* 68(2):364-383.
Clasen, D.R.
   1994   Project STREAM: Support, training and resources for education able minorities. Pp. 1-21 in *Contexts for Promise: Noteworthy Practices and Innovations in the Identification of Gifted Students*, C. Callahan, C.M. Tomlinson, and P.M. Pizzat, eds. Charlottesville, VA: University of Virginia, Curry School of Education.
Clausen, J.A.
   1967   Mental deficiency: Development of a concept. *American Journal of Mental Deficiency* 71:727-745.
   1968   A comment on Halpern's note. *American Journal of Mental Deficiency* 72:950.
   1972   Quo vadis, AAMD? *The Journal of Special Education* 6:51-60.
Clay, M.M.
   1993   *Reading Recovery: A Guidebook for Teachers in Training*. Portsmouth, NH: Heinemann.
Clifford, G.J., and J. Guthrie
   1988   *Ed School: A Brief for Professional Education*. Chigago, IL: University of Chicago Press.
Cohen, D.K.
   1970   Immigrants and the schools. *Review of Educational Research* 40(1):13-27.
Cohn, J.F., S.B. Campbell, and S. Ross
   1991   Infant response in the still-face paradigm at 6 months predicts avoidant and secure attachment at 12 months. *Development and Psychopathology* 3:367-376.
Cohn, J.F., R. Matais, E.Z. Tronick, D. Connell, and K. Lyons-Ruth
   1986   Face-to-face interactions of depressed mothers and their infants. *New Directions for Child Development: Maternal Depression and Child Disturbance* 34:31-46.

Coie, J., and M. Jacobs
    1993   The role of social context in the prevention of conduct disorder [Special Issue].
            Development and Psychopathology 5(1/2):263-276.
Coie, J.D., and G. Krehbiel
    1984   Effects of academic tutoring on the social status of low-achieving, socially rejected
            children. *Child Development* 55(4):1465-1478.
Colangelo, N.
    1985   Counseling needs of culturally diverse gifted students. *Roeper Review* 8:33-35.
Cole, K.N., P.S. Dale, P.E. Mills, and J.R. Jenkins
    1993   Interaction between early intervention curricula and student characteristics. *Exceptional Child* 16:17-28.
Cole, M., J. Gay, J.A. Glick, and D.W. Sharp
    1971   *The Cultural Context of Learning and Thinking*. New York: Basic Books.
Cole, M., and S. Scribner
    1977   Crosscultural studies of memory and cognition. Pp. 229-271 in *Perspectives on the Development of Memory and Cognition*. R.V. Kail, Jr., and J.W. Hagen, eds. Mahwah, NJ: Erlbaum Associates.
Cole, M., D.W. Sharp, and C. Lave
    1976   The cognitive consequences of education. *Urban Review* 9:218-233.
Coleman, J.S., E.Q. Campbell, C.J. Hobson, J. McPartland, A.M. Mead, F.D. Weinfeld, and R. L. York
    1966   *Equality of Educational Opportunity*. Washington, DC: U.S. Department of Health, Education, and Welfare.
Coleman, M., and S. Vaughn
    2000   Reading interventions with students with emotional and behavioral disorders: A review with implications for research and practice. *Behavioral Disorders* 25(2):93-104.
Coleman, M.R., and J.J. Gallagher
    1992   *Report on State Policies Related to Identification of Gifted Students*. Chapel Hill, NC: University of North Carolina, Gifted Education Policy Studies Program.
College Board
    1999   *Reaching the Top: A Report of the National Task Force on Minority High Achievement*. New York: College Board Publications.
Collins, M., and Tamarkin, C.
    1982   *Marva Collins' Way*. Los Angeles: Jeremy P. Tarcher.
Colvin, G., E. Kameenui, and G. Sugai
    1993   Reconceptualizing behavior management and school-wide discipline in general education. *Education and Treatment of Children* 16(4):361-381.
Conduct Problems Prevention Research Group
    1999a   Initial impact of the Fast Track Prevention Trial for Conduct Problems: I. The high-risk sample. *Journal of Consulting and Clinical Psychology* 67:631-647.
    1999b   Initial impact of the Fast Track Prevention Trial for Conduct Problems: II. Classroom effects. *Journal of Consulting and Clinical Psychology* 67:648-657.
Conger, R.D., K.J. Conger, and G.H. Elder, Jr.
    1997   Family economic hardship and adolescent adjustment: Mediating and moderating processes. Pp. 288-310 in *Consequences of Growing Up Poor*. G.J. Duncan and J. Brooks-Gunn, eds. New York: Russell Sage Foundation.
Conger, R.D., K.J. Conger, G.H. Elder, Jr., F.O. Lorenz, R.L. Simons, and L.B. Whitbeck
    1992   A family process model of economic hardship and adjustment of early adolescent boys. *Child Development* 63:526-541.

Conley, D., and N. Bennett
  2000   Is biology destiny? Birth weight and life chances. *American Sociological Review*
          65(June):458-467.
Connery, A.R.
  1987   A Description and Comparison of Native American and Anglo Parents' Knowledge
          of Their Handicapped Children's Rights. Unpublished doctoral dissertation. North-
          ern Arizona University, Flagstaff.
Cook, P.J., and J. Ludwig
  1998   The burden of "Acting White": Do Black adolescents disparage academic achieve-
          ment? Pp. 375-400 in *The Black-White Test Score Gap*, Christopher Jencks and
          Meredith Phillips, eds. Washington, DC: Brookings Institution Press.
Cooper, C. M.
  1983   Administrators' Attitudes Toward Gifted Programs Based on the Enrichment Triad/
          Revolving Door Identification Model: Case Studies in Decision-making. Unpub-
          lished Ph.D. dissertation, University of Connecticut, Storrs, CT.
Cornell, D.G., C.M. Callahan, L.E. Bassin, and S.G. Ramsey
  1991   Affective development of accelerated students. Pp. 74-101 in *Academic Accelera-
          tion of Gifted Children*, W.T. Southern and E.D. Jones, eds. New York: Teachers
          College.
Correa, V.I.
  1989   Involving culturally diverse families in the educational process. Pp. 130-144 in
          *Meeting the Needs of Culturally and Linguistically Different Students: A Hand-
          book for Educators*. S.H. Fradd and M.J. Weismantel, eds. Boston: College Hill.
Cost, Quality, and Outcomes Study Team
  1995   *Cost, Quality, and Child Outcomes in Child Care Centers, Public Report* 2nd ed.
          Denver, CO: Economic Department, University of Colorado at Denver.
Council for Children with Behavioral Disorders
  1987   *Definition and Identification of Students with Behavioral Disorders*. Reston, VA:
          CCBD, a Division of the Council for Exceptional Children.
  1989   Best assessment practices for students with behavioral disorders: Accommodation
          to cultural diversity and individual differences. *Behavioral Disorders* 14:263-278.
  1990   Position paper on provision of services to children with conduct disorders. *Behav-
          ioral Disorders* 15:180-189.
Council for Exceptional Children
  2001   *Study of Personnel Needs in Special Education (SPeNSE)*. [Online]. Available: http:/
          /www.spense.org/description.html [Accessed March 17, 2001].
Council of State Directors of Programs for the Gifted
  1999   *The 1998 State of the States Gifted and Talented Education Report*. Denver, CO:
          Council of State Directors of Programs for the Gifted.
Cowan, P.A., C.P. Cowen, M.S. Schulz, and G. Heming
  1994   Prebirth to preschool family factors in children's adaptation to kindergarten. Pp.
          75-114 in *Exploring Family Relationships with Other Social Contexts*. R.D. Parke
          and S.G. Kellam, eds. Hillsdale, NJ: Lawrence Erlbaum.
Coyne, M.C., E.J. Kame'enui, and D.C. Simmons
  2001   Prevention and early intervention in beginning reading: Two complex systems.
          Learning Disabilities Research and Practice 16:62-73.
Crawford et al. v. Honig
          No. C-89-0014 RFP U. S. District Court, Northern District of California, Com-
          plaint for Declaratory Judgment, May 1988; Order, September 29, 1989; Memo-
          randum and Order, August 31, 1992.

Cromwell, R., R. Blashfield, and J. Strauss
1975 Criteria for classification systems. Pp. 4-25 in *Issues in the Classification of Children*, N. Hobbs, ed. San Francisco, CA: Jossey-Bass.
Cummings, E.M., and P.T. Davies
1994 Maternal depression and child development. *Journal of Child Psychology and Psychiatry* 35(1):73-112.
1999 Depressed parents and family functioning: Interpersonal effects and children's functioning and development. Pp. 299-327 in *Advances in Interpersonal Approaches: The Interactional Nature of Depression*. T. Joiner and J.C.Coyne, eds. Washington, DC: American Psychological Association.
Cunningham, K., K. Cunningham, and J.C. O'Connell
1986 Impact of differing cultural perceptions on special education service delivery. *Rural Special Education Quarterly* 8(1):208.
Cunningham, M.
1999 African American malesí perceptions of their community resources and constraints: A longitudinal analysis. *Journal of Community Psychology* 27:569-588.
Currie, J.
2000 Early Childhood Intervention Programs: What Do We Know? Working Paper from the Children's Roundtable. Washington, DC: Brookings Institution.
Cutler, J.A.
1982 Attribution style, depression and behavior disorders of childhood. *Dissertation Abstracts International* 42, 9-B. (University Microfilms No. AAT 8203745).
Damasio, A.R., and H. Damasio
1983 The anatomic basis of pure alexia. *Neurology* 33:1573-1583.
Danziger, S., M. Corcoran, S. Danziger, C. Heflin, A. Kalil, J. Levine, D. Rosen, K. Seefeldt, K. Siefert, and R. Tolman
2000 Barriers to the employment of welfare recipients. In *Prosperity for All? The Economic Boom and African Americans*, R. Cherry and W.M. Rodgers, III, eds. New York: Russell Sage Foundation.
Darling-Hammond, L.
1997 *The Right to Learn: A Blueprint for Creating Schools That Work*. San Francisco California: Jossey-Bass.
Darling-Hammond, L., and L. Post
2000 Inequality in teaching and schooling: Supporting high quality teaching and leadership in low income schools. Pp. 127-168 in *A Notion at Risk: Preserving Public Education as an Engine for Social Mobility*. R.D. Kahlenberg, ed. New York: The Century Foundation Press.
Dasen, P.R.
1975 Concrete operational development in three cultures. *Journal of Cross-cultural Psychology* 6:156-172.
1977a Are cognitive processes universal? A contribution to cross-cultural Piagetian psychology. In *Studies in Cross-Cultural Psychology* (Vol. 1) N. Warren, ed. London: Academic Press.
Dasen, P.R., ed.
1977b *Piagetian Psychology: Cross-Cultural Contributions*. New York: Gardner Press.
Dasen, P.R., and A. Heron
1981 Cross-cultural tests of Piaget's theory. Pp. 295-341 in *Handbook of Cross-Cultural Psychology: Developmental Psychology Volume 4*. H.C. Triandis and A. Heron, eds. Boston: Allyn & Bacon.
David, R., and J. Collins, Jr.
1997 Differing birth weight among infants of US-born Blacks, Africa-born Blacks, and U.S.-born Whites. *New England Journal of Medicine* 337:1209-1214.

Davidson, R.G.
  1993   OraL Preparation for Literacy: Mothers' and Fathers' Conversations with Preco-
         cious Readers. Doctoral dissertation, Graduate School of Education of Harvard
         University, Cambridge, MA.
Dawson, G., and S. Ashman
  2000   On the origins of a vulnerability to depression: The influence of the early social
         environment on the development of psychobiological systems related to risk for
         affective disorder. In The Effects of Adversity on Neurobehavioral Development:
         Minnesota Symposia on Child Psychology, Vol. 31, C.A. Nelson, ed. Hillsdale, NJ:
         Lawrence Erlbaum.
Dawson, G., H. Panagiotides, K. Grofer Klinger, and D. Hill
  1992   The role of frontal lobe functioning in the development of infant self-regulatory
         behavior. Brain and Cognition 20:152-175.
de Haan, M., P. Bauer, M. Georgieff, and C. Nelson
  2000   Explicit memory in low-risk infants aged 19 months born between 27 and 42
         weeks of gestation. Developmental Medicine and Child Neurology 42:303-312.
de la Rocha, O.L.
  1986   The reorganization of arithmetic practice in the kitchen. Anthropology and Educa-
         tion Quarterly 16(3):193-198.
Dean, W., and J. Morgenthaler
  1990   Smart Drugs and Nutrients. Santa Cruz, CA: B. & J. Publications.
Dean, W., J. Morgenthaler, and S. Fowkes
  1993   Smart Drugs II: The Next Generation. Menlo Park, CA: Health Freedom Publica-
         tions.
Dee, T.S.
  2001   Teachers, Race and Student Achievement in a Randomized Experiment. Working
         Paper 8432. Washington, DC: National Bureau of Economic Research.
Dejerine, J.
  1891   Sur un cas de cécité verbale avec agraphie, suivi d'autopsie. C. R. Société du Biologie
         43:197-201.
Delcourt, M.A.B., B.H. Loyd, D.G. Cornell, and M.D. Goldberg
  1994   Evaluation of the effects of programming arrangements on student outcomes. (Re-
         search Monograph 94108). Storrs, CT: University of Connecticut, National Re-
         search Center on the Gifted and Talented.
Delgado-Gaitan, C.
  1990   Literacy for Empowerment: The Role of Parents in Children's Education. New
         York: Falmer.
Delpit, L.D.
  1988   The silenced dialogue: Power and pedagogy in educating other people's children.
         Harvard Educational Review 58(3):280-298.
DeMeis, D.K., and R.R. Turner
  1978   Effects of students' race, physical attractiveness, and dialect on teachers' evalua-
         tions. Contemporary Educational Psychology 3:77-86.
Demb, J., G. Boynton, and D. Heeger
  1998   Functional magnetic resonance imaging of early visual pathways in dyslexia. Jour-
         nal of Neuroscience 18:6939-6951.
Denning, C.B., J.A. Chamberlain, and E.A. Polloway
  2000   An evaluation of state guidelines for mental retardation: Focus on definition and
         classification practices. Education and Training in Mental Retardation and Devel-
         opmental Disabilities 35:119-134.

Deno, S.L., and L.S. Fuchs
    1987   Developing curriculum-based measurement systems for data-based special educa-
            tion problem solving. *Focus on Exceptional Children* 23(6):1-24.
Denson, R., J.L. Nanson, and M.A. McWatters
    1975   Hyperkinesis and maternal smoking. *Canadian Psychological Association Journal*
            20:183-187.
Depaulo, B.A., J. Tang, W. Webb, C. Hoover, K. Marsh, and C. Litowitz
    1989   Age differences in reactions to help in a peer tutoring context. *Child Development*
            60:423-439
Deshler, D.E., and J.B. Schumaker
    1986   Learning strategies: An instructional alternative for low-achieving adolescents. *Ex-
            ceptional Children* 52:583-590.
Detterman, D.K., and M.H. Daniel
    1989   Correlations of mental tests with each other and with cognitive variables are high-
            est for low IQ groups. *Intelligence* 13:349-359.
Diana v. State Board of Education
            No. C-70-37 RFP U. S. District Court, Northern District of California, Consent
            Decree, February 3, 1970.
Dickstein, S., R. Seifer, K.D. Magee, E. Mirsky, and M.M. Lynch
    1998   Timing of Maternal Depression, Family Functioning, and Infant Development: A
            Prospective View. Paper presented at the Biennial Meeting of the Marce Society,
            June 1998, Iowa City, Iowa.
Digest of Education Statistics
    1999   Selected Characteristics of Public School Teachers: Spring 1961 to Spring 1996
            [Chart]. [Online]. Available: http://nces.ed.gov/ [Accessed March 13, 2001].
Dillon, D.R.
    1989   Showing them that I want them to learn and that I care about who they are: A
            microethnography of the social organization of a secondary low-track English read-
            ing classroom. *American Educational Research Journal* 26(2):227-259.
DiMaggio, P.
    1982   Cultural capital and school success: The impact of status culture participation on
            the grades of U.S. high school students. *American Sociological Review* 47:189-201.
Dingman, H.F., and G. Tarjan
    1960   Mental retardation and the normal distribution curve. *American Journal of Mental
            Deficiency* 64:991-994.
Dodge, K.
    1993   The future of research on conduct disorders. *Development and Psychopathology*
            5(1/2):311-320.
Doll, E.E.
    1962   A historical survey of research and management of mental retardation in the United
            States. Pp. 21-68 in *Readings on the Exceptional Child*. E.P. Trapp and P. Himmel-
            stein, eds. New York: Appleton-Century-Crofts.
Doll, E. E., ed.
    1967   Historical review of mental retardation 1800-1965: A Symposium. *American Jour-
            nal on Mental Deficiency* 72:165-189.
Dolstra, L.A.
    2000   *Ethnic and Gender Comparisons of Students Nominated for Pre-referral Interven-
            tions: Do Differences Exist?* Master of Arts Thesis, University of California, River-
            side.

Donahue, P.L., R.J. Finnegan, A.D. Lutkus, N.L. Allen, and J.R. Campbell
  2001   *The Nation's Report Card: Fourth Grade Reading 2000.* Washington DC: U.S. Department of Education, National Center for Educational Statistics, Office of Educational Research and Improvement.
Donahue, P.L., K. Voelkl, J. Campbell, and J. Mazzeo
  1999   *NAEP 1998 Reading Report Card for the Nation and the States.* Washington, DC: U.S. Department of Education, Office of Educational Research and Improvement.
Doris, J.
  1986   Learning disabilities. Pp. 3-52 in *Handbook of Cognitive, Social, and Neuropsychological Aspects of Learning Disabilities*, Vol. 1. S.J. Coci, ed. Hillsdale, NJ: Erlbaum.
  1993   Defining learning disabilities: A history of the search for consensus. Pp. 97-115 in *Better Understanding Learning Disabilities: New Views from Research and Their Implications for Education and Public Policies.* G. Lyon, D. Gray, J. Kavanagh, and N. Krasnegor, eds. Baltimore: Paul H. Brookes.
Downey, G., and J.C. Coyne
  1990   Children of depressed parents: An integrative review. *Psychological Bulletin* 108(1):50-76.
Doyle, W.
  1986   Content representation in teachers' definitions of academic work. *Journal of Curriculum Studies* 18(4):365-380.
Dressler, W.
  1985   Extended family relationships, social support, and mental health in a southern Black community. *Journal of Health and Social Behavior* 26:39-48.
Drummond, T.
  1994   *The Student Risk Screening Scale (SRSS).* Grants Pass, OR: Josephine County Mental Health Program.
Dube, E.F.
  1982   Literacy, cultural familiarity, and "intelligence" as determinants of story recall. Pp. 274-292 in *Memory Observed: Remembering in Natural Contexts.* U. Neisser, ed. San Francisco: Freeman.
Duimstra, D., C. Johnson, C. Kutsch, B. Wang, M. Zentner, and S. Kellerman
  1993   A fetal alcohol syndrome surveillance pilot project in American Indian communities in the Northern Plains. *Public Health Reports 1993* 108:225-229.
Duncan, B.B., S.R. Forness, and C. Hartsough
  1995   Students identified as seriously emotionally disturbed in day treatment: Cognitive, psychiatric, and special characteristics. *Behavioral Disorders* 20:238-252.
Duncan, G.J., and J. Brooks-Gunn, eds.
  1997a *Consequences of Growing Up Poor.* New York: Russell Sage Foundation.
  1997b Income effects across the life span: Integration and interpretation. Pp. 596-610 in *Consequences of Growing Up Poor.* New York: Russell Sage Foundation.
Dunn, H.G., and A.K. McBurney
  1977   Cigarette smoking and the fetus and child. *Pediatrics* 60:772.
Dunn, L.M.
  1968   Special education for the mildly retarded: Is much of it justifiable? *Exceptional Children* 35:5-22.
Durrer, B., and T.F. McLaughlin
  1995   The use of peer tutoring interventions involving students with behaviour disorders. *B.C. Journal of Special Education* 19(1):20-27.

Dusek, J.B, and G. Joseph
  1983   The basis of teacher expectancies: A meta-analysis. *Journal of Educational Psychology* 75:177-185.

Dweck, C.S.
  2000   *Self-theories: Their Role in Motivation, Personality, and Development.* Philadelphia: Taylor & Francis.

Ebrahim, S.H., E.T. Luman, R.L. Floyd, C.C. Murphy, E.M. Bennett, and C.A. Boyle
  1998   Alcohol consumption by pregnant women in the United States during 1988-1995. *Obstetrics and Gynecology* 92:187-192.

Eden, G.F., J.W. VanMeter, J.M. Rumsey, J.M. Maisog, R.P. Woods, and T.A. Zeffiro
  1996   Abnormal processing of visual motion in dyslexia revealed by functional brain imaging. *Nature* 382:66-69.

Edin, K., and L. Lein
  1997   *Making Ends Meet: How Single Mothers Survive Welfare and Low Wage Work.* New York: Russell Sage Foundation.

Education of All Handicapped Children Act of 1975
  20 U.S.C. §1400 *et seq.* (statute); 34 CFR 300 (regulations published in 1977).

Egan, O., and P. Archer
  1985   The accuracy of teachers' ratings of ability: A regression model. *American Educational Research Journal* 22:25-34.

Elbaum, B., and S. Vaughn
  2001   Can school-based interventions enhance the self-concept of students with learning disabilities? *Elementary School Journal* 101(3):303-329.

Elbaum, B., S. Vaughn, M.T. Hughes, and S.W. Moody
  1999   Grouping practices and reading outcomes for students with disabilities. *Exceptional Children* 65(3):399-415.
  2000   How effective are one-to-one tutoring programs in reading for elementary students at risk for reading failure? A meta-analysis of the intervention research. *Journal of Educational Psychology* 92(4):605-619.

Elias, R., Y. Hirao, and C. Patterson
  1975   Impact of present levels of aerosol Pb concentrations on both natural ecosystems and humans. Pp. 257-271 in *International Conference on Heavy Metals in the Environment, Vol. 2.* Ann Arbor: University of Michigan.

Elliott, M.
  1998   School Finance and Opportunities to Learn: Does Money Well-Spent Enhance Students' Achievement? *Sociology of Education* 71:223-245.

Elliott, S.N., Barnard, J., and Gresham, F.M.
  1989   Preschoolers' social behavior: Teachers' and parents' assessments. *Journal of Psychoeducational Assessment* 7:223-234.

Ellis, E.S., D.D. Deshler, B.K. Lenz, J.B. Schumaker, and F.L. Clark
  1991   An instructional model for teaching learning strategies. *Focus on Exceptional Children* 23(6):1-24.

Elmore, R.F., and D. Burney
  1997   *Investing in Teacher Learning: Staff Development and Instructional Improvement in Community School District #2, New York City.* CPRE/NCTAF Joint Report. New York: National Commission on Teaching and America's Future and Consortium for Policy Research in Education.

Engeström, Y.
  1987   *Learning by Expanding.* Helsinki: Orinta-Konsultit Oy.
  1990   *Learning, Working and Imagining: Twelve Studies in Activity Theory.* Helsinki: Orinta-Konsultit Oy.

Englert, C.S., and T.E. Raphael
1988   Constructing well-formed prose: Process, structure, and metacognitive knowledge. *Exceptional Children* 54(6):513-520.

Englert, C.S., T.E. Raphael, and T.V. Mariage
1994   Developing a school-based discourse for literacy learning: A principled search for understanding. *Learning Disability Quarterly* 17(1):2-32.

English, P.B., B. Eskenazi, and R.E. Christianson
1994   Black-White differences in serum cotinine levels among pregnant women and subsequent effects on infant birthweight. *American Journal of Public Health* 84:1439-1443.

Ensminger, M.E., Kella, S.G., and B.R. Rubin
1983   School and family origins of delinquency: Comparisons by sex. Pp. 73-97 in *Prospective Studies of Crime and Delinquency*. K.T. Van Dusen and S.A. Mednick, eds. Boston: Kluwer-Nijhoff.

Entwisle, D., and K. Alexander
1992   Summer setback: Race, poverty, school composition, and mathematics achievement in the first two years of school. *American Sociological Review* 57:72-84.

Epstein, J.L.
1996   Advances in family, community, and school partnerships. *Community Education Journal* 23(3):10-15.

Epstein, M.H., F.A. Polloway, J.R. Patton, and R. Foley
1989   Mild retardation: Student characteristics and services. *Education and Training of the Mentally Retarded* 24:7-16.

Ernhart, C.B., S. Scarr, and D.F. Geneson
1993   On being a whistleblower: The Needleman case. *Ethics and Behavior* 3(1):73-93.

Escobedo, T.H., and J. Huggins
1983   Field dependence-independence: A theoretical framework for Mexican-American cultural variables? In *Early Childhood Bilingual Education: A Hispanic Perspective*. T.H. Escobedo, ed. New York: Teachers College Press.

Essman, W.B., ed.
1987   *Nutrients and Brain Function*. London: Karger.

Etzel, R.A., and S.J. Balk, eds.
1999   *Handbook of Pediatric Environmental Health*. Elk Grove Village, IL: American Academy of Pediatrics.

Evertson, C.M., J. Brophy, and T.L. Good
1972   *Communication of Teacher Expectations: First Grade. Report 91.* Austin: University of Texas, Research and Development Center for Teacher Education.

Evertson, C.M., and C.H. Randolph
1989   Teaching practices and class size: A new look at an old issue. *Peabody Journal of Education* 67:85-105.

Eysenck, H.J., and S.J. Schoenthaler
1997   Raising IQ level by vitamin and mineral supplementation. Pp.363-392 in *Intelligence, Heredity, and Environment*, R.J. Sternberg and E. Grigorenko, eds. Cambridge, UK: Cambridge University Press.

Faden, V., B. Graubard, and M. Dufour
1997   The relationship of drinking and birth outcome in a U.S. national sample of expectant mothers. *Paediatric and Perinatal Epidemiology* 11:167-180.

Fagerheim, T., P. Raeymaekers, F. Tonnessen, D. Pedersen, L. Tranebjaerg, and H. Lubs
1999   A new gene (DYX3) for dyslexia is located on chromosome 2. *Journal of Medical Genetics* 36:664-669.

Farran, D.C.
1990 Effects of intervention with disadvantaged and disabled children: A decade review. Pp. 501-539 in *Handbook of Early Childhood Intervention*. J.P. Shonkoff and S.J. Meisels, eds. New York: Cambridge University Press.

Feiring, C., B. Louis, I. Ukeje, M. Lewis, and P. Leong
1997 Early identification of gifted minority kindergarten students in Newark, NJ. *Gifted Child Quarterly* 41:76-82.

Feldman, R.S., L. Devin-Sheehan, and V. Allen
1976 Children tutoring children: A critical review of research. Pp. 235-249 in *Children as Teachers: Theory and Research on Tutoring*. V. Allen, ed. New York: Academic Press.

Felton, R.H., C.E. Naylor, and F.B. Wood
1990 Neuropsychological profile of adult dyslexics. *Brain and Language* 39(4):485-497.

Feng, H., and G. Cartledge
1996 Social skills assessment of inner city Asian, African, and European American students. *School Psychology Review* 25: 227-238.

Ferguson, R.F.
1991 Paying for public education: New evidence of how and why money matters. *Harvard Journal of Legislation* 28:465-498.

Ferguson, R.F., and H.F. Ladd
1996 How and why money matters: An analysis of Alabama schools. Pp. 265-298 in *Holding Schools Accountable: Performance-Based Reform in Education*, H.F. Ladd, ed. Washington, DC: Office of Educational Research and Improvement, U.S. Department of Education.

Fergusson, D.M., J.E. Fergusson, L.J. Horwood, and N.G. Kinzett
1988a A longitudinal study of dentine lead levels, intelligence, school performance, and behavior. Part I. Dentine lead levels and exposure to environmental risk factors. *Journal of Child Psychology and Psychiatry* 29:781-792.
1988b A longitudinal study of dentine lead levels, intelligence, school performance, and behavior. Part II. Dentine lead levels and cognitive ability. *Journal of Child Psychology and Psychiatry* 29:783-809.
1988c A longitudinal study of dentine lead levels, intelligence, school performance and behavior. Part III. Dentine lead levels and attention/activity. *Journal of Child Psychology and Psychiatry* 29:811-824.

Fergusson, D.M., L.J. Horwood, and M.T. Lynsky
1993 Maternal smoking before and after pregnancy: Effects on behavioral outcomes in middle childhood. *Pediatrics* 92(6):815-822.
1994 The childhoods of multiple problem adolescents: A 15-year longitudinal study. *Journal of Child Psychology and Psychiatry* 35:1123-1140.

Figueroa, R.A.
1983 Test bias and Hispanic children. *Journal of Special Education* 17:431-440.

Filipek, P.
1996 Structural variations in measures in the developmental disorders. Pp. 169-186 in *Developmental Neuroimaging: Mapping the Development of Brain and Behavior*. R. Thatcher, G. Lyon, J. Rumsey, and N. Krasnegor, eds. San Diego,CA: Academic Press.

Finn, J.D., and C.M. Achilles
1999 Tennessee's class size study: Findings, implications, misconceptions. *Educational Evaluation and Policy Analysis*, 21:97-109.

Finucci, J.M., and B. Childs
    1981   Are there really more dyslexic boys than girls? Pp. 1-9 in *Sex Differences in Dyslexia*. A. Ansara, N. Geschwind, M. Albert, and N. Gartrell, eds. Towson, MD: Orton Dyslexia Society.

Fischer, K.W., D.H. Bullock, E.J. Rotenberg, and P. Raya
    1993   The dynamics of competence: How context contributes directly to skill. In *Development in Context: Acting and Thinking in Specific Environments*. R. Wozniak and K.W. Fischer, eds. New Jersey: Lawrence Erlbaum.

Fletcher, J.M.
    1998   IQ discrepancy: An inadequate and iatrogenic conceptual model for learning disabilities. *Perspectives* Winter:10-13.

Fletcher, J.M., D.J. Francis, S.E. Shaywitz, G.R. Lyon, B.R. Foorman, K.K. Stuebing, and B.A. Shaywitz
    1998   Intelligent testing and the discrepancy model for children with learning disabilities. *Learning Disabilities Research and Practice* 13(4):186-203.

Fletcher, J.M., and G.R. Lyon
    1998   Reading: A research based approach. In *What's Gone Wrong in America's Classrooms*. W. Evers, ed. Stanford, CA: Stanford University, Hoover Institution.

Fletcher, J.M., S.E. Shaywitz, D.P. Shankweiler, L. Katz, I.Y. Liberman, K.K. Stuebing, D.J. Francis, A.E. Fowler, and B.A. Shaywitz
    1994   Cognitive profiles of reading disability: Comparisons of discrepancy and low achievement definitions. *Journal of Educational Psychology* 86:6-23.

Flugum, K.R., and D.J. Reschly
    1994   Prereferral interventions—quality indexes and outcomes. *Journal of School Psychology* 32(1):1-14.

Flynn, J., and M. Rahbar
    1994   Prevalence of reading failure in boys compared with girls. *Psychology in the Schools* 31:66-71.

Flynn, J.R.
    1984   The mean IQ of Americans: Massive gains. *Psychological Bulletin* 95:29-51.
    1987   Massive IQ genius in 14 natives: What IQ tests really measure. *Psychology Bulletin* 101:171-191.

Fobih, D.K.
    1979   The Influence of Different Educational Experiences on Classificatory And Verbal Reasoning Behavior of Children in Ghana. Unpublished doctoral dissertation, University of Alberta, Canada.

Foorman, B.R., J.M. Fletcher, and D.J. Francis
    2001   Early reading assessment. In *Testing America's Schoolchildren*, W. Evert, Ed. Stanford, CA: Stanford University, Hoover Institution.

Foorman, B.R., and Schatschneider, C.
    In   Measuring teaching practices in reading/language arts instruction and their relation
    press   to student achievement. In *Reading in the Classroom: Systems for Observing Teaching and Learning*. Baltimore, MD: Paul H. Brookes.

Ford, D.Y.
    1995   *Correlates of Underachievement Among Gifted and Non-Gifted Black Students*. (RBDM). Storrs, CT: University of Connecticut, National Research Center on the Gifted and Talented.
    1996   *Reversing Underachievement Among Gifted Black Students*. New York: Teachers College Press.

Fordham, S.
    1988   Racelessness as a factor in black students school success: Pragmatic strategy or
            pyrrhic victory? *Harvard Educational Review* 58:54-84.
Forness, S.
    1992a   Broadening the cultural-organizational perspective in exclusion of youth with so-
            cial maladjustment. *Remedial and Special Education* 13:55-59.
    1992b   Legalism versus professionalism in diagnosing SED in the public schools. *School
            Psychology Review* 21(1):29-34.
Forness, S.R., L. Bennett, and J. Tose
    1983   Academic deficits in emotionally disturbed children revisited. *Journal of American
            Academy of Child Psychiatry* 22(2):140-144.
Forness, S.R., and J. Knitzer
    1990   *A New Proposed Definition and Terminology to Replace "Serious Emotional Dis-
            turbance" in Education of the Handicapped Act.* Alexandria, VA: Workgroup on
            Definition, the National Mental Health and Special Education Coalition, c/o Na-
            tional Mental Health Association.
    1992   A new proposed definition and terminology to replace "serious emotional distur-
            bance" in Individuals with Disabilities Education Act. *School Psychology Review*
            21:12-20.
Foster, H.
    1997   The enigma of low birth weight and race. *New England Journal of Medicine*
            337:1232-1233.
Franca, V.M., M.M. Kerr, A.L. Reitz, and D. Lambert
    1990   Peer tutoring among behaviorally disordered students: Academic and social ben-
            efits to tutor and tutee. *Education and Treatment of Children* 13(2):109-128.
Francis, D.J., S.E. Shaywitz, K.K. Stuebing, B.A. Shaywitz, and J.M. Fletcher
    1996   Developmental lag versus deficit models of reading disability: A longitudinal, indi-
            vidual growth curves analysis. *Journal of Educational Psychology* 88(1):3-17.
Frankel, K.A., and R.J. Harmon
    1996   Depressed mothers: They don't always look as bad as they feel. *Journal of the
            American Academy of Child and Adolescent Psychiatry* 35(3):289-298.
Frankenberger, W., and K. Fronzaglio
    1991   States' definitions and procedures for identifying children with mental retardation:
            Comparison over nine years. *Mental Retardation* 29:315-321.
Franklin, M.E.
    1992   Culturally sensitive instructional practices for African American learners with dis-
            abilities. *Exceptional Children* 59(2):115-122.
Frasier, M.M., S.L. Hunsaker, J. Lee, V.S. Finely, J.H. Garcia, D. Martin, and E. Frank
    1995   *An Exploratory Study of the Effectiveness of the Staff Development Model and the
            Research-Based Assessment Plan in Improving the Identification of Gifted Eco-
            nomically Disadvantaged Students.* (Research Monograph 95224). Storrs, CT: Uni-
            versity of Connecticut, National Research Center on the Gifted and Talented.
Frede, E.C.
    1998   Preschool program quality in programs for children in poverty. Pp. 77-98 in *Early
            Care and Education for Children in Poverty: Promises, Programs, and Long-Term
            Outcomes*, W.S. Barnett and S.S. Boocock, eds. Buffalo, NY: SUNY Press.
Frentz, C., F.M. Gresham, and S.N. Elliott
    1991   Popular, controversial, neglected, and rejected adolescents—Contrasts of social
            competence and achievement differences. *Journal of School Psychology* 29(2):109-
            120.

Frick, P.J.
1998   *Conduct Disorders and Severe Antisocial Behavior.* New York, NY: Plenum Press.

Frick, P.J., B.B. Lahey, R. Loeber, M. Stouthamer-Loeber, M.A.G. Christ, and K. Hanson
1992   Familial risk factors to oppositional defiant disorders and conduct disorder: Parental psychopathology and maternal parenting. *Journal of Consulting and Clinical Psychology* 60(1):49-55.

Fried, P.A.
1992   Clinical implications of smoking: Determining long-term teratogenicity. Pp. 77-96 in *Maternal Substance Abuse and the Developing Nervous System,* I.S. Zagon and T.A. Slotkin, eds. New York: Academic Press.

Fried, P.A., C.M. O'Connell, and B. Watkinson
1992a   60- and 72-month follow-up of children prenatally exposed to marijuana, cigarettes, and alcohol: Cognitive and language assessment. *Journal of Developmental and Behavioral Pediatrics* 13:383-391.

Fried, P.A., B. Watkinson, and R. Gray
1992b   A follow-up study of attentional behavior in 6-year-old children exposed prenatally to marijuana, cigarettes, and alcohol. *Neurotoxicology and Teratology* 14:299-311.

Friedman, R.F., J.E. Ween, and M.L. Albert
1993   Alexia. Pp. 37-62 in *Clinical Neuropsychology. (3rd ed.).* K.M. Heilman and E. Valenstein, eds. New York: Oxford University Press.

Fuchs, D., and L.S. Fuchs
1992   Limitations of a feel-good approach to consultation. *Journal of Educational and Psychological Consultation* 3:93-97.
1994   Inclusive schools movement and the radicalization of special education reform. *Exceptional Children* 60:294-309.

Fuchs, D., L.S. Fuchs, and P. Fernstorm
1993   A conservative approach to special education reform: Mainstreaming through transenvironmental programming and curriculum-based measurement. *American Educational Research Journal* 30:149-177.

Fuchs, L.S., and D. Fuchs
1986   Effects of systematic formative evaluation: A meta-analysis. *Exceptional Children,* 53:199-208.
1989   Enhancing curriculum-based measurement through computer applications: Review of research and practice. *Journal of School Psychology* 18(3):317-327.
1996   Combining performance assessment and curriculum-based measurement to strengthen instructional planning. *Learning Disabilities Research and Practice* 11:183-192.
1998   Treatment validity: A unifying concept for reconceptualizing the identification of learning disabilities. *Learning Disabilities Research and Practice* 13(4):204-219.
2001   Principles for prevention and intervention of mathematics difficulties. *Learning Disabilities Research and Practice* 16:85-95.

Fuchs, L.S., C.L. Hamlett, and D. Fuchs
1997   *MBSP Basic Reading Manual* (2nd ed.). Macintosh version [Computer software]. Austin TX: PRO-ED.

Fulton, M., G. Raab, G. Thomson, D. Laxen, R. Hunter, and W. Hepburn
1987   Influence of blood lead on the ability and attainment of children in Edinburgh. *Lancet* 1:1221-1226.

Furlong, M., and M. Karno
1995   Review of social skills rating system. Pp. 967-969 in *The Twelfth Mental Measurements Yearbook.* J.C. Conoley and J.C. Impara, eds. Lincoln: University of Nebraska-Lincoln, The Buros Institute of Mental Measurements.

Gabarino, J.
  1982   *Children and Families in the Social Environment.* New York: Aldine.
Gagne, F.
  1985   Giftedness and talent. *Gifted Child Quarterly* 29:103-112.
Gaines, M.L.
  1990   Accuracy of Teacher Prediction of Elementary Student Achievement. Paper prepared for the annual meeting of the American Educational Research Association.
Galaburda, A.M., G.F. Sherman, G.D. Rosen, F. Aboitiz, and N. Geschwind
  1985   Developmental dyslexia: Four consecutive patients with cortical anomalies. *Annals of Neurology* 18(2):222-233.
Galinsky, E., C. Howes, S. Kontos, and M. Shinn
  1994   *The Study of Children in Family Child Care and Relative Care.* New York: Families and Work Institute.
Galler, J.R., F. Ramsey, G. Solimano, and W. Lowell
  1983   The influence of early malnutrition on subsequent behavioral development. II. Classroom behavior. *Journal of the American Academy of Child Psychiatry* 22:16-22.
Gallimore, R., C.N. Goldenberg, and T.S. Weisner
  1993   The social construction and subjective reality of activity settings: Implications for community psychology. *American Journal of Community Psychology* 21:537-559.
Galton, F.
  1869   *Hereditary Genius: An Inquiry into Its Laws and Consequences.* London: MacMillan.
Gandara, P.
  2000   Interventions for Excellence: What We Know about Nurturing High Ability in Underrepresented Students. Unpublished paper, University of California, Davis.
Gandara, P. and D. Bial
  2001   *Paving the Way to Postsecondary Education: K-12 Intervention Programs for Underrepresented Youth.* Washington, DC: National Center for Education Statistics.
Gandara, P., M. Mejorado, D. Gutierrez, and M. Molina
  1998   Final Report of the High School Evaluation, 1994-1998. Unpublished manuscript, University of California, Davis.
Garber, H.L.
  1988   *The Milwaukee Project: Preventing Mental Retardation in Children at Risk.* Washington, DC: American Association on Mental Retardation.
Garces, E., T. Duncan, and J. Currie.
  2000   *Longer Term Effects of Head Start.* Labor and Population Program Working Paper Series 00-20, Washington, DC: RAND.
Garcia, E.
  1994   *Understanding and Meeting the Challenge of Student Diversity.* Boston, MA: Houghton Mifflin.
Garcia, E.E.
  1992   Linguistically and culturally diverse children: Effective instructional practices and related policy issues. Pp. 65-86 in *Students at Risk in At-risk Schools: Improving Environments for Learning.* H.C. Waxman, J.W. deFelix, J.E. Thomas, and H.P. Baptiste, Jr., eds. Newbury Park, CA: Sage.
Gardner, H.
  1983   *Frames of Mind: The Theory of Multiple Intelligences.* New York: Basic Books.
  1999   Are there additional intelligences? The case for naturalist, spiritual, and existential intelligences. Pp. 111-131 in *Education, Information, and Transformation,* J. Kane, ed. Englewood Cliffs, NJ: Prentice Hall.

Garrett, P., N. Ng'andu, and J. Ferron
  1994 Poverty experiences of young children and the equality of their home environ-
       ments. *Child Development* 65:331-345.
Gaskins, I.W., L.C. Ehri, C. Cress, C. O'Hara, and K. Donnelly
  1997 Analyzing words and making discoveries about the alphatice system: Activities for
       beginning readers. *Language Arts* 74(3):172-184.
Gay, G.
  1990 Achieving educational equality through curriculum desegregation. *Phi Delta
       Kappan* 70:56-62.
  2000 *Culturally Responsive Teaching: Theory, Research, and Practice.* New York: Teach-
       ers College Press.
Gelfand, D.M., D.M. Teti, S.A. Seiner, and P.B. Jameson
  1996 Helping mothers fight depression: Evaluation of a home-based intervention pro-
       gram for depressed mothers and their infants. *Journal of Clinical Child Psychology*
       25(4):406-422.
Gentry, M., and S.V. Owen
  1999 An investigation of the effects of total school flexible cluster grouping on identifica-
       tion, achievement, and classroom practices. *Gifted Child Quarterly* 43:224-243.
Georgiewa, P., R. Rzanny, J. Hopf, R. Knab, V. Glauche, and W. Kaiser
  1999 fMRI during word processing in dyslexic and normal reading children.
       NeuroReport 10:3459-3465.
Gerald, D.E., and W.J. Hussar
  2000 *Projections of Education Statistics to 2010.* Washington, DC: National Center for
       Education Statistics Annual Report Program.
Gerber, M.M.
  1999/ An appreciation of learning disabilities: The value of blue-green algae. *Exeptionality*
  2000 8:29-42.
Gersten, R.
  1985 Direct instruction with special education students: A review of evaluation research.
       The Journal of Special Education 19:41-58.
Gersten, R., and S. Baker
  1998 Real world use of scientific concepts: Integrating situated cognition with explicit
       instruction. *Exceptional Children* 65(1):23-35.
  2000a What we know about effective instructional practices for English-language learn-
        ers. *Exceptional Children* 66(4):454-470.
  2000b The professional knowledge base on instructional practices that support cognitive
        growth for English-language learners. Pp 31-79 in *Contemporary Special Educa-
        tion Research*, R. Gersten, E. Schiller, and S. Vaughn, eds. Mahwah, NJ: Erlbaum.
  2001 Teaching expressive writing to students with learning disabilities: A meta-analysis.
       Elementary School Journal 101(3):251-301.
Gersten, R., D.W. Carnine, and W.A. White
  1984 The pursuit of clarity: Direct instruction and applied behavior analysis. In *Focus on
       Behavior Analysis in Education.* W. Heward, T.E. Heron, D.S. Hill, and J. Trap-
       Porter, eds. Columbus, OH: Charles Merrill.
Gersten, R., E.P. Schiller, and S. Vaughn, eds.
  2000 *Contemporary Special Education Research.* Mahwah, NJ: Erlbaum.
Gersten, R., J. Williams, L. Fuchs, and S. Baker
  2001 Teaching reading comprehension strategies to students with learning disabilities: A
       review of research. *Review of Educational Research* 71(2):279-321.
Geschwind, N.
  1965 Disconnection syndromes in animals and man. *Brain* 88:237-294.

Gettinger, M.
  1988   Methods of proactive classroom management. *School Psychology Review* 17(2): 227-242.

Geva, E., and L.S. Siegel
  2000   Orthographic and cognitive factors in the concurrent development of basic reading skills in two languages. *Reading and Writing* 12,(1/2), 1-30.

Giannarelli, L., and J. Barsimantov
  2000   Child Care Expenses of America's Families. Occasional Paper Number 40 in *Assessing the New Federalism* project. Washington, DC: Urban Institute.

Gilbert, S.E., and Gay, G.
  1989   Improving the success in school of poor Black children. Pp. 275-291 in *Culture, Style, and the Educative Process*, B.J. Robinson Shade, ed. Springfield, IL: Charles C. Thomas.

Gilger, J.W., I.B. Borecki, S.D. Smith, J.C. DeFries, and B.F. Pennington
  1996   The etiology of extreme scores for complex phenotypes: An illustration using reading performance. Pp. 63-85 in *Developmental Dyslexia. Neural, Cognitive, and Genetic Mechanisms*, C.H. Chase, G.D. Rosen, and G. F. Sherman, eds. Baltimore, MD: York Press.

Ginsburg, H.P., and A.J. Baroody
  2002   *Test of Early Mathematics Ability (3rd ed.)(TEMA-3)*. Austin, TX: Pro-Ed.

Gleason, M.M., G.T. Colvin, and A.L. Archer
  1991   Interventions for improving study skills. Pp. 137-160 in *Interventions for Achievement and Behavior Problems*, G. Stoner, M. Shinn, and H.M. Walker, eds. Silver Spring, MD: National Association of School Psychologists.

Goldenberg, C., L. Reese, and R. Gallimore
  1992   Effects of literacy materials from school on Latino childrens' home experiences and early reading achievement. *American Journal of Education* 100:497-537.

Goldstein, A.P., Sprafkin, R.P., N.J. Gershaw, and P. Klein
  1980   *Skillstreaming the Adolescent: A Structured Learning Approach to Teaching Prosocial Skills*. Champaign, IL: Research Press.

Goldstein, H., C. Arkell, S.C. Ashcroft, O.L. Hurley, and M.S. Lilly
  1975   Schools. Pp. 4-61 in *Issues in the Classification of Children: Volume 2*, N. Hobbs, ed. Washington, DC: Jossey-Bass.

Good, R.H. III, and R.A. Kaminski
  1996   Assessment for instructional decisions: Toward a proactive/prevention model of decision-making for early literacy skills. *School Psychology Quarterly* 11(4):326-336.

Goodlad, J., R. Soder, and K. Sirotnick
  1990   *Places Where Teachers Are Taught*. San Francisco, CA: Jossey-Bass.

Goodnow, J.J.
  1962   A test of milieu effects with some of Piaget's tasks. *Psychological Monographs* 76:(36, Whole No. 555).
  1976   The nature of intelligent behavior: Questions raised by cross-cultural studies. In *The Nature of Intelligence*, L.B. Resnick, ed. Hillsdale, NJ: Lawrence Erlbaum.

Gordon, R.A.
  1980   Examining labeling theory: The case of mental retardation. Pp. 111-174 in *The Labeling of Deviance: Evaluating a Perspective*, W.R. Gove, ed. Beverly Hills, CA: Age.

Gottfredson, D.C.
  1990   Changing school structures to benefit high-risk youths. Pp. 246-271in *Understanding Troubled and Troubling Youth*, P.E. Leone, ed. Newbury Park: Sage Publications.

Gottfried, A.W., ed.
1984 *Home Environment and Early Cognitive Development: Longitudinal Research.* New York: Academic Press.

Gottlieb, J.
1981 Mainstreaming: Fulfilling the promise? *American Journal of Mental Deficiency* 86:115-126.
1992 *Individual Development and Evolution: The Genesis of Novel Behavior.* New York: Oxford University Press.
1999 Comparison of students referred and not referred for special education. *The Elementary School Journal* 99(3):187-199.

Gottlieb, J., M. Alter, and B.W. Gottlieb
1999 General education placement for special education students in urban schools. In *Inclusion: The Integration of Students with Disabilities*, M.J. Coutinho and A.C. Repp, eds. Belmont, CA: Wadsworth Publishing Co.

Gottlieb, J., M. Alter, B.W. Gottlieb, and J. Wishner
1994 Special education in urban America: It's not justifiable for many. *The Journal of Special Education* 27:453-465.

Gottlieb, J., B.W. Gottlieb, and S. Trongone
1991 Parent and teacher referrals for a psychoeducational evaluation. *The Journal of Special Education* 25:155-167.

Gottlieb, J., and S. Weinberg
1999 Comparison of students referred and not referred for special education. *The Elementary School Journal* 99:187-199.

Gough, P.B., and W.E. Tunmer
1986 Decoding, reading, and reading disability. *Remedial and Special Education* 7:6-10.

Grabe, W.
1991 Current developments in second language reading research. *TESOL Quarterly* 25:375-406.

Graden, J.L., J.E. Zins, and M.J. Curtis, eds.
1988 *Alternative Educational Delivery Systems: Enhancing Instructional Options for All Students.* Washington, DC: National Association of School Psychologists.

Graham, S., K.R. Harris, and L. Larsen
2001 Prevention and intervention of writing difficulties for students with learning disabilities. *Learning Disabilities Research and Practice* 16:74-84.

Gray, S.W., B.K. Ramsey, and R.A. Klaus
1982 *From 3 to 20: The Early Training Project.* Baltimore: University Park Press.

Greenfield, P.M.
1974 Comparing dimensional categorization in natural and artificial contexts: A developmental study among the Zinacantecos of Mexico. *Journal of Social Psychology* 93:157-171.

Greenfield, P.M., and C.P. Childs
1977 Weaving, color terms and pattern representation: Cultural influences and cognitive development among the Zinacantecos of southern Mexico. *Interamerican Journal of Psychology* 11:23-48.

Greenough, W.T. and J.E. Black
1992 *Induction of Brain Structure by Experience—Substrates for Cognitive Development. Child Psychology* 24:155-200.

Greenwald, E.A., H.R. Persky, J.R. Campbell, and J. Mazzeo
1999 *NAEP 1998 Writing Report Card for the Nation and the States.* Washington, DC: U.S. Department of Education.

Greenwood, C.R., J.J. Carta, and D. Kamps
  1990   Teacher versus peer-mediated instruction. Pp. 177-206 in *Children Helping Children*, H. Foot, M. Morgan, and R. Shute, eds. Chichester, England: John Wiley.
Greenwood, C.R., B. Terry, C.A. Utley, D. Montagna, and D. Walker
  1993   Achievement, placement, and services: Middle school benefits of classwide peer tutoring used at the elementary school. *School Psychology Review* 22(3):497-516.
Gresham, F.M.
  1985   Utility of cognitive-behavioral procedures for social skills training with children: A critical review. *Journal of Abnormal Child Psychology* 13(3):411-423.
  1991   Conceptualizing behavior disorders in terms of resistance to intervention. *School Psychology Review* 20:23-26.
  1999   Noncategorical approaches to K-12 emotional and behavioral difficulties. Pp. 107-138 in *Special Education in Transition: Functional Assessment and Noncategorical Programming*, D.J. Reschly, W.D. Tilly III, and J.P. Grimes, eds. Longmont, CO: Sopris West.
  2001   Responsiveness to Intervention: An Alternative Approach to the Identification of Learning Disabilities. Paper prepared for the Office of Special Education Programs. Learning Disabilities Initiative, Office of Special Education Programs, U.S. Department of Education, Washington, DC.
Gresham, F.M., and S.N. Elliot
  1990   *Social Skills Rating System—Teacher*. Circle Pines, MN: American Guidance Service.
Gresham, F.M., K.L. Lane, and K. Lambros
  2000   Comorbidity of conduct and attention deficit hyperactivity problems: Issues of identification and intervention with "fledgling psychopaths." *Journal of Emotional and Behavioral Disorders* 8(2):83-93.
Gresham, F.M., K.L. Lane, D.L. MacMillan, and K.M. Bocian
  1999   Social and academic profiles of externalizing and internalizing groups: Risk factors for emotional and behavioral disorders. *Behavioral Disorders* 24:231-245.
Gresham, F.M., and G.H. Noell
  1999   Functional assessment as the cornerstone for noncategorical special education. Pp. 49-80 in *Special Education in Transition: Functional Assessment and Noncategorical Programming*, D.J. Reschly, W.D. Tilly III, and J.P. Grimes, eds. Longmont, CO: Sopris West.
Gresham, F.M., and J.C. Witt
  1997   Utility of intelligence tests for treatment planning, classification, and placement decisions: Recent empirical findings and future directions. *School Psychology Quarterly* 12:249-267.
Griffin, S., R. Case, and A. Capodilupo
  1995   Teaching for understanding: The importance of central conceptual structures in the elementary mathematics curriculum. Pp. 121-151 in *Teaching for Transfer: Fostering Generalization in Learning*, A. Mckeough, I. Lupert, and A. Marini, eds. Hillsdale, NJ: Lawrence Erlbaum.
Griffin, S.A., and R. Case
  1996   Evaluating the breadth and depth of training effects when central conceptual structures are taught. *Society for Research in Child Development Monographs* 59:90-113.
  1997   Rethinking the primary school math curriculum: An approach based on cognitive science. *Issues in Education* 1(3):1-49.
  1998   Re-thinking the primary school math curriculum: An approach based on cognitive science. *Issues in Education* 4(1):1-51.

2000   *Number Worlds: A Pre-K-2 Mathematics Program (4 Levels)*. Durham, NC: Number Worlds Alliance Inc.

Griffin, S.A., R. Case, and R.S. Siegler
1994   Rightstart: Providing the central conceptual prerequisites for first formal learning of arithmetic to students at-risk for school failure. Pp. 24-49 in *Classroom Lessons: Integratuing Cognitive Theory and Classroom Practice*, K. McGilly, ed. Cambridge, MA: MIT Press.

Grigorenko, E.L., F.B. Wood, M.S. Meyer, L.A. Hart, W.C. Speed, A. Shuster, and D.L. Pauls
1997   Susceptibility loci for distinct components of developmental dyslexia on chromosomes 6 and 15. *American Journal of Human Genetics* 60:27-39.

Grossman, H.J., ed.
1973   *Manual on Terminology and Classification in Mental Retardation*. Washington, DC:American Association on Mental Deficiency, Special Publication Series No. 2.
1977   *Manual on Terminology and Classification* (Rev. ed.). Washington, DC: American Association on Mental Deficiency.
1983   *Classification in Mental Retardation* (3rd rev.). Washington, DC: American Association on Mental Deficiency.

Grossman, H.J., and G. Tarjan, eds.
1987   *AMA Handbook on Mental Retardation*. Chicago, IL: American Medical Association.

Guadalupe Organization v. Tempe Elementary School District No. 3
No. 71-435 (D. Ariz., January 24, 1972) (consent decree).

Gueguen, C., G. Lagrue, and J. Janse-Marec
1995   Effect of smoking on the fetus and the child during pregnancy. *Journal de Gynecologie, Obstetrique et Biologie de la Reproduction.* 24:853-859.

Guo, G., J. Brooks-Gunn, and K.M. Harris
1996   Parental labor-force attachment and grade retention among urban black children. *Sociology of Education* 69:217-236.

Guralnick, M.J., ed.
1997   *Effectiveness of Early Intervention*. Baltimore, MD: Paul H. Brookes Publishing.

Gutierrez, R., and R.E. Slavin
1992   Achievement effects of nongraded elementary schools: A best evidence synthesis. *Review of Educational Research* 62:333-376.

Guyer, B., J. Martin, M. MacDorman, R. Anderson, and D. Strobino
1997   Annual summary of vital statistics—1996. *Pediatrics* 100:905-918.

Hack, M., N. Klein, and G. Taylor
1995   Long-term developmental outcomes of low birth weight infants. Pp. 176-196 in *The Future of Children–Low Birth Weight*, R. Behrman, ed. Los Angeles: The Center for the Future of Children, David and Lucile Packard Foundation.

Hall, J.W.
1972   Verbal behavior as a function of amount of schooling. *American Journal of Psychology* 85:277-289.

Hallahan, D.P., and J.M. Kauffman
1997   *Exceptional Children: Introduction to Special Education* (7th ed.). Boston: Allyn & Bacon.

Haller, E.J.
1985   Pupil race and elementary school grouping: Are teachers biased against black children? *American Educational Research Journal* 22:465-483.

Hallgren, B.
1950   Specific dyslexia (congenital word blindness): A clinical and genetic study. *Acta Psychiatrica* 65:1-279.

Hankin, J., J. Sloan, I. Firestone, R. Ager, P. Sokol, and S. Martier
    1993   A time series analysis of the impact of the alcohol warning label on antenatal drinking. *Alcohol and Clinical Experimental Research* 17:284-289.

Hanushek, E.A.
    1994   Money might matter somewhere: A response to Hedges, Laine, and Greenwald. *Educational Researcher* 23(4):5-8.
    1997   Assessing the effects of school resources on student performance: An update. *Educational Evaluation and Policy Analysis* 19(2):141-164.

Hardy, J.B., and E.D. Mellits
    1972   Does maternal smoking during pregnancy have a long-term effect on the child? *Lancet* 2:1332-1336.

Haro, R., G. Rodriguez, and J. Gonzales
    1994   *Latino Persistence in Higher Education: A 1994 Survey of University of California and California State University Chicano/Latino Students.* San Francisco: Latino Issues Forum.

Harrell, R.F., E. Woodyard, and A.I. Gates
    1955   *The Effects of a Mother's Diet on the Intelligence of Offspring.* New York: Bureau of Publications, Teachers' College, Columbia University.

Harris, K.R., and M. Pressley
    1991   The nature of cognitive strategy instruction: Interactive strategy construction. *Exceptional Children* 57:392-404.

Harrison, P.H., and B. Robinson
    1995   Best practices in assessment of adaptive behavior. Pp. 753-762 in *Best Practices in School Psychology III* (3rd Ed.), A. Thomas and J. Grimes, eds. Washington DC: National Association of School Psychologists.

Harrison, P.L., and T. Oakland
    2000   *ABAS, Adaptive Behavior Assessment System: Manual.* San Antonio, TX: Psychological Corporation.

Harry, B.
    1992   Making sense of disability: Low-income, Puerto Rican parents' theories of the problem. *Exceptional Children* 59(1):27-40.

Harry, B., N. Allen, and M. McLaughlin
    1995   Communication versus compliance: African-American parents' involvement in special education. *Exceptional Children* 61:364-377.

Harry, B., and M. Anderson
    1994   African American males in special education: A critique of the process. *The Journal of Negro Education* 63(4):602-619.

Harry, B., M. Kalyanpur, and M. Day
    1999   *Building Cultural Reciprocity with Families: Case Studies in Education.* Baltimore, MD: Paul H. Brookes Publishing Co.

Hart, B., and T.R. Risley
    1992   American parenting of language learning children: Persisting differences in family-child interactions observed in natural home environments. *Developmental Psychology* 28:1096-1105.
    1995   *Meaningful Differences in the Everyday Experience of Young American Children.* Baltimore, MD: Paul H. Brookes Publishing Co.

Haskins, R.
    1989   Beyond metaphor: The efficacy of early childhood education. *American Psychologist* 44(2):274-282.

Hatzakis, A., A. Kokkevi, K. Katsouyanni, K. Maravelias, J.K. Salaminious, A. Kalandidi, A. Koutselinis, K. Stefanis, and D. Trichopoulis
  1987 Psychometric intelligence and attentional performance deficits in lead-exposed children. Pp. 204-209 in *Proceedings of the 6th International Conference on Heavy Metals in the Environment*, S.E. Lindberg and T.C. Hutchinson, eds. Edinburg: CEP Consultants.

Hauser-Cram, P., D.E. Pierson, D.K. Walker, and T. Tivnan
  1991 *Early Education in the Public Schools.* San Francisco: Jossey-Bass.

Hawkins, J.D., R.F. Catalano, and J.Y. Miller
  1992 Risk and protective factors for alcohol and other drug problems in adolescence and early adulthood: Implications for substance abuse prevention. *Psychological Bulletin* 112(1):64-105.

Heath, S.B.
  1982 Questioning at home and at school: A comparative study. Pp. 102-131 in *Doing the Ethnography of Schooling: Educational Anthropology in Action*, G. Spindler, ed. New York: Holt, Rinehart & Winston.
  1983 *Ways with Words: Language, Life and Work in Communities and Classrooms.* Cambridge, UK: Cambridge University Press.
  1989 Oral and literate traditions among Black Americans living in poverty. *American Psychologist* 44(2):367-373.

Hebbeler, K., and M. Wagner
  2000 Representation of Minorities and Children of Poverty Among Those Receiving Early Intervention and Special Education Services: Findings from Two National Longitudinal Studies. Paper prepared for the Commission on Behavioral and Social Sciences and Education, National Academy of Sciences, Washington, DC.

Heber, R.F.
  1959 *A Manual on Terminology and Classification in Mental Retardation.* Pineville, LA: American Association on Mental Deficiency.
  1961 *A Manual on Terminology and Classification in Mental Retardation.* Pineville, LA: American Association on Mental Deficiency.

Hedges, L.V., R.D. Laine, and R. Greenwald
  1994 Does money matter? A meta-analysis of studies of the effects of differential school inputs on student outcomes. *Educational Researcher* 23:5-14.

Heflinger, C.R., V.J. Cook, and M. Thackrey
  1987 Identification of mental retardation by the System of Multicultural Pluralistic Assessment: Nondiscriminatory or nonexistent? *Journal of School Psychology* 25:177-183.

Hehir, T.
  1996 Office of Special Education policy letter. *Individuals with Disabilities Education Report* 23:341.

Heim, A.S.
  1998 Gifted students and the right to an ability-appropriate education. *Journal of Law and Education* 27:131.

Helburn, S.W., ed.
  1995 *Cost, Quality, and Child Outcomes in Child Care Centers, Technical Report.* Denver, CO: Department of Economics, Center for Research in Economic and Social Policy, University of Colorado at Denver.

Helenius, P., A. Tarkiainen, P. Cornelissen, P.C. Hansen, and R. Salmelin
  1999 Dissociation of normal feature analysis and deficient processing of letter-strings in dyslexic adults. *Cerebral Cortex* 4:476-483.

Heller, K.A., and N.J. Schofield
   2000   International trends and topics of research on giftedness and talent. Pp. 123-137 in
           International Handbook of Giftedness and Talent (2nd ed.), K.A. Heller, F.J.
           Monks, R. J. Sternberg, and R.A. Subotnik, eds. Oxford, UK: Elsevier.
Heller, K.A., and A. Ziegler
   1996   Gender differences in mathematics and the sciences: Can attributional retraining
           improve the performance of gifted females. *Gifted Child Quarterly* 40:200-210.
Hendrick, I.G., and D.L. MacMillan
   1989   Selecting children for special education in New York City: William Maxwell, Eliza-
           beth Farrell, and the development of ungraded classes. *Journal of Special Educa-
           tion* 22(4):395-417.
Herman, R., D. Aladjam, P. McMahon, E. Masem, I. Mulligan, O. Smith, A. O'Malley, S.
Quinones, A. Reeve, and D. Woodruff
   1999   *An Educator's Guide to Schoolwide Reform*. Washington, DC: American Institutes
           for Research.
Hernandez-Reif, M., and T. Field
   2000   Preterm infants benefit from early interventions. Pp. 297-325 in *WAIMH Hand-
           book of Infant Mental Health: Infant Mental Health in Groups at High Risk,* J.D.
           Osofsky and H.E. Fitzgerald, eds. New York: John Wiley & Sons.
Hersh, R., and H. Walker
   1983   Great expectations: Making schools effective for all students. *Policy Studies Review*
           2:147-188.
Hess, R.D., and V. Shipman
   1965   Early experiences and socialization of cognitive modes in children. *Child Develop-
           ment* 36:869-886.
Hiebert, J.
   1986   *Conceptual and Procedural Knowledge: The Case of Mathematics*. Hilldale, NJ:
           Lawrence Erlbaum.
Hilliard, A.G., III
   1992   The pitfalls and promises of special education practice. *Exceptional Children* 59:
           168-172.
Hinshaw, S.
   1992a   Academic underachievement, attention deficits, and aggression: Comorbidity and
           implications for intervention. *Journal of Consulting and Clinical Psychology* 20(6):
           893-903.
   1992b   Externalizing behavior problems and academic underachievement in childhood and
           adolescence: Causal relationships and underlying mechanisms. *Psychological Bulle-
           tin* 111:127-155.
Hinshelwood, J.
   1917   *Congenital Word-Blindness*. Chicago: Medical Book Co.
Hockenbury, J., J.M. Kauffman, and D.P. Hallahan
   1999-   What is right about special education? *Exceptionality* 8(1):3-11.
   2000
Hodgkinson, H.L.
   1995   What should we call people? Race, class, and the Census for 2000. *Phi Delta
           Kappan* 77:173-179.
Hoff-Ginsberg, E.
   1991   Mother-child conversation in different social classes and communicative settings.
           Child Development 62:782-796.
Hoff-Ginsberg, E., and T. Tardif
   1995   Socioeconomic status and parenting. Pp. 161-187 in *Handbook of Parenting*, Vol.
           4, M.H. Bornstein, ed. Mahwah, NJ: Lawrence Erlbaum.

Hoffman, E.
  1975   The American public school and the deviant child: The origins of their involvement. *Journal of Special Education* 9:415-423.
Honig, A.S., and J.R. Lally
  1982   The Family Development Research Program: A retrospective review. *Early Childhood Development and Care* 10:41-62.
Horacek, H.J., C.T. Ramey, F.A. Campbell, K.P. Hoffman, and R.H. Fletcher
  1987   Predicting school failure and assessing early interventions with high-risk children. *Journal of the American Academy of Child Psychiatry* 26:758-763.
Horner, R.H.
  1994   Functional assessment: Contributions and future directions. *Journal of Applied Behavior Analysis* 27:401-404.
Horner, R.H., and E.G. Carr
  1997   Behavioral support for students with severe disabilities: Functional assessment and comprehensive intervention. *The Journal of Special Education* 31:84-104.
Horwitz, B., J.M. Rumsey, and B.C. Donohue
  1998   Functional connectivity of the angular gyrus in normal reading and dyslexia. *Proceedings of the National Academy of Sciences* 95:8939-8944.
Hosp, J.L., and D.J. Reschly
  2002a Regional differences in school psychology practice. *School Psychology Review* 31:11-29.
Hosp, J.L., and D.J. Reschly
  2002b Predictors of restrictiveness of placement for African American and Caucasian students. *Exceptional Children* 68:225-238.
Howes, C.
  2000   Social-emotional classroom climate in child care, child-teacher relationships and children's second grade peer relations. *Social Development* 9(2):191-205.
Howes, C., C.E. Hamilton, and L.C. Phillipsen
  1998   Stability and continuity of child-caregiver and child-peer relationships. *Child Development* 69(2):418-426.
Howes, C., C.C. Matheson, and C.E. Hamilton
  1994   Children's relationships with peers: Differential associations with aspects of the teacher-child relationship. *Child Development* 65(1):253-263.
Howes, C., and M. Olenick
  1986   Family and child care influences on toddler compliance. *Child Development* 57:202-216.
Howes, C., and E.W. Smith
  1995   Relations among child care quality, teacher behavior, children's play activities, emotional security, and cognitive activity in child care. *Early Childhood Research Quarterly* 10(4):381-404.
Howes, C., M. Whitebrook, and D. Phillips
  1992   Teacher characteristics and effective teaching in child care: Findings from the National Child Care Staffing Study. *Child and Youth Care Forum* 21(6):399-414.
Hudley, C., and S. Graham
  1993   An attributional intervention to reduce perr-directed aggression among African American boys. *Child Development* 64:124-138.
Hughes, C.A., and J.B Schumaker
  1992   Test-taking strategy instruction for adolescents with learning disabilities. *Exceptionality* 2:205-221.

Hunt, E.
  1997   Nature vs. nurture: The feeling of *vuja de*. Pp. 531-551 in *Intelligence, Heredity, and Environment*, R.J. Sternberg and E. Grigorenko, eds. Cambridge, UK: Cambridge University Press.
Hunt, J.
  1961   *Intelligence and Experience*. New York: Ronald Press.
Hunter, J., M.A. Urbanowicz, W. Yule, and R. Lansdown
  1985   Automated testing of reaction time and its association with lead in children. *Inernational Archives of Occupational Environmental Health* 57(1):27-34.
Huston, A.C., V. McLoyd, and C. Garcia Coll
  1994   Children and poverty: Issues in contemporary research. *Child Development* 65:275-282.
Idol, L., and J.F. West
  1987   Consultation in special education. 2. Training and practice. *Journal of Learning Disabilities* 20(8):474-494.
Ikeda, M.J., W.D. Tilly, J. Stumme, L. Volmer, and R. Allison
  1996   Agency-wide implementation of problem solving consultations: Foundations, current implementation, and future directions. *School Psychology Quarterly* 11(3): 228-243.
Improving America's Schools Act
  1994   20 U.S.C. § 6301 *et seq*.
Individuals with Disabilities Education Act
  1997,   20 U. S. C. 1400 *et seq*. (Statute). 34 C.F.R. Part 300 (Regulations).
  1999
Irvine, J.J.
  1990   *Black Students and School Failure: Policies, Practices, and Prescriptions*. New York: Greenwood.
Ilrwin, M.H., and K.H. McLaughlin
  1970   Ability and preference in category sorting by Mano school children and adults. *Journal of Social Psychology* 82:15-24.
Jackson, G., and C. Cosca
  1974   The inequality of educational opportunities in the Southwest: An observational study of ethnically mixed classrooms. *American Educational Research Journal* 11(3):219-229.
Jacobson, S.W., G.G. Fein, J.L. Jacobson, P.M. Schwartz, and J.K. Dowler
  1984   Neonatal correlates of prenatal exposure to smoking, caffeine, and alcohol. *Infant Behavior and Development* 7(3):253-265.
Jencks, C., M. Smith, H. Acland, M.J. Bane, D. Cohen, H. Gintis, B. Heynes, and R. Mickelson
  1972   *Inequality*. New York: Harper & Row.
Jensen, A.R.
  1974   Interaction of level I and level II abilities with race and socioeconomic status. *Journal of Educational Psychology* 66:99-111.
  1980   *Bias in Mental Testing*. New York: Free Press.
  1998   The g factor and the design of education. pp. 111-131 in *Intelligence, Instruction, and Assessment*, R. J. Sternberg and W. M. Williams, eds. Mahwah, NJ: Lawrence Erlbaum.
Jenson, W.R., H.N. Sloane, and K.R. Young
  1988   *Applied Behavior Analysis in Education: A Structural Approach*. Englewood Cliffs, NJ: Prentice Hall.

Johnson, D.W., and R.T. Johnson
   1981   Effects of cooperative and individualistic learning experiences on interethnic inter-
          action. *Journal of Educational Psychology* 73:444-449.
Johnson, D.W., R.T. Johnson, and B. Taylor
   1993   Impact of cooperative learning on high-ability students' achievement, self-esteem,
          and social acceptance. *The Journal of Social Psychology* 133:839-844.
Johnson, D.W., R.T. Johnson, M. Tiffany, and B. Zaidman
   1983   Cross-ethnic relationships: The impact of intergroup cooperation and intergroup
          competition. *Journal of Educational Research* 78:75-79.
Johnson, J.
   1969   Special education and the inner city: A challenge for the future of another means of
          cooling the mark out. *Journal of Special Education* 3:241-251.
Jones, R.L., ed.
   1988   *Psychoeducational Assessment of Minority Group Children: A Casebook.* Berke-
          ley, CA: Cobb & Henry.
Judy, J.E., P.A. Alexander, J.M. Kukikowich, and V.L. Willson
   1988   Effects of two instructional approaches and peer tutoring on gifted and non-gifted
          sixth-grade students' analogy performance. *Reading Research Quarterly* 23:236-
          256.
Juel, C.
   1988   Learning to read and write: A longitudinal study of 54 children from first through
          fourth grades. *Journal of Educational Psychology* 80:437-447.
Jussim, L., and J. Eccles
   1995   Naturally occurring interpersonal expectancies. *Review of Personality and Social
          Psychology* 15:74-108.
Jussim, L., J. Eccles, and S. Madon
   1996   Social perception, social stereotypes, and teacher expectations: Accuracy and the
          quest for the powerful self-fulfilling prophecy. Pp. 281-388 in *Advances in Experi-
          mental Social Psychology,* Vol. 28, M.P. Zanna, ed. San Diego, CA: Academic
          Press.
Kagan, J., R.E. Klein, G.E. Finley, B. Rogoff, and E. Nolan
   1979   A cross-cultural study of cognitive development. *Monographs of the Society for
          Research in Child Development* 44:(5, Serial No. 180).
Kain, J.F., and K. Singleton
   1996   Equality of educational opportunity revisited. *New England Economic Review*
          (May/June):87-114.
Kamps, D., T. Kravits, J. Rauch, J.L. Kamps, and N. Chung
   2000   A prevention program for students with or at risk for ED: Moderating effects of
          variation in treatment and classroom structure. *Journal of Emotional and Behav-
          ioral Disorders* 8:141-154.
Kanner, L.
   1964   *A History of the Care and Study of the Mentally Retarded.* Springfield, IL: Charles
          C. Thomas.
Kaplan, S.N.
   1979   *Providing Programs for the Gifted and Talented: A Handbook.* Ventura, CA: Su-
          perintendent of Schools.
Karnes, F.A., and R.G. Marquardt
   2000   *Gifted Children and Legal Issues.* Scottsdale, AZ: Gifted Psychology Press.

Karoly, L.A., P.W. Greenwood, S.S. Everingham, J. Hoube, M.R. Kilburn, C.P. Rydell, M. Sanders, and J. Chiesa
  1998   *Investing in Our Children: What We Know and Don't Know About the Costs and Benefits of Early Childhood Interventions.* Washington, DC: RAND.
Karweit, N.L.
  1989   Effective preschool programs for students at risk. Pp. 75-102 in *Effective Programs for Students at Risk,* R.E. Slavin, N.L. Karweit, and N.A. Madden, eds. Needham, MA: Allyn & Bacon.
Kauffman, J.M.
  1993   How we might achieve the radical reform of special education. *Exceptional Children* 60(1):6-16.
  1997   *Characteristics of Emotional and Behavioral Disorders of Children and Youth* (6th ed.). Upper Saddle River, NJ: Prentice-Hall.
Kaufman, A.S., and J.E. Doppelt
  1976   Analysis of WISC-R standardization data in terms of the stratification variables. *Child Development* 47(1):165-171.
Kavale, K.A., and S.R. Forness
  1999   Effectiveness of special education. Pp. 984-1024 in *The Handbook of School Psychology* (3rd Ed.), C.R. Reynolds and T.B. Gutkin, eds.New York: John Wiley & Sons.
  2000   Policy decisions in special education: The role of meta-analysis. Pp. 281-326 in *Contemporary Special Education Research: Syntheses of the Knowledge Base on Critical Instructional Issues,* R. Gersten, E.P. Schiller, and S. Vaughn, eds. Mahwah, NJ: Lawrence Erlbaum.
Kay, P.J., ed.
  1999   *Preventional Strategies That Work: What Administrators Can Do to Promote Positive Student Behavior.* Burlington, VT: University of Vermont, Department of Education.
Kazdin, A.
  1993   Treatment of conduct disorders: Progress and directions in psychotherapy research. *Development and Psychopathology* 5(1/2):277-310.
Kazdin, A.E.
  1987   Treatment of antisocial behavior in children: Current status and future directions. *Psychological Bulletin* 102:187-203.
Kazimour, K., and D. Reschly
  1981   Investigation of norms and concurrent validity for the Adaptive Behavior Inventory for Children. *American Journal of Mental Deficiency* 85:512-520.
Kearins, J.M.
  1981   Visual spatial memory in Australian aboriginal children of desert regions. *Cognitive Psychology* 13:424-160.
Keating, D.P., and C. Hertzman, ed.
  1999   *Developmental Health and the Wealth of Nations.* New York: Guilford Press.
Keeping, J.D., J.M. Najman, J. Morrison, J.S. Western, M.J. Andersen, G.M. Williams
  1989   A prospective longitudinal study of social, psychological and obstetric factors in pregnancy: Response rates and demographic characteristics of the 8556 respondents. *British Journal of Obstetrics and Gynaecology* 96:289-297.
Kellam, S.G., X. Ling, R. Merisca, C.H. Brown, and N. Ialongo
  1998a   The effect of the level of aggression in the first grade classroom on the course and malleability of aggressive behavior into middle school. *Development and Psychopathology* 10, 165-185.
  2000   Erratum. *Development and Psychopathology* 12:107.

Kellam, S.G., L.S. Mayer, G.W. Rebok, and W.E. Hawkins
  1998b The effects of improving achievement on aggressive behavior and of improving aggressive behavior on achievement through two prevention interventions: An investigation of causal paths. Pp. 486-505 in *Adversity, Stress and Psychopathology*, CN 27, B. Dohrenwend, ed. New York: Oxford University Press.

Keller, H.R.
  1988 Children's adaptive behaviors: Measure and source generalizability. *Journal of Psychoeducational Assessment* 6:371-389.

Kenny, D.A., F.X. Archambault, and B.W. Hallmark
  1995 *The Effects of Group Composition on Gifted snd Non-gifted Elementary Students in Cooperative Learning Groups.* (Research Monograph 95116). Storrs, CT: University of Connecticut, National Research Center on the Gifted and Talented.

Keogh, B.K., S.M. Major, and H.P. Reid
  1978 Marker variables—search for comparability and generalizability in the field of learning disabilities. *Learning Disability Quarterly* 1(3):5-11.

Kerr, M.M., and C.M. Nelson
  1989 *Strategies for Managing Behavior Problems in the Classroom* (2nd ed.). Columbus, OH: Merrill.

Kessler, R., J. House, and J. Turner
  1987 Unemployment and health in a community sample. *Journal of Health and Social Behavior* 28:51-59.

Kiely, J.L., K.M. Brett, S. Yu, and D.L. Rowley
  1994 Low birthweight and intrauterine growth retardation. Pp. 185-202 in *From Data to Action: CDC's Public Health Surveillance for Women, Infants, and Children*, L.S. Wilcox and J.S. Marks, eds. Atlanta, GA: U.S. Department of Health and Human Services, Public Health Service, Centers for Disease Control and Prevention.

Kim A.M.
  1999 Functional analysis and treatment of problem behavior exhibited by elementary school children. *Journal of Applied Behavior Analysis* 32(2):229-332.

Kirk, S.
  1962 *Educating Exceptional Children.* Boston: Houghton Mifflin.
  1963 Behavioral Diagnosis and Remediation of Learning Disabilities. Paper presented at the Exploration into the Problems of the Perceptually Handicapped Child Conference, Evanston, IL.

Klee, L., D. Kronstadt, and C. Zlotnick
  1996 Foster care's youngest: A preliminary report. *American Journal of Orthopsychiatry* 67:290-298.

Klingberg, T., M. Hedehus, E. Temple, T. Salz, J. Gabrieli, M. Moseley, and R. Poldrack
  2000 Microstructure of temporo-parietal white matter as a basis for reading ability: Evidence from diffusion tensor magnetic resonance imaging. *Neuron* 25:493-500.

Klingner, J., and B. Harry
  2001 Understanding the Complexity of Disproportionate Representation: Multiple Perspectives. Paper presented at the Annual Conference of the Council for Exceptional Children. Kansas City, MO.

Knitzer, J., Z. Steinberg and B. Fleish
  1990 *At the Schoolhouse Door: An Examination of Programs and Policies for Children with Emotional Problems.* New York: Bank Street College of Education.

Knupp, R.
  1988 *Improving Oral Reading Skills of Educationally Handicapped Elementary School-aged Students Through Repeated Readings.* ERIC Document Reproduction Service No. ED 297275. Columbus, OH: ERIC.

Kochanek, T.T., R.I. Kabacoff, and L.P. Lipsitt
  1990   Early identification of developmentally disabled and at-risk preschool children. *Exceptional Children* 56(6):528-538.
Krueger, A.B, and D.M. Whitmore
  2001a *Would Smaller Classes Help Close the Black-White Achievement Gap?* Industrial Relations Section Working Paper #451, Princeton University.
  2001b The effect of attending a small class in the early grades on college test-taking and middle school test results: Evidence from Project STAR. *Economic Journal* 111:1-28.
Kucan, L., and I.L. Beck
  1997   Thinking aloud and reading comprehension research: Inquiry, instruction, and social interaction. *Review of Educational Research* 67:271-299.
Kulik, C.L. and J.A. Kulik
  1982   Effects of ability grouping on secondary school students: A meta-analysis of evaluation findings. *American Educational Research Journal* 19:415-428.
Kulik, J.A.
  1992   *An Analysis of the Research on Ability Grouping: Historical and Contemporary Perspectives* (RBDM 9204). Storrs, CT: University of Connecticut, National Research Center on the Gifted and Talented.
Kulik, J.A., and C.C. Kulik
  1984   Effects of accelerated instruction of students. *Review of Educational Research* 54:409-425.
  1987   Effects of grouping on student achievement. *Equity and Excellence* 23:22-30.
  1991   Ability grouping and gifted students. Pp. 178-196 in *Handbook of Gifted Education*, N. Colangelo and G. Davis, eds. Needham Heights, MA: Allyn and Bacon.
  1992   Meta-analytic findings on grouping programs. *Gifted Child Quarterly* 36: 73-77.
  1997   Ability grouping. Pp. 230-242 in *Handbook of Gifted Education (2nd ed.)*, N. Colangelo and G. Davis, eds. Needham Heights, MA: Allyn & Bacon.
Kusche, C.A., and M.T. Greenberg
  1994   *The PATHS Curriculum.* Seattle: Developmental Research and Programs.
Lacy, W.B., and E. Middleton
  1981   Are educators racially prejudiced?: A cross-occupational comparison of attitudes. *Sociological Focus* 14:87-95.
Lambert, N.M.
  1981   Psychological evidence in *Larry P. v. Wilson Riles*: An evaluation by a witness for the defense. *American Psychologist* 36:937-952.
Lancy, D.
  1983   *Cross-Cultural Studies in Cognition and Mathematics.* New York: Academic Press.
Landesman-Dwyer, S., and I. Emanuel
  1979   Smoking during pregnancy. *Teratology* 19:119-126.
Lane, K.L.
  1999   Young students at risk for antisocial behavior: The utility of academic and social skills interventions. *Journal of Emotional and Behavioral Disorders* 7:211-223.
Lane, K.L., M.E. Beebe-Frankenberger, K.M. Lambros and M. Pierson
  2001a Designing effective interventions for children at-risk for antisocial behavior: An integrated model of components necessary for making valid inferences. *Psychology in the Schools* 38(4):365-379.
Lane, K.L., T. O'Shaughnessy, K.M. Lambros, F.M. Gresham, and M. Beebe-Frankenberger
  2001b The Efficacy of Phonological Awareness Training with Students Who Have Externalizing and Hyperactive-Inattentive Behavior Problems. *Remedial and Special Education.*

Lane, K.L., J. Umbreit, and M. Beebe-Frankenberger
   1999   Functional assessment research on students with or at risk for EBD: 1990 to the present. *Journal of Positive Behavior Interventions* 2:101-111.
Lane, K.L., and J. Wehby
   In   Addressing antisocial behavior in the schools: A call for action. *Academic Ex-*
   press   *change Quarterly.*
Laosa, L.M.
   1979   Inequality in the classroom: Observational research on teacher-student interactions. *Atzlan* 8:51-66.
Lareau, A.
   1989   *Home Advantage: Social Class and Parental Intervention in Elementary Education.* New York: Falmer.
Lareau, A., and E.M. Horvat
   1999   Moments of Social Inclusion and Exclusion: Race, Class, and Cultural Capital in Family-School Relationships. *Sociology of Education* 72:37-53.
Larry P. v. Riles, 343 F. Supp. 1306 (N.D. Cal. 1972) (preliminary injunction) *affirmed* 502 F.2d 963 (9th Cir. 1974); 495 F. Supp. 926 (N.D. Cal. 1979) (decision on merits) *affirmed* (9th Cir. No. 80-427), Jan. 23, 1984) Order modifying judgment, C-71-2270 RFP, September 25, 1986).
Larson, K.A.
   1989   Task-related and interpersonal problem-solving training for increasing school success in high-risk young adolescents. *Remedial and Special Education* 10:32-41.
Lave, J.
   1977   Tailor-made experiments and evaluating the consequences of apprenticeship training. *The Quarterly Newsletter of the Laboratory of Comparative Human Development* 1:1-3.
   1988   *Cognition in Practice: Mind, Mathematics and Culture in Everyday Life.* Cambridge, England: Cambridge University Press.
Lazar, I., R. Darlington, H. Murray, J. Royce, and A. Snipper
   1982   Lasting effects of early education: A report from the Consortium of Longitudinal Studies. *Monographs of the Society for Research in Child Development* 47:2-3, Serial No. 195.
Lazar, I., R. Hubble, H. Murray, M. Rosche, and J. Royce
   1977   *The Persistence of Preschool Effects: A Long-Term Follow up of Fourteen Infant and Preschool Experiments, A Summary.* Washington, DC: U.S. Department of Health, Education and Welfare, Administration of Children, Youth, and Families.
Lefkowitz, M.M.
   1981   Smoking during pregnancy: Long-term effects on the offspring. *Developmental Psychology* 17:192-194.
Lefly, D.L., and B.F. Pennington
   1991   Spelling errors and reading fluency in compensated adult dyslexics. *Annals of Dyslexia* 41:143-162.
Legislative Office of Education (LOEO) of Ohio
   1998   *Head Start's Impact on School Readiness in Ohio: A Case Study of Kindergarten Students.* Columbus, OH: Ohio State Legislative Office of Education Oversight.
Lennon, M.C., J.L. Aber, and B.B. Blum
   1998   *Program, Research, and Policy Implications of Evaluations of Teenage Parent Programs.* New York: Research Forum on Children, Families, and the New Federalism.
Lester, B.M., L.L. LaGasse, and R. Seifer
   1998   Drug abuse: Cocaine exposure and children: The meaning of subtle effects. *Science* 282(5389):633-634.

Leung, B.
   1986   Psychoeducational assessments of Asian students. Pp. 29-35 in *Exceptional Asian Children and Youth*, M.K. Kitano and P.C. Chinn, eds. Reston, VA: Council for Exceptional Children and Youth.

Levin, E.D, and T.A. Slotkin
   1998   Developmental neurotoxicity of nicotine. Pp. 587-615 in *Handbook of Developmental Neurotoxicology*, W. Slikker and L.W. Chang, eds. San Diego: Academic Press.

Levin, E.D., A. Wilkerson, J.P. Jones, N.C. Christopher, and S.J. Briggs
   1996   Prenatal nicotine effects on memory in rats: pharmacological and behavioral challenges. *Developmental Brain Research* 97:207-215.

Levine, D.U., and A. Ornstein
   1989   Research on classroom and school effectiveness and its implications for improving big city schools. *Urban Review* 21:81-94.

Leviton, A., D. Bellinger, E.N. Allred, M. Rabinowitz H. Needleman, and S. Schoenbaum
   1993   Pre- and post-natal low-level lead exposure and children's dysfunction in school. *Environmental Research* 60:30-43.

Lewis, M.
   1997   *Altering Fate: Why the Past Does Not Predict the Future*. New York: Guilford.

Lewis, T.J., and C. Daniels
   2000   Rethinking school discipline through effective behavioral support. *Reaching Today's Youth* 4:43-47.

Liberman, I.Y., and D. Shankweiler
   1991   Phonology and beginning to read: A tutorial. In *Learning to Read: Basic Research and Its Implications*, L. Rieben and C.A. Perfetti, eds. Hillsdale, NJ: Lawrence Erlbaum.

Lloyd, J.W., D.G. Bateman, T.J. Landrum, and D.P. Hallahan
   1989   Self-recording of attention versus productivity. *Journal of Applied Behavior Analysis* 22:315-323.

Lloyd, K.M., M. Tienda, and A. Zajacova
   2001   *Trends in Educational Achievement of Minority Students Since Brown vs. Board of Education*. Princeton, NJ: Princeton University.

Lochman, J.E., and K.A. Dodge
   1994   Social-cognitive processes of severely violent, moderately aggressive, and nonaggressive boys. *Journal of Consulting and Clinical Psychology* 62:366-374.

Lock, W.R., and L.S. Fuchs
   1995   Effects of peer-mediated reading instruction on the on-task behavior and social interaction of children with behavior disorders. *Journal of Emotional and Behavioral Disorders* 3(2):92-99.

Lockart, G.
   1996   Grouping Practices and Their Effects on Middle Level Gifted Students. Unpublished paper, Education, Southern Illinois University at Edwardsville.

Loeber, R., T.J. Dishion, and G.R. Patterson
   1984   Multiple gating: A multistage assessment procedure for identifying youths at risk for delinquency. *Journal of Research in Crime and Delinquency* 21:7-32.

Lonigan, C.J., S.R. Burgess, and J.L Anthony
   2000   Development of emergent literacy and early reading skills in preschool children: Evidence from a latent-variable longitudinal study. *Developmental Psychology* 36:596-613.

Lou, Y., P.C. Abrami, J.C. Spence, C. Poulsen, B. Chambers, and S. d'Apollonia
1996   Within-class grouping: A meta-analysis. *Review of Educational Research* 66:423-458.

Lowe, J., and L. Papile
1990   Neurodevelopmental performance of very-low-birth-weight infants with mild, peri-ventricular, intraventricular hemorrhage. *American Journal of Diseases of Children* 144:1242-1245.

Lozoff, B., E. Jimenez, J. Hagen, E. Mollen, and A.W. Wolf
2000   Poorer behavioral and developmental outcome more than 10 years after treatment for iron deficiency in infancy. *Pediatrics* 105(4):E51.

Lozoff, B., E. Jimenez, and A. Wolfe
1991   Long-term developmental outcome of infants with iron deficiency. *New England Journal of Medicine* 325:687-976.

Lozoff, B., A. Wolfe, E. Mollen, and E. Jimenez
1997   Functional significance of early iron deficiency (Abstract). *Pediatric Research* 41:15A.

Luchow, J. P., T.K. Crowl, and J.P. Kahn
1985   Learned helplessness: Perceived effects of ability and effort on academic performance among EH and LD/EH children. *Journal of Learning Disabilities* 18(8):470-474.

Luckasson, R., ed.
1992   *Mental Retardation: Definition, Classification, and Systems of Support.* Washington, DC: American Association on Mental Retardation.

Luckasson, R., D.L. Coulter, E.A. Polloway, S. Reiss, R.L. Schalock, M.E. Snell, D.M. Spitalnik, and J.A. Stark
1992   *Mental Retardation: Definition, Classification, and Systems of Support* (9th Ed.). Washington DC: American Association on Mental Retardation.

Lucker, G.W., D. Rosenfield, J. Sikes, and E. Aranson
1976   Performance in an interdependent classroom: A field study. *American Educational Research Journal* 13:115-123.

Luke, B., N. Mamelle, L. Keith, F. Munoz, J. Minogue, E. Papiernik, and T. Johnson
1995   The association between occupational factors and pre-term birth: A United States nurses' study. *American Journal of Obstetrics and Gynecology* 173:849-862.

Lundberg, I., J. Frost, and O. Petersen
1988   Effects of an extensive program for stimulating phonological awareness in pre-school children. *Reading Research Quarterly* 23(3):263-284.

Lynch, E.W., and R. Stein
1987   Parent participation by ethnicity: A comparison of Hispanic, Black, and Anglo families. *Exceptional Children* 54:105-111.

Lyngbye, T., O.N. Hansen, A. Trillingsgaard, I. Beese, and P. Grandjean
1990   Learning disabilities in children: Significance of low-level lead exposure and con-founding factors. *Acta Paediatrica Scandinavica* 79(3):352-360.

Lynn, R.
1990   The role of nutrition in secular increases in intelligence. *Personality and Individual Differences* 11:273-275.

Lyon, G.R.
1996   Learning disabilities. *The Future of Children: Special Education for Students with Disabilities* 6:56-76.

Lyon, G.R, J.M. Fletcher, S.E. Shaywitz, B.A. Shaywitz, J.K. Torgesen, F.B. Wood, A. Schulte, and R. Olson
  2001   Rethinking learning disabilities. Pp. 259-288 in *Rethinking Special Education for a New Century*, C.E. Finn, Jr., A.J. Rotherham, and C.R. Hokanson, Jr., eds. Washington, DC: Thomas B.Fordham Foundation.

Maag, J.W., and K.W. Howell
  1992   Special education and the exclusion of youth with social maladjustments: A cultural-organizational perspective. *Remedial and Special Education* 13:47-52.

Maccoby, E., and J. Martin
  1983   Socialization in the context of the family: Parent-child interaction. Pp. 1-101 in *Handbook of Child Psychology*, Vol. Four, E.M. Hetherington, ed. New York: John Wiley & Sons.

Mace, F.C.
  1994   The significance and future of functional analysis methodologies. *Journal of Applied Behavior Analysis* 27(2):385-392.

Mackie, R.
  1969   *Special Education in the United States: Statistics 1948-1966.* New York: Teachers College Press.

MacMillan, D.L., and S. Borthwick
  1980   The new educable mentally retarded population: Can they be mainstreamed? *Mental Retardation* 18(4):155-158.

MacMillan, D.L., and S.R. Forness
  1998   The role of IQ in special education placement decisions: Primary and determinative or peripheral and inconsequential? *Remedial and Special Education* 19:239-253.

MacMillan, D.L., F.M. Gresham, and K.M. Bocian
  1998a   Discrepancy between definitions of learning disabilities and school practices: An empirical investigation. *Journal of Learning Disabilities* 31:314-326.
  1998b   Curing mental retardation and causing learning disabilities: Consequences of using various WISC-III IQs to estimate aptitude of Hispanic students. *Journal of Psychoeducational Assessment* 16:36-54.

MacMillan, D., F.M. Gresham, and S. Forness
  1996a   Full inclusion: An empirical perspective. *Behavioral Disorders* 21(2):145-159.

MacMillan, D.L., F.M. Gresham, M.F. Lopez, and K.M. Bocian
  1996b   Comparison of students nominated for prereferral interventions by ethnicity and gender. *The Journal of Special Education* 30:133-151.

MacMillan, D.L., F.M. Gresham, and G.N. Siperstein
  1993   Conceptual and psychometric concerns about the 1992 AAMR definition of mental retardation. *American Journal on Mental Retardation* 98(3):325-335.
  1995   Heightened concerns over the 1992 AAMR definition. *American Journal on Mental Retardation* 100:87-97.

MacMillan, D.L., F.M. Gresham, G.N. Siperstein, and K.M. Bocian
  1996c   The labyrinth of I.D.E.A.: School decisions on referred students with subaverage general intelligence. *American Journal on Mental Retardation* 101:161-174.

MacMillan, D.L., C.E. Meyers, and G.M. Morrison
  1980   System-identification of mildly mentally retarded children: Implications for conducting and interpreting research. *American Journal of Mental Deficiency* 85:108-115.

MacMillan, D.L., and D.J. Reschly
  1996   Issues of definition and classification. Pp. 47-74 in *Handbook of Mental Deficiency: Psychological Theory and Research* (3rd ed.), W. MacLean, ed. Hillsdale, NJ: Lawrence Erlbaum.

1998   Overrepresentation of minority students: The case for greater specificity or recon-
        sideration of the variables examined. *The Journal of Special Education* 32:15-24.

MacMillan, D.L., G.N. Siperstein, and F.M. Gresham
1996d   Mild mental retardation: A challenge to its viability as a diagnostic category. *Ex-
        ceptional Children* 62:356-371.

Madden, J., P. Levenstein, and S. Levenstein
1976   Longitudinal IQ outcomes of the mother-child home program. *Child Development*
        46:1015-1025.

Maher, C.A.
1982   Behavioral effects of using conduct problem adolescents as cross-age tutors. *Psy-
        chology in the Schools* 19:360-364.
1984   Handicapped adolescents as cross-age tutors: Program description and evaluation.
        Exceptional Children 51:56-63.

Mandler, J.M., S. Scribner, M. Coke, and M. DeForest
1980   Cross cultural invariance in story recall. *Child Development* 51:19-26.

Marion, R.
1981   *Educators, Parents, and Exceptional Children*. Rockville, MD: Aspen.

Marquardt, R.G., and F.A. Karnes
1989   The courts and gifted education. *West's Education Law Reporter* 50:9.
1996   The courts and gifted education revisited. *West's Education Law Reporter* 113:539,

Marquis, J.G., R.H. Horner, E.G. Carr, A.P. Turnbull, M. Thompson, G.A. Behrens, D.
Margito-McLaughlin, M. McAtee, C.E. Smith, K.A. Ryan, and A. Doolabh
2000   A meta-analysis of positive behavior supports., Pp. 137-178 in *Contemporary Spe-
        cial Education Research*, R. Gerstein, E. Schiller, and S. Vaughn, eds. Mahwah, NJ:
        Lawrence Erlbaum.

Martens, B.K., and S.Q. Kelly
1993   A behavioral analysis of effective teaching. *School Psychology Quarterly.* 8:10-26.

Martorell, R.
1998   Nutrition and the worldwide rise in IQ scores. Pp. 183-206 in *The Rising Curve*, U.
        Neisser, ed. Washington, DC: American Psychological Association.

Mash, E.J., and L.G. Terdal
1988   *Behavioral Assessment of Childhood Disorders: Selected Core Problems*. New
        York: Guilford Press.

Mastropieri, M.A., V. Jenkins, and T.E. Scruggs
1985   Academic and intellectual characteristics of behavior disordered children and youth.
        Pp. 86-104 in *Severe Behavior Disorders of Children and Youth*, R.B. Rutherford,
        Jr., ed. Reston, VA: Council for Children with Behavior Disorders.

Mastropieri, M.A., and T.E. Scruggs
1998   Constructing more meaningful relationships in the classroom: Mnemonic research
        into practice. *Learning Disabilities Research and Practice* 13:138-145.

Mathes, P.G., D. Fuchs, L.S. Fuchs, A.M. Henley, and A. Sanders
1994   Increasing strategic reading practice with Peabody ClassWide Peer Tutoring. *Learn-
        ing Disabilities Research & Practice* 9:44-48.

Mathes, P.G., and L.S. Fuchs
1993   Peer-mediated reading instruction in special education resource rooms. *Learning
        Disabilities Research & Practice* 8:233-243.
1994   The efficacy of peer tutoring in reading for students with mild disabilities: A best-
        evidence synthesis. *School Psychology Review* 23:59-80.

Mathes, P.G., D.C. Simmons, and B.I. Davis
1992   Assisted reading techniques for developing reading fluency. *Reading Research and
        Instruction* 31:70-77.

Mayer, G.R.
   1995   Preventing antisocial behavior in the schools. *Journal of Applied Behavioral Analysis*, 28:467-478.
McCarty, T.L., R.H. Lynch, S. Wallace, and A. Benally
   1991   Classroom inquiry and Navajo learning styles: A call for reassessment. *Anthropology and Education Quarterly* 22:42-59.
McConaughy, S., and R. Skiba
   1993   Comorbidity of empirically based syndromes in matched general population and clinical samples. *School Psychology Review* 22:421-436.
McConaughy, S.H., P.J. Kay, and M. Fitzgerald
   2000   How long is long enough? Outcomes for a school-based prevention program. *Exceptional Children* 67:21-34.
McFadden, A.C., G.E. Marsh, B.J. Price, and Y. Hwang
   1992   A study of race and gender bias in the punishment of school children. *Education and Treatment of Children* 15(2), 140-146.
McGee, R., and W.R. Stanton
   1994   Smoking in pregnancy and child development to age 9 years. *Journal of Pediatrics and Child Health* 30(3):263-268.
McIntosh, R., S. Vaughn, J. Schumm, D. Haager, and O. Lee
   1993   Observations of students with learning disabilities in general education classrooms. *Exceptional Children* 60(3):249-261.
McIntyre, T.
   1993   Behaviorally disordered youth in correctional settings: Prevalence, programming, and teacher training. *Behavioral Disorders* 18:167-176.
McLaughlin, B.
   1987   *Theories of Second Language Learning.* London: Edward Arnold.
McLoyd, V.C.
   1997   The impact of poverty and low socioeconomic status on the socioemotional function of African-American children and adolescents: Mediating effects. Pp. 7-34 in *Social and Emotional Adjustment and Family Relations in Ethnic Minorities*, R. Taylor and M. Wang, eds. Mahwah, NJ: Lawrence Erlbaum.
McLoyd, V.C., T.E. Jayarante, R. Ceballo, and J. Borquez
   1994   Unemployment and work interruption among African American single mothers: Effects on parenting and adolescent socioemotional functioning. *Child Development* 65:562-589.
McLoyd, V.C., and B. Lozoff
   2001   Racial and ethnic trends in children's and adolescents' behavior and development. Pp. 311-350 in *America Becoming: Racial Trends and Their Consequences*. Division of Behavioral and Social Sciences and Education. N. Smelser, W.J. Wilson, and F. Mitchell, eds. Washington, DC: National Academy Press.
McNaughton, D.
   1994   Measuring parent satisfaction with early intervention programs: Current practice, problems, and future perspectives. *Topics in Early Childhood Special Education* 14:26-48.
McNeil, C.B., S. Eyberg, T.H. Eisenstadt, K. Newcomb, and B. Funderburk
   1991   Parent-child interaction therapy with behavior problem children: Generalization of treatment effects to the school setting. *Journal of Clinical Child Psychology* 20(2): 140-151.
McWilliam, R.A., L. Tocci, and G. Harbin
   1995   *Services Are Child-Oriented and Families Like It That Way—But Why?* Chapel Hill: Early Childhood Research Institute on Service Utilization, Frank Porter Graham Child Development Center, University of North Carolina.

Mehan, H., A. Hartwick, A., and J.L. Miehls
   1986   *Handicapping the Handicapped: Decision-Making in Students' Educational Careers.* Stanford, CA: Stanford University Press.

Meisels, S.
   1987   Uses and abuses of developmental screening and school readiness testing. *Young Children* (January):4-8.

Meisels, S.J.
   1996-   Using work sampling in authentic assessments. *Educational Leadership:* 60-65.
   1997   (Winter)

Melnick, S., and D. Pullin
   1999   *Teacher Education and Testing in Massachusetts: The Issues, the Facts, and Conclusions for Institutions of Higher Education.* Boston, MA: Association of Independent Colleges and Universities of Massachusetts.

   2000   Can you take dictation? Prescribing teacher quality through testing. *Journal of Teacher Education* 51:262-275.

Melnick, S.L., and K.M. Zeichner
   1998   Teacher education's responsibility to address diversity issues: Enhancing institutional capacity. *Theory into Practice* 37(2):88-95.

Mercer, C.D., L. Jordan, D.H. Allsopp, and A.R. Mercer
   1996   Learning disabilities definitions and criteria used by state education departments *Learning Disability Quarterly* 19:217-232.

Mercer, J.
   1973a   *Labeling the Mentally Retarded.* Berkeley and Los Angeles, CA: University of California Press.
   1973b   The myth of 3% prevalence. Pp. 1-18 in *Sociobehavioral Studies in Mental Retardation,* G. Tarjan, R,K. Eyman, and C.E. Meyers, eds. Washington, DC: Monographs of the American Association on Mental Deficiency, No. 1.
   1979a   *System of Multicultural Pluralistic Assessment Technical Manual.* San Antonio, TX: Psychological Corporation.
   1979b   In defense of racially and culturally nondiscriminatory assessment. *School Psychology Digest* 8:89-115.

Mercer, J.R.
   1970   Sociological perspectives on mild mental retardation. Pp. 378-391 in *Social-Cultural Aspects of Mental Retardation,* H.C. Haywood ed. New York: Appleton-Century-Crofts.

Merton, R.
   1948   The self-fulfilling prophecy. *Antioch Review* 8:193-210.

Mervasch, Z.R.
   1991   Learning mathematics in a different mastery environment. *Journal of Educational Research* 84:225-231.

Meyer, M.S., and R.H. Felton
   1999   Repeated reading to enhance fluency: Old approaches and new directions. *Annals of Dyslexia* 49:283-306.

Meyers, C.E., P.E. Sundstrom, and R.K. Yoshida
   1974   The school psychologist and assessment in special education. *School Psychology Monographs* 2:(No. 1).

Mickelson, R.A.
   1990   The attitude-achievement paradox among Black adolescents. *Sociology of Education* 63:44-61.

Milich, R., T.A. Widiger, and S. Landau
   1987   Differential diagnosis of attention deficit and conduct disorders using conditional probabilities. *Journal of Consulting and Clinical Psychology* 55(5):762-767.

Miller, G.E., K. Brehm, and S. Whitehouse
  1998   Reconceptualizing school-based prevention for antisocial behavior within a resiliency framework. *School Psychology Review* 27:364-379.
Miller, J.G.
  1997   A cultural-psychology perspective on intelligence. Pp. 269-302 in *Intelligence, Heredity, and Environment*, R.J. Sternberg and E. Grigorenko, eds. Cambridge, UK: Cambridge University Press.
Miller, L.S.
  2000   Minority High Academic Achievement Patterns and Their Implication for the Gifted and Talented Education Community. Paper prepared for the National Academies' Committee on Minority Representation in Special Education and Gifted and Talented Programs. Washington, DC.
Miller, S.
  1995   *An American Imperative*. New Haven: Yale University Press.
Miller-Jones, D.
  1989   Culture and testing. *American Psychologist* 44(2):360-366.
Mills v. Board of Education
      348 F. Supp. 866 (D.D.C. 1972).
Mills, C.J., K.E. Ablard, and L.E. Brody
  1993   The Raven's progressive matrices: Its usefulness for identifying gifted/talented students. *Roeper Review* 15(3):183-186.
Mlawer, M.A.
  1993   Who should fight? Parents and the advocacy expectation. *Journal of Disability Policy Studies* 4(1):105-115.
Molnar, A., P. Smith, J. Zahorik, A. Palmer, A. Halbach, and K. Ehrle
  1999   Evaluating the SAGE program: A pilot program in targeted pupil-teacher reduction in Wisconsin. *Educational Evaluation and Policy Analysis* 21(2): 165-177.
Montague, M., J. Bergeron, and E. Lago-Delello
  1997   Using prevention strategies in general education. *Focus on Exceptional Children* 29:1-12.
Moody, S.W., S. Vaughn, M.T. Hughes, and M. Fischer
  2000   Reading instruction in the resource room: Set-up for failure. *Exceptional Children* 66(3):305-316.
Moore, C.L., and P.M. Retish
  1974   Effect of the examiner's race on black children's Wechsler Preschool and Primary Scale of Intelligence IQ. *Developmental Psychology* 10(5):672-676.
Moore, K.A., M. Zaslow, M.J. Coiro, S. Miller, and E. Magenheim
  1995   *The JOBS Evaluation: How Well Are They Faring? AFDC Families with Preschool-Aged Children in Atlanta at the Outset of the JOBS Evaluation*. New York: Manpower Demonstration Research Corporation.
Morris, D.
  1980   Assessing word awareness in the beginning reader: An alternative strategy (Occasional Paper No. 2). (ERIC Document Reproduction Service No. ED 230922). Lanham, MD: ERIC.
Morris, R.D., K.K. Stuebing, J.M. Fletcher, S.E. Shaywitz, G.R. Lyon, D.P. Shankweiler, L. Katz, D.J. Francis, and B.A. Shaywitz
  1998   Subtypes of reading disability: Variability around a phonological core. *Journal of Educational Psychology* 90:347-373.
Morrison, J., G.M. Williams, J.M. Najman, M.J. Anderson, and J.D. Keeping
  1993   Birthweight below the tenth percentile: The relative and attributable risks of maternal tobacco consumption and other factors. *Environmental Health Perspectives Supplement* 3:275-277.

Mosteller, F., R.J. Light, and J.A. Sachs
  1996   Sustained inquiry in education: Lessons from skill grouping and class size. *Harvard Educational Review* 66(4):797-842.
Moyer, S.B.
  1982   Repeated reading. *Journal of Learning Disabilities* 15:619-623.
Msall, M.E., J.A. Bier, L.L. LaGasse, M. Tremont, and B. Lester
  1998   The vulnerable preschool child: The impact of biomedical and social risks on neuro-developmental function. *Seminars in Pediatric Neurology* 5(1):52-61.
Munoz, H., D. Romie, E. Palazuelos, T. Mancilla-Sanchez, J. Meneses-Gonzales, and M. Hernandez-Avila
  1993   Blood lead level and neurobehavioral development among children living in Mexico City. *Archives of Environment and Health* 48(30):132-139.
Murnane, R.J., and F. Levy
  1996   Evidence from fifteen schools in Austin, Texas. Pp. 93-96 in *Does Money Matter? The Effect of School Resources on Student Achievement and Adult Success*, G. Burtless, ed. Washington, DC: Brookings Institution Press.
Murnane, R.J., J.D. Singer, J.B. Willett, J.J. Kemple, and R.J. Olsen
  1991   *Who Will Teach? Policies That Matter.* Cambridge, MA: Harvard University Press.
Murray, L., and P.J. Cooper
  1997   Editorial. Postpartum depression and child development. *Psychological Medicine* 27:253-260.
Naeye, R.L., and E.C. Peters
  1984   Mental development of children whose mothers smoked during pregnancy. *Obstetrics Gynecology* 64:601-607.
National Association of State Directors of Special Education
  1999   *Child Count Variations and Anomalies Across States.* Washington, DC: Author.
National Cancer Institute
  2000   *The Nation's Investment in Cancer Research: A Plan and Budget Proposal for Fiscal Year 2002.* Rockville, MD: Author.
National Center for Education Statistics (NCES)
  1997a *America's Teachers: Profile of a Profession, 1993-94.* Washington, DC: U.S. Department of Education.
  1997b *Schools and Staffing Survey: Characteristics of Stayers, Movers, and Leavers: Results from the Teacher Follow-up Survey, 1994-95.* Washington, DC: U.S. Department of Education.
  1998   *National Education Longitudinal Study, 1988.* Ann Arbor, MI: Inter-university Consortium for Political and Social Research.
  2000   *The Condition of Education 2000: Racial-Ethnic Distribution of Public School Students.* Washington, DC: U.S. Department of Education.
  2001   *Number of Newly Hired Public School Teachers Needed for 11 Years from 1998-99 to 2008-09, by Continuation Rate Used and Teacher Total Assumption.* Washington, DC: U.S. Department of Education.
National Center for Health Statistics
  1998   *Health, United States, 1998 with Socioeconomic Status and Health Chartbook.* Hyattsville, MD: U.S. Department of Health and Human Services.
National Clearinghouse for Professions in Special Education
  2001   *Employment Opportunities Are Excellent.* [Online]. Available: http://www.cec.sped.org/cl/research_library/employment-1.html [Accessed March 17, 2001].
National Commission on Teaching and America's Future (NCTAF)
  1996   *What Matters Most: Teaching for America's Future.* New York: Author.

National Institute of Child Health and Human Development
  1996   Characteristics of infant child care: Factors contributing to positive caregiving. *Early Childhood Research Quarterly* 11(3):269-306.
  1997a   The effects of infant child care on infant-mother attachment security: Results of the NICHD study of early child care. *Child Development* 68:860-879.
  1997b   Poverty and patterns of child care. Pp. 100-131 in *Consequences of Growing Up Poor*, J. Brooks-Gunn and G.J. Duncan, eds. New York: Russell Sage.
  1997c   Mother-child interaction and cognitive outcomes associated with early child care: Results from the NICHD Study. Poster symposium presented at the Biennial Meeting of the Society for Research in Child Development, April, 1997, Washington, DC.
  1999   Effect Sizes from the NICHD Study of Early Child Care. Paper presented at the Biennial Meeting of the Society for Research in Child Development, April 1999, Albuquerque, NM.
  2000   *Report of the National Reading Panel. Teaching Children to Read: An Evidence-based Assessment of the Scientific Research Literature on Reading and Its Implications for Reading Instructions.* (NIH Publication No. 00-4769). Washington, DC: U.S. Government Printing Office.
National Research Council
  1982   *Placing Children in Special Education: A Strategy for Equity.* Panel on Selection and Placement of Students in Programs for the Mentally Retarded, Committee on Child Development Research and Public Policy, K.A. Heller, W.H. Holtzman, and S. Messick, eds. Commission on Behavioral and Social Sciences and Education. Washington, DC: National Academy Press.
  1992   *Assessing Evaluation Studies: The Case of Bilingual Education Strategies.* Panel on Review Evaluation Studies of Bilingual Education, Committee on National Statistics, M.M. Meyer and S.E. Feinberbg, eds. Washington, DC: National Academy Press.
  1993   Lead exposure to sensitive populations. Pp. 99-141 in *Measuring Lead Exposure in Infants, Children, and Other Sensitive Populations.* Committee on Measuring Lead in Critical Populations, Board on Environmental Studies and Toxicology, Commission on Life Sciences. Washington, DC: National Academy Press.
  1996a   *Fetal Alcohol Syndrome: Diagnosis, Epidemiology, Prevention, and Treatment.* Committee to Study Fetal Alcohol Syndrome, Division of Biobehavioral Sciences and Mental Disorders. K. Stratton, C. Howe, and F. Battaglia, eds. Washington, DC: National Academy Press.
  1996b   *The Use of IQ Tests in Special Education Decision Making and Planning: Summary of Two Workshops.* Board on Testing and Assessment. P. Morison, S. White, and M. Feuer, eds. Commission on Behavioral and Social Sciences and Education. National Academy Press.
  1997a   *Educating One and All: Students with Disabilities and Standards-Based Reform.* Committee on Goals 2000 and the Inclusion of Students with Disabilities, L.M. McDonnell, M.J. McLaughlin, and P. Morison, Eds. Washington, DC: National Academy Press.
  1997b   *Improving Schooling for Language-Minority Children: A Research Agenda.* D. August and K. Hakuta, eds. Washington, DC: National Academy Press.
  1998   *Preventing Reading Difficulties in Young Children.* Committee on the Prevention of Reading Difficulties in Young Children, Commission on Behavioral and Social Science and Education, C.E. Snow, M.S. Burns, and P. Griffin, eds. Washington, DC: National Academy Press.

1999a   *Making Money Matter: Financing America's Schools.* Committee on Education Finance, H. F. Ladd and J. S. Hansen, eds. Washington, DC: National Academy Press.

1999b   *High Stakes: Testing for Tracking, Promotion, and Graduation.* J.P. Heubert and R.M. Hauser, eds. Washington, DC: National Academy Press.

1999c   *Improving Student Learning: A Strategic Plan for Education Research and Its Utilization.* Washington, DC: National Academy Press.

2000a   Family resources. Pp. 267-296 in *From Neurons to Neighborhoods.* Committee on Integrating the Sciences of Early Childhood Development, Board on Children, Youth and Families, J.P. Shonkoff and D.A. Phillips, eds. Washington, DC: National Academy Press.

2000b   *Promoting Health.* Committee on Capitalizing on Social Science and Behavioral Research to Improve the Public's Health, Division of Health Promotion and Disease Prevention, B.D. Smedley and S.L. Syme, eds. Washington, DC: National Academy Press.

2000c   *Neurons to Neighborhoods.* Committee on Integrating the Sciences of Early Childhood Development, Board on Children, Youth and Families, J.P. Shonkoff and D.A. Phillips, eds. Washington, DC: National Academy Press.

2001a   *Eager to Learn: Educating our Preschoolers.* Committee on Early Childhood Pedagogy, Division of Behavioral and Social Sciences and Education, B.T. Bowman, M.S. Donovan, and M.S. Burns, eds. Washington, DC: National Academy Press.

2001b   *New Horizons in Health: An Integrative Approach.* Committee on Future Directions for Behavioral and Social Sciences Research at the National Institutes of Health. B.H. Singer and C.D. Ryff, eds. Washington, DC: National Academy Press.

2001c   *Testing Teacher Candidates: The Role of Licensure Tests in Improving Teacher Quality.* Committee on Assessment and Teacher Quality, Center for Education, Board on Testing and Assessment, K.J. Mitchell, D.Z. Robinson, B.S. Plake, and K.T. Knowles, eds. Washington, DC: National Academy Press.

National Research Council and Institute of Medicine

1998   *Educating Language-Minority Children.* Committee on Developing a Research Agenda on the Education of Limited-English-Proficient and Bilingual Students, D. August and K. Hakuta, eds., Commission on Behavioral and Social Sciences and Education. Washington, DC: National Academy Press.

Needleman, H.L.

1993   Reply to Ernhart, Scarr, and Geneson. *Ethics and Behavior* 3(1):95-101.

2000   Childhood Exposure to Lead: Mechanisms, Consequences and Interventions. Unpublished paper prepared for the Division of Behavioral and Social Sciences and Education (DBASSE), National Academy of Sciences, Washington, DC.

Needleman, H.L., C. Gunnoe, A. Leviton, R. Reed, H. Peresie, C. Maher, and P. Barrett

1979   Deficits in psychologic and classroom performance of children with elevated dentine lead levels. *New England Journal of Medicine* 300:689-695.

Needleman, H.L., J.A. Riess, M.J. Tobin, G.E. Biesecker, and J.B. Greenhouse

1996   Bone lead levels and delinquent behavior. *Journal of the American Medical Association* 275:363-369.

Needleman, H.L., A. Schell, D. Bellinger, A. Leviton, and E.N. Allred

1990   The long-term effects of exposure to low doses of lead in children: An 11-year follow-up report. *New England Journal of Medicine* 322:83-88.

Neisser, U., ed.

1982   *Memory Observed: Remembering in Natural Contexts.* San Francisco: Freeman.

1998   Introduction: Rising test scores and what they mean. In *The Rising Curve: Long-Term Gains in IQ and Related Measures,* U. Neisser, ed. Washington, DC: American Psychological Association.

Neisser, U., G. Boodoo, T.J. Bouchard, A.W. Boykin, N. Brody, S.J. Ceci, D.F. Halpern, J.C. Loehlin, R. Perloff, R.J. Sternberg, and S. Urbina
    1996   Intelligence: Knowns and unknowns. *American Psychologist* 51:77-101.
Nelson, J.R., A. Johnson, and N. Marchand-Martella
    1996   Effects of direct instruction, cooperative learning, and independent learning practices on the classroom behavior of students with behavioral disorders: A comparative analysis. *Journal of Emotional and Behavioral Disorders* 4(1):53-62.
Nelson, J.R., D.J. Smith, L. Taylor, J.M. Dodd, and K. Reavis
    1991   Prereferral intervention: A review of the research. *Education and Treatment of Children* 14:243-253.
Newcomb, A.F., W.M. Bukowski, and L. Pattee
    1993   Children's peer relations: A meta-analytic review of popular, rejected, neglected, controversial and average sociometric status. *Psychological Bulletin* 113(1):99-128.
Newmann, F.M., and Associates
    1996   *Authentic Achievement: Restructuring Schools for Intellectual Quality*. San Francisco, CA: Jossey-Bass.
Nishioka, V.
    2001   *Similarities and Differences in the Personal and Ecological Characteristics of Middle School Boys with Emotional Disturbance, Learning Disabilities, and Social Maladjustment*. Eugene: Institute on Violence and Destructive Behavior, University of Oregon.
Nokes, C., C. van den Bosch, and D. Bundy
    1998   *The Effects of Iron Deficiency and Anemia on Mental and Motor Performance, Educational Achievement, and Behavior in Children*. Washington, DC: International Nutritional Anemia Consultative Group.
Nuñes, T.
    1994   Street intelligence. Pp. 1045-1049 in *Encyclopedia of Human Intelligence* (Vol. 2), R.J. Sternberg, ed. New York: Macmillan.
Nunes, T., A.D. Schliemann, and D.W. Carraher
    1993   *Street Mathematics and School Mathematics*. Cambridge, England: Cambridge University Press.
Nye, B., L.V. Hedges, and S. Konstantopoulos
    1999   The long-term effects of small classes: A five-year follow-up of the Tennessee class size experiment. *Educational Evaluation and Policy Analysis* 21:127-142.
Nystrand, M., and A. Gamoran
    1988   *A Study of Instruction as Discourse*. Washington, DC: U.S. Department of Education, Office of Educational Research and Improvement.
Oakes, J.
    1985   *Keeping Track: How Schools Structure Inequality*. New Haven, CT: Yale University Press.
O'Connor, R.
    2000   Increasing the intensity of intervention in kindergarten and first grade. *Learning Disabilities Research and Practice* 15(1):43-54.
O'Connor, R.E., A. Notari-Syverson, and P.F. Vadasy
    1998   *Ladders to Literacy: A Kindergarten Activity Book*. Baltimore, MD: P.H. Brookes.
Offord, D.R., R. J. Alder, and M.H. Boyle
    1986   Prevalence and sociodemographic correlates of conduct disorder. *American Journal of Social Psychiatry* 6:272-278.
Offord, D.R., H.C. Kraemer, A.E. Kazdin, P.S. Jensen, R. Harrington, and J.S. Gardner
    1998   Lowering the burden of suffering from child psychiatric disorder: Trade-offs among clinical, targeted, and universal interventions. *Journal of the American Academy of Child and Adolescent Psychiatry* 37(7):686-694.

Ogbu, J.U.
  1987   Variability in minority school performance: A problem in search of an explanation. *Anthropology and Education Quarterly* 18:312-334.
Ogden, C.
  1998   Third National Health and Nutrition Examination Survey. Unpublished analysis. Atlanta: Centers for Disease Control and Prevention.
Olds, D.L., J.J. Eckenrode, C.R. Henderson, Jr., H. Kitzman, J. Powers, R. Cole, K. Sidora, P. Morris, L.M. Pettitt, and D. Luckey
  1997   Long-term effects of home visitation on maternal life course and child abuse and neglect: Fifteen-year follow-up of a randomized trial. *Journal of the American Medical Association* 278(8):637-643.
Olds, D.L., C.R. Henderson, Jr., H. Kitzman, J.J. Eckenrode, R. Cole, R. Tatelbaum, J. Robinson, L.M. Pettitt, R. O'Brien, and P. Hill
  1998   Prenatal and infancy home visitation by nurses: A program of research. Pp. 79-130 in *Advances in Infancy Research*, Vol.12, C. Rovee-Collier, L.P. Lipsitt, and H. Hayne, eds. Stamford, CT: Ablex Publishing Company.
Olds, D.L., C.R. Henderson Jr., R. Tatelbaum, and R. Chamberlin
  1986   Improving the delivery of prenatal care and outcomes of pregnancy: A randomized trial of nurse home visitation. *Pediatrics* 77:16-28.
Olenchak, F.R., and J.S. Renzulli
  1989   The effectiveness of the schoolwide enrichment model on selected aspects of elementary school change. *Gifted Child Quarterly*, 33:36-46.
Olson, K., and L. Pavetti
  1996   *Personal and Family Challenges to the Successful Transition from Welfare to Work.* Washington, DC: The Urban Institute.
Olweus, D.
  1991   Bully/victim problems among school children: Basic facts and effects of a school based intervention program. Pp. 411-446 in *The Development and Treatment of Childhood Aggression*, D. Pepler and K. Ruben, eds. London: Lawrence Erlbaum.
Oppenheim, D., A. Sagi, and M.E.Lamb
  1988   Infant-adult attachments on the kibbutz and their relation to socioemotional development 4 years later. *Developmental Psychology* 24:427-433.
Orlosky, D.E., ed.
  1988   *Society, Schools, and Teacher Preparation. A Report on the Future Education of Teachers* (Teacer Education Monograph No. 9) Washington, DC: ERIC Clearinghouse on Teacher Education.
Orton, S.
  1925   Word-blindness in school children. *Archives of Neurology and Psychiatry* 14:581-615.
O'Shea, L.J., P.T. Sindelar, and D.J. O'Shea
  1987   The effects of repeated readings and attentioned cues on the reading fluency and comprehension of learning disabled readers. *Learning Disabilities Research* 2:103-109.
Oswald, D.P., M.J. Coutinho, and A.M. Best
  2000   Community and School Predictors of Over Representation of Minority Children in Special Education. Paper prepared for the Harvard University Civil Rights Project, Conference on Minority Issues in Special Education, November 17, 2000, Cambridge, MA.
Oswald, D., M.J. Coutinho, N. Singh, and A. Best
  1998   Ethnicity in special education and relationships with school related economic and educational variables. *Journal of Special Education*, 32:194-206.

Padula, R.G.
 1997   The plights of Connecticut's brightest students: *Broadley v. Meriden Board of Education. Connecticut Law Review* 29:1319.
Pagani, L., B. Boulerice, and R.E. Tremblay
 1997   The influence of poverty on children's classroom placement and behavior problems. Pp.311-339 in *Consequences of Growing Up Poor*, G.J. Duncan and J. Brooks-Gunn, eds. New York: Russell Sage Foundation.
Palincsar, A.S., and A.L. Brown
 1984   The reciprocal teaching of comprehension-fostering and comprehension-monitoring activities. *Cognition and Instruction* 1:117-175.
Pallas, A.M., D.R. Entwistle, K.L. Alexander, and M.F. Stluka
 1994   Ability-group effects: instructional, social, or institutional? *Sociology of Education* 67:27-46.
Parrish, T.B., C.S. Hikido, and W.J. Fowler, Jr.
 1998   *Inequalities in Public School District Revenues.* (NCES 98-210.) Washington, DC: National Center for Education Statistics, U.S. Department of Education.
Passow, A.H., and R.A. Rudnitski
 1993   *State Policies Regarding Education of the Gifted as Reflected in Legislation and Regulation* (CSR93302). Storrs, CT: University of Connecticut, National Research Center on the Gifted and Talented.
Patrick, J., and D. Reschly
 1982   Relationship of state educational criteria and demographic variables to school-system prevalence of mental retardation. *American Journal of Mental Deficiency* 86:351-360.
Patterson, G., B.D. DeBarshye, and E. Ramsey
 1989   A developmental perspective on antisocial behavior. *American Psychologist* 44:329-335.
Patterson, G.R.
 1986   Performance models for antisocial boys. *American Psychologist* 41:432-444.
Patterson, G.R., Reid, J.B., and T.J. Dishion
 1992   *A Social Learning Approach IV: Antisocial Boys.* Eugene, OR: Castalia.
Pattishall, E.N., G.L. Strope, and R.A. Etzel
 1985   Serum cotinine as a measure of tobacco smoker exposure in children. *American Journal of Diseases of Children* 139(11):1101-4.
Patton, J.M.
 1992   Assessment and identification of African-American learners with gifts and talents. *Exceptional Children* 59:150-159.
 1998   The disproportionate representation of African-Americans in special education: looking behind the curtain for understanding and solutions. *Journal of Special Education* 32(1):25-31.
Patton, J.M., and R.L. Braithwaite
 1984   Obstacles to the participation of Black parents in the educational programs of their handicapped children. *Centering Teacher Education* 34-37.
Patton, J.M.
 1990   The nature and extent of programs for the disadvantaged gifted in the United States and territories. *Gifted Child Quarterly* 34(3):94-96.
Paule, M.G.
 1998   Maternal drug abuse and adverse effects on neurobehavior of offspring. Pp. 617-629 in *Handbook of Developmental Neurotoxicology*, W. Slikker and L.W. Chang, eds. San Diego: Academic Press.
Paulesu, E., J.F. Demonet, F. Fazio, E. McCrory, V. Chanoine, and N. Brunswick
 2001   Dyslexia—Cultural diversity and biological unity. *Science* 291:2165-2167.

Peacock Hill Working Group
  1991   Problems and promises in special education and related services for children and youth with emotional or behavior disorders. *Behavior Disorders* 16(4):299-313.
Peisner-Feinberg, E.S., and M.R. Burchinal
  1997   Relationships between preschool children's child care experiences and concurrent development: The Cost-Quality, and Outcomes Study. *Merrill-Palmer Quarterly* 43(3):451-477.
Peisner-Feinberg, E.S., M.R. Burchinal, R.M. Clifford, M.L. Culkin, C. Howes, S.L. Kagan, N. Yazejian, P. Byler, J. Rustici, and J. Zelazo
  2000   *The Children of the Cost, Quality, and Outcomes Study Go to School: Technical Report.* Chapel Hill, NC: Frank Porter Graham Child Development Center, University of North Carolina at Chapel Hill.
Pelham, W.E., S.W. Evans, E.M. Gnagy, and K.E. Greenslade
  1992   Teacher ratings of DSM-III-R symptoms for the disruptive behavior disorders: Prevalence, factor analyses, and conditional probabilities in a special education sample. *School Psychology Review* 21(2):285-299.
Pennington, B.F., and J.W. Gilger
  1996   How is dyslexia transmitted? Pp. 41-61 in *Developmental Dyslexia: Neural, Cognitive, and Genetic Mechanisms*, C.H. Chase, G.D. Rosen, and G.F. Sherman, eds. Baltimore, MD: York Press.
Pennsylvania Association for Retarded Children v. Commonwealth of Pennsylvania
  343 F. Supp. 279 (E. D. Pa. 1972).
Phillips, S.
  1983   *The Invisible Culture.* New York: Longman.
Phillips, D.A., M. Voran, E. Kisker, C. Howes, and M. Whitebook
  1994   Child care for children in poverty: Opportunity or inequity? *Child Development* 65:472-492.
Phillips, S.
  1972   Participant structures and communicative competence: Warm Springs children in community and classroom. In *Functions of Language in the Classroom*, C.B. Cazden, V.P. John, and D. Hymes, eds. Columbia: Teachers College Press.
Phinney, J.S.
  1996   When we talk about American ethnic groups, what do we mean? *American Psychologist* 51(9):918-927.
Pianta, P.C., and S.L. Nimetz
  1991   Relationship between children and teachers: Associations with classroom and home behavior. *Journal of Applied Developmental Psychology* 12:379-393.
Picone, T.A., L.H. Allen, P.N. Olsen, and M.E. Ferris
  1982a Pregnancy outcome in North American women. II. Effects of diet, cigarette smoking, stress, and weight gain on placentas, and on neonatal physical and behavioral characteristics. *American Journal of Clinical Nutrition* 36:1214-1224.
  1982b Pregnancy outcome in North American women. I. Effects of diet, cigarette smoking, and psychological stress on maternal weight gain. *American Journal of Clinical Nutrition* 36:1205-1213.
Pierce, C.
  1994   Importance of classroom climate for at-risk learners. *Journal of Educational Research* 88:37-42.
Plomin, R.
  1997   Identifying genes for cognitive abilities and disabilities. Pp. 89-104 in *Intelligence, Heredity, and Environment*, R.J. Sternberg and E. Grigorenko, eds. Cambridge, UK: Cambridge University Press.

Pollitt, E., H. Ma, H. Harahap, et al.
  1994   Stunting and delayed motor development in rural west Java. *American Journal of Human Biology* 6(5):627-635.
Polloway, E.A., M.H. Epstein, J.R. Patton, D. Cullinan, and J. Luebke
  1986   Demographic, social, and behavioral characteristics of students with educable mental retardation. *Education and Training of the Mentally Retarded* 21:27-34.
Posner, J.K.
  1982   The development of mathematical knowledge in two West African societies. *Child Development* 53:200-208.
Posner, J.K., and A.J. Barody
  1979   The development of mathematical knowledge in two West African societies. *Child Development* 10:479-496.
Powell, C., and S. Grantham-McGregor
  1989   Home visiting of varying frequency and child development. *Pediatrics* 84:157-164.
Powless, D.L., and S.N. Elliott
  1993   Assessment of social skills of Native American preschoolers: Teachers' and parents' ratings. *Journal of School Psychology* 31:293-307.
Pressley, M., R. Brown, P.B. El-Dinary, and P. Afflerbach
  1995   The comprehension instruction that students need: Instruction fostering constructively responsive reading. *Learning Disabilities Research & Practice* 10:215-224.
Price-Williams, D., W. Gordon, and M. Ramirez
  1967   Manipulation and conservation: A study of children from pottery-making families in Mexico. Pp. 106-121 in *Memorias del XI Congreso Interamericano de la psicologia* Mexico City. Tegucigalpa: Colegio Hondureno de Economistas.
Price-Williams, D.R., W. Gordon, and M. Ramirez, III
  1969   Skill and conservation: A study of pottery-making children. *Developmental Psychology* 1:769.
Prieto, A.G., and S.H. Zucker
  1981   Teacher perception of race as a factor in the placement of behaviorally disordered children. *Behavioral Disorders* 7(1):34-38.
Puma, M., N. Karweit, C. Price, A. Ricciuti, W. Thompson, and M. Vaden-Kiernan
  1997   *Prospects: Final Report on Student Outcomes.* Washington, DC: U.S. Department of Education.
Purcell, J.H.
  1994   *The Status of Programs for High Ability Students* (CRS94306). Storrs, CT: The National Research Center on the Gifted and Talented, University of Connecticut.
Quay, H.C., and D.R. Peterson
  1983   *Manual for the Revised Behavior Problem Checklist.* Coral Gables, FL: University of Miami.
Quint, J.C., J.M. Bos, and D.F. Polit
  1997   *New Chance: Final Report on a Comprehensive Program for Young Mothers in Poverty and Their Children.* New York: Manpower Demonstration Research Corporation.
Quiroga, T., and Z. Lemos-Britton, E. Mostafapour, R.D. Abbott, and V.W. Berninger
  2002   Phonological awareness and beginning reading in Spanish-speaking ESL first graders: Research into practice. *Journal of School Psychology* 40(1):85-111.
Ramey, C.T., D.M. Bryant, B.H. Wasik, J.J. Sparling, K.H. Fendt, and L.M. LaVange
  1992   Infant Health and Development Program for low birth weight, premature infants: Program elements, family participation, and child intelligence. *Pediatrics* 89:454-465.

Ramey, C.T., and S.L. Ramey
  1998   Early intervention and early experience. *American Psychologist* February:109-120.
Ramey, C.T., S.L. Ramey, and R.G. Lanzi
  2000   Intelligence and experience. Pp. 83-115 in *Environmental Effects on Cognitive Abilities*, R.J. Sternberg, ed. Los Angeles: Lawrence Erlbaum.
Ramey, S.L., and C.T. Ramey
  1992   Early educational intervention with disadvantaged children—To what effect? *Applied and Preventive Psychology* 1:131-140.
  1994   The transition to school: Why the first few years matter for a lifetime. *Phi Delta Kappan* 76(3):194-198.
  1999   Early experience and early intervention for children "at risk" for developmental delay and mental retardation. *Mental Retardation and Developmental Disabilities Research Reviews* 5:1-10.
  2000   Early childhood experiences and developmental competence. In *Securing the Future*, S. Danziger and J. Waldfogel, eds. New York: Russell Sage Foundation.
Ramey, S.L., and G.P. Sackett
  2000   The early care-giving environment: Expanding views on non-parental care and cumulative life experiences. Pp. 365-380 in *Handbook of Developmental Psychopathology*, A. Sameroff, M. Lewis and S. Miller, eds. New York: Plenum Publishing Company.
Ramirez, D.J., S.D. Yuen, D.R. Ramey, and D.J. Pasta
  1991   *Final Report: National longitudinal Study of Structured-English Immersion Strategy, Early-Exit and Late-Exit Transitional Bilingual Education Programs for Language-Minority Children. Volumes I and II.* San Mateo, CA: Aguirre International.
Rantakallio, P.
  1983   A follow-up study up to the age of 14 of children whose mothers smoked during pregnancy. *Acta Paediatrica Scandinavica* 72(5):747-753.
Rashotte, C.A., and J.K. Torgesen
  1985   Repeated reading and reading fluency in learning disabled children. *Reading Research Quarterly* 20:180-188.
Raven, J.
  1990   *Raven Manual Research Supplement 3:American and International Norms–Neuropsychological Uses.* Oxford: Oxford Psychologists Press.
Recruiting New Teachers
  2000   The Urban Teacher Challenge: Teacher Demand and Supply in the Great City Schools. [Online]. Available: http://www.rnt.org/quick/utc.pdf [Accessed March 20, 2001].
Reece, C.M. et al.
  1997   *NAEP 1996 Mathematics Report Card for the Nation and the States.* Washington, DC: U.S. Department of Education.
Reid, J.B., and J.M. Eddy
  1997   The prevention of antisocial behavior: Some considerations in the search for effective interventions. Pp. 343-356 in *Handbook of Antisocial Behavior*, D.M. Stoff, J. Breiling, and J.D. Maser, eds. New York: John Wiley & Sons.
Reid, J.B., J.M. Eddy, R.A. Fetrow, and M. Stoolmiller
  1999   Description and immediate impacts of a preventative intervention for conduct problems. *American Journal of Community Psychology* 24(4):483-517.
Reid, J.B., and G.R. Patterson
  1989   The development of antisocial-behavior patterns in childhood and adolescence. *European Journal of Personality* 3(2):107-119.

Reis, S.N.
  1981   An Analysis of the Productivity of Gifted Students Participating in Programs Using the Revolving Door Identification Model. Unpublished Ph.D. dissertation, The University of Connecticut, Storrs, CT.
Renzulli, J.S.
  1977   *The Enrichment Triad Model.* Mansfield Center, CT: Creative Learning Press.
Renzulli, J S., and S.M. Reis
  1985   *The Schoolwide Enrichment Model: A Comprehensive Plan for Educational Excellence.* Mansfield Center, CT: Creative Learning Press.
  1994   Research related to the Schoolwide Enrichment Model. *Gifted Child Quarterly* 38:2-14.
Repetti, R.L., and J. Wood
  1997   Effects of daily stress at work on mothers' interactions with preschoolers. *Journal of Family Psychology* 11(1):90-108.
Reschly, D., and M. Lamprecht
  1979   Expectancy effects of labels: Fact or artifact? *Exceptional Children* 46:55-58.
Reschly, D.J.
  1981   Psychological testing in educational classification and placement. *American Psychologist* 36:1094-1102.
  1988a Minority MMR overrepresentation: Legal issues, research findings, and reform trends. Pp. 23-41 in *Handbook of Special Education: Research and Practice* (Vol. 2), M.C. Wang, M.C. Reynolds, and H. J. Walberg, eds. Oxford, England: Pergamon Press.
  1988b Special education reform: School psychology revolution. *School Psychology Review* 17:459-475.
  1988c Minority MMR overrepresentation and special education reform. *Exceptional Children* 54:316-323.
  1988d Assessment issues, placement litigation, and the future of mild mental retardation classification and programming. *Education and Training of the Mentally Retarded* 23:285-301.
  1992   Mental retardation: Conceptual foundations, definitional criteria, and diagnostic options. Pp. 23-67 in *Developmental Disorders: Diagnostic Criteria, and Clinical Assessment.* S.R. Hooper, G.W. Hynd, and R.E. Mattison, eds. Hillsdale, N.J.: Lawrence Erlbaum.
  1996   Identification and assessment of children with disabilities. *The Future of Children: Special Education for Children with Disabilities* 6(1):40-53.
  1997   Utility of individual ability measures and public policy choices for the 21st century. *School Psychology Review* 26:234-241.
  2000   Assessment and eligibility determination in the Individuals with Disabilities Act of 1997. Pp. 65-104 in *IDEA Amendments of 1997: Practice Guidelines for School-Based Teams,* C.F. Telzrow and M. Tankersley, eds. Bethesda, MD: National Association of School Psychologists.
Reschly, D.J., and D.N. Bersoff
  1999   Law and school psychology. Pp. 1077-1112 in *The Handbook of School Psychology* (3rd ed.), C.R. Reynolds and T.B. Gutkin, eds. New York: John Wiley & Sons.
Reschly, D.J., and F.J. Jipson
  1976   Ethnicity, geographic locale, age, sex, and urban-rural residence as variables in the prevalence of mild retardation. *American Journal of Mental Deficiency* 81:154-161.

Reschly, D.J., and R.J. Kicklighter
   1985   Comparison of Black and White EMR Students from Marshall vs. Georgia. Paper presented at the Annual Convention of the American Psychologist Association, Los Angeles, ERIC ED 271 911.
Reschly, D.J., R.H. Kicklighter, and P. McKee
   1988   Recent placement litigation, Part III: Analysis of differences in Larry P., Marshall, and S-I and implications for future practices. *School Psychology Review* 17:37-48.
Reschly, D.J., and W.D. Tilly III
   1999   Reform trends and system design alternatives. Pp. 19-48 in *Special Education in Transition: Functional Assessment and Noncategorical Programming*, D.J. Reschly, W.D. Tilly III., and J.P. Grimes, eds. Longmont, CO: Sopris West.
Reschly, D.J., W.D. Tilly, III, and J.P. Grimes, eds.
   1999   *Special Education in Transition: Functional Assessment and Noncategorical Programming*. Longmont, CO: Sopris West.
Reschly, D.J., and S.M. Ward
   1991   Use of adaptive measures and overrepresentation of black students in programs for students with mild mental retardation. *American Journal on Mental Retardation* 96:257-268.
Reschly, D.J., and M.S. Wilson
   1990   Cognitive processing vs. traditional intelligence: Diagnostic utility, intervention implications, and treatment validity. *School Psychology Review* 19:443-458.
Reschly, D.J., and J.E. Ysseldyke
   1995   School psychology paradigm shift. Pp. 17-31 in *Best Practices in School Psychology III*, A. Thomas and J. Grimes, eds. Washington DC: National Association of School Psychologists.
Reschly, D.J., and J.E. Ysseldyke
   2002   Paradigm shift: The past is not the future. Pp. 3-20 in *Best Practices in School Psychology IV*, A. Thomas and J. Grimes, eds. Bethesda, MD: National Association of School Psychologists.
Resnick, D.P., and M. Goodman
   1994   American culture and the gifted. Pp. 109-121 in *National Excellence: A Case for Developing America's Talent. An Anthology of Readings*, P.O. Ross, ed. Washington, DC: U.S. Department of Education.
Reynolds, A.J.
   1994   Effects of a preschool plus follow-on intervention for children at risk. *Developmental Psychology* 30:787-804.
Reynolds, A., J.A. Temple, D.L. Robertson, and E.A. Mann
   2001   Long-term effects of an early childhood intervention on educational achievement and juvenile arrest. *Journal of the American Medical Association* 285(18):2339-2346.
Reynolds, C.R.
   1985   Measuring the aptitude-achievement discrepancy in learning disability diagnosis. *Remedial and Special Education* 6:37-55.
Reynolds, C.R., P.A. Lowe, and A.L. Saenz
   1999   The problem of bias in psychological assessment. Pp. 549-595 in *The Handbook of School Psychology* (3rd ed.), C.R. Reynolds and T.B. Gutkin, eds. New York: John Wiley & Sons.
Rice, D.C.
   1998   Developmental lead exposure: neurobehavioral consequences. Pp. 539-557 in *Handbook of Developmental Neurotoxicology*, W. Slikker and L.W. Chang, eds. San Diego: Academic Press.

Richards, C.M., D.K. Symons, C.A. Greene, and T.A. Szuszkiewicz
   1995   The bidirectional relationship between achievement and externalizing behavior problems of students with learning disabilities. *Journal of Learning Disabilities* 28(1):8-17.
Rieben, L., and C.A. Perfetti
   1991   *Learning to Read: Basic Research and Its Implications.* Hillsdale, NJ: Lawrence Erlbaum.
Riksen-Walraven, J.M.
   1978   Effects of caregiver behavior on habituation rate and self-efficacy in humans. *International Journal of Behavioral Development* 1:105-130.
Robinson, A.
   1991   *Cooperative Learning and the Academically Gifted Student.* (RBDM9106). Storrs, CT: University of Connecticut, National Research Center on the Gifted and Talented.
Robinson, G.E., and J.H. Wittebols
   1986   *Class Size Research: A Related Cluster Analysis for Decision Making.* Arlington, VA: Educational Research Service.
Robinson, H.B., and N.M. Robinson
   1965   *The Mentally Retarded Child.* New York: McGraw-Hill.
Robinson, N.M., R.D. Abbott, V.W. Berninger, J. Busse, and S. Mukhopadhyay
   1997   Developmental changes in mathematically precocious young children: Longitudinal and gender effects. *Gifted Child Quarterly* 42:145-158.
Robinson, N.M., R.A. Weinberg, D. Redden, S.L. Ramey, and C.T. Ramey
   1998   Factors associated with high academic competence among former Head Start children. *Gifted Child Quarterly* 42:148-156.
Robinson, S.S., and R.G. Dixon
   1992   *Language Concepts of Low- and Middle-Class Preschoolers.* Ames, IA: Iowa State University of Science and Technology.
Rockwell, S.
   1993   *Tough to Reach Tough to Teach: Students with Behavior Problems.* Reston, VA: Council for Exceptional Children.
Rodriguez, E.M.
   1998   *Preparing Quality Teachers: Issues and Trends in the States.* Denver, CO: State Higher Education Executive Officers.
Rogers, K.B.
   1989   A content analysis of the literature on giftedness. *Journal for the Education of the Gifted* 13:78-88.
   1991   *The Relationship of Grouping Practices to the Education of the Gifted and Talented Learner.* (RBDM 9102). Storrs, CT: University of Connecticut, National Research Center on the Gifted and Talented.
Roggman, L.A., J.H. Langlois, L. Hubbs-Tait, and A. Riesner-Danner
   1994   Infant day-care, attachment, and the "file drawer problem." *Child Development* 65(5):1429-1443.
Rogoff, B., and P. Chavajay
   1995   What's become of research on the cultural basis of cognitive development? *American Psychologist* 50(10):859-877.
Rogoff, B., and J. Mistry
   1985   Memory development in cultural context. Pp. 117-142 in *Cognitive Learning and Memory in Children*, M. Pressley and C. Brainerd, eds. New York: Springer-Verlag.
Rogoff, B., and K.J. Waddell
   1982   Memory for information organized in a scene by children from two cultures. *Child Development* 58:1224-1228.

Roncagliolo, M., M. Garrido, T. Walter, P. Peirano, and B. Lozoff
 1998 Evidence of altered central nervous system development in young iron-deficient anemic infants: Delayed maturation of auditory brain stem responses. *American Journal of Clinical Nutrition* 68:683-690.

Rose, T.L.
 1984 Effects of previewing on the oral reading of mainstreamed behaviorally disordered students. *Behavioral Disorders* 10:33-39.

Rosenthal, R., and L. Jacobson
 1968 *Pygmalion in the Classroom.* Austin, TX: Holt, Rhinehart & Winston.

Ross, B.M., and C. Millsom
 1970 Repeated memory of oral prose in Ghana and New York. *International Journal of Psychology* 5:173-181.

Ross, G., S. Boatright, P. Auld, and R. Nass
 1996 Specific cognitive abilities in 2-year-old children with subependymal and mild intraventricular hemorrhage. *Brain and Cognition* 32:1-13.

Ross, P.O.
 1994 Introduction to descriptions of Javits grant programs. *Gifted Child Quarterly* 38:64.

Roth, R., ed.
 1999 *The Role of the University in the Preparation of Teachers.* Philadelphia, PA: Falmer Press.

Rothstein, R.
 2000 Equalizing education resources on behalf of disadvantaged children. Pp. 31-92 in *A Notion at Risk: Preserving Public Education as an Engine for Social Mobility*, R.D. Kahlenberg, ed. New York: The Century Foundation Press.

Rumsey, J.M., P. Andreason, A.J. Zametkin, T. Aquino, C. King, and S.D. Hambruber
 1992 Failure to activate the left temporoparietal cortex in dyslexia. *Archives of Neurology* 49:527-534.

Rumsey, J.M., K. Nace, B. Donohue, D. Wise, J.M. Maisog, and P. Andreason
 1997 A positron emission tomographic study of impared word recognition and phonological processing in dyslexic men. *Archives of Neurology* 54:562-573.

Rush, D., Z. Stein, and M. Susser
 1980 *Diet in Pregnancy.* New York: Alan R. Liss, Inc.

Russ, S., B. Chiang, B.J. Rylance, and J. Bongers
 2001 Caseload in special education: An integration of research findings. *Exceptional Children* 67(2):161-172.

Russell, S., and C. Ann
 1985 Interventions for behaviorally disordered students: A quantitative review and methodological critique. *Behavioral Disorders* 10(4):239-252.

Ruth, W.
 1996 Goal setting and behavior contracting for students with emotional and behavioral difficulties: Analysis of daily, weekly, and total goal attainment. *Psychology in the Schools* 33:153-158.

Rutter, M.
 1979 Protective factors in children's responses to stress and disadvantaged. Pp. 49-74 in *Primary Prevention of Psychopathology, Vol. 3: Social Competence in Children*, M.W. Kent and J.E. Rolf, eds. Hanover, NH: University Press of New England.
 1985 Resilience in the face of adversity. Protective factors and resistence to psychiatric disorder. *British Journal of Psychiatry* 147:698-711.

Rutter, M., and W. Yule
 1970 Reading retardation and antisocial behavior-the nature of the association. Pp. 240-255 in *Education, Health and Behaviour*, M. Rutter, J. Tizard, and K. Whitmore, eds. London: Longman.

Sackett, G.P., M.F.S.X. Novak, and R. Kroeker
  1999   Early experience effects on adaptive behavior: Theory revisited. *Mental Retardation and Developmental Disabilities Research Reviews* 5:30-40.
Saigal, S., P. Szatmari, P. Rosenbaum, D. Campbell, and S. King
  1991   Cognitive abilities and school performance of extremely low birth weight children and matched term control children at age 8 years: A regional study. *Journal of Pediatrics* 118(5):751-760.
Salend, S.J., and M.R. Nowak
  1988   Effects of peer-previewing on LD students' oral reading skills. *Learning Disability Quarterly* 11:47-53.
Salinger, T., and E. Chittenden
  1994   Analysis of an early literacy portfolio: Consequences for instruction. *Language Arts* 71:446-452.
Salmelin, R., E. Service, P. Kiesila, K. Uutela, and O. Salonen
  1996   Impaired visual word processing in dyslexia revealed with magnetoencephalography. *Annals of Neurology* 40:157-162.
Sameroff, A.
  2000   Ecological perspectives on developmental risk. Pp. 3-33 in *WAIMH Handbook of Infant Mental Health, Vol. 4: Infant Mental Health in Groups at High Risk*, J.D. Osofsky and H.E. Fitzgerald, eds. New York: John Wiley & Sons, Inc.
Sameroff, A., and M. Chandler
  1975   Reproductive risk and the continuum of caretaking casualty. Pp. 187-244 in *Review of Child Development Research* (4th ed.), F.D. Horowitz, ed. Chicago: The University of Chicago Press.
Sameroff, A.J.
  1993   Models of development and developmental risk. Pp. 3-13 in *Handbook of Infant Mental Health*, C.H. Zeanah, ed. New York: Guilford Press.
Sameroff, A.J., R. Seifer, and M. Zax
  1982   Early development of children at risk for emotional disorder. *Monographs of the Society for Research in Child Development* 47 (Serial No. 199).
Samuels, J.S.
  1987   Information processing abilities and reading. *Journal of Learning Disabilities* 20:18-22.
Sanders, W.L., and J.C. Rivers
  1996   *Cumulative and Residual Effects of Teachers on Future Student Academic Achievement.* Knoxville: University of Tennessee.
Sandoval, J.
  1979   The WISC-R and internal evidence of test bias with minority groups. *Journal of Consulting and Clinical Psychology* 47:919-927.
SAS Institute, Inc.
  1992   *SAS User's Guide: Statistics, Version 6 Edition.* Cary, NC: Author.
Sattler, J.M., and J. Gwynne
  1982   White examiners generally do not impede the intelligence test performance of black children: To debunk a myth. *Journal of Consulting and Clinical Psychology* 50(2):196-208.
Scarborough, H.S.
  1984   Continuity between childhood dyslexia and adult reading. *British Journal of Psychology* 75:329-348.
  1990   Very early language deficits in dyslexic children. *Child Development* 61:1728-1743.
Scarborough, H.S., L.C. Ehri, R.K. Olson, and A.E. Fowler
  1998   The fate of phonemic awareness beyond the elementary school years. *Scientific Studies of Reading* 2:115-142.

Scarr, S.
  1997   Behavior-genetic and socialization theories of intelligence: Truce and reconcilia-
          tion. Pp. 27-31 in *Intelligence, Heredity, and Environment*, R.J. Sternberg and E.
          Grigorenko, eds. Cambridge, UK: Cambridge University Press.
Scarr, S., and L. McCartney
  1988   Far from home: An experimental evaluation of the mother-child home program in
          Bermuda. *Child Development* 59:531-543.
Schieffelin, H.S., and E. Ochs
  1983   A cultural perspective on the transition from prelinguistic to linguistic communica-
          tion. Pp. 115-131 in *The Transition from Prelinguistic to Linguistic Communica-
          tion*, R.M. Golinkoff, ed. Hillsdale, NJ: Lawrence Erlbaum.
Schoenthaler, S.
  1991   *Improve Your Child's IQ and Behaviour*. London: BBC Books.
Schoenthaler, S., W. Doraz, and J. Wakefield
  1986a   The impact of low food additive and sucrose diet on academic performance in 803
          New York City public schools. *International Journal of Biosocial Research* 7:189-
          195.
  1986b   The testing of various hypotheses as explanations for the gains in national stan-
          dardized academic test scores in the 1978-1983 New York City Nutrition Policy
          Modification Project. *International Journal of Biosocial Research* 8:196-203.
Schweinhart, L., H. Barnes, D. Weikart, W.S. Barnett, and A.S. Epstein
  1993   Significant benefits: The High/Scope Perry Preschool study through age 27. *Mono-
          graphs of the High/Scope Educational Research Foundation*, Number 10. Ypsilanti,
          MI: The High/Scope Press.
Schweinhart, L.J, and D.P. Weikart
  1993   Success by empowerment: The High/Scope Perry Preschool Study through age 27.
          Young Children 49:54-58.
  1997   Lasting differences: The High/Scope preschool curriculum comparison study
          through age 23. *Monographs of the High/Scope Education Research Foundation*
          12. Ypsilanti, MI: High Scope Press.
Sciarillo, W., A. Alexander, and K. Farrell
  1992   Lead exposure and child behavior. *American Journal of Public Health* 82:1356-
          1360.
Scott, M.S., P. Perou, R. Urbano, A. Hogan, and S. Gold
  1992   The identification of giftedness: A comparison of white Hispanic, and black fami-
          lies. *Gifted Child Quarterly* 36:131-139.
Scribner, S.
  1974   Developmental aspects of categorized recall in a West African society. *Cognitive
          Psychology* 6:475-494.
  1975   Recall of classical syllogisms: A cross-cultural investigation of error on logical
          problems. Pp. 153-173 in *Reasoning: Representation and Process in Children and
          Adults*, R.J. Falmagne, ed. New York: John Wiley & Sons.
  1977   Modes of thinking and ways of speaking: Culture and logic reconsidered. Pp. 483-
          500 in *Thinking*, P.N. Johnson-Laird and P.C. Wason, eds. Cambridge, UK: Cam-
          bridge University Press.
Scruggs, T.E., and M.A. Mastropieri
  1988   Acquisition and transfer of learning strategies by gifted and nongifted students.
          Journal of Special Education 22:133-152.
  1990   The case for mnemonic instruction: From laboratory research to classroom applica-
          tions. *Journal of Special Education* 24:7-32.

Scruggs, T.E., M.A. Mastropieri, C. Jorgensen, and J. Monson
  1986   Effective mnemonic strategies for gifted learners. *Journal for the Education of the Gifted* 9:105-121.
Scruggs, T.E., and R.T. Osguthorpe
  1986   Tutoring interventions with special education settings: A comparison of cross-age and peer tutoring. *Psychology in the Schools* 23(2):187-193.
Seelman, K., and S. Sweeney
  1995   The changing universe of disability. *American Rehabilitation* 21(Autumn-Winter):2-13.
Seifer, R., A.J. Sameroff, S. Dickstein, G. Keitner, I. Miller, S. Rasmussen, and L.C. Hayden
  1996   Parental psychopathology, multiple contextual risks, and one-year outcomes in children. *Journal of Clinical Child Psychology* 25(4):423-435.
Serdula, M., D.F. Williamson, J.S. Kendrick, R.F. Anda, and T. Byers
  1991   Trends in alcohol consumption by pregnant women: 1985 through 1988. *Journal of the American Medical Association* 1991(265):876-879.
Serpell, R.
  1977   Strategies for investigating intelligence in its cultural context. *The Quarterly Newsletter of the Institute for Comparative Human Development* 1:11-15.
Shankweiler, D., I.Y. Liberman, L.S. Mark, C.A. Fowler, and F.W. Fischer
  1979   The speech code and learning to read. *Journal of Experimental Psychology: Human Learning and Memory* 5(6):531-545.
Shankweiler, D., S. Crain, L. Katz, A.E. Fowler, A.M. Liberman, S.A. Brady, R. Thornton, E. Lundquist, L. Dreyer, J.M. Fletcher, K.K. Stuebing, S.E. Shaywitz, and B.A. Shaywitz
  1995   Cognitive profiles of reading-disabled children: Comparison of language skills in phonology, morphology, and syntax. *Psychological Science* 6(3):149-156.
Shapiro, E.S., and T.R. Kratochwill, eds.
  2000   *Behavioral Assessment in Schools: Theory, Research, and Clinical Applications* (2nd ed.). New York: Guilford Press.
Share, D.L.
  1995   Phonological recoding and self-teaching: Sine qua non of reading acquisition. *Cognition* 55:151-218.
Share, D.L., R. McGee, and P. Silva
  1989   IQ and reading progress: A test of the capacity notion of IQ. *Journal of American Academy of Child and Adolescent Psychiatry* 28:97-100.
Share, D.L., and K.E. Stanovich
  1995   Cognitive processes in early reading development: Accommodating individual differences into a model of acquisition. *Issues in Education* 1:1-57.
Sharp, D., and M. Cole
  1972   Patterns of responding in the word associations of West African children. *Child Development* 43:55-65.
Sharp, D., M. Cole, and J. Lave
  1979   Education and cognitive development: The evidence from experimental research. *Monographs of the Society for Research in Child Development* 44(1-2 Serial No. 178).
Sharp, E.Y.
  1983   *Analysis of Determinants Impacting on Educational Services of Handicapped Papago Students.* Tucson: University of Arizona, College of Education. (ERIC Document Reproduction Service No. ED 239 468).
Shaywitz, B., S. Shaywitz, K. Pugh, R. Fulbright, W. Mencl, P. Skudlarski, R. Constable, J. Fletcher, G. Lyon, and J. Gore
  2001   The neurobiology of dyslexia. *Clinical Neuroscience Research* 1(4):291-299.

Shaywitz, B.A., S.E. Shaywitz, K.R. Pugh, W.E. Mencle, R.K. Fullbright, P. Skudlarski, R.T. Constable, K.M. Marchine, J.M. Fletcher, G.R. Lyon, and J.C. Gore
In   Disruption of posterior brain systems for reading in children with developmental
press   dyslexia. *Biological Psychiatry.*

Shaywitz, B.A., T.R. Holford, J.M. Holahan, J.M. Fletcher, K.K. Stuebing, D.J. Francis, and S.E. Shaywitz
1995   A Matthew effect for IQ but not for reading: Results from a longitudinal study. *Reading Research Quarterly* 30(4):894-906.

Shaywitz, S.
1998   Current concepts: Dyslexia. *The New England Journal of Medicine* 338(5):307-312.

Shaywitz, S., B. Shaywitz, K. Pugh, R. Fulbright, W. Mencl, R. Constable, P. Skudlarski, J. Fletcher, G. Lyon, and J. Gore
In   The neuropsychology of dyslexia. In *Handbook of Neuropsycholology (2nd ed.,*
press   *vol. 7: Child Neuropsychology)* S. Segalowitz and I. Rapin, eds. Amsterdam: Elsevier.

Shaywitz, S., B.A. Shaywitz, K.R. Pugh, R.K. Fulbright, R.T Constable, and W.E. Mencl
1998   Functional disruption in the organization of the brain for reading in dyslexia. *Proceedings of the National Academy of Sciences* 95:2636-2641.

Shaywitz, S.E.
1996   Dyslexia. *Scientific American* 275(5):98-104.

Shaywitz, S.E., M.D. Escobar, B.A. Shaywitz, J.M. Fletcher, and R. Makuch
1992   Evidence that dyslexia may represent the lower tail of a normal distribution of reading ability. *New England Journal of Medicine* 326(3):145-150.

Shaywitz, S.E., J.M. Fletcher, J.M. Holahan, A.E. Shneider, K.E. Marchione, K.K. Stuebing, D.J. Francis, K.R. Pugh, and B.A. Shaywitz
1999   Persistence of dyslexia: The Connecticut Longitudinal Study at adolescence. *Pediatrics* 104:1351-1359.

Shaywitz, S.E., B. Shaywitz, J.M. Fletcher, and M.D. Escobar
1990   Prevalence of reading disability in boys and girls: Results from the Connecticut Longitudinal Study. *Journal of the American Medical Association* 264:998-1002.

Sheeber, L.B., and J.H. Johnson
1994   Evaluation of a temperament-focused, parent-training program. *Journal of Clinical Child Psychology* 23(3):249-259.

Shepard, L.A., M.L. Smith, and C.P. Vojir
1983   Characteristics of pupils identified as learning disabled. *American Educational Research Journal* 20:309-331.

Sheppard, S., and L.S. Kanevsky
1999   Nurturing gifted students' metacognitive awareness: Effects of training in homogeneous and heterogeneous classes. *Roeper Review* 21:266-271.

Shinn, M.R.
1998   *Advanced Applications of Curriculum-Based Measurement.* New York: Guilford Press.

Shinn, M.R., R.H. Good III, and C. Parker
1999   Pp. 81-106 in *Special Education in Transition: Functional Assessment and Noncategorical Programming.* D.J. Reschly, W.D. Tilly III, and J.P. Grimes, eds. Longmont, CO: Sopris West.

Shinn, M.R., G. Tindal, D.A. Spira, and D. Marsten
1987   Special education referrals as an index of teacher tolerance: Are teachers imperfect tests? *Exceptional Children* 54(1):32-40.

Shinn, M.R., G.A. Tindal, and D.A. Spira
  1987   Special education referrals as an index of teacher tolerance: Are teachers imperfect tests? *Exceptional Children* 54:32-40.
Shore, B.M., D.G. Cornell, A. Robinson, and V.S.Ward
  1991   *Recommended Practices in Gifted Education: A Critical Analysis.* New York: Teachers College Press.
Shore, R.
  1997   *Rethinking the Brain: New Insights into Early Development.* New York: Families and Work Institute.
Shores, R., P. Gunter, and S. Jack
  1993   Classroom management strategies: Are they setting events for coercion? *Behavioral Disorders* 18(2):92-102.
Siegler, R.S., and M. Robinson
  1982   The development of numerical understandings. Pp. 241-312 in *Advances in Child Development and Behavior*, H.W. Reese and L.P. Lipsitt, eds. New York: Academic Press.
Sigel, I.E.
  1993   Educating the young thinker: A distancing model of preschool education. Pp. 237-252 in *Approaches to Early Childhood Education*, J.L. Roopnarine and J.E. Johnson, eds. Columbus, OH: Merrill/Macmillan.
Sigman, M., C. Neumann, A.A. Jansen, and N. Baribo
  1989   Cognitive abilities of Kenyan children in relation to nutrition, family characteristics, and education. *Child Development* 60:1463-1474.
Sigman, M., and S.E. Whaley
  1998   The role of nutrition in the development of intelligence. Pp. 155-182 in *The Rising Curve*, U. Neisser, ed. Washington, DC: American Psychological Association.
Silva, P.A., P. Hughes, S. Williams, and J.M. Faed
  1988   Blood lead, intelligence, reading attainment, and behavior in eleven-year-old children in Dunedin, New Zealand. *Journal of Child Psychology and Psychiatry* 29:43-52.
Simos, P., J. Breier, J. Fletcher, E. Bergman, and A. Papanicolaou
  2000   Cerebral mechanisms involved in word reading in dyslexic children: A magnetic source imaging approach. *Cerbral Cortex* 10:809-816.
Sindelar, P.T.
  1987   Increasing reading fluency. *Teaching Exceptional Children* 19:59-60.
Skiba, R., and K. Grizzle
  1991   The social maladjustment exclusion: Issues of definition and assessment. *School Psychology Review* 20:577-585.
Skiba, R., K. Grizzle, and K.M. Minke
  1994   Opening the floodgates? The social maladjustment exclusionary and state SED prevalence rates. *Journal of School Psychology* 32(3):267-282.
Slavin, R.E.
  1987   Ability grouping and student achievement in elementary schools: A best-evidence synthesis. *Review of Educational Research* 57:293-336.
  1989   Class size and student achievement: Small effects of small classes. *Educational Psychologist* 24:106.
Slavin, R.E., and N.A. Madden
  1999a Effects of bilingual and English as a second language adaptations of Success for All on the reading achievement of students acquiring English. *Journal of Education for Students Placed at Risk* 4(4):393-416.

1999b *Success for All/Roots and Wings: Summary of Research on Achievement Outcomes.* (Report No. 41). Washington, DC: Center for Research on the Education for Students Placed at Risk.

Slavin, R.E., N.A. Madden, L.J. Dolan, B.A. Wasik, S. Ross, L. Smith, and M. Dianda
1996 Success for All: A summary of research. *Journal of Education for Students Placed at Risk* 1(1):41-76.

Slavin, R.E., N.A. Madden, N.L. Karweit, L. Dolan, and B.A. Wasik
1992 *Success for All: A Relentless Approach to Prevention and Early Intervention in Elementary Schools.* Arlington, VA: Educational Research Service.

Smith, J.R., J. Brooks-Gunn, and P.K. Klebanov
1997 Consequences of living in poverty for young children's cognitive and verbal ability and early school achivement. Pp. 132-189 in *Consequences of Growing Up Poor*, G.J. Duncan and J. Brooks-Gunn, eds. New York: Russell Sage Foundation.

Smith, L.J., S.M. Ross, and J.P. Casey
1994 *Special Education Analyses for Success for All in Four Cities.* Memphis: University of Memphis, Center for Research in Educational Policy.

Smith, M.J., and A.S. Ryan
1987 Chinese-American families of children with developmental disabilities: An exploratory study of reactions to service providers. *Mental Retardation* 25(6):345-350.

Smith, M.L.
1980 Teachers' expectations. *Evaluation in Education* 4:53-56.

Snow, C.E., and M. Paez
In   The Head Start classroom as an oral language environment: What should the per-
press   formance standards be? In *The Head Start Debates*, E. Zigler and S. Styfco, eds. New Haven: Yale University Press.

Snow, R.
1995 Validity of IQ as a Measure of Cognitive Ability. Paper prepared for the National Academies' Board on Testing and Assessment.

Snowling, M.J.
1981 Phonemic deficits in developmental dyslexia. *Psychological Research* 43:219-234.

Sontag, J.C., and R. Schacht
1994 An ethnic comparison of parent participation and information needs in early intervention. *Exceptional Children* 60(5):422-433.

Spencer, M.B.
1995 Old issues and new theorizing about African American Youth: A phenomenological variant of ecological systems theory. Pp. 37-70 in *Black Youth: Perspectives on Their Status in the United States*, R.L. Taylor, ed. Westport, CT: Praeger.
1999 Social and cultural influences on school adjustment: The application of an identity-focused cultural ecological perspective. *Educational Psychologist* 34(1):43-57.

Sprague, J., G. Sugai, and H. Walker
1998 Antisocial behavior in schools. Pp. 451-474 in *Handbook of Child Behavior Therapy, Ecological Considerations in Assessment, Treatment, and Evaluation,* S. Watson and F. Gresham, eds. New York: Plenum Press.

SRI International
1995 *National Longitudinal Transition Study of Students in Special Education.* Menlo Park, CA: SRI.

Sroufe, L.A., N Fox, and V. Pancake
1983 Attachment and dependency in developmental perspective. *Child Development* 54(6):1615-1627.

St. John, N.
1971 Thirty-six teachers: Their characteristics and outcomes for Black and White pupils. *American Educational Research Journal* 8:635-648.

Stahl, S.
   1999   Why innovations come and go: The case of whole language. *Educational Researcher* 8:13.
Stanbury, J.B.
   1998   Prevention of iodine deficiency. Pp. 167-201 in *Prevention of Micronutrient Deficiencies*, C.P. Howson, E.T Kennedy, and A. Horwitz, eds. Washington, DC: National Academy Press.
Stanley, J.C.
   1984   Use of general and specific aptitude measures in identification: Some principles and certain cautions. *Gifted Child Quarterly* 28:177-180.
Stanovich, K.E.
   1986   Matthew effects in reading: Some consequences of individual differences in the acquisition of literacy. *Reading Research Quarterly* 21:360-407.
Stanovich, K.E., and L.S. Siegel
   1994   Phenotypic performance profile of children with reading disabilities: A regression-based test of the phonological-core variable-difference model. *Journal of Educational Psychology* 86:24-53.
Starko, A.J.
   1986   The Effects of the Revolving Door Identification Model on Creative Productivity and Self-Efficacy. Unpublished Ph.D. dissertation, The University of Connecticut, Storrs, CT.
Stecher, B., G. Bohrnstedt, M. Kirst, J. McRobbie, and T. Williams
   2001   Class-size reduction in California: A story of hope, promise, and unintended consequences. *Phi Delta Kappan* 82(9):670-674.
Steele, C.M.
   1997   A threat in the air: How stereotypes shape intellectual identity and performance. *American Psychologist* 52:613-629.
Steele, C.M., and J. Aronson
   1995   Stereotype threat and the intellectual test performance of African Americans. *Journal of Personality and Social Psychology* 69:797-811.
Stein, J., and V. Walsh
   1997   To see but not to read; The magnocellular theory of dyslexia. *Trends in Neurosciences* 20(4):147-152.
Stein, Z.A., and H. Kassab
   1970   Nutrition. Pp. 269-282 in *Mental Retardation*, J. Worlis, ed. New York: Grune and Stratton.
Steinberg, L.
   1996   *Beyond the Classroom: Why School Reform Has Failed and What Parents Need to Do*. New York: Simon and Schuster.
Steinberg, Z., and J. Knitzer
   1992   Classrooms for emotionally and behaviorally disturbed students: Facing the challenge. *Behavioral Disorders* 17:145-156.
Sternberg, R.J.
   1981   Intelligence and nonentrenchment. *Journal of Educational Psychology*, 73:1-16.
   1988   *The Triarchic Mind: A New Theory of Human Intelligence*. New York: Viking.
   1997   *Successful Intelligence*. New York: Plume.
   1999   The theory of successful intelligence. *Review of General Psychology* 3(4):292-316.
Sternberg, R.J., and P.R. Clinkenbeard
   1994   The triarchic model applied to identifying, teaching, and assessing gifted children. *Roeper Review* 17:255-260.

Sternberg, R.J., M. Ferrari, P. Clinkenbeard, and E.L. Grigorenko
    1996   Identification, instruction, and assessment of gifted children: A construct validation
            of the triarchic model. *Gifted Child Quarterly* 40:129-137.
Sternberg, R.J., E.L. Grigorenko, D. Ngorosho, E. Tantubuye, A. Mbise, C. Nokes, and D.A.
Bundy
    1999   Hidden Intellectual Potential in Rural Tanzanian School Children. Manuscript sub-
            mitted for publication.
Sternberg, R.J., B. Torff, and E.L. Grigorenko
    1998a   Teaching triarchically improves school achievement. *Journal of Educational Psy-
            chology* 90:374-384.
    1998b   Teaching for successful intelligence raises school achievement. *Phi Delta Kappan*
            79:667-669.
Sternberg, R.J., K. Nokes, P.W. Geissler, R. Price, F. Okatcha, D.A. Bundy, and E.L.
Grigorenko
    2001   The relationship between academic and practical intelligence: A case study in Kenya.
            Intelligence 29(5):401-418.
Stiles, K.M., and D.C. Bellinger
    1993   Neuropsychological correlates of low-level lead exposure in school-age children: a
            prospective study. *Neurotoxicology and Teratology* 15(1):27-35.
Stipek, D.J., and R.H. Ryan
    1997   Economically disadvantaged preschoolers: Ready to learn but further to go. *Devel-
            opmental Psychology* 68(5)(Oct):507-517.
Stoolmiller, M., J.M. Eddy, and J.B. Reid
    2000   Detecting and describing preventative intervention effects in a universal school-
            based randomized trail targeting delinquent and violent behavior. *Journal of Con-
            sulting and Clinical Psychology* 68:296-306.
Storch, S.A., and G.J. Whitehurst
    In   The role of family and home in the development of literacy in children from low-
    press   income backgrounds. Pp. 53-71 in *New Directions for Child and Adolescent De-
            velopment: No 92,* W. Damon, P.R. Birtto, and J. Brooks-Gunn. San Francsico:
            Jossey-Bass.
Stowitschek, C.E., A. Hecimovic, J.J. Stowitschek, and R.E. Shores
    1982   Behaviorally disordered adolescents as peer tutors: Immediate and generative ef-
            fects on instructional performance and spelling achievement. *Behavioral Disorders*
            7:136-148.
Strauss, A., and H. Werner
    1942   Disorders of conceptual thinking in the brain injured child. *Journal of Nervous and
            Mental Disease* 96:153-172.
Strauss, R.P., and E.A. Sawyer
    1986   Some new evidence on teacher and student competencies. *Economics of Education
            Review* 5(1):41-48.
Streissguth, A., F. Bookstein, and H. Barr
    1996   A dose-response study of the enduring effects of prenatal alcohol exposure, birth to
            fourteen years. Pp. 141-168 in *Alcohol, Pregnancy, and the Developing Child,* H.
            Spohr and H. Steinhausen, eds. Cambridge, UK: Cambridge University Press.
Stringfield, S., M.A. Millsap, E. Scott, and R. Herman
    1996   The Three Year Effects of 10 Promising Programs on the Academic Achievement of
            Students Placed At Risk. Paper presented at the American Educational Research
            Association, New York City, New York.
Suchman, J. R.
    1962   *The Elementary School Training Program in Scientific Inquiry.* Champaign, IL:
            University of Illinois.

Sullivan, O T.
    1980   Meeting the Needs of Low-Income Families with Handicapped Children. Washington, DC: US Department of Health and Welfare, National Institute of Education. (ERIC Document Reproduction Service No. ED 201 091).

Swanson, H.L.
    1999   Intervention Research for Adolescents with Learning Disabilities: A Meta-Analysis of Outcomes Related to High-Order Processing. Washington, DC: U.S. Department of Education.

Swanson, H.L., and M. Hoskyn
    1998   Experimental intervention research on students with learning disabilities: A meta-analysis of treatment outcomes. Review of Educational Research 68:277-321.

Swanson, H.L., M. Hoskyn, and C. Lee
    1999   Interventions for Students with Learning Disabilities: A Meta-analysis of Treatment Outcomes. New York: The Guilford Press.

Swartz, J.P., and D.K. Walker
    1984   The relationship between teacher ratings of kindergarten classroom skills and second-grade achievement scores: An analysis of gender differences. Journal of School Psychology 22:209-217.

Symons, D.K.
    1998   Post-partum employment patterns, family-based care arrangements, and the mother-infant relationship at age two. Canadian Journal of Behavioural Science 30(2):121-131.

Talcott, J., C. Witton, M. McLean, P. Hansen, A. Rees, G. Green, and J. Stein
    2000   Dynamic sensory sensitivity and children's word decoding skills. Proceedings of the National Academy of Sciences 97:2952-2957.

Tallal, P.
    2000   The science of literacy: From the laboratory to the classroom. Proceedings of the National Academy of Sciences 97:2402-2404.

Tapp, J.T., J.H. Wehby, and D.N. Ellis
    1995   A multiple option observation system for experimental studies: MOOSES. Behavior Research Methods, Instruments and Computers 27:25-31.

Tarjan, G., S.W. Wright, R.K. Eyman, and C.V. Keeran
    1973   Natural history of mental retardation: Some aspects of epidemiology. American Journal f Mental Deficiency 77:369-379.

Telzrow, C.F., K. McNamara, and C.L. Hollinger
    2000   Fidelity of problem-solving implementation and relationship to student performance. School Psychology Review 29(3):443-461.

Tharp, R.G., and R. Gallimore
    1988   Rousing Minds to Life: Teaching, Learning, and Schooling in Social Context. Cambridge, UK: Cambridge University Press.

Tilly, W.D. III., T.P. Knoster, and M.J. Ikeda
    2000   Functional behavioral assessment: Strategies for behavioral support. Pp. 151-198 in IDEA Amendments of 1997: Practice Guidelines for School-Based Teams, C.F. Telzrow and M. Tankersley, eds. Bethesda, MD: National Association of School Psychologists.

Tilly, W.D. III., D.J. Reschly, and J.P. Grimes
    1999   Disability determination in problem solving systems: Conceptual foundations and critical components. Pp. 285-321 in Special Education in Transition: Functional Assessment and Noncategorical Programming, D.J. Reschly, W.D. Tilly III, and J.P. Grimes, eds. Longmont, CO: Sopris West.

Tobias, S., M. Zibrin, and C. Menell
   1983   Special education referrals: Failure to replicate student-teacher ethnicity interaction. *Journal of Educational Psychology* 75:705-707.
Tobin, T.
   1992   Educating students with behavioral disorders: Best practices. *Topics in Behavior Disorders: Issues, Controversies, and Trends* 1:35-48.
Todd, A.W., R.H. Horner, and G. Sugai
   1999   Self-monitoring and self-recruited praise: Effects on problem behavior, academic engagement, and work completion in a typical classroom. *Journal of Positive Behavior Interventions* 1:66-76.
Tomlinson, C.A.
   1999   *The Differentiated Classroom: Responding to the Needs of All Learners.* Alexandria, VA: Association for Supervision and Curriculum Development.
Tomlinson, C.A., C.M. Callahan, and K.M. Lelli
   1997a Challenging expectations: Case studies of high-potential, culturally diverse young children. *Gifted Child Quarterly* 41:5-17.
Tomlinson, C.A., T.R. Moon, and C.M. Callahan
   1997b Use of cooperative learning at the middle level: Insights from a national survey. *Research in Middle Level Education Quarterly* 20(4):37-55.
Tomlinson, J.R., N. Acker, A. Canter, and S. Lindborg
   1977   Minority status, sex, and school psychological services. *Psychology in the Schools* 14(4):456-460.
Top, B.L., and R.T. Osguthorpe
   1987   Reverse-role tutoring: The effects of handicapped students tutoring regular class students. *Elementary School Journal* 87:413-423.
Torgesen, J.K.
   1995   *Phonological Awareness: A Critical Factor in Dyslexia.* Baton Rouge, LA: Orton Dyslexia Society.
   2000   Individual differences in response to early interventions in reading: The lingering problem of treatment resisters. *Learning Disabilities Research and Practice* 15(1): 55-64.
Torgesen, J.K., A.W. Alexander, R.K. Wagner, C.A. Rashotte, K.K.S. Voeller, and T. Conway
   2001   Intensive remedial instruction for children with severe reading disabilities: Immediate and long-term outcomes from two instructional approaches. *Journal of Learning Disabilities* 34:33-58.
Toth, S.L., D. Cicchetti, J. MacFie, A. Maughan, and K. Vanmeenen
   2000   Narrative representations of caregivers and self in maltreated pre-schoolers. *Attachment and Human Development* 2(3):271-305.
Townsend, B.
   2000   The disproportionate discipline of African American learners: Reducing school suspensions and expulsions. *Exceptional Children* 56(3):381-391.
Tran, X.C.
   1982   *The Factors Hindering Indochinese Parent Participation in School Activities.* San Diego, CA: San Diego State University, Institute for Cultural Pluralism. (ERIC Document Reproduction Service No. ED 245 018).
Tresch Owen, M., and M.J. Cox
   1988   Maternal employment and the transition to parenthood. Pp. 85-119 in *Maternal Employment and Children's Development: Longitudinal Research*, A.E. Gottfried and A.W. Gottfried, eds. New York: Plenum Press.

Trivette, C.M., C.J. Dunst, K. Boyd, and D. Hamby
  1996   Family-oriented program models, helpgiving practices, and parental control ap-
          praisals. *Exceptional Children* 62:237-248.
Tronick, E.Z., and M.K. Weinberg
  1997   Depressed mothers and infants: Failure to form dyadic states of consciousness. Pp.
          54-81 in *Postpartum Depression and Child Development*, L. Murray and P.J. Coo-
          per, eds. New York: Guilford Press.
Trueba, H., L. Jacobs, and E. Kirton
  1990   *Cultural Conflict and Adaptation: The Case of Hmong Children in American Soci-
          ety.* New York: Falmer.
Turnbull, A.P., and H.R. Turnbull
  2000   *Families, Professionals, and Exceptionality,* 4th ed. Columbus, OH: Merrill.
Tuthill, R.W.
  1996   Hair lead levels related to children's classroom attention-deficit disorder. *Archives
          of Environmental Health* 51:214-220.
Tyack, D., and L. Cuban
  1995   *Tinkering Toward Utopia: A Century of Public School Reform.* Cambridge, MA:
          Harvard University Press.
Tyson, K.
  1998   Challenging the "Burden of 'Acting White'": Missing Links in the Explanation of
          Black Academic Performance. Presentation at the American Sociological Associa-
          tion Annual Meeting, San Francisco, CA, August 1998.
Umbreit, J.
  1995   Functional assessment and intervention in a regular classroom setting for the dis-
          ruptive behavior of a student with attention deficit hyperactivity disorder. *Behav-
          ioral Disorders* 20:267-278l.
U.S. Bureau of the Census
  1950   *United States Census of Population: 1950, Vol. IV: Special Reports, Part 3.*
          Washington, DC: U. S. Department of Commerce.
  2000   *National Population Projections: I, Summary Files.* Available http://www.census.
          gov/population/www/projections/natsum-T3.html [November 20,2001].
U.S. Department of Education
  1993   *National Excellence: A Case for Developing America's Talent.* Washington, DC:
          U.S. Government Printing Office.
  1997   *1994 Elementary and Secondary School Civil Rights Compliance Report: National
          and State Projections.* Washington, DC: DBS Corporation, Office for Civil Rights.
  1998   *To Assure the Free Appropriate Public Education of All Children with Disabilities,
          Individuals with Disabilities Education Act, Section 618.* Twentieth Annual Report
          to Congress on the Implementation of the Education of the Individuals with Dis-
          abilities Education Act. Washington, DC: Office of Special Education Programs,
          Author.
  1999   *1997 Elementary and Secondary School Civil Rights Compliance Report: National
          and State Projections.* Washington, DC: DBS Corporation, Office for Civil Rights.
  2000   *To Assure the Free Appropriate Public Education of All Children with Disabilities.*
          Twenty-second Annual Report to Congress on the Implementation of the Individu-
          als with Disabilities Education Act. Washington, DC: U.S. Department of Educa-
          tion.
  2001   *The Longitudinal Evaluation of School Change and Performance in Title I Schools:
          Final Report.* Washington, DC: Planning and Evaluation Service, U.S. Department
          of Education.
U.S. Department of Health, Education, and Welfare
  1972   *Education of the Gifted and Talented.* Washington, DC:Author.

U.S. Department of Health and Human Services
  1995   The JOBS Evaluation: How Well Are They Faring? AFDC Families with Pre-
         school-Aged Children in Atlanta at the Outset of the JOBS Evaluation. Washing-
         ton, DC: U.S. Department of Health and Human Services.
  1999   Access to Child Care for Low-income Working Families. Washington, DC: U.S.
         Government Printing Office.
  2001a Youth Violence: A Report of the Surgeon General. Rockville, MD: U.S. Depart-
         ment of Health and Human Services, Centers for Disease Control and Prevention,
         National Center for Injury Prevention and Control; Substance Abuse and Mental
         Health Services Administration, Center for Mental Health Services; and National
         Institutes of Health, National Institute of Mental Health.
  2001b Building Their Futures: How Early Head Start Programs Are Enhancing the Lives
         of Infants and Toddlers in Low-Income Families. Summary Report. Washington,
         DC: U.S. Department of Health and Human Services. The Commissioner's Office
         of Research and Evaluation and the Head Start Bureau, Administration on Chil-
         dren, Youth, and Families.
U.S. General Accounting Office
  1997   Head Start: Research Provides Little Information on Impact of Current Program.
         (Report No. HEHS 97-59.) Washington, DC: Author.
  1998   Head Start Programs: Participant Characteristics, Services and Funding. (Report
         No. HEHS-98-65.) Washington, DC: Author.
  1999   Lead Poisoning: Federal Health Care Programs Are Not Effectively Reaching At-
         Risk Children. (Report No. HEHS-99-18.) Washington, DC: Author.
  2000   Early Education and Care: Overlap Indicates Need to Assess Crosscutting Pro-
         grams. (Report No. HEHS-00-78.) Washington, DC: Author.
U.S. President's Task Force on Environmental Health Risks and Safety Risks to Children
  2000   Eliminating Childhood Lead Poisoning: A Federal Strategy Targeting Lead Paint
         Hazards. Washington, DC: Author.
Upah, K.R. and W.D. Tilly
  2002   Best practices in designing, implementing and evaluating quality interventions. In
         Best Practices in School Psychology IV, A. Thomas and J. Grimes, eds. Washing-
         ton, DC: National Association of School Psychologists.
Useem, E.L.
  1992   Middle schools and math groups: Parent's involvement in children's placement.
         Sociology of Education 65(4):263-279.
Valdes, G., and R.A. Figueroa
  1994   Bilingualism and Testing: A Special Case of Bias. Norwood, NJ: Ablex Publishing.
Valencia, R.R., and L.A. Suzuki
  In   Intelligence Testing and Minority Students: Foundations, Performance Factors, and
  press Assessment Issues. London: RoutledgeFalmer.
Van Acker, R., and E. Talbott
  1999   The school context and risk for aggression: Implications for school-based preven-
         tion and intervention efforts. Preventing School Failure 44:12-20.
van den Boom, D.C.
  1994   The influence of temperament and mothering on attachment and exploration: An
         experimental manipulation of sensitive responsiveness among lower-class mothers
         with irritable infants. Child Development 63:840-858.
van Ijzendoorn, M.H., S. Goldberg, P.M. Kroonenberg, and O. Frenkel
  1992   The relative effects of maternal and child problems on the quality of attachment: A
         meta-analysis of attachment in clinical samples. Child Development 63:840-858.
  1995   Journal of Child Psychology and Psychiatry 36(2):225-248.

Van Oers, B.
   1998   From context to contextualizing. *Learning and Instruction* 8(6):473-488.
VanTassel-Baska, J.
   2000   Theory and research on curriculum development for the gifted. Pp. 345-366 in *International Handbook of Giftedness and Talent* (2nd ed.), K.A. Heller, F.J. Monks, R. J. Sternberg, and R.A. Subotnik, eds. Oxford, UK: Elsevier.
VanTassel-Baska, J., G. Bass, R. Ries, D. Poland, and L.D. Avery
   1998   A national study of science curriculum effectiveness with high ability students. *Gifted Child Quarterly* 42:200-211.
VanTassel-Baska, J., L. Zuo, L.D. Avery, and C.A. Little
   2002   A curriculum study of gifted student learning in the language arts. *Gifted Child Quarterly* 46(1):30-45.
Vaughn, S., and B.E. Elbaum
   1999   The self-concept and friendships of students with learning disabilities: A developmental perspective. Pp. 81-110 in *Developmental Perspective on Children with High Incidence Disabilities*. R. Gallimore, L. Bernheimer, D.L. MacMillan, D.L. Speece, and S. Vaughn, eds. Mahwah, NJ: Lawrence Erlbaum.
Vaughn, S., R. Gersten, and D.J. Chard
   2000   The underlying message in LD intervention research: Findings from research syntheses. *Exceptional Children* 67(1):99-114.
Vaughn, S., S. Moody, and J.S. Schumm
   1998   Broken promises: Reading instruction in the resource room. *Exceptional Children* 64(2):211-226.
Vellutino, F.R., D.M. Scanlon, E.R. Sipay, S.G. Small, R. Chen, A. Pratt, and M.B. Denckla
   1996   Cognitive profiles of difficult-to-remediate and readily remediated poor readers: Early intervention as a vehicle for distinguishing between cognitive and experiential deficits as basic causes of specific reading disability. *Journal of Educational Psychology* 88:601-638.
Ventura, S.J., J.A. Martin, S.C. Curtin, F. Menacker, and B.F. Hamilton
   1999   Births: Final data for 1999. *National Vital Health Statistics Reports* 49(1).
Ventura, S.J., J.A. Martin, S.C. Curtin, T.J. Mathews, and M.M. Park
   2000   Births: Final data for 1998. *National Vital Health Statistics Reports* 48(3).
Viteri, F.E.
   1998   Prevention of iron deficiency. Pp. 45-102 in *Prevention of Micronutrient Deficiencies*, C.P. Howson, E.T Kennedy, and A. Horwitz, eds. Washington, DC: National Academy Press.
Vygotsky, L.
   1986   *Thought and Language*. Cambridge, MA: MIT Press.
Vygotsky, L.S.
   1962   *Thought and Language*. Translated by E. Haufmann and G. Vakar. Cambridge: MIT Press.
   1978   *Mind in Society: The Development of Higher Psychological Processes*. Cambridge, MA: Harvard University Press.
Wadsworth, S.J., J.C. DeFries, J. Stevenson, J.W. Gilger, and B.F. Pennington
   1992   Gender ratios among reading-disabled children and their siblings as a function of parental impairment. *Journal of Child Psychology and Psychiatry* 33(7):1229-1239.
Wagenknecht, L.E., G.R. Cutter, N.J. Haley, et al.
   1990   Racial differences in serum cotinine levels among smokers in the Coronary Artery Risk Development in (Young) Adults Study. *American Journal of Public Health* 80:1053-1056.

Wagner, R.
2000   Preventing reading failure. Paper prepared for the Commission on Behavioral and Social Sciences and Education, National Academy of Sciences.

Wagner, R., and J. Torgesen
1987   The nature of phonological processes and its causal role in the acquisition of reading skills. *Psychological Bulletin* 101:192-212.

Wahlsten, D., and G. Gottlieb
1997   The invalid separation of effects of nature and nurture: Lessons from animal experimentation. Pp. 163-192 in *Intelligence, Heredity, and Environment*, R.J. Sternberg and E. Grigorenko, eds. Cambridge, UK: Cambridge University Press.

Wald, J.
1996   Diversity in the special education teaching force. *NCPSE News* 1:1-6.

Walker, H.M., A. Block-Pedego, B. Todis, and H. Severson
1991   *School Archival Record Search*. Longmont, CO: Sopris West.

Walker, H.M., G. Colvin, and E. Ramsey
1995   *Antisocial Behavior in School: Strategies and Best Practices*. Pacific Grove, CA: Brooks/Cole.

Walker, H. M., K. Kavanagh, B. Stiller, A. Golly, H.H. Severson, and E.G. Feil
1998   First step to success: An early intervention approach for preventing school antisocial behavior. *Journal of Emotional and Behavioral Disorders*, 6(2):66-80.

Walker, H.M., and S.R. McConnell
1995   *The Walker-McConnell Scale of Social Competence and School Adjustment*. Florence, KY: Thomson Learning.

Walker, H.M., V. Nishioka, R. Zeller, H. Severson, and E. Feil
2000   Causal factors and partial solutions for the persistent under-identification of students having emotional and behavioral adjustment problems in the context of schooling. *Diagnostique*.

Walker, H.M., and H. Severson
1992   *Systematic Screening for Behavior Disorders: Technical Manual*. Longmont, CO: Sopris West.
2001   Developmental prevention of at-risk outcomes for vulnerable antisocial children and youth. In *Interventions for Children with or at Risk for Emotional and Behavioral Disorders*, K.L. Lane, F.M. Gresham, and T.E. Oshaughnessy, eds. Boston: Allyn & Bacon.

Walker, H.M. and H.H. Severson
1990   *Systematic Screening for Behavior Disorders (Ssbd): User's Guide and Technical Manual*. Longmont, CO: Sopris West.

Walker, H.M., M.R. Shinn, R.E. O'Neill, and E. Ramsey
1987   A longitudinal assessment of the development of antisocial behavior in boys: Rationale, methodology, and first year results. *Remedial and Special Education* 8(4):7-16.

Walker, H.M., J.R. Sprague, D.W. Close, and C.M. Starlin
1999   What's right with behavior disorders: Seminal achievements and contributions of the behavior disorders field. *Exceptionality*.

Wang, M.C., G.D Haertel, and H.J. Walberg
1994   What helps students learn? *Educational Leadership*. 51:74-79.

Wasik, B.A., C.T. Ramey, D.M. Bryant, and J.J. Sparling
1990   A longitudinal study of two early intervention strategies: Project CARE. *Child Development* 61:1682-1696.

Wasik, B.A., and R.E. Slavin
1993   Preventing early reading failure with one-to-one tutoring: A review of five programs. *Reading Research Quarterly* 28:178-200.

Wasserman, G., B. Jaramilo, P. Shrout, and J. Graziano
  1995   Lead Exposure and Child Behavior Problems at Age 3 Years. Paper presented at the
          1995 Society for Research in Child Development, Indianapolis, IN.
Waxman, H.C., and S.L. Huang
  1997   Classroom instruction and learning environment differences between effective and
          ineffective urban elementary schools for African American students. *Urban Education* 32:7-44.
Webber, J.
  1992   A cultural-organizational perspective on special education and the exclusion of
          youth with social maladjustment: Second invited reaction to Maag and Howell
          paper. *Remedial and Special Education* 13:60-62.
Webber, J., and B. Scheuermann
  1997   A challenging future: Current barriers and recommended action for our field. *Behavior Disorders* 22(3):167-178.
Webber, J., B. Scheuermann, C. McCall, and M. Coleman
  1993   Research on self-monitoring as a behavior management technique in special education
          classrooms: A descriptive review. *Remedial and Special Education* 14:38-56.
Webster-Stratton, C.
  1989   Systematic comparison of consumer satisfaction of three cost-effective parent training
          programs for conduct problem children. *Behavior Therapy* 20(1):103-116.
  1998   Preventing conduct problems in Head Start children: Strengthening parental competencies. *Journal of Consulting and Clinical Psychology* 66(5):715-730.
Webster-Stratton, C., M. Kolpacoff, and T. Hollingsworth
  1988   Self-administered videotape therapy for families with conduct-problem children:
          Comparison with two cost-effective treatments and a control group. *Journal of Consulting and Clinical Psychology.* 56(4):558-566.
Webster-Stratton, C., S. Mihalic, A. Fagan, D. Arnold, T. Taylor and C. Tingley
  2001   The incredible years series. In *Blueprints for Violence Prevention,* D.S. Elliott, Series Ed. Boulder, CO: Center for the Study and Prevention of Violence, Institute of
          Behavioral Science, University of Colorado at Boulder.
Wehby, J., F. Symonds, J. Canale, and F. Go
  1998   Teaching practices in classrooms for students with emotional and behavioral disorders: Discrepancies between recommendations and observations. *Behavior Disorders* 24(1):51-56.
Weikart, D.P., J.T. Bond, and J.T. McNeil
  1978   The Ypsilanti Perry Preschool Project: Preschool Years and Longitudinal Results
          Through Fourth Grade. Monographs of the High/Scope Educational Research
          Foundation.
Weitzman, M., S. Gortmaker, and A. Sobol
  1992   Maternal smoking and behavior problems of children. *Pediatrics* 90(3):342-349.
Wells, E.A., D.M. Morrison, M.R. Gillmore, R.F. Catalano, B. Iritani, and J.D. Hawkins
  1992   Race differences in antisocial behaviors and attitudes and early initiation of substance use. *Journal of Drug Education* 22:115-130.
Wendland-Carro, J., C.A. Piccinini, and W.S. Millar
  1999   The role of an early intervention on enhancing the quality of mother-infant interaction. *Child Development* 70(3):713-721.
Werthamer-Larsson, L., S.G. Kellam, and L. Wheeler
  1991   Effect of first grade classroom environment on child shy behavior, aggressive behavior, and concentration problems. *American Journal of Community Psychology* 19:585-602.

Wertsch, J.V.
1998   *Mind as Action.* New York: Oxford University Press.
West, J., K. Denton, and L.M. Reaney
2001   *The Kindergarten Year: Findings from the Early Childhood Longitudinal Study, Kindergarten Class of 1998-99.* Washington, DC: National Center for Education Statistics.
West, J., K. Denton, and E.G. Hausken
2000   *America's Kindergartners: Findings from the Early Childhood Longitudinal Study, Kingergarten Class of 1998-99, Fall, 1998.* Washington, DC: National Center for Education Statistics.
West, J.F., and L. Idol
1987   School consultation, 1. An interdisciplinary perspective on theory, models, and research. *Journal of Learning Disabilities* 20(7):388-408.
Westberg, K.L., F.X. Archambault, Jr., S.M. Dobyns, and T.J. Salvin
1993   *An Observational Study of Instructional and Curricular Practices Used with Gifted and Talented Students in Regular Classrooms.* (Research Monograph 93104.) Storrs, CT: The University of Connecticut, The National Research Center on the Gifted and Talented.
White, B.Y., and J.R. Frederiksen
1998   Inquiry, modeling, and metacognition: Making science accessible to all students. *Cognition and Instruction* 16(1):3-118.
White, K.R.
1991   *Longitudinal Studies of the Effects and Costs of Early Intervention for Handicapped Children: Final Report, October 1, 1985-December 31, 1990.* Logan: Utah State University, Early Intervention Research Institute.
White, K.R., and G.C. Boyce, eds.
1993   Comparative evaluations of early intervention alternatives [Special Issue]. *Early Educational Development* 4.
White, W.A.T.
1988   A meta-analysis of the effects of direct instruction in special education. *Education and Treatment of Children* 11:364-374.
Whitebook, M., C. Howes, and D.A. Phillips
1990   *Who Cares? Child Care Teachers and the Quality of Care in America.* Final report of the National Child Care Staffing Study. Oakland, CA: Child Care Employee Project.
Whitehurst, G.J., and J.E. Fischel
2000   A developmental model of reading and language impairments arising in conditions of economic poverty. Pp. 53-71 in *Speech and Language Impairments in Children: Causes, Characteristics, Intervention, and Outcome.* D. Bishop and L. Leonard, eds. East Sussex, UK: Psychology Press.
Whitehurst, G.J., and G.M. Massetti
In   How Well Does Head Start Prepare Children to Learn to Read? To appear in *The*
press   *Head Start Debates (Friendly and Otherwise),* E. Zigler and S.J. Styfco, eds. New Haven, CT: Yale University Press.
Wiegmann, D.A., D.F. Dansereau, and M.E. Patterson
1992   Cooperative learning: Effects of role-playing and ability on performance. *Journal of Experimental Education* 60:109-116.
Williams, G.M., M. O'Callaghan, J.M. Najman, W. Bor, M.J. Andersen, and D. Richards
1998   Maternal cigarette smoking and child psychiatric morbidity: A longitudinal study. *Pediatrics* 102(1).

Williams, S., J. Anderson, R. McGee, and P.A. Silva
   1990   Risk factors for behavioral and emotional disorder in preadolescent children. *Journal of the American Academy of Child and Adolescent Psychiatry* 29:413-419.
Willis, S.
   1972   Formation of Teachers' Expectations of Students' Academic Performance. Unpublished doctoral dissertation: University of Texas, Austin.
Wilson, M.S., J.M. Schendel, and J.E. Ulman
   1992   Curriculum-based measures, teachers' ratings, and group achievement scores: Alternative screening measures. *Journal of School Psychology* 30:59-76.
Winebrenner, S.
   2000   *Teaching Gifted Kids in the Regular Classroom: Strategies and Techniques Every Teacher Can Use to Meet the Academic Needs of Gifted and Talented* (Rev. Ed). Minneapolis: Free Spirit Press.
Winick, M., K. Meyer, and R., Harris
   1975   Malnutrition and environmental enrichment by adoption. *Science* 190:1173-1175.
Winneke, G., A. Brockhaus, and R. Baltissen
   1977   Neurobehavioral and systemic effects of long-term blood lead elevation in rats, I. Discrimination learning and open-field behavior. *Archives of Toxicology* 37:247-263.
Winneke, G., A. Brockhaus, U. Ewers, U. Kramer, and M. Neuf
   1990   Results from the European multicenter study of lead neurotoxicity in children: Implications for risk assessment. *Neurotoxicology and Teratology* 12:553-559.
Winneke, G., and V. Kramer
   1984   Neuropsychological effects of lead in children: Interaction with social background variables. *Neuropsychobiology* 11:195-202.
Winneke, G., V. Kramer, A. Brockhaus, U. Ewers, H. Kujanek, H. Lechner, and W. Janke
   1983   Neuropsychological studies in children with elevated tooth-lead concentrations. II. Extended study. *International Archives of Occupational and Environmental Health* 51(3):231-252.
Wolery, M., D.B. Bailey, and G.M. Sugai
   1988   *Effective Teaching: Principles and Procedures of Applied Behavior Analysis with Exceptional Students.* Boston: Allyn and Bacon.
Wong, B.Y. L.
   1999   Metacognition in writing. Pp. 183-198 in *Developmental Perspectives on Children with High-Incidence Disabilities*, R. Gallimore, L.P. Bernheimer, D.L. MacMillan, D.L. Speece, and S. Vaughn, eds. Mahwah, NJ: Elbaum.
Woods, S.B., and V.H. Achey
   1990   Successful identification of gifted racial/ethnic group students without changing classification requirements. *Roeper Review* 13(1):21-26.
World Health Organization
   1992   *International Statistical Classification of Diseases and Related Health Problems* (10th Ed.). Geneva: Author.
Yell, M.L.
   1992   A Comparison of Three Instructional Approaches on Task Attention, Interfering Behaviors, and Achievement of Students with Emotional and Behavioral Disorders. Unpublished doctoral dissertation. *Dissertation Abstracts International* 53(09): 3174. (University Microfilms No. 9236987).
Youngs, R.C., and W.W. Jones
   1969   *The Appropriateness of Inquiry Development Materials for Gifted Seventh Grade Children.* Normal, IL: Illinois State University. (ERIC Document Reproduction Service No. ED 32702).

Ysseldyke, J., and B. Algozzine
1983 LD or not LD: That's not the question! *Journal of Learning Disabilities* 16:29-31.

Yule, W., and R. Lansdown
1981 Blood lead concentrations and school performance. *British Medical Journal* 283:1336.

Yule, W., R. Lansdown, I.B. Millar, and M. Urbanowicz
1981 The relationship between blood lead concentration, intelligence, and attainment in a school population: A pilot study. *Developmental Medicine and Child Neurology* 23(5):567-576.

Yule, W., M.A. Urbanowicz, R. Lansdown, and I.B. Millar
1984 Teachers' ratings of children's behavior in relation to blood lead levels. *British Journal of Developmental Psychology* 2:295.

Zable, M.K.
1992 Responses to control. *Beyond Behavior* 4:3-4.

Zeanah, C.H., N. W. Boris, and J.A. Larrieu
1997 Infant development and developmental risk: A review of the past 10 years. *Journal of the American Academy of Child and Adolescent Psychiatry* 36(2):165-178.

Zeichner, K., S. Melnick, and J.L. Gomez
1996 *Currents of Reform in Preservice Teacher Education.* New York: Teachers College Press.

Zeskind, P.S. and C.T. Ramey
1981 Preventing intellectual and interactional sequelae of fetal malnutrition: A longitudinal, transactional, and synergistic approach to development. *Child Development* 52(1):213-218.

Zetlin, A., M. Padron, and S. Wilson
1996 The experience of five Latin American families with the special education system. *Education and Training in Mental Retardation and Developmental Disabilities* 31:22-28.

Ziegler, A., and T. Raul
2000 Myth and reality: A review of empirical studies on giftedness. *High Ability Studies* 11:113-136.

Zigler, E.
1967 Familial mental retardation: A continuing dilemma. *Science* 155:292-298.

Zigler, E., D. Balla, and R. Hodapp
1984 On the definition and classification of mental retardation. *American Journal of Mental Deficiency* 89:215-230.

Zigler, E., and R.M. Hodapp
1986 *Understanding Mental Retardation.* New York: Cambridge University Press.

Zigmond, N.
1993 Learning disabilities from an educational perspective. Pp. 251-272 in *Better Understanding Learning Disabilities: New Views from Research and Their Implications for Education and Public Policies,* G.R. Lyon, D.B. Gray, J.F. Kavanaugh, and N.A. Kraznegor, eds. Baltimore, MD: Paul H. Brookes.

Zigmond, N., and J.M. Baker
1994 Is the mainstream a more appropriate educational setting for Randy? A case study of one student with learning disabilities. *Learning Disabilities Research and Practice* 9(2):108-117.

1995 Concluding comments: Current and future practices in inclusive schooling. *Journal of Special Education* 29(2):245-250.

Zigmond, N., J. Jenkins, L.S. Fuchs, S. Deno, D. Fuchs, J.N. Baker, L. Jenkins, and M. Coutinho
  1995   Special education in restructured schools: Findings from three multi-year studies. *Phi Delta Kappan* March:531-540.
Zirkel, P.A., and P.L. Stevens
  1986   The law concerning public education of gifted students. *West's Education Law Reporter* 34:353.
Zucker, S.H., and A.G. Prieto
  1977   Ethnicity and teacher bias in educational decisions. *Instructional Psychology* 4:2-5.
Zucker, S.H., A.G. Prieto, and R.B. Rutherford
  1979   Racial determinants of teachers' perceptions of placement of the educable mentally retarded. *Exceptional Child Education Resources* 11:1.
Zutell, J.
  1996   The directed spelling thinking activity (DSTA): Providing an effective balance in word study instruction. *The Reading Teacher* 50:98-108.

Biographical Sketches

Christopher T. Cross (*Chair*) is president of the Council for Basic Education in Washington, DC. Previously he served as director of the Education Initiative for the Business Roundtable, as the president of the Maryland State Board of Education, and as the assistant secretary for educational research and improvement, U.S. Department of Education. He has served on the National Research Council's Board of International Comparative Studies in Education and on the Committee on Program Evaluation in Education. He has published numerous articles on education policy and served on a variety of boards of education associations. He has an A.B. in political science from Whittier College and an M.A. in government from California State University at Los Angeles.

Carolyn M. Callahan is a professor in the Curry School of Education, University of Virginia, and also associate director of the National Research Center on the Gifted and Talented. She teaches courses in the area of education of the gifted and is executive director of the summer enrichment program. She has authored numerous articles, book chapters, and monographs on the topics of creativity, the identification of gifted students, program evaluation, and the issues faced by gifted females. She has received recognition as outstanding faculty member in the Commonwealth of Virginia and was awarded the distinguished scholar award from the National

Association for Gifted Children. She is a past president of the Association for the Gifted and the National Association for Gifted Children. She serves on the editorial boards of *Gifted Child Quarterly*, the *Journal for the Education of the Gifted*, and *Roeper Review*.

M. Suzanne Donovan (*Study Director*) is a program officer at the National Research Council's Division of Behavioral and Social Sciences and Education. Her work focuses on education and public policy. She is currently associate director of the Strategic Education Research Partnership and study director of a project that will produce a volume for teachers titled *How Students Learn: History, Math and Science in the Classroom*. She was coeditor of two previous NRC reports: *How People Learn: Bridging Research and Practice*, and *Eager to Learn: Educating Our Preschoolers*. She has a Ph.D. from the University of California at Berkeley School of Public Policy and was previously on the faculty of Columbia University's School of Public and International Affairs.

Beth Harry is professor of special education in the Department of Teaching and Learning at the University of Miami. Formerly she was associate professor at the University of Maryland, College Park. Her research has focused on parent-professional relationships related to disabilities and on the issue of ethnic disproportionality in special education. Her studies of parental perspectives and experiences, funded by the Office of Special Education Programs (OSEP), focused on ethnic minority parents of children with disabilities, with a particular focus on black and Hispanic families. Her current research, also funded by OSEP, uses ethnographic research methods to examine the process by which minorities become overrepresented in special education programs. Her teaching reflects her combined interest in special education, multicultural education, family issues, and qualitative research methods. A native of Jamaica, she has bachelor's and master's degrees from the University of Toronto, Canada, and a Ph.D. in special education from Syracuse University.

Samuel R. Lucas is associate professor of sociology at the University of California, Berkeley. He currently serves on the technical review panel for the Education Longitudinal Study of 2002 and the sociology advisory panel of the National Science Foundation. He coauthored *Inequality by Design: Cracking the Bell Curve Myth* with five colleagues in the Sociology Department at Berkeley; the book received a Gustavus Myers Center award for the study of human rights in North America in 1997. His book on tracking, *Tracking Inequality: Stratification and Mobility in American High Schools*, received the Willard Waller award in 2000 for the most outstanding book in the sociology of education for 1997, 1998, and 1999. He received a bachelor's degree from Haverford College in 1986, was awarded a National Science Foundation Minority Graduate Fellowship in 1988, and completed a Ph.D. in sociology from the University of Wisconsin-Madison as a Ford Foundation minority doctoral dissertation fellow in 1994.

Donald L. MacMillan is professor of education at the University of California, Riverside. He has conducted research on problems in measuring disproportion in the representation of minorities in special education programs and on mainstreaming minority children. He has published widely on special education issues for the past 30 years, particularly in the area of mental retardation. He has also conducted research on issues of identification and assessment of children with learning disabilities. Among his many awards, he received the career research scientist award from the Academy on Mental Retardation, the research award from the Council for Exceptional Children in 1990, the outstanding research award from the special education special interest group of the American Educational Research Association in 1998, the education award of the American Association on Mental Retardation in 1990, and the Edgar A. Doll award from Division 33 of the American Psychological Association in 1989. He has an Ed.D. from the University of California, Los Angeles.

Margaret J. McLaughlin is associate director of the Institute for the Study of Exceptional Children and Youth at the University of Maryland at College Park, where she directs several national projects related to school reform and special education. Her recent research publications examine the extent to which students with disabilities and special education programs interact with school reform initiatives, including standard assessments and new accountability systems. She served as cochair of the National Research Council's Committee on Goals 2000 and the Inclusion of Students with Disabilities. She has a Ph.D. in education from the University of Virginia.

Diana Pullin is an attorney, professor, and former dean of the School of Education at Boston College. As a practicing attorney, she has represented school districts, teachers' unions, parents, students, and educators in a broad range of matters concerning education law, civil rights, and employment, and she is best known for representing a class of students that successfully challenged Florida's requirement that students pass a minimum-competency test in order to graduate. Her research and teaching focus on education law, particularly testing. She served as a member of the National Research Council's Committee on Goals 2000 and the Inclusion of Students with Disabilities. She has a J.D. and a Ph.D., the latter in education, from the University of Iowa.

Craig Ramey is director of the Civitan International Research Center and professor of psychology, pediatrics, sociology, nursing, maternal and child health, and neurobiology at the University of Alabama at Birmingham. He is also director of the university's affiliated program for developmental disabilities. He has conducted extensive research on early interventions for young, high-risk, and disabled children, including work in the Carolina Abecedarian Project—a longitudinal and multidisciplinary approach to the prevention of developmental retardation. He has developed curricula for infant development and for early intervention with low-birthweight infants. He has also written books on parenting focused on building a child's foundation for life in the early years. Among his many awards are the Chautauqua award for outstanding contribution to the field of developmental disabilities and the American Psychological Association's award for exemplary prevention programs. He has a Ph.D. in life-span developmental psychology from West Virginia University.

John B. Reid is executive director of the Oregon Social Learning Center and director of the Oregon Prevention Research Center. He has published widely on assessment methodology and the development of conduct problems and delinquency and has developed and evaluated several family- and school-based interventions for the prevention of delinquency, child abuse, and substance use. He has a Ph.D. in psychology from the University of Oregon.

Daniel Reschly is professor of education and psychology at the George Peabody College, Vanderbilt University, where he chairs the Department of Special Education. He has conducted extensive research on assessments of disabilities in minority children and youth, school psychology professional practices, system reform, and legal issues in special education. From 1975 to 1998 he directed the Iowa State University School Psychology Program and achieved the rank of distinguished professor of psychology and education. Among his many awards are three National Association of School Psychologists distinguished awards and the Stroud award. He served on the National Research Council's Committee on Goals 2000 and the Inclusion of Students with Disabilities, and he is chair of its Committee on Disability Determination in Mental Retardation. He has a Ph.D. in psychology from the University of Oregon.

Robert Rueda is professor in the Division of Learning and Instruction in the School of Education at the University of Southern California. His research interests include the sociocultural basis of learning and instruction, with a focus on academic achievement (especially reading) in at-risk, language minority students and students with mild learning disabilities. He has also conducted research on children's acquisition and uses of literacy and teaching and learning issues related to the academic achievement of language minority students in public school settings. He has a Ph.D. in educational psychology and special education from the University of California, Los Angeles.

Bennett A. Shaywitz is professor of pediatrics and neurology and director of pediatric neurology at the Yale University School of Medicine. His research uses functional magnetic resonance imaging (fMRI) to study children with dyslexia, and he currently leads a research group that is using this technology to investigate the neural basis of reading, dyslexia, and most recently mathematics disability. These ongoing studies have resulted in the first demonstration of sex differences in the functional organization of the brain for higher cognitive function. Recently he and his colleagues have used this technology to discover differences in brain organization and function in children and adults with dyslexia, and he now uses fMRI to study how the brain changes as children with dyslexia are taught to read. He is a member of the Institute of Medicine. With his wife, Sally Shaywitz, he was the recipient of the 2001 Leonard Apt lectureship of the American Academy of Pediatrics and the 2001 inaugural Samuel T. Orton and June Lyday Orton lectureship of the International Dyslexia Association.

Margaret Beale Spencer is professor of education and psychology at the University of Pennsylvania. She also serves as director of the Center for Health, Achievement, Neighborhood, Growth, and Ethnic Studies (CHANGES) and the W.E.B. Du Bois Collective Research Institute at the university. She is the principal investigator for the center's multiethnic longitudinal studies, including project PAC (Promotion of Academic Competence), a five-year longitudinal project that represents a sample of extremely impoverished, southern, inner-city, and mostly male adolescents. Her research interests include exploring the predictors of resiliency by examining the interface between physiological functioning, socioemotional development, and undergirding cognitive processes as linked to context character. She focuses on gender, race, and ethnic patterns in her program of developmental research, which has been published as edited volumes, as well as numerous articles and chapters. She serves on several editorial review boards and as a board member and trustee of the National 4-H Council and the Foundation for Child Development. She has a Ph.D. in child and developmental psychology from the University of Chicago.

Edward Lee Vargas currently serves as superintendent for the Hacienda La Puente Unified School District in Los Angeles County, California. Formerly he was superintendent of the Ysleta Independent School District, the highest-achieving of all large urban districts in Texas, and has 25 years of experience as a teacher, diagnostician, school psychologist, site administrator, and in various central office leadership positions in special education, including service as an assistant superintendent. He has provided leadership to school systems in Albuquerque, New Mexico, Santa Ana, California, and Texas. He was a member of the NRC Committee on Goals 2000 and the Inclusion of Students with Disabilities. He has bachelor's and master's degrees from the University of New Mexico and a doctorate in educational studies from the University of Washington.

Sharon Vaughn is the Mollie V. Davis professor at the University of Texas, Austin. Her areas of research and professional expertise include reading for children with learning and behavioral problems, social development and self-concept of children with learning and behavior problems, and the development of inclusion programs that address academic success for all children in general education classrooms. She worked as a public school teacher from 1973 to 1980. She has a Ph.D. in education and child development from the University of Arizona.

Index